Imperial Twilight

Imperial Twilight

*The Opium War and
the End of China's Last Golden Age*

STEPHEN R. PLATT

Alfred A. Knopf
NEW YORK 2018

THIS IS A BORZOI BOOK
PUBLISHED BY ALFRED A. KNOPF

Published in the United States by Alfred A. Knopf,
a division of Penguin Random House LLC, New York,
and distributed in Canada by Random House of Canada,
a division of Penguin Random House Canada Limited, Toronto.

www.aaknopf.com

Knopf, Borzoi Books, and the colophon are registered
trademarks of Penguin Random House LLC.

Library of Congress Cataloging-in-Publication Data
Names: Platt, Stephen R., author.
Title: Imperial twilight : the Opium War and the End of
China's Last Golden Age / by Stephen R. Platt.
Description: New York : Alfred A. Knopf, 2018. | "A Borzoi book." |
Includes bibliographical references.
Identifiers: LCCN 2017028172 | ISBN 9780307961730 (hardcover) |
ISBN 9780307961747 (ebook)
Subjects: LCSH: China—History—Opium War, 1840–1842. | China—
History—19th century. | China—Foreign relations—19th century.
Classification: LCC DS757.5 .P55 2018 | DDC 951/.033—dc23
LC record available at https://lccn.loc.gov/2017028172

Jacket image: *View of the Canton Factories* (detail) by
William Daniell, ca. 1805. Bridgeman Images
Jacket design by John Vorhees
Maps by Mapping Specialists, Ltd.

Manufactured in the United States of America
First Edition

For Francie, Lucy, and Eliot

Desolate castle, the sky, the wide desert.
There is no wall left to this village.
Bones white with a thousand frosts,
High heaps, covered with trees and grass;
Who brought this to pass?
Who has brought the flaming imperial anger?
Who has brought the army with drums and with kettle-drums?
Barbarous kings.
A gracious spring, turned to blood-ravenous autumn . . .

—LI BO (701–762), TRANS. EZRA POUND,
"Lament of the Frontier Guard"

Weave a circle round him thrice,
And close your eyes with holy dread,
For he on honey-dew hath fed
And drunk the milk of Paradise.

—SAMUEL TAYLOR COLERIDGE,
"Kubla Khan"

Contents

———◆———

RUSSIA

QING EMPIRE

Beijing
Tianjin

Yellow R.

KOREA

Sea of Japan

Chusan
East China Sea

Ningbo

Yangzi R.

Canton
Macao

Taiwan (Formosa)

INDIA

Calcutta

BRITISH INDIA

SIAM (THAILAND)

COCHIN-CHINA (VIETNAM)

Bombay

Arabian Sea

Bay of Bengal

Bangkok

Manila

South China Sea

PACIFIC OCEAN

Singapore

INDIAN OCEAN

Sumatra

Batavia

Sunda Strait

Java

Amsterdam Island

The Route of HMS *Lion*
to China in 1792

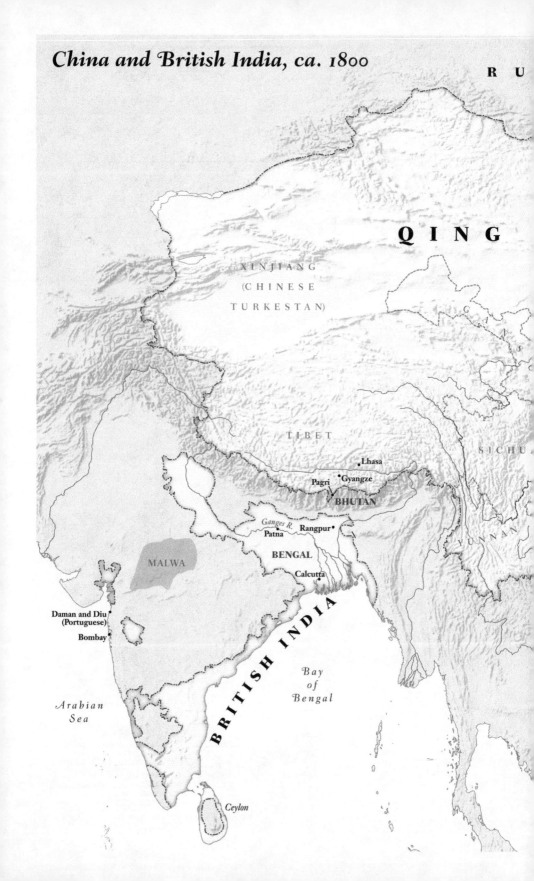

China and British India, ca. 1800

R U

QING

XINJIANG
(CHINESE
TURKESTAN)

TIBET

SICHU

Lhasa

Pagri •Gyangze

BHUTAN

Ganges R. Rangpur •

Patna

BENGAL

Calcutta

YUNNAN

MALWA

Daman and Diu
(Portuguese)

Bombay

BRITISH INDIA

*Bay
of
Bengal*

*Arabian
Sea*

Ceylon

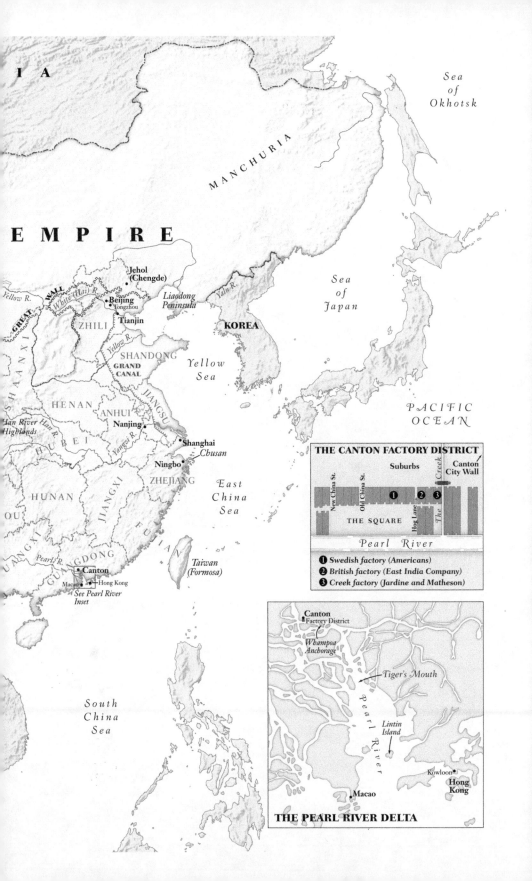

I A

EMPIRE

MANCHURIA

Sea of Okhotsk

Jehol
(Chengde)

Yellow R. GREAT WALL *White (Hai) R.*
Beijing
Tongzhou
Tianjin
ZHILI

Liaodong
Peninsula

Yalu R.

KOREA

Sea of Japan

SHANDONG
GRAND
CANAL

Yellow R.

Yellow Sea

SHAANXI

HENAN

ANHUI

Han River Highlands

HUBEI

Nanjing

JIANGSU

Shanghai
Chusan

Ningbo

ZHEJIANG

East China Sea

PACIFIC OCEAN

HUNAN

JIANGXI

Yangzi R.

OU

UANGXI

FUJIAN

Pearl R.

GUANGDONG

Canton

Macao Hong Kong

See Pearl River Inset

Taiwan (Formosa)

South China Sea

THE CANTON FACTORY DISTRICT

Suburbs

New China St.

Old China St.

Canton City Wall

The Creek

① ② ③

THE SQUARE

Hog Lane

Pearl River

❶ *Swedish factory (Americans)*
❷ *British factory (East India Company)*
❸ *Creek factory (Jardine and Matheson)*

Canton
Factory District

Whampoa Anchorage

Tiger's Mouth

Pearl River

Lintin Island

Kowloon

Hong Kong

Macao

THE PEARL RIVER DELTA

Introduction: Canton

If you stand outside the wall, it is impossible to gauge the size of the city. Canton is built on a plain, so the low, flat buildings of brick and wood that lie inside are invisible from where you stand. The wall is thirty feet high and crenellated, built from large blocks of sandstone at its base and smaller bricks above. It stretches as far as you can see in either direction, with forts visible on top at regular intervals, cannons peering outward. Near you is one of the twelve massive wooden gates that open into the city, a shadowed cave guarded by soldiers and horsemen. The gates creak open each morning at dawn, and close again each evening around 9 p.m. Not that you will be allowed in. As a foreigner, you are stopped at the gate and turned away. You will not see the fantastic warren of narrow streets inside, paved with thick slabs of granite. You will not see the dense brick houses with their sloping tiled roofs, the vast examination hall with its thousands of cells, the lavish mansions, the temples, the gardens, or the government offices that lie within.[1]

Instead, you stay outside and wander back through the suburbs, the sprawling and amorphous settlements surrounding the wall where you could walk for miles without any sense of their coming to an end. It is steamy weather, so humid your sweat seems to just blend into the air around you. The paved streets are twisting and so very narrow that you can sometimes touch the walls on both sides at the same time. The buildings here, fronted with fragrant carved wood, are mostly two stories high, with tall shutters on the windows. Above you, laundry hangs to dry on lines stretched across the top of the alley, creating a canopy effect. It is hard to hear over the din of the hawkers and the shouting of porters and chair-bearers as they try to push their way through. Everywhere is the press of humanity—people traveling on foot or carried in sedan chairs, lounging in the alleyways, eating in open-air restaurants as street performers and beggars ply them for money.

If there are other foreigners about in the suburbs you might over-hear a few snatches of Pidgin English, the local trading language. It is a hybrid of the Cantonese dialect of the city and the European tongues native to the foreigners who come to trade here ("pidgin" means "business"). For the most part it is made up of English words, sometimes with a bit of Hindi or Portuguese, set to Chinese grammar and pronunciation. It is a meeting ground between vastly different languages and will take some getting used to. Fragments of it will be absorbed back into English—having a "look-see" or eating "chow," asking someone to hurry up "chop-chop" or telling them "Long time no see." In its full-blown form it is a colorful singsong of a language. "I saw a man eating" becomes "My look-see one piecee man catchee chow-chow." "He has no money" translates to "He no hab catchee dollar." "You belongy smart inside" means "You're very smart."

A Canton street scene

Vertical signs hang from the sides of most buildings with Chinese characters announcing what is for sale in the shops on the ground floor. You can't read them. But you may be relieved to see that some stores have signs written out in English letters to lure you in. You enter one of these shops through a tall central doorway flanked by two large open windows. It is cooler inside, out of the sun. There is a counter near one of the windows, piled with writing materials. A clerk flips the beads of an abacus rapidly with one hand while he writes down calculations with the other. It is quiet except for the clicking of the abacus. The shop is crammed to the rafters with silk of every description.

Back out in the alley you continue on your way, past shops selling tea, medicine, porcelain, a hundred other goods. A great deal of money changes hands here. There are craftsmen and artists—cabinet makers, blacksmiths, tailors, painters. The painters work in oil, on glass or canvas. They can produce Chinese or European images for you with equal skill, easily replicating anything you bring to them. They will even hold sittings for a visitor like yourself to get your portrait painted. Some of the foreigners say their oil portraits aren't always so flattering. But as the joke goes, when they complain the painters just tell them, "No hab got handsome face, how can hab handsome picture?"

It is not a clean city—though neither, for that matter, are London or Boston. It is especially filthy near the Pearl River, which is where we are headed. The sluggish water of the canals feeding into the river is thick with sewage and refuse from the nearby houses. Rows of sampans are tied up several deep in the river, where the boat people live. Piles of garbage are strewn along the bank. The smell of refuse stewing in the humid warmth is something you will stop noticing in time.

Now we come to the factory district at the edge of the river. This is where you belong.

What you will notice first as you enter from along the river is the relatively enormous amount of open space before you. You have seen nothing like it in the tightly packed suburbs, where alley gives way to alley and there are no open public areas (the great gardens of the suburbs are private and lie behind walls). But here is a wide expanse of hard-trodden dirt with space to walk around freely. This plaza of reclaimed land—the square, as it is known—slopes gently down to a muddy riverfront densely crowded with ships. The ships here are all small ones, for the river is fairly shallow; all of the giant oceangoing vessels you might have expected to see are about ten miles downriver at a deeper anchorage called Whampoa.

There are small groups of Chinese wandering around on the open square, and if you turn away from the water you will see what they have come for. Jarringly out of place in comparison to the low wooden houses of the suburbs, here is an imposing row of thirteen large buildings of brick and granite, higher than anything you have yet seen in Canton—higher even than the city wall. They are distinctly European in appearance, with columned verandas and terraces. Several have tall flagpoles out front that fly the national flag of a Western country: Britain, France, the United States.

These are the factories, where the foreigners live. In spite of the name, they are not sites of manufacturing (a "factor" is a term from India meaning a trader). They contain living quarters, warehouses, and offices. Each one has a Chinese "compradore," or chief steward, who staffs it with a small army of servants—cooks, valets, butlers, even menial servants to pull the ropes that keep the ceiling fans spinning in this oppressive heat. They keep the factories well supplied with food and other necessities. Some have a few head of livestock or a milk cow on hand. If a factory is inhabited by a single national group, it gets to fly its flag out front. The ones without flags host a variety of foreign businessmen, many from India.

For the most part the factory buildings have been built touching one other to economize on space, but there are three gaps between them—short, busy streets filled with single-story Chinese shops. Even on this small scale there are important gradations, better or worse parts of "town." The more respectable alleys are New China Street and Old China Street—toward the left if you face the factories from the water. About twelve feet wide, they have orderly rows of retail stalls and tailor shops, a place for temporary visitors to pick up souvenirs and get clothing made. The less respectable alley, a narrower and dirtier one off to the right, is called Hog Lane, and it is mainly crammed with bars catering to foreign sailors from the ships down at Whampoa, who occasionally get a few days of shore leave, which—as

The foreign factories at Canton and the square in front of them

in any other port they might encounter—they mainly spend getting drunk. The Chinese proprietors of the bars have adopted English names like "Jolly Jack" and "Tom Bowline." Their liquor shacks are so tiny they don't have benches or a bar per se, just a rope over which a sailor can hang by his armpits and drink until he passes out.

In all the compound, it is the British factory that is most striking. Larger than the others, it has its own fenced-in space in front that reaches all the way down to the riverbank. Standing out in front under the limp Union Jack on this sultry afternoon you can see the factory's broad, columned terrace with a view up and down the river, where the merchants of the East India Company can enjoy their tiffin and sometimes catch a bit of a breeze. If you go through the front gate, past the vigilant Chinese guard with his rattan cane, entering through the shade of the veranda, you will find upstairs a European world that might make you forget where you are. Along the wide hallways you will find counting rooms, tea-tasting rooms, and parlors.

There is a chapel with a spire that holds the only public clock in the compound. There are well-appointed living apartments, a dining hall with room for more than a hundred guests, a billiard room, a library of four thousand books.

Looking around inside the vast, chandeliered British dining hall—the portrait of a king on one wall, a former ambassador on another—drinking your sherry as a bustling crowd of servants prepares to serve a dinner of roast beef and potatoes with gravy, you could be forgiven for imagining you had stumbled into some colonial outpost. But this is not India. The British are not in charge here. The Chinese are. These buildings are, all of them, owned by Chinese merchants, who rent them out to the foreign traders so they will have a place to stay and do their business. The armies of servants answer to their Chinese superiors, not to those they wait on. They report what goes on with the guests. Watched over at all times, the foreigners feel sometimes like grubby infants—coddled and helpless, attended always by their nurses. They need permission to do just about anything.

As opulent as these surroundings may be, the residents sometimes feel that they have volunteered to become prisoners here. Despite the feeling of open space outside on the square, the compound is quite limited in size. It runs for just three hundred yards along the waterfront, and between the square out front and the extensive factory buildings behind, it is about two hundred yards deep. The longer you are here, the smaller it will feel. Foreigners are not permitted to go into the city itself, and they can only wander through the very nearest parts of the suburbs. Farther on, and throngs of young boys will materialize to throw rocks at them and call them foreign devils. Even farther, and Chinese soldiers will come to escort them gently home. Every ten days a small group is allowed to take the air in a nearby garden. Other than that, this is their gilded cage. There is nothing else like it in the world. The entire formal trade of Europe and America with China, the largest empire in existence, goes on here in a space of just twelve acres—less, some like to point out, than the footprint of one of the pyramids in Egypt.

You may not want to spend too many years of your life here, but as you see it in the early 1830s, Canton hardly seems the kind of place to start a war.

No event casts a longer shadow over China's modern history than the Opium War. Sparked by an explosive series of events that took place in the Canton factory compound in 1839, the war would end in 1842 with China's humiliating defeat and a treaty all but dictated by the British aggressors, setting a disastrous pattern for the century to come. Textbooks in China on "modern" history, as a rule, take the Opium War as their starting point, the moment when China left its traditional past behind and was dragged forcibly into the world of European imperialism. The war occupies that place not because it was so destructive; in fact, it was relatively small and contained. It caused none of the large-scale social dislocation that China's major internal wars of the nineteenth century like the Taiping Rebellion did. It did not topple the ruling dynasty or even remotely threaten to do so. There weren't even that many battles fought.

But the symbolic power of the Opium War is almost limitless. It has long stood as the point when China's weakness was laid bare before the world, the opening of a "Century of Humiliation" in which Western (and later Japanese) predators would make war on China to bully it into granting territorial concessions and trading rights. It marked a sea change in relations with the West—the end of one era, when foreigners came to China as supplicants, and the dawn of another, when they would come as conquerors. And it carries especially strong power because China unquestionably had the moral high ground: as remembered since, and as charged by critics at the time, Great Britain unleashed its navy on a nearly defenseless China in order to advance the interests of its national drug dealers, who for years had been smuggling opium to China's coast against the laws of the country. The shocking grounds of the war have provided the very foundation of modern Chinese nationalism—from the overthrow of the Qing dynasty in 1912 and the rise, first of the Republic, and then the People's Republic of China, the Opium War has stood for the essence of everything modern China has tried to leave behind: weakness, victimhood, shame.

Because we live in a world so heavily shadowed by this memory, it has been easy for westerners of more recent generations to imagine that this was always the case—that weakness and victimhood were somehow inherent to China's nature. Through the twentieth century, China was a poor, vulnerable, and frequently chaotic nation that never seemed a contender for power. A third-world nation in the eyes of the wealthier countries, it was alternately a pariah or an object of sympathy. For that reason, the country's worldly aspirations of the late twentieth and early twenty-first centuries—to play a leading role in the UN, to host the Olympics, to put a man on the moon—were initially viewed by outsiders almost with bemusement, as if it were an overly ambitious upstart forgetting its proper place. That bemusement has now given way to alarm in many quarters as China strengthens its naval power to unprecedented levels and lays claim to vast swaths of contested maritime territory, asserting its power in ways completely unknown to living memory.

But over the long term, China is anything but an upstart. And as its economic and military power today grow far beyond anything it seemed capable of in the twentieth century, it is coming to resemble far less the weak, bullied nation that suffered the Opium War than the confident and central empire that preceded it. If we take this war not as a beginning but as an ending, and shift our sights instead back into the era before it took place, back before that ostensible dividing line with the modern era, we find a China that was powerful, prosperous, dominant, and above all envied. The memory of that lost era looms ever larger in China today, as a reminder of its potential (some would say rightful) place in the world, a nostalgic vision of what it could be once again.

This is a book about how the Opium War came to be—that is, how China declined from its eighteenth-century grandeur and how Britain became sufficiently emboldened to take advantage of that decline. The central question of the war, as I see it, is not how Britain won, for that was never in serious doubt—in military terms the Opium War pitted the most advanced naval power in the world against an empire with a long and vulnerable coastline that had not needed a seagoing navy in more than a hundred years and so did not have one. Rather, the central question is a moral one: how Britain could have come to fight such a war in China in the first place—against, it should be noted, savage criticism both at home and abroad.

A sense of inevitability has always been projected backwards onto this era in hindsight, as if the war were always meant to be, but when viewed in the light of its own time the Opium War could hardly have been more counterintuitive. Aside from the audacity of sending a small fleet and a few thousand troops to make war on the world's largest empire, critics at the time pointed out that Britain was putting its entire future tea trade at risk for only the vaguest and least justifiable of goals. It seemed paradoxical in the 1830s that a liberal British government that had just abolished slavery could turn around and fight a war to support drug dealers, or that proponents of free trade would align their interests with smugglers. If we revisit these events as they actually unfolded, rather than as they have been reinterpreted afterward, we find far more opposition to this war in Britain and America on moral grounds, and far more respect for the sovereignty of China, than one would otherwise expect.

One reason a reader might not expect such opposition to this war is that we too easily forget how much admiration China used to command. Because of its great strength and prosperity in the late eighteenth century, Europeans viewed China in a dramatically different light than they did the other countries of the East. At a time when India was an object of British conquest, China was an object of respect, even awe. Occasional calls for the use of naval power to advance trade there were struck down as self-defeating, while British traders in Canton who made trouble were generally ordered home or at least reminded to behave themselves. In commerce, China held all the cards. In stark contrast to the British Orientalist vision of India in the late eighteenth century—lost in the past, childlike and divided, a prize to be captured and controlled—China represented instead a strong, unified empire and another living civilization.

For that reason, readers who are familiar with the East India Company as a force of imperial conquest in India will find a very different face of it in China. When young Britons went to work for the Company overseas, it was India that attracted the military adventurers, the administrators, those with dreams of empire. The bean counters, by contrast, went to Canton. (And remarkably, it should be noted that in the early nineteenth century those bean counters in their quiet factories served the Company's bottom line in London far better than the conquerors of India did.) Even as goods—especially cotton and later opium—flowed steadily from India to China, there was almost no professional circulation between the two regions, where Company agents developed largely separate worldviews. When visitors acculturated to British India intruded into the separate world of Canton, they would often cause problems—not just with the Chinese, but with their more experienced countrymen as well.

The Opium War would force those two worlds together, tainting the old admiration and respect for China with a taste for blood. The war would never be universally popular in Britain, however, and fierce opposition to the use of force in China would linger for a long time afterward (another controversial China war in the 1850s would entail the dissolution of Parliament and new elections to disempower the British lawmakers who tried to stop it). Nevertheless, by the time the war finally began, an ongoing collision of two competing worldviews—between those British who respected China's power and prosperity and those who said it was no more enviable than India—reached a crucial threshold.

Thus, while the Opium War was ultimately a war over trade, the story of its origins is, to a significant degree, the story of how the grand mystery of China faded in the cold light of knowledge as British subjects first began to learn the language and explore the interior of the country—and, pursuant to those projects, how the admiring Western views of China that were so prevalent in the late eighteenth century came to be eroded over time by disillusionment and contempt. Within that shift lies the key to understanding how Britain's government could come to a point in 1839 where it was willing to consider, for the first time in two hundred years, the use of violence to further its economic ends there.

Western histories of the Opium War for general readers have long told the story with a wink as the predictable triumph of West over East, a lesson taught to a childish people who dared to look down on the British as barbarians and tried to make them "kowtow" (a loaded term that used to indicate a specific ceremony of kneeling before the Qing emperor but now lives on in our language with the general meaning of "showing obseqious deference"). In such accounts, China typically appears as an unchanging backdrop, a caricature of unthinking traditions and arrogant mandarins stuck in the ancient past who are incapable of appreciating the rise of British power.[2]

With this book, I aim instead to give motion and life to the changing China that lay beyond the confines of Canton in the early nineteenth century—the rebellions, the spread of corruption, and the economic troubles that preoccupied the country's rulers and formed the wider context for the issues of foreign contact that lie at the story's center. Though the Chinese of this era have long been depicted as oblivious to the outside world, that is a false view. Coastal officials in China were fully aware that they had no capacity to resist a European navy; they knew what the British were capable of if given cause for war. Their naiveté, such as it was, resulted not from ignorance but from their faith in the stabilizing power of trade—in particular, their assumption that as long as the British enjoyed profitable commerce in Canton they would never have reason to resort to violence (a belief that was shared along the way, incidentally, by nearly everyone in the British government who had a say in the matter).

On the Western side of my story is a cast of British and American sojourners who tried to get beyond their limited confines in Canton— traders, explorers, missionaries, government agents, and smugglers who, for a variety of reasons both commendable and not, tried to see, contact, and understand more of the country than they were supposed to. Together, they embodied the long Western dream of opening China—"opening" here not to mean that China was always and universally closed (it was not), but to capture how it was experienced by the British and Americans of the late eighteenth and early nineteenth centuries. They were tightly restricted in their ability to conduct trade, they were forbidden to learn the Chinese language, and they were kept within exceptionally close boundaries with no ability to travel farther into the empire or interact with the general population. Some wished it were otherwise, and their efforts in that direction would have great repercussions.

On the Chinese side, meanwhile, this is the story of an empire in decline from a lofty, almost unimaginable height—a wealthy, powerful, civilized state controlling roughly a third of the world's population, riven by internal pressures of overpopulation, official corruption, and sectarian dissent (all three of which, notably, count again among the Chinese government's most pressing concerns today). The characters on this side will include emperors and officials who tried to maintain the order of the state, rebels and others at the fringes of society who tried to subvert it, and reform-minded Confucian scholars who—far from clinging blindly to tradition—proposed creative and pragmatic solutions to the problems of their time. Together, the Chinese and Western sides of the story are meant to give the reader a broader vision of this grand eclipse of empires in the early nineteenth century—China, crossing its meridian and entering into a long decline, while Britain rose to new nationalistic heights through its victories in the Napoleonic Wars and beyond. The Opium War was the point where those two arcs finally crossed.

In closing, a word on inevitability. Although this early age of contact between China and the West has long been treated in retrospect as if it were somehow always destined to end in war, it was not. The Opium War did not result from an intractable clash of civilizations, as it would later be framed in the West. Neither did it represent the culmination of some grand imperial master plan, as it is generally understood in China. To nearly all parties concerned, including even the government ministers who launched it, the war was all but unthinkable until it actually began. The truth is that over the long term, the foreigners and Chinese who came together at Canton found far more common ground than conflict. This book will have much to say about the individuals who made the war possible, but they are by no means the whole story. It is also a book about the many others, now mostly forgotten, who stood against the more familiar currents of their time and can remind us how differently the course of events might have gone—among them British activists who opposed the opium trade, Chinese scholars who counseled pragmatism in foreign relations, and Americans whose relationships with their Chinese counterparts set a more positive pattern than most of the British. As we look to the future of our own era, with China's arc once again ascendant, such figures are every bit as important for us to remember as the ones who caused all the trouble.

Imperial Twilight

The Journey of James Flint

———◆———

In the summer of 1759, James Flint sailed up the coast of China and almost didn't come back. He was at the time the only Englishman who knew how to speak and write in Chinese, a talent that made him extremely valuable to the small community of East India Company traders who lived for a few months of the year in the factories outside the port city of Canton. Those British traders, known as "supercargoes," had recently learned that the emperor would no longer allow them to visit other cities up the coast, which frustrated them not only because they wanted access to multiple Chinese ports for the sake of competition, but also because the senior customs official in Canton (known to them as the "hoppo") was corrupt. He regularly demanded bribes from them and charged higher duties than he was supposed to. Their only recourse, as they saw it, was to try to appeal directly to the emperor in Beijing, in hopes that he might discipline the hoppo and allow them access to one or two other ports for their trade. As Flint was the only one among them who could communicate in Chinese, it fell to him to bring their appeal north.

James Flint's path to learning Chinese had not been in any way a product of his own hopes or interests. As a child in England, he had been adopted in the 1730s by a ship's captain named Rigby who

The Canton factories in the late eighteenth century

brought him halfway around the world to the trading enclave of Canton and left him there, just a boy at the time, with instructions to learn the local language so he might make himself useful and perhaps get a job with the East India Company. Rigby then sailed away, intending to reunite with the boy sometime in the future. It was three years before young James finally heard from Rigby again, in a letter summoning him to Bombay. James took passage from Canton, but Captain Rigby died in a shipwreck not long after writing the letter, and by the time James got to India there was no one there to greet him. The British administrators in Bombay, at a loss as to what to do with the orphan boy, put him back on a ship to Canton, alone and penniless.[1]

With no money for a passage back to England, and nobody to care for him there even if he could get back, young James found a home with the East India Company's supercargoes. He grew up over the years under their guardianship in Canton and the nearby Portuguese settlement of Macao—an adolescent, then a young man with a long

Chinese braid, who dressed like the English when their ships were in port but wore clothes like the Chinese when they were not. He had no family but the East India Company, no home but the hybrid trading world in the small compound outside the broad stone walls of Canton where the foreigners stayed. Along with his native English he learned to speak the local dialect of Cantonese and a bit of the official dialect of Mandarin, and he could read and write in Chinese as well.

It was, as Captain Rigby had hoped, enough to make him a living. The British ships that came and went from Canton paid Flint a respectable fee to negotiate their terms of trade with local merchants. Without him, they had to rely on native translators, who charged high fees and usually took the side of their Chinese patrons. When discussions got thorny, the native translators were useless. The British supercargoes had long wanted one of their own kind to represent them in their business dealings, someone they could trust to put their interests first, and with Flint they finally had that. In time he was made a supercargo himself, and by 1759 when the others sent him up the coast to try to reach the emperor, he had put in more than twenty years of service at Canton.[2]

Flint sailed from Macao on the morning of June 13, 1759, on the *Success*, a little English snow with an eight-man crew and three servants, their course set for the port of Ningbo midway up the coast. He carried a formal petition in Chinese, addressed to the emperor, that his Chinese teacher had helped him write. Along with asking the emperor to investigate the Canton hoppo, Flint's petition also requested permission for the British to trade at Ningbo, which was closer to the centers of production of tea and silk (and closer to the northern climates where there might be a better market for English woolens than at subtropical Canton). The British had traded at Ningbo in the past and knew that the merchants there still wanted their business—Flint himself had ascertained as much during a series of short voyages up to the city a few years earlier. But the officials in Canton were jealous of other ports siphoning off their business. And the government in Beijing enjoyed a steady income from the taxes on land transport for all of the goods that were carried down to Canton, income that would be lost if the trade went on in more convenient places. For those reasons, and to keep foreign relations focused and closely supervised, the emperor seemed intent on restricting the British to Canton alone.[3]

The initial stage of the voyage was unpromising. Upon his reaching Ningbo in late June, the officials in the port told Flint that his ship was forbidden to remain there. Flint pleaded that he carried a petition for the emperor, asking that the officials at least forward it for him to Beijing, but they would not accept it or even allow anyone from his ship to disembark. They told him to go back to Canton. He could not do that, though; it was impossible to sail back down against the winds in that season, and would be until September at least, when the strong southwest monsoon that swept up the coast of China during the summer months would reverse itself. So, absent any welcome from shore, Flint gave up on Ningbo and the *Success* continued on its plaintive course northward into the unknown.

On July 10, after two more weeks of feeling its way up the coast without a chart, the *Success* finally arrived at the broad, turbid mouth of the White River in northern China (known today as the Hai River), the maritime gateway to the inland city of Tianjin. Beyond Tianjin, a road led overland to Beijing. An official from one of the large forts that guarded the shallow river's mouth came out in a junk to inform Flint that his ship was forbidden to proceed inland. But everything was negotiable, and after some further conversation the official said perhaps he could represent Flint's case to his colleagues in Tianjin. For a fee, he could tell them that the *Success* hadn't come on purpose but had simply been blown to this part of the coast by foul weather, and in that case Flint might be allowed up the river. The price he named for his services was 5,000 Chinese taels, a bribe worth nearly $7,000 at the time, or about $200,000 in today's currency. Flint protested that he didn't have that much money on board, but the official said he wouldn't risk his position for anything less than half that sum. He gave Flint one night to think about it.[4]

Flint could not turn back. Aside from the adverse winds that made a southbound cruise impossible, the unsanctioned voyage of the *Success* up the coast would soon become known to the jealous officials down in Canton, who, if they knew the English had failed to get the attention of the emperor, were likely to become even more antagonistic. So Flint finally gave in and offered the man 2,000 taels—less than he had demanded, but still an astronomical bribe. He would pay two-thirds down, the remainder when he left. The official was true to his word, and on July 21, Flint continued upriver to Tianjin, where the senior official in charge of the city gave him a polite reception. Less polite, though, were the ordinary residents of Tianjin, who got into such a commotion over the arrival of a foreign ship that soldiers had to be called in to prevent a mob from storming it. An official transmitted Flint's petition to the emperor in Beijing, and Flint himself was moved into housing on land to wait for a response, in a Buddhist temple surrounded by guards to protect him from the mobs. There were twenty of them, which proved barely enough to keep the locals at bay.

A response from the capital came one week later. As much as Flint was given to know of its contents, the emperor had been moved by the foreigners' complaints about corruption at Canton and was appointing a commissioner to investigate the hoppo. So Flint's petition had been at least partially successful. Indeed, the British complaints about excessive customs charges at Canton were welcome to the ears of an emperor keenly interested in maintaining control over the remote distances of his vast empire, who knew that legitimate reports of official misconduct were far more difficult to come by than bland cover-ups.

Since Flint was the complainant, though, he was made responsible for seeing the accusations through. The emperor ordered him to leave the *Success* and its crew behind at Tianjin, and rather than sail back down the coast with them in the autumn as he had planned, he was to proceed immediately overland to Canton in the company of the imperial commissioner in order to provide him with proof of the hoppo's corruption. Flint and the commissioner left the next morning, beginning a journey down the north–south axis of the empire along an inland route through China never before traversed by an Englishman. Flint did not leave a record of what he saw, but he arrived safely in Canton six weeks later. The *Success* and its crew, however, would never be heard from again.[5]

Regrettably for James Flint, it turned out that there was more to the emperor's response than he knew. The hoppo was indeed removed from office and replaced by someone more honest, but beyond that, the emperor had also been disturbed by Flint's audacity in circumventing the established channels of communication. In particular, Flint had sailed an English ship into ports where foreign vessels were forbidden, and he had submitted a petition in Chinese directly to the sovereign despite having no rank or status within the empire.

And so it was that another edict arrived, not long after Flint got back to Canton, ordering his arrest for those crimes.[6] The local authorities at Canton gladly took him into custody and locked him up in a jail at the edge of Macao. As he languished there for months, and as those months turned into years, the British supercargoes were completely powerless to secure his release—or even to visit him, for that matter. At one point during his long incarceration, the Qing governor in Canton went so far as to write a letter to the king of England extolling the Chinese government's generosity in merely sentencing James Flint to prison, calling his punishment "such amazingly gracious treatment that he should think of it with tears." He said that all the British who had come to China for trade "have been so drenched with the waves of the imperial favour that they should leap for joy and turn towards us for civilization!"[7]

The only sense in which Flint's treatment might be termed "gracious" was in how it compared to the fate of his Chinese teacher. As the emperor saw it, Flint could not have made his voyage, and thus could not have committed his various crimes, if native Chinese subjects had not helped him learn the language and write the petition. They were the ones most to blame. And so, by the emperor's further orders, on the same day that James Flint was arrested, his Chinese teacher was taken into custody as well and decapitated.[8] The teacher's head was then hung on display as a public warning to any other Chinese at Canton who might in the future think of helping one of the foreign traders learn their language. Flint was finally released in November 1762, after three years in prison, at which point the local authorities put him forcibly onto a British ship and banished him from China forever, thereby rendering useless the one valuable skill he had managed to acquire in the term of his unfortunate life.

Some Chinese accounts maintain that James Flint died immediately after his release from prison, but he did in fact manage to live on, if obscurely, in England. Sources are thin, but he makes an appearance, happily enough, in January 1770 teaching Benjamin Franklin how to make tofu.[9] So his knowledge did not go entirely to waste. Nevertheless, the failure of Flint's petition and his deportation from China marked the end of any hope that the English East India Company would be allowed to venture beyond the narrow confines of the port of Canton. For more than eighty years after Flint's arrest—an age handed down to posterity as the "Canton era"—all legal British, French, Dutch, Indian, and American trade with the entire, enormous empire of China was formally restricted to that one single southern port with its tiny, seasonal compound for foreigners. It was the lone point of sanctioned commercial contact between maritime westerners and mainland Chinese, a symbol both of the Qing dynasty's power to dictate international trade on its own terms and—to the British and other foreigners who suffered the same limiting conditions—of the disdain the emperor felt for them. The East India Company traders had tried to ask for more, but after the dismal outcome of Flint's petition they realized that the wisest course of action was simply to stop complaining and be thankful for what they had.

There were good reasons why the East India Company did not do anything else that might put their little foothold in China at risk. In the eyes of Europeans in the late eighteenth century, the empire of the Qing dynasty was an unequaled vision of power, order, and prosperity. It had long been, as Adam Smith described it in 1776 in *The Wealth of Nations*, "one of the richest, that is, one of the most fertile, best cultivated, most industrious, and most populous countries in the world." Smith believed China to have been at a stable climax of development for eons—at least as far back as Marco Polo's visit in the thirteenth century—which meant that although it did not have the capacity to develop any further (an advantage he reserved largely for Europe), it nevertheless showed no signs of retreating from its pinnacle of prosperity. "Though it may perhaps stand still," he insisted, "[China] does not seem to go backwards."[10]

Enlightenment champions of reason saw in China the model of a moral and well-governed state that needed no church—a secular empire, founded on rational texts and ruled by scholars. "Confucius," wrote Voltaire with admiration in his *Philosophical Dictionary* of 1765, "had no interest in falsehood; he did not pretend to be a prophet; he claimed no inspiration; he taught no new religion; he used no delusions."[11] In reading extracts from Confucius's works, Voltaire concluded, "I have found in them nothing but the purest morality, without the slightest tinge of charlatanism." The state that had been founded on those works was, he believed, the oldest and most enduring in the world. "There is no house in Europe," he observed, "the antiquity of which is so well proved as that of the Empire of China."

China's political unity in the later eighteenth century was dazzling not just to British economists and French philosophers but to Americans as well, once they began to emerge as a nation of their own. In 1794, a U.S. citizen of Dutch descent, who had served as interpreter for an embassy from the Netherlands to China, dedicated the published account of his voyage to George Washington, celebrating in particular "the virtues which in your Excellency afford so striking a resemblance between Asia and America." China was for him the standard by which Western countries could be measured: Washington was virtuous because he exhibited some of the qualities of a Qing dynasty emperor. The highest hope that the writer could muster for the future of his new nation was that Washington, in his "principles and sentiments," might procure for the United States "a duration equal to the Chinese Empire."[12]

These were not just Western fantasies. China in the eighteenth century was not only the most populous and politically unified empire on earth, but also the most prosperous. The standard of living in its wealthy eastern and southern cities was easily a match for the companion regions of western Europe, as was life expectancy. To measure by the consumption of luxury goods such as sugar and tea, the quality of life in eastern China in the 1700s appears to have left Europe behind.[13] At the same time, however, due to the Qing government's tight strictures on foreign trade and residence, China was also seen from outside as impossibly guarded and remote, "the only civilised nation in the world," as one British writer put it, "whose jealous laws forbid the intrusion of any other people."[14] The immense riches of the empire were—to the eternal frustration of westerners—always just out of reach.

The southern port city of Canton, as China's primary point of contact with the oceangoing West, thus took on an especially intense air of mystery. One early account of the city by a French traveler, published in London in 1615, described Canton as a vast and secretive metropolis, "the principall Cittie of all *China*, . . . beyond which there is no passage; say any body what hee will to the contrary." No European had ever made it into China beyond the city of Canton, he wrote, "except (as they say) six *Jesuits* . . . of whom there was never since heard any newes, nor is their hope ever to see their returne."[15]

British trade in the city had gotten off to an appropriately rocky start in June 1637, when a Captain Weddell arrived off Macao, the Portuguese settlement eighty miles down the Pearl River delta from Canton, leading a small fleet of English merchant ships and bearing a letter from King Charles I requesting commerce with China. The Portuguese refused to allow Weddell's fleet to land at Macao, so he led his ships up the river toward Canton until they were blocked at the "Tiger's Mouth," a strategic strait in the Pearl River with several major forts that guarded the onward passage to the city. Holding back the main body of his fleet, Weddell sent ahead a single, heavily armed pinnace with fifty men on board to "seeke For speech and trade with the Chineses."[16] The pinnace, lacking a native pilot, felt its way carefully upriver until a fleet of twenty Chinese war junks arrived to turn it back. Before making the English leave the river, however, the admiral of the Chinese fleet invited two of them to discuss what they had come for. When the pinnace returned to Weddell's fleet a few days later, it happily reported that the Chinese admiral, while expressly forbidding them to come to Canton, had promised the British a license to trade alongside the Portuguese at Macao.[17]

When the Portuguese were presented with this news, however, they still refused to let Weddell's ships anchor at Macao, no matter what the admiral had told them. After a pause for counsel, Weddell decided to head back up the river and force his way to Canton. This time he sailed his entire fleet up through the Tiger's Mouth, drawing fire from Chinese defenders on both shores and responding with broadsides of his own. A landing party managed to capture one of the Chinese forts, running up the English colors and looting its guns before burning down all of the buildings inside. During a lull in the fighting, the Chinese invited a few of the English to come up to Canton for negotiations, but the talks soured and several men were taken prisoner. Captain Weddell then proceeded to make war, "laying waste towns and villages," as one account put it, "and burning several of their vessels."[18] In the end, the Chinese capitulated and said they would allow the English to trade directly at Canton. Weddell's spirited efforts proved unnecessary, though, for the Ming dynasty collapsed just seven years after his voyage and Canton was largely destroyed during the wars of Manchu conquest that followed the founding of the Qing dynasty in 1644. It would be nearly eighty years before English trade with Canton could be established on any kind of a regular basis.[19]

Even as Captain Weddell tried to open trade in Canton at gunpoint, he had no idea how important this port would eventually become to his country. Notably, it was one of the merchants who sailed in Weddell's fleet in 1637—Peter Mundy by name—who left the first written record of an Englishman drinking a cup of tea. Just before the hostilities broke out, Mundy noted that some locals along the Pearl River "gave us a certaine Drinke called Chaa" ("cha" being the Chinese name for tea), "which is only water with a kind of herbe boyled in itt." He wasn't terribly impressed, noting clinically, "It must bee Drancke warme and is accompted wholesome."[20]

Weddell's merchants had come in search of sugar and ginger at Canton, and tea was an unknown product. But by the time the East India Company began sending its ships to China in earnest in 1717, along with purchasing the more familiar commodities of copper, porcelain, and raw silk, the ships' masters were also instructed to bring back "Tea as much as the Ship can conveniently stow."[21] By 1725 the Company would be importing 250,000 pounds of tea into England from Canton per year, displacing silk as the primary object of trade with China. Through the eighteenth century Britain's appetite for the drink continued to grow at an enormous rate, and the import figures kept climbing, growing nearly 10,000 percent by 1805, at which point the Company would be shipping home 24 million pounds of tea per year. It became England's national beverage, "practically a necessary of life" as some in government described it, and in 1784, Parliament passed a law requiring the East India Company—which enjoyed a complete monopoly on all British trade with China—to hold a year's supply of it in strategic reserve at all times.[22] The only place in the world where the British could obtain their tea was in China, and the only place in China they could buy it was in Canton.

So it would remain, quietly, for thirty years after Flint's arrest, until the autumn of 1792—when the British government, flush with pride in its rising industrial revolution, and hoping that the emperor might finally be convinced to reconsider his limitations on foreign trade, took it upon itself to send an emissary to China to try to open the country's gates for real.

PART I

Gracious Spring

CHAPTER I

A Time of Wonder

On the morning of September 26, 1792, several days of cold English rain came to an end, a light wind picked up from the north, and HMS *Lion*, a sixty-four-gun ship of the line, unfurled its sails and weighed anchor to depart the harbor at Spithead. It was a time of peace for Great Britain, and the First Lord of the Admiralty felt he could spare the vessel for a two-year voyage to China to ensure that Lord Macartney, the ambassador who sailed on board, would arrive at the court of the Chinese emperor in a suitably impressive fashion.[1] The *Lion* carried four hundred passengers and crew, and was accompanied for its journey by the *Hindostan*, a fifty-six-gun East Indiaman (a merchant ship of the East India Company's fleet, armed as well as many a naval man-of-war), which carried the members of Macartney's large entourage who couldn't fit as passengers on the *Lion*, as well as most of the six hundred crates and packages of cargo that he was bringing to China as gifts for the emperor. If the voyage should meet with success, Macartney would be the first ambassador from Great Britain ever to pay his respects in China; his lone would-be predecessor, a Lieutenant Colonel Charles Cathcart, had sailed from England five years earlier but died at sea on the long outbound journey.[2]

Macartney had had a long if somewhat rocky career as a diplomat. A courtly and determined man with a square jaw and sharp eyes, he had been knighted at age twenty-seven and in his younger years served as an envoy to Russia, where he would have been made ambassador if he hadn't managed to seduce not one but two women of Empress Catherine's court while in the country.[3] By the time of the embassy to China he was middle-aged and a bit on the portly side, but still considered a fine example of British manhood. Since Russia, he had served as governor of Grenada and spent a contentious term as governor of Madras. At the end of his service in Madras he was offered, but declined, the governor-generalship in Bengal. Macartney was proud and optimistic, and imagined himself fully prepared to accommodate the strange customs and practices of the country to which the king now sent him.

In excited anticipation of the Oriental splendor of the Chinese court—at least as he had read about it in fanciful accounts and extrapolated from his experiences in India—Macartney had prepared the most colorful and grandiose outfit he could muster: "a suit of spotted mulberry velvet," as his valet described it, "with a diamond star, and his ribbon; over which he wore the full habit of the order of the Bath, with the hat, and plume of feathers, which form a part of it."[4] Dressed up like a peacock, he felt certain to make a grand impression in a country that he, and most of his entourage, to say nothing of his countrymen, had only ever encountered in their imaginations.

Macartney's mission was a joint venture of the British government and the East India Company, the latter of which bore its costs. Its primary goal was the expansion of British trade into Chinese ports north of Canton—the same request James Flint had brought to the emperor more than thirty years earlier, with such discouraging results (though some, including Macartney himself, believed that if Britain had sent a royal ambassador to Beijing back in 1759, rather than a mere interpreter, things might have gone differently).[5] Nevertheless, the situation for British traders in China had improved considerably in the intervening years. By 1792, the East India Company's share of the Canton trade had grown to eclipse that of all of its continental rivals. The young United States had sent its first trading ship to Canton in 1784, almost immediately upon achieving independence, but compared to the mighty fleet of the East India Company, which sent six ships to Canton for every one of theirs, the upstart Americans still posed no competition worth speaking of.[6]

Best of all for the East India Company, in 1784 the British government had dramatically lowered its tariff on tea imports to combat smuggling from Europe, reducing the tax from upwards of 100 percent to a flat 12.5 percent across the board, so profits were pouring in. The Company's tea imports had tripled, and British cotton textiles were selling well to Chinese merchants in exchange. The London *Times* in 1791 noted hopefully that the China trade was "in the most flourishing state. All English Manufactures find a ready sale there; and the Chinese begin to think that our cottons are superior to their own."[7] Thus the Company itself was actually quite lukewarm about the embassy. Its directors were comfortable in their supremacy, suitably rich, and deeply aware of precedent (or rather the lack thereof) in their direct relations with the Chinese throne. They worried that any new requests from Britain might be taken as impertinence, offending the emperor and damaging rather than advancing their trade in Canton. But industrialists in northern England were demanding expanded markets for their goods, so an optimistic home secretary made sure that the mission went forward against the Company's misgivings.[8]

The sailing routes from England to Macao and Canton in south China were well known thanks to a long history of direct trade, but the *Lion*'s planned course beyond Canton, up the coast of China and through the Yellow Sea to Beijing, was as yet uncharted by European sailors. So to command the *Lion*, Macartney chose a Royal Navy captain, Sir Erasmus Gower, who had been around the world twice and was experienced at the careful business of navigating large ships through unknown waters. No expense was spared; the government gave Gower the freedom to choose all of his own officers, of whom he brought an outsized complement of what one member of the embassy proudly described as "young gentlemen, of the most respected families, glowing with all the ardour and enterprise of youth."[9]

Dangers aside, the unknown nature of the waters through which they were planning to sail was one of the main attractions of the voyage, an ancillary goal of which was to gather naval intelligence.

The Yellow Sea was bordered by both the Qing Empire and Korea, and "no fairer occasion," one passenger noted, "could offer for penetrating into it, and adding so much to marine knowledge, without creating suspicion or giving offence to the court of Beijing."[10] After all, there was no way for Macartney to get to Beijing without sailing through that unknown sea, unless he were somehow to disembark in Canton and travel a thousand miles overland to the capital with his entire retinue and many tons of fragile baggage. If nothing else, a basic chart of the coastline would open the way for other British ships in the future, of which they hoped there would be many.

The essential strategy of Macartney's mission was reflected in the presents that crowded the hold of the *Hindostan*. Some were industrial goods—textiles and manufactures—that the British hoped Chinese traders might be induced to purchase, thus opening new avenues of commerce. Even more important, though, were the scientific and mechanical gifts, which represented the most recent technological developments in Europe. The British assumed that these were unknown in China, and since the public at home viewed them with wonder there was no reason to think they would amaze and delight the Chinese any less. Macartney, and the British government, hoped that the mission's technical marvels (to say nothing of the combined 120 guns of the *Lion* and *Hindostan*) would gently impress upon the emperor of China the power of British civilization and, consequent to that, convince him of the great value and importance of the two countries' trade.

Among those presents was a gigantic planetarium that had taken thirty years to build and was deemed "the most wonderful piece of mechanism ever emanating from human hands."[11] There were giant lenses of every description. There were globes of the stars and earth, two carriages even more ornate than the king's own (one for the emperor's use in summer and the other for winter), "chemical and philosophical apparatuses," several brass field guns, a sampling of muskets and swords, howitzer mortars, two "magnificent" lustres (elaborate chandeliers that could illuminate a room) packed in fourteen cases, vases, clocks, an air pump, Wedgwood china, artwork depicting everyday life in England, paintings of military battles on land and sea, portraits of the royal family, and other articles worth a total of £14,000.[12] Beyond just impressing the Chinese with the greatness of British science and industry, the *Times* expressed a wish that men of letters could go along with Macartney as well. "We could almost wish Boswell were to take a trip with them to China," it said, "provided he kept, during the voyage, a literary log book."[13]

The embassy's mechanical expert was a Scot named James Dinwiddie, an astronomer and natural philosopher. He was responsible for the elaborate planetarium as well as the demonstrative

A hopeful image of Macartney being welcomed
into the wonders of China

experiments—including a diving bell and a hot-air balloon—that he planned to show off to Macartney's Chinese hosts. The balloon was a new invention, and it was dangerous (one could fall out, crash, get swept away by a storm, explode if using hydrogen, or strand oneself in a treetop), and in England Dinwiddie refrained from going up in one himself. Nevertheless, by the time of Macartney's embassy he had established himself as one of the foremost experts on such devices in Europe. He was just the man, in the later words of his grandson, "to surprise the Chinese with the power, learning, and ingenuity of the British people," and when the ambassador invited him along to China he immediately said yes, resolving that he would make his very first ascent in a balloon in Beijing, for the benefit of the Chinese emperor and the awe of his people.[14]

The ships' most important cargo of all, however, was a letter from King George III to Qianlong, the emperor of China. It was a wondrous example of overblown diplomatic language in which the British monarch bent over backwards to address Qianlong as he imagined Qianlong might wish to be addressed. Thus King George referred to him as "the Supreme Emperor of China . . . worthy to live tens of thousands and tens of thousands thousand years." He declared that the English had come to China not for conquest (which was true), and neither had they come for mere profit (which was not). Rather, he claimed, Britain's sole purpose in sending the mission was for the sake of discovery and to better their own civilization. He spoke of China in the most glowing terms. "Above all," he insisted, "our ardent wish has been to become acquainted with those celebrated institutions of your Majesty's populous and extensive empire which have carried its prosperity to such a height as to be the admiration of all surrounding nations."[15]

The king's lofty language wasn't just a show for his royal counterpart—it appeared in his private instructions to Macartney as well. There, he described the Chinese as "a people, perhaps the most singular upon the globe, among whom civilization had existed, and the arts been cultivated, through a long series of ages, with fewer interruptions than elsewhere."[16] Likewise, the chairman and deputy chairman of the East India Company in London, in a separate private communication to Macartney, referred favorably to "the known character of the Emperor for wisdom, justice and equity."[17] The corruption and difficulty of working with local officials in Canton was well known, but the British in both government and trade at this time shared a deep admiration for China's overall imperial system of governance and faith in the personal virtue and wisdom of its ruler.

———

One of the most challenging obstacles to mounting the mission had turned out to be language. Macartney needed an interpreter, but in 1792, as far as the organizers of the mission could tell, there was not a single person in Britain or any of its far-flung territories who could speak Chinese.[18] James Flint had recently died, and in the thirty years since his arrest and banishment the East India Company had given up encouraging its personnel to study the language. When in the country, they relied entirely on native interpreters, but nobody knew for sure whether any of those linguists had a vocabulary sufficient for diplomatic niceties, nor whether they would even be willing to accompany a foreigner to Beijing given the well-known fate of Flint's Chinese teacher.

The job of finding an interpreter fell to Macartney's longtime secretary, Sir George Leonard Staunton, an old friend who would be the number-two-ranking member of the embassy. Staunton, a baronet, was a physician with an inordinately large nose who saw the quest for a Chinese interpreter as a fine chance to improve the education of his eleven-year-old son, George Thomas Staunton, who had never in his life seen a Chinese person but would be coming along as Macartney's page. Young George (who shared his father's nose) was a sickly and timid child, and Staunton had determined that what the boy lacked in physical strength he would make up for in education and worldliness. Perhaps to compensate for having been absent in India with Macartney for the first four years of the boy's life, Staunton doted on his son and made him into something of a philosophical experiment. He took him to scientific lectures, hired private tutors instead of enrolling him in ordinary schools, forbade him to read fairy tales, and tried to indoctrinate him with a grounded love of the natural world. The two traveled throughout England to see and learn about the latest developments in agriculture, mining, and manufacturing—a living education if there ever was one.

It was toward this end that he brought the boy along with him on his hunt through Europe in the winter and spring of 1792 to find someone who could speak Chinese. Catholic missionaries from the continent had in small numbers been traveling to and from China since the early seventeenth century, and were generally the only thread other than trade to link those two ends of the world. Staunton's best hope of finding one was in Italy, which had long been a base for the Jesuit missions to China until they were driven out by Qianlong's grandfather in the early eighteenth century (and later suppressed in Europe as well). The Vatican was said to employ a handful of educated Chinese to curate its collection of Oriental manuscripts, so that was their fallback destination. But France was closer, so for their first step father and son sailed the Channel in the wet chill of January 1792 and took a carriage overland from Calais to see if they could scrounge up a returned missionary in Paris.

France was just three years fresh from its revolution when they arrived, and they found an atmosphere of excitement and novelty, friendly peasants wearing tricolor cockades in their hats to celebrate the new nation (a nation the Stauntons never imagined would so soon be at war with their own). They paid their respects to King Louis XVI and Marie Antoinette—out of power, but not yet guillotined—and visited the ruins of the Bastille. They listened to speeches at the Society of the Jacobins, toured the gardens of Versailles, and admired how the Palais-Royal had been converted into shops for ordinary people. They did not, however, find anyone who could speak Chinese. There were two institutes for foreign missions in Paris, one housing nobody who had ever been to China, the other containing just one, an old Catholic missionary who had come home some twenty years earlier. Even if he hadn't almost entirely forgotten the language, he insisted that he "was not disposed to visit that distant country again, on any terms."[19]

The urgency of their business pressed them onward, through Germany and then down to Italy, where, after a difficult midwinter crossing of the Alps, they arrived in Rome only to find that their information was out of date. The Vatican, it turned out, had not employed any Chinese scholars in a very long time. But in a turn of luck, the British ambassador at Naples managed to succeed on their behalf. He pointed them to a Roman Catholic College of the Propaganda, which had been founded in 1732 to educate the young Chinese boys European missionaries tended to bring home with them like so many botanical specimens.[20] The college trained the boys in religion so they could eventually return to their home country as Catholic missionaries in their own right. When the Stauntons arrived, they found four such students, now men in their early thirties, who were conversant in Latin and Italian along with their native Chinese, and who wished very much to go home.[21] Staunton engaged two of them ("of amiable manners, and of a virtuous and candid disposition," he believed) to join the embassy as interpreters.[22] The two men came back with Staunton and his son to England that summer, lived with them in London, and then set sail with the embassy to China in September.

The *Lion* and *Hindostan* would be ten months at sea. From England they sailed southward to the Portuguese island of Madeira, then Tenerife in the Canary Islands off Morocco to take on a load of wine for the voyage. They were accompanied at the outset by a small tender brig, the *Jackall*, which promptly got separated from them and, they assumed, wrecked (though it would turn up again months later, after they were almost to China and had purchased another to replace it).[23] They were traveling in a familiar corridor and had regular contact, speaking to British Indiamen on their way home, passing French and American whalers. They then continued southwest across the full span of the Atlantic to Rio de Janeiro, which young George Staunton was pleased to discover was "not so hot nor so infested with venemous serpents" as his mother had led him to believe.[24] Then came the longest leg of their voyage, catching the prevailing winds to sail back eastward across the southern Atlantic, around the Cape of Good Hope at the southern tip of Africa, and back up through the Indian Ocean to the Sunda Strait between Java and Sumatra in modern-day Indonesia.

In contrast to the ships' crews, who worked with little sleep under harsh and dangerous conditions, subject always to the bosun's whip, there was little for the gentlemen passengers to do on board the ships during the long, queasy voyage. But they managed to while away the time reading and conversing, listening to Macartney's musicians, drinking tea, and watching for curiosities of nature—unknown birds and fish, strange patterns of weather and lights in the night sky. There were occasional floggings for them to view, crew members being punished for drunkenness and other infractions. They could take exercise on the quarterdeck, counting their paces to ensure mile-long walks on the small platform. Sometimes they were able to go ashore on a volcanic island and boil a fish in a hot spring or shoot at exotic species.

Approaching one such island, Amsterdam Island in the remotest heart of the Indian Ocean more than two thousand miles from the nearest continent, its waters teeming with sea snakes and large codlike fish, they were startled to see two men up on a hill waving a handkerchief on a stick. They naturally assumed the men were shipwrecked, but it turned out they actually lived there on purpose. There were five of them altogether on the rocky island, three Frenchmen and two Americans from Boston. A French ship had left them there six months earlier with a contract to spend a year and a half procuring seal skins for eventual sale in Canton. They had forged a makeshift life for themselves on the island in the interim, building a hut of stones and clearing a path across a hill that separated them from their hunting grounds, where they had already managed to bludgeon and skin eight thousand seals. They still had a year left on their contract before the ship would finally come and pick them up to bring them to China. After a brief visit, the *Lion* and *Hindostan* left them to their grim work. The ships weighed anchor at night, the island receding behind them aglow in the dim light of its volcano.[25]

With encouragement from his father, little George Staunton occupied himself for much of the voyage with the interpreters, taking basic lessons in Chinese until he was able to hold short conversations and write a few characters. The elder interpreter, known as "Padre Cho," turned out to be cantankerous and foul-tempered. The other was more agreeable, however, a Mr. Jacobus Li with northern Chinese features, who could converse in Italian as well as his native tongue and intended to avoid censure in China by passing himself off as a foreigner. He dressed in a European uniform, accessorized with a cockade and sword. His Chinese surname Li meaning "plum," he was known to the English—unnecessarily, given the ease of pronouncing his actual name—as "Mr. Plumb."[26]

The ships of Macartney's embassy were cursed with terrible luck on their outbound journey. Perhaps it was the albatross one of the gentlemen shot at the island of Tristan da Cunha, deep in the southern Atlantic. A heavy gale blew up the night afterward, ripping loose the *Lion*'s anchor and nearly dashing the ship on the rocks. They survived that catastrophe, but as they made their way around the Cape of Good Hope and then up into Southeast Asia, the companies on board were plagued with accidents and disease. On March 28, the *Hindostan*'s cook died of a fever. The next day Macartney's carpenter was killed by natives while washing linen on shore. The day after that, a sailor died of illness. This was while they were sailing through the region where Lieutenant Colonel Cathcart, Macartney's predecessor, had died of fever on the failed embassy to China five years earlier. On April 1, they reached the island where Cathcart was buried, and Macartney and Captain Gower went ashore to see the wooden monument by the water that marked his grave. The next day, a servant on the *Hindostan* died of fever, and four days later a sailor fell from a mast into the water and drowned. The day after that another sailor died of fever. On April 12 the purser of the *Lion* died of illness. On April 23, another sailor fell from the masthead and was lost.[27]

As they made their way up into Southeast Asia they could begin to feel the gravitational pull of China. Their contact with the European ships of the Atlantic had long before given way to the vast emptiness of the Indian Ocean, but now as they reached modern-day Indonesia they entered the outer domain of Chinese shipping—gorgeous, elaborately worked seagoing junks with ribbed sails that plied the water routes from coastal China down to Vietnam, Malaysia, Java, and Sumatra to their west, the Philippines and the Spice Islands to their south, routes they had been navigating for more than a thousand years.[28] Chinese-built ships began to dominate the anchorages and settlements where the embassy stopped for water and provisions long before the *Lion* reached China itself. At the Dutch colony of

Batavia (modern-day Jakarta) they found a city of two hundred thousand people, half of whom, they were told, were Chinese—itinerant
merchants, fishermen, and settlers alike. In contrast to the indigenous
peoples of the various islands and ports along their journey, whom the
British uniformly considered to be savages, the Chinese settlers represented to them another civilization. They "appear to be a quiet and
industrious people," one passenger on the *Lion* noted with approval,
a far cry from the "savage and ferocious disposition" of the natives.[29]

The ships first touched Chinese territory at the Ladrones Islands near
Macao on June 20, 1793. Staunton took a small boat to the Portuguese
settlement for a couple of days to gather news from the East India
Company's supercargoes (who lived in Macao in the off-season until
they were allowed back to Canton in the fall). He returned to the *Lion*
delighted to share the news that the emperor had responded favorably
to Britain's proposal to send an embassy, and the officials up the coast
had been notified to attend to their needs on the way to Beijing. Even
better, the supercargoes had been told that the emperor was positively "impatient" for Macartney's arrival and greatly looked forward
to "the curious and valuable presents" they had brought for him.[30]
Staunton also reported, in a boost to British pride, that the Dutch and
Portuguese were extremely jealous. On the downside, however, he
heard that the value of the embassy's gifts had been greatly exaggerated in certain Chinese accounts, so there was a danger that the actual
presents might come as a disappointment.[31]

Padre Cho left them at Macao. He feared being arrested by the
Qing government for having gone abroad, so he went ashore and
refused to continue on to Beijing with the embassy. Only Mr. Plumb,
in his European disguise, stayed on as interpreter, though a few
Chinese-speaking European missionaries hitched a ride from Macao,
hoping to gain residence in Beijing where thirty or so French, Italian, and Portuguese Catholics had been retained over the years as
technical advisers to the emperor. Those missionaries in the capital
served as mathematicians and astronomers for the most part, and they
were strictly forbidden to proselytize. They also had to relinquish any

claim on ever returning home, so it was a lifelong calling with little hope of success or remuneration. Nevertheless, there had always been a few who felt driven to join their number.

With approval to proceed, the embassy began working its way up the coast. They were now off their charts, and the coastal features had no European names, so they went ahead and named them after themselves—Cape Gower, after the captain of the *Lion*. Cape Macartney. Staunton's Island. When they stopped for provisions and to take on pilots, the Chinese officials they encountered seemed welcoming and ready to meet their needs. Still, their course was not smooth. A gale blew up as they plied the Yellow Sea off north China, pitching the ship so violently that two more men were lost overboard, one of them a musician from Macartney's band. After the wind calmed, the fog settled in, blocking all view of land, or the ships of each other. As night fell the *Hindostan* hove to rather than risk, as one passenger put it, "a thick night in an unknown sea, and where islands so unexpectedly appear." Disease was spreading on the ships. Two of Macartney's guards died. More than a hundred men were on the *Lion*'s sick list.[32]

With so much at stake after the long and treacherous voyage, and after such a massive investment of capital in the ships, crews, passengers, and gifts, Macartney was determined that nothing should go wrong. As the *Lion* and *Hindostan* neared their final landfall, he sent around instructions on how to act in China. In them, he admonished everyone—crew, officers, passengers—to be on their absolute best behavior. They now represented Great Britain, he told them. Their conduct in China would determine how their countrymen would be treated there in the future. The whole success of the embassy depended on "gaining the good-will of the Chinese." But past tensions at Canton had, he was told, convinced the Chinese that the British were "the worst of the Europeans," and so it was the job of every man on the English ships to display "conduct diametrically opposite" and impress the Chinese anew with England's great civilization.[33]

The Chinese, Macartney explained in his instructions, were a fiercely unified nation where even the lowest members of society "were supported by their superiors in all their differences with foreigners." It was a country where those in power were "ready to avenge [the] blood" of any of their subjects who suffered conflict with an outsider.

So he insisted that even with the poorest people they encountered, his men must exercise "caution and mildness in every intercourse or accidental meeting." If anyone dared to commit a crime or harm a Chinese person while in the country, he warned, they should expect no help from him.[34]

Along with worrying about the conduct of those who accompanied him, Macartney also fretted constantly about whether he might make a wrong impression himself. On that count, the possibility that the gifts might be insufficient nagged at him. As the *Lion* sailed up the coast he coerced various gentlemen into giving up personal objects they had brought along (which they had intended to sell for profit at Canton) and donate them to the general pool of embassy gifts. To his horror, he later found out that in addition to the general embassy gifts, he was also supposed to bestow his own personal gifts on the emperor and the emperor's sons and some of the ministers, and he didn't have anything for them. So he pressured the captain of the *Hindostan* into selling him several watches he had brought along.[35] Macartney would never have classified Britain as a lesser power, but China was an empire to be reckoned with—vast in size, politically unified, prosperous almost beyond imagination. And so Lord Macartney, the first Englishman to visit the court of China's emperor, came as a supplicant, hoping to gain favor by his good behavior.

All of the worries, the preparation, and the endless voyage seemed justified as the *Lion* finally touched shore in north China and the long-dreamt-of land came into view. Macartney was overcome with delight. He imagined himself entering some unknown Eden, gazing enchanted at lands never before seen by European eyes. In his diary he noted the beauty of fields that "smiled under the hand of industry." The buildings appeared to him like drawings from books, built in an exotic style "by no means displeasing to the eye." But it was the people who really captivated him: throngs of half-naked children who ran along the shore to watch the ships, full-grown men "well-looking, well-limbed, robust and muscular." He imagined himself Shakespeare's Miranda. "How beauteous mankind is!" he wanted to bellow over the water. "Oh, brave new world that has such people in it!"[36]

The *Lion* and *Hindostan* were too large to continue once they reached the mouth of the shallow White River, so Macartney gave Captain Gower orders to wait for him with the ships at the island of Chusan partway down the coast, and they began offloading their cargo into flat-bottomed junks the Chinese provided for their inland journey. The men of the embassy wilted in the late-summer humidity, mosquitoes buzzing relentlessly around them, the air thick with the smell of mud and decay. But some indication of the hospitality they were to receive at court came as they took on supplies. They were given provisions, compliments of the emperor, that included twenty bulls, one hundred sheep, one hundred pigs, a thousand fowls, several thousand melons and pumpkins, one thousand cucumbers, one hundred and sixty sacks of rice, huge quantities of flour and steamed buns, and twenty-two crates of dried peaches. Some of the foodstuffs were suited to a different cuisine than the British were accustomed to, but they soon discovered that the soft Chinese steamed buns weren't so bad if you sliced them up and made them into toast.[37]

The embassy made its grand entrance into China on the White River, sailing on a fleet of thirty-seven imperial junks with a military escort. People ran out from villages to watch them, men and women alike—the men with shaved heads and long braids, the women with their feet bound (and not hidden away from sight as the British had expected; Macartney's artist noted that they "stumped along as publickly as they would in any country town in England"). When the wind ran against their course and they could not make sail, trackers on shore hauled the ships upriver manually, phalanxes of strong men leaning forward into harnesses of wood, singing as they pulled together. The soldiers of the military escort marched on the banks alongside, matching pace with the junks. When the ships anchored for the night, the soldiers pitched camp on the opposite shore, keeping watch through the dark from their bonfires. In the towns they passed, musicians played for them with horns and drums and gongs, and at the great city of Tianjin, soldiers at attention lined the banks of the river for a full mile.[38]

From Tianjin, the embassy sailed onward to the canal terminus of Tongzhou, where their baggage was offloaded onto carts and wheelbarrows for the overland leg to Beijing. They would stop at the capital only briefly, though, for the emperor had gone north to his summer residence in Jehol to escape the heat, and they would need to follow him there. It would be another six-day journey northward beyond the capital. They left the fragile scientific gifts in the imperial palace outside Beijing, fearing they might be broken by further travel, and James Dinwiddie stayed behind to oversee the assembly of the planetarium and lens displays so the emperor could view them when he came back to Beijing in the fall. After resting for a few days, they continued onward to the north, passing on September 5 through a gate of the Great Wall of China. The wall was crumbling, for it had been built to keep out the tribes of the north, but now one of those tribes ruled the empire, so it served no defensive purpose anymore. Little George Staunton helped himself to a few stones that had fallen from it. Macartney was impressed; he reckoned the wall to be "the most stupendous work of human hands," probably greater in extent than all of the other forts in the world put together. Its construction, he remarked in his journal, was a sign of "not only a very powerful empire, but a very wise and virtuous nation."[39]

Beyond the Great Wall, they continued northward into Manchuria—or "Tartary," as they called it—the original realm of the emperor's people. Here, they found a much smaller population and a complete absence of large towns. The hills were sharp, reminding Macartney of the Swiss Alps. The air was cooler than in China proper, crisp in the mornings, and the route wended darkly through shadowed mountain valleys, ascending slowly northward toward the summer residence of the emperor. They bumped along roughly on unsprung wooden carts over roads meant more for horses and footmen than carriages, past sparse forests of dwarf oak and walnut trees that dotted the southern faces of the slopes, past villages of isolated hill people who stared silently at them. They stopped for rest one night at a nearly abandoned palace, an imperial way station that seemed home only to squirrels.[40]

Macartney continued to worry about the gifts. As they traveled north, Mr. Plumb told him that in Tianjin there had been a report that the British were bringing along several magical gifts for the emperor. Among them were supposedly an enchanted pillow that could transport you to faraway countries in your sleep, a living elephant the size of a cat, a songbird as big as a chicken that could eat six bushels of charcoal a day, and several twelve-inch-tall men "in form and intellect as perfect as grenadiers."[41] The imaginary gifts may have sounded more marvelous to Chinese ears than planetaria and lenses, and Macartney tried to laugh off the report, but it did risk the emperor's disappointment if he should look in vain among Macartney's crates for the little men and enchanted pillow that were promised.

At last, an early departure on September 8 brought them into range of the emperor's summer quarters. They had been traveling for nearly a year since their departure from England in the autumn of 1792, and the success or failure of the embassy would likely be decided in the next few days. They stopped a mile from the imperial residence to primp and reassemble themselves for presentation, then

The Great Wall of China

set forth for the final leg of the journey in a makeshift parade formation with as much pomp as they could muster. The English soldiers
and cavalry led the way on foot, followed by a two-by-two procession
of servants, musicians, scientists, and various gentlemen. Bringing up
the rear were the elder George Staunton in a palanquin, and finally
the ambassador himself, accompanied by young Staunton, in a post-
chaise trailed by a little turbaned African boy one of the gentlemen
had brought along.[42]

The earnest paraders arrived around ten in the morning at their
designated quarters, a low-slung palace of wood and stone with eight
great steps leading up to it. But no one was there to greet them.
Macartney had been given to believe that he would be welcomed on
arrival by the imperial minister of state, a Manchu named Heshen
whom the British knew as the "Grand Choulaa" (there was in fact
no such title, though it would take Western diplomats about fifty
years to confirm that).[43] However, Heshen was nowhere to be seen.
Macartney assumed that he must have been delayed for some reason
and would be along shortly, so the soldiers made preparations to fall
into line, and the British traveling party arranged itself in formation
in front of the building, waiting ceremoniously to greet the "Grand
Choulaa" when he arrived. An hour passed that way. Then another
hour, and still he did not come. Most of the time they just stood there
waiting for him, though occasionally they would launch into an abortive parade if someone important-looking approached nearby, but
none of them turned out to be him. After six hours of standing in
formation with no sign of the imperial minister, they finally lost heart
and went inside for their dinner.[44]

In the end, it was Macartney who had to go find the "Grand Choulaa"
himself, which set an uncomfortable tone for the opening of relations. Nevertheless, over the next several days, mountains of gifts
were exchanged. The British presented their rugs, woolens, and cottons. The emperor's representatives in turn gave them an abundance
of luxurious fabrics—velvets, silks, satins—along with embroideries,
hundreds of fans, jade, a huge assortment of expensive porcelain, lac-
querware, and large quantities of top-quality tea.[45] It was in these gifts,

however, that we find the contradiction at the heart of the embassy. For the British sought to impress. They brought the finest products of their science and technology, their burgeoning industry, and their purpose was to awe the Chinese with their advancement. But this was not how embassies traditionally worked in the Qing Empire. When embassies from neighboring countries came to Beijing—from Thailand, Vietnam, especially Korea—they came to trade. While Macartney wished to negotiate for more advantageous policies in the future, and hopefully gain approval to station a permanent British minister in the capital, for the Asian diplomats who came to visit the emperor the embassy itself *was* the opportunity for trade. Thus the large quantity of high-quality trading goods that the emperor gave to the British— the silks, the porcelain, the tea. He expected that these were what they wanted above all, so they could bring them home and sell them.

Furthermore, the embassies that came from tributary states like Vietnam and Korea did not come to impress the throne; they came to seek the emperor's approval, which gave them political power back home. To demonstrate their government's legitimacy in the eyes of the powerful Qing emperor was (at least in China's eyes) to argue for their own sovereign's right to rule in his own country. And to gain this approval, they paid tribute. They readily performed the so-called kowtow before the emperor in the manner of his own ministers— a prescribed ritual of nine kneeling bows to the ground (three sets of three) to humble themselves in his presence. And it made perfect sense to do so, because in their recognizing the supremacy of the emperor of China, the eminent power in Asia, he would recognize *their* supremacy within their own, smaller countries. Whether or not such emissaries actually considered their own countries to be inferior, it was still in their best interests to follow the court's protocol. But such a relationship could hardly have been further from Lord Macartney's expectations, and it was on this issue of ceremony that the weak pageantry of the British embassy began to unravel.

Initially Macartney did not realize that he was supposed to prostrate himself before the emperor. Nor, when it was explained to him, was he willing to do so. Despite his great admiration for the prosperity and civilization of the Qing Empire, he viewed Qianlong as an equal to the king of England, entitled only to the same show of respect he would give to his own sovereign. Since Macartney would not perform anything so abject as the kowtow before his own king, he felt he could not do so before Qianlong either. In any case, he expected that the ceremony would be waived in his case, and submitted a request to that effect in advance, which he had been told was approved. But on the embassy's arrival at Jehol, Heshen denied ever having seen the request, and insisted Macartney should perform the full kowtow before the emperor. Imperial officials assured Macartney that it was just for show, "a mere exterior and unmeaning ceremony," and urged him to go forward with it.[46]

The negotiations were thorny. Macartney insisted that he would "readily" perform the ceremony of nine kneeling bows as long as it was reciprocal—that is, if a Chinese official would do exactly the same before the king of England (or rather, before the portrait of King George that Macartney had brought along).[47] Failing such reciprocity, he insisted there should be a different ceremony for "equal" states like Britain (as he, but not they, considered it), to distinguish his own powerful country from mere tributary states like Korea. In that vein, he proposed to bend on one knee before Qianlong and bow his head once, as he would do for the king of England. To Macartney's great relief, that proposal was accepted. He could now look forward to his audience with the emperor, to productive discussions of new trade privileges, and hopefully to a long residence in the capital. And that was to say nothing of what he expected would be the heightened respect for the English more widely in China once it became known that their ambassador—theirs alone—did not have to kowtow before the emperor.[48]

After a few more days of waiting, Macartney finally learned that the emperor would see him on September 14, nearly a week after their arrival. Heshen the "Grand Choulaa" still had never come to Macartney's own residence to pay his respects, which was irritating from a protocol standpoint, though lesser officials consoled Macartney that Heshen hadn't visited only because there wasn't enough room in Macartney's quarters to fit his entourage (also, they said evasively, he had hurt his foot).[49] But now that didn't seem to matter; the British diplomat would have his audience with the emperor of China, and the members of the embassy could finally enjoy a taste of success in their mission.

At three o'clock in the morning on the appointed day, the ambassador was whisked away in a palanquin, dressed in his full regalia of mulberry velvet suit, diamond star, and plume of feathers. He was followed through the dark by his suite and musicians, also done up in their best, who tried to march in formation behind him until they realized they couldn't keep up with the quick-footed Chinese porters who carried Macartney's litter, at which point they began running after him, breaking ranks as they got mixed up in various herds of pigs and donkeys that crowded the early-morning road.[50]

The servants, musicians, and gentlemen in their sweaty disarray were abandoned near the entrance to the emperor's ceremonial tent. Macartney entered, carrying above his head a jewel-encrusted golden box containing the letter from King George, accompanied by George Staunton in a scarlet Oxford gown (calculated, as misguidedly as Macartney's own outfit, to win the admiration of the "scholarly" Chinese), as well as Staunton's son and Mr. Plumb their interpreter.[51] By Macartney's own account, inside the tent he ascended the steps to the emperor's throne, knelt on one knee as agreed, and presented him with the box (also, awkwardly, some of the watches). The emperor did not seem in the slightest chagrined that the ritual had been changed. The elder Staunton later wrote that Qianlong's eyes were "full and clear, and his countenance open," in contrast to the "dark and gloomy" demeanor they had expected.[52]

The letter from King George had been rendered into Chinese with the assistance of the European missionaries in the capital. Their translation preserved the king's language of lofty admiration, even amplifying it, so what Qianlong actually read was not just that he was "worthy to live tens of thousands and tens of thousands thousand years" from the original but also that he "*should* rule" for that long, an endorsement that was absent from the original. The translators also weeded out potentially offensive references to Christianity, deleting for example a reference by the king to "the blessings which the Great God of Heaven has conferred upon various soils and climates." Furthermore, they rendered the letter into standard honorific form,

elevating the word "China" one line above the rest of the text whenever it appeared, and elevating all references to the emperor three
lines above the rest. In the form in which Qianlong read it, the letter
scarcely appeared to come from the pen of a sovereign who considered himself to be Qianlong's equal.[53]

Macartney was nearly overcome by the ornate pageantry of the
audience tent—the tapestries and carpets, the rich draperies and lanterns, "disposed with such harmony," he wrote in his journal, "the
colors so artfully varied."[54] It was as if he were inside a painting. The
"commanding feature" of the ceremony, he recalled dreamily, was
"that calm dignity, that sober pomp of Asiatic greatness, which European refinements have not yet attained." The only flaw to intrude
upon Macartney's Orientalist reverie was that he was not the only
ambassador in attendance. There were in fact several others from
various tributary states, including six Muslims from near the Cas-

The emperor arriving at his tent for the audience. Macartney in his fancy suit,
along with Staunton in his Oxford regalia and Staunton's son are at lower right.

pian Sea and a Hindu from Burma, "but," he noted jealously, "their appearance was not very splendid." Unlike Macartney, they all readily performed the kowtow.

The most unexpected moment during the audience, in which the British would take great pride, was that Qianlong offhandedly asked Heshen if any of the English could speak Chinese. That was when George Staunton's son stepped forward. Thanks to his studies with Padre Cho and Mr. Plumb on board the *Lion*, the sickly boy had mastered a few phrases of Chinese, and now he climbed the steps to the throne and bravely put them to use with the emperor. Young George did not say much (according to his own diary, "He wanted I should speak some Chinese words to him, which I did, thanking him for his presents"),[55] but it was enough that his father and Macartney could come away from the audience believing that the twelve-year-old boy was a prodigy who had impressed the elderly sovereign with his fluent mastery of the Chinese language. The truth be what it may, the boy's words were certainly enough to charm, and Qianlong gave him a small embroidered purse from his own waist as a token of his esteem.[56] Little George Staunton was thus anointed as the first Englishman since James Flint to cross the wall of language between Britain and China. Whether he wanted it to or not, that moment would set in play his entire future career.

———

After the audience, Macartney and his retinue were allowed to stay at Jehol for a few days. They took part in the emperor's birthday banquet, viewed the gardens, watched a fireworks display, and attended several opera performances—one of which, unbeknownst to them, was an idealized drama of the British embassy in which the narrator at one point announced that "the country of England, gazing in admiration at your imperial majesty, sincerely presents tribute to your court."[57] Soon, however, they were told it was time to leave Jehol and go back to Beijing. On September 21, the day of their departure, yet another of Macartney's entourage died, a gunner named Reid. Perhaps to console himself, Macartney blamed it on the dead man's intemperate appetite, noting disapprovingly that Reid had eaten forty apples that morning at breakfast. But even if Macartney refused to entertain the likelihood that his entourage suffered from a contagious disease, his hosts did not, and a certain amount of the hurry with which they were urged along was, according to gossip in the palace, because the emperor worried that the members of the British embassy might infect his court.[58]

Meanwhile, down in Beijing, the mechanist-mathematician-balloonist Dinwiddie had been busy preparing all of the instruments and scientific demonstrations for the return of the emperor from Jehol at the end of September. With help from the European missionaries of the capital who acted as his interpreters, he filled a grand hall of the imperial palace just outside the city of Beijing with the embassy's planetarium, lenses, lustres, globes, clocks, air pump, and reflecting telescope. He didn't envy the missionaries at all. It wasn't just that they had agreed never to return home, or that they were so strictly limited in where they could travel, but also their letters were read, and as foreigners they were especially susceptible to the intrigues of the court and could be ruined at whim. It was a distasteful and pathetic existence. But at least they were company, and could help him with interpretation. Before long, though, they seemed to grow tired of helping him, and then stopped coming altogether. He had no way to know it, but they had been ordered to have no more contact with the embassy.[59]

After much scrambling to assemble the lenses in their various frames and set the gigantic planetarium in motion, Dinwiddie had everything ready for the emperor's visit. The gifts were all arrayed along one wall of the palace hall, "a very Beautifull appearance, much admired by the Chinese," thought young Staunton, who saw them along with some of the palace servants when he got back from Jehol.[60] The emperor, however, would not be quite so admiring. He came to view the display on October 1, when the arrangements had only barely been finished. To Dinwiddie's eye (as he secretly watched the emperor's reflection in a mirror), Qianlong showed no particular emotion as he toured the hall. After looking at the lenses and reflecting telescope for what Dinwiddie judged to be about two minutes, he pronounced them "good enough to amuse children," and left.[61]

The emperor was finished, but at least the "Grand Choulaa" Heshen and some of the court officials came back to watch Dinwiddie's demonstrations. He started with a few mechanical experiments and the air pump, to little effect. A second round of demonstrations included showing how the giant lens could be used to melt copper coins. Heshen used it to light his pipe as a joke, much to the delight of his entourage, and seemed disappointed to learn that it could not be used to incinerate an enemy's city. The high point of the afternoon was when a eunuch stuck his finger into the beam and burned it, to great merriment all around.

But that was it. Dinwiddie had planned on conducting several more days of demonstrations leading up to the grand finale of his hot-air balloon flight over Beijing. Likewise, Macartney had expected that he and the gentlemen would winter over in the capital so he could continue his "negotiations" before eventually returning to Canton in the spring.[62] Instead, without warning, on October 6 the emperor ordered the entire embassy to leave immediately, before the cold should set in. Everything had to be packed up at once—no small feat since many of the larger shipping crates had been broken up and reworked into furniture by the embassy's carpenters. There would be no diving-bell demonstration. Dinwiddie would not get to strike awe into the people of China by floating over them in a balloon, impressing them forever with Britain's mastery of the natural world. Instead, the lustres and planetarium were hastily broken down and shoved back into their remaining packing boxes by the palace staff—despite the protests of a near-hysterical Dinwiddie that they weren't being careful enough.

For the other members of the embassy, it was every man for himself through a frantic night of repacking their trunks and crates, trying to find space to store the new gifts they had received, arguing by gesticulation with Chinese servants whose language they couldn't understand. Then, on October 7, the whole affair was over, and the embassy was sent from the capital. It was on the way out from Beijing that it finally dawned on them that the mission was not in fact a success. Rather, they were being turned out on their collective ear. As one embittered British servant put it, "We entered Beijing like paupers;

we remained in it like prisoners; and we quitted it like vagrants."[63]
Palace servants were already tearing down all the decorations in the
guest quarters before the British had even left the grounds.[64]

Macartney had no idea how deeply he had offended the emperor with
his "negotiations." As early as September 10, four days prior to the
audience, Qianlong was already so furious about the English ambassador's dithering over ritual and his attempts to drag out his time
in Jehol that he issued an edict to his ministers of state expressing
"great displeasure" with the British and declaring that he would no
longer show them any extra favors. They could keep the gifts that
were planned for them, he said, and hold the meetings that had been
promised, but otherwise they were cut off. He said that he had originally planned to let Macartney stay for a while to enjoy the sights
in Jehol, but given the "presumption and self-importance" displayed
by the English ambassador, he had decided that Macartney and his
retinue should be sent from Jehol immediately after the banquet,
then escorted from Beijing after having a day or two to pack their
belongings. "When foreigners who come seeking audience with me
are sincere and submissive, then I always treat them with kindness,"
Qianlong wrote. "But if they come in arrogance, they get nothing."[65]

The surface politesse of entertaining the embassy had gone ahead
despite the tension behind the scenes, but on a practical level Macartney's mission was doomed; he just didn't realize it yet. On October 3,
a few days before they were ordered out, Macartney received Qianlong's response to the letter from King George: an edict on imperial yellow silk, rejecting all of the British requests. Fortunately for
Macartney, he couldn't read it. The request to have a British ambassador remain at the capital, said Qianlong, was (in the language of the
translation later prepared for the king) "not consistent with the Customs of this our Empire, and cannot therefore be allowed." Qianlong
acknowledged that foreign missionaries had been allowed to live in
Beijing, but pointed out that anyone wishing to adopt such a position
"must immediately put on the Chinese dress, dwell with the Society
assigned to him, and cannot return to his Country." Such an arrange-

ment, he observed, even if he approved it for Macartney, would be quite contrary to what the king hoped to achieve. Trade was in fine hands, said Qianlong, and there was no need to change more than a century of precedent just to please one country.[66]

Qianlong pointed out that he had already given the British embassy an abundance of gifts, and they should simply be grateful and go home. As far as the British presents, on which the Company had spent so much money and about which Macartney had worried for so much of his voyage, Qianlong noted that he had accepted them not because he actually wanted them, but merely as "Tokens of your own affectionate Regard for me." In truth, he went on, "As the Greatness and Splendor of the Chinese Empire have spread its Fame far and wide, and as foreign Nations, from a thousand Parts of the World, crowd hither over mountains and Seas, to pay us their Homage, and to bring us the rarest and most precious offerings, what is it that we can want here?" In words that would sting the British for a generation, he added, "Strange and costly objects do not interest me. . . . We possess all things. I set no value on objects strange or ingenious, and have no use for your country's manufactures."[67]

Because he could not read the edict at the time and did not understand the rejection it contained, Macartney remained hopeful. Later that same day he pressed for a letter to be given to Qianlong, translated into Chinese by Mr. Plumb and copied by little George Staunton, in which he listed even more boldly than before his primary requests: for new ports to be opened to the British; for an island on the coast they could use as a storage depot for their goods; and for privileged and protected terms of trade in Canton, among other concessions. The emperor's response to that letter—in a second edict addressed to the king of England—was, as one might expect, even more blunt. It coincided with the order for the British embassy to leave, and Macartney received it on his way out from the capital.

The essential, underlying point of Qianlong's second edict was that Great Britain had no leverage with him. He laid out the long-term economic relationship of the two countries in his own terms. "The products of our empire are abundant," he wrote to King George, "and there is nothing we do not have. So we have never needed trade with foreign countries to give us anything we lacked." However, he went on, the tea, porcelain, and silk that China produced were "essential needs" for countries like England that did not have them, and so out of grace the dynasty had long permitted foreign merchants to come to Canton to purchase such goods, "to satisfy your needs and to allow you to benefit from our surplus."[68] Trade, in other words, was—and had always been—entirely a favor on China's side. England, he reminded the king, was only one of many countries that came to trade in Canton, and if he gave Britain special treatment, then he would have to give it to all the others as well.

Nevertheless, Qianlong did not propose to punish King George for his naiveté in making these requests, and he noted that it was entirely possible Macartney had acted without the king's permission. Instead, Qianlong expressed his sympathy for remote England—whose people, he observed, were so unfortunate as to live far away beyond an expansive waste where they were ignorant of the civilization of China. So he did not revoke any of Britain's existing privileges, but he did go through every single one of Macartney's requests to explain in each case why he could not possibly grant them. He also suggested that the British had betrayed their own ignorance by even making such requests in the first place.

Macartney had entertained extremely high hopes, and his failure to gain advantage in the Chinese court burned him. He wound up having quite a lot of time to brood on things before he sailed home, for it turned out that Captain Gower had been forced to take the *Lion* back down to Macao for the sake of his crew, a huge number of whom were sick, and so there was no ship waiting to convey him back to the south (the *Hindostan* remained, but Macartney complained that there wasn't room on it for everyone, and the crowding would only worsen the chances of disease).[69] With the emperor's permission, Macartney and his companions were escorted on a two-month inland journey along canals and rivers and over mountain passes to Canton—repeating the slow passage of James Flint after his farewell to the *Success* in 1759.

In Macartney's journal after Beijing, on the way back down to Canton empty-handed, his earlier wide-eyed admiration gave way to a new undertone of anger. "Can they be ignorant," he wondered in late October, "that a couple of English frigates would be an overmatch for the whole naval force of their empire, that in half a summer they could totally destroy the navigation of their coasts and reduce the inhabitants of the maritime provinces, who subsist chiefly on fish, to absolute famine?" Separately he fantasized that Britain could, from its territories in India, trigger a revolt in Tibet. Or British naval vessels could destroy the Tiger's Mouth forts guarding the river passage to Canton with just "half a dozen broadsides." They could "annihilate" the Canton trade, and the millions of Chinese employed in that trade "would be almost instantly reduced to hunger and insurrection."[70]

But—and this was an extremely important caveat—he also realized full well that if Britain showed any aggression toward China, the emperor could simply shut down their trade. Were that to happen, worried Macartney, "the blow would be immediate and heavy," and the economies of England and British India would suffer immeasurable damage with no recourse. The China trade was the lifeblood of the British Empire, and so he admitted to himself that the idea of showing force or trying to conquer territory in China, no matter how appetizing it might be to his wounded pride, was "too wild to be seriously mentioned." Given the current state of the two empires, he concluded that the best course for Britain was patience. "Our present interests, our reason, and our humanity," he concluded, "equally forbid the thoughts of any offensive measures with regard to the Chinese, whilst a ray of hope remains for succeeding by gentle ones."[71]

The Macartney mission ended as an embarrassment. Later critics would decry the "strange want of decent and manly spirit by which it was distinguished," charging that the most prominent feature of this first embassy from Great Britain to China was that it "acknowledged the inferiority of its country."[72] After the *Lion* and *Hindostan* returned home, the senior members of the embassy took their time preparing official accounts of the journey for publication, but they were beaten to the press by Macartney's valet, who quickly published a much more candid account than anything they would write—and unlike Macartney and Staunton, he, as a servant, had no vested interest in upholding the dignity of either the government or the Company. The servant's

A satirical cartoon of Macartney kneeling before
Qianlong and presenting his "gifts"

unvarnished narrative was an immediate success, going through three
reprintings in its first year alone.[73]

Macartney became a standing joke. Caricatures of him circulated, an awkward figure abasing himself before plump, overbloated
Chinese officials. The satirist John Wolcot, writing as Peter Pindar,
ridiculed him in a poem titled "Ode to the Lion Ship of War, on her
return with the Embassy from China," which begins:

> Dear Lion, welcome from thy *monkey* trip;
> Glad is the Bard to see thee, thou good Ship;
> Thy mournful ensign, half way down the staff,
> Provokes (I fear me much) a general laugh!
>
> . . .

Say, wert thou not *asham'd* to put thy prow
Where Britons, dog-like, learnt to crawl and bow?
Where *eastern* majesty, as hist'ry sings,
Looks down with smiles of scorn on *western* kings?[74]

Macartney did not endure his embarrassment silently, however. He had his own version of events, which centered on the arrogant obliviousness of the Chinese throne. And whatever the results of the embassy may have been, he was now recognized as one of the very few Englishmen qualified to speak of China. His pronouncements after he returned home to England were, if anything, even more resentful than what he had penned on the later part of his journey. He wrote a series of observations for the use of the British government and the East India Company—short essays on China's people, its economy, its agriculture, science, legal system, and so on—the unifying theme of which was that the empire was far less prosperous or stable than Europeans had previously imagined.

He had begun to explore this idea in his journal in Canton just before the voyage home. "The empire of China is an old crazy first-rate man of war," he mused, "which a fortunate succession of able and vigilant officers has contrived to keep afloat for these hundred and fifty years past; and to overawe their neighbors, merely by her bulk and appearance." China's grandeur and power, he came to believe (or wanted to believe), was illusory—or at least, it was a relic from the past that was now lost. "She may perhaps not sink outright," he wrote, continuing his nautical metaphor, "she may drift some time as a wreck, and will then be dashed in pieces on the shore; but she can never be rebuilt on the old bottom."[75]

His judgment on this matter darkened the longer he thought about it (and, it should be noted, the more bruising his dignity suffered once he was back in England). Against those in the West who imagined China to be a model of stable and virtuous government, Macartney described it instead as "the tyranny of a handful of Tartars over more than three hundred millions of Chinese." And those Chinese subjects, he predicted ominously—fed at least in part by his own wish to see the Manchu emperor humbled—would not suffer "the odium of a foreign yoke" for much longer. A revolution was coming.[76]

He did not stop there. China's day of reckoning was not just inevitable, he believed, it was imminent. "I often perceived the ground to be hollow under a vast superstructure," he wrote, "and in trees of the most stately and flourishing appearance I discovered symptoms of speedy decay." The huge population of ethnic Chinese (that is, the Han Chinese) were "now recovering from the blows that had stunned them; they are awaking from the political stupor they had been thrown into by the Tartar impression, and begin to feel their native energies revive. A slight collision might elicit fire from the flint, and spread the flames of revolt from one extremity of China to the other." The destruction of the Qing dynasty's great empire would be a savage affair, he predicted, attended by "horrors and atrocities." And it would come soon. "I should not be surprised," he concluded, "if its dislocation or dismemberment were to take place before my own dissolution."[77]

These were words written in resentment and anger by a man who had only traveled in the country for a few months. Macartney knew little of China's history or the conditions in the interior of the empire beyond the threadlike path of his own journey. He could not speak the language or read the country's books, he had no network of informants or advisers, and his understanding was irretrievably colored by his own national pride. And yet he would turn out to be more correct than he had any right to be.

CHAPTER 2

Black Wind

———◆———

The Qianlong emperor had always been larger than life. When he was eleven years old, long before he came to the throne, he was on a hunting trip with his elderly grandfather, the Kangxi emperor, when a wounded bear charged at him. The boy did not move or show any fear. He simply sat there on his pony, cool and impassive, while his grandfather shot the bear and saved his life.[1] According to the story that was handed down, that was when Kangxi decided to name Qianlong's father as his heir, to ensure that this boy—out of all of his dozens of grandsons—would one day rule China. Qianlong was enthroned in 1735 at the age of twenty-four and would rule longer than any Chinese emperor ever had, or ever would again. He presided over massive frontier wars in Central Asia and sponsored cultural projects of a scale unimaginable in the West. (At a time when there were more book titles in China than in the rest of the world combined, he oversaw the compilation of a literary encyclopedia that ran to more than thirty-six thousand volumes in length and would fill a large room.) He was an accomplished and prolific classical poet and a renowned practitioner of calligraphy, and with a firm hand for government and a taste for over-the-top displays of power and beneficence he guided the empire to its apex of prosperity.

The first Qing rulers had begun the work of carving out their empire's borders after the conquest of Beijing from the Ming dynasty in 1644. Over generations they expanded westward into Central Asia, beyond the original heartland of the fallen Ming, assimilating new territories in the southwest and the island of Taiwan to the east. But it was not until Qianlong's reign in the eighteenth century that the Qing Empire reached its fullest flower, largely setting the boundaries for the Chinese state that exists today. At its peak under Qianlong, the empire reached all the way from Manchuria in the northeast to the provinces of Guangxi and Yunnan in the southwest, and from Taiwan off the eastern coast deep into Central Asia with the territories of Xinjiang and Tibet in the far west. It was an empire of four and a half million square miles, larger than all of Europe put together.

When Macartney came to pay his respects, Qianlong was just turning eighty-two. He was a sturdy man with drooping eyes, slight jowls, and a long mustache. His reign had been long enough that he was the same ruler who sat on the throne at the time of James Flint, the same who had originally ordered British trade confined to Canton. By the time of the Macartney embassy, Qianlong had ruled China for nearly fifty-eight years. He was not alone in his longevity either, for his grandfather Kangxi had reigned for sixty-one years, from 1661 to 1722, the two of them forming the backbone of one of the most powerful dynasties in China's long history.

No matter what impression the British were left with, Qianlong was no narrow provincial. The pointed line in his edict to King George III that "strange and costly objects do not interest me"—to say nothing of his dismissal of Dinwiddie's lenses and planetarium as "sufficient to amuse children"—were primarily a matter of posturing. He had learned the virtue of outward indifference to exotic foreign objects from the *Book of Documents*, one of the Confucian classics, which said, "When he does not look on foreign things as precious, foreigners will come to him; when it is real worth that is precious to him, his own people near at hand will be in a state of repose."[2] Privately, however, Qianlong was deeply fascinated by Western inventions. He had a cherished collection of seventy intricate English clocks gathered over the years, and had written poetry on the loveliness of foreign glass as well as several poems about telescopes. He periodically

Qianlong in his old age

addressed edicts to the customs commissioner in Canton asking him to send European goods or artisans to the capital. He was a patron of the Catholic missionaries he employed at court as astronomers and cartographers, and though he allowed them little freedom, he valued the skills they brought. When James Dinwiddie was assembling the scientific equipment that Qianlong would so publicly dismiss, he did so without knowing that the emperor had actually ordered the missionaries to watch closely what Dinwiddie was doing so they could replicate his work after he was gone.[3]

Qianlong was likewise a connoisseur of European art, and had in the past kept an Italian named Giuseppe Castiglione as court painter to create European paintings of Chinese scenes for him, even portraits in oil of the emperor himself. In the 1740s he commissioned Castiglione and a French Jesuit to design and build a grand series of marble buildings in his palace outside Beijing in a rococo European style, replete with fountains and soaring columns, the rooms of which he decorated with Western artifacts. So he was scarcely unappreciative of European manufactures or aesthetics, and in any case he had in his lifetime experienced far more contact with Europeans than any king of England ever had with subjects of China. Above all, though, Qianlong knew the value of China's foreign trade at Canton, because a significant portion of the tariff income it generated went toward underwriting the lavish expenses of the imperial household.[4]

On the larger scale of the imperial economy, foreign trade was crucial during Qianlong's reign because it was the empire's primary source of silver—of which China was the largest net importer in the world, and had been since the 1600s. Foreign traders, mainly British and later American, brought silver dollars in exchange for some of the tea and silk they purchased at Canton, and from there it circulated inland, where it helped to stabilize what would otherwise have been a precarious economy. For two contrary forces were at work in the China that Macartney visited. The first was that the population had risen dramatically over the preceding several decades. Thanks to the general peace and prosperity that marked Qianlong's reign, families bore increasing numbers of children. Hardy new crops imported from the New World like corn and sweet potatoes allowed the cultivation of formerly unused land, which in turn made it possible for more of those newly born children to survive. The result was an unprecedented population boom during Qianlong's reign, in which the population of the empire doubled in size between the 1740s and the early 1790s. By 1794 there were between three and four hundred million people living in China, or one-third of the entire world's population.[5]

The other, contrary, force at work during Qianlong's reign was the state's inability to increase its revenues in proportion to the rapid growth of the population it had to govern. Roughly 80 percent of the government's income came from land taxes, which were assessed on farmers and landlords independently of how many people actually lived on a given parcel. In 1712, Qianlong's grandfather, the Kangxi emperor, in a grand gesture of confidence in his dynasty's rule (as well as to win support from influential landowning gentry), had promised that the land taxes would never be raised again. Qianlong, as Kangxi's grandson, was bound by filial piety to respect that promise. But by the late eighteenth century, that meant that the dynasty's primary source of revenue had barely risen with the conquest of mostly inarable new territory, while heavy population growth in China's fertile southern and eastern regions had led to dangerous overcrowding in the cities, great pressure on the land, and a broad migration of settlers into less hospitable regions of the country that lacked established government oversight. With such strict limits on its tax revenue, the dynasty was unable to expand the size of the government bureaucracy to levels appropriate for maintaining control over such a large and shifting population. In that context, the steady flow of silver coming in at Canton from foreign trade, as one of the few alternative sources of government income, became all the more crucial for undergirding a system that was threatening to burst at the seams.

The combination of a growing population and a stagnating government also caused a crisis for the hundreds of thousands of literate elites in the empire who hoped to become officials. For more than a thousand years, officials in China had been chosen for government work on the basis of anonymous examinations that tested their knowledge of the Confucian classics. The hope behind that system was that those who served in government would, by such means, gain their positions purely by virtue of their own personal talents, rather than through family connections or the influence of wealth. Furthermore, as Confucius had placed the virtues of loyalty and righteousness at the center of his teachings, successive emperors trusted that officials who had been indoctrinated from youth with Confucian morals would, once they were posted to their jobs in the provinces, prove loyal and righteous even without direct supervision from the capital.

To outsiders, the Chinese examinations had always been one of the most admired facets of Chinese civilization. Eighteenth-century French philosophers hailed them as a model of meritocracy free from the pernicious influence of heredity or the church. Voltaire wrote, "The human mind certainly cannot imagine a government better than this one where everything is to be decided by the large tribunals, subordinated to each other, of which the members are received only after several severe examinations." Montesquieu, admiring how China's scholar-officials were steeped in Confucian morals, wrote that they "spent their whole youth in learning them, their whole life in the practice. They were taught by their men of letters, and . . . China was well governed." In the mid-eighteenth century there had been calls in British popular magazines to establish a meritocratic exam system in England like the one in China, a wave that would culminate in 1806 with the East India Company's establishment of a competitive exam of its own in London, inspired largely by what its traders had learned of the Chinese system in Canton. The Company's exams selected men for service in India, and would in turn become the foundation of the British government's own civil service exams when they were established in the mid-nineteenth century.[6]

For all the admiration of the Chinese examinations by outsiders, however, by the late eighteenth century the system was beginning to fail. It had always been extremely difficult to pass the exams, but as the population expanded in the Qianlong reign there were far more candidates than before who wanted to take part in the competition, and proportionally fewer government jobs with which to reward them. The competition became more and more fierce, and great numbers of talented candidates were left behind, creating a glut of highly educated men with few career prospects. They generally found unsatisfying work as tutors, secretaries, and bureaucratic underlings, unreliable jobs that required a high level of literacy and education but were transient and depended entirely on the patronage of their individual employers. These men were failures in the eyes of their parents, many of whom had spent lavish sums on their sons' educations in hopes of their becoming officials and bringing power and prestige to the family.

Furthermore, even those scholars who did manage to pass the examinations might still have to wait ten or twenty years before a position in the imperial bureaucracy opened up to them through normal channels. By consequence, the system of civil appointments became fertile ground for bribery schemes. Those who controlled the appointments demanded huge fees from qualified candidates before they would give them a position—in essence, forcing them to purchase their jobs, and then often making them pay yearly sums to hold on to them. As the practice spread, great numbers of officials began their careers in heavy financial debt to their superiors—debts they were expected to make up for by squeezing bribes from their own inferiors or finding other ways (such as embezzlement) to supplement their meager salaries and pay for the fees and gifts that were required of them.

At the lowest levels, where the vast imperial governing apparatus reached the level of the common people, this pyramid of graft resulted in widespread petty oppression and outright cruelty by minor officials towards the populations they governed—especially the peasants and those on the margins of society, who were most vulnerable to their extortions. Such victims had little or no effective legal recourse if they were harassed or beaten or had their meager property taken by greedy officials. All they could really do, if they were desperate enough, was to revolt.

In the spring of 1794, as the *Lion* was departing from Macao for its voyage back to England, a rumor was making its way through the mountainous counties of north-central China that a "True Master" had appeared in Shanxi province. The Master was marked, it was said, with the character for the sun imprinted on his left hand and the character for the moon on his right—together they formed the character "Ming," the name of the previous dynasty (and thus a marker of rebellion against the Qing). According to the rumor, a great boulder in the village of the Master's birth had suddenly split open one day, revealing a scripture hidden inside that read:

> A black wind will blow for a day and a night.
> It will destroy men beyond number.
> White bones will be piled into mountains, and
> Blood will flow to become an ocean.[7]

An apocalypse was coming, said those who carried the rumor through central China. The only way to escape destruction was to memorize the scripture from the rock and begin chanting it—and then to start stockpiling guns, swords, and powder in preparation to support the Master's uprising. A date was set for the spring of 1796, two years later, when the black wind would blow and all would rise up together to destroy the world of old and usher in a new age.

A peasant named Zhang Zhengmo, who lived in a remote, mountainous county of western Hubei province in north-central China, was one of many who heard the rumor that spring and believed it.[8] He was thirty-two years old at the time, and heard it from an itinerant sect leader named Bai from a northern county, who explained to him that the True Master's doctrine was a branch of the White Lotus teachings. White Lotus sects had been around for hundreds of years in rural China, a loose conglomeration of religious groups with certain shared tenets from Buddhism and Daoism but a variety of competing teachers. Most of the time, the White Lotus sects were harmless, their practices centering on promises of faith healing and protection from misfortune. But their religion was also, by varying degrees, a millennial one: it contained a prediction of apocalypse, and its followers believed in a second coming of Buddha, who would return in the form of a bodhisattva named Maitreya to destroy the world of corruption and suffering. Maitreya would annihilate the government and the disbelievers and build a new utopia to reward those who helped bring about the "turning of the kalpa," as the coming apocalypse was called.

This undercurrent of potential violence in the religion was well known to the government, for White Lotus sects had sparked uprisings of various sizes all the way back through the Ming era—some even linked them to the rebellion that brought the Ming dynasty to power in the first place. The new strains of the religion that began to emerge in the early 1790s—around the time of Macartney's visit, though far from the regions where he and his entourage traveled—were, however, far more virulent than most. Their message was more urgent, their appeal more attractive in a time of uncertainty.

Zhang Zhengmo became a convert, and Bai the traveling sect leader became his teacher, explaining the True Master's doctrine to him and helping him plan for his next steps. Zhang donated what small amounts of money he could to his teacher, and started hoarding weapons. He also began actively recruiting other disciples to become his own students just as he himself had first been recruited: by telling them the tale of the True Master's coming, and asking those who believed him to start raising money, to collect weapons, and finally to go forth and continue spreading the word to others.

———

The region of China where Zhang Zhengmo lived was an internal frontier of the empire, a heavily mountainous territory where the provinces of Hubei, Sichuan, and Shaanxi pressed up against one another and where government control had always been tenuous. Known as the Han River Highlands for the fierce tributary of the Yangzi River that carves a deep path through it, the region had an inhospitable topography that ensured it was one of the last areas in central China opened up to settlement. Its society was less firmly grounded as a result. Dense with old-growth forests and steep, heavily vegetated hills, it was attractive to the fringes of Chinese society—bandit gangs lived comfortably there, and criminals could easily find sanctuary.

But it was also, because of its late development, one of the few regions left in eighteenth-century China with excess land for clearing and cultivation. The population boom of Qianlong's reign saw a massive influx of poor settlers, pioneers driven from the crowded southern and eastern parts of the empire who meticulously cleared its hillsides to plant crops, or who took up occupations in the hills making charcoal or working as hired laborers. By the time Zhang Zhengmo came to adulthood there, the region's population had grown many times over and pressures on the land had increased beyond what it could possibly support, forcing competition between settlers over water and other necessary resources.[9] Fitting with its tradition as a frontier society, such conflicts were more often than not settled with violence.

The Han River Highlands were a fearful and unstable place to live in the late eighteenth century, with little security from the region's scant government supervisors, and so the White Lotus warnings of a coming apocalypse—and the promise of safety for those who followed their teachings—found ready acceptance among the settlers. By 1794 the government was aware of the increased sect activity in the region and knew in general terms that religious groups were planning for some kind of insurrection, so provincial authorities went to work trying to dismantle the White Lotus cells before they could cause trouble. The crackdown began in 1794, focusing initially on groups based in the neighboring provinces of Sichuan and Shaanxi and then expanding into Hubei. There was nothing subtle about Qianlong's instructions for handling the White Lotus. In an edict in September of that year, he ordered that all captured sectarians should be punished according to the nature of their guilt. For spiritual leaders, that meant execution by cutting them into pieces. Those who spread the White Lotus teachings or played major roles in stirring up trouble would be beheaded. Mere followers, Qianlong ordered, should be arrested and shipped off to Manchuria as slaves.[10]

As instructed, the local government authorities (such as they were, for government presence had always been thin and so much of the work was done informally by village headmen) began organizing forces to round up White Lotus practitioners. Within a few months they had managed to arrest twenty teachers and more than a hundred of their followers. However, the brutality of their exhaustive house-to-house searches only made the tense situation worse. There were not enough regular troops to support such a broad operation, so local thugs were hired to conduct the searches. They demanded bribes of guilty and innocent people alike, threatening to have them arrested as sectarians if they didn't pay up. Those who somehow managed to prove that they were not White Lotus followers—or at least who paid the thugs what they asked—were given placards to put on their doors marking them as "good people." Everyone else, however, remained suspect, vulnerable to the gangs hunting for religious sect members, fearful of the savage punishments that would follow if anyone were to accuse them of being religious subversives.[11]

Like many others who shared his newfound spiritual beliefs, Zhang Zhengmo heard about the searches and abandoned his home before the inspection gangs could reach him. He returned to his native county, nearby in the same province, where he had a greater chance of secrecy and knew the lay of the land better. He continued recruiting followers as he went. By the late winter of 1796—just three years after Macartney's dire prediction that a revolution was about to explode in China—Zhang had converted, by his estimate, more than a thousand other men and women to his religion. His planning had been patient, but on the fifteenth of February, still two months from the planned date for the general uprising, he learned that local authorities were mounting a renewed crackdown that seemed likely to reach him.[12] Fearing arrest, he preempted their arrival. He called his immediate followers together and told them the time had come.

Zhang's followers took to the roads, where they soon joined up with other cells that had grown around other recruiters with whom he had contacts. In just a few days, more than ten thousand White Lotus believers converged under Zhang's leadership, carrying swords, guns, powder, and other supplies on their backs. They plundered villages to take supplies, conscripting their residents and stealing their food. This caused no moral discomfort to Zhang's followers, because unbelievers, as they had been taught, would be destroyed when Buddha returned anyhow, so there was no reason to refrain from harming them now. Amassing forced conscripts and new converts, and soon numbering upward of twenty thousand, they set up barricades to block the roads from government soldiers. Then they took to the hills.

The first base for Zhang Zhengmo's army was the mountain estate of a wealthy convert, but Zhang worried that the site was too vulnerable to attack, so he led his followers deeper into the mountains, to a strategic pass he knew they could hold. They built a camp with thousands of shacks of grass and wood, planting white banners and adopting white headbands to identify themselves as rebels.[13] For weapons, they had swords and knives, along with an arsenal of three hundred matchlock rifles and six cannons carved from chestnut wood, which they supplemented by preparing hundreds of poison-tipped crossbow arrows. They set up a perimeter defense, laying makeshift land mines along the paths leading through the mountains to their camp and building a series of stone guard towers, manned by sentries equipped with guns and cannons as well as hewn logs and heavy rocks to crush attackers.[14]

In spite of the two years of advance preparation, however, they were poorly led. Zhang Zhengmo was reluctant to take his followers down from the hills, fearing that they would be slaughtered by the government soldiers who surely waited for them in the forested valleys below. So they dug in and remained in place as the months passed, sending down occasional raiding parties to bring back supplies. Winter gave way to spring, then summer, and in the dense heat of June a plague killed two or three thousand inside the camp.

By July they were still unable to move, but Zhang knew from his scouts that a cordon of government troops was slowly closing in. He burned his name registers in hopes that some of his followers could escape without leaving a record of their involvement. They had no real master; Zhang realized that he was no proper religious teacher. He had never even laid eyes on the rumored True Master, though the others all thought he had. They looked to him alone for guidance, so he lied to them, showing them an old sword he happened to own and telling them it had been given to him personally by the True Master. He tried to give them what faint hope he could.

When he had called for the uprising to begin, Zhang Zhengmo thought that all of the White Lotus followers from miles around would come to join them. But after the initial stage they had stopped coming, so he guessed that the others must have been captured and killed. There was no longer anywhere for his followers to go to escape, and no one who was coming to help them. Maitreya had not come. The kalpa had not turned. He held out for two months longer, but when the government troops finally broke through to his encampment in September, he led his followers in kneeling down before them in surrender.

Before Zhang Zhengmo was executed, a government interrogator demanded to know why he and his followers had rebelled. "You are all peasants," the interrogator said. "You receive the blessings of the emperor. He relieves you of taxes and tribute grain. He relieves your debts. When there is a flood or a drought he gives you aid. You have a human heart, and you should feel gratitude and abide by the laws. So why, under the banner of these evil teachings, did you start a rebellion? In the end, what was it you *wanted*?" Zhang did not contradict him (facing imminent execution, he had little choice). "We have indeed received blessings from the emperor," he replied. "We had warm clothes and could eat our fill. We were peasants, and we were grateful."[15]

But, Zhang went on, he had not initially joined the White Lotus for any reason of anger or seditiousness. "It was at a time when I was ignorant, that I first began to practice this religion," he told his questioner. "It was only because I wanted to encourage people to do good deeds and to avoid misfortune. But then the investigations and arrests intensified, and I saw that when people who practiced our religion were captured, all of them were charged with heavy crimes. So I became afraid." In other words, it was the vicious crackdown on the White Lotus sect that caused him to rebel. This was the crux of his confession, and it would be repeated many times over by others in his same situation—the only reason he rose up against the government, he said, was because he was afraid of it.

Taken alone, Zhang Zhengmo's rebellion might have been unremarkable—one of a long history of attempted peasant uprisings, reckless bursts of defiance against cruel local officials that typically ended with pathetic failure and in most cases brutal execution of the leaders. But Zhang and his followers had not been nearly so alone as they thought. Unknown even to those who were caught up in it, as soon as Zhang Zhengmo launched his own uprising, the "black wind" had begun to spread. The vast range and appeal of the apocalyptic rumors that had seized Zhang's imagination and redirected the course of his own life only became known for real once the spring of 1796 arrived and he took up his arms. As the news from Zhang's county spread by word of mouth through the province, other uprisings began exploding spontaneously all through the hill counties of the Han River Highlands. He didn't know it, but he was the spark that had set the woods aflame. By the time the government soldiers broke through into Zhang Zhengmo's camp, his home province of Hubei was fully engulfed and waves of rebellion were spreading across the unprotected borders into the neighboring provinces of Sichuan and Shaanxi. By the time the government forces finally captured him, the White Lotus uprisings had already spread so far and so quickly that in the grand scheme of things he no longer mattered at all.

———

On February 9, 1796, the first day of the lunar new year and just six days before Zhang Zhengmo's uprising began, Qianlong gave up his throne. The abdication had been planned for a long time, as far back as his enthronement in 1735, soon after which he had issued an edict saying that he hoped to rule for as long as his grandfather Kangxi had—sixty-one years—but no longer. Keeping his word, on the surface at least, at the close of his sixtieth year as emperor he staged an elaborate ceremony of abdication in which he formally stepped down from power and his son Jiaqing was made the new ruler of the empire.

The abdication, however, was meaningless. Jiaqing was indeed enthroned as emperor, and beyond the confines of the capital all calendars recorded the new year as Jiaqing Year 1. But within the capital, which was the place where the emperor really mattered, it was the beginning of Qianlong Year 61. Two calendars were kept, two sets of imperial annals, one reflecting the new emperorship of Jiaqing, and the other the continued reign of Qianlong as the "supreme retired emperor." Qianlong thus continued to rule in reality while his son ruled only in name. Jiaqing was a figure with no real power, and there was nothing he could do about it.

It might have been better for China if the abdication had been sincere. For as effective a ruler as Qianlong had been in his prime, already by the time of the Macartney mission in 1793 he was nearing the end of his useful reign. Not that the British travelers noticed any outward signs of weakness. Macartney judged him to be "of great bodily strength . . . little afflicted with the infirmities of age," and along with noting his "full and clear" eyes, Staunton wrote that he "marched firm and erect." [16] But they only met him briefly and were distracted by the novelty of the grandeur in which they found themselves. Others who spent more time at court in the years to follow would see something different. The year after Macartney's visit, a Korean diplomat reported to his superiors that the emperor was acting erratically. Among other odd behaviors, on one occasion he ordered breakfast immediately after having finished his breakfast. He appeared to be slipping into senility. Three years later, in 1797, another Korean envoy reported that in the evening Qianlong could no longer remember what had happened in the morning, or what he had done the day before.[17]

One of the great dangers of a weak emperor in China was that factions from within the court could vie for power—not to usurp the emperor directly, but to assume imperial powers in his name. Such a process began to play out in the final years of Qianlong's rule, accelerating with the decline in his mental clarity. The official who quite masterfully insinuated himself into the real seat of power in Qianlong's dotage was Heshen, the Manchu courtier whom the British had known as the "Grand Choulaa." Heshen had first caught the Qianlong emperor's eye in 1775, when he was a young imperial bodyguard stationed at the gate to the inner court of the Forbidden City. He was an effete and startlingly good-looking man. A Korean who saw him in 1780 described him as "elegant in looks, sprucely handsome in a dandified way that suggested a lack of virtue."[18] Within a year of their first encounter, Qianlong was fully smitten with Heshen and gave him a stunning series of promotions, including an appointment to the Grand Council—the elite inner circle of the emperor's advisers, which operated outside of the regular government's supervision and could in some cases act in the emperor's name.[19]

Over the two decades that followed, Heshen held on to his special position as Qianlong's favorite minister and steadily accumulated greater powers and influence. In 1780, at the age of thirty, he was made president of the Board of Revenue, one of the six branches of the imperial government, with oversight of the imperial treasury. In that same year his son married Qianlong's favorite daughter, joining their families together. In 1784 he became president of the Board of Civil Affairs, another of the six branches of the government, with oversight of the entire system of civil service appointments. His relationship to the elderly emperor was so close that as Qianlong's faculties began to slip, Heshen increasingly spoke and acted on his behalf. By the 1790s, even an outside observer like George Staunton could see that Heshen "enjoyed, almost exclusively, the confidence of the emperor," and that he "might be said to possess, in fact, under the emperor, the whole power of the empire."[20]

As it happened, Heshen was also terrifically corrupt. In a time when corruption was eating through the ranks of government like a disease, he was unrivaled in the sheer audacity and extravagance of his misconduct. Through his positions of power in the capital during the 1780s and 1790s he was able to treat large swaths of the government bureaucracy as his own personal patronage network. Far from the Chinese ideal of government by humble scholars selected on the basis of virtue through merit-based exams, the officials he put into place in—to give just one example—the Yellow River Conservancy, which handled all funding for flood control over the course of China's second-longest river, were chosen by himself, and he expected them to pay him handsomely for the privilege. The conservancy presented ample opportunity for embezzlement from the roughly six million taels of silver the government spent each year on preventing the Yellow River from flooding, and by the tail end of the eighteenth century, with Qianlong drifting away and Heshen ascendant, only about one-tenth of the funds the government gave the conservancy actually made it into public works projects. The rest went to enriching the officials themselves, who spent the money on elaborate banquets and expensive gifts for Heshen. Even worse for those peasants who suffered in the broad floodplain of the river known for its destructiveness as "China's Sorrow," the officials in the Yellow River Conservancy found that it was in their best interests to allow the river to breach its dikes periodically, just to make sure that government funds would continue flowing into their pockets.[21]

Heshen's corruption was vividly apparent to others at court, but to make an accusation against him or anyone in his inner circle was to invite ruthless punishment from him in retaliation. A truly upright Confucian official would accept such risk of unjust punishment stoically, but to make an accusation against Heshen also risked the far more grievous effect of criticizing the emperor himself for having trusted Heshen, which amounted to saying in effect that Qianlong had lost control of his government. If some thought it, none dared say so publicly. Thus the criticisms of conscientious officials were

reserved for those lower down on the ladder of power, provincial officials attached to Heshen, while he himself remained untouchable.[22]

When the White Lotus rebellion began to spread, its remarkable
speed and range were only partly attributable to the fact that there
were so many more believers preparing for the apocalypse than even
an individual sect leader like Zhang Zhengmo could have imagined.
The other reason, in a perilous harmony with the first, was that there
were also far fewer government forces on hand to respond to the initial uprisings than there should have been. Due to an outbreak of
violence between Han Chinese settlers and the Miao minority group
in Hunan province to the south of Hubei in 1795, most of the regular
government forces that would normally have been stationed in the
region of the first White Lotus uprisings had been transferred down
to Hunan. The transfers left only skeleton garrisons in Zhang's native
province, entire counties with fewer than a hundred government soldiers each.[23]

Officials throughout the province were caught unprepared. In
one county seat about a hundred miles northwest of where Zhang
Zhengmo holed up with his followers, a scant force of a few dozen
imperial soldiers with insufficient weapons faced a much larger army
of rebels that massed outside the city's walls in preparation to invade.
Wildly outmatched, the ranking city official was reduced to ordering
the townspeople to start carving sticks of wood into clubs and cutting bamboo into sections to be used as makeshift gun barrels. He
put the women and children to work rolling stones into place to but-
tress the city's wall, and assembling firebombs. Across the province,
overwhelmed and underprepared government forces resisted the
rebels with whatever weapons they could muster—matchlock guns,
fireballs, giant stones, vats of boiling water. They called for reinforce-
ments from neighboring provinces. But the rebellions were too much
for them to control.[24]

With such a severe shortage of imperial soldiers, local gentry in
the various towns began taking self-defense into their own hands,
raising small, improvised militias by hiring peasants and giving them

weapons. These mercenary forces did little to help anyone other than their own masters, however. One witness in a town about thirty miles north of Zhang Zhengmo's camp recalled seeing a private militia arrive on the scene, the gentryman on horseback and dressed richly in furs, escorted by private soldiers carrying pikes and swords. Rather than setting up some kind of defense for the town, however, they looted it. "The so-called militia soldiers," wrote the witness, "just continued the work of stealing everything the refugees had left behind in their houses. There wasn't an empty hand anywhere . . . if the White Lotus rebels are like an ordinary comb, the private militia are the fine-toothed one."[25] And those were the more disciplined groups. Other "militias" he saw were just gangs of bandits, who dressed themselves in red sashes on which they had written the characters for "village militia." They killed with impunity—entire families when they felt like it—and if anyone asked then why they had killed someone they would just say that they had found them in possession of a piece of white cloth, which proved they were part of the rebellion.[26]

The rebels were all called "White Lotus" by the government, but they had many other names for themselves, for in reality they represented a wide range of religious sects that had little direct contact with one another. Nevertheless, although these separate sects had originally competed with each other for members and funding before the rebellion, once it was under way they coalesced in common resistance to their shared enemy: the Qing government. "The officials oppress, and the people rebel" became the slogan of the White Lotus rebellion writ large, painted on banners and written in proclamations, a constant incantation in the confessions of captured White Lotus followers no matter what their backgrounds. And it was a vicious cycle, for as the government redoubled its efforts to extinguish the sects, their justification to rebel became all the more strong, and their uprisings all the more fierce.[27]

———

Although the rebellion did not begin until after Qianlong abdicated his throne, there was no question that he would be the emperor to direct its suppression; he did not trust his son Jiaqing with such responsibilities. But Qianlong saw religious uprisings as local problems that should be dealt with by local forces. To him, internal unrest was of a far lower degree of danger to the empire than a frontier war, so he denied requests to send in the elite Manchu forces that had been almost universally victorious against the Qing dynasty's enemies in Inner Asia. Instead, he required provincial officials to use their own resources to combat the religious sectarians.[28] Even though he would not send elite government troops, however, he did give the local officials generous financial support—which he could do because coming into the White Lotus rebellion the Qing treasuries were flush with a surplus of more than seventy million taels of silver.

Failing to secure the deployment of Manchu troops from the capital, and short on regular forces, provincial officials followed the lead of local gentry and began to organize their own militias of armed peasants, on a larger scale than the privately led forces that had preceded them. At the outset of the rebellion, these government militias were still modest—a few hundred informal soldiers in most counties, sometimes as many as a few thousand. But as the rebellion spread into neighboring provinces and the military funding from Beijing increased, their numbers exploded. By 1798, the province of Hubei would have nearly four hundred thousand militiamen registered on its books, while the neighboring provinces of Sichuan and Shaanxi each raised their own militia armies of comparable size. In concert with the roughly one hundred thousand regular army soldiers transferred in to fight the rebellions, the three provinces reported a total of more than one million men in arms spread across the entire White Lotus war zone. In just two years, the uneasy border society of settlers in the Han River Highlands had broken down into almost complete militarization.[29]

Far from proving effective against the rebellion, however, these legions of militia soldiers did far more harm than good. Militia soldiers could come from any background, as reliable and stable as farmers, or as rootless and unknowable as unemployed migrants, and a substantial number were petty criminals who joined the militia ranks for the good pay that was offered—pay that was equal to or better than the salaries of the regular military, without the long-term commitment or the same kind of discipline. It was an attractive option for anyone who wanted to take advantage of the breakdown of order—safer, at any rate, than individual banditry, and it came with license to carry weapons. Also, since the militia soldiers had no allegiance beyond the money they were paid, under the right conditions they readily defected to the side of the rebels. This happened with such frequency that by the later years of the war, half the White Lotus armies were thought to be made up of former militia troops.[30]

Among the regular government troops, furthermore, cowardice and poor discipline reigned. The governor-general of Sichuan province reported with disgust that when government forces went into battle they made the militia charge in ahead of them and then hung back where they would be safe. If the militiamen got turned back by the rebels and started to run away, the government soldiers just ran after them. He described the kinds of false victories that were being reported—where government soldiers would wait for the rebels to move on from a camp, and then after the rebels had been gone for a few days they would start firing their cannons and charge in, murdering innocent refugees from nearby villages and setting their bodies up in the abandoned camp to make it look like they had been rebels. In fact, he said, the two sides scarcely even encountered each other: "Where the rebels are, there are no government forces; and where the government forces are, there are no rebels." In the final count, the depredations and abuses of the government troops were so awful that the peasants had begun calling them the 'Red Lotus,' because they were even more violent and murderous than the rebels were.[31]

Meanwhile, Qianlong's deepening senility, coupled with his insistence on maintaining personal control over the campaign, meant that the real command of the dynasty's war against the White Lotus fell into the hands of Heshen, who treated it as the greatest opportunity for self-enrichment of his entire career. As Qianlong obsessed over details of the fighting, reading reports night and day—so worried, according to his son, that he was barely able to sleep or eat—Heshen was able to control what information would or would not reach him. He provided Qianlong with fictionalized reports of victories against the rebels to make it seem as if the campaign was progressing well, and prevented him from seeing reports of setbacks and defeats. He installed his protégés in key military positions and created honors to reward them for victories that never occurred. He whitewashed the massacre of civilians by government troops, channeled military funds into his own pockets as well as those of his followers, and protected incompetent officers who paid him tribute.[32]

For the first three years of the war, Heshen effectively controlled the central government's disbursement of military funds, and under his patronage an extraordinary level of fiscal corruption crept into the White Lotus campaign. It would later turn out that a substantial portion of the hundreds of thousands of militia soldiers who had been recruited to fight the White Lotus did not in fact exist. Military officials had been padding their rosters with fake names so they could pocket the salaries of the nonexistent soldiers (along with the funds for the equipment they did not need and the food they would never eat). Furthermore, for the militia soldiers who *did* exist and were killed fighting the rebels, corrupt officers found ways to embezzle their death benefits, which in many cases never reached their families—thus also creating a perverse incentive for officers to have more of their soldiers die in battle. Militia-related expenses claimed the lion's share of the exorbitant military funds the central government funneled into the White Lotus war, and at least half of those funds, the Jiaqing emperor would later determine, were siphoned off by corrupt military commanders before they could ever be spent on the war itself.[33]

The violence and tenacity of the White Lotus uprisings were thus tightly intertwined with the corruption of the government. Rebel leaders blamed cruel and self-serving officials for having forced them to revolt in the first place, while dishonest military officials in turn botched the suppression so badly that they fanned the rebellions to greater and greater heights. If the slogan of the rebels was "The officials oppress, and the people rebel," in time a good number of upright officials loyal to the dynasty would come to see the war in exactly the same terms. As one loyalist scholar described the corruption of officials in Hubei during the years leading up to the war, "At first they nibbled away like worms, gradually taking more and more until they were gulping like whales. In the beginning, their embezzlements could be reckoned in hundreds and thousands of taels, but presently nothing less than ten thousand would attract notice. Soon amounts ran to scores of thousands, then to hundreds of thousands, then to millions."[34] Another supporter of the dynasty declared that among the lower-level officials, "Not even two or three out of ten behaved uprightly."[35] Such critics maintained that there was no way the Qing government could suppress the White Lotus uprisings until it cracked down on its own corrupt bureaucrats, who continued to give the insurgents a justification to rebel.[36]

———————

Qianlong had expected an easy victory against the White Lotus. In falsifying so much of their expenditures, the commanders in the field created on paper what should have been a rout, with hundreds of thousands of militia soldiers mobilized to suppress sectarian groups that numbered only in the thousands or tens of thousands. Yet the war did not end. After all of the positive reports of victory that Heshen had forwarded to him, Qianlong was maddened and confused by the refusal of the White Lotus leaders to submit. The war weighed on him, obsessed him in his final years, occupied his full attention—or at least what remained of it in his decline. "I left my rule," he wrote sadly in a poem in 1798, "but still I work diligently at government. And now I see that in these past two years it has only gotten worse."[37]

By the time Qianlong reached the end of his long life, in 1799, the cost of fighting the relentless White Lotus rebellions had already reached nearly one hundred million taels of silver—a monstrous sum equal to two entire years of the imperial government's revenue.[38] It had completely exhausted the huge treasury surplus that predated the war, but there was no end in sight. It was the most expensive campaign the dynasty had ever fought, and its lack of success broke Qianlong's spirit. After his unparalleled reign—the longest and one of the most successful in China's history—he died in a position of helplessness, the treasuries emptied, the moral foundations of the empire shifting like sand beneath him.

CHAPTER 3

The Edge of the World

———

Five hundred miles to the south of the Han River Highlands, the grand port city of Canton was isolated from the turmoil of the ongoing rebellion but not from the rising tide of corruption that had helped provoke it. Given the vast amounts of money that traded hands in Canton—it was the third-largest city in the world at the time, surpassed only by London and Beijing—official appointments there were plum positions, some of the ripest in the empire for individual graft.[1] Canton was the capital of populous Guangdong province and home to a large civil government overseen by a provincial governor, then, above him, a governor-general. The governor-general was responsible for both Guangdong and neighboring Guangxi province, and he answered directly to the emperor—but as the saying went, "Heaven is high, and the emperor is far away." The governor's lavish offices and mansion were inside the city of Canton itself, while the governor-general, though formally based in a different town, also kept offices in Canton and spent much of his time there.

Foreign trade followed a separate path of authority than the civil government. At the level of actual face-to-face commerce, a small group of Chinese commercial families known as the Hong merchants, typically numbering about a dozen, were given a monopoly over commerce with foreigners. All Western trade had to come through them—if you were a foreign ship's captain, your cargo would have to be guaranteed by one of the Hong merchants before you could sail up the river to Canton. Only that Hong merchant could rent you warehouse space, and he alone was supposed to be able to arrange with you for the purchase of whatever tea or silk you wished to bring home. Personal relationships were key, and a close friendship with an individual Hong merchant was an immensely valuable boon for any foreigner involved in the Canton trade. However, the Hong merchants were also accountable for the conduct of all personnel on the ships that they guaranteed. So if a drunken sailor got into a fight with a local Chinese, an event that happened with some frequency, it was the Hong merchant who was held responsible.

With such a small number of Hong merchants controlling the full trade of China with Great Britain, America, and the European continent, the opportunities to get rich were abundant. However, the Hong merchants also had to manage enormous business risks. They had to calibrate gigantic shipments of tea from the Yangzi River valley more than seven hundred miles away, ensuring the quality and amount of the product, orchestrating its packing and transportation on rivers and overland to Canton, making sure that it all arrived on time for loading onto the foreign ships that sailed once a year. They had to bear the risk of market fluctuations as poor weather, floods, and crop shortages—and, now and then, rebellions—drove up prices on commodities for which they had contracted with foreign traders. From the other direction they had to bear the risk of falling demand for fashionable import products (like seal skins) that they purchased from abroad.

Above all, though, their access to capital made them primary targets for exactions by the government—large, involuntary donations to support military campaigns and disaster relief. Sometimes the amounts involved could be huge; their "contributions" to the White Lotus campaign, for example, amounted to more than three million taels of silver (worth more than four million dollars at the time, which the Jiaqing emperor celebrated as if the donations had been voluntary). The Hong merchants thus comprised some of the richest men in China, but they also went bankrupt with great regularity. And this

The house and gardens of a wealthy Chinese merchant in Canton

cycle was difficult to escape, for an individual Hong merchant was not allowed to resign without permission from the very officials who squeezed him.

The senior superintendent of foreign trade at Canton was the imperial customs commissioner, known to foreigners as the hoppo, whose offices were located just to the north of the factory compound. He reported directly to the Board of Revenue in Beijing, and all of the Hong merchants were responsible to him. It was the hoppo who was responsible for ensuring a proper flow of tariff income to the capital, and of all the government positions in Canton, his was the one with the greatest opportunities for self-enrichment.

The hoppos were often unpopular with the foreign traders at Canton, and they hardly fared better in the eyes of their Chinese contemporaries. A popular Chinese novel published in 1804 and set in Canton, *Mirage*, gives a clear enough picture of how the holders of this office were seen by the cynical Chinese around them. The story's villain was a newly arrived hoppo named Master He—who, the novel tells us, "had schemed to be the superintendent of the Canton Customs for the sole purpose of getting rich and indulging in sex."[2] The story begins with his arrival in the city, saddled with enormous debt from the bribes he had paid to get his position. His first order of business was to make good on his debts by arresting all of the Hong merchants, charging them with corruption, and threatening them with beatings and exile until they came up with a huge payment of several hundred thousand taels—which was worth more than the actual value of their businesses.

———

The foreign traders in their comfortable factories were only dimly aware of the White Lotus rebellion that raged deep within China's interior in the mid-1790s, and so, knowing as little as they did of events closer by, their much greater concern was that Britain and France had gone to war. In January 1793, the Jacobins beheaded Louis XVI, sending a shock wave through the monarchies that had initially welcomed France's revolution. Eleven days later, the French Republic declared war on Great Britain—a war that, through changes of leadership and shifting alliances, would embroil the two powers and span the globe in its fighting for the better part of the next twenty-two years. Macartney had learned about the events in France while he was still in Beijing, from, of all people, Padre Cho, the interpreter who had abandoned them in Macao, who had come to Beijing by an interior route to avoid association with the foreign embassy and brought the latest news from Canton. Captain Gower of the *Lion* learned of the declaration of war while he waited on the coast for Macartney, and on his way down to Macao he even managed to capture a French-flagged vessel as a prize. Unfortunately for the five seal hunters the British embassy had encountered on remote Amsterdam Island during their outbound voyage, that French ship was the one that was supposed to retrieve them when their contract was up. Its capture by the *Lion* left them stranded on their island in perpetuity.[3]

The naval war stretched to every corner of the world that a French or British ship might sail, so for Macartney's homeward journey the *Lion* took on escort duty for a convoy of thirteen East Indiamen, including the *Hindostan*. Captain Gower drew up a line of battle for the ships, which together carried two thousand sailors and an arsenal of nearly four hundred cannon, with the heavily armed *Lion* at the center of the line.[4] The collective force of the China fleet was formidable enough to scatter any French vessels and pirates they encountered on the way home, and the millions of pounds' worth of cargo they carried remained safe even as the dangers of the war mounted. The *Lion* and its convoy were still rounding the Cape of Good Hope in late May 1794 when, six thousand miles to their north, the largest naval battle of the war was being fought between British and French fleets totaling more than fifty enormous ships of the line. The "Glorious First of June," as it would be remembered, was a British triumph in which Earl Howe's Channel fleet decimated a tenacious force of Republicans defending the path of a grain convoy from America. The *Lion* and its charges were fortunate to avoid such fighting themselves, though they did encounter Howe's victorious fleet in the English Channel as they neared home.[5]

Canton may have been far from the crucial battles between Britain and France, but it still felt the effects of the European conflict. For one thing, the war spelled the end of a meaningful French presence in China. France's commerce at Canton had always been weak in comparison to its trade in Cochin-China (modern-day Vietnam), but that commerce diminished further after the revolution, then all but disappeared once the war was fully under way. The neutral Americans readily filled in the gap, sending more ships to make up for the reduction of French activity and eventually taking over the defunct French factory in Canton as their own, raising the Stars and Stripes on the pole in front where the tricolor had once flown (an occasion on which one especially spiteful Yankee declared, "We raise the fortunes of the United States on the wreckage of France").[6]

More ominously, the war brought a new and sustained British military presence to the vicinity of Canton. The East India Company's China fleet contained some of the richest prizes on the ocean, laden with silver on their voyage to Canton and crammed with valuable cargoes of tea and silk on their way home, so the advent of war meant the arrival of Royal Navy cruisers in Chinese waters to protect and escort the Indiamen as they came and went. They were a destabilizing force. In the past, relations between the British and Chinese in Canton had always been conducted by civilians—the Company supercargoes on the one hand, and the Hong merchants on the other, who in turn represented the foreign merchants to the hoppo and provincial officials. That system worked, and generations of trust and predictability had been built in to it. But the British warships did not answer to the East India Company, and their captains did not take orders from merchants, so their looming presence was unsettling to all concerned.

The flash point for trouble turned out to be Macao, the Portuguese settlement eighty miles south of Canton. Macao was not a Portuguese colony per se, being Chinese territory governed ultimately by the Qing Empire, but in a unique arrangement the Portuguese had been granted the right to live there since the sixteenth century (originally for helping the Ming dynasty with pirate suppression), and they were allowed to exercise their own government over the port city. The local Portuguese maintained control over the comings and goings of foreign ships from Macao, as well as authority over who could and could not live there. Since foreigners were not permitted in Canton outside the immediate trading season of the fall and winter months, Macao was a crucial base for half of the year. Also, the Chinese did not permit foreign women to come to the Canton factory compound (to make sure the traders did not become too comfortable there and attempt to settle down), so any foreign merchant who brought his family with him to China would have to station his wife and children year-round in Macao and visit with them during the off-season.

The Portuguese had long been a neutral presence in Macao, a waning power that did not pose any competition for trade. But in June 1801 Portugal signed a treaty with France that included a provision that all Portuguese ports would be closed to the British. Suddenly Macao mattered. The Admiralty in London worried that the French would send a fleet to take control of the port, and either (at best) exclude the British from residence there, to the detriment of their trade, or (at worst) use it as a base from which to attack British shipping in south China. To head off those disasters, they authorized Lord Wellesley, the governor-general in Bengal, to send a naval fleet from India to preempt the feared arrival of French troops.[7]

The East India Company supercargoes balked. Writing to Wellesley and the Admiralty, they warned of "dangerous consequences" if
the British should threaten naval action in Chinese waters. They, far
better than their countrymen in India and England, understood that
any interference with Macao would not just involve the British and
Portuguese, but could easily draw in the Chinese government as well.
However, their letters did not arrive in time, and a fleet of six British
warships arrived all the same in March 1802. When the Portuguese
refused to allow the fleet to anchor at Macao to blockade the city
peacefully, its commander threatened to attack.

The supercargoes tried to stand in the way. They were adamant
that conflict with the Chinese must be avoided at all costs (the prospect of losing their trade, the only reason for their presence in Asia,
terrified them). Writing to the Company's directors in London, they
warned that "the only and invariable rule of Conduct, to be observed
[in China] . . . was on no occasion to give offense to the Chinese
government."[8] Nevertheless, against their protests the British naval
commander insisted on trying to open negotiations. In a message to
the governor-general in Canton, he explained that the British fleet
was peaceful and had only come to protect Macao against the aggressions of the French. The governor-general did not believe him—and
neither did the Jiaqing emperor, who after he read the governor-
general's report from Canton called the British commander's justification "lying words." "We do not have to lend any credence to these
comments," said Jiaqing, "because the intention of the English was no
more than to dissemble their project to take the town."[9] He ordered
the governor-general to ensure that Britain's warships were sent away,
and the governor-general accordingly shut off the fleet's access to
food supplies and fresh water.

Tensions would have risen from there, but much to the relief of
the traders in Canton, the news soon arrived from Europe of the signing of the Treaty of Amiens—which ended, at least temporarily, the
hostilities between Britain and France. The British fleet stood down
and, after waiting for the monsoon to shift, sailed back to India and
left Canton and Macao in peace.[10]

When the Macartney mission had failed in 1793, Macartney himself wasn't the only one personally disappointed by the outcome. His secretary, George Staunton, had agreed to come along largely because he expected to stay on afterward as the British minister at Beijing. In accepting that prestigious role, Staunton had turned down a less prestigious but more lucrative position offered to him at the same time, to be president of the "select committee" of the East India Company's supercargoes at Canton. The president of the select committee, also known as the "taipan" or chief, was the top-ranking Company figure in Canton, a situation that would be certain to make him a fortune and likely buy him a seat in Parliament when he returned home. But when faced with the choice between money and prestige, Staunton had gambled on prestige and lost. After Qianlong refused to allow the British to station a permanent diplomat at his capital, George Staunton had to return home to England as empty-handed as Macartney, regretting that he hadn't taken the position in Canton instead. His only hope was that a shift in Company personnel at the factory, or a second attempt at an embassy, might eventually call him back to China again.

It was not to be. Staunton suffered a stroke soon after his return home that left him partially paralyzed, unable to take part any longer in public life. His dreams of a China fortune and a seat in Parliament were shattered. But at least he still had his son, the boy who had spoken to the emperor in Chinese. After that audience, Staunton had decided the boy's linguistic ability might give him some prospects in the future, so when the mission was passing through Canton on its way out of China he had hired two Chinese servants to come back with him to England and continue young George's instruction at home. After the stroke, he pinned all of his thwarted plans and hopes on the boy, relying on him to do what the father no longer could. And so in 1798, after more than a decade with young George at his side, traveling the world with him and molding the boy in his own image, Staunton put his unhappy child back onto the *Hindostan* to sail once again for Canton—this time all alone—knowing that he would probably never see him again.[11]

To judge by his letters on the voyage that followed, the younger George Staunton seems to have had no real notion of why he was going back to China. He followed his father's instructions dutifully, though. He brought his Chinese servants along with him so he could study for a few hours each day on the ship, insisting that they should only speak to him in Chinese, and his reading ability progressed to the point that he could start working through the *Romance of the Three Kingdoms,* one of the classics of Chinese literature. He learned enough, furthermore, to understand that there were multiple dialects at work—the residents of Canton all spoke Cantonese, which was unintelligible to someone who spoke the Mandarin dialect of the court. If he was going to use his Chinese to talk to officials, he realized, his servants from Canton would not be much help.

Staunton was eager to please his father, who had set him on the task of learning Chinese, but he admitted in letters home that everyone thought it was a waste of time. The supercargoes who accompanied him on the *Hindostan,* he wrote, "express a very contemptible idea of the use and advantage of the knowledge of the Chinese language to the Company's servants in China."[12] It was a conservative community within the British factory, which did not value those who broke with past practice—especially if what they were doing might risk good relations with the Hong merchants and the officials in Canton. So he worried about being alienated from his colleagues. "I hope to succeed as well as any other," he wrote, "and as to my knowledge of the Chinese . . . [it] will certainly tend to make the situation somewhat pleasanter or somewhat less pleasant to me than to others, which [circumstances] only will determine."[13] He was, however, not at all eager to learn the answer to that question, and actively dreaded his arrival. In July the captain told him they should reach Canton in about five more months. "I am, perhaps, the person on board, the least anxious for that event," he told his parents.[14]

When young George Staunton, now eighteen years old, finally did arrive in the little world of the Canton factory compound on January 22, 1800, the door opened onto what he would later describe as "the most gloomy period of my life."[15] With help from Lord Macartney, his father had managed to finagle him a position at the East India Company's factory as a writer. It was the lowest of jobs available, poorly paid and extremely boring (consisting mostly of weighing crates of tea and copying documents), but offering significant prospects for advancement. The positions at Canton were the richest patronage positions the East India Company in London had to offer, and even the lowly writerships normally went only to sons of the Company's powerful directors.[16] Despite young George's nascent skills in Chinese—in which the Company showed no interest whatsoever—it had taken all of the elder Staunton's social capital to get his son the job.[17]

It was a bleak life for such a sheltered young man. As an only child educated mostly by his father, George had rarely associated with anyone his own age—or for that matter, with anyone outside of his own home. Even his one brief period of study at Cambridge prior to his departure for Canton had given him little social contact because his parents moved there so he could continue living with them instead of in his college; in any case, his father soon pulled him from the university in anger because the faculty didn't give his son a prize in Latin.

The Canton factories

Now Staunton was severed for the first time from his domineering father—who sent a long, wistful letter after him promising the boy that all this was for his own good, that he should only stay as long as necessary to come home with a fortune, and that he could always return earlier if he just couldn't bear it. Not only was he somehow to make a home in a strange country, but among the rowdy bachelor luxuries of the Company quarters—the drinking, the boyish frolicking, the long dinner parties that lasted until dawn—he felt completely out of place. The "coarseness and freedom of manners" of the other Englishmen in Canton embarrassed him. Also, despite his father being a baronet, he was not of the same social circle as the sons of directors, which made him something of a pariah from the outset. As he later put it sadly, "I am fully conscious that I was not at first generally popular." [18]

The work quickly consumed him, though—endless copying of bills, letters, diaries, dispatches, and consultation books, and attending at the weighing of teas—so there was little time to brood about what to make of his life. But when he did brood, he had three primary goals, two of which were straightforward and the other less so. The straightforward ones were, first, to learn the work and do it well enough that he could eventually get promoted into the ranks of the supercargoes, which would boost his salary significantly. And second, because he did not relish the idea of waiting patiently for such a promotion, he wanted to find some means of alternate income, separate from his Company job. The writer position paid very little and he didn't expect to be able to go home again until he had made so much money that he would never have to come back.

There weren't many ways to make money on the side if you were a Company writer. If you had the connections, you could act as the Canton agent for one of the major private firms in India that sent cargoes to Canton. (Though the East India Company had a monopoly on direct trade between England and China, as well as between England and India, its monopoly did not apply to the third leg of the triangle, the so-called country trade between India and China.) Another way to generate income without taking time away from your Company duties was to loan money to the Hong merchants, who always needed capital and paid between 15 and 18 percent interest. But Staunton had neither connections in India nor large sums of capital to invest. So in hopes of accelerating his return home to England, he asked his father to send him as much money as he could, even to borrow more from friends to add to the sum, so that young George could invest it with the Hong merchants. Specifically, he hoped that his father might be able to raise £10,000, which would be equivalent to nearly a hundred years of his starting salary.[19]

Staunton's other goal, the less straightforward one, was to figure out what to do with his Chinese language ability. He admitted that it was unlikely to help in any trade-related capacity—the supercargoes all told him that, repeatedly. He learned with disappointment that there was an Englishman already in Canton, a private merchant by the name of Beale, who could speak Cantonese fluently but didn't derive any advantage from it; of course, he couldn't speak Mandarin, or read and write as Staunton was learning to do, but still his example was uninspiring. Despairing of any encouragement from the Company, Staunton banked everything on the hope that Great Britain would send another embassy to Beijing—the one instance in which he could imagine all of his hard work paying off. On that count he was pleased to learn of the death of Qianlong, because the beginning of Jiaqing's proper reign seemed like a fine time for Britain to try again to send an ambassador, and he hoped that Jiaqing might be more favorable toward foreigners than his father had been. Nothing materialized, however, and the Company—as it always had—worried that an embassy might cause more harm than good. One prominent director held simply that it was "most advisable to let the government of China alone."[20]

It was the tensions around the Royal Navy presence in Chinese waters that gave Staunton his first opening. Just a few months after his arrival, local Chinese authorities ordered the arrest of several sailors from a British man-of-war, HMS *Providence*, for having shot at a boat full of Chinese men, one of whom appeared likely to die from his wounds. The captain of the *Providence*, John Dilkes, refused to hand his men over and said that they had only been defending their ship—the Chinese they shot were thieves, he insisted, who had come up alongside the *Providence* at night to cut the ship's anchor cable. Not only did Dilkes refuse to hand over his men, but he demanded that the Chinese arrest the thieves and punish them.

Under normal circumstances, the supercargoes would probably have grudgingly followed past practice—which was, in short, to hand over the ostensibly guilty parties in order to preserve the trade. The starkest precedent was in 1784 when a British ship had fired a salute that accidentally killed two Chinese. After much protest, the gunner was finally handed over by the Company and executed. The supercargoes regretted the outcome, but they were in no position to push the issue, and the Chinese authorities had the power to shut down their trade. This time, however, the accused sailors were from a navy ship, and Captain Dilkes made it very clear that he was in no way answerable to the supercargoes; as a "King's officer," he told them, he "could not . . . submit to their interference or mediation."[21] This was, as he saw it, an issue between the king of England, represented by himself, and the emperor of China. The Company had no say in the matter.

Staunton volunteered his services, and wound up being asked by the Canton governor-general to interpret for Captain Dilkes and the accused in a Chinese court within the city. It was an utterly unprecedented event—Staunton described even the fact that the Chinese *had* a written code of laws as a "discovery."[22] Fortunately it went well, and eventually the sailors were set free, mainly because after forty days the Chinese victim had not died, so they were no longer liable for charges of murder. The irascible captain of the *Providence* was not fully pleased with the outcome, however, and taunted the Company supercargoes for what he saw as their craven groveling before the Chinese authorities. "I beg leave to congratulate you," he wrote to them, "upon this recorded acknowledgment of your entire independence of His Majesty's Service."[23] However, it was the first time that such a conflict between foreign sailors and Chinese had been settled respectably in a court of law.

The case was eye-opening. It turned out, for one thing, that the law against teaching Chinese to foreigners did not necessarily apply to the foreigners themselves (or at least it wasn't enforced in that way), for Staunton was not punished for speaking Chinese. Quite the opposite, he had been actively welcomed as interpreter, and one imperial official who spent some time chatting with him even com-

A Chinese painting of British sailors on trial in a Chinese court of law.
George Staunton is furthest left of the foreigners in white shirts and
dark coats on the left-hand side.

plimented him on his fluency, telling him that in three more years
he might "acquire sufficient perfection," as Staunton wrote happily
to his father.[24] The only real negative for Staunton was that some of
the Hong merchants seemed resentful toward him afterward, as he
had proven he was now capable of going behind their backs to the
officials.

Furthermore, the incident with the *Providence* was enough to convince the president of the select committee, a man named Hall, that
not only should Staunton continue in his study of Chinese, but also
that the Company should pay for it, even if the directors in London
hadn't approved. Hall had seen, for the first time, how Staunton's
ability to use the language might in certain situations give leverage to
the otherwise powerless foreigners in Canton. Staunton had gotten

a glimpse, as it were, beyond the walls that surrounded the traders in their little enclave. He had engaged in direct communication with Chinese officials without the mediation of the Hong merchants, and in this instance at least, there seemed to be no backlash.

With Hall's financial support and encouragement, Staunton redoubled his efforts to learn Chinese. He couldn't study in Canton itself—where, he told his father, he was "unable to find anyone acquainted with the Chinese language in its purity, and bold enough at the same time to give me lessons on it."[25] But he did manage to secure a teacher in the comparatively free setting of Macao for the summers, a Chinese Roman Catholic who knew Latin and the Mandarin court dialect. He started reading imperial edicts and lists of regulations. At the expense of the Company he also purchased a copy of the entire Qing legal code, in 144 volumes, and began slowly to translate it into English with help from his teacher. For the first time since James Flint, there was a British interpreter in Canton, and his interests went well beyond just the negotiations for trade. It was the beginning of something, though Staunton didn't yet know where it might lead.

———

George Staunton's melancholy first two years in Canton ended—or shall we say culminated—in 1802 with the news that his father was dead. The elder George Staunton had actually passed away quite a bit earlier, but it took half a year for word to reach his son in China. Sadly, most of the letters the young man had written—asking his father to raise funds for him to invest, relaying his victories in first using his Chinese—were never read by the man to whom he addressed them. Staunton wound up being allowed to visit home much earlier than expected, but for more dismal reasons than he had hoped.

From 1802 until 1804, Staunton was back home in England on leave from the Company, to prove his father's will and take over the family estates in Ireland (he also inherited at this time his father's baronetcy, and became Sir George). Even in the absence of his father he found a sympathy back home he hadn't felt in China. Lord Macartney took a paternal interest in him, and said he would treat him like his own son. In December 1802, Macartney took young Staunton for an audience with King George and Queen Charlotte. With Macartney's patronage and on the strength of his studies in Chinese he was made a fellow of the Royal Society and elected to the Literary Club, a group founded by Samuel Johnson whose past members included Adam Smith and Edward Gibbon. He greatly enjoyed being with his mother. And by the time he sailed back to Canton in June 1804 the Company had promoted him to supercargo. With his inheritance, and a substantial salary increase from the promotion, things looked up for him financially. He wished he didn't have to go back, though, and still considered life in China to be a "painful sacrifice."[26]

Staunton was at least comforted to know that his time in Canton would not be eternal. As supercargo he would have a guaranteed leave in a few more years, and if his advancement through the factory's ranks continued, it would be just a matter of time before he had enough money to come home for good. Although he had managed to convince the select committee in Canton that it was important to have someone on their side who could speak and read Chinese, he had no intention of spending the rest of his life being the person to do that for them. So while he continued his studies after his return and worked diligently on his translation of the Qing legal code, he otherwise looked forward to finding a way to share the load with someone else. But newcomers in Canton were few and far between, and those who came under the Company's auspices had no interest in learning the language. In 1807, however, two unexpected new arrivals would change Staunton's luck.

———

If you were a westerner who wanted to go to live in Canton in the early 1800s, you did not have many choices. If you were British, you could try to become a writer for the East India Company like George Staunton did, which was close to impossible unless you came from the right family. Alternatively, you could ship off to India with a private firm and try to bluster your way past the objections of the Company staff in Canton by getting yourself made consul for some other country like Sweden or Denmark, which was the only way to subvert the

Company's monopoly on British citizens trading with China. (Beale, the private English trader who spoke Cantonese, for example, was technically consul for Prussia.) If you were American, you didn't have to worry about the East India Company's monopoly, but unless you had the funds to buy and outfit your own ship you had to get a position with one of the very few, extremely small, and closely held New England firms that kept a permanent representative in Canton. The way to do that, even more so than with the East India Company, was through birth or marriage into the right family. And finally, no matter where you came from, if you did not have a job with one of the existing companies lined up in advance, your options were almost nonexistent. The China trading ships did not as a rule take passengers.[27]

Initially this was not a great problem, because there were essentially no British or Americans who dreamed of traveling to China for any reason other than trade. Even those who did go for trade spent most of their time in the country, like George Staunton, looking forward to the day when they could return home. But something shifted at the opening of the nineteenth century, thanks in large part to the many travelogues and memoirs about China that were published by the members of the Macartney mission. Those books made the country seem a less impossible destination and began for the first time to attract travelers who had purposes other than commerce in mind.

The first arrival of this new generation was a playful and spirited young eccentric from Norfolk, England, named Thomas Manning. An Anglican rector's son with a ruddy complexion and jet-black hair, Manning had studied mathematics at Cambridge but never graduated because he refused to take examinations. Sometime around 1801, for reasons he never fully explained, he started to be "haunted with the idea of China," as a friend put it.[28] In his own words, Manning became obsessed with "the design of attempting to explore that country myself, and by my own observations and researches . . . to dissipate some of the obscurity and doubt which hangs over its moral and civil history."[29]

Since there was no way to learn Chinese in England, the would-be explorer Manning traveled to Paris in 1802 to study with a Dr. Joseph Hager at the Bibliothèque Nationale, who had examined various Jesuit texts and claimed to have unlocked a grand theory to

Thomas Manning

explain the Chinese written character (a theory later revealed to be bunk).[30] Whatever useful knowledge Manning might have gained from Hager, however, the peace of Amiens broke down the following summer, hostilities resumed, and he was made a prisoner of war until the fall of 1804 when he escaped France with, allegedly, the only passport ever granted to an English prisoner by Napoleon.[31] A great self-promoter, Manning intimated that the reason Napoleon let him go was because the general supported Manning's intended exploration of China and admired him as "a man who had destined himself to voyages of discovery."[32] Once safely back in England, however, Manning was still no closer to China. In frustration, he turned to studying medicine. He was "melancholy," noted a friend, "and seems to have something in his head which he don't impart."[33]

Manning was well connected in Britain's literary world, being a close Cambridge friend of the essayist Charles Lamb, who himself was intimate with the poets William Wordsworth and Samuel Taylor Coleridge. Lamb was delighted and titillated by the sheer outlandishness of Manning's plan to go to China. "For God's sake don't think any more of 'Independent Tartary,'" he wrote to Manning in

February 1803, at a point when Manning thought he might enter the Qing Empire from the north, through Russia. "I tremble for your Christianity. They will certainly circumcise you." On an even more histrionic note, Lamb added, "My dear friend, think what a sad pity it would be to bury such *parts* in heathen countries, among nasty, unconversable, horse-belching, Tartar-people! . . . The Tartars, really, are a cold, insipid, smouchy set. You'll be sadly moped (if you are not eaten) among them. Pray *try* and cure yourself."[34]

Ultimately, Manning wound up setting his sights on Canton, where he hoped to study Chinese with George Staunton before smuggling himself into the country. He had no position with the East India Company to get him there, but he did have his connections. Joseph Banks, the eminent natural scientist and president of the Royal Society, wrote a letter on his behalf to the directors of the East India Company to recommend him for a secret mission of exploration. Banks noted that Manning would have no hope of success unless he could blend in perfectly: he must learn to dress like a Chinese, act like one, and speak with no accent at all—all of which he hoped Manning could learn in Canton. "I take a deep interest in the fate of this very amiable young man," wrote Banks, "both on account of his mild character and the energies of his mind."[35] On the strength of Banks's endorsement, the directors granted Manning free passage on an East Indiaman departing in 1806, along with permission to live in the British factory as a doctor once he arrived.[36]

Manning did not want for self-esteem, and his audacity in hoping to sneak into China was companion to a faith that he was simply smarter than most people. "My greatest want is good society," he wrote with ennui during the passage to China, tiring of how much everyone on the ship fawned over his brilliance. "I am among a set of grossly ignorant people. The rogues soon found out my superiority of acquirements, and they now will give me credit for knowing what I am really ignorant of."[37] He began to grow a beard, as if to underscore his nonconformity and set himself apart from the merely ordinary passengers on the ship. By the time he arrived, the beard would be half a foot long, lovingly groomed, and still growing. Eventually it would reach down to his waist. "China! Canton!" wrote Charles Lamb to him as he sailed, in a letter otherwise filled with theater gossip and the latest on Coleridge (who had recently come to live with Lamb). "Bless us—how it strains the imagination and makes it ache!"[38]

In January 1807, Manning arrived at Canton and immediately sought out George Staunton, to whom Joseph Banks had given him a glowing letter of introduction. Staunton was already a great admirer of Banks, who had been a close friend of his father's and helped prepare the Macartney mission (which Banks had hoped in vain would return with the means to cultivate tea in British India, by bringing back either tea plants, Chinese tea farmers, or both).[39] So Staunton was delighted to welcome Manning to Canton—here, at last, was another Englishman who wanted to learn Chinese. The select committee, for its part, was skeptical of Manning's likelihood of exploring China, but they still let him take up residence in the factory. "Although we entertain but a very faint hope of his success," they conceded, ". . . the consequence might be rather favourable than otherwise to the public service."[40]

The other new arrival in 1807 was a round-faced son of a boot-tree maker from Northumberland named Robert Morrison, a twenty-five-year-old with a mop of thick, curly black hair who came to Canton for entirely different reasons than Manning and against even greater odds. Like Manning, Robert Morrison did not have a job with the Company—nor did he want one—but being from a lower social class he also did not have any connections to speak of. Morrison was trying to get to China not because it called to him personally in any particular way but because the directors of the London Missionary Society had seen fit to appoint him as the first Protestant missionary there. They did not, however, have any clear plan for how he should accomplish that. Catholic missionaries from the European continent had been going to China for generations, but by this time the Chinese government had outlawed their activities, so only the few who were kept by the emperor in Beijing were allowed to reside legally in the country. The rest lived in secret and risked violent persecution if discovered. Furthermore, many of them were French, and since Morrison was a Protestant rather than a Catholic, even aside from the tensions of the ongoing war between their countries or the religious crackdowns of the Chinese government, he knew that he would have no help from their channels.

Neither, for that matter, would he have any help from his own kind, because no Protestant missionary had ever gone to China before—and the East India Company rather liked it that way. Morrison noted ruefully in his diary in December 1806, while he was trying to get permission to travel on a Company ship to Canton, that "strong prejudices existed in England and in all parts of India where the British influence extended against missionary exertions."[41] Most of the Company's directors viewed missionaries as sanctimonious troublemakers who could easily upset the local authorities, so they refused Morrison passage on any of the Company's ships—the only civilian vessels that sailed between England and China. It was an unpromising start for a man who, as his instructions from the London Missionary Society informed him, was supposed to "go far hence to the Gentiles, as an ambassador of the Prince of Peace."[42]

Morrison settled on taking passage to New York—the wrong direction, but where he hoped to find an American ship that would bring him to Canton. On January 8, 1807, just before he left England (and just as Thomas Manning was landing comfortably in Canton), Morrison was ordained as a minister in preparation for his journey. It was as if he were going off to war. "I have now to buckle on my armour," he wrote in his diary. "O! to be enabled 'to deny myself, to take up my cross,' and to follow the Lamb fully!" Denial would indeed describe much of what was to come. It was a disastrous 109-day passage across the Atlantic, marked by storms and fire and snow so heavy he couldn't see the bow of the ship. He fought back fear and depression on the way, trying to rein in his resentment at the hopelessness of his mission. ("Were it not for God," he wrote in his diary, "I should sink under this pressure.") He tried preaching to the ship's crew, but nobody would listen to him. Arriving at New York, he disembarked only to find that there were no ships there, either, that were willing to take him to Canton.[43]

In despair, Morrison left New York and took a rough wagon ride down to Philadelphia, where he finally found one ship whose owners were willing to give him a berth—but only at the price of $1,000 for his passage, which was more money than the London Missionary Society had given him to fund his entire mission, let alone his journey to Canton. The Americans, however, turned out to be far more sympathetic to missionaries than the British. An enthusiastic network of American Protestants took him in, giving him places to stay and introducing him to others like himself, one of them a missionary to the Cherokee in Tennessee. They also agitated on his behalf, and they had influence. One managed to persuade a ship's captain in New York to give him passage to Canton, at the cost only of his food (for which another of the Americans paid). And despite his not being a citizen of the United States, they even managed to prevail upon the secretary of state, James Madison, to write him a letter of introduction to the U.S. consul in Canton asking him to do anything he could to help.[44] Morrison sailed in May and arrived in Canton 113 days later in September 1807, eight months after he left England.

The warm glow of Morrison's reception in America had faded by the time he reached China, where he faced the bleak reality of his situation. His fellow British refused to let him live in their factory in Canton. The Portuguese, being that they were Catholics, did not want him in Macao. And he hadn't quite understood how difficult it would be to find someone in Canton to teach him the language until one of the foreigners explained that the Chinese could be put to death for doing so.[45] So he turned to George Staunton as the only man who could possibly help him. The Royal Society president, Joseph Banks, had given Morrison a letter of introduction to Staunton just as he had done for Thomas Manning, and Morrison delivered that letter when he arrived. However, Banks had made a more confidential assessment of Morrison's prospects in the letter he wrote for Manning several months earlier. After having sung Manning's praises as an explorer so brave that he held "even Death itself in contempt," Banks had mentioned offhandedly that there was also a missionary on his way from England, and about him he was far less enthusiastic. "My own opinion," he wrote, "leans to the probability of his obtaining the crown of martyrdom much more readily than a single convert to the Cross."[46]

George Staunton was intending to return to England in January 1808 for his second term of home leave, so he was cheered by the appearance of these two new students of Chinese. Since the factory would otherwise be without a Chinese interpreter during his two-year absence, he was eager to hand his mantle to Manning and Morrison—if, that is, they could be convinced to take it. In any case, he had only a few months to help them get settled before his departure, after which they would be left to their own devices.

Manning was a straightforward case, for he had come with the blessing of the directors in London and already had a position with the Company. Staunton set him up with a teacher and let him get to work on his studies right away. He was a popular figure around the factory and a great talker who seemed happy to have gained a toehold at the edge of China. But he was also restless. Manning was only learning Chinese for the sake of his planned explorations, so working for the factory was just the means to an end, and he did not want to stay in Canton any longer than necessary.

Morrison's case was far more complicated. Staunton was eager to help him when he arrived in Canton, and offered to set him up with his own teacher, but the directors of the Company had been adamant that a missionary could not be allowed to live in the British factory, so the first issue became finding him a home. Fortunately, Morrison had his letter of introduction from James Madison. The American consul, a Rhode Island merchant named Edward Carrington, arranged for Morrison to live sub rosa in the American factory for the first few months after his arrival, sharing an apartment with the merchants of the ship on which he had come out. In order to stay there he had to pretend to be an American rather than a British citizen. He also had to stretch his small budget to rent out an extra room to keep his Chinese papers and books where none of the servants who came and went from the factory might see them.[47]

George Staunton introduced him to a tutor, a Roman Catholic named Abel Yun who spoke fluent Latin and came secretly to his quarters each day—though Morrison, whose money was rapidly running out, worried that Yun wanted to be paid too much. He also worried about the unexpectedly high prices he had to pay for food, for laundry, for a servant boy, for firewood, and especially for candles. He eventually moved into a dank ground-floor room of the American factory with cheaper rent. He also tried to save money—and, he hoped, set a cultural example—by eating only Chinese food, using only chopsticks, and wearing only Chinese clothes. He tried to become as Chinese as possible, even to the point of growing a braid and letting his fingernails grow. But the culture shock wore him down, and when he became ill he finally gave up and started shaving again, cut his nails, lopped off his braid, and resumed wearing his black preacher's clothes from England. By then it was clear that he had to find financial support of some kind.

Fortunately for Morrison, a new president of the select committee, John Roberts, was sympathetic to his mission. It wasn't mere benevolence behind Roberts's support, though—his desire to help Morrison was wrapped up in his own fairly bigoted views of the Chinese, which were rather more contemptuous than the norm for a man in his position. A superior-minded Christian, Roberts hoped that Morrison might succeed in translating the Bible so he could give it to his Confucian counterparts and tell them, sneeringly, "This volume *we* deem the best of books."[48] Roberts became Morrison's patron during his first year in China, providing the young missionary with a house in Macao for the off-season and, by his lofty standing as president of the Company's select committee, preventing the Portuguese from driving Morrison out.[49] On moral grounds it was something of a devil's bargain, though. Morrison was uncomfortable having to rely so heavily on a man of trade—a man driven more by greed than by charity, more by arrogance than humility. He had been shocked by the opulent life of the supercargoes when he first arrived in Canton. "It would be impossible," he wrote in a letter home, "for me to dwell amidst the princely grandeur of the English who reside here."[50] And yet there he was, living in a home provided by the most powerful and rich of them all. But without John Roberts's patronage Morrison could never have gotten established, so he was grateful. It was not the last such compromise he would make.

As the Napoleonic Wars ground on, the importance of the East India Company's trade in China climbed sharply. Though Britain had in the 1780s reduced its tax on tea imports to 12.5 percent to combat smuggling from continental Europe, the country's pressing need for funds to finance its naval war against France forced the government to begin squeezing the East India Company harder once again—and it was able to do so, in part, because the vast presence of British land and naval forces during the war made smuggling into England virtually impossible.[51] The British government started raising its tax on the Company's tea in 1795, during the third year of the war, and continued pushing it upward every year or two. In 1802 the tax on tea imports reached 50 percent and then, in 1806, 96 percent (it would climb to an even 100 percent in 1819).[52]

At the same time, the Company's income from the China trade was completely swamping its revenues from India: in the first decade of the 1800s, the imports from Canton provided two-thirds of the entire sales income of the East India Company in London. By the latter part of that decade the China portion of its trade was bringing in record profits while the India trade operated in some years at a net loss.[53] The effect was, first, to create a huge increase in the government's tax revenue from the China trade—to the point that by some estimates as much as one-tenth of Britain's national revenue derived from the trade at Canton.[54] By corollary, the growing reliance of the British government on its tax revenues from the Company's tea also meant that the stability of affairs in Canton became a matter of serious national interest. Any interruption to the China trade could interfere with Britain's ability to finance its war.

And so when tensions from the global conflict coalesced once again around Macao in 1808, the situation escalated far more quickly and dangerously than it had in 1802. The spark was a similar one: the British in Canton heard a rumor that France was sending troops to occupy Macao. This time, however, the British would respond even more preemptively, a reflection that the nature of the war had changed in the six years since 1802. By 1808, Napoleon had subsumed nearly the entire European continent into his Continental System, to the exclusion of British trade. In the summer of 1807 he defeated Russia as well, and the British had recently learned with great alarm that Napoleon was proposing to Tsar Alexander that they go on to attack India together.[55] Meanwhile, although Britain held the upper hand on the oceans, French cruisers were everywhere. In Southeast Asia in particular, the French had a major naval force near Java and exercised virtual control over the port of Manila in the Philippines.[56] All of which meant that Britain's China trade, with Macao as one of its two keys, was not only more important but also more vulnerable than it had ever been before.

In contemplating the prospect of renewed hostilities over Macao, the British and the Chinese both had the precedent of 1802 to guide them. To the Qing government, the lesson of 1802 was that the Canton governor-general's firm resolution in cutting off supplies to the British fleet had worked. The ships had left soon after. Notwithstanding the external factor of the Treaty of Amiens, the departure of the British fleet from Macao in 1802 had been reported to Jiaqing as a victory for the dynasty.[57] So it was clear to the Chinese government that if trouble should arise again it only needed to hold firm and the British would back down. Meanwhile, the British supercargoes in Canton and the directors of the East India Company in London had been relieved to avoid any harm to their trade in 1802 and remained wary of their inability to control the forces of the Royal Navy. For them, the lesson of 1802 was that they should do everything possible to avoid provoking the Chinese government. Both sides thus acknowledged that China had the upper hand—which was, in its way, a recipe for peace.

However, not everyone understood the precedent of 1802 in the same way. In particular, John Roberts, the new president of the select committee (and Robert Morrison's patron), saw in the renewed tensions of 1808 a chance for Britain to seize an advantage over the local authorities. In his opinion, the lack of more forceful action on the Chinese side in 1802—the very fact that Chinese troops had not opened fire on the British fleet when it first refused to leave—were proof that the Qing government had no effective means (or will) to counter a display of British force. The others on the select committee came to agree with him, or at least followed his lead. And so in March 1808 the committee wrote secretly to Lord Minto, the new governor-general of Bengal, that they did not think there would be any consequences if the British should send in another naval fleet and this time capture Macao. "Should it appear expedient to counteract any intentions of the Enemy by anticipating them in the possession of [Macao]," they wrote, ". . . in our opinion neither embarrassment to our affairs or any serious opposition are to be apprehended on the part of the Chinese Government." [58] In fact, they even speculated that the Chinese authorities might welcome a British presence in Macao, since the Royal Navy would undoubtedly be better than the Portuguese at suppressing pirates. Later, Roberts added his assurance that "any objections or impediments on the part of the Chinese will be of a temporary nature." [59]

A naval fleet under Rear Admiral William Drury, the commander of British naval forces in India, arrived in September 1808. This time, however, there would be no Treaty of Amiens to resolve the situation externally. The British were also without an interpreter, as Staunton had already left for England before the tensions erupted. Thomas Manning apparently did not yet have strong enough language skills. Thus in spite of the insistence of the directors that the Company staff should have nothing to do with missionaries, they were reduced to asking Robert Morrison to help with translation. He declined on principle, however; the London Missionary Society had sent him to China to save the souls of the Chinese, not to act as some kind of diplomatic interpreter. It turned out to be a good decision on his part, for the Portuguese priest the British wound up hiring in his place was arrested by the Chinese authorities in Macao, stripped naked, and beaten. So vicious was his treatment at the hands of the Chinese, even after his release from prison, that the select committee eventually had to pay to send him to Brazil for his own safety.[60]

Events unfolded quickly. On September 11, 1808, Drury sent a letter informing the Portuguese governor at Macao that he intended to occupy the city. The Portuguese governor refused him and appealed to the Chinese governor-general for protection. On September 21, Drury landed three hundred marines who quickly took control of Macao's shore batteries, against much protest but no physical resistance from the Portuguese. In response, the Chinese governor-general ordered a shutdown of British trade in Canton, forcing the Indiamen of the Company fleet—which were still fully laden with their cargoes from England—to remove themselves to Macao along with the supercargoes, who had to abandon their factory in Canton. Drury then called in seven hundred more troops from India to shore up his position at Macao.[61]

Following the script from 1802, the Chinese governor-general then warned that if the British marines did not withdraw, the fleet and all British residents in Macao would be cut off from food supplies. At that point in the escalation, Drury balked. He had not intended to start a war, nor did his orders authorize him to do so. But John Roberts egged him on, insisting that the Chinese were in the wrong and Drury should acknowledge "the impossibility of giving way to the Chinese so long as they persevered in their haughty conduct." A few days later, Roberts suggested that Drury should open fire to intimidate the governor-general. Drury ignored him.[62]

When the reports of the British invasion of Macao reached the Jiaqing emperor in Beijing, he was furious. He issued an edict to the governor-general in Canton that "such a brutal eruption at Macao indicates an affrontery without limit," dismissing completely Drury's claim that his force was merely trying to protect Macao from the French. "To invoke such a pretext is to freely insult the Chinese empire," Jiaqing wrote. "It is important in any case to raise considerable troops, attack the foreigners, and exterminate them. In this way, they will understand that the seas of China are forbidden to them."[63] In response to the emperor's orders, and in the surest sign yet that this would not be a repeat of 1802, the governor-general called up eighty thousand Chinese troops at Canton and ordered all of the coastal forts in the vicinity to prepare for war. Word reached Drury that Chinese troops were under orders to kill any Englishmen who remained behind in Canton and burn their ships.

Roberts tried to get Drury to bluff, saying he should threaten war without meaning to go through with it. He felt sure that this would be enough to scare the Chinese into submission. If Drury backed down, Roberts warned, it would only teach the Chinese that they could push the British around at will. It would "completely satisfy [them] of the hold they have upon us by means of our Trade." But this time, in contrast to 1802, the roles of the Company and navy were reversed. This time, it was the naval commander who counseled prudence. "Threats without meaning is not my manner of proceeding," Drury responded in anger to Roberts. "It is scratching with a pin or squirting dirty water, and is the disguise of impotence." He warned Roberts of two grave dangers if the British should refuse to withdraw from Macao. First, that it might stir up the popular, nationalist sentiment of the Chinese, "which is always furious, implacable, irresistible." He pointed out that the invasion of Macao had "already irritated the Chinese to acts of hostility" and insisted that they must "avoid lighting that spark of enthusiasm which a breath would blow into flames and which," he admonished Roberts, "the Chinese are not destitute of, however contemptible they are in your mind." [64]

Furthermore, Drury knew there was an even greater danger to British interests than roiling the popular anger of the Chinese people. It was the exact same specter that had broken through Macartney's own vengeful musings on how easily a handful of British warships could wreak destruction on China's coast. Namely, that if Britain should threaten military action on Chinese soil, the emperor could simply shut down their Canton trade for good—and if he did so, Admiral Drury warned, it "would exclude the English forever, from the most advantageous monopoly it possesses in the Universe."

So Admiral Drury backed down. He refused to risk starting a war with China because he believed it could never end in peace. Against the continued goading of John Roberts (who when Drury wouldn't threaten war, tried to do so himself, twice, with no effect), Drury asked for a détente, sending word to the governor-general that he would remove his troops from Macao and leave with his ships as long as the trade in Canton might be restored. The governor-general concurred. Drury even went so far as to acknowledge the offensiveness of his own actions and, to his own testament, commended the moral grounds of the Chinese governor-general's response—which, Drury wrote, had been "dictated by Wisdom, justice and dignified manhood, in support of those Moral Rights of Man, of Nations, and of Nature, outraged and insulted." [65]

Drury withdrew his marines from Macao, and six days later the

Qing governor-general restored trade in Canton. The Company ships returned to their anchorage at Whampoa and began unloading their cargoes of woolens, cotton, and silver, and the supercargoes moved back into their factory. Tea was bought, and the taxes would flow again into the British government's coffers. The dominant mood on the British side was relief. In India, Lord Minto was quick to point out that he had never authorized Drury to make war in China, insisting that "it was never in our contemplation to suggest the prosecution of actual Hostilities." He said he "highly approved" of Drury's decision to retreat.[66]

Back in London, meanwhile, the directors of the East India Company were likewise relieved that serious conflict had been avoided at Canton, but they were astounded that John Roberts seemed to have forgotten all of the lessons of 1802. He had, they declared, recklessly endangered "the property . . . of the Company[,] their footing in China and the most valuable trade they possess."[67] They said they would rather see France in possession of Macao than suffer the risk of a rupture with the Chinese government. They agreed with Drury that a war with China would be purely self-defeating, and to underline that point they voted unanimously to fire John Roberts for having done his very best to start one.

Roberts was removed as president of the select committee and recalled home, while the rest of the committee were demoted and replaced with more junior personnel. Still, their lot was better than that of their Chinese counterparts. Contrary to Staunton's hopes that the new emperor would be more favorably minded toward foreigners than his father had been, Jiaqing was outraged that his soldiers hadn't shown more muscle when the British first landed their troops at Macao. Disgusted with the timidity of his officials at Canton for not having used the full forces at their disposal, he removed the governor-general from office and sent him into exile in the empire's godforsaken northwestern frontier. He likewise punished several other lower officials, blaming them for being too compromising with the British—and thus making it perfectly clear to those who succeeded them just what sort of position the emperor expected them to take in the future.[68]

CHAPTER 4

Sea and Land

———

The Jiaqing emperor did not have an enviable start to his reign. A broad, heavyset man with a talent for archery, he was left to clean up the problems of corruption and rebellion that had begun to unsettle the empire in his father's dotage. After the honor of learning in 1795 that Qianlong had chosen him, the fifteenth son, as heir apparent, Jiaqing had been forced to suffer the ignominy of being enthroned in 1796 only to find that all decisions would still be made by his father and his father's personal advisers like Heshen. Already verging on forty years of age at the time, a conscientious and eager aspirant to the throne, Jiaqing ruled for his first three years in name only, a ceremonial actor openly defied by the ministers of his retired father and treated like a puppet. "When the retired emperor is happy, he is happy," wrote one observer at court. "When the retired emperor laughs, he laughs."[1] To judge by Jiaqing's later actions, however, he was clear-eyed enough to see exactly where the worst problems lay. It was just that as long as his father was alive, he was powerless to do anything about them.

When Qianlong finally died in 1799, one of Jiaqing's first major acts—only a day after the "supreme retired emperor's" death—was to order Heshen's arrest. After a swift and widely publicized trial, the Board of Punishments found the old emperor's favorite minister guilty of a long list of corruption-related charges and sentenced him to death. In keeping with his rank and the favor of the late emperor, Heshen was allowed to strangle himself with a silk cord—a privilege considered more honorable than, say, beheading. But while his high-profile execution may have been cathartic, serving as a decisive sign that a new emperor was in power, there was little it alone could do to stem the spreading rot of corruption.

In the trial and its aftermath, Heshen was in effect blamed for all of the sins of the age, as if he alone had managed to drag the entire imperial bureaucracy down into the depths of self-interest and graft during Qianlong's later years. Documents of the trial, as well as separate assessments of Heshen's wealth, revealed the truly fantastic scale of his misdeeds. Most pertinent to his execution were the political crimes. Among them: revealing to Jiaqing in advance that Qianlong had chosen him as heir (claiming that it was his own doing, to cultivate the heir apparent's loyalty); hiding military reports on the White Lotus rebellion from the emperor; removing names from the rosters of officials in line for promotion; and fabricating imperial edicts.[2]

But it was the astounding wealth Heshen had accumulated in the course of his two decades in power that really confounded the imagination. First there was his sprawling mansion of 730 rooms, flanked by separate east and west wings with more than 300 rooms each. Then there was his secondary residence, with 620 rooms of its own. There were his landholdings, totaling more than 120,000 acres of productive farmland (nearly two hundred square miles). There were extravagances that hinted at his lavish lifestyle: seventy-two silver place settings for banquets, two hundred pairs of gold chopsticks, five hundred pairs in silver. He had entire storehouses of jewels and jade and ginseng. He owned ten banks, ten pawnshops with millions of taels in capital, and another storehouse just to hold his pearls. One wall of his main residence turned out to be filled with nearly five thousand pounds of pure gold bullion. Forty tons of silver was buried in the basement. He had other stores of silver as well, vast ones including millions of ounces of silver ingots and foreign silver dollars. Estimates of the total value of Heshen's property reached as high as eight hundred million taels of silver—an impossible sum worth, for comparison, roughly $1.5 billion at the time, or four times the entire gross domestic product of the United States.[3] Less sensational (and surely more accurate) figures still put the value of his property at somewhere around eighty million taels—more than the entire treasury surplus that preceded the White Lotus war and enough to make him as wealthy as the emperor himself.

With Heshen's very public trial and execution, Jiaqing had an opening to mount a wide-scale campaign against official corruption, which a good number of his advisers wanted to see. Many identified corruption as the greatest danger facing the dynasty, more fundamental even than rebellion, insofar as they blamed corrupt officials for having provoked the White Lotus uprisings in the first place. After making a grand display of punishing Heshen, however, Jiaqing let the campaign peter out. By doing so, he risked allowing the graft-driven government culture to continue unimpeded, but he sensed even greater dangers if he should cast a wider net. He knew how easily an anticorruption campaign could lose control and become a general purge, for almost nobody was innocent. Officials would readily testify against their personal enemies, turning them in for any number of crimes, but there was no way to know where the process would end (or whether, once it was done, it would leave enough honest men of talent behind to run any kind of a government). The Qing administration would get bogged down further, old scores would be settled, and the fractiousness of the officials would only worsen.[4]

That did not, however, mean that nothing changed with Heshen's execution. One subtle but important shift in Jiaqing's early reign was that Han Chinese scholars—that is, ethnic Chinese Confucians, who had been fully subordinate to the Manchus since the founding of the dynasty—became bolder and more outspoken in addressing the empire's problems. They started to critique the government's policies and suggest solutions, even when their advice was not wanted. The Manchu emperors of the Qing dynasty had long been suspicious of private Chinese scholarly associations—poetry societies, Confucian academies, and the like—where Han scholars could meet to discuss political problems. Even when they were motivated only by patriotism, they could become antagonistic if their advice was not followed. Such associations had been banned outright in the seventeenth and eighteenth centuries, but under Jiaqing's reign at the opening of the nineteenth century the climate began to thaw.[5]

It was the Heshen case that first provoked the shift. Unhappy with the Jiaqing emperor's refusal to mount a purge of Heshen's followers, in 1799 a nervous and insomniac Confucian scholar named Hong Liangji broke with precedent and wrote a bold letter to the Jiaqing emperor demanding reform. The emperor, he wrote, should dig deeper into the problem of corrupt officials. He should restore moral government and redeem the respect that officials had once enjoyed from the public but no longer did. The emperor should choose his advisers more carefully, for he was "frequently misled by buffoons and intimate associates." Hong Liangji admitted in the course of the harshly critical letter that he did not have sufficient rank to address the emperor directly (a mentor submitted it for him to a prince, who passed it on to the sovereign). But nevertheless he refused to remain quiet: "The country," he wrote, "cannot be left without *someone* who dares speak out in the face of opposition."[6] He then went on—for pages upon pages, for thousands of characters—to identify a litany of problems that faced the dynasty, and to spell out how the Jiaqing emperor as a ruler had failed to deal with them.

Even an emperor who was not, like Jiaqing, anxious about his authority at the start of his proper reign would have bristled at such a cutting and uninvited critique. And so, as his ancestors would have done as well, Jiaqing had Hong Liangji arrested. The Board of Punishments almost immediately sentenced Hong to death for "extreme indecorum."[7] But then Jiaqing had an unexpected change of heart. Instead of allowing the execution to proceed, he instead commuted Hong Liangji's death sentence and merely banished him to Chinese Turkestan in the far west. By letting him live—even if in exile—he sent a signal that such criticism would be, if not strictly tolerated, at least not punished by death. To other scholars more judicious in holding their tongues, Hong Liangji became a vision of romantic virtue, the archetype of an upright official unafraid to speak the truth to his ruler. As he traveled out to Turkestan for his exile, crowds turned out to cheer for him at every stop along the way. It was, they sensed, the dawn of a new era.[8]

To his great credit, Jiaqing realized that he needed advice and guidance, even needed to hear criticism. The disturbances in the empire were simply too complex and unsettling for him to rule as a confident authoritarian like his father. So in the spring of 1800, half a year after sending Hong Liangji into exile, he pardoned the scholar and allowed him to come back to the capital. Not only that, but Jiaqing also publicly apologized for having punished him in the first place. He had been wrong, the emperor announced, to condemn an honest official who was merely trying to correct his ruler's faults. Jiaqing let it be known that he had not destroyed the original letter in which Hong Liangji criticized him—in fact, he said, he kept it by his bedside so that he would always be reminded of its contents. There had been a terrible drought that year in Beijing, which, like other natural disasters in China, was taken to be a potential sign of Heaven's displeasure with the emperor. According to the imperial records, on the day that Jiaqing officially pardoned Hong Liangji, the rain finally began to fall again.[9]

The first order of business for the newly empowered sovereign in 1799 was to finish the war against the White Lotus. The day after Qianlong's death, Jiaqing issued an edict naming the suppression of antigovernment religious sects as the dynasty's most urgent priority. Although Qianlong's previous victories over internal rebellions had always been achieved within months, wrote Jiaqing, the White Lotus alone had dragged on for years and cost tens of millions of taels. Jiaqing said that his most important duty was to carry forward the work of his father, whose final days had been haunted by the desire for victory. "I have now received the weight of the empire," Jiaqing wrote, "and every day that passes with the war still unfinished is a day that I must bear the guilt of being an unfilial son."[10] He railed against the corruption of the military officers in the campaign, accusing them of dragging out the war merely in order to increase their own profits. He laid blame for the insurrection at the feet of the dynasty's own civil servants, for their extortions from the peasants below them. "The peasants enjoy few fruits from their labor," wrote Jiaqing in sympathy, "so how can they possibly supply such insatiable demands? It is the local officials who provoked these rebellions."

Jiaqing began by removing corrupt and incompetent military officials from command, trying to restore some kind of account-ability and integrity to the war effort. The grim reality, though, was that given the circumstances of the time he had an exceptionally thin pool of talent to draw from.[11] Most of the great Manchu generals of his father's generation had passed on or were too old to lead a campaign. Those in the younger generation were comparatively soft from having grown up in such a prosperous age. Among them were a great number tainted by association with Heshen and his network of patronage, who couldn't be fully trusted. But at least a small number of the old guard remained, the great warriors who had won so many hard-fought campaigns for Qianlong.

The best of them was a broad-shouldered, chiseled Manchu field commander named Eldemboo. He was fifty-one years old in 1799 when Jiaqing picked him to lead the White Lotus suppression—on the older side to lead a campaign, but he was incorruptible, expe-rienced, and ruthless. He represented the foundations of the Qing dynasty's military strength—a forceful, hard-bitten man of arms, a concentration of physical power in contrast to the cerebral bureau-crats who governed the empire. He, like those Manchu warriors who had gone before him, was the dark fist of brute strength that lay behind the gentle and refined demeanor of the emperor and his civil officials. Yet so far apart did he live from that cultured world that he could not even read or write in Chinese, only the Manchu language.

Eldemboo's career read like a summary of Qianlong's great expansion of the empire: conscripted in 1768 at the age of twenty to fight the Burmese in southern Yunnan province, he had served in the crushing of an ethnic Tibetan rebellion in Sichuan in the 1770s and a Muslim uprising in Gansu province in 1784. He helped put down a rebellion on Taiwan in 1787, and served in the far west in the early 1790s in major wars against the Gurkhas in Tibet and Nepal. In 1797, promoted to lieutenant general, he led the suppression of the Miao ethnic uprising in Hunan province that preceded the outbreak of the White Lotus. Eldemboo was clean of connections to Heshen, and Jiaqing promoted him to assistant commander of the war against the White Lotus rebels as part of an upper-level recalibration in early 1799. In September of that same year, Jiaqing put him in charge of the entire campaign.[12]

The fundamental problem for the government's campaign was mobility. The rebels needed little more than hand weapons, and they could get everything else they required from villages as they traveled. When on the move, they didn't need elaborate camps, and they were accustomed to the landscape of mountains and heavy forests. They could come and go like birds. The government troops, on the other hand, were far larger in number, and plundered from villagers at their own peril, so they had to carry all of their food with them—along with their matchlock muskets, powder, shot, bows, arrows, and all of their other necessities, which meant heavy loads for the regular soldiers, as well as a long train of porters. That wouldn't be such a hardship if they were experienced, but most of the government soldiers had been transferred from other parts of the empire and were unaccustomed to the mountainous terrain. Their progress through the unforgiving territory where the rebels made their bases was slow and exhausting.[13]

As a result, the government commanders in the early part of the war had preferred to set up regular outposts, stationing bodies of soldiers in fixed positions, a lazy strategy that proved nearly useless against the highly mobile bands of rebels who moved through the countryside around them. Even competent officers were loath to take their men in pursuit of the enemy into dangerous territory like the old-growth forests of the Hubei-Sichuan border region (where, it was said, among unseen valleys of ancient trees dating back to the time of "wilderness and chaos," there were spiders as large as cartwheels that fed on tigers).[14] In the winter of 1800 one of Jiaqing's handpicked generals, a young, bookish Manchu named Nayancheng, explained his reluctance to take his army into these woods. "The rebels' tracks run here and there but they don't come out of the ancient forest," he reported to Jiaqing. "The dense trees block everything and you can't see more than a hundred feet in any direction. To make it worse, the weather is bitterly cold and the snow drifts reach several feet in places, so we can't even build fires and burn the woods to flush the rebels out."[15]

Jiaqing was intensely frustrated by the excuses and foot-dragging of his commanders. "Nayancheng's military force is hardly inadequate," he responded angrily in this case. "How can you have more than ten thousand crack government troops at your disposal, along with several tens of thousands of militia forces, yet get so bogged down trying to pursue just a couple of thousand rebels into the forest and wipe them out?"[16] By the summer, Jiaqing would strip Nayancheng of his military duties and recall him to Beijing, transferring his forces to the command of the veteran Eldemboo—who, unlike the younger and softer generals, was unafraid of harsh terrain and weather, and perfectly willing to endure the same outdoor hardships as his men.[17]

The dynasty's war against the White Lotus was in its essence a counterinsurgent war, and it needed a new strategy to suit the reality that the rebels were deeply blended into—and drew their continued strength from—the local peasant populations. With Qianlong's passing and the execution of Heshen, Jiaqing was open to a new approach, and the strategy by which Eldemboo would ultimately win the war for him was called *jianbi qingye*, meaning literally "fortify the walls and clear the countryside."[18] A progenitor of the "strategic hamlet" system used with less effect in the early years of American involvement in the Vietnam War, it relied on two primary efforts. First, to separate off the "good" peasants who were as yet unaffected by the rebels' ideology and move them into concentrated places of safety—a succession of heavily fortified encampments every ten or twenty miles, known as *baozhai* ("walls and ramparts")—where some of them would be armed and trained as a militia to defend the camp. Second, to "clear the countryside" by moving all of the grain harvests and food stores into those same fortified encampments where the people would take refuge, thus denying the rebels any source of food or other supplies.[19] The hope was that the rebels, unable to scavenge food from the emptied countryside, would be forced to come out of hiding to engage the far superior armies of the government.[20]

Under Eldemboo's command, the *jianbi qingye* strategy was implemented widely throughout the war zone. Hundreds of fortified camps were built across the afflicted provinces, with heavy walls and moats to surround them.[21] As for the local militias that defended the *baozhai*, they would not be taken on campaign like the ones that had caused so much trouble in the earlier years of the war. Their only role would be to protect their own families and those of their neighbors, which kept them relatively honest and removed the worst excesses of their forebears: the looting and abusing of local populations, their tendency to collaborate with the rebels. With the "good" population concentrated in their *baozhai*, defended by their own militia units, Eldemboo's Manchu and Chinese troops were then free to campaign at will through the afflicted provinces—which, in their cleared state, became an open field for combat. Despite occasional setbacks (which, unlike his predecessors, he reported honestly to the throne), Eldemboo began racking up a string of victories over the weakened and fragmenting rebel forces.

By the beginning of 1803, Eldemboo's campaign had moved into its final phase, the brutal mopping up of the remnants of the broken rebellion and the beginning steps to demilitarize and disarm the local militias. But Jiaqing warned his generals not to relax their vigilance too soon. "Though the main disease is cured," he wrote, "there are boils and sores that remain." Jiaqing demanded the complete annihilation of the White Lotus survivors: "If even a single rebel is left alive," he wrote, "it would be enough for them to keep spreading and growing."[22] They heeded his instructions, ruthlessly, and by the late summer of 1803 Jiaqing's commanders were finally able to report to him that after eight years of effort the extermination of the White Lotus sects in the main three provinces of the rebellion was for all intents and purposes complete.[23]

In the early spring of 1804, Eldemboo traveled back to Beijing, where he returned his carved seal of authority to the Jiaqing emperor, signifying that the war was over. It would be the last victory in his long career, however—the grizzled general died the next year at the age of fifty-seven, and with him passed a generation. The Manchu general had served his emperor well, though, and by 1805, for the first time, Jiaqing could address the future of his empire without the ongoing drain of resources to the gigantic White Lotus war.[24]

It was a bitter victory. Going just by the official reports of casualties, a Chinese historian writing a few decades later estimated that several hundred thousand rebels had been killed in the course of suppressing the White Lotus. As for the numbers of government soldiers and militiamen killed—let alone the masses of civilians who died of violence, starvation, or suicide—he admitted there was no way to know for sure.[25] There is also no way to know just how many of the "rebels" killed by government forces were actually believers in the White Lotus religion, as opposed to innocent bystanders, forced conscripts, or followers of other secretive religions who were caught up in the suppression. But Jiaqing could at least take solace in the fact that the rebellion had been brought under control and there was peace again in the central provinces (as much, at least, as there had been before the war).

Order more widely in the empire, however, was still elusive. During the years when the dynasty was concentrating all of its military and financial resources on the White Lotus suppression in the central provinces, vacuums of power had opened up elsewhere in the country—which created openings for other disturbances of different kinds, far from the central war zone. The largest of these ancillary rebellions, which in 1805 still lay in the way of Jiaqing's path to restoring order and security to China, had emerged not in the mountains of the interior but at the edge of the sea where the westerners were.

———

For many people in south China, the line between the land and water was blurred from birth. In cramped urban areas like Canton there were "floating cities" of tens of thousands of boat people, poor families who could not afford land or rent, who were born, died, and lived their entire lives on narrow boats lashed together seven or eight deep at the riverbanks, rarely setting foot on dry land. Unlike those who lived on land, the boat families did not bind their daughters' feet, and much of the labor—steering, hawking, collecting laundry from foreign ships to wash—was done by the women. Poor as it was, in this transitional world between the hard land and the boundless sea there was far greater equality to be found between women and men.

It was from this floating world in Canton that a young woman named Shi Yang first emerged in the early nineteenth century. Her early years are murky, but it is known that she worked as a prostitute in one of the floating brothels for which Canton was famous throughout China—"flower-boats," by their more poetic names, where the wealthy could squander their riches on wine and singsong girls. No accurate image of her has ever been found, but she was rumored (predictably, given what came later) to have been gorgeous. In 1801, Shi Yang married one of her clients, a successful pirate captain named Zheng Yi. In the years that followed, Shi Yang would bear him two sons and adopt a third who was older. More important, she would help Zheng Yi to unite six rival pirate fleets into a large confederation that by 1805 totaled somewhere in the neighborhood of seventy thousand sailors on four hundred ships in an organized body of pirates more than twice the size of the Spanish Armada. When Zheng Yi died in a storm at sea in 1807, Shi Yang installed her adopted son (who would later become her second husband) as commander of the largest fleet in the confederation, the red banner fleet, which operated on the southern coast around Canton. Then she assumed the supreme command of the confederation herself.[26]

It was easy for a fisherman to become a pirate in those days. One didn't need to be a hardened desperado to start out, just to have encountered difficult times and be willing to rob from another family or village in order to improve things for one's own. A band of pirates could be born from nothing more than a handful of fishermen with shared hard luck, possessing little more than a cluster of rowboats and a few knives. But with those boats and knives they could capture a small trading junk and take command of it. Often some of the crew would stay on to join them. As they repeated the process (if they managed to avoid capture), their ranks would grow. Their ships would increase in size and number as they traded up and took on larger risks. They would buy cannons for the ships. With success, they would attract more followers—especially in a time of widespread difficulty like the early 1800s with its overpopulation, when so many of the poor chafed at the oppressions of government officials and despaired of making a living on land. Eventually the most talented and charismatic of the leaders commanded large fleets with major ships carrying fifteen or more guns. One flagship seen by a foreign witness mounted thirty-eight guns on deck, two of them long twenty-four-pounders.[27]

The core of Shi Yang's fleets had taken form as Chinese mercenary navies in a Vietnamese rebellion in the 1780s. Those predatory fleets were let go after the rebellion failed in 1799, after which they returned to China with their battle-hardened organizations and began assimilating smaller bodies of pirates. It was a welcome coincidence that their return overlapped with the Qing dynasty's efforts to put down the White Lotus rebellion in the interior, for not only was the empire's military attention directed inland at the time, but the dynasty also borrowed heavily from its coastal forces to help shore up the beleaguered armies in the White Lotus region. Just as the transfer of dynastic forces to Hunan to fight the Miao Rebellion had preceded the White Lotus, tens of thousands of soldiers from the Chinese coast were transferred inland to fight the White Lotus in the years leading up to the major pirate campaigns. Meanwhile, millions of taels of silver were collected from the Hong merchants in Canton to help pay for the White Lotus campaigns—funds that would have served those merchants far better had they been invested instead in local maritime defense.[28]

Even if the dynasty hadn't been so heavily bogged down with the White Lotus, it had little immediate capacity to respond to the rise of piracy. This was not because China's government was inherently unable to counter enemies along the coast, but simply because the country had not faced a serious coastal threat for more than a hundred years, since the time of Qianlong's grandfather Kangxi. Kangxi's response to that previous threat, however, showed what the regime was capable of if the emperor so chose. Back then, in the 1660s, the young Qing dynasty was just twenty years past its conquest of Beijing and still only partially in control of the empire. It faced a pirate navy of more than a thousand ships and 150,000 sailors that had declared open rebellion against the Manchus and called for the restoration of the Ming dynasty. Kangxi had just come to the throne, a mere boy at the time, and he and his advisers recognized that the dynasty's Manchu forces, which were mounted on horseback, could not possibly hope to master such a large force of pirates on water. So rather than fighting them head-on, Kangxi instead ordered the evacuation of China's entire southeastern coast.

Nearly a thousand miles of shoreline, from Zhejiang province in the east all the way down to Canton in the south and beyond, was emptied of its inhabitants so the Ming-loyalist pirate fleet would have nowhere to find supplies or conscripts. The evacuation began in 1661 with a zone three miles wide, increasing to ten miles the following year. Lines were drawn (soldiers stretched ropes to mark them), and the population living between the boundary lines and the shore were forced at spearpoint to abandon their homes and villages and move inland, carrying whatever of their possessions they could manage. Behind them, the farms were dug up and the fishing boats and villages burned, leaving nothing for the pirates to find on land except military camps.

The evacuation in the 1660s was horrific from a humanitarian standpoint: a forced relocation of millions of people, leading their farm animals on a slow exodus, carrying the elderly on their backs, into cities and inland regions where they had no land rights and no clear way to make a living. "There was wailing everywhere," wrote an observer at the time. "The sight was too painful to watch."[29] But as a military strategy it succeeded. The pirate fleet, unable to obtain supplies on the Chinese coast, abandoned mainland China and sailed across the Taiwan Strait to conquer the Dutch colony that then existed on Formosa (modern-day Taiwan). The coastal evacuation order would be enforced in most areas for more than twenty years, which was how long it took for the Qing dynasty to build a navy sufficient to cross the strait and destroy the pirates on their new base. Once the pirate armada was defeated, the dynasty incorporated Taiwan into its empire and the millions of people who had been removed from the coast were finally allowed to return home.

That victory was so decisive and complete that China's coast would enjoy a long era of peace afterward. Through the eighteenth century, the only real security issues China's coastal communities faced were small-scale amateur pirates—poor fishermen, typically, who sailed up the coast to make trouble in the off-season when the winds wouldn't allow them to go to sea. They hardly merited a centralized military response. In times of need, coastal communities raised their own funds to build watchtowers and guardhouses, and hired local police forces to protect their markets against the predations of bandits— local measures that, up to the early 1800s, were fully sufficient.[30] By

the time the new pirate confederation rebelled against the government, the dynasty had not needed an oceangoing navy for more than
a hundred years and the ships it had built to conquer Taiwan had long
ago rotted away.

The Qing military was thus completely unprepared to confront
the rise of Shi Yang's armada, which nearly rivaled the scale of the
great Ming-loyalist fleet of old. The empire's coastal forces in the
early 1800s depended mainly on lumbering "rice-carrier" junks,
which were originally used for shipping and could only sail close to
shore. They were far inferior to the swift, well-handled seagoing vessels of Shi Yang's pirates, and poorly armed by comparison. While the
imperial boats were typically manned by forty to eighty sailors with a
handful of mismatched cannons, the larger pirate vessels carried hundreds of crewmen and sometimes dozens of large guns.

Further, in reflection of the Qing navy's long-standing irrelevance, its forces had little funding and morale was low. Commanders
could not coordinate with one another, the skills of the sailors and
captains were amateurish, and payrolls were usually in default. Ships
that were lost in battle or wrecked in storms generally couldn't be
replaced, and (in reflection of the corruption of the time) even basic
repairs could go unmade due to dockside embezzlement, so only a
portion of the fleet was ever seaworthy. Indeed, when the pirate fleets
first rose up, the Qing forces were so scant and weak that officials in
charge of coastal defense were reduced to hiring local fishermen and
other civilians with nonmilitary craft to supplement their fleets.[31]

The results were disastrous. Qing naval patrols feared contact
with Shi Yang's pirates, even to the point of sabotaging their own ships
to avoid going to sea. Others hid from the pirate vessels in secret harbors and filed false reports with their superiors reporting grand victories. On the rare occasions on which they did engage the pirates in
battle, they almost always lost.[32] It wasn't until 1805—after the White
Lotus rebels were finally suppressed—that the Jiaqing emperor was
finally able to concentrate his attention on the pirates, but even then
it took time for the government to find its footing.

By 1808, when the conflict with Admiral Drury broke out at
Macao, Shi Yang's pirate network controlled virtually the entire eastern and southern coastlines of China. Aside from the more familiar

predations of raiding ships, stealing their cargoes, and holding their crews for ransom, they developed an institutional side as well: collecting tribute (effectively, taxes) from seagoing communities along the coast, which were paid at a series of offices the pirates maintained on land. They also worked a huge protection racket, selling passes to guarantee safe passage to fishermen and cargo shippers, who should they fail to purchase a pass were almost certain to be boarded. They were professional to the point that if a body of pirates accidentally plundered a vessel carrying a pass from another fleet, their chief would make them return all of the stolen goods along with money for damages.[33]

Senior officials in Canton tried to expand their local naval forces, with unimpressive results. In 1808, the pirates killed a new provincial commander in chief who had been sent to Canton to suppress them. By the end of that year Shi Yang's pirates had destroyed nearly half the ships in the provincial navy. In 1809, in a major effort by newly built Qing forces, forty imperial junks rigged with extra weapons were launched to attack one of the pirate fleets, but in their very first encounter, twenty-eight of the government ships were captured, while the rest turned tail and fled to safety. By August of that year, the pirates were bold enough to post public notices on land threatening to attack Canton itself.[34]

Unlike in central China where the dynasty battled alone against the White Lotus rebels, however, there was another force at work off the China coast: namely, the Western traders—especially the gigantic East India Company ships with their Royal Navy escorts and modern gunnery. And whereas the White Lotus were so far inland as to be invisible to the British and Americans who plied the waters between Canton and Macao, the pirates struck them where they lived. Shi Yang's pirates were just as willing to attack foreign ships as Chinese ones, provided the situation worked to their advantage (an isolated ship, preferably undermanned or crippled by a storm)—and on approach they were indistinguishable from any of the other junks that crowded the Canton waterways, so it was impossible to keep them at a distance. Just like the captains of Chinese ships, then, foreign merchants also had to pay protection fees to the pirates at their offices in Macao and Canton to ensure safe passage, fees that they rationalized as a form of insurance.[35]

The pirates also occasionally took foreign hostages, who left some of the most vivid accounts we have of life in their ranks. An Englishman named John Turner, first officer on a ship from Bombay, was captured near Macao in December 1806 and held for nearly six months. He described the spartan day-to-day existence of the pirates—their cramped and filthy boats where he, like the pirates themselves, had a space only eighteen inches wide and four feet long in which to sleep. His diet consisted mostly of rice and dried fish. The Qing authorities were notoriously brutal to captured pirates (one practice was to nail their hands together instead of using rope to bind them), and Turner witnessed firsthand how readily the pirates returned the favor. One official from a captured government boat, he wrote, was nailed to the deck by his feet and beaten by the pirates, then taken on shore and cut into pieces. "The others," he wrote, "I believe, were treated in a similar manner."[36] Hostages who weren't officials were treated better, and many stayed on for service with the pirates afterward if their ransoms weren't paid. Those who tried to escape generally met with gruesome ends.

As for Turner himself, the pirates made it clear that if he couldn't get his employers to pay a $30,000 ransom he would have to join their crew as a gunner or they would kill him too. After five and a half months of captivity he managed to negotiate the ransom down to $2,500, which an Englishman in Canton (Beale, the Prussian consul and Cantonese speaker) paid to secure his release. During his captivity, Turner tried to understand why the pirates did what they did, and the only answer they ever gave him echoed the answers that the White Lotus rebels gave their own questioners, namely that officials in their home districts were so corrupt and abusive that they had left to go to sea and find safety with the pirates.[37] It was the same refrain: the corruption and cruelty of low-level Qing officials had forced them to become outlaws, just as they forced the White Lotus to become rebels. The officials oppressed, and the people rebelled.

Another Englishman, named Richard Glasspoole, was captured in 1809 and concurred in the cruel violence of the pirates—who, he wrote, were "so savage in their resentments and manners that they frequently take the hearts of their enemies and eat them with rice."[38] The Canton governor-general instituted a coastal embargo to try to block supplies from getting to the pirate ships, which succeeded only in driving the pirates inland along the complex riverways of Guangdong province. Glasspoole was witness as his ship took him upriver inland far beyond the range of the boats associated with the foreign trade, through a landscape of ruined towns and villages. The river valleys were outlaw territory, he noted, where entire villages paid tribute to the pirates, their populations singing songs to the fleet from shore as its hundreds of ships passed them on the river. The pirates attacked other towns with impunity, rowing in and landing under cover of night, then burning down the government buildings and demanding promises of annual tribute from the locals, threatening otherwise to destroy the entire town. Tribute was paid in silver dollars and in kind: rice, roasted pigs, sugar. When the pirates encountered government soldiers, they made Glasspoole and the other foreign hostages join the fighting with their European muskets—"which," he noted sardonically, "did great execution" against Qing soldiers armed mainly with bows and arrows and ancient matchlock guns.[39]

Because the problem of coastal piracy affected foreign as well as Chinese shipping, it offered grounds for international cooperation between the naval forces present in south China. Both the Chinese and Europeans, after all, had a shared interest in freeing the coast from the scourge of piracy, and the Western ships—especially the British naval vessels, finely tuned from their ongoing war with France—had the potential to be far more devastating against the pirate fleets than the slipshod and jury-rigged Qing naval forces.

Jiaqing, however, made it clear to his ministers that the suppression of pirates was a matter of imperial prestige. As he saw it, even a small reliance on foreign aid would be an embarrassment, tantamount to admitting that the dynasty was unable to secure its own territory. In March 1805, after learning that the British were sending gunships to protect their merchant vessels against pirate raids as they sailed up to Canton, he wrote in a scathing edict that "if foreign-

ers get plundered by pirates after they have already entered Macao—
a port in our internal waterways—then how can we *not* be a laughing-
stock to them?"[40] He ordered the governor-general to redouble his
efforts to strengthen the region's coastal defenses and discipline the
imperial soldiers "so the pirate traitors will take themselves far away,
the foreigners will have nothing to fear, and the maritime border will
be peaceful." In the same edict, he referred to a recent letter from
King George in which the British monarch had said vaguely that he
would be glad to provide any services the dynasty might require. Jiaqing took that as a veiled offer of military assistance, which he found
insulting. "Apparently he has heard of occasional instances of robbery
on the ocean and thinks we might need his military power to join
with our own," Jiaqing wrote. "Do we now have to borrow help from
vassal states to eliminate pirates?!" Nine months later, in a response
to the king, he told him bluntly, "We have no need for the services of
your state."[41]

Nevertheless, the pride of the emperor in Beijing and the pragmatism of the officials on the ground in Canton—who actually had to
deal with the enormous pirate problem up close—were two different
things. Jiaqing had seen only paintings of European naval ships, but
many of the officials in Canton had been on board them and were
perfectly aware of how useful they might be against the pirates. Since
those officials were ultimately answerable to the emperor, however,
any direct (or at least recorded) effort on their part to recruit military
aid from foreigners risked punishment from Beijing if it should be
revealed. So while they did begin asking for help, politics dictated that
they be secretive and informal about doing so. The foreigners they
approached, however, wanted neither secrecy nor informality; they
wanted credit for their aid, and they wanted leverage for commerce.

By the time Shi Yang reached the peak of her power in 1809,
relations between the Chinese and Western traders were back on
decently strong footing again after the mess of the Drury incident.
(Drury, incidentally, in the course of trying to justify his invasion of
Macao, claimed at one point that he had been sent to help China
fight pirates—a claim that Jiaqing called "utter nonsense.")[42] In
August 1809, pirate forces put chase to five different American ships
in the vicinity of Macao and captured a Portuguese vessel belonging

to the governor of Timor.[43] That same month, the Hong merchants in Canton privately purchased a little English brig of 108 tons, the *Elizabeth*, which they planned to outfit for pirate suppression at their own expense.[44] They also commissioned a foreign ship, the three-hundred-ton *Mercury*, and staffed it with fifty American volunteers, though it was too small to be very effective.[45] The new governor-general, a man named Bailing, found himself in an intensely awkward position. His predecessor had just been sent into exile by Jiaqing for being too gentle with the British. He knew he was supposed to maintain a hard line against foreigners. Yet he also knew that their help against the pirates could be extremely useful.

A promising opportunity materialized in September 1809 with the arrival of the sixty-four-gun *St. Albans*, a Royal Navy ship of the line on convoy duty escorting a fleet of twelve East Indiamen. The captain of the *St. Albans* was Francis Austen, an officer of great accomplishments (whose talents nevertheless paled in comparison to those of his younger sister, Jane Austen). A few weeks after his arrival in Canton, a mid-level official visited Austen at the British factory and asked him informally, on behalf of the governor-general, if he would organize and lead a naval campaign against the pirates. Given that the Company's ships wouldn't be needing his services until their return voyage several months hence, Austen said he was open to the idea. But he did have two conditions: first, that he be allowed to sail freely to and from Canton without a pass (which was normally required of foreign warships), and second—the sticking point—that since he was in effect being asked to kill Chinese subjects, he needed the governor-general to give him a formal written invitation. But he was strongly inclined to help, and even offered advice on how to better equip Qing naval junks to make them more effective (chauvinistic advice it was, though: along with outfitting the junks with Western guns, he also recommended they be manned by European sailors instead of Chinese).[46]

An appointment was set for Captain Austen to meet in person three days later with Governor-General Bailing at the hoppo's offices just outside the factory compound. Austen was not happy about what ensued. Expecting courtesy appropriate to the magnitude of the favor that was being asked of him and his country's service, he complained afterward that he was instead made to wait "nearly half an hour in a close dirty kind of lobby, exposed to the stare of every blackguard who could squeeze himself into the passage leading to it."[47] Bailing never showed up. Instead, he asked the hoppo to meet with Austen in his place, which Austen refused, wanting to deal only with the imperial governor-general rather than a mere customs official. Austen finally left the hoppo's offices in a huff, demanding that if the governor-general wanted to see him, he should come find him in the British factory. Given that he had no idea of the pressure Bailing was under from a watchful emperor in Beijing who considered foreign aid a sign of weakness, Austen simply chalked up the governor-general's failure to attend the meeting to "imbecility, and a struggle between pride and the conviction of his own inability to arrest the progress of the pirates."[48] There would be no follow-up.

———

The Qing forces did, in the end, bring the pirates to heel without significant help from outside, and they did so on their own terms. The way they accomplished this was a sharp contrast to the forceful military suppression of the White Lotus, with its armies in the tens of thousands, in that it invoked the other major tool in the dynasty's arsenal: namely, forgiveness, and the lure of a peaceful and settled life in China. Once the White Lotus war was over, the government began shifting resources into developing stronger naval capacities on the coast near Canton—which, in conjunction with coastal embargoes to break the pirates' supply lines, started to gain traction by late 1809. Newly built and freshly armed government fleets fought pitched battles with the pirates on water, sometimes involving more than a hundred ships and lasting for days. Such measures alone, however, could not prevail. "The pirates are too powerful," as one Chinese admiral wrote plaintively, "we cannot master them by our arms; the pirates are many, but we are few . . . we are unable to engage with this overpowering force."[49]

It was the other side of the dynasty's strategy that ultimately prevailed. To complement its military effort, the provincial government put up proclamations offering amnesty to pirates who surrendered peacefully. It was an attractive offer for outlaws who otherwise faced only the prospect of execution if they should be captured. As embargoes made life on the water more difficult, food supplies became scarce. (The English prisoner Glasspoole had nothing but boiled caterpillars and rice for an entire three-week stretch, and described his captors eagerly devouring the rats in the ship's hold.)[50] Combined with the government's steadily increasing military presence on both sea and land, fractures began to appear in the large pirate alliance. Lesser captains who turned themselves in were quickly rewarded by the government and then unleashed on their former comrades.

By the end of 1809, under growing pressure, a rift broke out between the leaders of the two largest fleets—the red fleet under Shi Yang's adopted son Zhang Bao, and the black fleet under a rival. Fearing an attack, the head of the black fleet drew up a petition of surrender to ask the government for clemency. "We now live in a very populous age," he wrote; "some of us could not agree with their relations, and were driven out like noxious weeds. Some after having tried all they could, without being able to provide for themselves, at last joined bad society. Some lost their property by shipwrecks; some withdrew into this watery empire to escape from punishment." In the familiar lament of the time, he claimed that his men had become pirates only because a crumbling society had driven them into a life of crime. And now, like wayward children, they wanted to come back home. "It was from necessity," he went on, "that the laws of the empire were violated, and the merchants robbed of their goods. . . . But now we will avoid these perils, leave our connections, and desert our comrades; we will make our submission."[51]

Alarmed at the prospect of the black fleet's leader joining the government's forces against her, Shi Yang took the government's offer of amnesty herself. In February 1810, she landed at Canton with a small number of women and children from the red fleet, and met with Bailing at his offices to negotiate a surrender. Bailing, according to one account of the meeting, told her he was "commanded by the humanity of his Majesty's government not to kill but to pardon you."[52] Zhang Bao, Shi Yang's adopted son and the commander of the red fleet, turned himself in shortly afterward. The Qing officials welcomed him with gifts of food and money for his men, and—rather than being arrested or cut into pieces—he was made a lieutenant in the imperial navy. Some of his men joined him in service to the government, while others were given money to renounce their past crimes and resettle themselves into new lives on land, welcomed back into the imperial fold.

Thus, in contrast to the scorched-earth destruction of the White Lotus, the Qing government brought the pirates back under control largely by means of aggressive persuasion. Rather than mounting enormous armies and militias as it had done in the land war in central China, the dynasty addressed the pirate threat on the coast with only modest improvements to its navy, relying more heavily on embargoes and offers of amnesty that were far more cost-effective. Zhang Bao would continue to serve the dynasty as a loyal officer until his death in 1822. Shi Yang, the prostitute who had risen to command a fleet of seventy thousand pirates, would live out the rest of her life as a civilian in Canton, running a gambling house and living in peace until she came to her natural death in 1844 at the age of sixty.[53]

An optimistic rendering of imperial forces "pacifying" the pirates in 1809

. . .

By 1810, the empire was back on a much more secure footing than in the final years of Qianlong's reign. Jiaqing's chosen commanders had suppressed the rebellion of the White Lotus in the interior and calmed the problem of coastal pirates on the periphery. They had demonstrated the continued ability of the huge Qing government bureaucracy, given sufficient time, to adapt to new threats and defeat them. Internal security aside, there were no serious border conflicts with the empire's neighbors, and after the brief problem with the fleet under Admiral Drury—which, notably, had ended because the British feared provoking a war with China—there was peace with the foreign traders who called at Canton as well. Jiaqing had slowed down the spiraling decline of his father's final days, overseeing at least a partial return of order. It was far from perfect, but there was room for optimism.

However, a more global recalibration of power was under way. In the years when China's government was developing its capacities to deal with internal rebellions, mobilizing gigantic land armies to fight deep-rooted insurgents in the interior, Great Britain had been focused ruthlessly on developing its sea power. Both empires expended huge amounts of money on military actions during this time—China spending as much as two hundred million taels on its eight-year White Lotus suppression, Great Britain spending the equivalent of about twelve times that on its twenty-two-year war with France—but Britain, even though it ran up a monstrous national debt that reflected more than two-thirds of its war expenses, would come out of its contest in 1815 strengthened and invigorated.[54] By the time Britain defeated Napoleon it had doubled the size of the Royal Navy, building it into the most powerful maritime force in the world, a tool it could easily repurpose for the control of a vast and profitable waterborne empire spanning much of the globe (and to which many new strategic outposts had been added in the war's course). By 1820, the British Empire would exercise control over a quarter of the world's population, coming nearly to rival the size of China.[55] Meanwhile, China, battling enemies within its own borders and along its own coast, losing much of its war funding to corruption, would, though likewise victorious, emerge from this era weakened rather than strengthened.

Victory over internal rebellions, moreover, held scarcely the same unifying prestige as victory over a foreign enemy, and the Qing dynasty did not, after the suppression of the White Lotus, enjoy the same rising faith in its national strength that Britain did after defeating Napoleon. Quite the opposite, in fact. The banner of rebellion against the Manchus had flown for eight years by the end of the White Lotus war, then continued under Shi Yang's fleets, damaging imperial prestige and giving encouragement to other disaffected groups within the empire. Furthermore, the economic costs of fighting these wars—especially the White Lotus—would significantly hinder the Qing government going forward.

As the full accounts of the White Lotus war started to come clear, Jiaqing slashed the budgets of the military and instituted strict cost-control measures to prevent a repeat of the widespread embezzlement that plagued the army under Qianlong and Heshen.[56] Such measures would stanch the dangerous bleeding of government funds, but they also ensured that the Qing dynasty's military would in the future have less funding, wield older weapons, and suffer from lower morale than it had enjoyed back when Qianlong was at his prime. The dynasty's forces were still the preeminent military power in Asia, and they still had deep resources on which they could rely in times of emergency, but by 1810 the emergencies seemed to be over. In expectation that the coming era would be one of peace for the empire, and facing an economic reality that was bleaker than he would have hoped, Jiaqing effectively mortgaged the future improvement of China's military to preserve the near-term stability of its government.

———

The British actually did, in the end, offer a more selfless assistance to help China fight its pirates. In 1810, Lord Minto in India prepared a squadron of warships and a detachment of artillery that he proposed to send to China to work with the Company's ships in destroying Shi Yang's fleets. By the time his offer was received in Canton, however, it was no longer needed. Bailing, the governor-general, was busy negotiating the surrender of the remaining pirates, and the governor below him responded to Lord Minto on August 12, 1810, that the pirates were "separated, exterminated and at rest: the whole number is reduced to profound tranquility, so that there is no need for assistance." [57]

There was peace in the South China Sea, no help needed from the Royal Navy. However, a chance for meaningful cooperation between two empires with deeply shared interests in the prosperity of trade at Canton had been lost. Jiaqing could go forward in confidence that his dynasty's military forces were self-sufficient and had no need for outside aid in strengthening themselves to maintain the security of south China. The British, for their part, could go on believing that Jiaqing was barely able to keep control over the mutinous elements within his own empire, but that he was too proud and oblivious to ask for their help.

CHAPTER 5

Points of Entry

While George Staunton was home in England on leave in 1809, he began to lobby for a second embassy to Beijing. In a letter to the chairman of the East India Company, he proposed that Britain should send a royal ambassador to repair the damage Admiral Drury had caused when he invaded Macao. Specifically, Staunton thought the new ambassador should reassure the Jiaqing emperor that the British government had never authorized Drury's actions and did not sanction hostility of any kind toward China, an empire with which it wanted only "the most amicable and mutually beneficial relations."[1] The ambassador could even be provided with British government documents translated into Chinese, he suggested, to prove his case and restore the Jiaqing emperor's good opinion of Great Britain. Even if that were all the ambassador accomplished, Staunton said he would count the mission as a success. As for other possibilities—the expansion of trade into new ports, exchanges of ambassadors, and so on—there was no way to tell what might come; it depended on the negotiating skills of whomever was sent. And at that point, Staunton's roundabout proposal finally made it clear who he thought that person should be. If the king's ambassador, he wrote, "should happily have the opportunity, such as never yet has been afforded, of conversing unreservedly and without the aid of Interpreters, with those who influence the Emperor's Councils . . . it will not be too much to expect the most important and beneficial results." The key words there were "without the aid of interpreters": the ambassador, he believed, should be himself.

The proposal met with interest. Staunton had a well-connected patron named John Barrow, an old friend of his father's who had been along on the Macartney mission and was now second secretary of the Admiralty, who tipped him off secretly that he was "almost certain" to be sent to Beijing as a royal ambassador and should expect to be summoned immediately.[2] Sure enough, Staunton soon found himself called in for a meeting with the chairman of the Court of Directors at the East India Company's headquarters on Leadenhall Street in London. Swelling with pride, he entered the august edifice of the East India House, newly expanded to represent the Company's rising status as a territorial power—in he went, past the fluted Ionic columns of the sixty-foot entrance, passing below the figure of Britannia riding a lion (flanked by a smaller figure of Asia, riding a camel), into the smoky, candlelit warren of hallways and stairwells within—eager to hear the news he had been hoping for since his parents first put him on the *Hindostan* back to Canton.[3]

On being called into the chairman's office, however, Staunton was instead informed soberly that the directors felt it would be inappropriate for the British embassy to be led by an employee of the East India Company. The embassy was intended to represent the king of England, not the merchants, and they believed Staunton's presence would confuse the issue. The news came as a withering shock. Even forty years later when writing his memoirs he still burned from his "mortification" on that day, certain he had been "extremely ill-used" and probably "the victim of some unworthy intrigue."[4] At the time, the only salve for his wounded pride was of the spiteful kind: the plans for that mission were eventually scuttled, so at least nobody else got to be the ambassador to China.

In spite of the setback, Staunton continued working to build his reputation as Britain's first real authority on China. In 1810, during the same visit home, he published the translation of the Qing legal code he had been working on for nearly a decade. It was the first

The East India House

major work ever to be translated directly from Chinese into English and greatly strengthened his claim to expertise. Though the book's importance, it should be noted, had less to do with the details of the code itself or the quality of the translation than with what it sought to reveal about China on the larger scale. Of all the texts Staunton could have translated, he believed that the legal code provided the best possible window into the workings of Chinese society, containing within its lines the "system and constitution of the Government, the principles of its internal policy, its connection with the national habits and character, and its influence upon the general state and condition of the people in that country."[5]

At the time when Staunton published his book, the admiring visions of China that had been current at the time of the Macartney mission were on the wane in some quarters. The seeds of disaffection had been planted by the publications from that very mission, some of whose members hinted that China was not the faultless vision of Eastern perfection they had expected. Macartney's own grim predictions of a coming revolution in China, though unpublished while he was still alive, had recently been made public along with other portions of his China diary after his death in 1806.[6]

At the same time, the years of war against France, intensified by British anti-Catholic sentiment, had tarnished the old Jesuit accounts of China that French Enlightenment philosophers had used to celebrate China as a model of stable and enduring government. In the Napoleonic era, British distrust of the French bled over into distrust of Frenchmen from the past—especially those like Voltaire whose writings also lay behind the Revolution. As one British writer put it in 1810, "Nothing can exceed the *gullibility* of the French *philosophistes*, except that of those who were misled by them." Under the illusions cast by French writers about China, he went on, "the world remained pretty generally persuaded of the vast perfection to which the Chinese nation has attained in the progress of the sciences, and especially in the arts of government, until the embassy of Lord Macartney, and the accounts of that embassy . . . open[ed] the eyes, of Englishmen at least, to the imposture under which they had laboured."[7]

With his book on Chinese law, Staunton acted as a British successor to the continental Jesuits of earlier centuries, casting China in a more flattering light for his own era. His view of the country was on the whole a positive one (as perhaps it could only be, given the degree to which he had yoked his career to it). He described China in the book's preface as an empire that was relatively enlightened, ruled by laws that were clearly defined and (for the most part) rational. It was obviously very different from Europe, he wrote, but there was a great deal for Europeans to admire in its civilization. Along with what he saw as the disinclination of China's government to conquer foreign countries, he singled out for praise "the sobriety, industry, and even intelligence of the lower classes," "the almost total absence of feudal rights and privileges," and "the equable distribution of landed property." All of these positive features of Chinese society, he explained, derived from "a system of penal laws, if not the most just and equitable, at least the most comprehensive, uniform, and suited to the genius of the people for whom it is designed, perhaps of any that ever existed."[8]

Staunton wanted especially to set China apart from—and above—the other "Oriental" civilizations of South Asia and the Near East with which Western readers who didn't know better might confuse it. Though he never questioned the superiority of Britain, he felt that the shortcomings of China's civilization were primarily due to its lacking Christianity. Otherwise, he argued, China was clearly superior to the other cultures of the Orient, including India. He disputed a recent theory advanced by a missionary in Bengal that the Chinese language had originally derived from Sanskrit: to the contrary, argued Staunton, China's great legacy of written history, its calendars, its inventions, and its technology had no counterpart among the Hindus. While the Chinese had been in possession of "a code of laws, founded on good sense and practical wisdom" for a very long time, Hindustan was, as he described it, a "miserable country, where passive millions drag a feeble existence under the iron rod of a few crafty castes."[9] And as for the Chinese government of his own day, Staunton depicted the Jiaqing emperor as a sober and talented ruler, a decisive monarch whose destruction of Heshen displayed a "political courage and sagacity which are requisite in the character of a monarch of a great and powerful empire."[10]

A few of the reviewers followed his lead. The *Quarterly Review* carried an especially glowing evaluation of Staunton's work, calling it "an extraordinary book in every point of view."[11] That review, however, was penned (anonymously, as was the practice) by Staunton's patron and friend John Barrow, the same who had tipped him off that he was likely to be named ambassador—and, awkwardly enough, the man to whom Staunton had dedicated the book. A more objective critic in the *Edinburgh Review* at least supported Staunton on the superiority of China to other non-Western cultures. He remarked on the "great reasonableness, clearness and consistency" of the Qing code of laws, which he saw as being free from "the monstrous *verbiage* of most other Asiatic productions—none of the superstitious deliration, the miserable incoherence, the tremendous *non sequiturs* and eternal repetitions of those oracular performances." He pronounced it to be "a calm, concise, and distinct series of enactments, savouring throughout of practical judgment and European good sense."[12]

Others would not be so kind. Staunton had no control over how the book was interpreted once it was printed, and his translation of the Qing dynasty's legal code inadvertently stirred up a lurking undercurrent of hostility—not toward Staunton himself, who was generally applauded for his accomplishment—but toward China. The finely detailed laws of the Qing code, with their many gradations of corporal punishment (specifying, among other things, exactly what size of bamboo cane a convict should be beaten with, and for how many times), struck some reviewers as the mark of an empire whose people were no more the beneficiaries of enlightened governance than a common ship's crew. The *Critical Review*, for its part, completely upended Staunton's intention to build a stronger appreciation for China, offering instead that after reading his book, "We are ourselves strongly inclined to consider the Chinese as a much more unimprovable race than any of the South Sea savages."[13]

Contrary to Staunton's own intentions, several of his reviewers discovered in the Qing legal system an unbridgeable divide between China's civilization and their own. One suggested that to impose such a harsh legal code on people like the British would be "the most base and cruel of all atrocities."[14] Others held that the civilizations of China and Europe were so far removed that their peoples merited (indeed, deserved) to live under completely separate systems of law and punishment. The distinction was not an issue of sovereignty but of race—the justness of the particular legal system depended on the nature of the individual being judged, not on where he or she might at that moment reside, or what government ruled that territory. It was but a short step from there to a further conclusion—one that these writers did not broach, but others would in time—that even on Chinese soil it would be nothing short of atrocity to hold an Englishman subject to Chinese law.[15]

———

Robert Morrison was dismayed by what he saw all around him in Canton. Idolatry. Incense-burning. Moon-worship. A people damned by their ignorance of Christ. He was not a lighthearted man, nor a forgiving one. Portraits of the missionary show him with a faint smile on his lips, muttonchop sideburns reaching down his jaw, a shock of curly black hair brushed back from his round face. In one, he is attended by Chinese assistants bent over their papers and working so diligently that they can't, apparently, take the time to look up at the portraitist. It is unclear how much he actually smiled, though. He was a relentlessly driven man whose calling was the subject of ridicule, even hostility, from many of his fellow westerners.

"And so, Mr. Morrison," a ship's owner once teased him, "you

Robert Morrison and his assistants

really expect that you will make an impression on the idolatry of the great Chinese empire?"

"No, sir," replied the humorless Morrison. "I expect God will."[16]

Morrison's mission was founded on the expectation that he would never be allowed into China proper, so his primary instructions were, first, to learn the written language, and then to translate the Bible into Chinese. Books could travel where preachers could not, and the London Missionary Society had faith that if Robert Morrison could just somehow render the Christian Gospel into Chinese, then China would eventually become a Christian country. In that, Morrison's new Protestant mission diverged significantly from its Catholic predecessors. The Catholics did not generally believe in translation—converts had to learn Latin if they wanted to read the Bible themselves, and the rituals of the church required that foreign missionaries or ordained Chinese priests had to be present inside the country to attend to their converts, to hear confessions and say mass. In contrast, the London Missionary Society, which represented an inclusive potpourri of Protestant denominations, believed that all a person needed was a book of scripture, in a language he or she could read, and that would be enough to become a practicing Christian. As a preacher in Salem, Massachusetts, put it while raising money for Chinese translation work in 1812, "During the dark days of popery, the reign of mystic Babylon, the Bible had been denied to the laity; it was little read, and less understood by the clergy. At length, being translated and printed in English, it became the grand instrument of the Reformation."[17]

The idea for a Protestant mission to China had originated with an English minister named William Moseley who in 1798 sent around a circular calling for the formation of a "Society for translating the Holy Scriptures into the languages of the most populous Oriental Nations"—by which he meant China and India—based on his concern that the great "Heathen Countries" of the world were damned by their ignorance of the Christian Gospel. Until they should have access to the scriptures in their native language, said Moseley, "the three hundred and thirty millions of China . . . will continue to sit in darkness and in the shadow of death."[18]

Moseley was inspired by the Macartney mission, which ostensibly proved, by the successful translation of George III's letter to Qianlong, that accurate translations into Chinese from English could in fact be made—something many had thought impossible. Further encouragement came a few years later, when Moseley discovered in the holdings of the British Museum a manuscript in Chinese of unknown providence, whose Latin description indicated that it contained the four Gospels. In early 1804 when George Staunton was home in England to settle his father's estate, Moseley engaged him to examine the mysterious manuscript, hoping that if Staunton could read it and determine that it was accurate—and that it didn't contain any kind of a "popish turn," as one concerned bishop put it—it could be published and used as the basis for a new China mission. Over the course of several visits to the museum, trying to discern whether the Chinese text had been based on the authorized English text or the Latin Vulgate, Staunton determined in the end, much to Moseley's disappointment, that it was based on the Vulgate, and probably written by a Jesuit.[19]

The text at the British Museum being problematic, and the potential expense of publishing a Chinese book in England being in any case unthinkable (in the absence of any kind of Chinese type, an artist illiterate in the language would have had to re-create every single character in the text like a little picture), Moseley's supporters backed out. There was also a parallel problem that even if the book were published there was no way to disseminate it in China except by way of the Catholic missionaries, who would surely never agree to hand out a Protestant text. Moseley's plan—on which, he insisted repeatedly, rested the eternal souls of fully one-third of the human race—would only work if there were Protestants in China. So finally the London Missionary Society stepped in to take over the project, and decided that they would send Robert Morrison to Canton to learn the language, to make a full translation of the Bible himself, and eventually to figure out some way to get it published in large numbers and distributed within China. In its own way, it was a more ambitious and impossible-seeming mission than anything a mere explorer like Thomas Manning could have concocted.

. . .

Morrison was less tender than other Christian missionaries of his time, said one man who knew him: "His piety had the bark on—theirs was still in the green shoot."[20] And he was solitary, though not by choice. There had originally been two Protestant missionaries slated to come to China, but the other, a man named Brown, pulled out before their departure because he could not stand working with Robert Morrison. "We cannot be fit associates in the same mission," wrote Brown to the directors of the London Missionary Society; "as for love and affection, I believe there has been little on either side."[21] Morrison regretted the solitude, and was lonely in China. Almost nobody wrote to him from England. During his first year he sent more than two hundred letters to family, friends, and missionary colleagues. He received just two in return.[22]

In the autumn of 1808, however, Morrison found love. Her name was Mary Morton and she was eighteen years old at the time, eight years younger than Morrison. He met her in Macao, where he was living in the house John Roberts had provided for him. Her father was an Irish surgeon in the Royal Navy who had brought his family with him to live in Ceylon for seven years, and they were stopping at Macao on their way back home. Morrison wooed her nervously over the course of a few months. As he dined with her family and led them in prayer, he was hobbled by guilt that he should be working on his Chinese instead. His courtship succeeded, however, and on the afternoon of February 20, 1809, just as her family were preparing to depart from Macao and return home, Mary Morton and Robert Morrison were married. For once, he was happy.[23]

Driven as he was by his devotion to God, Morrison's study of Chinese was grueling and single-minded. Mary joined him initially, but she could not keep up. When conditions permitted, he studied with his tutors for eight or more hours a day, every day of the week except for the Sabbath (when he would read the Jesuit Gospel translation from the British Museum, which he had copied to bring with him to China). It did not take long before he reached his mentor George Staunton's level of ability in the written language and left his counterpart Thomas Manning behind.[24] He also surpassed both of them in his speaking ability, for while Staunton and Manning aimed only to learn Mandarin, for the sake of communicating with imperial officials, Morrison hoped to convert ordinary people. Thus he learned to speak the local dialect of Cantonese as well.

Morrison's teachers were a ramshackle crew. Abel Yun, the teacher Staunton had set him up with in Macao, was a Roman Catholic from north China who spoke Mandarin but, since he had been educated by Catholic missionaries, could write only Latin and was illiterate in Chinese characters. Another teacher of sorts was Morrison's servant boy, who taught him to speak Cantonese, though Morrison regretted that the boy came from the countryside and spoke with such a thick accent that people from the city said they couldn't understand him. His most esteemed teacher, an elderly scholar he called Mr. Li, had spent twelve years in Portugal training with the Jesuits to become a priest before quitting to get married. After leaving the Jesuits he returned to Canton and became a merchant, but found little success. He was fluent in written Chinese but had no future as a scholar, and by the time he agreed to be Morrison's teacher he was seventy years old and nearly bankrupt.[25]

Morrison's goal of translating the entire Bible was a mammoth project that he expected would take much of his lifetime, if he should complete it at all—King James, after all, had employed fifty-four translators working simultaneously, whereas Morrison toiled mostly alone. But he had a subsidiary goal that would turn out to be much more important for the other English speakers around him in Canton: namely, to try to make it easier for those who came after him to learn Chinese. Within a year of his arrival in Canton, he had already prepared a basic vocabulary of Cantonese, which he sent back to London so future missionaries could study it in advance. His larger aspiration in that field, however, was to prepare a Chinese-English dictionary—one that could be as comprehensive as possible, that could be used to decipher any kind of text that might exist in China. Nothing like it had ever existed.

It was on account of Robert Morrison's language work that the East India Company finally took notice of him. In spite of the overt hostility of the London directors to his presence in Canton, to say nothing of his own pious disdain for the men of commerce, the select committee needed an interpreter while Staunton was away. Morrison, for his part, quite desperately needed a source of income, especially if he was to support a family. And so in February 1809, on the very day of Morrison's wedding in Macao, John Roberts (the orders for whose removal were still making their way from England) offered him a position as the Company's Chinese interpreter with a salary of £500 per year—the same as George Staunton's salary at the time and equal to all of the money Morrison had spent in his first year in China. Even more valuable than the salary, the job also came with an invitation to live in the British factory in Canton.[26]

It was a potentially scandalous arrangement—the servant of God working for the disciples of Mammon—but Morrison could see no other way that he could stay in China or continue his work. And from the other side, with George Staunton home on leave in England, there was nobody else in Canton who could provide the select committee with the stream of translated edicts and regulations to which they had become accustomed. (There was Thomas Manning, of course, but compared to Morrison his translations were difficult to read and by his own admission he spoke Chinese "very imperfectly.")[27] After the withdrawal of Drury's fleet there seemed to be no more danger of getting embroiled with the Chinese authorities, so Morrison could look forward to doing his translation work for the Company quietly and safely from within the factory, with pen and paper. Thus the newly married preacher decided to swallow his moral qualms, and, knowing full well that he might be savaged by the missionary community back home for doing so, he accepted the position.

The London Missionary Society, as it turned out, would be far more accepting of the arrangement than the East India Company. A rumor did pass around certain missionary circles in England that Morrison "had deserted the cause for which he had left his home and country," but the directors of the society accepted the pragmatic necessity of his working for the Company. If nothing else, it relieved them of the burden of trying to fund him.[28] The directors of the East India Company, however, were furious to learn that their Canton factory had employed a missionary, and they ordered that Morrison be fired as soon as George Staunton returned to China from his leave in 1810. But John Roberts's successor as president of the select committee considered Morrison just as valuable as Roberts had, so he defied the orders. Reasoning that the directors in London couldn't possibly understand how useful Morrison's language services were, he told them the select committee intended to keep Morrison on its payroll unless the directors should issue further orders for his termination. It was convenient, for his purposes, that letters took roughly six months to travel each way between Canton and London—meaning that it would be another year before he could hear back from them.[29]

Morrison's acceptance into the British factory at Canton turned out to be a mixed blessing. On the one hand, it greatly advanced his language work, especially his progress on the dictionary. He was even able to take on a few students: some of the junior writers from the factory, along with Beale, the independent British trader who spoke Cantonese, and a young Dutchman who had been rescued from pirates.[30] However, his work for the Company was exhausting in its own right and cut deeply into the time he would otherwise have spent on his missionary projects. He had no time or energy to try to convert the local Chinese, and all of his efforts toward the Bible translation had to be kept secret, because even his supporters on the select committee did not want him working openly on religious texts in the factory.

Most painfully, though, since Chinese regulations did not allow foreign women to live in Canton, Mary had to stay behind in Macao without him. Macao had a much larger Western community than Canton—several thousand people, compared to a few dozen in Canton—but almost all of them were Portuguese, which was a problem not of language (for Mary could speak some Portuguese) but of religion: they were Catholic, and Mary, the Protestant missionary's wife, had almost no friends there. The Qing government did not permit free travel between Canton and Macao, so Morrison could only be with her in the summer. Even then, due to his frosty relations with the other Europeans their house was, in his words, a "lonely, solitary" one.[31] From late autumn through the spring she was entirely alone, and the newly married couple were reduced to corresponding by letter despite being closer by distance than New York and Philadelphia.

The times they did spend together were intimate, though, and in the summer of 1810 they welcomed a child. They christened him James, but he died a day after his birth, and Mary nearly followed him. In a cruel reminder of their isolation within the community, the Portuguese refused to allow Mary and Robert to bury their son in

Macao's lone foreign cemetery, on the grounds that it was only for Catholics. So they buried the newborn instead on a hillside, all by himself. Mary had already shown a propensity toward depression, which worsened with her isolation and pregnancy. With the loss of her child, she nearly slipped over the edge. "She walks in darkness," wrote Morrison to a friend, quoting Isaiah, "and has no light." [32]

The early nineteenth century was a terrible time to be a Christian in China. The imperial government recognized only blurry distinctions between unorthodox religions (when it recognized any distinctions at all), so the war against the White Lotus sects gave way to a crackdown on Catholics as well—who, aside from the short-leashed European advisers in the emperor's court, lived and practiced in secret. In 1805, Jiaqing issued an edict expressly forbidding the publication of Christian texts, at which time the wooden printing blocks for over two hundred books composed by the Catholic missionaries in Beijing were burned. Over the years that followed, his suppression of Christian religious activity escalated, and by 1812 he would designate the printing of Christian tracts a crime punishable by death. In 1815 a Catholic missionary who had been living secretly in Hunan province was strangled, as were all of his converts. The same year, an elderly French missionary was executed in Sichuan and his severed head was sent on a tour of the nearby districts as a warning. [33] Nevertheless, against the rising current of danger Morrison kept at his work.

By 1811, Morrison was able to convince a Chinese printer in Macao to begin producing a few small biblical tracts for him, printed with false covers to evade detection (a precaution the printer took on his own initiative). First came a Chinese translation of the Acts of the Apostles, in 1811, then the Gospel of Saint Luke and a tract on redemption the following year. Morrison had no converts to give his little books to, however, just his teachers, whom he tried in vain to woo away from Catholicism during their Sabbath breaks from work. Nevertheless, he happily reported his success to the directors of the London Missionary Society back in England to reassure them that his work for the East India Company had not derailed his missionary efforts completely.

His bragging nearly got him thrown out of the British factory. The London Missionary Society proudly reported Morrison's progress on his tracts in its 1814 annual report, a copy of which—in an uncharacteristic fit of playfulness—they forwarded to the East India Company's headquarters in London. When the Company's directors learned that Morrison was producing illegal religious tracts while working in their factory, they sent new, unequivocal orders for the select committee to fire him at once. They condemned Morrison's "mistaken Zeal," declaring that no matter how useful he had been as an interpreter, "he has not only been guilty of great imprudence on his own part but has put at risk the interests of the East India Company." They warned that he could cause "serious mischief" to British trade as a whole if his illegal activities were discovered.[34]

Still, the select committee did not want to lose Morrison's translation services, so once again they defied the directors' orders to get rid of him. In their reply to London, they assured the directors that Morrison was in fact so completely ineffective as a missionary—he hadn't, they pointed out, managed to baptize even a single convert during his several years in Canton—that he posed no real danger of discovery. They were certain that his Gospel tracts would never gain any kind of wide distribution. They also promised that if the Chinese government should ever actually take notice of Morrison's missionary work, they would sever ties with him at that time. In the end, the directors wound up deferring to the judgment of their personnel on the ground in Canton and allowed them to keep Morrison on as their interpreter. Morrison, for his part, wrote to the directors of the London Missionary Society and asked them to please be more prudent in the future.[35]

———

While George Staunton and Robert Morrison were each trying to open a British pathway into China through the figurative gate of language, it was left to Thomas Manning to attempt an entry of the literal kind: by land. Manning's romantic vision of exploration, however, turned out to be more elusive than he had hoped. The select committee did its best to help him when he first arrived, even submitting a petition to the hoppo in November 1807 to propose that Manning might go to Beijing as a scientist—the accepted route for Catholic priests to be allowed into China—but the hoppo refused to forward their petition to the capital. He told them the emperor already had plenty of European scientists and didn't need any more. Agitated and impatient, Manning took passage to Vietnam a few months later on an East India Company survey vessel tasked with charting the islands of the South China Sea, in hopes that he could get into China by somehow joining a Vietnamese embassy to Beijing (for which purpose he brought along a Vietnamese outfit as a disguise). When that didn't work out either, he returned grumpily to Macao and threw himself back into his language studies. In that area, at least, he began to make progress. "The veiled mysteries of the Chinese language gradually open upon my view," he wrote to his father in August 1808. He would do a bit of translation work for the Company in Staunton's absence, and put his medical training to use in a doctor's practice, but mostly he just bided his time, letting his beard grow and waiting for a better opportunity to come along.[36]

In the winter of 1810 he finally made his move. Leaving Canton that February, he took passage on a ship bound for Calcutta in the British-controlled territory of Bengal. By this time he had decided to dress only in colorful silk Vietnamese-style clothing, which he had tailors make for him in Canton. His beard, a midnight shade of black, was more than a foot long, carefully coiffed, and proudly untouched by a razor, though he did trim back the mustache portion a bit once he got to India to make it easier to eat soup.[37] (The other English were somewhat offended by his beard, but that didn't bother him. "There is no accounting for some people's want of taste," he told his father.)[38] The select committee gave him a letter of introduction to Lord Minto the governor-general, explaining that Manning had been learning Chinese in preparation to enter the country. They expressed faith that "whatever can tend to encrease the general knowledge of the Language and Customs of China, will prove of essential service to the interests of the Hon'ble Company, and our Country."[39]

In Calcutta, Manning began scouring the bars of the city for a Chinese interpreter—a "munshi," as Manning would call him, using the Persian term for secretary—who could accompany him on the next stage of his journey, the plans for which he kept closely guarded.

When not trolling for a Chinese interpreter, he linked up with a small group of Orientalist missionary scholars in Calcutta who held forth on religion and their various theories of the origins of Hindu and Chinese civilization over argumentative dinner parties that carried regularly into the wee hours of the morning.[40] They were fine company, though when it came to their ideas about China he found them "a little weak in the upper story."[41]

In time, he found one willing candidate to be his munshi, a Chinese man named Zhao who was a Roman Catholic convert and had worked in the past for one of the Hong merchants in Canton. By his own account, Zhao had come to Calcutta the year before to work in a bar owned by a Chinese proprietor. As it happened, his employer died right about the time Manning started coming around asking about an interpreter, so he decided to throw in his lot with the bearded Englishman in his Vietnamese clothes.[42] On October 11, 1810, Manning posted a cryptic letter to Charles Lamb. "Just going to leave Calcutta for God knows where!" he wrote.[43] Then he disappeared.

His goal was Tibet. If he couldn't get into China through Canton, he reasoned, he would try to enter through the empire's western frontier. In September 1811, nearly a year after his final letter to Lamb and after preparations of which he left almost no record, Manning and his "munshi" crossed over the border into Bhutan from Rangpur, leaving the British territory of Bengal far behind them to the south.[44] Ahead of them lay the Himalayas. The two men traveled on foot, with a local guide and porters for their baggage. The paths along which they hiked were narrow and heavy with rocks, and in the lowlands they had to ford cold streams that came up to their waists. But as they made their way farther along up the switchbacks into the mountains, the crossings gave way to narrow, swinging rope bridges that spanned the dizzying chasms below.

About two weeks into the mountains of Bhutan, Manning began having trouble with his munshi. On setting out from the town of Paro on October 16—on horseback now—he found that Zhao had apparently sold his spoons, which were silver, and replaced them with pewter ones. Their guide, and an unnamed "slave" who served him, seemed to be part of the deal. Manning demanded that they go back to Paro to retrieve the spoons, but the others all refused. It was a minor issue on its surface, but it awakened Manning to his own vulnerability. "It was not the value," he wrote in his diary, "but the example. I am in bad, bad hands."[45] The next day, with snowbound peaks just coming visible in the distance, his misgivings deepened. "The Chinaman is as cross as the devil and will not speak," he wrote. It later turned out that there had been a misunderstanding. The munshi had fallen off his horse and was angry because he thought Manning didn't care. Manning hadn't seen it happen. They patched things up and continued on.

They traveled upward and northward through Bhutan, following a pilgrimage trail that carved its slow way along the edge of steep winding cliffs. At night Manning and his munshi slept in sheds or deserted houses when they could find them, outdoors when they could not. By mid-October they were waking up to frost in the mornings, and the trail wound still higher into the labyrinthine mountains. Finally, on October 21, they crossed the border from Bhutan into Tibet, reaching the frontier town of Pagri unchallenged. It had been five years since his departure from England, but Manning was finally inside the Qing Empire.

Manning did not try to hide himself in Pagri, though he also did not advertise the fact that he was English. He even paid a visit to the local Chinese magistrate, who was quite civil. His munshi, however, was visibly agitated at being back inside the Qing domain. "He is always discontented and grumbling," noted Manning.[46] The magistrate paid his own visit to Manning after he had been in town a few days, and tried to sound him out as to where he had come from. He asked Manning if he were a Muslim and Manning said that no, he ate pork. The magistrate's interpreter, he noticed, refrained from translating his little joke.

Just as the British of the Macartney mission had sensed such clear distinctions of civilization between the Chinese settlers and the indigenous peoples they encountered along their way through Southeast Asia, Manning too saw a vast cultural gulf between the Chinese and the Tibetan "natives" they governed. "Chinese politeness, even in the common soldiers, forms a great contrast with the barbarians of this place," he wrote in Pagri. The Chinese represented civilization to him, the Tibetans something much lower. "The Chinese are really civilized, and do not live like cattle," he wrote farther on in the journey; "it is a comfort, after having lodged in smoke and dirt with the native animals of Tibet, to take shelter in a Chinaman's house, where you are sure of urbanity and cleanliness at least." He was, for his generation, the first to see China properly as an empire—here, where the Chinese, themselves ruled by the Manchus, had conquered Tibet and set up control over its people more than fifteen hundred miles from their own capital in Beijing. Compared to Canton, where all of the Chinese seemed alike to foreigners and could be imagined as some kind of monolithic society, Manning found in Tibet a stark polarity between the ruling and subject races that wasn't so far different from the colonial world his own people were building a few hundred miles to the south. The resonance was not lost on him. "The Chinese lord it here like the English in India," he wrote in his diary in Pagri.[47]

Manning and his munshi were treated remarkably well in the border town. The magistrate gave them food and arranged permission for them to continue onward. Having figured out that Manning was English (or at least that he had come from an English territory), he said he would be interested in opening a line of trade between Tibet and India through Bhutan. Manning thought that was a fine idea too, but he had no authority to negotiate an agreement on the Company's behalf. He thought the British authorities should have given him, a Chinese speaker, some kind of diplomatic commission before he left India. "What use are their embassies," he wrote scornfully in his diary, "when the Ambassador can't speak to a soul, and can only make ordinary phrases pass through a stupid interpreter? . . . Fools, fools, fools, to neglect an opportunity they may never have again!"[48]

When word spread in the town that Manning was a physician, some Chinese soldiers came to see him for various treatments. His ministrations were effective enough that they asked him to travel onward with them. And so when Manning and his munshi moved on from Pagri, leaving on horseback at four o'clock on a bitterly frosty November morning with snow visible in the mountains around them, they rode in the company of a Qing imperial army unit. The soldiers and the officers who led them were immensely friendly to Manning. They shared their food, loaned him sheepskin clothing to fight off the cold, and pitched a tent for him and the munshi when they camped.

The soldiers' commander, whom Manning referred to as "the General," was a half-Manchu officer from Sichuan who came often to sit with Manning and smoke his pipe, sometimes playing songs for him on his lute while one or two of the soldiers sang opera. Manning enjoyed the General's wine (if not so much his cooking), and the General for his part enjoyed lounging in Manning's quarters in the sunshine of a morning, going on at length about the old days and how much tougher and hardier the imperial soldiers used to be when he was young, back in the time of Qianlong. He was quite taken with Manning's long beard, seeming, in Manning's words, "as if he never could sufficiently admire it." At one point Manning brushed it out to its full, glorious length for him, and when the General "saw its tapering shape descending in one undivided lock, he . . . declared he never had seen one nearly so handsome."[49] Manning enjoyed the fraternity of his new companions. One afternoon, as they came upon a broad, frozen lake, he was disappointed not to have brought along his skates so he could show off for them.

Relations with his munshi, on the other hand, weren't so good. Manning took to calling Zhao "his sublime crossness" for his tendency to explode with anger. It came to the point, he wrote, that they spoke to each other as little as possible "in order that no quarrel might ensue."[50] At one point, Zhao broke down and asked why Manning had even brought him along. He said Manning should just have left him in India. Their frictions were at least partly due to the munshi's personality—he considered the Tibetans uncivilized, and didn't think too highly of Manning's culture either—but as a Qing subject, he was in genuine danger if he should be discovered as a Catholic, to say nothing of being a lowly man from Canton who had traveled to India and Tibet without permission and escorted a European secretly over the border. He had good reasons for being testy.

The General and his soldiers said goodbye at Gyangze, a town about a hundred miles from Pagri where the road to Lhasa turned northeast. Manning and his munshi continued toward the capital with just a guide, who soon abandoned them. Onward they rode on broken horses through barren valleys below high, snowbound mountains, along rivers of icewater and up steepening roads marked by piles of white stones. In early December, their faces blistered by the high-altitude sun, they descended into a plain and finally saw the Tibetan capital of Lhasa sparkling in the distance.

Manning was the first Englishman ever to lay eyes on the city (and the last for the remainder of the nineteenth century). His only European predecessors were a pair of Catholic missionaries who had reached the city two hundred years earlier. From a distance, at least, it was the Shangri-La of fables. The grand Potala Palace where the Dalai Lama lived loomed high and white on a hill above the city, visible from miles off, more magnificent in appearance than he had even imagined it could be. But some of the magic was lost on approach. A ceremonial gate they passed through on the road to the city had gilt decorations that caught the sun from afar, but up close the ornaments seemed imbalanced and off-kilter to Manning, reminding him of "pastry work" or "gingerbread architecture." The blindingly white palace itself was like a hive, swarming with monks in gorgeous robes of deep maroon, but the city below it was poor and rough. The houses were "begrimed with smut and dirt." Wild dogs with mangy and ulcerated skin ran freely in the streets, growling and digging about for food. In spite of himself, Manning sensed a deep strangeness to the place, an unreality. "Even the mirth and laughter of the inhabitants I thought dreamy and ghostly," he recalled. "The dreaminess no doubt was in my mind, but I never could get rid of the idea."[51]

On the advice of his munshi, Manning pretended to be a Buddhist lama from India, one who happened to be versed in medicine. He hid the fact that he could speak or read Chinese, since it would make the presence of an interpreter suspicious. He also hid that he could speak English, so the two of them only communicated openly in Latin (in which both were fluent, it being the confluence of Manning's Cambridge education and the munshi's childhood training by a Roman Catholic missionary). This led to a long chain of interpretation when Manning spoke to Tibetans: someone would first have to translate from Tibetan into Chinese, then Manning's munshi would translate the Chinese into Latin for him, and he would have to respond in Latin, back along the chain. To avoid standing out—and because he decided he liked it—he performed the kowtow before Chinese and Manchu officials whenever he was asked (a lesser version than that reserved for the emperor, touching the head to the ground three times rather than nine). In fact, he said, he found it so restful to kneel down to the ground after all the walking he had to do that he tried to kowtow as much as possible—including in front of high-ranking Tibetans (which offended his munshi, who said no Chinese would ever do that).[52]

Manning was granted an audience with the Dalai Lama on December 17, 1811. To get to it, he had to climb up hundreds of steps carved into the side of the mountain on which the Potala Palace was built, steps that gave way in time to ladders on which he continued climbing up through the nine floors of the palace, its air rich with the smoke of incense and yak-butter lamps, to reach the high roof with its breathtaking view over the city and the broad, vast plain to the deep blue-white mountains in the distance.[53] A monk escorted him into a smooth-floored reception hall built onto the roof, walls hung with tapestries and its ceiling held up by high, strong pillars. Sunshine streamed down through a skylight. In the middle of the hall, on a throne supported by carved lions, he found a young boy in maroon robes and a pointed saffron hood who appeared to be about seven years old (he had, in fact, just turned six). Manning knelt down before the Dalai Lama and performed the kowtow.

Manning still had his beard, but he had shaved the top of his head in preparation for the audience, so that the boy could lay hands on him. The normally impish Englishman was quieted in the lama's presence. "His face was, I thought, poetically and effectingly beautiful," wrote Manning. "He was of a gay and cheerful disposition; his beautiful mouth perpetually unbending into a graceful smile, which illuminated his whole countenance. Sometimes, particularly when he had looked at me, his smile almost approached to a gentle laugh." They made polite small talk. The Dalai Lama asked about his journey. Manning asked for Tibetan Buddhist books, and asked if someone who spoke Chinese could teach him their contents, though he was gently rebuffed. It wasn't the conversation that mattered, though, but simply the fact of being in the Dalai Lama's presence. Unlike Macartney's audience with Qianlong, there was no power relationship in play, no hidden challenge, no posturing. Just curiosity. And friendliness. All of Manning's playful cynicism vanished. "I could have wept through strangeness of sensation," he wrote afterward. "I was absorbed in reflections when I got home."[54]

.   .   .

Manning's experience with the imperial government at Lhasa, by contrast, came as a lurching shock. The senior Qing official in the Tibetan capital, known by the Manchu title of "amban," was the closest thing there was to an imperial governor-general in the region. Tibet was a protectorate, meaning that it enjoyed a certain measure of internal autonomy, while China controlled it militarily. The Dalai Lama was Tibet's political and religious leader, but most major decisions had to be filtered through and approved by the Manchu amban, who also exercised full control over Tibet's foreign relations. It was thus the amban's office that took a more sinister notice of Manning's arrival and began sending agents to investigate him and the munshi. Visitors claiming to be friends came to visit their rented rooms at all hours. They made awkward conversation, long outstayed their welcomes, and opened doors to poke around where they weren't invited.

At one point, the amban called Manning in for a face-to-face interrogation. It was a relatively civil interview, but he came straight out and told Manning that he thought he was either a Catholic missionary or a spy. He just wasn't sure which. As for the latter possibility, he revealed that he was not only aware of but worried about Britain's conquest of territory in India and its implications for Tibet. "These Europeans are very formidable," he told Manning—unsure of where exactly he fit in, trying to draw him out. "Now one man has come to spy the country he will inform others. Numbers will come, and at last they will be for taking the country from us." [55]

This particular amban, Manning was mortified to learn, harbored a special loathing for the British. The only reason he was stationed in Tibet was because the Jiaqing emperor had removed him from his previous position, a vastly preferable one in Canton, after Admiral Drury's invasion of Macao in 1808. He was one of the officials the emperor had punished for being too soft on foreigners. So he considered the British to be the architects of his professional downfall: in his mind, they were the sole reason why he was stuck in this remote, semibarbaric Himalayan wasteland instead of enjoying the luxuries and riches of Canton.

Manning worried about being recognized as English (rather than just a British subject from India, as he was pretending). He wore Chinese glasses as a disguise. And he took pains to hide the fact that he had ever been to Canton, let alone that he had worked for the East India Company's factory there—which might trigger God knew what kind of reaction from the vindictive amban. Even if the amban himself didn't recognize Manning, one of the secretaries he had brought from Canton might. Or they could simply have known there was an Englishman with a long beard who could speak Chinese. Manning knew the Qing officials were concerned about him; there were rumors that he and the munshi were to be tortured. A comet with a brilliant tail had appeared during the season before his arrival, lingering brightly on the horizon for months. The amban took it as an omen that something bad was coming to Lhasa. He told Manning he thought it might be him.[56]

After several days of interviews, the amban sent a report to the emperor in which he informed Jiaqing of his suspicion that Manning, who appeared to be a European, might actually be a Catholic missionary who had come to Tibet pretending to be a Buddhist but was really intending to spread Christianity in secret.[57] Though Manning and the munshi weren't privy to the amban's report, they heard rumors about its contents and the munshi was terrified. He worried that he might be executed. He thought Manning might be too.

Beijing was more than fifteen hundred miles away as the crow flew, so it would be months before the amban could hear back from the emperor and learn how Jiaqing wished for him to deal with the two suspicious travelers. So Manning and his munshi were effectively made prisoners, forced to winter over in Lhasa while waiting to learn what would happen to them. The munshi decorated his small room for the long term—little ribbons, a looking glass, a carved seal. Manning saw patients, and met several more times with the Dalai Lama. His money ran low, so he had to start selling his possessions—some cloth, a belt, handkerchiefs, a few bottles of cherry brandy he had brought along for gifts, an opera glass. Relations continued to sour with the munshi, who lost all patience with the neediness of his European charge; Manning, in turn, resented the munshi's "beastly, mulish behavior." It seemed all but certain that they would not be allowed to continue on freely into China proper. Mostly, though, Manning just hoped he would not be put to death. He tried not to envision the scene, but his mind kept getting pulled toward it. "I look round," he imagined, "I have no resource, no refuge; instruments of torture, instruments of execution are brought by florid, high-cheeked, busy, grinning, dull-hearted men . . ."[58]

Jiaqing's response finally arrived in late February 1812, just after the lunar new year. He agreed that it was reasonable to assume Manning was a Catholic missionary. "Recently, the western foreigners have spread out to every place, preaching their heretical Catholic teachings with the intention of stirring up trouble," he wrote; "they most certainly do not know their place. You should devote your attention to taking precautions against them." His primary concern was with Manning. "This foreigner Manning claims to be from the Calcutta tribe," he wrote. "But the territory of Calcutta is on the coast, and is connected by sea lanes to the West, where people are not Buddhist. So why would he come all this way to Tibet? Clearly he is just pretending to be a follower of Buddha and has come secretly as some kind of spy, trying to find a crack in the wall, intending to spread his teachings and delude the masses. You absolutely cannot allow him to stay in Tibet."[59]

Jiaqing ordered Manning to be deported, and further demanded that border security be stepped up in response to his incursion, to make sure no more westerners could get into Tibet from India. In the future, he said, any Europeans who came to the border pretending to be Buddhist pilgrims should be turned back. All things considered, deportation was a gentle punishment, but it was standard for foreigners who had not committed capital crimes. As for Manning's munshi, however—or, as Jiaqing called him ominously in the edict, "the Chinese traitor"—he was no foreigner. Jiaqing had him arrested in preparation for a trial. Manning last saw his munshi on the day after the emperor's edict arrived. He was in chains. There is no record of what they talked about. After their months of bickering travel together, they were never to see each other again.[60]

The journey to Lhasa marked both the culmination and the end of Thomas Manning's career as an explorer. He would never dare to repeat the attempt. But he had at least shown that China could, with the right preparation and at great risk, be entered. And he survived the journey, escorted back to the border at Pagri with an iron collar around his neck and finally released into Bhutan to make his way back to India.

In the bigger picture of Britain's embryonic ability to understand China, the basic impression Manning brought back from his journey into Tibet was a tantalizing one. It was an impression founded on the stark contrast between the warmth of Manning's reception by low-level officials, the General, the soldiers, and the Dalai Lama on the one hand, and, on the other hand, the harsh suspicion of the amban and the emperor above him. Beyond demonstrating that China's borders were porous, Manning brought back evidence that many of the Chinese and Tibetan subjects of the empire were in fact quite friendly and open to outsiders. They did not appear to be even remotely as antiforeign as the British had imagined—in fact, they seemed positively eager for trade and other kinds of commerce with westerners. The closed nature of China, Manning would testify a few years later before a parliamentary committee seeking to expand British trade, was due entirely to the jealousy of the reigning government. It had nothing to do with the people themselves.[61] Find some way to get past the emperor and the jealous mandarins, his experience suggested, and the ordinary people of China would welcome the British with open arms.

Back at Canton, meanwhile, Robert Morrison was struggling to balance the work of creating his dictionary with caring for his wife. After the death of their newborn son in 1810, a local doctor had pronounced her incurable, but her emotional condition stabilized and in 1812 they had another child—a girl, Rebecca, who survived. Mary seemed happier after her daughter's birth, less alone.[62] A son, John Robert, followed in April 1814, and the family grew, but mostly in Morrison's absence. As before, he was forced to be away from them during the long trading season, which also meant that while he was in Canton he could devote every ounce of his energies to his language projects.

His work on the Chinese-English dictionary, in particular, escalated as the years passed until it consumed nearly all of his waking hours, all of his guilt channeling itself into the manuscript on which he worked sometimes eleven or twelve hours a day for months on end, broken only by the weekly Sabbath. Mary's mental health declined again, and in January 1815, at the instigation of a British doctor, she finally took the children and went home to England. Morrison was left to work year-round without disturbance, but also without companionship.[63]

One of the practical difficulties of the dictionary that so consumed Morrison was how to publish it when it was done. The Gospel pamphlets he had worked on were written entirely in Chinese and meant only for Chinese readers, so they were best printed after the local fashion with traditional carved woodblocks in string-bound volumes. However, the dictionary's users would, hopefully, be English speakers from Britain and America, and the dense English printing it called for would be unfeasible with Chinese woodblocks. It needed a proper English press, but there was no such thing in China. As it turned out, though, the members of the select committee were so excited about the prospect of his dictionary and the subtle power they expected it would bring to the British in China that in 1814, as the manuscript for its first volume neared completion, they expended the lavish funds to import one for him from England.

When the president of the select committee at the time, a man named Elphinstone, asked the Court of Directors in London to send a printing press to China, he underscored how important Morrison's dictionary would be for the "English cause in China," as he termed it. The dictionary would make it possible for the British in Canton to communicate directly with officials and any number of local elites, he argued, and thus "gradually remove the ridiculous prejudices at present entertained against foreigners." It would ensure that the British "will be thought deserving of more respect and attention, as our character becomes better known."[64] In other words, the essential value of Morrison's Chinese-English dictionary, by his reasoning, would be to allow the British to make themselves better understood to the Chinese—not to make the Chinese better understood to them. But that was perhaps the best way to sell it, for the directors in London had no particular interest in learning more about China; what they wanted was to improve trade, and Elphinstone's vision promised just that. They approved.

The press, along with an English printer by the name of P. P. Thoms to operate it, arrived in Macao on a Company ship in 1814. Thoms brought with him a full set of English type and tens of thousands of blank metal shanks so he could get Chinese type cut by hand in Macao. The directors did not bother providing him with paper, since they knew that the Chinese made that commodity best. The only conditions the directors put on the printing press were, first, that it should stay in Macao rather than Canton (where it might rile the authorities or be confiscated), and second, that it should never be used to print religious works.[65] The first volume of the dictionary came out the following year in Macao in a beautiful quarto edition. In a sign of how far Morrison's relationship with the Company had come since it first refused to let him sail on its ships to Canton, he dedicated his dictionary to the Court of Directors of the East India Company, "by their much obliged, and very obedient humble servant, the author."[66]

A glance at the volume shows much of what Morrison had been up against. For one thing, at nearly a thousand oversize pages it was still only the first of nine planned installments, a fragment of the eventual whole. Chinese was a vast language. Morrison worked with the most complete Chinese dictionary in existence, the Kangxi Dictionary of 1716, compiled under Qianlong's grandfather, which contained forty thousand different characters (in contrast to the mere twenty-six letters of the Latin alphabet). No scholar in China would know them all—many of the characters in the Kangxi Dictionary were obscure, or variant forms of a similar character—but all had to be accounted for, arranged, and defined.

Furthermore, while each character was the rough semantic equivalent of a word in English, many could have multiple meanings or be used as part of a compound, and those variant meanings and compounds had to be defined as well. Then there were the allusions, for much of classical Chinese was incomprehensible without understanding the literary references—to the Confucian classics, to ancient historical texts, to poetry—that a highly educated Chinese reader would bring to the text. In other words, to make an effective dictionary Morrison not only had to account for tens of thousands of characters and the compounds in which they were commonly used, but he also had to provide a window into the deeper cultural context that gave them meaning. The work he attempted to create would therefore not be some mere handbook for deciphering official regulations or imperial edicts—it would, he hoped, be the key to an entire civilization.

Some of the characters could be defined easily in just a word or two (basic nouns, for instance). Others, however, depending on how culturally distant they were from similar concepts in English, could be far more complicated to explain. So, to give one example, the entry in Morrison's dictionary for the Chinese character meaning "to study" went on for a full thirty-nine pages of explanation. That was because to understand what the Chinese meant by "study," Morrison felt, one had to appreciate China's long tradition of Confucian scholarship and the centrality of education to its society and government. And so, along with giving a range of historical quotations to illuminate the character's basic meaning, Morrison went on to sketch out the general contours of Chinese education. He translated major points from the government regulations for the civil service examinations—descriptions of the content of the exams, how they were conducted, who could qualify to take them, how they were graded.

As part of his definition for the character, he also translated a list of one hundred rules from a Chinese academy, to give a sense of the Chinese reverence for learning. Among those rules: That students should bow first to Confucius upon entering the classroom, then to the teacher. That they should sit in order of seniority. That at the end of the day the youngest should be allowed to leave first and they must go directly home (where they must bow first to the household gods, then to their ancestors, then to their parents). Students were not to form groups or make plans to play together. They were to read out loud, but only in low voices. Students were not to speak the gutter language of the marketplace. When sitting, students were to be still, without crossing their legs or leaning to one side. When outside, they were not to frisk about or throw things. Students were to love their books and keep them from harm. They were to apply the teacher's lessons to their own conduct every day. On and on went the list, filling page after expensively printed page—all of it necessary, in Morrison's opinion, for the reader of his dictionary to grasp the essence of what "study" really meant in China.[67]

A call for subscriptions to the current and future volumes of Morrison's dictionary ran in some of the top literary magazines in London, announcing that although the full run would likely cost up to 20 guineas (about $2,000 today), it was worth the price not just because of the enormously long history that lay behind the Chinese language, but—and this was the most important point—because Chinese was a *living* language. It was not some dusty artifact like Latin or Sanskrit. It may have been classical, and ancient, but it was hardly obsolete—after nearly four thousand years it was still, the advertisement explained, "the written medium, in private and public life, in literature, in arts, and in government, of the most extensive empire on earth."[68] The *Asiatic Journal*, in British India, commended Morrison for making possible "the acquisition of the Chinese language, a task which the greater part will consider . . . positively unconquerable and terrific."[69] The *Quarterly Review* in London, which had given such an adulatory review to George Staunton's translation of the Qing legal code, recognized that Morrison's work was of an entirely different scale—his dictionary, they declared, would be nothing less than "the most important work in Chinese literature that has yet reached Europe." Hopefully, they added that "we most sincerely wish he may live to finish it."[70]

CHAPTER 6

Hidden Shoals

George Staunton finally got his embassy in 1816. Or at least he got *an* embassy—which, though he would not lead it (an honor that fell to one William, Lord Amherst), would nevertheless finally give him the chance to return to Beijing and complete the unfinished business of his father. By the time the new mission was announced to him in January 1816, Staunton had been back in Canton since 1810 and had finally completed his climb through the ranks of the factory. Through sheer doggedness and a few opportune retirements, he had attained the presidency of the select committee. He was the leader of the factory, the taipan, the preeminent British subject in Canton. It was a long way from his early days as a junior writer, far more prestigious and powerful (to say nothing of the roughly £20,000 it brought in each year, about two hundred times his starting salary). Despite having gained the respect of those below him in the factory, however, he never did become fully comfortable in their free-mannered bachelor community. He had tried at times to fit in—back in 1806, for a few months, he engaged in what he demurely referred to as "rather high play" with the others—but eventually his priggishness won out. He would have no remorse about leaving Canton when the time came, and by 1816 that time seemed to have come at last: he had made the fortune he had come for, and a prominent role in a British embassy to Jiaqing's court would surely cement his reputation in England. A permanent return—and perhaps even a seat in Parliament—were within his grasp.[1]

The proximate reason for the embassy was a sudden and sharp downturn in British-Chinese relations at Canton during 1813 and 1814, in which things got so bad that the British government saw "reason to apprehend the failure of the Commerce altogether."[2] Some of the frictions were purely local—the East India Company, for some reason, tried to give John Roberts a second chance in Canton, and the local Chinese officials protested. Separately, the emperor reduced the number of Hong merchants the British could trade with, and the supercargoes protested. The larger source of trouble, however, had a more distant cause: the outbreak of the War of 1812, which brought a bloom of violence between British and American ships to the waters around Canton. Whereas the Napoleonic Wars had mostly kept their distance due to the scarcity of French trade in south China, the Americans were second only to the British in the size of their commerce at Canton, so there was no way this time for the two enemies' ships to avoid each other.

Given the lack of U.S. Navy cruisers to convoy their merchant vessels after the war broke out, the Americans in south China relied on letters of marque and heavy armament, turning their merchant vessels into privateers. They also tried to avoid landing at the same time as the Company ships with their naval escorts, but the timing did not always work. In March 1814, the Royal Navy frigate *Doris* captured a three-hundred-ton American privateer, the *Hunter,* and brought her into Macao as a prize. Two months later, the *Doris* and three of its boats chased the American schooner *Russell* all the way up the Pearl River to the Whampoa anchorage, just a few miles shy of the city itself. They then exchanged fire at Whampoa with another American ship, the *Sphynx,* which they successfully boarded and captured. Tit-for-tat raids continued over the following months, with Americans capturing lightly armed British "country" ships sailing in from India and the British sometimes capturing them back—all above the angry, ongoing complaints of the Chinese authorities, which the westerners ignored. Finally, the Qing governor-general ordered supplies cut off to the *Doris* and threatened to suspend trade with the British and Americans until the two sides could behave themselves.[3]

The British supercargoes in Canton complained that, as always, they had no control over the actions of the Royal Navy—and, as always, those complaints met with disbelief on the Chinese side. Hostilities with the local authorities escalated quickly. A Chinese linguist working in the British factory was arrested and likely subjected to torture. The governor-general started refusing to read communications in Chinese from the supercargoes, a privilege to which they had become accustomed since Staunton's early days. Seeking leverage, and feeling themselves to be the wronged party, the British tested the value of their commerce to the Chinese government by taking the unprecedented move of shutting down their *own* trade and withdrawing their ships from Canton until they should be treated better.

There had been tensions before at Canton of a similar scale that had not resulted in the extravagantly costly measure of sending a royal embassy to Beijing to patch up relations. But while the problems in 1814 may have been more severe than usual, the crucial difference in this case was that by the time the East India Company began asking the government for an embassy, the Napoleonic Wars were ending. Amherst's departure for China came just six months after the Duke of Wellington's victory at Waterloo in June 1815, in which the twenty-two years of nearly continuous warfare between Britain and France finally came to an end. The East India Company could start planning for the world after the peace, and independently of anything happening at Canton, the directors wanted to make sure that France didn't send a postwar embassy to China before Britain did.

The two British missions would thus be bookends around the long era of war with France: as Macartney had departed for China during the last days of peace before its onset, the new mission, under Amherst, would come to announce its end. Amherst was instructed to tell the Chinese court that the prince regent (for George III had gone mad by this time and, unlike his counterpart Qianlong in his own dotage, no longer exercised power over the government) was "sensible how much the happiness of Nations depended on the cultivation of the habits of peace" and that "the pacification of Europe had appeared to him to present a most auspicious occasion" to send this embassy to China.[4] One of the underlying imperatives of Amherst's mission was to make sure the Chinese understood that Great Britain was now unrivaled as the dominant military power in Europe.

William Pitt Amherst was an odd choice to lead the embassy. A dull but well-mannered man who was untalented at public speaking, he was neither brilliant nor particularly handsome, but he hailed from an excellent family. He was the son of an aide-de-camp to the king, after whose death (when William was eight) he was raised by his uncle, Jeffrey Amherst, the famous commander in chief of the British army. The sum total of his diplomatic experience when he departed for China had been an ineffective ambassadorship to Sicily from 1809 to 1811, in which he tried but failed to bring rival factions of nationalists and the exiled monarchy of the Two Sicilies together. He played no public role after leaving that position in 1811, until he was unexpectedly called up to lead the embassy to China in 1816.[5]

The Amherst mission was explicitly conceived as an end run around the local authorities at Canton. The directors in London assumed (wrongly) that the troubles in Canton were a purely local matter and the Jiaqing emperor knew nothing about them. Their goal was to inform the emperor of what they saw as the outrageous behavior of his officials at the southern trading port, assuming (again, wrongly) that he would then discipline those officials and perhaps apologize for the treatment the British had suffered. Thus Amherst was instructed to avoid touching at Canton on his way to Beijing, since it was so likely that the hoppo and the governor-general would try to prevent the British from going over their heads. Even Staunton and the other factory personnel who joined the mission were to sail separately and rendezvous in secret with Amherst's ship, the forty-six-gun frigate *Alceste*, at some distance from Canton.

By the time the news of the coming embassy reached Canton in January 1816, however, Staunton was no longer sure that the timing was appropriate. The overt reason for sending Amherst to China—to defuse the tensions over British attacks on American shipping near Canton—was already moot. The War of 1812 had ended, and British warships were no longer lying in wait for American trading vessels.

(Not that their rivalry would cease; one leading American merchant, writing to his Canton agent from Boston to report the end of the war, predicted continued harassment at the hands of the British: "How far we shall, in time of peace, be permitted to pursue our former commerce, is a question difficult to decide," he wrote. "Great Britain has neither affection nor respect for us.")[6]

Staunton had managed to patch up relations with the local authorities through a round of tense but successful negotiations with a representative of the governor-general. Trade had been reopened—for, absent the interference of external forces, the trade at Canton tended to rebalance itself quite naturally, thanks to the shared interest of all concerned in seeing it prosper—and so by the time Staunton learned of Amherst's embassy, he worried that "much of what was of probable accomplishment, was already accomplished."[7] As always he had his dream of filling the shoes of his father, but he doubted whether there was anything the British might gain from sending an ambassador to Beijing to inform Jiaqing of their troubles in Canton. He feared instead that it might be a question of what they could lose.

The emperor, as it happened, was hardly oblivious to what was going on in Canton. In fact, Jiaqing not only knew about the tensions between the British and the local officials, but he also knew about George Staunton personally and had begun to wonder if he might be dangerous. In January 1815, the emperor had asked for an investigation into whether Staunton had anything to do with the *Doris* chasing the American schooner up to Whampoa. "There is an English foreigner named Staunton (*si-dang-dong*)," Jiaqing wrote, "who once came to the capital along with his country's tribute mission. He was youthful and cunning then, and on the way home he made careful maps of the terrain of our mountains and rivers. After getting to Canton he did not return to his home country, but instead stayed on in Macao. He has been there for twenty years now and is thoroughly proficient in Chinese. By regulation, foreigners who live in Macao cannot enter the provincial capital of Canton, but Staunton has now been there for so long that when new foreigners come, most of them look to him for guidance. I fear that before long he will cause trouble."[8] In light of that edict, some of the Hong merchants warned their friends in the British factory that Staunton should not accompany

Amherst's mission to Beijing—the emperor obviously did not want him coming to the capital again. Staunton, however, ignored them.[9]

Staunton had reconciled himself to the fact that the Company did not want the ambassador to be one of its own employees, but he still found himself bitter over the situation of rank within the mission: he complained to his mother that "my stature in it was not what it ought to be."[10] His position in Amherst's embassy would be intricately tied up with the memory of his father, and all of his language study had been tending toward the goal of returning to the Qing court in Beijing. By 1816, independently of his work with the Company, he rightly considered himself his country's leading expert on China. So he was profoundly offended when he found out that, including Amherst, there would be three commissioners in the embassy—and that he himself was likely to be ranked third, behind Amherst's secretary.

So it was that when Amherst arrived on the *Alceste* at their secret rendezvous off the sparsely populated island of Hong Kong in July 1816—far from the prying eyes of Canton—Staunton was so petulant about his rank that he initially refused even to speak to the ambassador. He would only communicate with him through his secretary. But Amherst very much wanted Staunton's expertise—not just in language, but also his familiarity with the government after such a long residence in Canton. Amherst himself, of course, had no experience with China at all. So he and his secretary cajoled Staunton, soothing his injured pride. The result of their negotiations was that Amherst elevated Staunton to the second rank in the embassy, ahead of his secretary.[11] That was the best Staunton could rightly hope for, and so—after insisting somewhat pedantically that Lord Amherst put the promotion into writing—he agreed to come along. He wrote immediately to his mother to share the good news: "You will perceive," he told her proudly, "that I am established the *Second*, and eventually on the death or absence of Lord Amherst *First* of the Embassy." Not that he was hoping for Amherst to die quickly (though perhaps he was), but even if Staunton didn't make the top rank he was still, he bragged to his mother in an Oedipal moment, outdoing his father. "Lord A[mherst]," he told her, "also said verbally, 'you are in a higher situation than your father was because you are actually found in the Commission of Embassy—whereas he was only Sec[retar]y of

Legation and eventual successor.' "[12] It was a fine distinction, but it would do.

Once satisfied that he should take part, Staunton brought everything he could to bear on the mission. He convinced Robert Morrison to come along as the lead Chinese interpreter, assisted by three of his language students from the factory (two of whom were junior writers and the other a physician). Thomas Manning, who had been living in India since his expulsion from Tibet, returned to Canton in May 1816 in hopes of joining up as well. Though Manning would eventually gain renown back in England as an explorer and scholar of China—his bust graces the library of the Royal Asiatic Society in London to this day—it was a vague sort of fame in his own time due to his indisposition to publish anything. Nevertheless, he wrapped himself in a mystique that drew others to him, and Staunton felt that his services would be crucial to the embassy.

By the time Manning got back to Canton, his mission (like Staunton's) had been accomplished as well as he could have hoped. The journey to Lhasa, while a triumph in its own right, nevertheless showed how difficult it would be to travel unseen through the rest of China, and the terror of his arrest left him unwilling to make another attempt. He was ready to return to England, just waiting for a good opportunity. Charles Lamb had been imploring him to come home, teasing him that after so many years abroad in the wilds of Asia he would be completely out of fashion in their London circle ("your jokes obsolete, your puns rejected with fastidiousness as wit of the last age"). In a touching letter on Christmas Day 1815, Lamb expressed his sorrow for Manning's long absence and the passage of time. "Come out of Babylon, oh my friend!" he wrote. "You must not expect to see the same England again which you left. Empires have been overturned, crowns trodden into dust, the face of the western world quite changed; your friends have all got old." [13]

As it did for Staunton, the Amherst mission thus offered Manning a timely capstone for his career in China—a journey to Beijing, no less—with the added boon that the *Alceste* could provide his passage home to England at the end. The only problem was that Lord Amherst refused to let him come along. Given his recent deportation from Tibet, Amherst worried that Manning's presence in the embassy might anger the emperor in Beijing. (In fact it wouldn't, but only because the Manchu amban in Lhasa, and the handlers of the Amherst mission, rendered Manning's English name into Chinese using different characters, so in the Chinese documents there was no way to link the explorer of Tibet to the interpreter for the British embassy.)[14]

The bigger issue, though, was Manning's beard. Amherst, with his gentlemanly sensibilities, was offended by Manning's free-spirited appearance. Staunton put up a fight on Manning's behalf. He told Amherst he regretted that "Mr. Manning's particular views did not permit him to conform entirely to the English costume," but assured him that the extensive beard reflected only Manning's "natural indolence" (as one of the writers described it) rather than any failure of character.[15] Manning, for his part, agreed to put aside his bright silk robes for the time being and dress like a proper Englishman, though he still refused to shave off his beard. Amherst finally gave in.

A deeper sense of entitlement surrounded the British mission to China in 1816 than the one under Macartney in 1793. The shift went along, to a large degree, with the post-Napoleonic surge of British national pride, the confidence of being the preeminent military and commercial power on earth. Some back home wondered why China did not seem to recognize this. A writer in the *British Review* expressed indignation that in China "even the East India Company, the most powerful mercantile association in the world, have no privileges to encourage, and no rights to protect them, more than the lowest adventurer from Portugal or America." In light of Britain's great strength, the unwillingness of China to grant special trading privileges made the country's leaders seem obtuse. "With the characteristic pride of semi-barbarians," the writer noted sarcastically, "the government of China professes to take no notice of such an insignificant affair as foreign commerce."[16]

Along with the general rise in British pride, though, there was something more subtle at work. The king's emissaries this time would not be, as Macartney and his suite had been, the first of their countrymen to visit China's capital—and so from the standpoint of exploration, a bit of the shine had come off. Henry Ellis, Amherst's secretary and the third-ranking member of the mission (after he was shunted down the ladder by Staunton), was especially unenthused. In his journal, which he described as "intended for the eye of private friendship," though he later published it, he apologized to his friends at the outset that he would likely have little of interest to tell them. Since Staunton's father and others on the Macartney mission had already written books about the country, he thought there was probably nothing left to tell.[17]

Ellis was the illegitimate son of the powerful president of the Board of Control—the cabinet minister who supervised the East India Company and thus British India—and he was jaded beyond his twenty-eight years from having spent more than a decade as a Company and government operative, sometimes secret, in India and Persia. His cynicism was born of the seeping imperialist view that the civilizations of the Far East were lost to history, begging for renovation by the British with their historic engines of progress and commerce. Once acquired, it was a difficult worldview to shake, and his conclusions after his voyage to China would be every bit as wearied as his mood going into it; which is to say, he would find exactly what he was looking for. "[My] curiosity was soon satiated and destroyed by the moral, political, and even local uniformity," he would write at the end of the journey. "Were it not therefore for the trifling gratification arising from being one of the few Europeans who have visited the interior of China, I should consider the time that has elapsed as wholly without return." After the long months of travel to and from the country, and the extensive labor of preparing his journal for publication, Ellis's summary pronouncement at the end of his five-hundred-page account was simply that China was a "peculiar but uninteresting nation."[18]

The British travelers this time had lower expectations than their predecessors. They came on a mission of friendship but were quicker to find fault, to take insult, to dismiss. They encountered the same landscapes, the same people (at least the children and grandchildren thereof) that Macartney had found so stirring in 1793 when he wanted to shout lines from Shakespeare across the water, but the intervening years had taken their toll on the scenes' romance. "The appearance of the country was miserable," wrote Robert Morrison at the site of one of Macartney's reveries; "nothing but low mud huts were seen on the banks of the river. Crowds of people were every where collected to gaze on us as we passed; they were all of a more dark and swarthy complexion than a stranger, who considered the latitude in which they lived, would have expected to find them."[19] Where Macartney had seen a brave new world, Morrison saw a country of dark heathens.

The members of Amherst's embassy were also bolder about asserting themselves. The presence of Staunton, Morrison, and Manning as interpreters meant that they could push the arguments they wished to make in the terms by which they understood them; they were not beholden to Chinese go-betweens. They probed beyond the boundaries their hosts had laid out for them, leading one critic back in England to complain that they "frequently ran riot, and rambled to considerable distances from the line of their route."[20] They also knew firsthand the weaknesses of the dynasty's military after watching the Qing navy flounder in its campaign to suppress piracy near Canton; the military gulf between Britain and China had never seemed so vast. They were also aware by this time of the terrible White Lotus rebellion that had shaken Jiaqing's early rule and how its suppression had nearly bankrupted the government. In a dispatch home, Amherst reported on how far the Qing dynasty seemed to have declined since Macartney's visit. In contrast to the "real power and authority" of Qianlong, Amherst wrote, the reign of his son Jiaqing was "frequently and very lately disturbed by insurrections of his subjects." Amherst noted as well the "disordered state of the Imperial Finances."[21] Overall, the members of the embassy in 1816 did not, as Macartney had, come as open-eyed admirers.

One result of this newly emboldened British attitude was a more aggressive charting of the coastline by Amherst's ships. Where the *Lion* and *Hindostan* had been largely content to wait for Macartney at the island of Chusan, Amherst's ships—accompanied by two East India Company surveying vessels, the aptly named *Discovery* and *Investigator*—divided forces and went to work immediately after dropping off the embassy and its baggage at the White River. On August 11, while the other vessels went south, the *Alceste* and *Discovery* took a northern route, sailing up past the point where the Great

Wall meets the sea and along the coast of Manchuria to make a partial circuit of the Yellow Sea, surveying the topography as they went. They sailed around the Liaodong Peninsula and then farther along up the Manchurian coast to the mouth of the Yalu River, where they passed beyond the frontier of the Qing Empire and entered Korean waters.

The *Alceste* and *Discovery* anchored at several villages and towns along the way so their officers could go on shore. Those officers took notes on population, on climate and geology, on the quality of the soil. They noted military installations (and the lack thereof), and sounded the depth of water in anchorages. They kept track of where they were welcomed and where they found hostility, whether the people were armed, whether they seemed prosperous, whether they were seagoing or bound to the land. They did this all with a single Chinese interpreter who could not read or write. At one village on the Korean coast, an elderly man—an official or chief, they thought—came aboard the *Alceste*, agitated, and tried to communicate with its officers using gestures. The interpreter could not understand him. He wrote something on paper. They could not read it. Later, back at Canton, they had it translated. It read, "I don't know who you are. What business do you have here?" Sometimes, in an act of blithe defiance, they handed out copies of Morrison's Bible tracts. And as Captain Gower had done before them, they gave names to the landmarks they encountered—a secret kind of ownership, translating the coastal geography onto a British map for the first time: Cape Charlotte. Leopold's Isle. Mount Ellis. Alceste Island.[22]

———

Lord Amherst and the Qing court both intended to use the earlier Macartney mission as a precedent, but unfortunately they did not agree on what exactly that precedent entailed. The ceremony of the kowtow—the ritual of nine kneeling bows with the head touched to the ground—had lurked behind the scenes for Macartney, but it only came to seem crucial to the British in hindsight. (Macartney, after all, had still been given an audience after saying he wouldn't perform it, and in any case the demands he brought were so brazen that performing the kowtow would not have made Qianlong any more likely to grant them.) Amherst came with what he knew were much more modest requests, which he hoped would be more welcome to the court than Macartney's. The British were no longer asking to station a permanent ambassador at the capital, and they weren't demanding open ports or an island warehouse. They just wanted some kind of provision for direct communication between the Company staff in Canton and a high-ranking committee with the ear of the emperor in Beijing, in order to circumvent any troubles that came up with the hoppo and the governor-general. They also wanted to be able to trade freely with other Chinese businessmen in Canton besides just the Hong merchants. So while both requests were anathema to the Chinese they dealt with day-to-day at Canton (who were extremely put out by the embassy), it was within the realm of possibility that the emperor might grant them. At least the Company hoped that he would.

This time, however, the ceremonial issue that had been a mere sideshow to Macartney's embassy took center stage. Almost as soon as the British ships anchored at the mouth of the White River in early August, a few weeks in advance of the planned audience at the imperial palace outside Beijing, the officials who came to escort Amherst to Beijing began asking him to practice his kowtow in front of a piece of yellow silk that represented the emperor, in order to show that he knew how to do it properly.[23] Lord Amherst's instructions from the British government were ambivalent on the subject: they told him to refer to Macartney's precedent, but also not to let any "trifling punctilio" get in the way of a successful audience with the emperor.[24] It was left up to him to do what he thought best. So the first time he was asked to practice his kowtow, Amherst simply referred to the example of Macartney: Macartney hadn't kowtowed, he said, and Qianlong had still received him in audience, so he should be able to do the same.

That was not how the Chinese government claimed to remember it, however. As one of the embassy's handlers, an official named Zhang, explained to Amherst, Macartney in fact *had* performed the kowtow in 1793, and that was why Qianlong had received him in audience. The Jiaqing emperor always followed the precedents of his ancestors, said Zhang, so Amherst would also have to kowtow if he wished to have an audience.[25] If that weren't enough, he also let on that Jiaqing *himself* remembered seeing Macartney perform the kowtow at Qianlong's birthday celebration (Jiaqing would have been thirty-two years old at the time, hardly a child with a fanciful memory).[26] The British, of course, had their own eyewitness on hand— George Staunton, who had been twelve years old in 1793 and who, for his own part, insisted that the kowtow had never taken place. The difference in written records being what it was, the issue of precedent thus came down to the emperor's word against Staunton's—not the sort of position a diplomat like Amherst would relish.

Jiaqing had already determined that Staunton was a devious character, and the handler Zhang, on behalf of the authorities above him, railed angrily to Robert Morrison about Staunton's duplicity. If Staunton was such an "expert" on China, he asked Morrison, then why hadn't he taught the ambassador how to perform the kowtow ceremony properly? Zhang said that according to information from Canton, Staunton lived a rich life down there with fine horses and luxurious apartments, and even possessed a large aviary (none of which was true, though old Beale, the ubiquitous Cantonese-speaking Prussian consul, actually did keep a rather fine aviary with peacocks and pheasants). He also said that the government was aware that Staunton had paid money to buy his position in the embassy. He was a fraud, said Zhang, and he was clearly lying to Amherst about what had happened during the Macartney mission.[27] Staunton was embarrassed to be singled out, and (as Amherst explained in a report home) "merely hinted at the imperfect recollection which he could retain of transactions which took place so long ago, and at so early a period of his life."[28]

It is worth considering the possibility that Jiaqing was right. Although the consistent narrative in England, common to all of the publications that came out of the Macartney mission, was that the ambassador refused to kowtow and only went down briefly on one knee before Qianlong, the twelve-year-old George Staunton's handwritten diary from that day recorded something more ambiguous. Describing the arrival of the emperor at his tent, carried in a gilt chair by sixteen bearers, the young Staunton wrote that "we went down upon one knee and bowed our heads down to the ground."

At some later point he went back and crossed out the words "to the ground." When Macartney approached the throne, accompanied by Staunton and his father and Mr. Plumb, young George wrote that they "walked up to the edge of the platform, and made the same ceremony as before." When he went up himself to Qianlong's throne, he said, "I went up and made the proper ceremony."[29]

The odd part of this is the crossing out of "to the ground"—which is the point that blurs the distinction between the British and Chinese rituals enough that Jiaqing could conceivably remember the British ambassador as having knocked his head on the ground before the emperor. It is likewise unclear just what the young Staunton meant by "the proper ceremony." At a separate point in his diary, during the banquet for the emperor's birthday three days after the audience (which was the specific instance where Jiaqing remembered seeing Macartney kowtow), Staunton noted that he was with Macartney and his father in the midst of an assemblage of two or three hundred officials and, "at a signall being made, we bent one knee and bowed down to the ground. We repeated this ceremony nine times with the other mandarins."[30] Whether on one knee rather than two, nevertheless, the bowing completely to the ground, repeated nine times in succession, was far more accommodating to the "proper ceremony" of the Qing court than anything reported in the British accounts of the embassy.

Macartney, for his part, admitted nothing of the kind in his own journal. Rather, he wrote quite specifically that everyone there bowed repeatedly "except ourselves."[31] One wants to credit the twelve-year-old Staunton with the ingenuousness of youth and take his diary as the more candid one—which, as it turns out, can in fact be done, for the adult Staunton in 1816, in spite of his claims of "imperfect recollection," eventually confided to Lord Amherst that, yes, although nobody admitted it when they got back to England, in fact Macartney *had* done a polite hybrid, repeating an almost-prostration nine times in order to approximate the proper Qing ceremony.[32] Given the loose, voluminous robes that hid most of Macartney's body from view, Amherst realized that his predecessor's nine repeated deep, kneeling bows would have been nearly indistinguishable from the kowtow when viewed from a distance.[33] It was clear how both sides could have come away from the audience claiming that Macartney's ritual performance had conformed to their own expectations.

As flexible as things might have been in 1793, however, in 1816 there appeared to be no room for accommodation (and that difference, Amherst believed, was a clear sign of Jiaqing's weakness in contrast to Qianlong's strength). As the frustrated Zhang handed Amherst off to higher-ranking handlers en route to Beijing, the demands intensified for him to practice his kowtow so that he "might not be at a loss when the day of presentation came." Think, those officials told Amherst, what harm might come to Britain's trade if the ambassador were refused an audience. Think of the embarrassment of Great Britain before other countries when the news got out that they had been rejected by the emperor. Some admonished Amherst to imagine the disappointment of his son (who accompanied him as page) if, after traveling such a long distance, he was denied the opportunity to meet the emperor of China. In a mood to make concessions, and hoping that the closer he got to Beijing the more likely it was that the audience with Jiaqing would take place, Amherst agreed that he would be willing to kneel down on one knee rather than two but still bow nine times, "for the sake of uniformity," or, if they preferred, kneel and rise nine separate times. He said it was more than he would do for any European sovereign, which seemed to please his conductors, at least temporarily. Amherst also offered to kiss the emperor's hand as he would his own king's, but the Chinese officials thought that was rather disgusting.[34]

The embassy's seniormost chaperone, whom the British knew as "the Duke," was a high-ranking Manchu named Heshitai, brother-in-law to the emperor, who received them at the canal port of Tongzhou for the final overland leg to the capital. He was especially adamant about the kowtow ceremony. "Heaven does not have two suns," he told Amherst and his interpreters on August 22, "and Earth does not have two rulers." If Amherst did not perform the kowtow exactly as expected—touching the head to the ground rather than just bowing, and kneeling on two knees rather than just one—then, the Duke threatened, he would be expelled from the capital without an audience and his gifts would be rejected. When Amherst protested through Morrison that the previous embassy had met with more flexibility, the

The anchorage at Tongzhou

Duke was dismissive: "The affairs of the last Embassy were its own affairs," he said; "those of the present Embassy alone are what we will converse about."[35]

In the end, Lord Amherst didn't really see what all the fuss was about, so on August 27, a few days before the planned audience, he decided that he would just go ahead and perform the kowtow as requested.[36] It seemed the polite thing to do, after all, to follow the customs of the court to which he had been sent. Given all the expense and the long journey, it did not seem to him like something worth risking an audience over—and since Jiaqing believed with good reason that Macartney had done it for Qianlong, it would be an insult for Amherst not to do the same. Henry Ellis, the secretary to the mission, agreed with Amherst completely. He did not see how hairsplitting distinctions between bowing and prostration, between kneeling on one knee or two, were in any way grounds for jeopardizing the goals of the embassy. For his part, as a budding imperialist fresh from India, it was less about being respectful than the fact that he considered all such Oriental customs to be, in his words, "absurd pretensions." Ceremonies like the kowtow, to his mind, were "ridiculous"—and thus meaningless—so what would be the harm in performing them for show, if it would get you what you wanted?[37] Many in England would agree with him.

As it turned out, the only person on the British side who cared deeply about the issue was George Staunton. It is hard to judge his motives—he claimed principle and national honor, but the memory of his father's failed mission, redeemed afterward only by the pride of not having submitted to the kowtow, was also at stake. If Lord Amherst were to succeed by abandoning the precedent of Macartney and Staunton's father (at least as they had claimed it), then the previous embassy might as well be written off completely, as if it had been led by a group of inflexible buffoons too stubborn to make diplomacy work. So when Amherst said that he planned to go ahead with the ceremony, Staunton begged him to wait. He asked for time to refer the question to the "Canton gentlemen"—a group that included Manning and Morrison and the three junior Company personnel who had come along. These men, he told Amherst, had a greater knowledge of China and therefore a keener sense of whether the kowtow would be damaging to British interests.

The deck was well stacked in Staunton's favor. All of the "Canton gentlemen" were either professionally subordinate to or personally indebted to him. Since he was the pathbreaker who had made their language studies possible, and was the reigning president of the select committee—who, furthermore, took this issue quite personally— there is little chance they would have contradicted him in front of Amherst. The three junior staff, as may be expected, agreed with him immediately. Manning, however, was "more qualified" in his agreement, Staunton admitted. He thought that in general it was fine to perform the kowtow (he himself had, after all, done it eagerly and repeatedly before the Dalai Lama), but he came to agree with Staunton that under the circumstances, with such uncivil pressure from their hosts, it might not be best for Amherst to give in. Robert

Morrison was the lone dissenter, stating that he saw no harm in it for the Company's interests.[38]

The majority was enough for Staunton to declare victory. "I reported these results to Lord Amherst and Mr. Ellis," he wrote in a private account, "and begged that they would accordingly consider my opinion as final."[39] They did. Deferring to Staunton's vaunted China expertise—and going against his own better judgment—Lord Amherst had his secretary Ellis draft a letter to the effect that the ambassador would be glad to kneel on one knee and bow however many times the emperor should like, and that he would "consider it the most fortunate occurrence of my life to be enabled thus to show my profound devotion to the most potent Emperor in the Universe," but nevertheless he "found it absolutely impossible" to perform the kowtow as specified. Morrison dutifully translated the statement into Chinese, and one of the junior linguists brought it to the Duke.[40]

———

The next morning, the travelers saw the last of their baggage and gifts offloaded from the river junks at Tongzhou in preparation for the final leg of their journey, twelve miles overland to the imperial palace outside Beijing. The air was full of optimism. A friendly message had come from the emperor, addressed to Amherst's son, apparently in memory of the general delight created by little George Staunton when he spoke Chinese with Qianlong in 1793. The Jiaqing emperor asked the boy how old he was, and whether he had read any Chinese books. He said he looked forward to seeing him in Beijing.[41] Once the transfer of the luggage was complete, the British travelers came ashore and were loaded into a Chinese caravan of sedan chairs and wooden wagons—all except for the three commissioners and Amherst's son, who rode in a British-made carriage that had been unpacked from their capacious baggage and was now drawn by four mules.

In the late afternoon with the sun headed lower in the sky, they set out with their handlers and a military guard along the wide, stone-paved road to the capital. The procession stopped just once, around seven in the evening, for dinner at a run-down hostel one of the trav-

elers described as being "just like the stable-yard of an inn," where
they sat down to what Amherst himself called a "disgusting repast"
of boiled, half-plucked fowl (intended, touchingly enough, to be an
approximation of English cuisine, at least as far as their Chinese hosts
understood it).[42] None found the dinner appetizing, but they were
still surprised and put out when their escorts hurried them onward
after only a short rest. The hour was getting late, they were told, the
sun was setting, and the gates to Beijing were always shut at night—
though the handler Zhang assured Staunton that the city's eastern
gate would be kept open for their arrival. Zhang also mentioned that
the emperor would receive Amherst on the morning after his arrival,
but that seemed too soon to Staunton, who ignored him, assuming it
was just a story he was making up to urge them along.[43]

A surreal journey followed. Night fell long before they reached
Beijing. Miles from the city, crowds of spectators began assembling
by the side of the road in the murky darkness to watch them, holding

A gate in the Beijing city wall

up little paper lanterns on sticks that cast a flickering yellow glow over their shadowed faces and the edges of the road. It was near midnight by the time the travelers reached the looming eastern wall of Beijing, so high they could barely make out its towers against the black sky above. The massive outer gate, contrary to what Zhang had promised, was shut. They could not enter the city. So they had to turn and continue their slow march along a rugged secondary road that circled the perimeter of the city wall, miles out of their original way through the pitch dark, at the pace of a man walking. The springless wooden carts of the caravan were so uncomfortable on the bumping, uneven path that several of the men simply got out and hiked the distance.

Traveling through the night without rest, the beleaguered embassy finally arrived at the imperial palace northwest of Beijing at dawn, disheveled and stinking. It was a beautiful scene in its way, ornate gardens illuminated by the rising sun, dim mountains visible in the distance. Most of the exhausted British entourage were told to wait behind while Amherst, Staunton, Ellis, and Morrison were brought forward with a few of the others and deposited into a small, elegant waiting chamber with windows on four sides, about seven by twelve feet, surrounded by a crowd of ministers wearing buttons of various rank, who were milling about and apparently waiting for something.[44]

It was then announced that Amherst's audience would take place immediately—in fact, he was already late for it and the emperor was at that moment mounting his throne in preparation to receive him. The ministers were all assembled and waiting (thus explaining the crowd outside of Amherst's chamber), and the Duke would be coming in a moment to escort Amherst into the audience hall for his long-awaited meeting with Jiaqing. At this, Amherst broke down. He wasn't ready, he protested. Not only was he bleary and unkempt, but his special outfit for the audience was still in his baggage, which hadn't arrived yet. (Amherst had brought his coronation robes for the occasion; Staunton, in emulation of his father, had gotten a tailor in Canton to replicate a Cambridge academic gown for him.) Amherst did not even have the letter from the prince regent that he was supposed to present to the emperor. He said he would not go.

The Duke soon arrived in a flurry of motion, clearing a path through the crowd of ministers. Amherst had to go to the audience, he said. Amherst, speaking through Robert Morrison, refused. The Duke argued with him, politely but firmly, and Amherst still refused. Finally, the Duke told him that if he must, he could even perform his own ceremony of kneeling. (It is worth noting that for all the fuss the British would eventually make over the kowtow, neither of their ambassadors was actually denied an audience for refusing to do it.) By then, however, Amherst had made up his mind firmly and refused to budge. The kowtow didn't matter; he wanted time to get cleaned up, and he needed his baggage. He wanted to rest.

The crowd of officials who had assembled for the audience began filing into Amherst's waiting chamber, jostling in their curiosity to get a look at the foreign ambassador and his retinue in their strange costumes, trying to overhear the argument between Morrison and the Duke. The air was close. Mandarins and servants of all ranks and ages pushed into the room while others filled the open windows, pressing for an angle to gratify their "brutal curiosity," as the unnerved Ellis termed it. A gnawing panic set in among the British, a feeling of being trapped. "They seemed to regard us rather as wild beasts than mere strangers of the same species with themselves," said Ellis.[45] Amherst's physician seethed, "We could not but be sensible that we were in the hands of a despotic and capricious government." The princes, officials, and eunuchs, he wrote, had "infested the apartment" and "looked upon us as a strange species of animal."[46]

Then it all went to hell. The Duke, summoning another official to help him, grabbed hold of Amherst by the arm as if to drag him on his way to the emperor. Amherst threw off their hands violently and shoved the surprised Duke backwards. Amherst's attendants leapt forward to his defense, reaching for their swords and getting ready, in Amherst's words, "to resist force by force."[47] The flustered ambassador, regaining a bit of his composure, quickly ordered his men to sheathe their weapons, fearing what might result. Desperate and claustrophobic, Amherst tried to push his way out of the room, but there were too many people, pressing in too close. He couldn't get out. It was the Duke who finally took pity on him. He snatched a whip from a guard and began violently beating the crowd of court officials and eunuchs to clear a path for Amherst to escape, knocking them to the ground as they scrambled to get out of the way of his lash.[48]

The audience, most assuredly, did not happen.

As it turned out, the melee at the waiting chamber wasn't even the worst of it. On the evening of November 13, while Amherst, Staunton, and the others were still making their slow journey back down to Canton via the inland route after failing to meet with the emperor, five hundred miles to their south the *Alceste*—back now from its surveying mission along the northern coast—was unleashing its full broadside of thirty-two-pounders against one of the Chinese forts guarding the Tiger's Mouth at the river entrance to Canton, blasting it into silence and killing a reported forty-seven Chinese soldiers as it pushed toward Whampoa under a sustained fire of dozens of cannons from shore.[49]

The *Alceste* had returned from its explorations earlier that month. Limping back to Canton due to storm damage, it anchored off an island in the Pearl River delta and its captain, a veteran Royal Navy officer named Murray Maxwell, requested permission to sail up to the Whampoa anchorage below Canton to make repairs before Lord Amherst returned from Beijing. Maxwell was, in response, taunted by a representative of the governor-general with the news that Amherst had been sent away from the capital without an audience. The local officials had won. No motion was made to give the *Alceste* permission to continue up to Whampoa.

After a week of waiting at the outlying island—where the *Alceste* was surrounded by war junks and supplies were only brought on board under cover of darkness—Captain Maxwell grew tired of being put off and decided to force his way up the river without a pass. Soon after the *Alceste* got under way, it was confronted by a Chinese fleet sent to turn it back. Maxwell and the Chinese ships exchanged a round of blank-shotted salutes, which quickly gave way to warning shots, and then to live fire. Then everything broke down as the *Alceste* ran out her guns and began blasting away at the Chinese coastal defenses, working her way up the river channel to the Whampoa anchorage where Captain Maxwell (who would be knighted when he got home) felt his ship belonged.

The *Alceste's* surgeon, at least, found the affair rather exciting—"The flashing of the guns on the glassy surface of the river, and the rolling echo of their reports along the adjoining hills, had a very grand and animating effect," he recalled. Despite the great number of Chinese killed by her guns, the *Alceste* suffered no casualties, just a couple of hullings and much damage to her rigging. When the shooting finally paused, Chinese boats continued to track the British ship carefully, but—perhaps in mutual realization that this was supposed to be a diplomatic visit—both sides refrained from further escalation.[50]

Neither side knew quite what to make of the British embassy's sudden turn toward disaster. To the British themselves, it seemed like a dream. Generally, the members of the embassy blamed Jiaqing. "We could only conjecture," wrote Amherst's physician, "that we had been hurried [out] and subjected to all kinds of indignity and inconvenience to suit the will of a capricious despot."[51] Jiaqing himself, meanwhile, was equally mystified. The embassy's handlers had misled him about Amherst's reluctance to kowtow, giving him no reason to imagine that the audience might not take place as planned. He thus had no idea why the British ambassador did not appear when he was expected (sickness was claimed, but when the emperor sent his own physician to attend to Amherst, he turned out to be perfectly healthy). So he initially blamed the rudeness entirely on Amherst himself, but after some investigation he determined that the debacle was in fact the fault of the escorting officials—above all, the Duke—who had been lying to him about Amherst's misgivings in order not to displease him. Jiaqing issued a scathing edict blaming the Amherst mission's handlers for incompetence and dishonesty, and referring them to the Board of Punishments for discipline.[52]

Most poignantly, though, far from being a "capricious despot" who didn't care a whit for foreign visitors, behind the scenes Jiaqing had in fact been quite determined to make sure the British visit went well. He was more willing to accommodate them than they knew. Three days before the aborted audience, he commented in an edict that the Duke should, if necessary, be flexible about whether Amherst would kowtow (indicating, as he did so, that his father Qianlong had shown at least some measure of accommodation to Macartney in 1793). "Do not be so severe and exacting about ceremonials that you lose track of the etiquette for managing foreigners," he instructed the Duke; "it was just like this in 1793, and we made the best of the situation then. Generally speaking, it is better to meet with them than to send them away."[53] Though Amherst and his entourage would blame Jiaqing's arrogance for the failure of the embassy, the emperor very much wanted to have a successful meeting, even if it meant compromising on the external trappings of ceremony. He too was disappointed that the British visit failed to result in a friendly audience.

As quickly as the acts of hostility burst forth, they were covered over by mutual embarrassment. When the *Alceste* reached Whampoa, its guns still stinking of powder, an official came down to the anchorage on the governor-general's behalf and welcomed the ship to Canton as if nothing had happened.[54] After the violence at the waiting chamber, Amherst was ushered politely on his way with no further mention of the scuffle that had broken out. When he first reached the riverboats at Tongzhou that would begin the mission's four-month inland journey back to Canton, a courier caught up to him with a conciliatory edict from the emperor, who sent some gifts for the king— a ceremonial jade scepter, some silk purses, a string of imperial beads. Jiaqing said that while he could not under such circumstances accept most of Amherst's presents, as a token of good faith he would keep the portraits Amherst had brought of the king and queen, as well as a book of prints and an atlas.

The edict that accompanied the presents, addressed to the king of England, was written the day after the failed audience when Jiaqing still blamed Amherst. In it, Jiaqing commended the king's "feelings of sincere devotion to me," as represented by his having sent an ambassador over such a long journey across the oceans to China. But he also regretted that "your ambassador, it would seem, does not understand how to practice the rites and ceremonies" of the Qing Empire. He made it clear that he did not consider this to be the fault of the king himself, just the result of a poorly chosen representative. Nevertheless, as if to ensure that the mutual embarrassment would not be repeated again, Jiaqing politely asked the king to please refrain from sending any more diplomats. "In the future," he wrote, "there is no reason you should have to send another ambassador from so great a distance and give him the trouble of crossing over the mountains and seas." If the king would just tend to the boundaries of his own empire, he said, and feel "dutiful submission" within his own heart, there would be no need for a British mission ever to come to China again.[55]

No matter how each side tried to paper it over, however, the Amherst mission was a catastrophe. Trade would continue unaffected, but new suspicions had been planted on both sides. Jiaqing was left wary. Troubled as he was by the ongoing problems of corruption and sedition within the empire, he had no desire to provoke a conflict with the British as well. But he was fully aware that they might be angered by their collision with his ministers, and was especially concerned (with good reason) about what Amherst's ships might have been up to after they left their designated anchorages without permission. One of the unintended outcomes of this ostensible mission of friendship was that the British came out of it seeming more sinister than they ever had before. From the other side, the great hopes of the East India Company and the British government for impressing upon the Jiaqing emperor their country's power in the new post-Napoleonic age, for securing his respect and goodwill, and for opening up a new line of communication beyond the narrow confines of Canton were all dashed. In a grand climax of poetic justice—perhaps the most fitting end possible for this travesty of a diplomatic mission—as the *Alceste* was carrying Lord Amherst and his retinue back to England, it slammed into an unseen rock and sank.

———

Back in England, the response to Amherst's mission was mainly disappointment, though tinged, depending on one's perspective, with a measure of either bemusement or indignation. The *Times*, for its part, leaned toward bemusement. It hadn't expected much to come of the "unfortunate" mission in the first place, and observed sarcastically that "the results of that brilliant embassage" did not afterward include any increase in British imports to China, nor any reduction in the price of tea to "gladden the breakfast-tables of the people of England." Overall, Amherst's embassy had "failed in the objects for which it was prepared and put forth by the British Government," said the paper, and "the political influence of England has not been either satisfactorily proved or successfully enforced, or, according to any human reasoning, much confirmed or extended." Indeed, in the *Times*'s opinion, the only useful product of the embassy was the series of detailed travel narratives that its members published afterward. Those it welcomed as the only sign of the mission having been in any way worthwhile.[56]

The sharpest denunciations of Amherst and his mission came from a new generation of free-trade advocates in Britain who dreamed of abolishing the East India Company's monopoly on commerce with China. As they saw it, Amherst was an arrogant fool who had offended the Chinese by his refusal to follow their customs. By fussing pointlessly over the kowtow, he had squandered a rare opportunity to expand British commerce. One such critic in the *Edinburgh Review*

The wreck of the *Alceste*

complained that the kowtow "does not appear much more humiliating than other court ceremonies" and insisted that Amherst should simply have done it. All of the troubles between Britain and China, he argued, could be traced back to individuals within the Company's factory in Canton—whether it be John Roberts goading Admiral Drury to invade Macao or George Staunton pressuring Amherst not to kowtow. With easy jobs free from competition, where they had "little or nothing to do" other than sit around and rake in money from their rich and exclusive trade, the Company's staff were, he insisted, sabotaging Britain's chances for a more productive relationship with the Qing Empire.

For contrast, he pointed to how well the Americans were faring in China with their total absence of a monopoly company. "The free and extensive traffic carried on by the Americans—an intercourse which is yearly increasing at our expense," he wrote, ". . . has never for a moment been interrupted by any quarrel or altercation with the Chinese or their government." The Americans never encountered the kinds of prestige-related problems the stodgy old East India Company did. To his mind, the obvious solution to the problem of relations with China was for the British government to abolish the monopoly and allow private British firms to compete freely for the business of Canton. "Let the Chinese trade, as soon as good faith and the laws will permit, be made free," he declared, "and we have no doubt whatever, either of its stability or its increase."[57] Such sentiments would only build in the years to come.

Others would take a more nationalistic tone, cheering Amherst for upholding Britain's honor even at the expense of improved relations with China. On that side, the same current of hostility that Staunton's book on the Qing law code had stirred up in 1810 rose anew. The *Quarterly Review*, examining Ellis's published journal, commended him for debunking the myth of Chinese civilization and revealing "in its true light . . . this government of sages, which Voltaire and his followers conspired to hold up as . . . an example for the general admiration of mankind."[58] Separately, it praised Amherst for not performing the kowtow, declaring that "the national character [has] been upheld by the refusal of Lord Amherst to comply with a disgusting and degrading ceremony." The British must continue to stand firm against the Chinese, it said, for "the less that is conceded to this pusillanimous and insolent people, the more will their fears for the consequence begin to operate."[59]

Down that road lay the fantasy of teaching China a lesson in respect—a resentful grumbling under the collective breath, the fodder for snide nationalistic quips about Jiaqing's failure to recognize the obvious power of the Royal Navy. John Wolcot, the satirist writing as Peter Pindar who had ridiculed Lord Macartney for humiliating himself before Qianlong ("Say, wert thou not *asham'd* to put thy prow / Where Britons, dog-like, learnt to crawl and bow?"), sharpened his pen again, but this time to take on the emperor rather than the ambassador. His humor in 1817 was of a darker variety than before, leading one reviewer to comment that in his "patriotic resentment" the well-known satirist's wit had become somewhat less funny.[60] As he addressed Jiaqing:

> Thou never didst vouchsafe, perhaps,
> To cast thine eye sublime on maps;
> And therefore, fancying thyself all-mighty,
> Has treated us with pompous scorn—
> . . .
>
> Know, should Old England's Genius frown,
> Her thunder soon would shake thy crown,
> Reduce thee from an eagle to a wren,
> Thine high Imperial pride to gall,
> Force thee to leap the Chinese wall,
> To feed on horse with Tartar tribes again.

Against such preening invocations of Britain's military dominance, more sober voices of caution were few. One, however, came from the very man who knew, more intimately than anyone else then alive, how fleeting a nation's presumed invincibility could be: Napoleon Bonaparte. In July 1817, Napoleon was living in exile on Saint Helena when he learned that Lord Amherst and his suite (who had been rescued from their shipwreck) would soon be landing at the island on their way home from China and hoped to have an audience with him. As he waited for their arrival, he chatted about the fate of the British embassy with his Irish physician, Barry O'Meara, who had accompanied the defeated general into exile.

Napoleon thought it was absurd that Amherst should have refused to kowtow. "Different nations have different customs," he told O'Meara. If the British wanted to send an ambassador to the Chinese court they should have told him to follow the customs of the Chinese. "You have no right to send a man to China to tell them, that they must perform certain ceremonies, because such are practised in England," he said. With a twinkle in his eye, the old general asked O'Meara what would have happened if the British custom were to kiss their king on his ass instead of his hand. When they got to China, would they have ordered the emperor to remove his trousers? All the British had accomplished with the Amherst mission was to lose the friendship of the Chinese over a ridiculous matter of protocol, he said, to the peril of their advantages in trade.[61]

O'Meara replied that it didn't matter if the British had the friendship of the Chinese. They had the Royal Navy.

And with that, the joking ended. Napoleon's eyes turned dark. "It would be the worst thing you have done for a number of years, to go to war with an immense empire like China," he told O'Meara. And his words that followed resonated with the fears of everyone who wondered quietly what might happen if the dragon, as it were, should be awakened. "You would doubtless, at first, succeed," Napoleon continued, ". . . but you would teach them their own strength. They would be compelled to adopt measures to defend themselves against you; they would consider, and say, 'we must try to make ourselves equal to this nation. Why should we suffer a people, so far away, to do as they please to us? We must build ships, we must put guns into them, we must render ourselves equal to them.' They would get artificers, and ship builders, from France, and America, and even from London; they would build a fleet," he said, "and, in the course of time, defeat you."[62]

PART II

The Milk of Paradise

CHAPTER 7

Boom Times

———◆———

Through the dusk of a mid-autumn evening in 1830, a young American threaded his way on a hired Chinese junk through the crowded anchorage at Whampoa on the way up to Canton. It was his first time in the country, but the image that impressed him most on his arrival had nothing to do with China itself. It was his competition: the trim, powerful line of the East India Company's trading fleet at rest at Whampoa—sixteen immense ships, as big as American frigates, heavily armed and manned. Quiet for the moment, the mammoth fleet projected a vision of discipline, strength, and unity to the American as he sailed past the anchorage in his little rented boat.[1]

The young man's name was John Murray Forbes, and he was seventeen, very much on the small side, the youngest of three brothers from the town of Milton, just south of Boston. If he hadn't precisely been born into the China trade, there was nevertheless little chance he could have avoided it. His father, a gout-ridden man who had never been a good provider, had died six years earlier when John was eleven, at which time it fell to his brothers, Robert Bennet Forbes and Thomas Tunno Forbes, nine and eleven years older than John, respectively, to support their mother and four sisters. Fortunately, they had a unique path open to them through an uncle. Their mother's older brother, Thomas Handasyd Perkins, was one of the wealthiest men in Boston and a renowned philanthropist. Most of his fortune, as it happened, had come from the China trade, in which he had played a major role on the American side since the time of George Washington's inauguration.[2]

John's older brothers Robert and Thomas took early apprenticeships under their rich uncle, starting out as clerks and runners in his counting house at Foster's Wharf in Boston before chasing more distant opportunities in his service. Robert, a natural sailor who loved climbing high up into a ship's rigging, chose the traveling side of the merchant's career. He went to sea for the first time at age thirteen on the *Canton Packet*, one of his uncle's ships, and by the precocious age of twenty had earned his own command as a captain on the Boston–China circuit. Thomas, older by a year and a half, was more inclined toward the sedentary side of the business, so he moved permanently to Canton, where by 1828 he was chief manager of their uncle's trading enterprise, Perkins & Co., and served as the U.S. consul. John, being so much younger than they, was sent at their expense to the Round Hill School, an experimental private academy in Northampton, Massachusetts, where he learned to play an early form of baseball, stood up to bullies, studied French and Spanish along with accounting, and tramped through the low, rolling hills and pine forests of the Connecticut River valley.

John had originally thought he might become a minister, but he lost his taste for the Bible in Northampton after having it shoved too much down his throat at school.[3] His thoughts often tended toward China, where he wondered if he would follow someday in his brothers' footsteps. He envied them—especially Thomas, who after their father's death was the closest thing to a patriarch in the family. The elder brothers had become wealthy enough in their China ventures to support their mother and establish one of their sisters independently, and John hoped eventually to do his part as well. From Canton, Thomas wrote to young John as a father would, giving him sober instructions on how to make his studies useful for a future in commerce, how to dress well without becoming a "Dandy," and how to choose the kinds of friends who would make him a gentleman. Mercifully, he also reminded him not to let the carefree joys of youth slip

The anchorage at Whampoa, facing upriver toward Canton

by. "Enjoy them all while you may," wrote Thomas in 1828, "for the time will come soon when they shall have passed away."[4]

That time came sooner than either expected. In the summer of 1829, Thomas was drowned in a gale near Macao. It took six months for the news to reach Boston, and within six months of that, John was on his way to China. The uncle's business had lost its manager in Canton, and John's family had lost its main provider. Robert, the middle brother, a bright-eyed young man with a rosy complexion and a squirrel of curly hair on top of his head, happened to be home in the United States at the time to outfit his own ship for the China trade, a barque called the *Lintin* (named after a small island in the Pearl River estuary about sixty miles south of Canton). When the *Lintin* launched at Medford, Massachusetts, that summer and Robert made for Canton on its maiden voyage, John—now all of seventeen years old and never to attend school again—sailed with him to take up their late brother's residence in the American factory.

. . .

The Canton where John Murray Forbes arrived in the autumn of 1830 was, on its surface at least, little changed since George Staunton had arrived there on the *Hindostan* at a comparably young age thirty years earlier. The narrow dimensions of the factory district were unchanged, though most of the buildings had been rebuilt after a fire in 1822. The rules that governed the lives of the compound's small population of a hundred or so foreigners were as strict as they had always been, and the visible objects of commerce—tea, silk, cotton— were also the same as before. The foreign community itself, however, was nearly unrecognizable. Most of the old guard were now gone. Staunton himself had returned to England in 1817 soon after the Amherst mission and in 1818 obtained the seat in Parliament that he, and his father before him, had always dreamed of—a purchased seat for a "rotten borough" with only a few dozen voters rather than a genuinely contested one, but still a seat nonetheless.[5] After an inconspicuous start to his parliamentary career, he had managed by this time to get himself appointed to the East India Committee of the House of Commons, where he hoped to begin putting his China expertise to work in the service of his country (as well as, of course, the interests of the Company that had served him so well).[6]

Others had moved on as well. Thomas Manning, the bearded eccentric, left with Amherst in 1817 and survived the *Alceste*'s shipwreck with the others. In England he joined the Royal Asiatic Society, which George Staunton cofounded with a Sanskrit scholar in 1823, and for a time he served as the society's honorary Chinese librarian. Charles Lamb welcomed him back to his London literary circle and loved him fiercely. "I am glad you esteem Manning," Lamb wrote to Samuel Taylor Coleridge in 1826, "though you see but his husk or shrine. He discloses not save to select worshippers, and will leave the world without any one hardly but me knowing how stupendous a creature he is."[7]

There were only a few left in Canton from before. Old Beale, the Cantonese-speaking private trader and nominal Prussian consul, was still kicking about. He had gone bankrupt in 1816 but still tended to his aviary in Macao, where by this time he had several hundred species including a rare bird of paradise and a parrot who could say, "Bring Polly a pot of beer."[8] A couple of the junior members of the British factory had grown into senior positions. But the unlikely doyen of the factory compound turned out to be Robert Morrison, who, alone among the first generation of British Chinese speakers, still lived in Canton with no plans to return home. He held court in Macao during the off-season, and in Canton he acted as the East India Company's senior interpreter as he had done now for twenty years. Thanks to his dictionary, the final volume of which was published in 1823, the ranks of the translators below him were growing steadily; in contrast to the days when Staunton was told it would be useless to know Chinese, the select committee now had a rule that all junior writers in the factory should study it. And thanks to Morrison's Bible—which was finally completed that same year—other Protestant missionaries were beginning to arrive in his wake, hoping somehow to get into China to further the work he had begun.

Morrison's wife, Mary, had felt strong enough to return to him from England with their two children in 1820, but within a year of her return to Macao she died of cholera. Since the Portuguese still would not let him use the Catholic cemetery, the Company staff purchased a small plot of land for him to open a Protestant cemetery in which to bury her.[9] He remarried in 1824 while traveling in England to raise support for his work in China, and his new wife (who would bear him several more children) had by 1830 settled down in Macao. His only living son from his first marriage, John Robert Morrison, lived with him in the British factory at Canton and followed in his father's footsteps—not as a missionary to the Chinese, for Morrison had mostly failed in that capacity, but rather as a linguist. In the same week that John Murray Forbes arrived, John Robert Morrison, by then sixteen years old, gained his first appointment as translator for the private British merchants in Canton.[10] If young Morrison carried on the secular side of his father's work, his older sister Rebecca continued the legacy of their mother insofar as she too was forbidden by virtue of being female from living in Canton. Like her mother before her, she had to stay behind in Macao during the trading season.

The most significant change in Canton was not so easily marked as the comings and goings of any given individual. What had changed most since the quiet days when Staunton first arrived was that there was now real competition afoot. By 1830, there were more private traders making their homes in the Canton factories than ever before, asserting their presence far more boldly, and finding far greater financial success. Among this growing community of free traders were Parsis from India, Armenians, a few Europeans, and various Scots and Englishmen who competed as best they could with the East India Company by wielding a range of spurious consulships to protect them from its monopoly on British residence in Canton. Then, of course, there were the Americans like the Forbes brothers. Collectively, the Americans and the private British now outnumbered the Company men more than two to one, and adding in the Parsis made that nearly five to one.[11] The rich and highly unified East India Company still presumed to dominate the social and commercial world of the Canton factory district, just as its fleet dominated the anchorage at Whampoa, but increasingly it did so against the competition and resentment of the other westerners and Indians among whom it operated. As one scornful American put it at this time, "by its improper interferences, and assumptions of superiority, [the Company has] earned the same dislike and unpopularity which a despotic and tyrannical government has entitled it to, in all other places where its influence extends."[12]

And yet, just as with the mighty fleet at which John Murray Forbes marveled on his arrival, the very size and unity of the East India Company also made it unwieldy and slow to react. Its mammoth strength opened spaces for independent operators like the Americans and private British in the "country" trade between India and Canton to get rich in its wake—buying and selling the goods the Company did not carry on its ships, sailing to the ports it did not supply, moving more quickly and nimbly through the spaces in its laboriously scheduled movements. And it is on this count that we find the very specific reason why John Murray Forbes sailed past the Company's grand fleet not on his brother's newly built ship the *Lintin*, on which he had come all the way from Boston, but instead on a hired Chinese boat—while the *Lintin*, it should be mentioned, was waiting at anchor some sixty miles away, at the outlying island after which it had been named, not daring to come any closer. It was the very same reason that lay behind the proliferation of private traders at Canton and the surge of competitive energy in the port. It was the reason why so many people were getting so rich, so easily. That reason was opium.

———

Robert Bennet Forbes, John's rosy-cheeked older brother, was a middleman in the drug trade. The *Lintin* he had just fitted out in Massachusetts was destined for use as a "receiving ship"—based off the southwest corner of Lintin Island, far from the reach of the authorities in Canton, he operated it as a floating warehouse for drug shipments. Foreign vessels coming in from India and elsewhere with cargoes of opium would stop first at Lintin, offload their chests of the drug onto Forbes's ship or another in the harbor, then proceed up to the Whampoa anchorage outside Canton with their holds empty of contraband and clean for inspection. In certain "money-changing shops" in the foreign compound, their captains or supercargoes could meet with the English-speaking agents of Chinese opium wholesalers (some, but not all, of whom were Hong merchants—since the trade was illegal, the Hong merchants' monopoly on foreign trade did not apply to opium as it did to tea). After agreeing on a price, the foreign merchants took payment for their opium, while the Chinese dealers sent their own men out to Lintin to retrieve the shipment from the holding vessel.[13]

Robert Bennet Forbes's job was a simple one. His cargo was not his own; he merely held it on consignment for other traders who had assumed the risk (storms, pirates, market fluctuations) of getting it to south China in the first place. Chinese smugglers took all of the responsibility for moving the drug inland and up the coast—and, eventually, for retailing it within China. They also took responsibility for bribing government officials to ensure that no inspections would be made at Lintin, or at least to make sure that such inspections would be announced well in advance. There were in fact Chinese warships stationed on the opposite side of Lintin Island from Forbes's ship, off the island's northeastern shore, but they were under a different county's jurisdiction than the smuggling anchorage and generally only sailed around the island in order to collect bribes from the smugglers before returning to the northeast again.[14] As captain of the *Lintin* receiving ship, Robert Bennet Forbes thus bore almost no risk at all. All he had to do was stay put and keep the opium safe, earning a commission for each chest he held. The hardest part of the job, for a young New Englander who loved to sail, was having to stay in one place all the time. For suffering that, he brought in an income that in today's currency was worth more than $800,000 per year.[15]

The basic fact was that the opium poppy grew very well in British India, which otherwise was a spectacularly unprofitable colonial venture (and which, without the rich profits from the Canton tea trade to offset its losses and debts, would likely have bankrupted the East India Company). European traders learned early on that there was a steady if small market for opium in China even though it was illegal there. As early as 1719 we can find the Chinese demand for the drug making an appearance in *The Farther Adventures of Robinson Crusoe*, Daniel Defoe's lesser-known sequel to his novel *Robinson Crusoe*, where Crusoe, who was rescued from his castaway fate in the previous book, made a run from Siam to China to sell opium, "a Commodity which bears a great Price among the Chinese, and which at that Time, was very much wanted there." Though Crusoe originally intended to sail north in China to sell it, he was advised to "put in at Macao, where we could not have fail'd of a Market for our Opium."[16]

There are more formal records of British traders carrying Indian opium to China by 1733, when the East India Company notified the captains of two of its ships of "the late severe laws enacted by the Emperour of China for the prohibition of Ophium," admonishing them that "you are neither to carry, nor suffer any of it to be carry'd in your Ship to China, as you will answer the contrary to the Hon'ble Company at your peril."[17] Going forward, the "Honourable Company" refrained from carrying any opium on its own ships, judging that the potential loss of its aboveboard tea trade was not worth the smaller reward to be gained from drug trafficking. That did not end the matter, however, but simply made an opening for independent operators who were more willing to take on the dangers of the illegal trade.

By the time of Macartney's arrival in 1793, a rogue commerce in Indian opium to China was well under way, established by private traders acting independently of the East India Company. The amounts they sold were relatively small, though, and only incidental to the overall commerce of the region. In any case, the British government had no interest in supporting or protecting them. Macartney's instructions acknowledged, "It is beyond a doubt that no inconsiderable portion of the Opium raised within our Indian Territories actually finds its way to China," but those instructions also said that if the emperor should, in the course of negotiating a treaty, ask for Britain's support in putting down the opium traffic, then Macartney should agree to do so "rather than risk any essential benefit" by trying to preserve it.[18] (But then there were, of course, no negotiations between Macartney and Qianlong, and no treaty, so no such request was ever made, let alone granted.)

By the early nineteenth century, the drug had long been established in China as a high-end luxury good, and despite various edicts condemning it, there seemed from the outside to be no social stigma to its purchase or use. When Thomas Manning was traveling in Tibet with "the General"—the half-Manchu military officer who so admired Manning's beard—Manning asked him what kind of gift he might like from India. The General immediately asked for some nice cloth and "a pound or two of opium."[19] Lord Amherst's diplomatic mission was openly solicited for the drug by an official during its inland journey back down to Canton in 1816, and his naturalist reported that while opium didn't seem to be sold openly in Chinese shops, he was told that it was in use, smoked with tobacco, "in all parts of the empire," and was considered "one of the greatest luxuries."[20]

Although the East India Company consistently avoided carrying opium to China on its own ships, that did not mean it did not take part in the trade. Rather, the Company's strategy was to dominate the supply side of the opium trade in India through a monopoly on production in Bengal, and then avoid risk by staying completely out of the smuggling enterprise at the Chinese end. At auctions in Calcutta, the Company would sell its opium to the country traders, who took responsibility for shipping the drug to Lintin Island and selling it to dealers in Canton. The proceeds from their sales—usually in the form of silver—would then typically be handed over to the East India Company's treasury at the British factory in Canton, either in return for bills of exchange the country traders could use to remit funds to

The East India Company's opium stacking room at Patna, India

India or England, or, if they had bought their cargo on credit, to pay back the Company what they owed from the Calcutta auction.

By such means, the East India Company could enjoy a constant flow of silver into its Canton treasury from the drug trade without ever transporting an ounce of opium to China itself. It had the best of both worlds, profiting enormously from the production and sale of the drug while still being able to present a clean face to the Chinese government for its regular trade. And as a side effect of this arrangement, in contrast to the heavy engagement of the East India Company's Bengal personnel in regulating and overseeing the production of opium in India, their counterparts in the British factory at Canton were so distant from the actual drug trade in China that a member of the select committee with nearly twenty years' experience in Canton could, in 1830, claim with a straight face that he had never seen a chest of opium in his life.[21]

As much as the East India Company wished to monopolize the supply of Indian opium, its control over production was not complete—and that would be the primary factor in a precipitous rise of opium imports into China that began in the 1820s. For the British controlled only a portion of the Indian subcontinent, primarily in the northeast. Farmers in the various states of central and western India outside of the East India Company's influence were perfectly free to grow poppies and process their own opium as they saw fit, which they transported to the west coast of India for export sale on independent terms. The same British and Parsi merchants of the country trade who bought and sold the Company's opium from Bengal (which was branded as "Patna") also, by the early 1800s, had begun to speculate in the rival product from the free territories of India (known as "Malwa" opium), which they shipped from Bombay and other ports on India's west coast.

Ideally, the East India Company wanted to keep a tight lid on Indian opium production in order to ensure that prices remained high at Canton. But it could only control the supply of Patna opium, and already by the early 1800s the competition from Malwa was beginning to undermine the Company's efforts to engineer the market. To reassert its control, the Company first tried to block shipments from Bombay (which was under British control), but the Malwa commerce simply moved northward to the Portuguese-controlled ports of Daman and Diu up the coast from Bombay, which were out of the Company's administrative reach.[22] By the late 1810s, growing sales of Malwa opium by the country traders were cutting so far into the overall Canton import market that the members of the East India Company's board of trade in Calcutta essentially threw up their hands and admitted failure. No longer would they try to choke off the Malwa trade in order to protect their monopoly; instead, fatefully, they decided to compete with Malwa head-on.

With its market share threatened, the Company began ramping up poppy cultivation in Bengal in 1820 and increasing production of its Patna opium in an attempt to drive the Malwa merchants out of business—seeking, in the words of the British governor-general in Calcutta, to furnish "a Supply on so enlarged a scale and on such reasonable terms as shall prevent competition."[23] At the same time, in a wildly misguided attempt to corner the market, the Company also began purchasing large amounts of Malwa opium itself—the main effect of which was to encourage even more production in the free states. The result was a dramatic increase in overall supply and a decline by nearly half in prices per chest for opium at the Calcutta auctions by the mid-1820s. The open field of competition between Patna and Malwa made for a heady and reckless time for the private traders in Canton. It also meant, significantly, that as Indian opium became less expensive to purchase in China, people beyond just the most wealthy could begin indulging in it, so the population of Chinese users expanded.[24] Ironically, if the East India Company had had its way, and if it had been able to maintain its failed monopoly in India, that expansion of opium usage in China might never have happened.

As for the progress of that expansion, in the years immediately following the Amherst mission the demand for foreign opium held steady at about four or five thousand chests per year (each chest holding about 133 pounds). However, sales of cotton from India, which had traditionally been the most important commodity at Canton on the British side, started to decline in the face of increased Chinese domestic production. By the early 1820s opium imports were rising sharply due to the Patna-Malwa competition even as cotton continued to slump, and in 1823 for the first time opium surpassed cotton as the largest Indian export to China. By the summer of 1828, opium was starting to seem like the only commodity left that could reliably secure a profit for the country traders. The flow of opium to Canton that year exceeded ten thousand chests, making up slightly more than half the value of all British imports into China—and, importantly, exceeding in value all of the tea the East India Company shipped back to England that year. Thanks to opium, the trade imbalance that had always operated in China's favor was starting to tip in the other direction.[25]

Yet the rise continued. By the 1830–31 season when John Murray Forbes arrived in Canton, opium imports reached 18,956 chests total—the size of the trade having nearly quadrupled in the course of a decade.[26] And that figure, it should be noted, represented only the opium imported from abroad: from India, mostly, with a small additional amount—about 8 percent of the whole—being Turkish opium imported by Americans (who trafficked in the cheaper variety from Turkey mainly because they faced no British competition for it). Those 18,956 chests did not include the much smaller but still meaningful amounts of opium grown and processed within China, or smuggled across China's western land borders in Central Asia. Nevertheless, they alone were enough to satisfy the annual needs of more than 150,000 habitual users.[27] In monetary terms, even accounting for the falling prices for opium—which were generally offset by the expansion of the Chinese consumer base—those 18,956 chests were worth nearly $13 million at the time, making for one of the most lucrative commodity trades in the world.[28]

———

The independent traders who did the real work of moving all the opium from India to China formed a community of their own in Canton to rival the Company's factory. Their leader was William Jardine, a hardheaded Scot with a degree in medicine from Edinburgh. Jardine got his start as a surgeon's mate for the East India Company, first sailing for India in 1802 just after his eighteenth birthday. When he eventually earned promotion from surgeon's mate to surgeon, he gained the privilege of a small space in the ship's hold to carry cargo on his own account, which he filled with badger-hair shaving brushes, lavender water, and macaroons. In time, he found that the strategies of trade were better suited to the workings of his mind than medicine, and its prospects more alluring than those of a ship's surgeon, so in 1817, after fifteen years in the East India Company's service, he quit to become a free merchant and throw his hat into the India-Canton country trade.[29]

The country trade, carried out in the shadow of the East India Company, was a highly restricted but profitable area of commerce. As the Company's monopoly applied to all British traffic between China and Europe, country traders like Jardine were only allowed to bring Indian products to Canton, and could only unload in India what they acquired from Canton—they were not allowed to trade in any European products at Canton, and were especially forbidden from shipping any Chinese tea or other commodities back to England. But the fact that India's produce included opium and cotton meant that they could still make a good living within those narrow limitations. Not that they were grateful to the Company for allowing the openings in which they worked, however. Generally speaking, they despised it.

Three years into his new life of commerce, Jardine met his lifelong partner, a fellow Scot of higher birth named James Matheson who had likewise been drawn into the country trade by the prospect of cotton and opium profits. The two men complemented each other's strengths—Matheson, who was twelve years younger than Jardine, was more temperamental and outspoken, more compelling as a writer. He also had money and better social connections back home. Jardine, by contrast, was more reserved and private but serious and purposeful, with a better head for business. Of the two, Matheson was the more willing to take big risks—in 1823 he tried unsuccessfully to corner the opium market at Canton, resulting in a glut and depression of prices—but then he, unlike Jardine, had family money to back him up if things went wrong. Jardine came from a more humble background and was a provider for his relatives back in Scotland, so he was the more conservative of the pair.[30]

In Canton, the two partners worked separately at first for firms founded by others, then together from 1828 onward, taking control of a firm called Magniac & Co., which they would in 1832 rename as Jardine, Matheson & Co. (It endures to this day as a major multinational conglomerate headquartered in Hong Kong, with more than four hundred thousand employees.)[31] Jardine and Matheson did much of their business as agents for Parsi and British opium merchants in Bombay and elsewhere in India, whose cargoes they would sell at Canton, where both of them eventually settled down to live in the "Creek factory" (named for its proximity to a creek at the edge of the compound), two doors down from the British factory where the East India Company was based. They were a hub for the community of British free traders, and in 1825 James Matheson even took upon himself the expense of importing a printing press to Canton, the first since the Company brought one for Morrison's dictionary, in order to publish the factory compound's first newspaper. Called the *Canton Register*, its purpose was to share shipping news and, more subtly, to advocate for the doctrine of free trade. To ward off the Company's monopoly on British residence at Canton, Matheson had an appointment as Danish consul, while Jardine (and their company as a whole) operated under protection of the Prussian flag, the consulship of which they inherited from old Beale, whose son came to work for them.[32]

Although Jardine and Matheson's social world in Canton was mostly British (and within that, mostly Scottish), their business partnerships were far more varied. Jardine's chief correspondent in India was a Parsi named Jamsetjee Jeejeebhoy, whose career trajectory had in some ways mimicked his own. The son of a poor family, orphaned at thirteen, Jeejeebhoy was born within a year of Jardine (who lost his own father at nine), and like Jardine he entered the China trade in hopes of finding a better life abroad. After his parents died, Jeejeebhoy moved to Bombay, where he worked for a bottle seller and began to learn English. He made his first voyage to Canton in 1799 as an apprentice to one of his cousins. Soon after, he began chartering his own ships with borrowed money for a succession of continuing trade voyages to China. In 1805, he and Jardine first crossed paths when Jeejeebhoy took passage to Canton on the same Company ship where Jardine was surgeon. Their ship was captured by a French frigate and both men were taken prisoner, then finally abandoned by their French captors at the Cape of Good Hope.[33]

Jardine and Jeejeebhoy made their separate ways home in 1805, but the contact appears to have held. After the misery of his imprisonment, Jeejeebhoy decided not to risk traveling to China anymore, instead sending cargoes under consignment to Canton to be dealt with by an agent—who by the early 1820s was usually William Jardine. With Jardine as his trusted partner, Jeejeebhoy could remain in Bombay while still reaping the rewards of the Canton trade. A bold speculator in cotton and opium—one of the boldest of his time—by 1822 he had amassed a huge fortune from his China ventures and was beginning to make Jardine a wealthy man as well.[34]

If there is any pattern to be found among the foreigners who got richest from the Chinese drug trade, it is that far from being stigmatized by their line of business, back home they would count among the most admired members of their respective societies. As with the Forbes brothers' uncle Thomas Handasyd Perkins and his many philanthropic projects in the Boston area, by the 1820s Jamsetjee Jeejeebhoy was making a name for himself as a philanthropist in Bombay, using the money he earned from opium speculation to found schools, hospitals, and other prominent public works.[35] Eventually even William Jardine would find himself in Parliament with the ear of the prime minister, though that is getting ahead of the story.

———

After John Murray Forbes arrived in Canton, he moved into the building where his uncle's business, Perkins & Co., was based—the so-called Swedish factory, five doors up from Jardine and Matheson (and which, despite its name, was entirely filled with Americans).[36] Like most other firms, Perkins & Co. had two faces: the aboveground trade in tea, silk, cotton, and other legal commodities that took place openly in Canton, and the underground trade in opium that took place at Lintin Island. Living in the Canton factory, John represented the legal, open side of Perkins's business. His account books from the time reflect mainly the purchase of tea and silks, sundries for the firm's staff (furniture, soap, chessmen), and fees for the Chinese linguists and servants the firm worked with. Opium appears only as a ghostly presence in the books: the day-to-day supplies for the *Lintin* receiving ship were included in his reckonings, as were occasional insurance fees for cargoes of Turkish opium—but never the sale thereof, nor any mention of opium from India.[37]

Perkins & Co.'s business was in disarray after Thomas Forbes's drowning in 1829, and even Thomas had only been entrusted with full control of the Canton office for a short time before his death. He had made arrangements that if anything should happen to him—knowing that it would be months before anyone else from the family could learn of the news, let alone reach Canton—then the firm's business should be entrusted temporarily to its chief American rival, a firm founded by a Connecticut orphan named Samuel Russell. By the time John Murray Forbes arrived, Thomas's bequest had set into motion a process that would ultimately result in the two rival houses—Perkins and Russell—deciding to merge permanently under the name of Russell & Co., forming an interest that would, upon its establishment in 1830, represent the largest American concern in China by far, coming in second only to the East India Company in the size of its legal trade at Canton.[38]

Americans had always done things differently in China. Without the unifying power of a monopoly company like the British had, the American firms were free traders from the start, working independently in competition with one another. This gave them less collective influence at Canton, but it also meant they had no national issues of prestige at stake in their trade so they avoided the kinds of embarrassment faced by the British during their two failed embassies under Macartney and Amherst. And although the China trade never comprised more than a small piece of America's overall commerce—in the early nineteenth century it represented only about 5 percent of U.S. foreign trade—the houses involved in it were few in number, and they were closely held by the families involved, so those Americans who managed to succeed in China were able to accumulate truly fabulous fortunes.[39]

In doing so, though, they had to be creative about how they went about things. With no commercial base in Asia like the East India Company's colony in India, the Americans were forced to work at a broader level, making longer voyages, buying and selling as they went in a so-called chain trade named for all the links along its way.[40] A typical American ship leaving Boston or New York in the early nineteenth century for Canton might first sail down around Cape Horn at the tip of South America, trading American and European goods for seal skins in the South Atlantic along the way, and then land at Mexico or Peru to sell as much of its remaining cargo as possible for silver, which was the most crucial commodity of all. Up to the mid-1820s, when bills of exchange on London began making it more convenient for Americans to buy Chinese goods on British credit than to carry physical specie to Canton, silver—mainly in the form of Spanish dollars—represented three-quarters of the value of all American imports into China.[41]

From Mexico and Peru, the ship could then continue on up the west coast of the North American continent to Oregon, where its crew would trade iron goods and textiles for sea otter pelts. So regular was this route that when Lewis and Clark first reached the mouth of the Columbia River in 1805, they found that the natives could already speak a bit of English thanks to the Canton fur trade (though their vocabulary, according to Lewis, consisted of little more than "musket," "powder," "shot," "knife," "damned rascal," and "son of a bitch"—which gives about as concise a portrait as can be had of the sailors who engaged in this trade).[42]

From the Pacific Northwest, the American ship could then set a southwest course to Hawaii or the Fiji Islands, where, if it was lucky, it might pick up some sandalwood to bring to Canton. Fair trade was one thing, but the uninvited harvesting of valuable natural resources could spark violence—one American on a ship collecting sandalwood in the South Pacific in 1811 recorded three of his shipmates being killed in a battle with natives on Fiji who "rosted and eat" them. (That unfortunate ship, the *Hunter*, did make it eventually to China, only to be captured at Macao by HMS *Doris* as part of the War of 1812's arrival to the region.)[43] After taking on sandalwood, the American vessel could continue across the Pacific and into Southeast Asia to barter for sea cucumber and other delicacies, then perhaps take on a load of rice or sugar at Manila before finally arriving at Canton with a cargo that bore almost no resemblance to the contents of its hold when it left America.[44]

The directors of Russell & Co., however, threw themselves into India as well. Beginning under Samuel Russell himself in the later 1820s and continuing aggressively under the merged firm after it added Perkins's business in 1830, Russell & Co. worked with several American brokers based in Calcutta to buy a piece of the British-dominated Indian opium trade. Within a year of the merger, the American firm was handling more than one-fifth of the Indian opium coming into China, posing serious competition to the British traders like Jardine and Matheson who sought to control the country trade.[45]

In light of later events, the British collectively would wind up receiving nearly all of the blame for this commerce. One-fifth, however, was hardly an insignificant share.

———

Everyone who lived in the Canton factory compound was aware that opium was technically illegal in the Qing Empire, but nobody knew quite what that meant. "Most of our readers know that Opium is strictly forbidden by the laws of China," observed James Matheson's *Canton Register* in April 1828. "Nevertheless [China] is the country, where the principal portion of the Indian Drug is consumed, together with a large quantity of what is produced in Turkey."[46] This was the paradox at the heart of their trade: they knew the commodity was forbidden, but they also knew it was welcome. To shun the opium trade on moral grounds meant giving up the easiest and most effective way to succeed at trade in China, whereas engaging in it carried almost no risk of punishment. For most, it was a temptation too attractive to resist.

And yet these men did not consider themselves immoral. In the following issue of the same paper, the editor complained about a practice whereby certain Western ships were dodging the tariffs they owed on legitimate, dutiable imports by offloading them onto Chinese vessels at Lintin and other islands instead of bringing them to Canton or Macao where they could be properly taxed by the Chinese government. The free-trading editor deplored this practice, writing that "in this age of civilization, and we are happy to think, of moral improvement also, we are unwilling to see any thing that can in the slightest degree detract from that distinguished character, which in former times, gained to the merchants, the title of 'Princes.'"[47] Which was to say that the great reputation of "merchant princes" for civilization and expansive moral virtue was apparently threatened by their avoidance of paying taxes. Selling opium, though, was perfectly fine.

Chinese government efforts to suppress the relatively open traffic were infrequent and halfhearted, in part because many officials were themselves opium users or otherwise involved in the traffic, so they had a vested interest in seeing the trade continue. Those on the coast who bore direct responsibility for controlling the inland flow of the drug were also the most ripe for being bribed by Chinese smugglers, and of course officials in Canton were no strangers to corruption. Jiaqing's abortive anticorruption campaign after Heshen's trial had done nothing to rein them in, and the rising supply of opium simply gave them a new source of income. From what the foreigners could see, Chinese enforcement was not just ineffective but almost non-existent.[48]

Nevertheless, despite its officially illegal nature, one of the Canton opium trade's most remarkable features was just how much international trust had been built into it at the wholesale level. Chinese, British, Parsi, and American traders came together from different continents and different languages to traffic in the drug with few written contracts and no protection from laws or their respective governments, their deals typically settled by little more than a handshake—and yet their trade was eminently safe, friendly, and civil. Complaints of cheating or thievery were almost nonexistent, as were incidents of violence between participants on either side. Perversely, it seemed to some observers almost a model for international relations on the grander scale; as one American put it in 1830, "Few men are better diplomatists than the merchants and Chinese brokers" of the Canton opium trade.[49] William Jardine, the dean of the British free traders, wrote to a friend back in England that the Canton opium trade was "the safest, and most Gentlemanlike speculation that I am aware of."[50]

Whether or not the British and American opium traders admitted there was any moral problem with their chosen profession, those back home were scarcely unaware of opium's harmful effects—not that European medicine had been terribly good at determining harmfulness, however. Even tea, for example, had long been criticized as a dangerous article. One 1706 London pamphlet by a certain Dr. Duncan, titled *Wholesome Advice Against the Abuse of Hot Liquors*, lumped tea together with coffee, hot chocolate, and warmed brandy in causing allegedly terrible harm to bodily organs. The abuse of hot drinks, Duncan wrote, "contributes very much to People the Kingdom of Death."[51] Even less forgiving was a pamphlet in 1722 titled *An Essay on the Nature, Use, and Abuse, of Tea*, which warned that the drink could "depauperate" the blood, its abuse causing a "Depression of the Spirits" that would leave the victim "oppress'd with Fears, Cares, and Anxieties."[52] It maintained that tea's worst effects were on women, causing "a Dimunition of their prolifick Energy, a Proneness to miscarry, and an Insufficiency to nourish the Child when brought into the World."[53]

There were also class-based attacks on tea in England, accusing the poor of spending so much on the drink that they ruined their lives (an argument that would echo in China as Confucian scholars eventually took up their own paternal crusades against opium use by the public). One anonymous British pamphleteer in 1777 condemned tea—along with sugar, white bread, butter, and other "modern luxuries"—as being "the foundation of almost all the poverty, and all the evils which affect the labouring part of mankind."[54] Above and beyond the wasting of scarce money, that author wrote, "It unstrings the nerves, it unbraces the constitution, dissolves nature, and destroys the *Englishman*." Under the influence of tea, he claimed, the "pleasing smiles" of English peasant girls gave way to a "haggard, yellow, meagre visage." They suffered "loss of appetite, sickness, and a puny race of children," and their families became "dead weight on the landed interest for life."

Such warnings did nothing to slow the spread and rising popularity of Chinese tea in England, but they did help muddle the British picture of opium—whose defenders typically claimed that it fell somewhere between tea and gin in the spectrum of harmfulness. As opium was known in Great Britain and the United States in the early nineteenth century, it was a perfectly legal medicinal product, freely sold by apothecaries, tobacconists, wine sellers, confectioners, and barbers.[55] Various liquid tinctures of opium were marketed as painkillers and remedies for coughs and intestinal disorders, sometimes even as a soothing tonic for teething babies (under such ominous names as "Mother Bailey's Quieting Syrup"). Opium drops, often mixed with wine in a form known as laudanum, were also well known as a convenient means of committing suicide if taken in a sufficient dose. John Murray Forbes, for one, nearly died as an infant when his mother gave him laudanum to combat seasickness.[56]

What was comparatively rare in the West, however, and never

caught on socially in the way that it did in China, was the recreational use of opium as a source of pleasure. England's most prominent opium addict of the 1820s and 1830s was a journalist named Thomas De Quincey, a self-described intellectual who had begun using the drug around 1804 and was swept into what he described as an "abyss of divine enjoyment" from which he barely managed to escape.[57] In 1821 he documented the horrors of his long addiction in a manuscript titled *Confessions of an English Opium-Eater*, which Charles Lamb helped him publish in four installments in the *London Magazine*.[58] In 1822, the magazine pieces were printed as a stand-alone book that would gain wide popularity and run through several editions. "I have struggled against this fascinating enthralment with a religious zeal," De Quincey wrote in the preface, "and have . . . untwisted, almost to its final links, the accursed chain which fettered me."[59]

Though the opium De Quincey used came from Turkey (as did all of that sold in England), it was China—and the "Orient" writ large—that figured most vividly in his terrifying visions. "I ran into pagodas," he wrote, "and was fixed, for centuries, at the summit, or in secret rooms; I was the idol; I was the priest; I was worshipped; I was sacrificed." China, to him, was the origin of an Oriental nightmare into which opium had dragged him, one of the sources for the hallucinations that haunted him after taking the drug. "I escaped sometimes," he wrote, "and found myself in Chinese houses, with cane tables, &c. All the feet of the tables, sofas, &c. soon became instinct with life: the abominable head of the crocodile, and his leering eyes, looked out at me, multiplied into a thousand repetitions."[60]

De Quincey's imagined China was a world of addiction, horror, and inescapable dreams, and he all but blamed the country itself for his drug-induced torments. If he should ever be forced to leave England and go live "among Chinese manners and modes of life and scenery," he wrote in one especially harsh passage, he would go insane.[61] From the deep associations De Quincey drew between his dream visions and the exotic otherworld of China, a reader would be hard-pressed to realize that the rising flow of opium at the time was not coming *out* of China, but going *into* it, and that the drug was being carried there for the most part by British hands.

There were less public addicts in England's literary world as well, including Samuel Taylor Coleridge, the mutual friend of Charles Lamb and Thomas Manning. Coleridge became friends with De Quincey in 1807 after he had already begun experimenting with opium himself. Coleridge's drug-induced hallucinations provided the visions behind some of his most enduring work—which, like De Quincey's own narcotic dreams, were sometimes set in an imaginary China. "Kubla Khan," one of the most haunting poems in the English language, was, as Coleridge scribbled at the end of one manuscript, "composed in a sort of Reverie brought on by two grains of Opium."[62] It begins with an invocation of the Mongol founder of China's Yuan dynasty, the predecessor to the Ming:

> In Xanadu did Kubla Khan
> A stately pleasure-dome decree:
> Where Alph, the sacred river ran
> Through caverns measureless to man
> Down to a sunless sea.

And it builds by the end into a mounting, hypnotic terror:

> I would build that dome in air,
> That sunny dome! those caves of ice!
> And all who heard should see them there,
> And all should cry, Beware! Beware!
> His flashing eyes, his floating hair!
> Weave a circle round him thrice,
> And close your eyes with holy dread
> For he on honey-dew hath fed,
> And drunk the milk of Paradise.

One of the first people to hear "Kubla Khan" was Charles Lamb, to whom Coleridge recited it in 1816 before it was published. The poem was a "vision," wrote Lamb to William Wordsworth afterward, "which said vision he repeats so enchantingly that it irradiates and brings heaven and elysian bowers into my parlour while he sings or says it."[63] The romance of his drug-induced dreams, however, led into a prolonged struggle against addiction that would torment the poet for the rest of his life and leave him at times unable to take part in public life or even leave his bed. Unlike De Quincey's very public addiction, Coleridge's struggle was a private one—at least until his death in 1834, when De Quincey (whose own career was faltering by then) wrote a long piece on his friend titled "Coleridge and Opium-Eating" in which he exposed the famous poet's crippling dependence for all the English-speaking world to read.[64]

Nevertheless, such powerful and widely read depictions of opium's power to consume a man and ruin his life did not impinge in any direct way on the brute fact of the foreign traffic at Canton, by which certain countrymen of the horrified readers of De Quincey's accounts—respectable ones, no less—were by the early 1830s pouring that very same drug into China in amounts totaling more than two and a half million pounds by weight each year. But that was happening far away, halfway around the world. And when those who sold it came back home, they did not speak of it.

———

As for the Canton foreign community of the time, what few voices of misgiving about opium can be found there came mainly from the small group who alone professed to care about the Chinese people themselves: namely, the Christian missionaries. But as the Protestants who came to China followed in the path of Robert Morrison, and as Morrison held such an important position working for the East India Company—the very body that orchestrated the opium trade from behind the scenes—the question of their own complicity was especially acute. In 1823, a young English missionary new to China wrote to Morrison that he considered the opium trade to be inconsistent with the morals of the Gospel. He said that he could not in good faith accept support from the merchants in Canton as Morrison had always done. "A Chinese author," the young missionary wrote, "says, that the truly 'virtuous man is one who sacrifices all earthly considerations to the maintenance of heavenly principles'; and shall I be less virtuous than a pagan? God forbid! Could I hold out the bread of life to the Chinese in one hand, and opium in the other? Could I bestow, with any propriety, in the service of religion, that money which accrued from the demoralization and consequent misery of a large portion of my fellow-creatures?"[65]

Unable to stomach the same compromises Morrison had made in order to stay in Canton, that young missionary wound up leaving China altogether, devoting himself instead to fighting what he saw as Britain's other great moral crime of the age: West Indian slavery. Those two terrible trades, he told Morrison—opium and slavery—had in common that no matter how abhorrent they were in the eyes of God, even the most respectable of Britain's trading houses did not hesitate to engage in them. There is no record of Morrison's response to his young friend. Beyond the occasional remark disparaging the Chinese for using too much of the drug, he found little to say on the matter of opium.

It wasn't just Morrison. Broadly speaking, the foreign community at Canton and Macao simply did not like to talk about opium in anything other than financial terms. Those who did question the morality of selling it generally weren't the ones who received profits from the trade, and they feared repercussions from those who did. An American working for Russell & Co., whose outspokenness had gotten him fired as editor of Matheson's *Canton Register* after just six issues, declared the amount of opium consumed in China in 1830 to be "startling." Fully convinced of the drug's addictive properties, he wrote that "those who habitually smoke opium, are in the intervals between the excitement of one dose and the period of its renewal, the most miserable and nerveless creatures, the artificial tone of their spirits being only purchased by their devotion to this destructive habit."[66] When a newly arrived missionary from Massachusetts named Elijah Bridgman sent home the first installment of his journal from Canton that same year, he added a warning in case his overseers should publish it. "Perhaps the paragraph on the *Opium Trade* had better be omitted," he told them, "for here it is a most delicate subject to touch upon—but it is *death* to China."[67]

———

Amid the thundering rise of opium into the 1830s, it is easy to lose track of the fact that there were still other viable models of foreign commerce at Canton that did not involve the smuggling of illegal drugs. John Murray Forbes, for one, had nothing directly to do with opium—not for any moral reason but simply because it was not part of his duties in Canton, where he helped with the legitimate side of Russell & Co.'s business and left the opium to his brother Robert at Lintin. John's lack of direct involvement with opium proved to be a great boon for his career, however, for although at seventeen he was too young to start out as anything more than a clerk at Russell & Co., his limited responsibilities for the firm left him free to accept other engagements in Canton—in particular, a part-time position as English-language secretary for one of the Hong merchants, a man by the name of Wu Bingjian who was known to the foreigners as Houqua.

Forbes got his introduction to Houqua from a cousin named John Perkins Cushing, twenty-six years older than he, who had been raised by their mutual uncle Perkins and had preceded John's older brothers in China. When Cushing first handed over the reins of the family business to Thomas Forbes in 1828, he told him that "Houqua as a man of business I consider the first in the Country." In a long memo advising Thomas on how to navigate the business community of Canton, Cushing repeated several times that Houqua was the only man one could work with on a basis of complete trust—and not just among the Chinese merchants, either. "With other foreigners in this place," he also wrote, "I should not be desirous of having any concerns in business."[68] Cushing had intended to retire for good in 1828, but after Thomas Forbes's death in 1829 he had rushed back to Canton to oversee the transition of Perkins & Co. to new management. He overlapped with John Murray Forbes for about a month, and in that time he introduced his young cousin and Houqua to each other, passing on their families' years of accumulated trust.

In a commerce driven by personal relationships, there was no individual in the Canton trade more influential than Houqua. He was in his mid-sixties at the time John met him, wizened and frail-looking beyond his years, with a long neck, drooping eyes, and pointed goatee. He struck John as an intellectual man, temperate and sedate. John's brother Robert described him as "a man of remarkable ability [who] in any community would have been a leader." Houqua handled all of

Houqua

the business of the East India Company factory in Canton, along with other foreign traders he chose to work with, and—notably—he was not only adamant about keeping his hands clean of the opium trade, but he also demanded the same of his foreign partners. (Later in his life, Robert Bennet Forbes would recall Houqua teasing him that among the three Forbes brothers, there was "only one bad man"— meaning Robert himself, for his work with opium at Lintin.)[69]

Representing as he did the best of the proper, legal trade at Canton, Houqua was revered by the foreign community for his honesty and business acumen. Teas marked with his imprimatur were considered the best that could be had in the world, and, uniquely among his countrymen, he became a household name in England and America. The name of Houqua, as a writer from a later generation put it, was "a symbol of the integrity of the Chinese . . . a mark of genuineness and excellence that few traders could do without."[70] Due entirely to Houqua's personal reputation, he reflected, "the honesty of the Chinese has become proverbial."

Houqua also happened to be likely the richest man in the world. The Americans in Canton reckoned his net worth to be $26 million in the early 1830s—a figure that, for comparison, far outstripped the fortune of John Jacob Astor, the wealthiest American of the time.[71] Houqua lived on an island across from the city proper, in a sprawling complex of buildings and gardens housing his own family and the families of his sons. As luxurious as his home was, however, his place of business in the factory compound was noted for being the opposite: severe, spartan, unadorned.[72]

It was in that spare office that John Murray Forbes went to work for Houqua as his secretary, supplementing his long hours of clerical work for Russell & Co. by helping the Hong merchant keep up with his English-language correspondence. Though Houqua was fluent in the Pidgin English of the port, with which he could easily communicate with any of the foreign traders in person, he needed a native interpreter to deal with the formal, written side of his commerce. Not that he cared much for contracts per se—one of his American trading partners insisted that after many years of dealing with the Chinese merchant, the only thing resembling a written contract he could find was a single small slip of paper with the words "forty thousand dollars, Houqua" written on it.[73] But Houqua did keep up a steady correspondence covering details of various transactions for tea and every other kind of commodity other than opium that was to be bought or sold in Canton.

Perhaps it was something about John Murray Forbes's youth, coupled with the inherited affection Houqua carried for his cousin and deceased brother, but John's service to Houqua soon expanded beyond just maintaining the merchant's letter book. Houqua came to trust young Forbes intimately, viewing him almost like a son and believing that Forbes understood his way of thinking better than any other foreigner.[74] Within the year, he was using Forbes as an agent to invest in shipping ventures of his own. In contrast to the largely one-way course of the traditional commerce, where foreign traders came and went in their ships while all transactions for the Chinese merchants took place on the ground in Canton, Houqua sent his own cargoes abroad for sale under his own terms, reaching beyond the confines of China and the Canton system. By the time John Murray Forbes turned eighteen, Houqua had him chartering multiple ships loaded with Houqua's own cargoes of tea, which sailed from Canton under papers that made them appear to be owned and controlled by Forbes alone. Houqua gave him a generous 10 percent commission, and by his own estimate John Murray Forbes soon had more than

John Murray Forbes, at a somewhat older age

half a million dollars of investment property under sail in his own name, underwritten entirely by Houqua.[75]

It was a swift path to growing up. "John is well and his character has become much matured by his intercourse with men," wrote his brother Robert to their uncle about a year after his arrival; "he's a general favourite and I trust will bye and bye make up to us in some manner for the miserable loss we have sustained."[76] Always John would live in the shadow of his dead brother Thomas, and always there would be the imperative to support their family. But he embraced the role. "I soon found myself playing a man's part," he later wrote with pride. He was starting to look the part as well: though a very small person who weighed little more than a hundred pounds, he was already going bald—which, he thought, made him look older than his actual age and gave him an additional measure of authority.[77]

In retrospect, one of the most remarkable things about the partnership between the old Hong merchant Houqua and the young American John Murray Forbes was how much it represented the great potential of the Canton era, and yet also showed by contrast what would be lost in the broader interactions between China and the Western nations of the time. The relationship between Houqua and Forbes was one of trust, affection, and respect. It worked to the advantage of both. It was personal, and it would be enduring. It did not involve any kind of conflicting systems of behavior or belief—commercial capitalism was for them a common language, one that, on the larger scale, Britain, America, and China spoke on a national level at the best times of their interactions. The foreign commerce at Canton—the legal side of it, at least—was necessary, it was profitable to many, and it connected countries and empires together in a way that gave advantage to all participants. In an era of Chinese-Western relations that would later be depicted almost entirely in terms of arrogance and antagonism, Houqua and Forbes represented something more hopeful at work.

CHAPTER 8

Fire and Smoke

The Jiaqing emperor's second son was still just a prince on October 8, 1813, when the palace was invaded. A slender thirty-one-year-old, Prince Mianning was studying as usual that morning in the palace school at the southeast corner of the Great Interior, the northern district of the Forbidden City in Beijing where the emperor's family lived in their peaceful isolation attended by eunuch servants. It was a deeply contained world. Near the school was a heavy wooden gate that controlled access through the thirty-foot red stone wall to the rest of the Forbidden City. Farther beyond, through another gate in another wall, lay the Imperial City where the Manchus lived, and beyond that, through yet another wall, was the Chinese city. Beyond that, finally, through the massive outer walls of Beijing, was China. The prince had recently returned from Jehol, the imperial summer retreat north of the Great Wall, and his father, the emperor, was expected home the next day.[1]

Outside of the Forbidden City's eastern gate with its broad steps and sloping yellow tile roof was a bustling street of tea and wine shops that catered to secretaries from nearby government bureaus and officials waiting for an audience. On this morning outside the eastern gate the shops were quieter than usual, given that the emperor was away, but still there were customers sitting around tables enjoying a leisurely morning of conversation. An astute observer might have noticed that some of those customers seemed anxious, a little out of place and unsure of themselves. Even the astute observer, however, would not have been able to see the headbands of white cloth they carried hidden under their clothing, or the knives.

The Manchu amban who had so feared Thomas Manning's arrival in Lhasa had not been the only one to see the great comet in the autumn of 1811 and wonder what it might mean. It had been visible around the world. In Russia, wrote Tolstoy in *War and Peace*, it "portended all kinds of horrors and the end of the world," presaging the bloody invasion of Russia by Napoleon. In the Mississippi Valley, its appearance preceded a series of mammoth earthquakes that devastated Missouri, rattling homes and ringing church bells as far away as Ohio and South Carolina. In Beijing, the imperial Board of Astronomy declared hopefully that the comet was a sign of glory for the dynasty, but not everyone believed that. In particular, the leaders of an offshoot of the White Lotus sect—which, despite the government's exhaustive efforts, had not in fact been fully suppressed—looked up at the sky and saw in that same gleaming comet a sign that the turning of the kalpa was finally at hand. On this early October morning in 1813, following two years of careful preparation after the appearance of that heavenly sign, the new sect's plan was finally ready to be put into action.[2]

Small groups of sect members had been arriving outside the eastern gate of the Forbidden City since midmorning in scattered order, dressed in ordinary clothes, whiling away their time buying breakfast or looking at curiosities in the street. Most had never been in Beijing before and were unfamiliar with its expansive warren of streets, so they relied on guides. One of the guides was a puppeteer who often came into the city for performances and knew his way around. Others, significantly, were eunuch servants from the imperial household, who had come to believe in the same White Lotus teachings as the others and secretly followed their same Master. Coming into the city that morning, the men had tried not to show their fear as they passed through the succession of gates—Chinese city, Manchu city—carrying their weapons under their clothing or hidden under baskets of persimmons and dates. Several lost courage and turned back before they even reached this place.

A little before noon, two eunuchs came out of the gate from the Forbidden City and entered one of the wine shops, where they sat down with one of these groups of men. They talked quietly with them. Then, at noon, they stood up and started walking back toward the open gate. This was the signal. Scattered patrons from the tea and wine shops along the street stood up in groups, pushing back their chairs and setting down their cups, and began following them toward the gate. There were about sixty of them in total. Some pulled out their white cloths and tied them around their heads. Two unfurled a banner reading "Entrusted by Heaven to Prepare the Way." Then they drew their knives and ran for the gate.

The guards spotted them coming, and once it dawned on them what was happening they frantically began wheeling shut the massive wood-and-iron doors of the gate. Some of the rebels heard the grinding sound of the doors and knew they wouldn't make it, so they tore off their white headbands and fled back through the narrow streets of the city, dropping their knives into canals or sewers as they ran. The gate slammed shut, but it wasn't quite in time. Five had made it through with the two eunuchs, and they disappeared, running, into the mazelike red-walled passages of the Forbidden City as the alarm went up that rebels were inside the imperial sanctum.

They made their way north, toward the Great Interior, the soft underbelly of the Forbidden City where the empress and the princes lived. Two guards appeared in their way with clubs. The intruders stabbed them with their knives, leaving them to bleed on the ground as they rushed onward. But the alarm was spreading. They were attacked again, and three were taken down; the other two (and the two eunuchs) continued racing northward toward the gate to the Great Interior, whose guards had left it unwatched at the noon hour, but once they got through it they were finally caught. One of the traitor eunuchs slipped away and disappeared, while the other turned on his charges and made a show of helping to capture them. Prince Mianning saw the scuffling, and took a cousin to go check on the empress in her quarters to make sure she was all right.

There was another group, however, that was mounting a mirror-image attack from the western gate, and it found better luck. On that side, the rebels rushed the gate against no opposition, shutting it behind them to keep soldiers from entering; about seventy of them made it through into the Forbidden City. Like the first group, they charged north toward the Great Interior, threading their way through the passages, attacking guards and palace staff who challenged them, picking up more eunuchs along the way who were part of their plot— which was, boldly enough, to take control of the Forbidden City and then, when the emperor arrived back from Jehol the next day, to murder him and his family.

The group coming from the west made it as far as the last gate standing between them and the inner quarters, but it had taken them too long. The gate was shut, the guards on full alert, and the invasion turned into a bloodbath as the rebels, cornered, turned and fought against guards who now rushed in from several quarters. They scattered and ran, looking for places to hide. A couple of them managed to scale the smooth wall, taking to the sloping yellow-tiled rooftops of the interior, traversing their way to the north in their hunt for the members of the imperial family.

Prince Mianning was still on his way to check on the empress when he heard the new commotion at the western gate. He saw a man up on a rooftop, a white cloth tied around his head. There were eunuchs running around below, but their only weapons were clubs. There were strict regulations against using firearms inside the Forbidden City, and the eunuchs couldn't get up the wall to catch him. The prince, however, took matters into his own hands. He sent a servant running to fetch his hunting musket and powder, regulations be damned. The rebel was still up on the roof when the servant got back. Loading and taking careful aim from where he stood, the prince shot the rebel and watched him fall from the wall. Then he ran into the neighboring courtyard where another rebel was up on a roof waving a white banner and shouting out to the others to climb the wall and follow him. Mianning reloaded, took aim again, and shot him dead.

The Jiaqing emperor arrived safely at the Forbidden City the following day, powerfully shaken by what had taken place. He issued a public edict to condemn the invasion. The tone was uncertain and penitent; Jiaqing blamed himself, as a good emperor would do, but said that he did not know what he had done to invite this attack on his family. "Our great Qing dynasty has ruled the empire for one hundred and seventy years," he wrote. "My ancestors, with their profound benevolence and favor, loved the people like their own children. . . . I have done nothing to harm or oppress the people. I do not understand what has changed." The fault must lie in himself, he went on, for somehow lacking in virtue, for somehow setting a poor example for those below him. "My ministers . . . have been lazy in their government, to the point of causing something like this to happen," he wrote, acknowledging the corruption of the time. Jiaqing pledged to correct himself in order to "relieve the anger of the people." The tone throughout was bleak. "My brush," he concluded, "traces the path shed by my falling tears."[3]

It took two days for the palace gendarmes to hunt down the rest of the invaders, who were cowering in their scattered hiding places. Those who hadn't already committed suicide were executed, as were the eunuchs who had plotted with them. Security was restored. But the fact remained: in spite of decades of government suppression, and despite the dynasty's ostensible victory in 1805 in its all-out war against the White Lotus rebels, the sect had not been eradicated. And while the rebellions of Qianlong's time had taken place hundreds of miles from the capital, now the rebels had penetrated all the way into the innermost recesses of the imperial city itself. Somehow they had recruited the emperor's own palace servants into their ranks. It was a fearful time to be ruler.

There was, at least, one thing in which Jiaqing could take solace on that day in 1813: the bravery of his son. Prince Mianning did not know it, but Jiaqing had already chosen him to be the sixth emperor of the Qing dynasty.

———

The invasion of the palace only worsened the image of the Qing as a dynasty in decline. Rumors spread in China that the rebels had been aided by members of the imperial family—that Jiaqing's own relatives had plotted to assassinate him—and even if the rumors were not true they still diminished Jiaqing's prestige and encouraged the perception of an aging emperor watching helplessly as his kingdom slipped further into corruption, plotting, and sedition. The rumors reached Canton easily, from where they traveled out into the English-speaking world. A British Indian newspaper in 1814 published a letter from a correspondent who reported confidently that three cousins of the emperor had taken part in the attempt to kill him along with the eunuchs and the rebels. From what that writer had heard, the emperor and his own corrupt family were at least partly to blame for inviting rebellion in the first place. "Whilst the Emperor was away from Beijing," he wrote, "he left his nine sons in charge. They are hedonists and opium smokers and only one or two show much promise as administrators of a great Empire."[4]

Rumors were rumors, though, and a British writer in Canton had no avenue to gain accurate knowledge of events inside the Forbidden City. From the writings Prince Mianning left for posterity, however, it appears that the stories were at least partly correct: Jiaqing's heir apparent was indeed an opium smoker. "Bored and tired," Mianning wrote on one occasion, "I ask the servant to prepare smoke and a pipe to inhale. Each time, my mind suddenly becomes clear, my eyes and ears refreshed. People in the past said that wine is endowed with all the virtues, but today I call smoke the satisfier. When you desire happiness, it gives you happiness."[5] He went on to write a poetic ode to the drug, which read in part:

> Inhale and exhale, fragrance rises,
> Ambience deepens and thickens.
> When it's stagnant, it is really as if
> Mountains and clouds are emerging from a distant sea.[6]

In 1820, as the opium trade from British India was about to begin its inexorable rise, the Jiaqing emperor died and that same young connoisseur—now to be known as the Daoguang emperor—took the throne. His personal experience of the pleasures of opium did not, however, make him any more indulgent toward the drug's use and sale. Rather the opposite—as if in knowing it so well, he feared its powers of seduction more than any of his ancestors had done.

———

The British had not introduced opium to China. Although it is unclear exactly when the drug first arrived, poppies were already being cultivated in China during the Tang dynasty in the eighth century.[7] The flowers had many uses—they were beautiful in their own right, and their shoots and seeds could be eaten as a delicacy (the latter being called "imperial rice"). By the twelfth century, Chinese medical texts listed a range of known uses for the plant, in suppressing coughs, curing intestinal ailments, and the like. They also noted that it was poisonous. Poppy cultivation continued to spread in China

The opium poppy

over the centuries that followed, and the variety of its medicinal uses expanded. By the fifteenth century, the Chinese term for the drug opium (*yapian*) first appeared, and both the Ming and early Qing dynasties taxed it as a legitimate medicinal product.[8]

The fateful change in China's relationship with opium came with the discovery that it could be mixed with tobacco and smoked— a means of ingestion that produced more euphoric effects than simply eating it. The practice of opium smoking first originated on the island of Java in the seventeenth century, from where the Dutch transmitted it to their (then) colony on Taiwan off the eastern coast of China. From Taiwan it spread via commercial traders to China's coastal provinces. By 1729, the smoking of the drug was prevalent enough in China that the Qianlong emperor's father, the Yongzheng emperor, issued an edict prohibiting it. He called for a ban on the use, sale, or transport of opium—though the harshest punishment (strangulation) was reserved not for the smugglers or smokers but only for the proprietors of opium dens. That was fitting, because Yongzheng's opium ban was just one of a series of edicts in which he condemned those who harmed public morality by seducing or confusing others— a series that also included bans on prostitution and the teaching of martial arts, as well as mandating the confinement of the insane. In any case, Yongzheng's opium ban was largely symbolic; there would be no more edicts against the drug for the rest of his reign, nor for the entire sixty-three-year reign of Qianlong. From the 1730s all the way up into the first decade of the nineteenth century, there is not a single known case of a clear-cut prosecution for opium offenses within the Qing Empire.[9]

It wasn't until the 1810s that Jiaqing would revive his grandfather Yongzheng's opposition to the drug. Prior to the Patna-Malwa competition that would so greatly increase its supply in the 1820s, opium was still an expensive and relatively rare commodity, a luxury for only the wealthiest to enjoy. After taking root in Canton and in prosperous cities in the east, Indian opium had migrated north (contained, some said, in the annual gifts sent to the capital from Canton), where it found a home among the abundant eunuch servants in Jiaqing's court. From the servants, who outnumbered the royal family they served by roughly forty to one, opium smoking spread easily enough to the imperial household members—like Prince Mianning—whom they tended.[10]

Jiaqing first expressed his concern about opium in 1810 when a smuggler was caught attempting to carry six containers of it into the capital. The emperor's primary concern, like that of his grandfather, was the demoralizing effect of the drug. "Opium has a most intense effect," he wrote at the time. "Those who smoke it can suddenly become excited and capable of doing whatever they want without restraint. Before long, it will steal their life and kill them."[11] By 1813 he noted with dismay that it was spreading further among the elite than he had previously known. Even imperial guards and government officials were using it. It was becoming socially respectable.[12]

After Jiaqing's death in 1820, Daoguang carried forward his father's opposition to the drug. Early in his reign, he called opium "a great harm to the customs and morals of the people" and demanded an end to coastal drug smuggling, targeting especially the corrupt officials who collected "taxes" (that is, bribes) to allow opium shipments through. "If there are traitors who try to collect taxes [on opium] to enrich themselves," Daoguang wrote, "or who personally smuggle it into the country, punish them immediately and severely in order to expunge this massing of insects."[13] But disturbing reports of the consequences of opium use continued to arrive. That same year, the head of the civil service examination in Beijing reported that there were opium-addicted scholars from the coastal provinces who had come north to take the exam, and who went through such convulsive withdrawals during the course of the three-day test that some of them died in the examination hall.[14]

It is unclear how many Chinese smokers of opium in the early nineteenth century were what we might call addicts. Some certainly were, but given how much was being imported they could not have been many relative to the size of the empire. By the start of Daoguang's reign in 1820, the nearly five thousand chests being imported from India each year were enough to support about forty thousand average habitual users empire-wide, or as many as one hundred thousand of the lightest daily smokers, so at most a few hundredths of a percent of the population.[15] Furthermore, most users at this time seem not to have been terribly debilitated by opium—they led productive lives and were not outcasts from their families or professions. Indeed, opium smoking was a generally open, public act and there were many socially encouraged reasons to take part in it. Medicinal reasons aside—and there were dozens of those—businessmen smoked opium to focus their minds and help them make smarter deals (at least they imagined that was the effect). Students smoked it for the clarity it brought, thinking it would help them succeed on the civil service examinations. For the stylish it was a relaxant to be offered to guests after dinner. For the privileged with little to do, like the eunuchs of the Forbidden City or Manchu courtiers with few responsibilities, it was an escape from boredom.[16]

Opium was, in other words, perfectly acceptable in respected circles. An aesthetic culture of gorgeously wrought pipes and other accessories grew up around its use by the wealthy, the very expense and extravagance of those tools elevating the act of smoking itself. The Chinese fashion for smoking, moreover, was quite profligate in comparison to the eating of the drug that went on in Britain; much was wasted in the process, and a smoker could easily go through an amount of opium in one day that would kill someone who ingested it directly.[17] For those in more humble situations who couldn't afford to smoke it themselves, employment in the opium trade still provided a chance for income as couriers and petty dealers.

From a purely economic standpoint opium had its advantages. Valuable and easy to carry (it was worth more than three hundred times its weight in rice), foreign opium was a very good business proposition for Chinese merchants in Canton.[18] Being illegal, it could be turned around quickly for a profit in silver—within a few days in most cases, as compared to tea, which involved large cultivation and transportation networks, and generally took half a year or more to produce a return on each year's investment. Since the Canton traders made more back from their customers inside China than they paid to the foreign suppliers, trading in opium also served as a convenient way for them to increase their own silver stocks, which they could then use to procure tea for sale to the foreigners. And though they had to pay bribes to officials, the illegal trade was otherwise, de facto, free from taxes.[19]

There is no evidence that the moral exhortations of the Daoguang emperor caught on with the general public in any meaningful way.[20] The widespread public opposition to opium on moral and public health grounds for which China would be known in the twentieth century was at this time entirely absent. Though perhaps the public's resistance to imperial moralizing was only to be expected; in the early seventeenth century, the Ming dynasty had tried to suppress tobacco for reasons very similar to the Qing dynasty's ban on opium—even to the point of ordering execution for anyone who cultivated or sold it—but they did not succeed.[21] By the time of the Qing dynasty, those prohibitions were long forgotten and tobacco was an accepted staple of daily life in China. There was no reason the Jiaqing or Daoguang emperors' edicts against opium should have been more likely to find success.

———

The Chinese of the early nineteenth century are often described as being uniformly insular and scornful of anything foreign, thanks mainly to an overly literal reading of the boilerplate language in Qianlong's edict to George III where he claimed that he did not value foreign things. But this was not really the case. For wealthy urbanites in China, Western goods were all the rage by the 1820s—furs, glass, intricate clocks, cotton textiles, and other products of the Canton import trade, which were highly sought after by those with sufficient money to buy them. Far from encountering any kind of disdain for foreign objects, Chinese retailers in the early nineteenth century found that attaching the adjective "Western" to their merchandise was in fact the key to a higher selling price.[22]

This consumer fashion for foreign products helps explain why the opium from British India became so popular in China. Against latter-day nationalist claims that the British came and forced opium down the throats of helpless Chinese consumers, there was in fact an existing system of domestic opium production in China already in place to compete with the import market at Canton (especially in the empire's western and southwestern provinces). There were also separate avenues for importing the drug overland from Central Asia—and opium from all of those sources was much cheaper than the Indian opium the British brought to Canton.[23] But opium was a luxury good, and its wealthy consumers weren't looking for a bargain; they were looking for status. Fashionable users of the drug in urban China preferred the opium from British India (the Patna, with its East India Company seal of quality) largely *because* it was "Western" and therefore seen as far more sophisticated to buy and smoke.[24]

By the late eighteenth century, when British traders began carrying Indian opium in meaningful quantities to Canton, they did so because they knew a market was already waiting for them there. They could not force the drug down anyone's throat—indeed, they couldn't even get themselves into the country; all they could do was to carry their opium to China's southern coast and sell it to Chinese agents. Everything from there on into the Qing Empire was entirely in Chinese hands. Moving forward into the nineteenth century, the extensive smoking of opium emerged as an almost uniquely Chinese social custom, the Canton market for the drug growing to become,

Opium smokers

primarily for domestic reasons, the most demanding in the world. If opium was illegal in name, it was almost never so in practice, a fact as apparent to outsiders calling at Canton as to insiders within the Qing Empire. As one British dealer testified to a government committee in 1830, "Every now and then there is a very strong edict issued against the trade; but, like other Chinese edicts, it is nearly powerless. It imposes a little difficulty perhaps for the moment, and enables the Mandarins to extort from the dealers."[25]

And so it was that the Western merchants who carried opium to Canton would insist to their dying days that they were merely filling a need they themselves had not created. Any moral questions concerning the opium trade, they maintained, were Chinese questions—for the Chinese themselves to ask and to answer. It was a self-serving view, but it contained at least a grain of truth. Given the utter powerlessness of foreign traders at Canton over the long term, especially since the days of James Flint, it was easy for them to make the case that they had no influence at all on the country or its laws or customs, and therefore they could not possibly be held responsible for the dark side of China's foreign trade.

By 1830, following a decade of rising imports and spreading usage, the Daoguang emperor's concern was giving way to alarm. "Opium is flooding into the interior," he wrote in an edict that January. "The multitude of users expands day by day, and there are more and more people who sell it; they are like fire and smoke, destroying our resources and harming our people. Each day is worse than the last."[26] He asked for reports from senior provincial officials on the state of the opium trade in their regions, and the accounts they sent back over the following year revealed a shocking level of drug use by government bureaucrats and their legions of assistants. One report said that in Zhili province in the north, "there are opium smokers everywhere, especially in the government offices. From the governor-general all the way down through the ranks of officials and their subordinates, the ones who do *not* smoke opium are very few indeed."[27] Other reports from across the empire—not just the coast, where the foreign traffic was centered—described networks of bribery, large numbers of users and petty dealers, smuggling vessels that could sail almost anywhere they wished, soldiers who were too addled by opium to fight.[28]

Opium smuggling in China was by this time an efficient and tightly choreographed enterprise. As soon as a deal was struck between a foreign importer and an agent in Canton, Chinese smuggling boats would be dispatched for Lintin Island. Known as "fast crabs" for their crowding of fifty to sixty oars, and locally called "glued-on wings" for their speed, these long and narrow boats were easily swift enough to leave any government pursuers behind.[29] A clerk from the Chinese agent's office would ride on board to supervise the unloading of the cargo from the foreign receiving ship, separating the contents of the chests into small matted parcels for ease of transport and weighing each ball to ensure proper quantity before bringing the shipment back to a depot.[30] The opium was then divided up to travel inland: on secondary waterways, along backwoods land routes and over mountains, on narrow paths through areas with scant official presence. A courier on foot could carry the drug easily under his clothes, or in larger amounts inside sacks of other commodities like grain or salt. Points of inspection were the most troublesome—getting past the gates of walled cities, crossing major bridges—but if a courier was familiar to the men who worked as inspectors and paid them bribes, he could pass unmolested. Opium was available everywhere; travelers could purchase small amounts of it easily at inns, even at some Buddhist temples. Shopkeepers in the towns and cities sold it under the table to improve business.[31]

The violence that was so conspicuously absent from the "gentlemanlike" world of the opium wholesale trade near Canton was by contrast very much present along the routes of transit into the country itself. The "fast crabs" were heavily armed to ward off government vessels along the riverways, and did not hesitate to fire their guns when approached. In coastal Fujian province, rival clans fought viciously for control over local opium markets, hiring mercenaries to protect their interests by force.[32] Throughout the empire, travelers carrying opium made a perfect target for robbers since the drug was at once expensive, easily carried, and simple to resell. Also, since it was illegal in the first place, imperial security forces were of no help to the victims in getting it back.

In response to the dramatic reports that reached him in 1831, Daoguang demanded greater efforts to suppress opium smuggling. But the government still proved incapable of getting at the larger forces behind the traffic: the clan- and regional-based syndicates that did the bulk of the wholesale buying, transportation, and resale of the drug. Beijing was unable to control them because—as in many similar cases worldwide—the drug kingpins showed themselves to be better providers for the locals in their areas of operation than the distant central government was. They gave rural people employment, income, and security, and by consequence the opium syndicates were both more respected and more feared locally than the remote powers of the state.

During the government's inland crackdowns, locals would close ranks to protect their own. In some cases village mobs attacked government enforcers who had been sent in to arrest opium dealers, driving them away. Prosecutions across the board were remarkably few, and prosecutions of the elite—scholars, wealthy merchants, syndicate members, corrupted officials—were all but nonexistent. The people who *were* arrested and tried on opium charges during Daoguang's reign tended to be marginal figures unprotected by local patronage: migrants living outside of their home region, poor shopkeepers and itinerant peddlers, ethnic minorities, people without influence or strong connections.[33]

Daoguang had been warned that this might be the case. Since official corruption was such an unavoidable fact in the empire, some of his advisers cautioned that any general campaign to stamp out opium smoking would be unlikely to change the actions of the people who were actually behind the trade, but it could easily prove harmful to the ordinary people who used the drug. One top provincial official warned in 1831 that stronger laws against smoking opium would do nothing but give underlings in the district government offices a new means of harassing commoners and extorting money from them under threat of enforcing those laws (a process similar to what unfolded during the late Qianlong era, when gangs of thugs went from house to house demanding bribes under the guise of hunting down White Lotus followers). Petty opium smokers were already suffering financial hardships, he warned, and punishing them would just make things worse—they would go bankrupt even sooner and their families would be broken up. He reminded the emperor that the whole point of having prohibition laws in the first place was to protect the people from harm, but if the laws became too harsh then the addicts would have no hope at all; their lives might as well already be over.[34] By that line of reasoning—which Daoguang, to judge by his actions, found appealing—leniency toward the common users of opium was the most benevolent approach, the sign of a ruler who truly cared about his people and wished to relieve their problems rather than compound them. It also, however, allowed usage to continue spreading unchecked through the general population.

——————

One man who grew up in this deteriorating world and wanted to do something to make it better was a scholar named Bao Shichen. Bao, who possessed deep-set eyes and a drooping mustache, was a self-made man. He was born in 1775 in a rural part of Anhui province in central China where his father had been a village schoolteacher, and though his father kept the family out of poverty, he did not provide much more than that. For several of his younger years, Bao Shichen supported his family by farming a rented plot of land and selling vegetables at a nearby market. But he also learned to read and write, and immersed himself in the Confucian classics that were the basis of the civil service examinations. In 1808, when he was in his early thirties, he passed the provincial examination in Anhui's capital. It was a great accomplishment, but that was as far as he could go. To qualify for a meaningful official position you had to pass the national examination in Beijing, which was only offered every three years. Though Bao would travel to the capital thirteen times over the course of his life to take that exam, he would fail it every time.[35]

Then again, Bao Shichen also did not have the strict focus on the traditional classics that might have gotten him further on the examinations. From an early age he had become distracted by the problems of his time. "I was born in the Qianlong reign," he once wrote to a friend, "and by the time I was a young student, everything was falling apart. Bribery was pervasive and open, the administration was contaminated and vile, and the people's energy was taut like a spring, as if there might be a rebellion."[36] Concerned by the economic problems and rising tensions of the society around him, Bao found himself drawn toward more practical kinds of scholarship that were not tested on the civil service exams—agriculture, law, the arts of war. While the exams privileged poetic skill and the writing of intricately constructed essays, Bao would in time become one of the leading figures in a field known broadly as "statecraft" scholarship, an informal movement of Confucians who were deeply concerned with real-world issues of administration and policy.[37]

Even though Bao Shichen could not become an official himself and would never have the ear of the emperor, he began writing policy essays that gained wide circulation among officials and other scholars who were also concerned about the apparent decline of the empire. Through those writings he would emerge as one of the most influential members of a new generation of well-connected Han Chinese scholars, many of whom were not directly affiliated with government. Like Bao, most of these scholars were graduates of the provincial-level exams but had not succeeded at the national level. Nevertheless, through their own social networks in academies and poetry societies, and by gaining employment as assistants and secretaries to high-level provincial officials, they began to exercise a greater collective influence from behind the scenes during the Jiaqing and Daoguang reigns than others of their kind had done since the beginning of the dynasty.

Bao Shichen and his fellow reform-minded Confucians were the intellectual descendants of Hong Liangji, the scholar Jiaqing had first sentenced to death and then pardoned after he wrote the emperor a long letter in 1799 calling for reform and the punishment of Heshen. Bao was nearly thirty years younger than Hong, but they were connected by a shared patron, and Bao agreed with the elder figure that Jiaqing should have undertaken a much larger overhaul of the civil service after Heshen's trial in order to root out corruption. Following in Hong Liangji's footsteps, Bao and the others in his generation were heirs to an age-old tradition of Confucian remonstrance against the errors of China's government, one in which the role of the scholar was not to follow the emperor blindly but to advise and guide him—and, when necessary, to correct him. Although Han Chinese scholars like themselves had been silenced under the Manchus since the days of the Yongzheng emperor, forbidden for generations from forming associations and meeting in groups, when Jiaqing pardoned Hong Liangji he had given them an opening to resume their roles from the past.

By the time Daoguang sat on the throne in the 1820s, this new generation of Chinese scholars was actively engaging in debates on a wide range of policy issues—food supply, grain transport, the management of water-control systems, monetary reform, and other matters of national interest that they believed the government was failing to manage properly. After the better part of a century of suppression they were cautious about being too outspoken—they shied away from direct criticism of the emperor, and were careful to avoid appearing to have too much influence—but in their academies and literary societies, and through writings that they circulated informally, they began to advocate various proposals for reform that they ultimately hoped the government would adopt and make into policy.[38] Among them, it was Bao Shichen who first began to sound warnings about the effect of the opium trade on China's economy.

Bao was, as many who admired him would be, intensely nativist and conservative. Like those in Britain who condemned tea for squandering the meager resources of England's poorer classes, he couched his initial concerns about opium in a wider critique of the economic costs of everyday luxuries in China. He believed there should be strict sumptuary laws to prevent people from wasting their money on unnecessary goods—for example, that citizens should only be allowed to wear simple clothing, and only in particular colors depending on their occupations.[39] Living at a time when chronic overpopulation made life difficult for the common subjects of the empire, he argued that growing luxury crops like tobacco, or grain for distilling alcohol, was a waste of land, labor, and fertilizer that should have been reserved for the growing of food instead.[40]

From tobacco and alcohol, Bao's attention turned naturally to opium, but he considered it to be a different kind of problem, because unlike tobacco and alcohol, which were fully supplied by domestic production, opium was a product of foreign trade. (He was in fact aware of the domestic production of opium in China, though through a technicality he believed that all Chinese opium was sold via Macao to foreigners for reimport, and thus counted as foreign.)[41] The problem of opium thus involved more than just the wasting of domestic resources, because it also opened an international vulnerability for the empire as a whole.

Bao Shichen had long been hawkish on foreign trade—as early as 1801, when he was still in his twenties, he advocated closing down the entire coastal import-export trade and expelling foreign merchants permanently from Canton. He also recommended at that time that foreign products like British textiles and clocks should all be banned and any Chinese who continued to import them should be beheaded.[42] By his own statistics (which were sketchy and almost absurdly impressionistic), he estimated that in 1820 there were a total of almost three million regular opium users in China, whom he believed collectively spent more than one hundred million taels of silver per year on their habit, a sum greater than the government's entire yearly tax revenue. (For comparison, the crushing cost of suppressing the White Lotus rebellion had been as much as two hundred million taels, spent over nearly a decade.) The financial cost of all that opium smoking was borne by the Chinese users, he argued, and all of the profit—as he saw it—went to British and American merchants. He thus warned that China's wealth was flooding out of the country into the hands of foreigners.[43]

The only way to make certain that China's silver would not leave the country, he argued, was to shut down the foreign import trade altogether. He admitted that by doing so the government would lose out on millions of taels' worth of annual tariff income it would otherwise have taken in through Canton. Nevertheless, he felt that the economic benefits to the people of China as a whole would be limitless. Bao knew that his proposal would be unpopular. "Some might worry that since we've had import markets for so long, if we suddenly close them down there could be trouble," he wrote. The foreign merchants, after all, would not take lightly to losing the source of their wealth. But to his mind (again, as a hard-nosed nativist) that was a baseless concern. "Of all the countries that come here to trade, the British are considered the most powerful," he wrote, "yet their territory and population don't even equal one hundredth of China's." He saw nothing to fear from the British from their tiny, faraway island, and maintained that the only reason any officials on the coast might warn about conflict was because they themselves were getting rich from foreign trade and didn't want it to end. He suggested that such officials were just exaggerating Britain's strength in order to browbeat the central government into leaving their region's commerce alone.[44]

Bao Shichen was only the first of his generation to suggest that foreign trade was causing long-term economic harm to China, and his early views would anchor the hardest line in the debate to follow. Others who came after him repeated the call for China to shut down foreign trade while amplifying Bao's basic points—that the trade at Canton was unnecessary for China, that it threatened to drain the empire of its silver. Another scholar in this vein, a man named Guan Tong who worked as a secretary in the offices of the Anhui provincial governor, targeted especially the fashion for foreign goods that was so prevalent among wealthy urban Chinese. Writing in the later 1820s, he argued that China's economy was threatened not just by opium, but by *everything* fashionable from abroad—woolen fabrics, clocks, glass, and so on. He gave a parable of a prosperous family (representing, of course, China) whose neighbor began to seduce it with exotic but useless objects for sale. The children of the family came to love those objects and in time gave all of their money to the neighbor, leaving the family with nothing. "Today," he wrote, "all of the foreign goods imported to China are what you would call intriguing and useless things. And yet for decades now, everyone has been raving decadently about 'foreign goods.' Even when it makes them poor, they continue to impoverish themselves just to take part in this fashion."[45]

Guan Tong argued that anything that was not traditionally Chinese was by definition unnecessary. When Chinese consumers bought foreign products they gave their wealth to outsiders, and in time they would wind up like the family in the parable. So in his opinion the Daoguang emperor's laws against opium weren't nearly enough—rather, China should ban *all* foreign goods and not just focus exclusively on drugs. Exchanging money for poppies or for foreign luxuries both equally "harm the people and sicken the country," he wrote. "But today, all we do is ban poppies and we do nothing about the rest; we know about the one, but we are ignorant of the other." His conclusion was stark: "Chinese and foreign merchants should have no commerce with each other. Any of their goods that remain in our country should be destroyed and not used. Anyone that goes against this should be treated as a criminal. Do this, and in just a few years China's wealth will be once again abundant."[46]

———

Against such calls for shutting down foreign trade, however, a very different set of opinions began to emerge from Canton itself. Most of the hard-liners had never muddied their hands with foreign affairs, but the scholars who lived and worked for long periods in Canton were more experienced. They understood more clearly the rewards and risks of the maritime trade, to say nothing of the naval strengths of the British—and because they understood those better, they were more cautious in advocating for changes to the system. It was one thing for a nativist from a distant part of China to recommend choking off relations with outsiders. Bao Shichen had never met a foreigner when he first called for the trade to be shut down. He had never seen one of their ships, and his livelihood at the time, as well as those of the people around him, did not depend on foreigners at all (though he would in fact put in a short stint at the hoppo's office in Canton later on, in 1826, after which his views would begin to moderate). The scholars based in Canton, however, knew just how much the region's economy had come to depend on trade with foreigners, and some of them worried about what might happen if it were to end.

One of the strongest responses to the opponents of foreign trade came from a man named Cheng Hanzhang who had served in a series of high offices, including as a provincial governor, and who had spent more than twenty years working in Canton. Although Cheng shared Bao Shichen's concerns about the loss of silver, he insisted nevertheless that foreign trade on the whole must be allowed to continue. While admitting that "of all the products that are made by foreign countries, nothing is a necessity for China," he pointed out that in a

typical year the Western merchants brought to Canton tens of millions of taels' worth of cotton and wool textiles, fragrant woods, metals like copper and tin, medicines, and other products, exchanging
goods for other goods with no need of actual silver to change hands.
"This is something that was never harmful to China in the past," he
observed. The only thing that departed from this pattern was opium,
which he called "a poison that the foreigners do not use themselves
but still sell to China, harming our people, consuming our wealth to
the tune of millions of taels per year, all secretly in exchange for silver
that will leave and never come back."[47]

Thus Cheng Hanzhang saw the same long-term risk of silver loss
to the opium trade that so worried Bao Shichen, but he strongly disputed the notion that the solution lay with shutting down all foreign
commerce. "Some," he wrote (and here he meant those who followed
Bao Shichen), "say that if we clamp down on the ports and major
sea lanes, and order customs to refuse to accept the foreigners' tariff
money, then we can prohibit them from coming." But it was absurd
even to conceive of shutting down foreign trade, he said. China simply
didn't have the military power to enforce such a ban. "Our coastline
is extremely long and there are places everywhere to land," he wrote.
"Even with a hundred thousand soldiers we could not police it."[48]

Nevertheless, the impossibility of closing the coastline was just a
prelude to his main concern, which was how the foreign traders might
react. "These foreigners have been trading with China for hundreds
of years already," he said. "If we were to suddenly cut them off, they
would unite and join their forces together to make trouble for us.
We would be ravaged by constant warfare and it would take decades
to restore peace." So not only was it unrealistic for China to enforce
a ban on foreign trade, but even attempting to do so was likely to
provoke a war—and he was far less sanguine than Bao Shichen about
what the outcome of such a war might be. To avoid a disastrous conflict, Cheng concluded, the foreign trade at Canton should be continued in all traditional commodities. Rather than trying to blame
foreigners for China's opium problem, he said, the Qing government
should redouble its efforts on the domestic front: work harder to
police smuggling, and try to reduce the demand for opium by treat

ing the users themselves, using public education to teach them how
to quit their habits.

———————

This burgeoning private debate about how the Chinese government
should deal with foreigners and the opium problem begs the question of just what the scholars involved actually knew about the other
countries involved. For none of them had been abroad, and while
Europeans had a limited familiarity with China via the writings of
Jesuit missionaries and the experiences of traders who had gone to
Canton, there was no similar movement in the other direction, no
sustained tradition of Chinese travelers to Europe or America who
could enlighten their countrymen back home. Few of the Chinese
scholars who discussed the merits and dangers of international trade
during Daoguang's reign had even been inside the compound where
the foreign merchants lived outside the Canton city walls. And yet
there was more information available to them than one might expect.

In the early 1830s as concerns were rising about foreign trade, at
least one Chinese scholar took it upon himself to make a serious study
of Great Britain as the most powerful of the countries that traded
with China. The scholar in question was a geographer named Xiao
Lingyu, a close friend of Bao Shichen (who wrote him a letter in 1826
predicting that within ten years the opium trade would cause problems on the coast as destructive as the pirate fleets that had plagued
the Ming dynasty).[49] Originally from Jiangsu province in the east,
Xiao worked in the customs bureau in Canton and spent some time
there gathering information about the British and their interactions
with China. He rooted around in local archives, conducted personal
interviews, and read various accounts by other scholars, pulling them
all together in 1832 into a treatise on the British that represented the
best knowledge of the time in China.[50]

Xiao Lingyu's account, titled, plainly enough, "An Account of
England," was remarkable for how much he was able to learn about
the British from Chinese sources—especially considering the common assumption that the Chinese of this time had no inkling what-

soever of British military power. Writing in the early 1830s, Xiao was able to give detailed and specific data on British ships that had been observed near Canton: how many guns they could carry, how many marines could ride on them, the arrangement of their sails, and how impressively they could navigate. He gave measurements for the height of their masts, the depth of their drafts, and the thickness of their wooden hulls. He described how their bottoms were coppered so they would not rot, and listed the variety of weapons they carried (long guns, short guns, repeating guns). In contrast to the matchlocks used in China, which required a burning piece of hemp to ignite the powder, he explained that the British possessed modern "self-firing" guns that used a piece of flint. He was especially awed by the British cannons—which, he explained, were aimed by using telescopes and could reach targets miles away. "They never miss," he wrote.[51]

Xiao Lingyu was also aware that those ships and guns were instrumental to Britain's quest for economic power. In a section on British imperial expansion he explained that India was a British colony, something not commonly understood in China at the time.[52] He explained as well that Britain controlled several islands and strategic ports in Southeast Asia, including most recently Singapore, which it had acquired in 1824. Britain had conquered those colonies with its navy, Xiao wrote, and now it received a regular share of their annual wealth in the form of "tribute and taxes." He thus understood that Britain's imperial expansion was motivated by trade and the search for profit (in contrast to the Qing Empire, whose expansion had been driven primarily by security needs, to pacify threats on its borders). And though Xiao Lingyu noted that the two empires butted heads where Tibet bordered on India, he sensed a more potent contact via Singapore since it was just a few days' sail from Canton—a fact about which Bao Shichen was especially worried, since there were Han Chinese subjects of the British in Singapore whom he feared could be used to infiltrate China in a way white Englishmen could never do.[53]

Given that Xiao Lingyu was using Chinese sources, the most accurate parts of his account related to interactions in Canton and the wider sphere of Chinese maritime trade in Southeast Asia; as he reached farther afield to describe British society itself, his ideas became somewhat more quaint. In England, he explained, women chose their own husbands and controlled household finances. Their husbands were not allowed to have concubines. "From the king on down," he wrote, "there is not a single person who does not value women more than men." He explained that the British had an alphabet rather than written characters (though he believed many of them could speak and write Chinese, a fact that would have pleased George Staunton), and since they "all believe in Catholicism or the Jesus-teachings" they used a Christian dating system. Britain's territory was great, wrote Xiao, but its fields were few. The British farmed with horses, and though they could grow beans and wheat, their national custom was to seek profit overseas (thus their excellence at building ships). Physically, they were tall, with blue-green eyes and red or yellow hair. When two men met, it was customary to remove their hats, and "to show the highest respect, they put their hand to their forehead" (that is, they saluted). In a reminiscence of the tensions over Macartney and Amherst, he explained that the British never knelt under any circumstances—even before their own king, he said, they remained standing.

Xiao Lingyu, significantly, did not consider opium to be a matter of concern for foreign relations. Rather, he saw it as a purely domestic problem and disputed those who tried to blame it on the British. "Some say the English sell opium to corrupt China," he wrote, "but the fashion for opium dates back only to the early 1800s and the English have been industriously making textiles and trading them at Canton for a great many decades now. Their woolen fabrics can be found everywhere; it is not as if they have only sold opium from the start. And if people in China did not smoke opium, then the English would not be able to sell it."[54]

Even as he absolved the British from blame for the opium trade, however, Xiao warned against underestimating their military strength. "Some also say that China would have no difficulty copying the excellence of Britain's ships and cannons," he went on. But he pointed out that during the Ming dynasty the Chinese had imported French cannons for use on the frontier but the officers and soldiers of the Chinese military were unable to operate them properly. Furthermore, those old guns weighed less than a hundred pounds each, while Britain's new brass cannons weighed thousands of pounds and were far more difficult to control. "If we don't have men who know how to use them," he wrote, "then I fear they could turn around and benefit the enemy."

Xiao then laid out a longer-term history of China's trading relations with the British, looking for lessons in how to deal with them. He wrote about James Flint's imprisonment in 1760, and the restriction of British commerce to Canton that followed. He listed the rules for foreigners in the factory compound. He wrote in detail about the Macartney mission in 1793 (which, in his words, came to present "tribute") and how Qianlong refused the British ambassador's demands. He wrote about Admiral Drury's invasion of Macao in 1808, suggesting that trade was China's most powerful weapon in determining the outcome of that crisis. In spite of Drury's intention to attack, he wrote, the English merchants themselves were "afraid" that the Chinese would not approve, and "did not dare" to openly occupy Macao. Once the invasion was under way, it was the closure of trade that struck fear into the hearts of the merchants and turned them against Drury. As Xiao quoted one angry British captain, "If you offend China and they shut down trade, then even if we capture Macao, what good would it do us?"

This was not, however, a blindly patriotic account of Chinese superiority. Although China had prevailed in its showdown with Drury—the closest the British and Chinese had ever come to war—Xiao made it clear that it was trade that had won the day: the British merchants were afraid of losing their market, so Drury left and commerce was restored. Yet China did not have a strong enough military option available as a fallback. As witnessed by the inability to control the native pirate fleets that rose up after Drury's departure, Xiao argued that China's naval forces near Canton were completely insufficient to defend the coast. "Our navy had no means to resist the pirates," he wrote, "yet the pirates themselves were quite fearful of the foreign ships." He judged that a single foreign ship was a match for at least ten native vessels. China's own coastal forces, in other words, were not even remotely comparable to what the British possessed.

The last episode in Xiao Lingyu's history was the Amherst mission, by which point he had become almost sympathetic to the earnestness of the British. Although he noted the ambassador's refusal to perform the kowtow, Xiao also described in detail the long and arduous journey to the capital that had preceded Amherst's aborted audience. Following on Jiaqing's condemnation of the "Duke" for forcing the audience at too-short notice, Xiao forgave Amherst for his various insults to the throne, explaining how the diplomat was exhausted after traveling through the night over stony roads, and that his ceremonial outfit had not arrived.

Xiao Lingyu was not aware, or at least he chose not to imagine, that there was any lasting resentment on the British side for the failure of Amherst's mission. His account ended with a banquet given by the Qing governor-general for Lord Amherst in Canton just before he sailed home. At the banquet, the governor-general explained how the emperor did not value exotic foreign things and so there was no need for England to send tribute anymore, adding that if the British felt they really must continue to send tribute, they could simply deliver it to Canton rather than going through the trouble of sending ships to the north (to which Amherst, according to Xiao, nodded agreement). The governor-general then reminded Amherst how valuable the China trade was to Great Britain: that Amherst's countrymen had been coming to Canton for a hundred years, that the market was worth tens of millions every year, that the British profited enormously from the trade—far more so, he said, than China did—and so they should do everything possible to ensure that the situation did not change.

In deciding to end his account of British-Chinese relations with Lord Amherst in 1817, besides just implying that the intervening years up to 1832 had been peaceful (which they had, for the most part), Xiao also gave Amherst—or at least Xiao's version of him—the final word. The account ends just after the governor-general's speech about the value of Chinese trade to Great Britain, with Lord Amherst responding, forthrightly, "China and my country both profit from this trade; we British are not the only ones who value it."[55] Xiao Lingyu thus ended on a relatively optimistic note: Lord Amherst, the British ambassador, acknowledging the great value his country attached to the trade at Canton, quibbling only that the commerce was beneficial to China as well (a fact that would be readily acknowledged by the Chinese traders of Canton, if not their government). Xiao—and by this point, his readers—knew full well that the British could not be controlled by military force. Britain's weapons were vastly superior to China's, their ships were incomparably stronger than the pitiful Qing navy, and their empire was expanding in Asia. Nevertheless, running through his full account was the promise that the British *could* be controlled through trade. From what Xiao Lingyu could tell about relations between the two countries by looking backward from 1832, whatever the tensions that had arisen over the years, it was obvious that the Canton trade was so important to the British financially that they would never do anything to risk losing it.

There is no reason he should ever have thought otherwise.

CHAPTER 9

Freedom

———◆———

The new round of troubles at Canton began, innocuously enough, with a new British factory chief who could not stand to be away from his wife. His name was Baynes, a "nervous, sickly man," as one woman in Macao described him.[1] He was a protégé of John Roberts, who had caused so much trouble back in 1808 by trying to goad Admiral Drury into attacking Canton. Baynes was just as inclined to support a hard line against the Chinese as Roberts had been (and so he was also just as completely at cross-purposes with the desire of the Company directors to maintain a peaceful trade). Baynes had become president of the select committee by staging a minor coup against his predecessor in 1829, unifying the junior members of the committee to demand that the Company withhold its trade from the Chinese until certain grievances were addressed by the hoppo. The president of the select committee opposed making threats against the Chinese authorities, which he saw as pointless and damaging, but he was outvoted by the three junior members led by Baynes. In frustration, he left Canton to return to England and the upstarts assumed power in his place.[2]

As it happened, the headstrong if sickly Baynes was blessed with the loveliest wife of all the men in the British factory, and he was resentful that she—like all of the other wives who had accompanied their husbands to China over the years—should have to stay behind in Macao during the October-to-April trading season while he was in Canton.[3] So in February 1830, he snuck her into Canton. Dressing her up in disguise, he brought her along when he sailed from Macao and smuggled her into the luxurious British factory to live with him. The plan sent the Western community of Macao into a tizzy; nobody had any idea what would happen. The rule against foreign women in Canton had never been tested. But to everyone's surprise, it seemed to turn out well (well enough, at least, that two more British wives soon went over to join her).

The Hong merchants, far from raising an alarm, came to pay Mrs. Baynes their respects and did their best to help keep her presence secret from the authorities—they were, after all, liable for the foreigners' behavior and could be punished for her being there. She even got to go out walking around a bit, which led to something of a mob scene as the local Chinese tried to crowd in for a glimpse of the Englishwoman—who, abandoning her travel disguise, went out dressed in full, unadulterated London fashion, puffy-sleeved dresses and all. Several entrepreneurial Chinese with boats on the river charged admission to see her.[4] But the authorities, who clearly knew she was there, did not press the issue, apparently considering it a minor enough matter to let pass. By April, she and the other two British wives were back safely in Macao, regaling anyone who would listen to them about their great adventure.

Not everyone was happy to listen to them, however. In particular, an American woman in Macao named Harriet Low found herself especially envious. Low was the most eligible Anglo-American bachelorette in town. A twenty-year-old from Salem, Massachusetts, she had come to Macao the previous year as a companion to her aunt, who was married to one of the partners in Russell & Co. In a rather catty diary Low kept for the sake of her sister back home (it was she who described Baynes as sickly), she noted that it wasn't *such* a big deal that all those Chinese people had turned out to see Mrs. Baynes. It wasn't as if the same thing wouldn't have happened if the tables were reversed. "Now I think the Chinese are much more civil than either American or English people would have been, if a China woman had

Harriet Low

appeared in our streets dressed in the costume of her country with little feet," she wrote in her diary. "Why she would be mobbed and hooted at immediately."[5]

Harriet Low was accustomed to being the belle of the ball in Macao, the center of a small social world of Anglo men and seasonally single wives set against an exotic backdrop of rolling sea views and Portuguese Catholic pageantry. Her little community was a constant parade of dinner soirées and singing parties at which she would dance quadrilles deep into the night. She had hordes of suitors—ship's captains came to woo her, as did the East India Company's chaplain (aggressively) and friends of various relatives from New England. The Forbes brothers, who worked with her uncle, were regular visitors when they were in town (she found the little balding one, John Murray Forbes, nice enough but "not much indebted to nature for beauty").[6] During the off-season when Robert Morrison was in residence she spent her Sunday mornings listening to his sermons, though not always with full attention. She became close friends with his daughter.

It was only when the British wives went to Canton that Harriet Low really felt her Americanness deeply—for they could go because they had the Company behind them. Her uncle's firm, Russell & Co., would never put its trade at risk for the sake of her freedom to travel about. Generally speaking, Harriet Low had always been mistrustful of the British, never having met one of them until she got to Macao. She had expected to dislike them for their notorious pomposity, but in time found them to be more genial and charming than she had assumed. In any case, the British wives were a significant part of her small social world in Macao and she did not take well to being left behind when they went to Canton. It was lonely enough already during the trading season when most of the men were gone, and she did not relish losing the women as well.[7]

When autumn came around again and trading resumed, Baynes decided to repeat his experiment. This time he brought his wife to Canton right at the opening of the season, arriving on October 4, 1830, though by that point the patience of the authorities had worn thin. A week after their arrival, the Qing governor-general ordered that Mrs. Baynes must leave Canton immediately, as per the regulations. Mr. Baynes ignored him. The governor-general pointed out that along with bringing women to Canton, foreigners had also been seen riding in sedan chairs, which was likewise forbidden. He ordered them to stop defying the rules of the compound. Still, Baynes stood his ground. In response, the governor-general's assistants plastered the factory district with notices in Chinese explaining how immoral the British had become, and calling upon the Hong merchants and Chinese linguists to do their best to teach them how to act like civilized people.

At that point, what should have been a harmless situation began to escalate out of control. The catalyst was a third party: a group of British free traders led by William Jardine and James Matheson. As private traders, there was little Jardine and Matheson loathed more than the Company, whose monopoly stood in the way of expanding their business to Europe. But if they couldn't ignore that monopoly, they could at least push the Company's select committee to take a more aggressive stance in representing their interests against the only thing they loathed even more—the Chinese government with its strict limitations on foreign trade. And whatever the outcome of that might be, they were always happy to help their Company rivals embarrass themselves.

The private British traders and the staff of the East India Company's factory may have been competitors but all of them were British, and that was the lever the private traders pulled. As soon as the governor-general's placards went up denouncing the British for their uncivilized behavior, Jardine and Matheson led a group of twenty-six private merchants in writing up a letter demanding that the East India Company do something about this allegedly terrible offense to their nation, charging that the governor-general's "grossly insulting" posters were "holding up Foreigners to the eyes of the Chinese, as an inferior and abject class."[8] Overblown of a reaction as it may have been, Baynes had no choice but to push the issue; if he didn't, he risked being branded a coward by the private traders (and, more importantly, by their newspaper, the *Canton Register*, which, they happened to mention in their letter, had subscribers throughout the British Empire).

Goaded to stand up for British honor, Baynes rallied the Company's translators and issued a remonstrance in Chinese to the governor-general, seeded with references from the Confucian classics, in which he protested the notion that the British were in any way uncivilized or unruly. He also asked that his wife be allowed to stay. "How does it accord with reason and the feelings of human nature to declare that the wife shall not accompany her husband and quietly reside in the factory with him!" he asked.[9] The governor-general responded on October 20—informally, in a verbal message relayed by Houqua—that Mrs. Baynes really must go. He asked Baynes to give a date by which his wife would return to Macao, and warned that if he refused to do so, soldiers might be sent to remove her from the factory.

The utterance of "soldiers" and "wife" in the same breath was enough to send Baynes over the edge. He immediately called for an armed force to protect his wife, and by the next morning one hundred British sailors from the Company's trading ships were landed at Can-

ton with carronades—"to resist," in the words of the select committee, "this menace of violating the Precincts of our Factory, hitherto
held sacred, to the utmost extremity." As if the governor-general's
troops were poised right at the gate to the English factory in preparation for spearing Mrs. Baynes through, the committee declared that
anything less than a forceful response to this threat "would be highly
injurious to the Interests and Honor of the British Nation of which
we are in this Country the Representatives." Jardine and his private
traders had managed to turn the situation into a national crisis, and
now it was no longer simply a matter of an impetuous Company
employee breaking the rules to spend more time with his wife. It was
now a defense of British national honor against the "menace" of the
Chinese government.[10]

The Qing governor-general, apparently mystified by Baynes's
overblown reaction, almost immediately issued a clarification via
Houqua that he didn't actually intend to send soldiers into the factory
on mere account of a foreign woman living there. But still Baynes held
his ground, demanding a promise in writing that the factory would
be untouched. Talking him down, the governor-general reminded
him that the regulations against women and sedan chairs had been in
place since 1760 and there was no reason they should suddenly have
changed. Finally, on October 31, claiming a victory of sorts (insofar
as his wife hadn't yet been hauled off), Baynes told the sailors to stand
down and had them return to their ships. The governor-general com-
plimented him for being penitent but reminded him to behave himself or trade would suffer. Baynes's destabilizing role came to an end
three weeks later, on November 23, when a Company ship arrived
from London carrying orders for his removal. Like Roberts before
him, Baynes was relieved of his duties in China and ordered home
along with his pretty wife.

In the midst of all this commotion, Harriet Low, not to be out-
done, managed to make the trip to Canton herself, along with her
aunt, the two of them establishing themselves as the first American
women to visit the city. They traveled in disguise under heavy robes
and hoods, and joined Low's uncle with the rest of the Russell & Co.
personnel in the Swedish factory. However, she, unlike the British
women, did not have any troops to protect her, and neither were the

Chinese merchants inclined to cover for her as they had done for Mrs. Baynes. One of the senior Hong merchants explained regretfully that he had already told the authorities that Mrs. Baynes's presence was necessary because Mr. Baynes was sick and needed her to care for him. He had passed off another English wife as being Baynes's cousin, saying that Baynes was in fact so sick he needed two attendants. For Low, however, he had nothing. "I no can talky sick any more," he apologized in Pidgin. "Now I know not what talky."[11]

Sure enough, Harriet Low was promptly ordered out of Canton, under threat that two Russell & Co. ships at Whampoa would not be allowed to unload their cargoes until she did. Her uncle had no intention of intervening on her behalf, so she took her aunt and left in a huff. "We shall have to go back to Macao," she complained, "while the English ladies stay here and enjoy themselves." Nevertheless, Low's brief glimpse of the all-male world of the Canton factories left her with a good impression. "You have no idea how elegantly these bachelors live here," she wrote to her sister. "I don't wonder they like it."[12]

Her presence reputedly caused quite the hullabaloo among those same bachelors, a number of whom had been living year-round in the factories and hadn't seen an unmarried American woman in years. A clerk from Russell & Co. described the antediluvian men of the American factory, unaccustomed to female company, tripping over one another as they tried to impress Low. "Old codgers were seen in immense coats, which had been stowed away in camphor trunks for ten or fifteen years," he wrote in his diary, "and with huge cravats on, and with what once were gloves"—all on their way to pay homage to Harriet and her aunt. When the two women left for Macao on November 30, all of the men in the American factory bustled down to the dock to see them off. After they were gone, one curmudgeon declared in relief that he hoped Canton wouldn't be "bothered with ladies" again, though the clerk noted in his diary that the complainer was "a notoriously crusty old fellow."[13]

So no harm came to Mrs. Baynes or Harriet Low, but the frictions between the British merchants and the Chinese authorities continued to build into 1831. The new select committee was not nearly so provocative as Baynes and his followers had been, but they were still vulnerable to being labeled cowards if they failed to stand up for their nation's honor. And the private traders kept pushing the issue. In December 1830, refusing to let go of the "insults" of the previous months (and angling, as always, for a way to damage the prestige of the Company), Jardine, Matheson, and this time forty-five other private traders in Canton joined together to send a petition to the House of Commons. Complaining that they had "long submitted in silence to the absolute and corrupt rule of the Chinese government," the private traders asked the British government to take a strong hand to put the trade at Canton on a new basis.

In light of the "total failure" of both the Macartney and Amherst embassies, as they put it, the petitioners argued that the "refinements of diplomacy" were useless in China. The Chinese government would never grant any concessions of its own free will; anything that had ever been gained, they offered, had been gained by standing up to it. "Even violence has frequently received friendly treatment," they said, "while obedience and conformity to its arbitrary laws have met only with the return of severity and oppression." They gave the example of Admiral Drury, who they said was humiliated after backing down in the face of Chinese threats and accomplished nothing. Yet the leader of the pirates who plagued China's coast afterward (meaning Shi Yang's adopted son Zhang Bao) was "invested with a robe of honour, and ultimately nominated to an important official situation." Which was to say that a British admiral who submitted to the authority of the Chinese government was "despised and treated with indignity," while a mere pirate who stood up to that government wound up being "ranked among the nobility of the land." The lesson was clear.[14]

The traders complained about the governor-general's placards depicting them as "a barbarous, ignorant, and depraved race, every way inferior." Bemoaning their lack of "free air and exercise" in the small Canton factory compound, denied the "sacred ties of domestic life" by the prohibition on women, they begged the British government to send a royal diplomat to supplant the East India Company in representing their interests in China. But given that China had refused to allow them to station a permanent ambassador in the country since the Macartney mission, the petitioners tiptoed around just how exactly they hoped Britain might establish him. They wouldn't come right out and say it, but the lawmakers who read their petition understood quite clearly that it was a veiled call for military force.

As the private British were writing to Parliament, the Company supercargoes were dealing with separate problems of their own. For years they had been trying to expand the small piece of land on which their factory rested (even though they had explicitly been told not to) by sinking wooden piles into the soft ground and building stone piers out into the river, seeking access to deeper water. They had even planted a shrubbery on the reclaimed land, of which they were quite proud. In May 1831, while they were in Macao for the off-season, they learned that the Canton governor had ordered their new shrubbery to be torn up and the reclaimed land with its piers demolished. At the same time they also learned that the governor had entered their factory in their absence, had poked around, and had reportedly called for a portrait of King George IV in the dining hall to be uncovered, then sat down with his back to it. The governor would later insist that he had no idea who the man in the portrait was (he said he assumed it was someone unimportant since it was at the end of the hall, whereas the place of honor for a Chinese portrait would have been at the center).[15] But no explanation could console them: the governor, as they understood, had insulted their former king.

Once again Jardine's private traders went on the offensive. In a resolution adopted on May 30, 1831, styling themselves "The British Merchants of Canton," they declared that the Canton governor's "gratuitous insult offered to the picture of the King of England," along with his "demolition" of the shrubbery, his "violent entry" into the Company factory, and other slights, demonstrated "a deliberate plan to oppress and degrade British Subjects."[16] The Company supercargoes took it from there. With enthusiastic support from their brethren in the private trade, they sent a ship to Calcutta with a letter asking the British governor-general to dispatch a naval fleet from India to uphold their nation's honor in China. They chased that ship with another to London carrying a secret letter for the East India Company's Court of Directors. "We have used every means available to us to preserve our national character and interests unimpaired," they warned the directors ominously. "If we fail, it can only be from want of sufficient power to maintain them."[17]

As an American watching from the sidelines while the crisis unfolded, John Murray Forbes's older brother Robert was tickled by the absurdity of the British grievances. In June 1831 he joked in a letter to his cousin John Perkins Cushing that the Qing governor "had the temerity to enter their Hall and turn his back to the King's portrait," adding, "Their grievances were thought matter of sufficient import to dispatch a ship to Calcutta."[18] Later, while waiting to see if a British fleet would arrive from India, he told his uncle that those same British traders who called for military intervention might well come to regret their actions. If the "belligerents," as he called them, should "get up the shadow of a War the drug trade will be very dull and there will be no means to pay for it." Without an opium trade, he imagined that "the 'British Merchants of Canton' who have been crying out for redress of imaginary wrongs will be very glad to see things going on as usual."

He then made a crucial point—one that others would make as well—that for all of its flaws, the Canton trade was in fact, in its jury-rigged and semilegal fashion, already one of the freest systems of commerce in the world. "Who would barter the present free trade in all description of goods," he asked, "for a regular commercial System of duties, entry permits and a myriad of forms like those in London. The facilities for trade have always been remarkable here and those who have had most experience are perfectly willing to *put up* with a continuation of the same."[19] The impatience of the British over their minor confrontations and perceived insults in China, to his mind, simply betrayed their ignorance of how good they really had it.

It wasn't just the foreign traders who were starting to test their boundaries. In the summer of 1831, around the time the British factory's shrubbery was being torn up, a twenty-seven-year-old missionary named Karl Gutzlaff was making his first attempt to get inside China. A dark-haired Prussian who was fluent in multiple languages and would marry a succession of Englishwomen (as well as flirting with Harriet Low, though pretty much everyone did that), Gutzlaff was, at his essence, a fusion of his forebears Robert Morrison and Thomas Manning.[20] Like Morrison, he was a zealous Protestant who had mastered spoken and written Chinese and felt himself called to bring the Gospel to the Chinese. He was thus deeply indebted to Morrison's groundbreaking work on the dictionary and Chinese Bible. But Gutzlaff was also imbued with "a love for adventure," as one colleague put it mildly, and so, like Thomas Manning (and very much unlike Morrison), he aimed to get into the country proper.[21]

Karl Gutzlaff in his Chinese disguise

He wanted to see China firsthand rather than suffer the confines of Canton—and to do that, he was willing to put on a disguise and risk his life by entering illegally.

Rather than bothering with Canton, Gutzlaff had spent his first years as a missionary in Southeast Asia—modern-day Malaysia and Thailand, especially—where he could work with more freedom among the overseas Chinese populations. From friends and converts he learned to speak the dialect of Fujian province on China's southeastern coast. In time, he gave himself a Fujianese name and even claimed to be a naturalized subject of the Qing Empire after allegedly getting himself adopted by a Fujianese family.[22] For the sake of travel, his disguise was far more promising than Thomas Manning's—with his dark eyes and swarthy complexion, his genius at picking up languages, dressed fully in Chinese clothes (and without a distracting beard), Gutzlaff could easily pass as a Chinese from Fujian. The only way in which he held back in his disguise was that he didn't grow a queue—the long braid that signified subservience to the Qing Empire. Instead he wore a head wrap, which he could remove when he needed to prove to someone that he was actually a foreigner.[23]

For his voyage up the China coast in 1831, Gutzlaff took passage on a native junk out of Bangkok, a 250-ton trading vessel bound for Tianjin with a Cantonese captain and a crew of fifty Chinese sailors. Like Manning, Gutzlaff made himself useful by serving as a physician. He also helped with navigation as the ship sailed up to China and then farther up the coast to Tianjin. His sleeping quarters in steerage were a fetid, cramped compartment barely large enough for him to lie down in, and he shared with the crew the same simple meals of rice, vegetables, and salt. In the space allowed for his cargo he carried some medicines and a "large quantity" of short Christian texts in Chinese that he planned to hand out as he traveled.

The Chinese ship's crew was remarkably indifferent to the presence of a foreign missionary on board their vessel, though Gutzlaff himself was less than charitable toward them. As a pious Christian, his entire purpose for the voyage was to spread the seeds of moral salvation, and he was repulsed by the degree of sin he found on board the ship—which, as he described it, was practically a floating opium den. The captain was "long habituated to opium-smoking," as were the pilot and his assistant. The ship's officers all "partook freely of this intoxicating luxury," which left them unfit for duty and often caused them to fall asleep on their watches. Meanwhile, the crew, left to their own devices, put the others to shame. When the vessel first made landfall in China, at a harbor some two hundred miles up the coast from Canton, a crowd of small boats pulled up alongside it to ply the crew members with opium, wine, and prostitutes. Gutzlaff wrote in dismay that "the disgusting scene which ensued, might well have entitled our vessel to the name of Sodom."[24]

Nevertheless, the dominant theme of Gutzlaff's voyage, at least as he reported it, was how remarkably welcoming everyone was to him along the way. The Chinese with whom he traveled were thrilled to be returning to their home country and "congratulated" him, he wrote, that he had finally "left the regions of barbarians, to enter the Celestial Empire." He received similar congratulations as the ship made its way north. In Tianjin he happened to run into some Chinese patients he had treated in Bangkok, who remembered him. "They lauded my noble conduct in leaving off barbarian customs," he wrote, "and in escaping from the land of barbarians, to come under the shield of the 'son of heaven.'" He was curious to learn what people along the coast thought about foreigners. Some told him the British were violent, others said they were good rulers at Singapore. Most of the people he talked to, though, didn't know much more than that Europe was "a small country inhabited by a few merchants who speak different languages, and who maintain themselves principally by their commerce with China."[25]

Laying the groundwork for future missionary work, Gutzlaff chronicled the grim spectacle of opium smoking in the ports he visited, along with the more traditional vices of prostitution and gambling. There was agitation, he reported: rumors said that Daoguang's heir apparent had died from an opium overdose, and the authorities were cracking down harder than ever. As with Thomas Manning, as soon as word got out that Gutzlaff was a doctor he was swamped with patients (though unlike Manning, he preached to them and sent them home with Christian tracts). One patron put him up in a grand house in Tianjin, where he treated large crowds of the afflicted until his medicines ran out, gaining wide notice; a wealthy man living across the street offered to purchase him outright for two thousand taels of silver, apparently in hopes that Gutzlaff would drum up business for his shop. Even some officials came to see him, mainly because they heard that he might know how to cure opium addiction.[26]

Gutzlaff's voyage was unexpectedly successful, the first journey up the coast and into the northern Chinese interior by a westerner since Amherst's mission, and the first without official sanction since James Flint. After a rough passage back down to Canton in December, Gutzlaff took leave of his sailor friends to make his way back to Macao (where, the Chinese sailors informed him, "many barbarians lived").[27] He arrived on December 13, and Robert Morrison was there to welcome him after his six-month journey. Gutzlaff's disguise had worked. His spoken Fujian dialect was fluent enough to convince even officials that he was a native. He had distributed his Gospel tracts, preached a bit, and managed to avoid arrest or deportation in the process. Even better, unlike Manning's journey to Tibet, his voyage held the promise of being repeated. Nothing like it had been done in living memory.

Back in 1810, Thomas Manning had been angry that the British government in India would not use his secret journey into Tibet as a means to try to open trade between Bengal and the western reaches of the Qing Empire. When Karl Gutzlaff went up the coast in 1831, however, times were beginning to change. A great many eyes had been watching him from Canton with interest.

———

It took six months for the pleas for help from the Canton traders to reach London, and when they finally got there the British government slapped them down, hard. Jardine and his followers got their most sympathetic hearing from the House of Commons (where it was said that they "were not only respectable, but were British subjects, promoting British prosperity in a remote quarter of the world"). The conclusion of that debate, however, was a straightforward one: no ambassador, let alone any naval fleet, should be dispatched to China to relieve their state of alleged distress. As one lawmaker put it, "There should on no account be even a threat of an appeal to arms, for the matter could easily be arranged by much better means." Charles Forbes, a Tory MP, suggested along the same lines as Robert Bennet Forbes (who was no relation) that the British merchants in China should be more appreciative of the status quo. He said he wished he could "ask those from whom this petition came, whether they would rather be treated there according to the laws of that empire, or according to the laws of Great Britain?" The answer, to his mind, was a simple one: in China they were able to smuggle freely without punishment; did they really want to exchange that for clear regulations and strict policing as in England?[28]

The House of Lords was even less sympathetic. In a discussion in December 1831 prompted by the news that the select committee had requested naval support from India, Earl Grey, the Whig prime minister, noted that "it did appear, that the factory at Canton had displayed a great deal of improper conduct." Lord Ellenborough, a recent president of the Board of Control that supervised the East India Company, pointed out how much revenue would be lost to British India if the Canton market should be shut down from these troubles—the East India Company would be crippled, unable to pay dividends and likely to default on its debt payments. And that was to say nothing of the millions of pounds per year in taxes that the British government would lose if the Company's tea imports to England were suspended. He wondered what was at stake that could possibly be worth such damage. "Far from complying with the request made for armed interference," he suggested, the government should instead "issue orders, directing the British merchants to obey the laws of the country in which they resided."[29]

Indeed, the voices of rebuke from back home were all but unanimous. Those in positions of responsibility in Britain roundly condemned the aggressive hopes of the merchants on the ground in Canton, telling them in a variety of ways that they had better start behaving themselves. The East India Company directors, for their part, wrote to the select committee to "decidedly condemn the requisition you made to the Bengal government, for the aid of Ships of War." As they later clarified: "We have no pretensions beyond the subjects of other nations to dictate to the Chinese government the principles upon which alone they are to carry on her trade with foreigners."[30]

The angriest and most pointed response of all, however, came from the First Lord of the Admiralty, James Graham. In a scathing letter to the British governor-general in India, he ripped the provocations of the Company supercargoes to shreds. The British traders in Canton, he insisted, "must not imagine that great national interests are to be sacrificed to their notions of self importance and to a spirit of haughty defiance mixed with contempt for the laws and customs of an independent people." He declared in the plainest language possible, "Trade with China is our only object; conquest there would be as dangerous as defeat, and commerce never prospers where force is used to sustain it. No glory is to be gained in a victory over the Chinese."[31]

———

It was a terribly inopportune time for the members of the British factory to be embarrassing themselves over trumped-up issues of national honor. For while Baynes was busy ferrying his wife back and forth to Canton and his successors were calling for gunboats to avenge their shrubbery, back home in Great Britain the East India Company's charter—in particular its long-standing monopoly on trade with China—was under a tremendous political attack. An alliance of rising industrial interests based in Liverpool, Manchester, Glasgow, and other manufacturing cities had determined that the Company's monopoly was the primary obstacle to selling more of their products to China, especially cotton textiles. If the monopoly were lifted, went their basic line of argument, and if private British firms were given the chance to trade freely and competitively between England and China, the market for British manufactured goods in Canton was certain to expand.

These nascent regional lobbying organizations had first tried to derail the East India Company's China monopoly back in 1813, the last time its charter had been up for renewal by Parliament, but they did not succeed then—although they did manage to get the trade between Britain and India opened up to private firms. Parliament drew the line at opening China, however, heeding strong arguments made by George Staunton that the trade with China was a unique situation—entirely different from India—and only the East India Company supercargoes had the experience and discipline to manage it. Staunton argued that since the Chinese government was so notoriously suspicious of foreigners, allowing independent British traders free access to Canton would likely provoke hostility from the local authorities and might damage the tea trade that was one of the Company's few sources of actual profit. Staunton insisted that the only way to avoid conflict and ensure a steady income from the commerce with China was to preserve the East India Company's monopoly, and in 1813 Parliament had agreed with him.[32]

This time around, however, the industrial lobbying interests began preparing years in advance for a much more forceful and tightly orchestrated campaign against the monopoly. In favor of their arguments, the sale of British textiles in India had increased several times over since India was opened to free trade in 1813, and by analogy it seemed obvious that even greater results could be achieved if the trade to Canton were opened as well. To the most zealous advocates of the doctrine of free trade, for whom it was nearly a religion, the destruction of the East India Company's monopoly was a matter of urgency not just for commerce but for the progress of civilization itself. As one partisan wrote in the *Edinburgh Review* in January 1831, "The Parliament of Great Britain have it now in their power to open new and boundless markets for the products of our artizans and they are called upon to assist in forwarding the civilisation of the Eastern world. . . . [The East India Company's monopoly] checks the spirit of improvement, paralyses industry, and upholds ignorance and barbarism in vast countries. Its abolition will redound to the advantage of every man in England, the 'gentlemen' of the factory only excepted."[33]

The free-trade lobbying societies this time were more numerous, more broadly representative, and far more professionally organized than they had been twenty years earlier. They enjoyed strong support from influential members of Parliament and ministers of the government, and they were single-minded in their enmity for the East India Company. Between February and July 1830, while Baynes was defi-

antly sneaking his wife into Canton for the first time, free-trade orga-
nizations across England and Scotland were swamping the House of
Commons with nearly two hundred petitions demanding that the
Company's monopoly on trade in China be brought to an end.[34]

Both houses of Parliament set up committees to investigate the
state of the East India Company's commerce with China, and one
of the strongest voices to come through in their hearings was that
the primary threat to Britain's economic interests in China was not
the Chinese government, nor even the East India Company per se,
but the United States. Speaker after speaker, coordinated by the free-
trade lobbies, charged that American firms were cutting deeply into
Britain's share of the China market because they could buy and sell
whatever they wanted, whenever they wished, while the private British firms had their hands tied by the East India Company and its
monopoly. They trotted out statistics showing how American trade
with China was growing at the expense of the British and argued that
if only their own country's private merchants were allowed full, unfet-
tered access to Canton, without the domineering interference of the
Company, then surely the Americans could be beaten back.

In response, defenders of the Company (who weren't nearly so
well organized) disputed the statistics on American trade, charging
that in fact what was called "American" was in many cases actually
British trade carried under consignment by American firms—or even
Chinese trade, as in the case of Houqua shipping his goods with John
Murray Forbes under the American flag. They also insisted that the
Americans would never have prospered so well without the presence
of the East India Company to keep the Chinese authorities "in check"
(as the Company's function was often described). Finally, there was
the question of just what exactly "free trade" even meant in the context of China. As one merchant pointed out, the British government
could only make the British side of the trade free; it had no power to
change the Chinese side. For two hundred years, Britain and China
had prospered in their mutual trade precisely because *both* sides used
monopolies as their points of contact: the East India Company on
the British side, and the Hong merchants of Canton on the other. If
Britain were to do away with its own monopoly, he worried, it would
mean nothing except confusion for the other side. China would still

have its Hong merchants. British trade would still, as before, be entirely confined to the port of Canton. How, he asked, could that be called "free"?[35]

In the end, though, the argument that ending the monopoly would claw back Britain's market share in China from the Americans rang true not just to the free-trade interests in Manchester and Liverpool but to the Americans themselves, and that helped to tip the balance of the debate. Americans in China knew, after all, just how well the Company's monopoly suppressed their potential British competitors. On that count, one of the most influential witnesses to come before the House of Commons committee was a man named Joshua Bates, a managing partner of Baring Brothers & Co., one of the oldest and most powerful merchant houses in London, who himself happened to be an American.[36] Bates had long been a correspondent with Perkins & Co. in Canton and was an old friend of John and Robert Forbes's cousin John Perkins Cushing as well as their deceased brother Thomas. Bates thus knew very well the kinds of opportunities Americans could avail themselves of in the shadow of the East India Company, and observed to the committee that the Perkins partners all returned home as "very wealthy" men.

Joshua Bates was certain what would happen if the Company's role should change. If the monopoly were lifted, he testified in March 1830, the American share of commerce at Canton would decline. The market for British goods in China was likely to increase dramatically because individuals, he believed, would do a much better job of pushing their wares than the bloated Company had done. He predicted that private British firms would eventually come to dominate the global tea trade, to the detriment of the Americans. The price of tea would come down in England, to the benefit of the entire British population. In time, Americans might even find it more economical to buy their tea at London rather than send ships all the way to China.[37]

The Company's supporters grilled him on issues of security. It was a fine thing to imagine an increase in overall trade, they said, but what about the role of the East India Company in ensuring the safety of Western trade at Canton? Bates stated that the Americans had never had any serious problems in Canton, and they needed neither protection nor representation. "The trade has always gone on very well," he said, "and without any difficulty." Asked whether the Chinese were an "anti-commercial people," as a witness in support of the Company had recently described them, Bates replied that at Canton they "seem to be very fond of trade" and "there is no unwillingness to deal with foreigners."

Viewed from Canton, the Americans most assuredly did not want to see the monopoly end. John Murray Forbes, for one, feared it would destroy much of Russell & Co.'s business, especially between Europe and China, where the Americans had previously faced no private British competition at all. He wrote to an uncle in February 1832 that "small as the foreign community here is, it is our world, and . . . the stoppage of the Company's trade would affect us more here than the appearance in Europe of a second Napoleon." At the time he wrote that letter, everyone in the Canton trading compound was still waiting to see if a naval fleet would arrive from India to support the British factory in its hysteria over the shrubbery and the king's portrait. Forbes noted to his uncle just how poorly timed the factory's manufactured crisis was, given the context; he didn't think it would result in a war, he said, but given the political climate back in London he thought "it may perhaps gain the casting vote against the continuance of the Company's monopoly."[38]

The East India Company directors mounted only a feeble resistance. They knew they faced daunting political odds: as soon as Earl Grey had assumed the prime ministership in 1830, the new president of the Board of Control, Charles Grant, informed the Company directors that as far as His Majesty's Government was concerned, their China monopoly was done for. A long fight in Parliament stood ahead of them, but for a range of reasons they did not put up much of a struggle. For one thing, they feared losing governing control over India, a threat Grey dangled before them to keep them quiet about the China monopoly. It also did not hurt that they were promised a 10.5 percent dividend to help purchase their complacency. Their weakness was intensely frustrating to the current and former members of the Canton factory, who felt themselves being sold out by their superiors in London. "The Directors are labouring hard to expire with as much discredit as possible," wrote one former factory chief to a colleague in Canton. "They will be humbugged by the Government, who will at length tell them they cannot resist the *popular voice* and they will throw them overboard like an old antiquated piece of machinery."[39]

The "popular voice" to which he referred was a crucial term at the time, for the debate over the Company's charter renewal in the early 1830s was taking place in a very different political atmosphere than the previous one in 1813 had. A major change was under way that had nothing to do with China but everything to do with the power of the manufacturing districts: namely, the upheaval of the Great Reform Act, a bill to increase the number of democratically elected seats in the House of Commons, especially in the rapidly growing centers of industry like Birmingham and Manchester that previously had had no constituencies of their own in Parliament. To make room for the new seats, the bill eliminated a great number of "rotten" boroughs with miniscule populations whose seats had traditionally been allotted by patronage and purchase. Against a backdrop of public agitation that the aristocracy feared might turn into a revolution, and amid great rancor and opposition from politicians—entailing as it did the disenfranchisement of many serving members of Parliament—the bill was finally forced through the House of Commons by Earl Grey's Whig party in 1832 on the heels of explosive public rioting in Bristol and elsewhere. Because the Reform Act would grant an unprecedented level of political power to the very industrial districts whose free-trade activists so fiercely opposed the Company's monopoly in China, once it was passed the Company no longer really stood a chance.

The East India Company still had George Staunton to defend it, though. Having served inconspicuously in the House of Commons since 1818, in 1830 Staunton was appointed to the committee investigating the East India Company's affairs and served there as something of a champion of its interests. Though the transcripts of their hearings do not identify the questioners by name, it was almost certainly Staunton who kept pressing the questions of security and stability, who kept reiterating the Company's role in keeping the corrupt and arbitrary local Chinese authorities in "check." That was, at any rate, a constant refrain of his own writings.

George Staunton's survival in Parliament through the turmoil of the Reform Act shows him to have been at least moderately adept at politics. Though his first seat in the House of Commons was for a rotten borough whose votes he purchased outright (the first of two such boroughs that would return him), by 1831 he was nimble enough to sense the inevitability of the changes under way. At least he realized what was at stake: "The question now is not how we shall improve the reform of our Representation," he wrote in his diary in the tumultuous fall of that year, "but how we shall prevent a Revolution."[40] Publicly, Staunton would eventually give his approval to the reform bill even though it meant eliminating his own seat. Any true support he felt for the cause, though, was purely abstract. Like many in such a position, he secretly resented it. "Although I always have and always shall disapprove of the entire Reform Bill," he wrote in his diary on December 10, 1831, "thinking that it will on the whole do more harm than good, introduce or aggravate more abuses, than it will either remove or alleviate, I am by no means confident that I shall continue to resist it."[41] In deference to the political winds, he kept his misgivings to himself, and later, like many in his situation, he would claim to have supported the noble cause of parliamentary reform all along.

With the passage of the reform legislation and the elimination of his previous seat, Staunton was forced to campaign for a democratic election for the first time in 1832 at the age of fifty-one, trying to gain a place in the new, reformed House of Commons. For the purposes of the campaign, he presented himself as a political independent, a "cordial" supporter of progressive Whig causes like the abolition of slavery (though quietly conservative in his stance on free trade). He insisted in campaign speeches that Britain's foreign policy should be "essentially *pacific*," though he hedged by adding that "no country can be secure in the enjoyment of peace, which is not also prepared to defend its rights and interests by war *when necessary*."[42] He said as little as possible about the East India Company and its charter.

Given Staunton's inexperience in the art of political persuasion, he was fortunate to be paired up for the election with a running mate whose ample charisma made up for his own shortcomings in that area: a well-connected liberal politician thirteen years his junior named Henry John Temple, best known as Lord Palmerston. Palm-

Palmerston

erston was a rising star of the Whig party with a splendid gift for effective (if "slipshod and untidy") oratory who had served since 1830 as foreign secretary in Earl Grey's government.[43] Staunton and Palmerston campaigned together for the two seats for South Hampshire in the elections of December 1832 in a contest that took a more vicious turn than Staunton had expected. "I was perfectly *astounded*," he later wrote, "by the virulence of the invectives with which I was assailed." (Of those invectives, one of the most hurtful, after his lifetime of social awkwardness, was that Staunton was "unpopular.") When the dust settled, though, Staunton and Palmerston won by a narrow margin.[44]

From his position in the reformed House of Commons, newly dominated as it was by the champions of free trade, George Staunton saw himself as standing all but alone against a current of public opinion that threatened to sweep away the Company and its older, proven ways in China. But in the management of the Canton trade (as he, but few others, saw it) lay the future of Britain's entire relationship with China, and Staunton considered himself personally responsible for the peaceful continuance of that relationship. For him, the Company represented order, stability, and dignity for the British in China. He was proud of having been part of the Canton factory for so long, from his early days arguing in a Chinese court to his leading role in convincing Lord Amherst to uphold Britain's dignity by refusing to kowtow. He feared what might happen if that force of tradition and stability should be removed.

Finding himself the vanguard of a cause that many considered to be lost, Staunton came to regret his shy nature and unconventional upbringing: his homeschooling, his lack of Cambridge or Oxford polish, his childhood with no friends other than his father and mother, all of his years as a wallflower in the Canton factory. They did not serve him well in the House of Commons. "Neither my habits nor my education," he admitted, "had well qualified me for the warfare of public discussion."[45] Although he commanded respect for his knowledge about China he was not, by any means, a compelling speaker.

In the spring of 1833, as the vote to terminate the Company's monopoly loomed, George Staunton swallowed his anxieties and moved a series of China-related resolutions in the House of Commons that he insisted would be necessary to ensuring a peaceful transition from monopoly to free trade in Canton. The foundation of those resolutions was Staunton's strong belief that the only thing that had ensured peace in the China trade over his lifetime had been the unity of the Company and its great familiarity and experience dealing with what he termed the "arbitrary," "oppressive," and "corrupt" agents of Chinese government at Canton.

Staunton feared the results of a free-for-all, where British traders who had no experience dealing with the Chinese would suddenly show up and get themselves into trouble at Canton, with no organized body to represent them or negotiate on their behalf. And so in his resolutions he proposed that the Company's role as mediator between the British and Chinese should only be allowed to lapse if a treaty could first be agreed upon with the Chinese authorities, one that would allow for a British government diplomat to be stationed in Canton to supervise the British community and represent its interests. Only then, he believed, could the trade go forward without a strong likelihood of the competing free traders provoking conflict or even a war with the Chinese.

Staunton tried repeatedly to bring his resolutions before the House of Commons for a debate. Twice he was scheduled to introduce them, but on both occasions he had to give up his allotted time to more pressing matters of national business (disappointing the *Times*, which considered Staunton's resolutions to be "well worthy of a distinct discussion").[46] Finally, on June 4, 1833, he got his chance. Nervously, he stood from his bench to deliver a lengthy prepared speech making the case for his resolutions. It was the first time that British relations with China had ever come before Parliament as a distinct question, he observed; for two hundred years, all responsibility for the relationship had been with the East India Company rather than the government. Apologizing for his lack of speaking ability, he assured the members present that he was nevertheless uniquely qualified to judge the situation in China. He reminded them of his long experience in commerce at Canton, his participation in both of Great Britain's embassies to Beijing, his ability to speak and read Chinese. Those experiences, he insisted, "have afforded me opportunities of information respecting that singular government and people, such as have probably fallen to the lot of no other European."[47]

In a shy voice that was unfortunately too quiet even for the reporters in the gallery above to make out much of what he was saying, Staunton tried to convince his listeners that any change to the trade in Canton would have to be gradual rather than sudden, and it would have to involve negotiations with the Chinese. Even if the monopoly were terminated, he argued, the Company's dominant role must be prolonged afterward as long as necessary to mediate between its own employees, the free traders, and the Chinese government. "It could not be expected," he said of the Company men and free traders, "that these conflicting parties would long live in harmony, nor could it be expected that either of them should be able to inspire the local authorities in China with respect, unless some higher power—some public representative were sent there to control both parties."[48]

As Staunton mumbled through his speech, pausing along the way to read aloud from a series of supporting documents, the less than captivated audience, already thin, was filtering out of the chamber. He was midway through an argument about how the presence of the Company kept the local Chinese authorities in check when he was interrupted. Someone motioned for a head count. Of the more than 650 members of the House of Commons who might have chosen to sit and listen to Staunton's speech that afternoon, there were not even forty left in the chamber—not enough to vote on his cherished resolutions—so the session abruptly ended. Staunton's carefully prepared speech was cut off mid-paragraph, never to be finished. Even for a man well acquainted with social embarrassment, he had never been so humiliated in his entire life.

Nevertheless, a sense of desperate urgency drove Staunton to fight through his humiliation and try one last time to get his resolutions adopted, by proposing them shortly afterward as a last-minute amendment to the bill on the East India Company's charter. They were immediately struck down without a vote. Charles Grant, the president of the Board of Control who was so antagonistic to the China monopoly, took issue with Staunton's faith that the East India Company supercargoes were the most capable representatives of the British in China. Actually, said Grant (in reference to events like those that had just transpired over the women and the shrubbery), the role of the Company supercargoes "was ambiguous and embarrassing, and occasionally, very invidious." Grant acknowledged Staunton's worries about the potential for future conflict between the British merchants and the Chinese authorities, but he said that was yet another reason why the monopoly must be abolished. The China trade was so important to Great Britain, Grant said, that "the exclusive privileges of carrying [it] on . . . ought not to be confined to one body of men."[49] Staunton's resolutions died a quiet legislative death, and the great momentum for opening Canton to free trade—without limitations—surged forward.

In the autumn of 1833, news reached Canton that the East India Company's monopoly would not be renewed when its charter expired the following May. Not only would the Company cease to control the

British traders at Canton, but according to the early intelligence William Jardine received—which turned out to be correct—it would no longer even be allowed by the British government to continue trading in China at all.[50] Come the spring of 1834, the East India Company that had dominated trade for more than a century in Canton would, for all intents and purposes, vanish.

CHAPTER 10

A Darkening Turn

———◆———

The final days of the East India Company's factory were an anxious time in Canton. For all the excitement of British investors preparing to leap into the newly opened China trade for the first time, those who had been in Canton for the long term were wary of the coming changes. Robert Morrison, for one, faced the fact that he would no longer have a job once the factory was dissolved. "Canton is greatly agitated by the new system. Hopes and fears alternate," he wrote in January 1834 to George Staunton, who had helped him find his footing in Canton back in 1807 when the Company still wanted to keep him out. The end of the monopoly, said Morrison, was "little short of a death-blow" to himself and the others who had made their careers in the British factory. He had read Staunton's speech from the House of Commons, the abortive one calling for a more gradual opening of the Canton trade, so he knew his old friend would sympathize when he said he worried about troubles that lay on the horizon—not so much for trade as for China itself. "How few," he told Staunton sadly, "consider the welfare of China in all their speculations about free trade."[1]

The Hong merchants were apprehensive as well. Though the East India Company was losing its monopoly on the British side, they would of course continue to hold theirs on the Chinese side, and it was unclear how the trade would function. "I fear we shall be overwhelmed with British goods of every description on the opening of the trades," wrote Houqua to John Murray Forbes, voicing the concern of many that the end of the monopoly would result in a hopelessly glutted market as British newcomers poured in without any rational control. Forbes was home in Boston at the time, where he would get married before returning to Canton and his duties at Russell & Co. later in the year. Houqua said he missed him and hoped for his safe return to China as soon as possible. "I shall be satisfied to see you here next season," he wrote, "when there may be something left for us to speculate upon, although the opening of the trade will be of no service to our operations."[2]

The country traders, heavily involved in opium as they were, had separate concerns. They welcomed the opening of legal trade between Canton and Britain (indeed, the very first private cargo of tea from China to London would go out under Jardine's name), but since the smuggling side of their operations had always been free of the East India Company's monopoly, the new era did not promise any new advantages. Rather, they braced themselves for a wave of Johnny-come-latelies who, to help support their entrance into the tea-for-textiles commerce at Canton, would surely try to muscle in on the opium trade at Lintin as well.

But Jardine and Matheson had been planning for this contingency for years. To circumvent the periodic gluts of opium at Canton that would only worsen under increased competition, they had been trying to find a way to do what their competitors could not: to get information, and opium, from India to China faster—and, if possible, to get it there in the off-season, against the yearly monsoon that had dictated the timetable of maritime commerce at Canton since the invention of sail. Toward that end they had tried chartering a steamship in 1829, the first to appear in East Asia, to carry a load of opium from Calcutta to Lintin for them. The experiment failed (it ran out of coal on the way), but in 1833 Jardine and Matheson invested in a special clipper called the *Red Rover*—small and narrow, with tall, raked masts and wide spars—that could beat so close to the wind it could make the passage from Calcutta to Canton against even the heaviest monsoon winds when conventional ships were grounded for the season. It would be the first of many, inaugurating the age of the "opium clipper," a unique vessel with an intensely specific purpose that would dominate the India-China opium trade for more than two decades to come.[3]

It was one thing to dominate the market at Lintin, but the holy grail, so to speak, was to find new markets entirely, up the coast and untouched by their competitors. To do that, a firm needed a ship with a captain willing to risk capture or attack by Chinese coastal forces, and—even more rare and valuable—it needed a Chinese interpreter willing to come along for the journey and negotiate the sale of the cargo. The most aggressive of the opium traders in Canton thus took a very keen interest in the missionary Karl Gutzlaff after his return in December 1831 from his secret journey up to Tianjin. He had proven that a voyage up the coast by a westerner without Chinese permission

A fleet of opium clippers on the Ganges River in India

could be pulled off. Or at least, he had shown that *he* could pull it off—for there was only one Karl Gutzlaff.

Remarkably, in 1832 it was the East India Company's factory—two years in advance of its dissolution—that took the radical step of funding Gutzlaff's second voyage up the coast. Without approval from London, the select committee hired him to escort a Company ship full of cotton textiles in search of new markets for British goods. Within weeks of returning from his first voyage north, Gutzlaff had signed on as interpreter for the Company's new mission. It was a convenient arrangement for him—he wanted to see more of the Chinese coast and distribute more religious tracts, and a Company ship would give him far more comfort and cargo space than the Chinese junk had. He could even bring full copies of Morrison's multivolume Chinese Bible along. Gutzlaff had no moral compunctions about working for the Company, as that path had already long been cleared for Protestant missionaries by Robert Morrison, even if Morrison himself would never have been daring enough to go to sea for them. (His son, John Robert Morrison, however, would—and was rather put out that Gutzlaff was chosen for the Company's mission over himself.)[4] Furthermore, since the ship would carry only cotton and wool textiles, Gutzlaff would not be implicated in any way by the opium trade he so loathed.

Gutzlaff's partner for the journey was a slippery character, a tall and handsome (if dissipated) thirty-year-old named Hugh Hamilton Lindsay who, like Gutzlaff, was yet another of Harriet Low's admirers, though she did not trust him much. "His sincerity is much to be doubted," she told her sister. "He is no favorite of mine."[5] An adventurer by nature and the son of one of the East India Company directors, Lindsay had worked for the Company in Canton since 1821 and had learned Chinese, though nowhere nearly as well as Gutzlaff. Their mission was meant to be a secret—even the directors in London knew nothing about it. Lindsay agreed to deny any involvement with the East India Company during the voyage, and to pretend instead to be a private British merchant who had been blown onto the Chinese coast by foul weather. The original plan was for Lindsay and Gutzlaff to sail on a Company ship named the *Clive*, but when its captain learned what they were up to he refused to take them. Casting about for a new vessel, Lindsay finally chartered a private ship at Lintin whose captain was willing to risk the voyage up the coast and was even eager to make charts along the way to improve the ones drafted during Lord Amherst's mission sixteen years earlier. The name of the ship under his command was, perfectly enough, the *Lord Amherst*.

The voyage of the *Lord Amherst* would take significantly longer than planned—leaving in February 1832, it did not get back to Macao until September, three months after its expected return. But it would accomplish much of what they had hoped. It carried Lindsay and Gutzlaff all the way up the coast of China and beyond, into Korea, repeating the circuit of the *Alceste* after it dropped off Amherst in 1816. Along the way, it took them into ports never before visited by the British, causing much alarm on the part of Qing coastal officials. The rumor from Canton that a British war fleet was coming to China had spread up and down the coast, and in the ports they visited, the first assumption of the local officials was that the *Lord Amherst* must be the vanguard of that fleet. But Lindsay had Gutzlaff with him, to sweet-talk and console the government officials they encountered, to convince them that the *Lord Amherst* had nothing to do with any navy. It was just a private ship in unfortunate straits, insisted Gutzlaff (who had no qualms about lying to further his missionary cause). All the men on board wanted to do, he insisted, was sell textiles.

Gutzlaff succeeded beautifully. While officials in each port insisted they must leave, those officials were so anxious to avoid conflict with foreigners that they often gave them supplies, even money, to go away. The closest the ship came to being attacked was the occasional firing of a blank shot. In person, the Qing officials were friendly and insisted they had no personal animosity toward Lindsay and Gutzlaff and the others on board their ship; they just wanted them to leave so the officials themselves wouldn't get in trouble with the emperor and lose their positions.

Meanwhile, they found merchants everywhere who were willing to defy the local authorities and meet secretly with them for trade. In contrast to the strained atmosphere at Canton, Lindsay reported "nothing but expressions of friendship and good will" from the villagers they met up the coast in their occasional forays onto land. In some places, he said, the locals even competed to see who could get Gutzlaff and the others to come into their homes and sit down for a bite to eat.[6]

Along with testing the demand for British textiles up the coast, the voyage of the *Lord Amherst* was also a propaganda mission. For Karl Gutzlaff, this meant Christian propaganda: he never went ashore without his pockets stuffed full of books and pamphlets. He handed out moral tracts in Chinese about the evils of gambling, opium use, and lying, distributed copies of Morrison's Chinese Bible, and preached in person whenever he could.[7] For Lindsay, by contrast, it was a chance to spread the gospel of free trade. His chosen weapon was a short work in Chinese titled "A Brief Account of the English Character," written by a Company employee and translated into Chinese by Robert Morrison, which informed its Chinese readers that in spite of what the Qing government might tell them, the British only wanted their friendship and commerce.

Lindsay wasn't supposed to have the pamphlet along. It was directly critical of the Chinese government, so the president of the select committee had refused to let him print it on the Company's press and ordered him to hand over any copies in his possession before leaving on his journey. But Lindsay lied to his more conscientious colleague, promising that he had no copies of the tract while actually bringing along five hundred of them in his luggage. He posted them on walls along the journey and handed them out in towns and villages whenever they went ashore.[8]

According to Lindsay's tract, which eventually reached the attention of the Daoguang emperor (who, to Robert Morrison's embarrassment if he had known, found it barely readable), the Chinese government had long "falsely represented" the British as having territorial ambitions. That was wrong, it said. In fact, Great Britain's territories were "already so large that the policy of its Government, is rather to diminish, than to enlarge them." It proudly described the great expanse of Britain's existing conquests—the territories in Europe and North America, the islands and strategic port cities like Singapore, the "hundred millions of subjects" in India. But these, it insisted, were only reasons to admire Britain, not to fear it. "The

Government of so great an Empire has no thirst for Conquest," it assured the reader. "The great object, and aim, is to preserve its subjects in a condition of happiness and tranquility."[9]

All the British had ever wanted in China, said Lindsay's tract, was peaceful and friendly trade. But they had been treated poorly in Canton—"heavily taxed and oppressed"—and the Chinese merchants they traded with were forced to pay bribes to officials. Lindsay was bringing the British case to the Chinese people themselves. "Why should not Chinese and English strive together?" his tract asked. Chinese merchants, officials, and everyday people should all just "treat foreigners with the respect and consideration to which they are entitled," it concluded. "Then indeed there will be peace, union, and harmony between the Native and British Community in China."

Though the voyage of the *Lord Amherst* had little effect in China beyond causing a flurry of agitated reports to the throne from coastal officials, in Great Britain and America it was a bombshell. For what Gutzlaff and Lindsay claimed to reveal in their accounts of the journey, which ran into multiple printings in Europe and the United States, was that China was no longer the closed empire of the past; the emperor was no longer fully in control, foreigners were no longer frozen out. Wishful as it may have been, the message Lindsay and Gutzlaff brought back—one that echoed Thomas Manning's experience in Tibet twenty years earlier—was that the ordinary people of China were perfectly friendly and open toward foreigners. The Chinese themselves wanted free trade, they insisted, and it was only the officials of the Qing government who stood in their way. In other words, the British represented the will of the Chinese people better than their own government did.

In essence, Lindsay and Gutzlaff had identified a wedge they believed could be driven right through the firmament of China: a natural alliance of British trade interests and the multitude of Chinese merchants with their desire for free commerce, both of them set against the jealous government of the Manchus. All of the exclusiveness, the restrictions, and the close management of trade that had defined the Canton commerce for so long were, Lindsay claimed, the products of a government that no longer enjoyed the full support of its subjects. A simple push from the outside and the whole system would topple from within.

There were joyous reactions to the *Lord Amherst*'s voyage in Britain and America. In London, the *Eclectic Review* declared that it "places the character of the natives altogether in a new light, and opens to us the most cheering prospect as to the possibility of wholly breaking down the partition which has for ages separated from civilized society a fourth portion of the human race."[10] The *Times* lauded Gutzlaff's revelations that "as a nation, China is politically weak," that its naval defenses were "contemptible," that the government had "no hold on the affections of the people," and that the officials were "cowardly, corrupt, and excessively cringing." But the ordinary people of China—the people!—were, the *Times* was delighted to report to its readers, "hospitable, kind, and eager to establish an intercourse with foreigners."[11]

In America, newspapers called Gutzlaff "one of the most extraordinary men of the age."[12] Legions of missionary writers quoted his potent declaration, "We are entirely erroneous about China." China was *not* a closed country, said Gutzlaff, but in fact "no country in Asia, ruled by native princes, is so easy of access."[13] According to believers on both sides of the Atlantic, be they believers in commerce or religion, the voyage of the *Lord Amherst* revealed the mysterious country of China in a new light: not as some impenetrable, reclusive empire but as a market for free commerce and a field for Christian conversion that was all but begging to be opened by the West.

In spite of all that, however, the *Lord Amherst*'s voyage was a very strange kind of mission for the East India Company's factory to have undertaken. For one thing, by violating the rules of the Canton system it departed from seventy years of established precedent. For another, it had no advance approval from back home. The Company's directors in London only found out about it after the fact, and when they did they were positively furious. In May 1833 they wrote a damning letter to the select committee in Canton expressing their fear that the journey would tarnish the honor of the East India Company and undermine British prestige in the eyes of the Chinese.

They were equally maddened by Lindsay's propaganda work.

Why *shouldn't* the Chinese have been alarmed at the *Lord Amherst's* approach, the directors asked, when Lindsay and the others were stealing up the coast "in disguise under foreign names . . . in direct violation of the laws and usages of the empire"? What would happen, they asked, if a Chinese vessel had attempted to do the same in Great Britain? What if a Chinese ship had come illegally to England, with an illegal cargo, and, when it was told to leave, had proceeded to "distribute throughout the coast papers complaining of the conduct of the Government, and calculated to incite the people against their rulers?" Britain would never tolerate such a provocation, said the directors, so "why then should we . . . act so decidedly in defiance of all common usage towards the Chinese, whose commerce we have sought and wish to retain?"[14]

But perhaps the voyage was never undertaken for the East India Company's sake in the first place. Although the future of the monopoly was still up in the air when the *Lord Amherst* departed in 1832, its termination was likely enough that Lindsay could simply have been betting on a future of free trade, using his erstwhile position in the Company to underwrite a voyage whose real value was to the free traders waiting in the wings. (The news of his voyage would in fact catch the tail end of the parliamentary debates, where it would be used as yet another battering ram against the monopoly.) Lindsay would become a free trader himself soon after the dissolution of the Company's factory, launching a private firm—Lindsay & Co.—that would give the others a run for their money.[15]

Furthermore, despite the *Lord Amherst's* journey being outwardly a project of the East India Company supercargoes, William Jardine appears to have had a significant hand in organizing it from behind the scenes. In a letter from January 1832, shortly before the mission was dispatched, Jardine mentioned to James Matheson, "I had made up my mind to Mr. Gutzlaff being engaged for the *Clive*"—the *Clive* being the first ship Lindsay attempted to sail on—which suggests that it was in fact Jardine who had decisive power over choosing the mission's interpreter.[16] The letter further indicated Jardine's involvement, telling Matheson that "the voyage required much management and great attention," and that Jardine was hopeful that Gutzlaff "may collect useful information for future purposes . . . but I shall be very much pleased when I hear of the safe return of the vessel." In any case, as galling as the *Lord Amherst*'s voyage was to the Company directors back home, the information it gathered was phenomenally useful for Jardine himself. For the bottom line of Lindsay's research into the opening of new Chinese markets was that while there was little demand for British textiles up the coast, just about everyone, everywhere he went, wanted opium.

The voyage would not be repeated. With the condemnation of the directors, followed soon after by the dissolution of the factory, there would be no more Company-sponsored vessels attempting the Chinese coast with innocuous cargoes of cotton textiles. Only drug smugglers would follow in the *Lord Amherst*'s wake. And so in 1833, failing any other means of travel, and giving the lie to every moral complaint he had ever made about the curse of opium in China, Karl Gutzlaff went to work for William Jardine. He agreed to ride Jardine and Matheson's smuggling ships and do their interpreting, and to sweeten the pill, they agreed to help underwrite the cost of his Christian publications. Displaying a stunning willingness to use any means necessary to pursue his "higher" calling, Gutzlaff was soon comfortably employed as Jardine and Matheson's chief interpreter, escorting their opium ships up and down the coast as they peddled their poisonous wares, handing out his little biblical tracts all along the way.

In the nearly two decades since Morrison had published the first installment of his dictionary, the collective ability of the British in Canton to read Chinese books and documents had advanced dramatically (less so the Americans, who, excepting the missionaries among them, saw little point in trying to get beyond the confines of the Canton trading system and so never bothered with the language). The *Canton Register* and other English-language newspapers that cropped up to compete with it carried regular translations from imperial edicts and notices from various government officials, as well as translated Chinese reports of major events in the provinces. Compared to the generations before them, the Western community in 1830s Canton thus had access to far more information about the country's interior. In 1832, Gutzlaff and a handful of other missionaries led by the American Elijah Bridgman even founded a magazine to try to bring this knowledge farther out into the English-speaking world. The *Chinese Repository*, as they called it, was dense with translations from Chinese history and literature, intended to stir up an interest among Western readers in the affairs of the Canton traders and especially the Protestant missionaries there.

From one direction, certain members of this new generation tried to use their increasing knowledge of China as a means to gain access where it hadn't been allowed before. Gutzlaff was the archetype of this process. When, for example, the opium ship *Sylph* anchored near Shanghai with Gutzlaff aboard in 1833, its crew sent out a small boat bearing a flag emblazoned with a quotation from Confucius about welcoming friends from afar. According to a report from the voyage, hundreds of people crowded down to the waterfront and "were exceedingly delighted" with the flag.[17] From a different direction, those who desired access to China beyond Canton—who wanted to "open" China, as the language generally went—wanted to translate Western texts as a means to influence the thinking of the Chinese and encourage them to skirt their government's limits on foreign contact.

For example, at one point in 1831 the *Register* reported on the desire of several merchants in Canton to have the "science" of political economy translated into Chinese. These proponents of free trade regretted that Adam Smith and John Stuart Mill were too obviously European and called for someone to write a treatise on free trade couched in the language of the Confucian classics.[18] What they wanted, in other words, was some way to use traditional Chinese texts to "teach" the Chinese the virtue of getting rich (missing the point, apparently, that the country's merchants had long ago discovered that virtue). An anonymous patron heeded their call and sponsored a contest for the best essay in Chinese on Western political economy, with a prize of £50, advising contestants to quote as much as possible from the Confucian classics so that their treatises on free trade would "carry conviction to the minds of Chinese readers."[19]

Karl Gutzlaff took this project to its highest level. He was a polyglot linguist with limitless patience for making translations, who in the course of his career would publish more than sixty works in

Chinese, along with others in English, Thai, Japanese, Dutch, and German.[20] And much to the delight of the Jardines and Mathesons of Canton, he saw almost no distinction between spreading British doctrines of free trade and spreading Christianity. Each, he believed, helped the other.[21]

In the range of his publications in Chinese, Gutzlaff borrowed a strategy the Jesuits had once used of translating works on science to convince their Chinese readers that those who believed in the proper God had also mastered the secrets of the natural world. In an 1833 letter to his American supporters, published by newspapers in Boston and New York, Gutzlaff pledged that he would write not just moral tracts to correct the "prejudices, bigotry and national pride" of the Chinese but also scientific works "to counteract their narrow-mindedness and to humble the pride of a *soi-disant* Celestial government." On the heels of his journey on the *Lord Amherst* he promised, in time, to undertake "a voyage which, if God grants success, will throw the whole interior of China open."[22]

In this grand vision of opening China, the Protestant missionaries indulged themselves in the language of a military campaign—conquest, attack, victory—an affectation that caught on among their supporters. Reporting on the departure of a new American missionary in the spring of 1834 who planned to help Gutzlaff in "penetrating the Chinese empire," the *Boston Recorder* related that the American would try to work in eastern China "while the indefatigable Gutzlaff attacks the Center." How long, the writer wondered, would it take before the two men would meet in the middle "as conquerors of this vast kingdom, [raising] the banner of *freedom* over the many millions of China?"[23]

This project of culture-as-warfare culminated in the founding at Canton, in 1834, of a "Society for the Diffusion of Useful Knowledge in China," led by Gutzlaff and Elijah Bridgman as Chinese secretaries, and with James Matheson and William Jardine as its first and second presidents, respectively. The society's avowed goal was to produce "intellectual artillery," as they called it—Chinese-language tracts with which to smash the walls of ideology that closed off the vast population of China to Western religion and trade. Violent as the society's rhetoric may have been, however, its founders believed—

deep down, fundamentally—that everything they did and hoped for was for the collective good of mankind.[24]

More deeply, though, the most aggressive of the free traders believed in the power of information and the written word to further not just the cause of commerce but also, if necessary, conquest. As the editor of Matheson's *Canton Register* put it, the right of the British to demand that China open up to free trade was the exact same right by which "the aborigines of North America and New Holland [were] driven from their *indisputable homes* by the governments of the United States and Great Britain"—namely, the right that "barbarism must vanish before civilisation, ignorance succumb to knowledge." That principle, he declared, was not just "a law of nature" but also "the will of God!"[25]

———

The question remained of what would happen to the trading system at Canton after the East India Company was removed from the scene. Ignoring George Staunton's warning that the Company's role in Canton must be preserved until a new system could be agreed upon with the Chinese, the British government went ahead with creating a new position, a "chief superintendent of trade," to take over from the Company's select committee in representing the British citizens in Canton. (All told, there would be a committee of three superintendents, two of whom were designated to be former Company men still in Canton, but the only one who really mattered was the chief who would be sent from London.) The chief superintendent would hold an ambiguous position, far below the status of an ambassador yet more official than the president of the select committee (in that he would answer to the British government rather than the Company). So although the superintendent was supposed to represent British interests in China, he would have no plenipotentiary powers to act independently on behalf of his country. And though he was supposed to supervise the free British traders at Canton, he would have no compulsive authority over them—which also meant that he would have no power to withhold their trade from the Chinese, which was the only bargaining lever the British had ever used with success.[26]

William Jardine worried that the position would go to George Staunton—who, even if he opposed its creation, was still the most qualified man in Great Britain to fill it. At one point, Jardine received news that Staunton had in fact been appointed superintendent, and he wrote immediately to James Matheson (then in Bombay) to say, "We consider this very so-so news, and would have preferred someone who had never served the Company in China."[27] Jardine's wariness of Staunton was tied up with a larger concern that the East India Company's influence would linger on even after its monopoly had ended, especially the model it had established for patient and (as he saw it) acquiescent relations with the Chinese authorities. Nobody then alive was more directly responsible for that model than George Staunton.

To the free traders, George Staunton was the enemy. Even before his opposition to ending the monopoly he had become notorious to Jardine's faction for allegedly sinking their December 1830 petition in which they claimed oppression at the hands of the Chinese government.[28] Given Staunton's opposition to free trade in China, his strong ties to the Company, and his longtime advocacy of a respectful, diplomatic approach to the Qing government, he was unlikely to look favorably on their smuggling concerns. Equally troubling, he was also unlikely to pursue the hard line Jardine wanted toward opening up new sites for British trade and pushing back against the power of the officials in Canton. What Jardine wanted in the new superintendent, in other words, was a free trader like himself, someone with no sympathies for the fading East India Company and its old-fashioned, overly scrupulous ways of doing things in China.

Jardine got his wish. The superintendency went in the end not to Staunton but to one William John Napier, a tall and gallant captain of the Royal Navy and veteran of the Napoleonic Wars whose specific qualifications to supervise trade in China amounted to exactly nothing. He had no experience in trade (though he sympathized, on principle, with the free traders). He also had no experience in diplomacy. And to complete the trifecta, he knew almost nothing about China prior to his departure. What he did have, though, was an excellent pedigree—he was the 9th Lord Napier, a Scottish nobleman descended from the mathematician who discovered logarithms—and he was a personal friend of King William IV, with whom he had been shipmates back in the day.[29]

Napier was not exactly humbled by the responsibilities of the office he sought. "The Empire of China is my own," he wrote triumphantly in his diary upon learning that his chief rival for the position had just withdrawn from consideration (that rival being not George Staunton, as it turned out, but Henry Ellis, Lord Amherst's cynical secretary). Napier fantasized about the power he might wield in China, which he understood (being off by an order of magnitude) to be an "enormous Empire of 40,000,000 [that] hangs only together by a spider's web." He contemplated what a "glorious thing" it would be to station a naval squadron along the coast, and "how easily a gun brig would raise a revolution and cause them to open their ports to the trading world." If he could just become the chief superintendent, thought Napier, then he could be the man to break China open.[30]

Given Napier's lack of qualification, and perhaps divining his less than charitable motivations in seeking the position in China, the prime minister, Earl Grey, was reluctant to give it to him. Grey dragged out the appointment process for several months, only to cave in the end under pressure from the king, who interceded forcefully on Napier's behalf.[31] Even then, after the appointment was made and Napier was preparing to depart, Earl Grey sent him a private letter to forestall what he apparently sensed (accurately) were the new superintendent's private ambitions. Politely, asking that Napier not take it as any kind of sign of distrust, the prime minister reminded him to exercise "the most careful discretion in all your dealings with the Chinese." Given the "jealous and suspicious character" of the Qing government and the Chinese people, Grey wrote, "Nothing must be done to shock their prejudices or to excite their fears."

Lord Napier was expected above all to keep the peace at Canton and do nothing to harm trade relations with the Chinese government. In all of his dealings with the Chinese, Earl Grey told him, "persuasion and conciliation should be the means employed—rather than anything approaching to the tone of hostile and menacing language." In the very worst case, should persuasion and conciliation fail him, Napier was to show "submission for a time" and wait for new instructions from home; he was forbidden on his own initiative to pursue "a vigorous enforcement of demands" no matter how "just" they might seem. Napier read that letter, even copied it into his notebook. He wrote back to Grey to say that he couldn't agree more. There is, however, little evidence that any of it sank in.[32]

Napier's instructions from Lord Palmerston at the Foreign Office, meanwhile, showed a similar desire to keep him on a short leash. Like the prime minister, Palmerston insisted that Napier's highest priority must be to prevent any kind of conflict with the Chinese. To that end, he forbade Napier in most cases to act on his own initiative or judgment—telling him, for example, that while it would be desirable to try to establish a line of communication with Beijing, since Napier was not an ambassador he should not actually go to Beijing himself, even if an opportunity arose, because he might "awaken the fears, or offend the prejudices" of the government. In the same vein, Palmerston asked Napier to find out if a survey could be made of the Chinese coast but added that Napier should not actually *make* such a survey, only write back to Palmerston to let him know whether it *could* be made. And even though Napier's arrival in China would signal the advent of a new system of relations between the British and Chinese at Canton—one that had never been discussed with, let alone approved by, the Chinese government—Palmerston instructed Napier not to negotiate with the officials there. If an opportunity for negotiation should arise, said Palmerston, Napier was simply to write home and then wait for further instructions as to how to proceed. Given the distance between Canton and London, any such further instructions would take about a year to reach him.[33]

Napier sailed from Plymouth on February 7, 1834, on the twenty-eight-gun *Andromache*, accompanied by his wife, Eliza, and two of his daughters (his other four children, including two sons, remained behind with governesses and tutors). Voyages to Canton were especially grueling for women, who had to stay sequestered in their cabins most of the time and, despite being months at sea, were still expected to keep up their appearances—a typical packing list would include at least seventy-two changes of underwear, since clothes couldn't be washed properly in salt water.[34] Lady Napier and her daughters were

violently seasick for the first several weeks of the voyage, while Lord
Napier, long accustomed to shipboard life, spent much of his time
during their five months at sea schooling himself on the situation in
Canton. He had a small library in his cabin that included eleven volumes of state papers and a long manuscript memoir prepared by the
East India Company on British-Chinese relations since 1600, all of
which Palmerston had given him for the Canton archives.[35] He also
had his own copies of several recent books on China, among them
an account of the Macartney mission by George Staunton's father,
Henry Ellis's account of the Amherst mission, and various recent
writings on China by Staunton himself and others.

Palmerston had made it strenuously clear to Napier that he was
not an ambassador (and when Napier asked just before his departure
if he could be supplied secretly with plenipotentiary powers, just in
case an opportunity to meet with the emperor arose, Palmerston flatly
refused). Nevertheless, it is evident from the journal Napier kept on
board the *Andromache* that in his own mind he was nothing less than
Macartney's and Amherst's successor. In his readings he focused
intently on the failings of those two previous embassies, with an eye
toward correcting them—especially the problems of Lord Amherst,
who Napier thought was doomed by having too many attendants and
gifts along, making his embassy "too cumbrous" to succeed.[36]

As for his readings, Napier was appalled that Amherst should
have refused to go to the audience with Jiaqing in 1816—especially
after the Duke had told him he wouldn't have to kowtow. "The unexpected and unasked for opportunity of a *private* audience was lost," he
wrote, "and why? merely because the Embassador during his journey
had separated himself from his Court dress and official Dispatch." As
Napier saw it, Amherst had botched his embassy through vanity over
his outfit and irresponsibility in not keeping better track of his documents. He faulted him with "culpable neglect." As for the kowtow
itself, Napier agreed with Henry Ellis that it was "merely a Court
ceremony" that did not imply Britain's subservience. He thought
Amherst had further bungled his mission by fussing so much over it
and listening to the advice of George Staunton and the other Company men. Such a ceremony, thought Napier, "*may be* and *ought to be*
performed by Foreigners seeking favour at that Court."[37] Given the

hoped-for opportunity, he planned to do things differently. (And it is worth noting here that, as counterintuitive as it might seem, those British who disdained China the most, such as Napier or Ellis, were generally the ones most in favor of performing the kowtow. By contrast, those who tried hardest to avoid it, like George Staunton, and Macartney before him, tended to be the ones with the greatest respect for the country.)

Napier's free-trade sympathies were already in place before he left Britain, and he read nothing on the way to China to improve his opinion of the East India Company. Indeed, there were only two figures in the entire history of British-Chinese relations he considered worthy of admiration. The first was Captain Weddell, the one who had blasted his way past the Tiger's Mouth forts in 1637 to open British trade at Canton for the first time. The second, of a piece with the first, was Captain Maxwell of the *Alceste*, who in 1816 had opened fire on those very same forts during the Amherst mission. In every other crisis, where British commanders or Company representatives had backed away from conflict with the Chinese, Napier judged that they had lost ground. As a naval captain himself it is perhaps natural that he would have sympathized with Weddell and Maxwell, but in any case the conclusion to which they led him was a powerful one. "Every act of Violence on our part," he jotted in his notebook, "has been productive of instant redress and other beneficial results."[38]

Those were issues of the past, though, and as Napier looked toward Britain's future in China he had two guides in his library: George Staunton, the voice of caution, on the one hand, and— very far away on the other hand—Hugh Hamilton Lindsay and his recently published account of the *Lord Amherst*'s secret voyage. As for Staunton, Napier despised him. Napier's position of superintendent only existed because the East India Company's monopoly had been revoked, and loyalty to the principles of his appointment aside, he believed the Company had long set a feeble example for British dealings with China. The Company directors were jealous of their trade and "thought of nothing more than pocketting their Dividends," he wrote, even as they had to pay high salaries to their agents in Canton "*as a set off* to the indignities they daily suffered." In other words, they cared nothing about honor and everything about money. George

Staunton was their figurehead and their most prominent public supporter, and so Napier (in a fact that would gratify Jardine) did not
trust him.

After reading through several of Staunton's shorter writings that
warned against the chaos that might be unleashed by free British
trade in China, Napier dismissed them out of hand and commented
that "it is clear that Sir George has only viewed the question as a
favourite Servant of the Company might have been expected to have
done. It is little more than a very unfortunate piece of special pleading
in behalf of the old interests." He questioned Staunton's diplomatic
legacy, especially his long-standing opposition to the kowtow ("why
not conform to the rules of the Court?" Napier wondered). As for
the speech in Parliament in 1833 in which Staunton was cut off while
warning about the necessity of a gradual transition from monopoly to
free trade in Canton, Napier judged it to be "nothing but the exuding
of a perverse spirit." He added, somewhat cruelly, "It is not surprising
that he did not 'get a hearing' in the House." All told, the new superintendent's opinion of George Staunton boiled down to, in his own
words, that "Sir George may be deeply versed in Chinese literature,
but in politics he is a Driveller."[39]

Napier was drawn instead to the other side, and nothing in his
readings excited him more than Lindsay's account of the voyage of the
Lord Amherst, with its claims that the Chinese people were oppressed
by an alien dynasty, that they liked foreigners, and that they wanted
free trade. The reports from Lindsay and Gutzlaff further convinced
Napier that his fantasy of a blockading squadron off the coast of China
was all that would be needed to force the Qing government to open
every port in China to British trade—which, Lindsay argued, had
been the natural state of things before Qianlong confined Western
commerce to Canton in 1760. "I see no reason," Napier wrote after
mulling over Lindsay's account, "why we should not use all means in
our power to oblige and coerce that intrusive government to restore
the old order of affairs, to respect the feelings and wishes of their
conquered people, and to conduct themselves towards *other nations* on
the principles of reciprocity as acknowledged by all civilised states."

If the British people wished it, Napier believed, it would be easy
enough to capture the Tiger's Mouth forts and "destroy every battery

and gunboat along the coast." The navy could at the same time mount a propaganda campaign like Lindsay's—to distribute pamphlets along the Chinese coast "assuring the people that we wage no war against them or their property." The Chinese people would flock to the side of the British, who (as Lindsay promised) shared their desire for free trade, and together the British and the Chinese people would turn against their common enemy, the Manchus who ruled the Qing dynasty. It would then be a simple matter, imagined Lord Napier in one of the most baldly imperialistic proposals any Briton had ever made about China, "to expel the Intruder *beyond the Wall* and restore the Chinese dynasty on our own terms." A new dynasty would reign in Beijing, put on the throne with British aid and answerable to British power behind the scenes. It would be a first step toward turning China into another India.

The *Andromache* arrived at Macao on July 16, 1834, in the midst of a brutal heat wave in which daily temperatures were topping ninety degrees in the shade.[40] Lord Napier disembarked, dressed proudly in his full naval captain's uniform in spite of the heat. It was just as the king had asked of him. Robert Morrison was there to greet Napier and his family at the Chinese customs house—nervously, for Morrison knew that Napier's arrival signaled the end of the Company's factory and therefore the end of his job of twenty-five years (for which the Company did not intend to give him a pension). Morrison assisted one of Napier's daughters in getting off the boat, and was flattered when Lady Napier mentioned that she knew his name already by reputation. That afternoon, Lord Napier assembled the factory members in Macao and read his commission aloud. To Morrison's relief, Napier asked him to serve as his official Chinese secretary—a step up from Morrison's position for the East India Company, for now he would work for the British government itself. He accepted eagerly, and Napier asked him to get rid of his preacher's gown and find a vice consul's uniform to wear instead.[41]

Napier tended to interpret his instructions as he saw fit, but on one minor point he chose to follow them to the letter: Palmerston had told him that when he got to China he should go straight to

Canton and announce himself directly to the Chinese authorities. It was an odd request, in that it contradicted the long-standing practice by which foreigners would wait in Macao for permission from the authorities to proceed to Canton, and then would communicate with the officials of the government only indirectly, through the medium of the Hong merchants. The wording of that passage in the instructions reflected only Palmerston's ignorance of how things worked at Canton, not any particular intent, but Napier took it perfectly literally.[42] Indeed, he was quite happy to ignore past practice because, as he saw it, he had been sent by the king (and imagined himself practically an ambassador), so he should have every right to travel where he wished, when he wished, and to address the officials of the Qing government as an equal.

Following those defective instructions, on July 23 Napier sailed onward to Canton with Morrison in tow, without asking for permission. They had to leave the *Andromache* at anchor below the Tiger's Mouth forts—in the "outer waters," as they were known—because foreign ships of war were not allowed past the forts into the Pearl River. They then proceeded the rest of the way up to Canton in a small cutter and arrived early in the morning of July 25. At the sweltering factory compound in Canton, Napier again read his commission aloud to an assemblage of British traders and gave a copy to the editor of the *Canton Register* for publication in his newspaper. Then he put Morrison to work composing a letter in Chinese to announce his arrival directly to the governor-general—again, following the arbitrary wording of his instructions to the letter.[43]

The governor-general, whose name was Lu Kun, would not accept the letter. Since Napier had come to Canton unannounced, without applying for a permit, Lu Kun had no idea what his business was, only that he had arrived in Macao on a warship and claimed to be in charge of British trade. The British at Canton had always had a taipan, a "chief merchant," the president of the select committee. And the taipans had, with rare exception, communicated only via the Hong merchants. This had been the practice for generations. Indeed, when Lu Kun's predecessor first learned that the East India Company's monopoly might come to an end, he was sufficiently concerned about disorder that he had the Hong merchants tell the British traders they must send home and have their government appoint a new taipan to represent them.[44] Napier, however, insisted that he was not a taipan—not some lowly merchant. He wanted to be treated differently. But he still had no permission to be there.

Lu Kun understood that Napier's arrival meant that the East India Company's role was at an end and a new set of regulations for trade were going to be needed. But he did not have the authority to establish any such regulations himself, without orders from the emperor. So he asked Houqua to meet with Napier, sound out his business, and report back so he could send a memorial (an official government dispatch) to Daoguang asking how trade should be handled going forward. Accordingly, on July 26 Houqua and a colleague visited Napier and explained the governor-general's request that he communicate through them as the British taipans had done in the past. But Napier brushed them off, saying that he didn't need their help. He said he preferred to communicate directly with the governor-general "in the manner befitting His Majesty's Commission and the honour of the British nation."[45] Ignoring Houqua, Napier then sent a delegation of British merchants through the suburbs to the Canton city gate to present his letter for delivery to Lu Kun.

Nobody would take it. After an hour of the British delegates standing outside the gate in the wilting heat while a succession of officials came and went, all of them refusing to accept Napier's message for delivery, Houqua arrived. He pleaded with them to go through himself instead. Following Napier's directions, they gave him the cold shoulder and kept waiting. After a while another official came along and, like the others, refused the letter. Houqua asked if he could just carry it in for them (an offer which Napier later described to Palmerston as "an insidious attempt" to circumvent his authority). Again they ignored him. After several more hours of waiting and chasing around fecklessly after other officials who happened to pass through the gate, the delegation gave up and returned back through the narrow streets of the suburb to the factory compound with Napier's Chinese letter undelivered.

The next day, Houqua came again to visit Napier (who had by this time taken an intense dislike to the elderly Hong merchant, imagining him full of "cunning and duplicity"). Trying to smooth the waters, Houqua suggested that Napier could perhaps just change the address on his message to the governor-general from "letter," which implied equality, to "petition," implying Napier's suppliant status. Napier was aghast. Houqua also shared some documents with Robert Morrison in which it turned out that a mischievous secretary somewhere along the line had given Napier a Chinese name that sounded vaguely like "Napier" but whose literal meaning, Morrison explained delicately, was "Laboriously Vile." Napier was even more aghast.[46]

And that was only part of it. Since Lu Kun did not know what title to use for Napier—being that he insisted he wasn't a taipan—he instead referred to the new chief superintendent as an *yimu*, a term meaning "headman" that was used for tribal chiefs and the like. In one of the more bizarre mistranslations of the time, someone rendered the characters for *yimu* into English literally, and out of context, as "Barbarian Eye." The title was inexplicable, but so, as the British thought, were many things about the Chinese. So nobody questioned it at the time (or later, except for George Staunton, who insisted that the term, properly understood, was actually a perfectly acceptable Chinese rendering of "Foreign Superintendent").[47] In any case, the bizarre translation turned what was at most a mildly derogatory term into something almost menacingly silly. The translated documents sent back to London were full of it, so Palmerston could sit down at his desk at the Foreign Office and puzzle over such constructions as "an English ship of war brought to Canton a Barbarian Eye," and "the said Barbarian Eye did not obey the old regulations." He could read the governor-general's accusation that "the said Barbarian Eye has not at all told plainly what are the matters he has come to attend to," and, when things got out of hand, that "the whole wrong lies on the Barbarian Eye."[48]

Napier's greatest error was that he did not understand that he was not dealing with "China" but rather with one individual official—a powerful one, the governor-general, but still one who was subject to losing his position if he should disappoint the emperor. It didn't matter what Lu Kun felt personally about how Napier communicated with him. What Lu Kun cared about was following established protocol and not inadvertently setting some new precedent, creating expectations in the British that might cause trouble down the road. He had no authority to negotiate a new system of communication or trade, and would do so at the peril of his career. Any of the Company veterans who remained in Canton could have explained to Napier that this was an impossible situation (and if Staunton were the superintendent, this is the point at which he would have retreated to Macao—had he even gone so far as Napier in the first place). But Napier did not trust the Company and he did not want the advice of anyone connected to it.

As it happened, the closest relationships Napier built among the British population in Canton were with the men most likely to advise *against* peaceful acquiescence to the demands of the Chinese government: namely, his fellow Scots Jardine and Matheson. With Jardine especially, who hailed from the same county in Scotland as he did, Napier struck up a quick friendship. Along with the other free traders in their camp (known to others in Canton as the "Scots faction"), Jardine and Matheson provided a social center for Napier in his new home, "a regular Scots party," as he described it. In a personal letter on August 6, he reminisced about how he "dined with Jardine—drank tea by starlight on a terrace on top of the house and had a long crack about Dumfriesshire." Jardine, he bragged, was "the first merchant here and said to be worth thousands and perhaps millions."[49] Writing home to Charles Grant, the president of the Board of Control, Napier insisted he kept his own counsel and was not influenced by any of the factions within the Canton British community, but he did confess that his views on China and trade matched so well with those of the prominent Scottish trader that it might appear he had "fallen into the hands of Jardine."[50]

Nearly lost in the middle of Napier's diplomatic tangle was that on August 1, suffering from an illness that had been bothering him since before the superintendent's arrival, Robert Morrison died at only fifty-two years old. Though in many ways Morrison had been a failure as a missionary per se, having converted no more than a dozen Chinese to Christianity after nearly thirty years of labor, he would be remembered as a larger-than-life figure: the pioneer of China missions, the one who first opened the gates for the masses of Protestants who would flock to China in the century to come. He left a troubling legacy, however, in the disconcerting marriage of convenience that made it possible for him to remain at Canton. With his language work he had made himself useful in a way that legions who came after him would repeat—indeed, the Protestant missionaries in China would always be deeply tied to the forces of trade and the state; they would be the interpreters, the enablers, the explorers. Morrison had lived a tenuous balance between his religious work and his service to the Company's trade (and in the end, to the government). But where others saw moral conflict, he plowed his way through and made his compromises and hoped always for the best. In some ways, though, it was better for him that he did not live to see what was to come.

———

By August 9, Napier was still unable to get his letter delivered to the governor-general and his nerves were starting to fray. He wrote to Palmerston, complaining of confusion over his instructions from home and expressing frustration over the constant demands that he leave Canton and return to Macao. His anger boiled over as he recounted an attempt by Houqua and some other Hong merchants to convene a general meeting where he was certain they would try to turn the British traders against him. He bragged of his defiance in staying put: his mere presence at Canton, he told Palmerston, was actually a sign of strength. There were reportedly forty thousand Chinese troops on garrison duty in the city who could toss him out anytime the governor-general wanted, yet they had not, which he attributed not to Lu Kun's forbearance but to the "imbecility of the Government."[51]

Napier did not suffer his humiliation easily, and his reports—a one-way conversation with Palmerston, given how long it would take for any response to get back to him—veered ever more dizzily away from the spirit of his instructions. On August 14, he declared to the foreign secretary that in dealing with a country like China, "His Majesty's Government [should not] be ruled by the ordinary forms prescribed among civilized people." Governor-General Lu Kun was a "presumptuous savage," he wrote. China's dynastic rulers weren't even Chinese, he told Palmerston, they were alien Manchus, and the Daoguang emperor himself was nothing more than an "intruder" in the country. The *real* people of China—that is, the Han Chinese, at least those who weren't government officials—all wanted British trade (of this, Lindsay and the ever-hopeful free traders had convinced him); it was just their illegitimate government that was holding them back. The Manchus may have been fierce and strong once upon a time, wrote Napier, but now, after generations of rule, they were "a wretched people, inconceivably degraded, unfit for action or exertion." [52]

What it all came down to, Napier told Palmerston, was that the British would be best off using their military power to force the Manchu government to open China's ports once and for all. Britain's government should tell the Daoguang emperor, "Adopt this, or abide the consequences." Napier admitted that those consequences might include "the horrors of a bloody war against a defenceless people," but if it came to that, he was certain that it could be pulled off without any loss of British life (of this, again, the free traders and Lindsay had convinced him)—"and," he insisted with the utmost confidence, "we have justice on our side." After less than three weeks in Canton as the new superintendent charged with maintaining a peaceful trading relationship, Napier had already made up his mind that what China really needed was a war.

For all of Napier's complaints about Chinese obstinacy, however, whenever Lu Kun made any show of compromise Napier gloated as if in triumph. On August 22, he learned from Houqua that the governor-general was sending three high-ranking prefectural officials to see him the next day, a concession Napier reported to Palmerston as "a strong instance of their vacillation, or want of steady purpose and determination." [53] But then the officials showed up late, and Napier was back to feeling insulted. He chastised them, through Morrison's son John Robert, that whereas in the past they had only dealt with the employees of a private merchant company, they were now dealing instead with "the officers appointed by His Britannic Majesty," who were "by no means inclined to submit to such indignities" as being made to wait for meetings to start. When they asked, on behalf of the governor-general, when he was planning to return to Macao, he responded stiffly that it would be decided "entirely according to his own convenience." After a tense and inconclusive meeting, one of the officials confided to him that it would be "very unpleasant were the two nations to come to a rupture." Bristling, Napier replied that it wouldn't necessarily be so unpleasant for the British.

Giving up on his government channels, and faced with a threat that trade would be suspended if he did not leave, Napier took his case to the people. Certain that all of the shopkeepers in Canton were rooting for him because they wanted free trade, he got Morrison's son to draft up a Chinese poster, which was lithographed and plastered all over the street corners near the factory compound on August 26. In the poster, Napier declared that he had been insulted and humiliated by the corrupt governor-general Lu Kun, whose "ignorance and obstinacy" were allowing the Hong merchants to shut down Britain's trade at Canton. Napier tried to turn the local Cantonese against the officials who governed them: "Thousands of industrious Chinese who live by the European trade must suffer ruin and discomfort through the perversity of their Government," he wrote. He promised that the only thing his people wanted was "to trade with all China, on principles of mutual benefit," and that the British would never rest until they reached that goal. The Qing governor-general would "find it as easy to stop the current of the Canton river, as to carry into effect the insane determination" of shutting down trade.[54]

It is unclear what Napier thought his poster would accomplish (a popular uprising of Chinese tailors and tea porters, apparently), but a propaganda battle in Chinese waged on the walls of Canton was not conducive to ending in his favor. The next day, another poster went up, this one from the Chinese authorities. "A lawless foreign slave, Napier, has issued a notice," it began. "We know not how such a dog barbarian of an outside nation as you, can have the audacious presumption to call yourself Superintendent." The tone went downhill from there, suggesting along the way that Napier's head should be cut off and displayed on a stake.

On the evening of September 4, Lord Napier was in the middle of dinner with five guests in the cavernous, nearly empty dining hall of the British factory when all of the servants in the complex rushed into the room at once to warn him that armed men had appeared at the front gate. Rising from the table with his guests, he trotted downstairs to find that Chinese soldiers had surrounded the building and a large crowd of onlookers was congregating in the plaza in front. An official was nailing an edict from the governor-general to the factory wall, announcing the official shutdown of trade and ordering all Chinese employees to vacate the British factory immediately. The large building quickly emptied of its servants, porters, and guards, leaving Lord Napier and his handful of companions all alone inside its echoing shell. Someone said the crowd was going to burn the factory down that night.[55]

So Napier called in the gunboats. He had two at his disposal, the *Andromache* and another called the *Imogene*, both sixth-rate Royal Navy frigates with fifty-four guns between them. Judging the crisis sufficiently extraordinary to defy his instructions from Palmerston and Grey to prevent British ships of war from entering the inner waters, Napier ordered them to force the passage of the Tiger's Mouth forts—whatever the resistance—and take up positions in Whampoa "for the more efficient protection of British subjects and their property." No longer the successor to Macartney and Amherst, he would now carry forth the legacy of Captains Weddell and Maxwell. After sending his instructions to the ships, he addressed a letter to the governor-general and Hong merchants declaring that they had "opened the preliminaries of war." Referring to his good friend King William IV, Napier warned that "His Imperial Majesty will not permit such folly, wickedness, and cruelty as [you] have been guilty of, since my arrival here, to go unpunished."[56] (Actually, Napier had no way to know just how wrong he was about that; the British government's response to his call for a war against China—which would not reach Canton until far too late—told him sharply to follow his instructions and behave. As the foreign secretary chided him, "It is not by force and violence that His Majesty intends to establish a commercial intercourse between his subjects and China.")[57]

Unfortunately for Napier, the ships of war caused less of a stir than he had hoped. They did indeed force the passage of the Tiger's Mouth, but due to adverse winds they got bogged down and were caught up in a long and stubborn exchange of cannon fire with the forts. In the heaviest fighting yet between Chinese and British forces, Napier's two frigates unloaded more than seven hundred rounds of shot into the Chinese defenses.[58] Two British sailors were killed and several more wounded before the forts were hammered into silence. But by the time the *Andromache* and *Imogene* finally dragged themselves into the anchorage at Whampoa, delayed further as Napier dithered over what orders to give them, Chinese forces had sunk heavy obstacles upriver to block their further progress toward Canton. So, despite the hostilities, the ships of war never got close enough to Canton to be visible from the factory compound and they failed to strike the awe and panic Napier intended.

Meanwhile, on the ground, the most damning problem for Napier was that the British merchants refused to follow his lead. They were of a dozen different minds as to how he should act, but mostly all they cared about was getting their trade reopened. Jardine and Matheson supported Napier's taking a hard line, but others did not, asking him instead to please give up and return to Macao, to obey the governor-general's orders so the ban on trade would be lifted. Some of them questioned whether Napier really had any authority at all, and said that if the Chinese would not recognize the chief superintendent then his mission had no purpose. They started sending him petitions to complain of the financial losses he was causing them.[59] Meanwhile, Governor-General Lu Kun made it clear that he had no issues with the merchants themselves—Napier alone was the reason why trade had been shut down, and normal commerce would resume if he left. Napier felt undermined by his own people. The merchants from Liverpool, Glasgow, and London, he complained to Palmerston, "care not one straw about the dignity of the Crown or the presence of a Superintendent."[60] Though Napier had assumed that the British free traders would all rally to him as their protector and champion, in the end they did not. Such was the nature of freedom.[61]

Embarrassed by the failure of his countrymen to fall into line behind him, Napier also felt desperately vulnerable inside the huge, empty factory building, out of reach of his gunboats and eating salt provisions from storage since the Chinese soldiers outside wouldn't let any food past his gate. He knew that he would bear the consequences if British trade suffered serious harm from his personal actions. He was also, coincidentally, starting to feel an illness of some kind coming on. So finally he backed down. The governor-general had called

The *Imogene* and *Andromache* forcing the passage of the Tiger's Mouth

his bluff; Napier had no power at all. On September 21, he sent word to his two gunboats that their services were no longer needed. Then he left Canton, his spirit broken. Trade resumed as normal a few days later. Britain's first chief superintendent of trade, the proud veteran of the Napoleonic Wars and personal friend of King William had, as he saw it, been brought low by the likes of Houqua and the "presumptuous savage" Lu Kun. After a slow and brutally uncomfortable five-day trip down from Canton with unexplained delays under heavy Chinese military escort, Napier arrived pale and feverish at Macao on September 26. Two weeks later he was dead.

CHAPTER II

Means of Solution

Conditions in China were getting worse under Daoguang's reign. By the time he took the throne, and to some degree beginning even with his father, Jiaqing, it becomes easier to speak of the empire each sovereign inherited rather than what he created or built. They, and the emperors and regents to follow, would have their successes—the dynasty would, after all, survive into the early twentieth century—but rarely did they leave China in a more solid position than they had found it. By the early nineteenth century, an inexorable process of decline was setting in, the slow setting of a sun that had reached its zenith under Qianlong in the late 1700s. Jiaqing had done his best, making strong efforts to rein in the corruption of the military and suppress the White Lotus and other rebellions. But under the rule of his son Daoguang, new problems would plague the empire even as old ones kept coming back in different forms.

Patronage, bribery, and embezzlement were the accepted norm among civil officials, especially in the lower orders. Population pressures on the land continued unabated, and Han Chinese settlers seeking an escape from the crowding continued to move into mountainous regions of the empire that had long been home to indigenous peoples, sparking incidents of ethnic violence. A breakdown of trust between the government and peasants worsened. The military was weakened by Jiaqing's cost-cutting measures after the White Lotus campaigns. Through the 1830s, internal rebellions erupted in different parts of the empire with regularity, every year or two—some led by religious sects similar to the White Lotus, others by rebel factions bonded together by regional or ethnic ties. The many divisions that ran naturally through a vast and diverse multiethnic empire were turning more frequently and more visibly into fractures.

Opium wove its way right through the tattering fabric of this restive society, the single most visible symbol of the Chinese government's inability to control its people. In spite of Daoguang's strong desire to control the drug, coastal enforcements on smuggling had failed so completely that by the later 1830s when a foreign ship materialized near the coast it would find not naval patrols but thousands of buyers standing along the shore and whistling to it in hopes that it would drop anchor and sell to them.[1] A major north–south land transport route for opium through Hunan province formed the locus of a series of uprisings that took place in central China in 1836, and imperial troops transferred inland to pacify them turned out to be such heavy users of opium themselves that they could barely fight. Ironically, they had acquired their drug habits in the course of their previous mission, which was to police the smugglers on the coast near Canton.[2]

China's rising domestic unrest caught the attention of foreigners in Canton, who worried about damage to tea and silk production from the disturbances in the interior. However, some of them also sensed opportunity in the ones that took place on China's periphery. In 1833, an explosive revolt of aborigines on Taiwan threatened Qing imperial control of the island for several months, in the midst of which it was announced in Britain's parliament that Taiwan had "declared its independence of the Chinese."[3] Some foreigners had already begun touting Taiwan as a potential British colony, a base from which they could conduct their trade with China free from the restrictions of Canton. They argued that, morally speaking, to take control of Taiwan would be nothing like trying to seize territory on the Chinese mainland, because Taiwan had been a Dutch possession prior to its conquest by Qianlong's grandfather Kangxi, so they judged it to be merely a colony of the Qing Empire rather than essential Chinese territory. According to one Canton English-language newspaper, the Taiwanese were a conquered people, "vassals of China; not willingly, but in consequence of bloody wars," and so even foreigners who opposed aggression toward China shouldn't object to the British taking control of the island, which the paper judged would be praiseworthy even if only for the sake of "ridding its people of the tyranny of the Chinese."[4]

While outbreaks of rebellion and interethnic violence were urgent threats to the government, they were still localized. More widespread by far, and therefore more insidious, were growing problems in the Chinese economy. By the mid-1830s, Daoguang's empire was cascading into depression. Grain prices deflated, driving down farming incomes. Unemployment rose and the government's already insufficient tax revenues declined. It became prohibitively expensive to build and maintain public works like flood-control dikes properly, which led to shoddy construction and neglected maintenance, giving way in turn to destructive episodes of flooding. To compound the failings of human government, nature sent China wildly unpredictable rains during several of those years, gutting agricultural productivity and afflicting parts of the empire with episodes of famine.[5]

There was nothing the government could do about the weather, but the root cause of the economic turmoil in the 1830s, and the problem from which many of the others grew, was a human one: China's monetary system had gone haywire. It was mainly a problem of currency, of which the Qing dynasty had two primary forms: copper for small transactions and silver for large ones. Copper came in minted coins (with holes through the middle so they could be strung on a loop for convenience), while domestic silver—nearly pure and known in English as "sycee"—was unminted, traded by weight in units of measurement called taels that were just under an ounce. In normal times, a tael of silver was worth a thousand copper coins, and, value for value, the excessive difficulty of moving large amounts of copper between provinces meant that silver was the medium through which all long-distance trade was conducted within the empire. Silver was also, significantly, the basis on which tax quotas were assessed. By contrast, copper was the medium of the rural marketplace and menial wages.[6] Nearly all of the income and savings of the lower classes of China—farmers, hired laborers, craftspeople—were in copper coins.

The crisis was that the value of silver had begun to rise sharply, and as it rose the exchange rate between silver and copper skewed out of control. From the ideal rate of 1,000 copper coins per tael of silver in the eighteenth century (even less at times, which was a boon for peasants since it meant their copper money was worth more), it had risen to 1,200 by the time Daoguang came to the throne. By 1830 it reached 1,365 copper coins per tael of silver and showed no signs of stopping.[7] Since taxes were assessed in a fixed amount of silver, which had to be purchased with copper currency, this meant that by the early 1830s the peasants of China had suffered a nearly 40 percent increase in their effective tax burdens for reasons none fully understood. And as with nearly every problem in the empire, the corruption of officials made a bad situation even worse, as tax collectors commonly charged even higher rates of exchange so they could pocket the proceeds. By the late 1830s, some regions were reporting copper–silver exchange rates as high as 1,600 to 1, with tax collectors independently demanding as much as 2,000 copper coins per tael of silver owed.[8] This dramatic decline in the worth of copper currency was disastrous for the general population, piling economic hardship on the poor who could scarcely bear it and sparking widespread tax protests that layered on top of all the other sources of dissent against the government. But although the emperor could occasionally grant tax amnesties to regions afflicted by floods or drought, the government quite desperately needed every tael of revenue it could get and so the exactions continued.

According to some Chinese scholars, in particular the admirers of Bao Shichen, the fundamental culprit was obvious: it was all the fault of foreign trade. As they saw it, the situation was just as Bao had predicted back in 1820 when he warned that China's silver would eventually disappear into the hands of foreign merchants. As the value of silver rose through the 1830s, it was an easy case to make that the metal was expensive because it was becoming scarce, and it was becoming scarce because it was pouring out of the country through

the commerce with foreigners—especially the foreign drug wholesalers. By that line of reasoning, the economic miseries of a peasant in
Jiangsu province, a thousand miles from the center of Western commerce in Canton, could nevertheless still be blamed on the foreign
ships that anchored at Lintin and Whampoa and plied their secret
courses up and down the Chinese coast.

They were partially correct. Payments to foreign opium dealers
were indeed made largely in sycee silver, which was illegal to export.
So in those transactions, domestic Chinese silver passed into the
hands of foreigners like Jardine and Matheson. However, foreigners
were also buying huge amounts of tea and other commodities from
the Hong merchants in Canton, so most of that silver should have
been able to flow right back into China via the aboveboard trade. The
catch, though, was that the Hong merchants refused to take sycee silver as payment for tea or silk. Since it was illegal to export sycee in the
first place, even to receive it *back* from a foreigner would implicate the
Chinese merchant with the taint of illegality. The Hong merchants
thus would only take silver in the form of Spanish dollars, the sole
legal currency for use in China's foreign trade (insofar as they originated outside the country). The odd cohabitation of legal and illegal
commerce at Canton thus meant that bulk sycee silver could come
out of China (illegally) but it had no way to go back in. As supplies
of it piled up uselessly in the hands of country traders, the East India
Company—aided by Jardine and Matheson—finally began shipping
it back to London, where it could simply be melted down and sold as
bullion, with the proceeds remitted to the opium traders' accounts in
India.[9]

Even with that outflow of sycee silver, however, the inflow of
Spanish dollars to purchase tea and silk at Canton should have been
able to maintain a relatively steady overall silver supply in China (and
in fact, since the late eighteenth century Spanish dollars had been
preferred even over native sycee in some of China's most important domestic markets).[10] But on that count, a range of forces far
beyond China's borders came into play. First, it had been American merchants who brought most of the silver to China in the early
nineteenth century (fully one-third of Mexico's entire silver output
between 1805 and 1834 was carried to China by Americans). But a

shift in U.S. government monetary policy in 1834 made silver more expensive for American merchants, so they switched abruptly to using bills of exchange—which were acceptable to the Hong merchants but resulted in a decline in the amount of tangible silver entering the country from abroad. With the drop in American imports, China, which for centuries had been the world's largest net importer of silver, unexpectedly turned into an exporter of the metal.[11]

In the even bigger picture, though, what the Chinese scholars who blamed foreign trade and opium for the scarcity of silver in China did not realize was that it wasn't just a Chinese problem: by the 1820s, silver was becoming scarce everywhere. Most of the world's supply at this time had come from mines in Spanish Mexico and Peru (thus the importance of the Spanish dollar), but national revolutions in Latin America that began in the 1810s shut down those mines and choked off the world's largest fonts of the precious metal. Global production of silver declined by nearly half during the 1810s—the same time its value began to creep upward in China—and it continued to decline during the decade that followed. The ramping up of the opium trade in 1820s China thus coincided fatefully with the onset of a global slump in silver output that would last for the next thirty years.[12]

Regardless of where the specific blame lay, it was a devastating confluence of economic forces for China: the loss of sycee through the opium smuggling trade, the global scarcity of silver after the Latin American revolutions, and the drying up of American silver imports into China together helped cause a catastrophic decline in the empire's supply of the metal. And it was a vicious cycle, for as silver became more valuable in China, wealthy families and businessmen would hoard it, removing even more from circulation and making the problem worse.

Given that most of these factors were beyond the ken of China's scholars and government officials, by the mid-1830s a consensus was emerging that the economic crisis was primarily, if not entirely, the fault of illegal foreign trade. And while the moral effects of opium smoking had long been disparaged by the emperor (if ignored by the people and most officials), it was becoming increasingly clear that the *economic* effects of the drug trade might be far more threatening to public order than anything having to do with public health or moral virtue. Even peasants who did not use or deal in opium, even those who lived hundreds of miles from the foreign trade on the coast, suffered the economic distress of their copper money plummeting in value. That distress could provide the fuel for new rebellions, even a revolution, and so the silver crisis—which was to say the opium crisis—finally emerged as the single most urgent problem for Daoguang's government.

The question remained of how to solve it. Shutting down foreign trade, as Bao Shichen had once recommended, was clearly unrealistic (even Bao himself no longer supported this position). As Cheng Hanzhang and others had warned, even if the Qing navy could police the entire coast—which it couldn't—closing down foreign trade entirely would likely provoke a war with Great Britain that China had no capacity to fight. Such warnings were confirmed by the relative ease with which Napier's two gunships had forced their way past the Tiger's Mouth forts in 1834, bringing home in shocking fashion the unpreparedness of Chinese forces to hold off Britain's ships of war, for those forts were supposed to be the strongest point of defense on China's southern coast. Governor-General Lu Kun tried to minimize the scale of the defeat in his reports, but Daoguang responded with a contemptuous edict ordering the degradation of the commander who led the defense of the Tiger's Mouth against Napier's ships. He also criticized Lu Kun for having "sacrificed the prestige of our nation and failed in the duties of his position," but allowed him to continue as governor-general under strict warning not to fail again.[13]

It was clear that military force was not an option for keeping the British under control. The only measure that had ever worked with them—and, importantly, it had worked yet again when Lu Kun stood his ground against Napier—was the threat of withholding trade. That threat, however, applied only to the commerce in tea and silk at Canton; the opium trade at Lintin and along the coast was so far outside the government's control that withholding it from the British was simply not an option. Of course, if the main problem was simply the loss of sycee silver, the government could have attacked it from the Chinese side by cracking down harder on domestic traffickers who sent silver out of the country—but many provincial officials were reluctant to try harder to suppress those domestic criminal networks out of fear that they would just provoke further incidents of mass local violence like the uprisings the dynasty could already barely contain.

As for solutions, Lu Kun reported on the sad state of military affairs to Daoguang in early November 1834, in a quiet moment after Napier had removed his war ships from Canton and returned to Macao (though before Lu Kun knew of the superintendent's death). It appeared that the tensions with the British had been settled, so the governor-general reflected on the bigger picture. "What the English rely on is nothing more than their ships," he told the emperor. "Those ships are large and strong and they can carry a great number of cannons. But our own naval vessels must be able to patrol in shallow coastal waterways so they cannot be as large as those of the foreigners."[14] Lu Kun worried that Chinese naval forces were unable to police foreign opium vessels—if the forces from one province drove one off, it would just sail out to sea and then return to another province to resume its selling. He worried especially that the British smugglers were becoming too familiar with the topography of China's coastline and could easily find their way around the ports and islands. "This is very wrong," he wrote.

He was tentative in his recommendations, though, mainly forwarding without endorsement various suggestions he heard around him in Canton. One idea was to open more ports. "Some say we should go back to the old regulations and let them trade at Fujian again," he wrote, "levying taxes and exchanging only goods for goods." In other words, the emperor could revert to the system in place before James Flint, before Qianlong restricted the British to Canton. Lu Kun presented that suggestion only secondhand, distancing himself from it in case it should displease the emperor. But there was another, even more radical idea floating around Canton, which Lu Kun also mentioned in passing, in just as noncommittal a way as the first. "Some others," he wrote, "say we should relax the ban on growing poppies."

Indeed, the idea had been gaining traction in certain academic and official circles in Canton that the most effective solution to the smuggling crisis would be for China to legalize opium. And despite his hesitancy in bringing it up to the emperor, Lu Kun was in favor of that policy.[15] The "presumptuous savage," as Napier had called him, was in fact a remarkably pragmatic and flexible administrator. He had successfully led the suppression of multiple internal rebellions and had earned his high position at Canton through skill and accomplishment. Far from being some kind of unthinking automaton, even as he was embroiled in his diplomatic head-to-head with Napier in 1834 he was already being won over to the sensibility of a new policy that would completely upend the measures Daoguang had pursued for his entire reign.

The specific argument that got Lu Kun's attention was an essay by a scholar named Wu Lanxiu who directed one of Canton's Confucian academies. In that essay, titled "The Alleviation of Suffering," Wu Lanxiu argued that to shut down foreign trade in order to stem the flow of silver would cause far worse problems for China than it would solve. "The countries of the Western seas have been sending their ships here to trade for over a thousand years," he wrote, "and westerners have lived in Macao for more than two centuries. The only ones that sell opium are the English. So should we cut off trade just with Great Britain? Or should we cut off trade with all of the Western countries?"[16] Cutting off trade with Britain alone would not solve the problem, he went on (presumably because other countries would step in to take their place). But given how many Chinese people were involved directly or indirectly with the legal foreign trade, if the government were to shut it down the blow to the domestic economy would be terrible. "Tens of thousands of our people who live along the southeastern coast will suddenly lose their jobs," he wrote. "They would have no means of making a living, and at best they would wind up banding together as criminals and pirates. At worst, they could start a rebellion. This is how major trouble in the southeast could begin." The economy of southeast China was, as he saw it, far more dependent on Western trade than critics nearer the capital imagined.

The solution, Wu Lanxiu argued, lay not in changing how China dealt with foreigners but in changing how it dealt with opium. He argued that the harsher the government's laws against the drug had become, the more counterproductive they had proven to be. "It's not as if the laws are not already strict, or the punishments not severe," he wrote, "yet the bad practices continue as before. Why? Because cor-

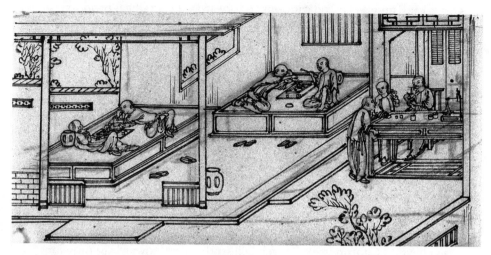

An opium den

rupt government staff use the laws to enrich themselves. The stricter the laws, the larger the bribes." There was, he believed, no realistic way under the imperial bureaucracy as it then existed to suppress opium by force of law—which suggested that the government's long-term obsession with punishment was misguided. "To an individual it may seem like opium is a major problem while silver is a small one," he wrote. "But from the perspective of the empire as a whole, it is opium that is minor. *Silver* is the major problem."

Wu Lanxiu argued that for the sake of ending the silver drain and rebalancing China's economy, the opium trade should be brought back into the open and treated like the commerce in any other commodity. "If you look at the old regulations, opium was taxed as a medicine," he wrote. "Why not order the foreign traders to pay this tax as before? Then they can exchange their opium directly with the Hong merchants for tea." If the transactions for opium took place in the open at Canton, then merchants would use only foreign dollars in their trade with outsiders, not Chinese sycee. Eventually the flow of silver would be reversed again and the currency crisis would end. "By such means, we can trade in all the goods of the world but still keep our silver in the country," he concluded. "In ten years, the economy will recover."

Lu Kun was far too cautious to forward such a radical proposal to Daoguang under his own name. Since it so dramatically contradicted the emperor's existing policy it was risky even for a senior provincial official like himself (especially as he had been put on notice for failing to keep Napier's ships from entering the Pearl River). But he was nevertheless, in the words of a contemporary, "filled with admiration" for Wu Lanxiu's essay.[17] Along with a handful of writings by other scholars from his academy arguing similar themes, Lu Kun in the end forwarded Wu Lanxiu's essay to the capital in the form of a small book bearing the innocuous title *The Private Views of the Canton Scholars*.

Without official endorsement, it was questionable whether Wu Lanxiu's proposal would gain any kind of consideration from the emperor, but at least Lu Kun ensured that it had a chance of reaching beyond Canton itself. Nevertheless, the trend toward suppression continued. That same year, Daoguang issued a new slate of harsher punishments for opium use. Existing punishments of officials would increase. Commoners and soldiers convicted of smoking opium would now be punished with one hundred strokes of the heavy cane and two months in the cangue (a plank of wood into which their neck and hands were locked, similar to the stocks of Puritan New England). The new punishments extended even to the users' families: if a young man was caught with opium, his father would be punished for the crime of failing to control and guide his children.[18]

———

In England, meanwhile, a different conversation on the Chinese opium trade was beginning to take shape. One effect of the intense debate over the East India Company's monopoly in the early 1830s had been that the opium trade finally came into public view in Great Britain. Witnesses before the East India committees of Parliament testified at length about the nature of the India and China trades, regaling the committee members with intricate descriptions of the overall smuggling commerce—how the opium was grown under Company monopoly in Bengal, how it was transported and sold at Lintin, how much money it brought in, and especially how much the Company had come to rely on the opium monopoly for its bottom line (convincingly enough that the House of Commons committee acknowledged, against George Staunton's protest, that "it does not appear advisable to abandon so important a source of revenue").[19]

As the full scale and moral implications of the illegal trade came to light, the traders involved did not find a warm reception. Indeed, the very fact of the opium commerce was raised as yet another reason why the East India Company's control over trade with China should be abolished. As James Buckingham, a champion of the free press in India who represented the industrial borough of Sheffield in the House of Commons, put it, the East India Company "cultivated this opium for no other purpose than for smuggling it into China, against the laws and edicts of the empire; and as had been truly said, of poisoning the health, and destroying the morals of the people of that country." It was painful, he said, "to think what a vast amount of evil had been already created by this trade."[20]

Although Jardine and his faction in Canton, and the industrialists in Great Britain, were technically on the same side of the free-trade issue, their moral principles varied widely. Buckingham (as with many of the industrialists) did not countenance the smuggling of contraband as part of his vision of what free trade really meant. In *his* vision of the future, since private merchants would be at liberty to carry ordinary British manufactures to China instead of just the "deleterious drug" from India, they would in time be able to abandon the opium trade completely. A "wholesome and reciprocally beneficial commerce would be created," he said, "instead of the mischievous and demoralizing traffic" that existed. He did not blame the individual country traders for selling opium, though—rather, he laid all guilt for the trade squarely on the East India Company. "It was they who furnished the opium from India," he said, "and their supercargoes at Canton who licensed the smugglers in China, so that the beginning and the end of this illicit and contraband trade was theirs."

With the lifting of the East India Company's monopoly, responsibility for the conduct of British opium traders in China shifted from the Company to the British government itself—little as that government wanted to deal with it. In 1833, with the end of the monopoly looming, a former president of the Canton select committee wrote an open letter to Charles Grant, the president of the Board of Control who had shepherded the free-trade legislation, to tell him, in so many words, that the British government now owned the problem of its national drug dealers. "To any friend to humanity it is a painful subject of contemplation that we should continue to pour this black and envenomed poison into the sources of human happiness and well-being," he wrote. "The misery and demoralization which it creates are almost beyond belief; but we console ourselves with the reflection, that if we did not poison the Chinese at this round rate, someone else would." [21] The breadth and scale of opium consumption in China, he warned Grant, were shocking: the Canton governor-general's palace had recently burned down because one of his secretaries had fallen asleep while smoking opium. He relayed Karl Gutzlaff's report that the Daoguang emperor's eldest son, the heir apparent, had died of an opium overdose. The country traders' imports of the drug from India had by 1833 reached twenty thousand chests per year—worth more than their imports of cotton and making up more than two-thirds of all the private commerce that went on in the shadow of the Company's tea monopoly. [22] The traffic was not about to go away of its own accord.

Nevertheless, the government initially tried to pretend the trade did not exist. Though Palmerston's instructions to Napier made euphemistic reference to the "adventures" of British traders who were sending ships up the coast, he told Napier not to encourage them, but, in keeping with the self-contradictory nature of those instructions, he also told Napier not to interfere with them either. Napier himself never expressed any concrete opinion on the subject; his only concern was Canton, where the "real" trade went on, not the amorphous world of Lintin and the coast. But public opposition was rising, especially among the missionary community (even Karl Gutzlaff, despite his work for Jardine, always condemned opium publicly). [23] In the liberal wave of 1830s Britain, an era of political reform, free trade, and surging moral campaigns, opium had few defenders. A stream of vivid and damning reports made its way back to England by way of personal letters and reprinted articles from the Canton and Calcutta press, describing in grim detail the misery of Chinese opium smokers. By 1834, emboldened by the successful abolition of slavery after a decades-long fight, some moralists in England began agitating for an end to what they were coming to think of as Britain's other great crime against humanity.

The first major broadside in the anti-opium movement came from a pair of activists, one a director of the London Missionary Society and the other a layman (a deliberate combination, to make the point that this wasn't just a religious cause), whose 1835 pamphlet *No Opium!* described itself as "the first public call for the Abolition of the Opium Trade."[24] The key word there was "abolition," for against those who claimed that the opium trade was no worse than selling tobacco, they argued that it should instead be understood in the same terms as the slave trade. "Our great manufacturers themselves will not long submit to the degradation of being identified abroad with smugglers," they predicted. "Public opinion will soon, and as surely, put down all such traffic, as it has annihilated the slave trade and slavery."[25]

The authors framed their pamphlet in commercial terms, arguing that opium undermined beneficial trade by keeping "real *goods* subordinate to the sale of poison," as well as lowering the character of the British in Chinese eyes. In the explicit language of free trade, they quoted an American merchant who charged that opium "destroys industry, and annihilates its products." Those who traded in it were no more respectable than if they "ministered to suicide in China," the authors wrote, supplying as they did "that which kills both the body and the soul at the same time."[26]

The authors acknowledged that some of their British readers might be surprised to hear the opium trade described in such depraved terms, given how rarely it had been discussed, let alone called a crime, in Great Britain. But they promised that this sense of newness would fade in time. They would continue to bring forward public evidence to back up their claims about the horror of opium, they promised, "until they are as familiar as the horrors of slavery and the Slave Trade." Britain's poisoning of China, as they saw it, should no longer be allowed to remain invisible. "'NO OPIUM!'" they declared, "must be made as loud and general a watch-word, as 'NO SLAVERY' was, if we would, as a nation, 'fear God or regard man.'"[27]

Jardine and Matheson, meanwhile, wasted no time in trying to capi-
talize on Lord Napier's death. The superintendent hadn't been in the
ground two months before they submitted a petition to the king in
council, demanding satisfaction for China's heinous insults to Lord
Napier and the British nation. Sixty-four British in Canton signed
it, a group that included several of their fellow opium smugglers (not
so described, of course), along with sundry employees of their firms
and some supportive ship's captains who happened to be in port at
the time. All coyness from their previous petition was abandoned.
This time they demanded, unequivocally and without mincing words,
a naval attack on China. They called on the king to send a full-
fledged ambassador, backed up by a war fleet, to demand reparation
for China's crimes—among which were the insults "wantonly heaped
upon" Napier by the authorities in Canton (whom they blamed for
his death); an ostensibly degrading reference to King William IV as
"reverently submissive" in a Chinese edict; and, in a truly baffling
contortion of logic, the "insult offered to your Majesty's flag" when
Chinese defenders had fired on the *Andromache* and *Imogene* as they
forced their way past the Tiger's Mouth forts.[28]

One of their petition's most pernicious claims—which would
become a mantra of sorts for the proponents of war—was that there
was no risk to Britain in undertaking such a mission. Even with just
a small force ("two frigates and three or four armed vessels of light
draft, together with a steam vessel, all fully manned"), they insisted it
would be a simple matter to blockade most of the waterborne trade
of the Qing Empire, "intercepting its revenues in their progress to
the capital, and . . . taking possession of all the armed vessels of the
country." Having thus promised that a fleet of six or seven British
vessels could capture the entire Chinese navy and cripple the trade of
an empire numbering more than three hundred million people, they
went on to assure the king that such an action would also be unlikely
to provoke a full-scale war with China. Rather, they insisted in yet
another bewildering flight of fancy, it would be "the surest course for
avoiding the danger of such a collision." In other words, the best and
perhaps only way to *avoid* a prolonged war with the Chinese was to
attack them immediately and decisively. With that petition—which
they wrote, organized, and were the first to sign—William Jardine

and James Matheson stepped forth from the shadows and staked out their clear position as the leaders of the war faction.

Outside of Jardine and Matheson's group, however, others in Canton did not see what all the fuss was about. Houqua, for one, thought the matter was already settled. As he explained to an American friend, "We have had great trouble with a high officer sent here from England who knew nothing of our customs and was not fortunate in his advisers. He ordered his vessels of war to commit certain outrages with the expectation of thereby intimidating our Government, but was at last compelled to yield every point and return to Macao."[29] The showdown was over, normal trade had resumed, and it seemed that life in Canton would go on as before.

In a similar vein, John Murray Forbes told a London correspondent that he didn't expect "any serious ill effects to the trade from the defeat of Lord Napier." Indeed, the superintendent's failure to intimidate the governor-general at Canton struck him as clear evidence that the cowardice of the Chinese had been exaggerated. Contrary to what Hugh Hamilton Lindsay and William Jardine would have others believe, it appeared the Chinese government was not likely to back down and grant concessions if threatened with violence. Forbes predicted that the British would abandon their demand for direct communication with the governor-general and "it will be found best to intrust British interests to a consul who shall negociate as other consuls have so long done with the Hong merchants."[30] In other words, a peaceful return to the status quo. (He was thus amused to learn that Jardine and Matheson's group were actually asking for a military strike intended, as he joked to his cousin, to "avenge the insult the governor-general put upon their beloved Sovereign in calling him 'heretofore Reverently Obedient and submissive.'")[31]

It did not help Jardine and Matheson's cause that the new superintendent, succeeding Napier, was a longtime Company man named John Davis who stiffly objected to their demand for reparations. He also detested them as a group—as one of his correspondents explained to Palmerston's undersecretary, Davis was "disgusted with the vulgar rabble of free-traders into whose hands Lord Napier was indiscreet enough to throw himself, and which in a great degree caused his ruin."[32] Davis had been one of George Staunton's underlings on the

Amherst mission in 1816, back when he was just a junior member of the factory, and the two had stayed close friends. A capable linguist, Davis had followed Staunton's example, though his interests tended more toward the translation of Chinese literature—poetry and fiction, mainly—rather than anything overtly political or (as some would have it) "useful." In 1829, he had published an ambitious two-volume translation of a classic Chinese novel, which he dedicated to George Staunton from "his very faithful friend and servant."[33] By 1834, Davis had become chief of the factory—the very last one, as it turned out. Nevertheless, he still got to be Napier's second on the new committee of superintendents, and when Napier died he took his place.[34]

Davis subscribed fully to Staunton's views on the China trade, especially his insistence that it should be conducted with caution and respect. Just a few days after Napier's death, Davis wrote to Staunton to tell him, in effect, that his failed parliamentary speech from 1833 had just been vindicated. Though Staunton had called for a gradual change to the system, one predicated on discussion and agreement with the Chinese authorities, Charles Grant had gleefully ignored Staunton's counsel and sent Napier straightaway to his doom. "Grant will learn that it had been better to have followed your advice," Davis confided, "and have had some previous negociation between the Govts." Davis himself had ridden on one of Napier's gunboats—a terrifying experience in which a man standing near him was killed—and he pointed out how useless the resort to force had been. The showdown accomplished nothing, and Napier still wound up following the governor-general's original orders to go back to Macao. Davis had little regard for the late superintendent. "Poor Lord Napier was very headstrong, and quite beyond the reach of advice," he told Staunton. "His was one of the weakest minds I ever met with."[35]

When Jardine and Matheson's faction sent their petition calling for war, Davis chased it with a report of his own, written in his new capacity as chief superintendent, in which he advised Palmerston to ignore them. "The crude and ill-digested Petition to His Majesty from a *portion* of the English traders at Canton (for some of the most respectable houses declined signing it)," he wrote, "is said to have been drawn up by a casual visitor from India, totally unacquainted with this country."[36] To judge by Palmerston's lack of response to the petition, Davis's words carried the day.

Davis, incidentally, was far more optimistic than the signatories of Jardine and Matheson's petition that the British could find a peaceful way out of the embarrassment Napier had caused. Knowing that the British government wanted "to avoid . . . a serious rupture with this country," Davis told Palmerston that a recent edict had made it clear that the Daoguang emperor also wanted to avoid any serious troubles.[37] Daoguang, he was pleased to report, had blamed the Napier affair not on the British but on the Hong merchants. The emperor had even expressed a measure of sympathy for the foreign traders, suggesting that they had been driven to "stir up disturbances" by the insufferable "grasping" of the Hong merchants.[38] As with the embarrassment of the Amherst mission, which Jiaqing had blamed publicly on his own ministers rather than the British ambassador, the Daoguang emperor likewise chose to assign blame for Napier internally rather than casting the British as some kind of enemy. In both cases, the way was thus paved for trade at Canton to resume as normal with no lingering mistrust directed at the British merchants. And indeed, after Napier's death that is exactly what happened.

Jardine and Matheson did not give up so easily, though. In March 1835, James Matheson had to sail home for medical treatment, and he took the occasion to escort Lord Napier's remains back to Scotland for reburial. He was adopting a pastoral role toward the family that Jardine had first established with Napier himself in Canton and continued with Napier's widow and her daughters as they grieved in Macao. ("Mr. Jardine will do anything to meet my wishes," wrote Lady Napier to a confidant in Scotland a few weeks after her husband's death. "I must ever be grateful to that gentleman . . . his kindness to me [has] been *very great* indeed.")[39] Jardine and Matheson raised some funds from their colleagues to build a monument to Napier in Macao, and Matheson planned to get the stone for it carved in England. Medical treatment aside, Matheson's most conspicuous role back home would be to advise Lady Napier, who had sailed home a few months earlier with her daughters, and to help her ensure a proper commemoration of Lord Napier's sacrifice. His less conspicuous role, intimately related to the former, was to insinuate himself as a representative of the family and use Napier's death as the casus belli to drum up support for a punitive expedition against China.

Once home, however, Matheson had a difficult time getting the attention of the government. Palmerston was occupied with other matters—China almost never commanded his focused attention—and Matheson kept getting put off in his efforts to meet with him. He wrote in dismay to Jardine that waiting for an audience with the foreign secretary was like waiting for a mandarin at the Canton city gate.[40] Having spent years as one of the largest fish in the small pond of the Canton factories, James Matheson held the China trade in the center of his worldview. Its problems dominated his mental landscape, so it was disorienting to find that back home nobody seemed to care about it. "The fact is, Jardine," he wrote, "people appear to be so comfortable in this magnificent country, so entirely satisfied in all their desires, that so long as domestic affairs, including markets, go right, they really cannot be brought to think of us *outlanders*."[41] The only thing that might make them snap to attention, he suggested, was if the China market should somehow run aground—if the import of tea should be interrupted, if the London merchants should suffer financial losses. Short of that, he told Jardine, "expect no sympathy here."

Matheson had no influence in the British government, but fortunately for him Lady Napier did. Palmerston had given the late superintendent's widow permission to address him at any time—a polite act of solicitation, perhaps, but she availed herself of it on numerous occasions to lobby for family friends and plead for greater recognition of her husband's service.[42] On July 14, 1835, she wrote an effusive letter to Palmerston introducing "my friend Mr. Matheson" and urging the foreign secretary to meet with him privately. Matheson was, she told Palmerston, "a man of the highest respectability—and of very *superior intelligence* and what he says may be *depended upon*." She described him as one of the top merchants in Canton, who had treated her husband Lord Napier warmly and "allowed no *selfish* or *temporary* interests to interfere with what he considered the liberal and true policy of England."[43] (By which she meant that Matheson and Jardine were among the few British merchants who did *not* tell Napier to give up and go back to Macao.) She would be deeply gratified, she said, if Palmerston would meet with him to learn the true state of affairs in China.

Matheson was using her—just as Jardine had used her husband to further his own ends in Canton—but underneath his business-related calculations his concern for Lady Napier was not entirely cynical. In a private letter to Jardine just after he first visited the widow at the looming mansion in Scotland where she stayed, Matheson showed a glimmer of genuine emotion. He described the shattered family: proud Lady Napier, broken in a way he was "grieved to see"; a glimpse of the uncertain new lord ("a dark lanky youth of sixteen"); Napier's eldest daughter, "pale and thin" from her ordeals. For their part, the Napier family never seemed to question the motives behind Jardine and Matheson's attentions to them. Napier's daughters told Matheson how fondly they remembered William Jardine, and one let on that she was stitching a pocketbook for him. ("But *this is a secret*," Matheson told Jardine, "and I promised not to tell you.")[44] His affection for the family, it would seem, was real. His desire for a war, however, was equally real.

Lady Napier's introduction finally opened the door for Matheson to meet with Lord Palmerston privately after nearly a month of waiting. Even then, however, it did not accomplish what he hoped, for Palmerston was hardly inclined to follow his advice. "Lord Palmerston. I have had an audience with him," he wrote curtly to Jardine afterward. "He has not had time to look into Chinese affairs, but the bent of his mind is not to interfere at present, but give time to see how the free trade will work on its present footing."[45] There would be no punitive expedition. Like the ministers of every British government before him, Palmerston trusted that the distant Canton trade would regain its balance naturally and the best course to follow was noninterference. It was not what James Matheson wanted to hear. It was, however, consistent. London and Beijing had in common that they had always preferred to let Canton take care of itself.

As it happened, Matheson was not working entirely alone. During the same months he was trying to get his foot into the door of

Palmerston's office, Hugh Hamilton Lindsay, the former Company supercargo who had chartered the *Lord Amherst*, was also in London trying to get Palmerston's ear for nearly the same purpose. Unlike Matheson, Lindsay was not an opium dealer (not yet, at least)—he was just a free trader at heart whose views all along had been more aggressive than the other East India Company men with whom he served. While Matheson was in London, Lindsay was there as well, sending long letters to Palmerston and seeking audiences of his own, giving similar arguments for why Napier's death was sufficient grounds for Britain to send a war fleet to Canton.

Matheson and Lindsay do not appear to have coordinated their efforts in any deliberate way, but they both shared the patronage of Lady Napier behind the scenes. Her husband had admired Lindsay's account of the *Lord Amherst* on his voyage out, and it had greatly influenced his view that China could easily be forced open. Lady Napier recognized that debt, though she preferred to view it in the opposite direction, and wrote to Lindsay with delight that his proposals to Palmerston were the very same that Lord Napier would have made, had he lived long enough—she was gratified, she said, to see in Lindsay's advice to Palmerston "proof of Lord Napier's sagacity and judgment that he should this early have seen what was the proper course to be pursued by this country." She supported Lindsay fully in his call for a war in the name of her husband, declaring that "if some show of apology is made, if we succeed in obtaining a commercial treaty, encreasing trade, intercourse, civilization and in God's good time *Christianity* will follow, and it will not be altogether in vain that Lord Napier sacrificed his health and life in the path he considered his duty and for his Country's advantage."[46]

James Matheson returned to China in the summer of 1836, empty-handed save for an extremely heavy marble column carved in honor of the late Lord Napier that would take 120 years to finally get erected.[47] Before leaving England, however, he planted a seed: a hundred-page pamphlet titled *The Present Position and Prospects of the British Trade with China*, the product of months of labor and research, in which he laid out the history of trade with China and made a strenuous case for the necessity of a British naval expedition. Having failed in the halls of government, he aimed instead for the public. Matheson started right off by describing the Chinese as "a people characterised by a marvellous degree of imbecility, avarice, conceit, and obstinacy" who nevertheless were blessed with the possession of "a vast portion of the most desirable parts of the earth."[48] His underlying argument was that such a people had no right to keep their "desirable parts" from the British; China must be opened or there would be no further trade at all.

He asked his readers to sympathize with the "intense anxieties, sufferings, and dangers" of their countrymen (like himself) who had long dared to engage in the China trade. They were "daily subjected to injuries and insults not merely of a harassing, but even of a horrible description." The Chinese called the British barbarians and looked down on them. Napier, he wrote, was "our unoffending representative," who was "destroyed" by his treatment at the hands of the Chinese. The British nation and its sovereign had been, through Napier, "treated with such disdain, and visited with such injuries, as they have never hitherto experienced, or chosen to endure." In all, he urged that the British government must take action for the sake of free trade and national dignity—the people of Britain must vindicate "our insulted honor as a nation," or else, in a dark reference to the kowtow, humble themselves "in ignominious submission, at the feet of the most insolent, the most ungrateful, the most pusillanimous people upon earth."[49]

Lindsay, too, took his case to the public by publishing one of his letters to Lord Palmerston advocating war—though he refused to call it a "war" because he was so confident that it would be short, inexpensive, and would succeed without embroiling the British in any kind of long-term conflict with China or harming the future trade (which, he promised, was "capable of almost unlimited increase"). Napier may have made mistakes, he acknowledged, but "the Chinese were predetermined to insult him." Lindsay denounced their "treacherous conduct" during Napier's evacuation from Canton, "which may justly be considered to have hastened, if not caused, his death." Britain had only two choices, he proposed: either to withdraw all political relations from China, or (his preferred approach) "a direct armed interference to demand redress for past injuries, and security for the future." Lindsay saw ample justification for the latter, on the grounds that "Lord Napier's death, when sent as the representative of our sovereign, was hastened, if not caused, by the treacherous and cowardly conduct of Chinese authorities."[50] They might as well have murdered him in cold blood.

The nearly simultaneous appearance of their pamphlets—Lindsay's the more bellicose, Matheson's the longer and more deeply thought out—made a strong case for a tightly focused war of retribution. To readers with slim knowledge of the actual course of events in China (most readers, that is), the case would seem fairly clear-cut. Britain had been wronged, its representative essentially murdered by arrogant Chinese officials who called him a "Barbarian Eye." But the nation's honor could easily be redeemed by dispatching a small fleet of ships that were already available to sail from India at little cost. And in the course of avenging their national honor, the British could advance their trade in China immeasurably, all with little or no risk at all. The picture Lindsay and Matheson drew was a tempting one.

It was George Staunton who came out to silence them. In response to their pamphlets advocating war, Staunton printed a tract of his own pointing out just how wrong—and more to the point, how "mischievous and dangerous"—Lindsay and Matheson's seductive views really were. Their claims that Britain could prevail with a small fleet were absurd, he said—considering the vast length of China's coastline, "a more gigantic and portentous scheme of national warfare cannot well be imagined." Beyond just dismissing the absurdity of Matheson and Lindsay's proposals for *how* a war with China should be conducted, Staunton especially deplored the grounds for *why* they thought Britain must fight. China was not some enemy, he said, but "a friendly power, with which, for upwards of an hundred years, we have carried on a most beneficial commercial intercourse." Furthermore, Lord Napier was not some innocent but an aggressor who fell on his own sword. The actions of the Chinese, as Staunton saw them, had been both predictable and reasonable when Napier so recklessly ordered his gunboats to force the passage of the Tiger's Mouth. Faced with "a couple of French frigates forcing their way up the Thames, and battering down Tilbry Fort," he offered, Britain would have done exactly the same.[51]

As for Lindsay and Matheson's predictions of the great expansion of trade that would follow from a treaty secured by war, Staunton acknowledged that of course it would be advantageous to have more ports in China opened to British trade. But, establishing himself as the voice of conscience toward China, he insisted that such concessions could only be granted voluntarily by the Chinese. There was no moral perspective from which an expansion of commerce by violence and war (or as it would later be known, "gunboat diplomacy") could, on the grounds offered by Matheson and Lindsay, be justified. It would "reflect only disgrace and discredit on our flag and name," he wrote, and alienate the British not only from the government of China but from its people as well. "To go to war—to engage in hostilities for the sake of obtaining such objects,—to endeavour to extort them by force from an independent state by the terror and sufferings which might arise to the people from our blockades and embargoes," wrote Staunton in anger, "seems to me outrageous, and quite unparalleled in the records of the comparatively civilized warfare of modern days."[52]

In the meantime, while Matheson and Lindsay were agitating unsuccessfully in London for a war, in China the domestic initiative to legalize opium was taking a dramatic step forward. Wu Lanxiu's essay on relaxing the opium ban had languished in Beijing after Lu Kun sent it to Daoguang in 1834, but in June 1836, around the time James Matheson was embarking for his voyage back to Canton, a vice minister in the Court of Imperial Sacrifices in Beijing named Xu Naiji—a high official of the central government with genuine influence, who was a four-year veteran of service in Canton and connected to the same networks as Wu Lanxiu—sent a memorial to the Daoguang emperor recommending the legalization policy in his own name and advising that it be implemented as soon as possible.

With Wu Lanxiu's essay as his foundation, Xu Naiji put together an extended argument in favor of making the opium trade legal in China. His proposal was not by any means a defense of opium itself, though, for he recognized how destructive the drug could be. "After it has been used for some time," he wrote, "the user must continue to smoke it at specific times; this is called 'addiction.' Time is squandered, the user stops working, and he comes to rely on the drug for his very survival."[53] Xu Naiji noted as well that opium had horrible physical effects—weak breath and a hollow body, ashen face and black teeth—yet even though its users could clearly see the harm it was doing to them, he wrote, they could still not stop themselves from using it. He believed that of course it should be prohibited if possible.

Xu Naiji's central argument, however, was that it was *not* possible to suppress opium, so the government must focus instead on mitigating the harm it caused. The policy of suppression had done nothing to stop the drug from spreading, he insisted. Although punishments had increased greatly over the years, nevertheless "the users have continued to multiply, to the point of filling nearly the whole empire." Whereas opium had once been openly traded for tea at Canton, now it was secretly purchased with illegal currency—leading to the drain of silver from China, the skewing of the exchange rate, and all the economic effects resulting therefrom. Furthermore, in spite of prohibition the trade in opium had grown enormously, from a few hundred chests per year in the early 1800s to more than twenty thousand at the time of his writing, with a total annual value of more than ten million taels of silver.

Responding to those who wanted to solve the problem by shutting down foreign trade at Canton, Xu Naiji repeated Wu Lanxiu's warning that doing so would put hundreds of thousands of southern Chinese out of work and cause social unrest. Furthermore, he pointed out that the foreigners could just take possession of an island in the outer waters and avoid Canton completely (which was, of course, exactly what some of them wanted to do). If that happened, then China's coastal merchants would gladly sail out to trade with them there and the Chinese government would lose the power to levy any taxes on the tea and silk trade. Finally, he pointed out just how much opium was being sold by foreign ships up and down the Chinese coast in spite of the government's best efforts to drive them off—which indicated that even if Canton should be closed to them, the British would still be able to go on selling their goods however they wished.

Xu Naiji, like others, believed that the Qing dynasty's recent laws against opium smoking had served primarily as a means for corrupt government workers to enrich themselves. From his years of experience in Canton he described the massive illegal trading entrepôt in the region: the foreign receiving ships at Lintin, the "fast crabs" and other armed smuggling vessels that connected them to the coast, the bribed military outposts and corrupted customs houses, the quick violence of the Chinese opium smugglers when challenged by government boats, the pirates who boarded unsuspecting ships by disguising themselves as officials hunting for opium. And through it all, he said, the common people were no help at all. "The commoners' fear of law and punishment is nothing compared to their desire for profit," he wrote. "There are times when the law has no effect on them at all."

As it pertained to those commoners, the most heartbreaking aspect of Xu Naiji's proposal was his grim acceptance that suppression was impossible, for which reason he essentially recommended that the government should abandon common opium addicts to their own self-destruction. In the future, as he saw it, the government should only pursue active prohibition efforts against public officials and soldiers—men who held positions of responsibility, whose impairment from opium might harm the public good. As for the multitudes of the common people (or at least those who could afford the drug), he said the government should "pay no regard" to whether they bought or used opium. China's problems had nothing to do with the loss of population, he said—new people were born every day, and opium did nothing to diminish the country's size. Opium smokers by nature were "lazy and shiftless with no aspirations." They died young, and even when they didn't they were still "worthless people." The government should not concern itself with them at all, he proposed. Instead, it should focus on salvaging China's economic resources. Opium addicts could be safely ignored, but the government must act immediately to stop the loss of silver.

Xu Naiji concluded that China's only option was to go back to the old system: opium should be taxed as a medicinal import. The Hong merchants should be allowed to take it in exchange for tea and other goods so that silver would not leave the country. Import duties on opium could be set lower than what the smugglers were paying in bribes to corrupt officials, which would ensure that they would voluntarily comply with the new regulations. Once the opium trade was brought fully into the open, the government could outlaw the export of silver in any form, either sycee or dollars. More than ten million taels a year would be saved, he reckoned. And while government officials and soldiers would be forbidden from indulging in opium at the peril of their jobs, the common people of China would be free to buy, sell, and use it as they saw fit. Faced with a choice between addressing the threat to China's economy from the loss of silver, and the threat to its public health from individual opium use, there was no question in his mind which was the more serious problem.

This time, the Daoguang emperor paid attention. After giving Xu Naiji's memorial a fair reading, in June 1836 he referred it to the authorities in Canton for deliberation. Lu Kun had died in office in 1835, and the new governor-general who replaced him was a man named Deng Tingzhen, a sixty-year-old scholar and veteran administrator. Deng had little experience in southern China, having served for the previous nine years as governor in Anhui province up on the Yangzi River, so he had no vested interest in foreign trade, but he was open to the needs of the port city. He was also aware of the region's vulnerabilities, and one of his first actions as governor-general had been to ask permission to strengthen the local coastal defenses.[54] Daoguang asked Deng Tingzhen to deliberate over the legalization proposal with his subordinates and with the hoppo who supervised trade, and then to report back to the throne with his own recommendations on the subject. This boded well for Xu Naiji, insofar as the very fact of the emperor's referring his memorial to Canton indicated that Daoguang was substantially in favor of implementing the plan.

In October, writing jointly with the Canton governor who served under him and the hoppo at the customs bureau, Deng Tingzhen sent a memorial to the Daoguang emperor giving his full and unreserved support to Xu Naiji's proposal. Along with voicing support for legalization, Deng also submitted a list of draft regulations to govern the new era of open trade in opium at Canton. "In setting regulations, it is important to accord to the nature of the times," he wrote, arguing that while Xu Naiji's proposal to legalize opium might have been a departure from recent precedent, it was perfectly appropriate to the circumstances, "motivated entirely by the needs of the times."[55]

Foreigners tended to imagine China's dynastic government as being stubbornly wedded to traditional, unchanging policies (and indeed this was sometimes the case), but Deng Tingzhen's memorial points to a rather different phenomenon that emerged when the emperor so desired—a deliberative government seeking pragmatic policies to suit actual conditions.

The autumn of 1836 thus found the highest-ranking imperial official at Canton laying the groundwork for a legalization of the opium trade. As he planned it, the receiving ships at Lintin and the smugglers along the coast would be welcomed back to Canton to exchange their wares directly for tea, paying low taxes that undercut the bribes and commissions the Chinese agents had been charging them. The legal and illegal branches of commerce that had existed so uneasily side by side for the past decade would finally be brought back together into a rational, unified system of trade under the supervision and control of the Qing government. The dangerous flow of silver out of China would be cut off, and the growing risk of a violent collision between foreign smugglers and Qing naval enforcers would be removed. In its way, it was the most hopeful moment in years for the peaceful future of the foreign trade at Canton.

CHAPTER 12

The Last Honest Man

———◆———

Few British officials were as intimately familiar with the brutality of slavery as Charles Elliot. A light-haired, thin-lipped captain in the Royal Navy, in 1830 he had been appointed "Protector of Slaves" in British Guyana, a newly created position in which he was supposed to investigate the most abusive practices of the British plantation owners and represent the interests of the slaves who suffered at their hands. The British government had outlawed the Atlantic slave trade in 1807, and the Royal Navy had long been tasked with enforcing that ban on the high seas, but in 1830 the *institution* of slavery was still legal in British territories even though a groundswell of popular support for emancipation meant that it would not remain so for long. Thus the British plantation owners in Guyana still controlled their slaves legally according to British law; they were merely forbidden to import any new ones. The colonial governor in Guyana had at least tried to improve the condition of the slaves in bondage—establishing rules forbidding certain kinds of excessive cruelty, mandating periods of rest from labor, providing a means for them to purchase their freedom, and creating the office of "protector" to defend their rights.

As Protector of Slaves, Charles Elliot had regular, close contact with men and women suffering horrific abuse at the hands of their

British masters. He did his best to serve them, interviewing the victims and trying to represent them legally against their tormenters in a colonial court. He sent home grim reports to the British government depicting the savage cruelty of the plantation managers toward the enslaved men and women who grew much of Britain's coffee, sugar, and cotton, detailing the punishments they inflicted with abandon. But it was in many ways a hopeless position. He was "desperately unpopular," as he described it, working constantly in opposition to British planters who resented him for interfering with their operations, yet he had little actual power to help the slaves under his protection. The experience hardened him into an abolitionist.[1]

Elliot could never have imagined how quickly he would have to transition from policing slave owners to supervising opium traffickers, but such was his lot. In 1833 the Whig government in Britain called him home from Guyana to advise them on the abolition of slavery, which was passed into law later that year on the same surge of liberal political energy that had carried through the Reform Act and toppled the East India Company's China monopoly. Once Elliot's expert advice to the government was given, however, he was no longer needed, and so Palmerston, who saw in him a convenient person at the right time, sent him almost immediately out in the other direction, accompanying Lord Napier to China. Elliot was appointed master attendant under Napier, a minor position in which he would supervise the British ships that anchored in the inner waters near Canton—really, little more than a glorified harbormaster. It was a pitifully low station, nothing to compare with that of chief superintendent.

Unlike Napier, Elliot had never asked to go to China (though in common with Napier, his assignment there would turn out to be the defining episode of his life). He thought the appointment as master attendant was beneath him, and it came with a low salary to match. "I feel all this to be a humiliation, and a very sore one too," he complained to his sister just before he left for China. He came from an illustrious family—one of his cousins was Lord Auckland, who would serve as First Lord of the Admiralty in 1834 and then governor-general of India, while another cousin was the 2nd Earl of Minto, who would succeed Auckland at the Admiralty in 1835. Elliot's own failure to achieve such stature despite his family connections made the lowliness of his position in China all the more regrettable. He suffered under debts he would never be able to pay off with the master attendant's salary, and was bitter about having to sacrifice his family's financial prospects for an arbitrary national cause, on a mission he had not chosen. "I go to this place . . . with a fixed determination to do all I can for my family and myself," he told his sister, "and to do for the public, not a whit more than my *barest duty.*"[2]

Elliot was a calculating man in his way, obsessively aware of how his actions would be interpreted back home, constantly angling for improvements to his career. And though he resented being sent off to China, he did sense an advantage of sorts in that it gave him "the touch of true bitterness and real selfishness, without which there is no success in this world."[3] In any case, most of his bitterness and disappointment came to be directed at Lord Napier, fifteen years his senior and incomparably higher than he in salary and prestige. Sarcastically, Elliot called him "My Emperor" behind his back, and his dislike of the superintendent extended to Napier's family as well. Lady Napier, in Elliot's letters, was "sly," her daughters "unmitigatedly disagreeable."[4] On the voyage over, Elliot was resentful that the arrogant Napier treated him and his wife with frigidity despite the fact that both men held equivalent rank in the navy.

All that changed after Napier's death. First, when John Davis took over from Napier he appointed Elliot as secretary to the committee of superintendents, a healthy promotion from master attendant. Davis took a strong liking to him, which pleased the career-minded Elliot to no end. In particular, Davis was drawn to what he saw as Elliot's pragmatic and flexible attitude, which he judged a necessary opposite to the headstrong rigidity by which Napier had caused so much trouble. In Elliot's own words, he was a sailor who when things went wrong knew "how to duck my head to the storm, and hope for better weather." Davis knew that because of his own East India Company background he wouldn't last long as chief superintendent—only as long as it would take for Palmerston to send someone without Company ties to replace him—so he resigned preemptively and left for home in January 1835. When he resigned, though, he lobbied Palmerston to make Elliot the new chief superintendent. Among Elliot's qualifications for the job (besides the implicit fact of his being untainted by connection with the East India Company), Davis emphasized that Elliot had the right kind of "temper"—a dig at the late Napier, who did not. Davis insisted that the situation in Canton would have been far better if Charles Elliot had been made chief superintendent in the first place instead of Lord Napier. "I really shall be uneasy for the state of affairs there unless Elliot is immediately put in charge," he told Palmerston.[5]

Palmerston agreed. Having recently fended off James Matheson's and Hugh Hamilton Lindsay's calls for a military intervention in China, Palmerston wanted to see a superintendent in Canton who could rein in the free traders and prevent them from causing serious trouble with the Chinese. He knew Elliot was the man to do that, based on reports Elliot had sent to a correspondent in the Foreign Office expressing hope that the government might take a firm hand with the British in China. Indeed, Palmerston's appointment of Elliot came just a week after he read one such report in which Elliot complained of "the very heedless temper at Canton" and warned that the most aggressive faction of the free traders was becoming dominant.[6]

Similar concerns had come to Palmerston's attention via merchants unaffiliated with the likes of Jardine and Matheson, such as an association of London merchants calling themselves the "East India and China Association" who petitioned him in June 1836 to send to China a commercial agent with "Judicial Functions" who could "prevent as far as may be practicable, the infraction of the Chinese Laws by British subjects."[7] Those who relied on the China market as a place to sell their goods were naturally concerned about the harm that might come to it from smugglers. Palmerston fully supported such measures, and after appointing Elliot superintendent he wrote to the Treasury in November 1836 to recommend that whatever the relationship between Great Britain and China might be in the future, the chief British agent on the ground must be given some kind of legal authority to control His Majesty's subjects in that region. Only by having the power to "enforce obedience" to regulations, he argued, could such a figure ensure "the peaceable maintenance of our commercial relations with the Chinese."[8] It was unclear, though, how such authority could be granted.

By the end of December 1836, Charles Elliot was happily in receipt of his new appointment from Palmerston. It had taken a bit of sleight of hand from the Foreign Office to arrange it, and some rejiggering of titles, so Elliot became "senior" (rather than "chief") superintendent of trade, but still he effectively took over the position first held by Napier. Due to budgetary concerns his salary was only half of Napier's—£3,000 rather than £6,000—but it was still more than he could believe, and easily enough to discharge his lingering debts.[9] His wife, who lived in Macao with their children (and was pregnant with another), could not have been more delighted with "Charlie," as she called him. He would make his mistakes in time, but as the year 1837 opened he was flying high.

With Napier out of the picture, Deng Tingzhen, the new governor-general, was able to start afresh with Charles Elliot, and the two found common ground with ease. In January 1837, Deng reported to the throne his receipt of a petition from Elliot (who, apparently for behaving well, was given a Chinese name, "Righteous Law," that wasn't derogatory in the slightest). In the petition, Elliot presented his credentials as the new superintendent of trade and explained that since the British trading ships carried many sailors who were ignorant of the Qing dynasty's regulations, he wished for permission to come to Canton and keep them in line. It was a replay of the encounter between Napier and Lu Kun, but this time around Elliot's approach was polite and respectful, it fit with protocol, it addressed Chinese interests, and it worked—proving, sadly, that none of Napier's bluster had been necessary in the first place. The emperor approved Elliot's petition, and the governor-general welcomed him to Canton to take up residence in the old British factory as the superintendent of trade, acting under the same regulations that had governed the taipans of the past. In Chinese he was referred to as a "consul" (*lingshi*), a respectable title that nobody could possibly confuse with a Barbarian Eye.[10]

It would not turn out to be an easy job, though Elliot's difficulties had less to do with the Chinese than with the other British. He promised to maintain a "conciliatory disposition" toward the Chinese government, he told Palmerston, but that was the opposite of what

Jardine and Matheson's faction wanted.[11] In that sense, his new role in China quickly began to resonate with his experience as protector of slaves in Guyana—in both cases, he understood the home government's intentions to be essentially benevolent, desiring him to rein in the depredations and scofflaw tendencies of British subjects overseas who sought profit at any moral cost. The merchants were "a rapacious and ravenous race of wolves," wrote his wife, "each howling after his prey."[12] Elliot warned Palmerston in January 1836 that the "peaceful and conciliatory policy" by which the British government wanted to promote its commercial intercourse with China was "not very generally approved amongst the fifty or sixty resident Merchants at Canton." On a personal note, he added with regret that his determination to put that policy into effect was "not the most popular task I could have proposed to myself."[13]

In his concern over how to keep peace at Canton without having any coercive power over British traders, Elliot was thrilled to hear the rumors that opium might be legalized. By early February 1837 he had in hand a full translation of Xu Naiji's memorial recommending an end to the opium prohibition, along with Governor-General Deng Tingzhen's positive response from the previous September. Excited, he wrote to Palmerston that those documents were "as remarkable a series of papers as has ever yet emanated from the Government of this country in respect to the foreign trade."[14] Some foreigners doubted whether the government of China would actually legalize opium, he admitted, but he was optimistic. Given the unwillingness of Chinese officials to take risks, he believed that Xu Naiji would never have submitted the memorial unless he knew there was already a strong faction at court in favor of it. Correctly, Elliot ascribed the legalization initiative to a fear of China losing control as more foreign ships plied its coast, along with worries about a continued loss of silver.

It is remarkable how much Elliot understood about imperial politics despite being new to China and having no understanding of the language at all. But he benefited from the legacy of Robert Morrison (and before him, George Staunton) in that he had ready access to reams of translations being prepared by the local English-language newspapers and the writers for the *Chinese Repository*, to say nothing of the official diplomatic translations undertaken by John Robert Morrison after his father's death. Nor was that all; while the Canton newspapers and young Morrison relied on Chinese documents that were shared with them by local contacts (especially the Hong merchants), an entirely separate stream of intelligence was coming in through Karl Gutzlaff, who in 1835 added the role of spy to his broad repertoire. Shifting his primary employment from Jardine and Matheson to the British government, Gutzlaff prepared long and detailed reports on the inner structures and systems of the Qing Empire: the imperial bureaucracy, social relations, the functioning of the economy, the organization of the military, and a range of other subjects. He based his reports on personal interviews from his clandestine travels up and down the coast, as well as broad reading in Chinese works on history and administration. The reports were sent home for Palmerston's benefit as well as being used by Elliot and others on the ground in Canton. They were intensely detailed—hundreds of pages in dense handwriting—and they provided a much deeper explanation of the workings of the Qing Empire than had ever before been available to the British.[15]

Not that all of those translators and interpreters served the same ends, however. While the newspapermen, especially the editor of Matheson's *Canton Register*, served the interests of free traders (including the opium smugglers among them), the writers for the *Chinese Repository* were mostly missionaries who frequently attacked those same smugglers' interests. There were regular grim reports on opium in the magazine, where one writer asserted, "There is no slavery on earth to name with the bondage into which opium casts its victim."[16]

Elliot had similar feelings about the opium trade, but for the sake of duty he suppressed his personal concerns in favor of the higher imperative of ensuring peaceful relations between the British traders and the Chinese authorities.[17] A couple of weeks after his first report on legalization to Palmerston, he wrote again to say that it appeared the government was already taking steps to relax the ban on the drug. Though he found the trade itself deplorable, he nevertheless hoped that its legalization "would afford His Majesty's Government great satisfaction."[18] Indeed, Elliot understood that the opium monopoly was quite valuable to the economy of British India. He regretted how heavily the Company had come to rely on opium production in Bengal, but at least it seemed that if Daoguang should endorse Xu Naiji's proposal to remove the Chinese ban it would put the trade on a more respectable footing. At least it would no longer necessitate smuggling. "The proposed measures of the Chinese Government seem to me to furnish the best hope for our safe extriction from an unsound condition of things," he told Palmerston. The opium trade was shaping up to be a national embarrassment for Britain, but its voluntary legalization by China could be their way out.

Meanwhile, as the British were entangling themselves ever more deeply in China, the Americans coursed along on their independent path with almost none of the tensions that faced their former colonial rulers. Their small population of sojourners continued to churn as always. Harriet Low, much to the dismay of the bachelors of Macao and Canton, returned home with her aunt and uncle in the autumn of 1833 and left many a disappointed suitor behind. Before she left, though, someone did manage to win her heart: an American named William Wood who published a local newspaper called the *Chinese Courier*, an oddball character with a lively wit and a predilection for writing doggerel and political commentary. He was the son of a prominent Shakespearean actor back in Philadelphia, and seems to have inherited his father's dramatic flair. The match wasn't what others expected; Harriet Low had a keen eye for beauty, while Wood was reputed to be one of the two ugliest Western men in China (his roommate at Russell & Co. described him as being so pockmarked that his face "resembled a pine cone").[19] But he was brilliant and funny, and he taught her to draw, and she fell completely in love with him. In Macao in the summer of 1832, they were secretly engaged to be married. When Low's uncle found out, however, he forced her to break off the engagement because he disapproved of Wood's financial prospects. She would eventually marry another man after her return from China, a banker from Boston who promptly hauled her off to live with him in London. The banker seemed more likely to give her financial security than the whimsical and romantic Wood could have, though in the end all he really gave her was five children to take care of before he went bankrupt and drank himself to death.[20]

Russell & Co. plowed ahead, with John Murray Forbes becoming a full partner in the firm on his return to China in 1834. Despite his continued youth (barely twenty-one years of age) and his diminutive size (128 pounds), he was already one of the major figures in the American China trade. "Now I am known as a partner of the most respectable American House in this part of the world," he wrote to his new wife back home in 1835, "and from having the management of a large business, I have acquired a confidence that would enable me to undertake any business in any part of the world."[21] He continued to manage Houqua's overseas investments under his own name, a service for which Russell & Co. took a cut, and his uniquely intimate, confidential relationship with the wealthy Hong merchant made him the envy of his peers. It was that friendship with Houqua, he confided to his wife, that was the real foundation of his success, giving him "great advantages over any one in Canton."[22] He told her he might already be rich enough to come home if instead of bothering with Russell & Co. he had just worked exclusively for Houqua from the beginning.

The ultimate goal for John Murray Forbes—as it had been for George Staunton and any number of other young men from Britain and America who came to Canton in the early nineteenth century to seek their fortunes—was simply to make enough money that he could return home permanently. But along the way Forbes had a better time of it in Canton than Staunton had, if only because he had none of Staunton's social hang-ups. The young New Englander made the best of it with his American friends, playing baseball (after getting a local craftsman to make him some bats and balls) and racing rowboats up and down the river against British and mandarin gigs alike. He procured a small sailboat to explore upcountry, and a pony on which to trot around the square in front of the factories. The expatriates, be they American or British, were like a gang of boys—for a while, the big game in town was leapfrog, played at all hours by fully grown men. Even "the gravest people of Canton," Forbes told his wife, could often be spotted hopping about and heaving themselves merrily over their squatting coworkers.[23] But no matter the ways he and the others found to pass their odd bits of leisure time, they all wanted most of all to go home.

Robert was the first of the two Forbes brothers to reach the point where he could do that. He had made up his mind to leave as early as April 1832, confident in his finances after two years running the *Lintin* receiving ship. His other reason for leaving, though, belied any Western claims that opium was harmless—he was suffering from poor health and finally realized that the thing making him sick was that he lived in a floating drug warehouse. He wrote to his uncle that "the effluvia of the Opium" was causing his illness, for every time he got away from the *Lintin* for a few days he felt like a new man. It was enough to convince him that "this climate and this mode of life will not answer."[24] So he sold his opium ship to Russell & Co. and returned home with the money he had made, ready to put it to work in Boston.

Robert turned out to be a better sailor than he was an investor, though, and he lived a lavish life back home that did not bode well for his continued fortune. Within a couple of years of his return, John Murray Forbes was sending his older brother outraged letters from Canton chastising him for the idiocy of his investments and the extravagance of his lifestyle. Indeed, Robert managed to lose most of the money he had made with his opium ship in risky investments that failed spectacularly in a financial panic that whipped through New England in the spring of 1837. The crash of 1837 caused widespread business and bank failures on both sides of the Atlantic—a wave of catastrophe that rolled onward to swamp many Western merchants in Canton as well, though Russell & Co. managed (barely) to survive as several of its competitors went under. Even after the worst initial shocks were past, though, it left a depression that would last for the next several years. It handily wiped out everything Robert had accumulated during his opium days, leaving him with the lone option of going back to Canton to try to start from the beginning again.

At least the timing of his return to China was convenient, for it followed not long after John Murray Forbes (much to Houqua's chagrin) finally amassed sufficient funds—$100,000, or a "moderate competency," as he described it—that he decided to return home too.[25] So with another turn of the revolving door, in the spring of 1837 he arrived home in New England a confident and relatively wealthy young man with a hundred thousand dollars of his own—and entrusted, furthermore, with half a million dollars of Houqua's own funds to invest in the United States as he saw fit—while his older brother Robert left for Canton early the following year a ruined man, glad to be able to take over the partnership at Russell & Co. his younger sibling had vacated.[26] It was thus Robert who would be in Canton when the crisis came, while John was safely home in Boston, starting to explore the new world of investments an industrializing American Northeast was just beginning to open up.

———

Much to Charles Elliot's concern, the Chinese government did not move forward with opium legalization as quickly as he had thought it would. In fact, through the spring and summer of 1837 the reality at Canton was that local authorities seemed to be taking even stronger interdiction measures against Chinese smugglers than they had before. These renewed efforts to suppress the opium traffic were especially mystifying because they were orchestrated by Deng Tingzhen—who, as Elliot and the others at Canton knew, personally supported legalization. Although Elliot had access to intelligence that was far better than anything available to previous generations, it still had its limits, but he did not fully appreciate that fact. He thought he knew and understood much more than he actually did. Despite ready access to government documents that circulated openly in Canton, and even despite Gutzlaff's personal interviews and wide research, much of what went on in China's central government was still a closed book.

One thing Elliot and the others did not seem to know was that quite soon after sending his memorial in support of Xu Naiji, Deng Tingzhen had received a whole series of edicts from the Daoguang emperor ordering him to renew his efforts to cut off the opium traffic at its Canton source and stop the outflow of silver. Xu Naiji's proposal for legalization was not in fact progressing as smoothly as Elliot thought. It was in limbo, neither advancing nor being rejected. It had met with some strong criticism from other officials at court, and for the time being the legalization plan was simply on hold. In the meantime, Daoguang wanted the existing laws enforced. Despite having expressed personal support for legalization, Deng was a man of duty and he readily followed Daoguang's orders while he waited for a final policy decision from the throne.[27]

This new crackdown came even as the opium trade was suffering from its own problems, bloated from too much competition after the end of the Company monopoly, the market already glutted by too many British, Indian, and American speculators—some of them betting on legalization with the same optimism as Charles Elliot (though for different reasons; they wanted profit, he wanted peace). As time went by with no implementation of Xu Naiji's proposals, however, it began to seem less and less certain to them what course the emperor would follow. "All hopes of the drug market being admitted on a duty have for the present vanished," William Jardine wrote to one of his coastal ship's captains on April 25, 1837. The investors in Calcutta, he wrote, were "anxious, beyond measure" because they had been banking on opium being accepted as a legal commodity, "as they had been led to believe it would be, by this time, from the correspondence of some of our neighbours."[28]

Through the summer of 1837 and into 1838 the opium trade all but collapsed in the face of strong enforcement efforts under Deng Tingzhen. With an energy never seen before, government agents chased down Chinese smugglers and destroyed their transport ships. They went after dealers on land, breaking the supply lines. Given the increasing dangers of the trade, Chinese smugglers demanded higher and higher fees from foreign wholesalers to carry their opium to the coast or upriver—fees that cut into already low prices as local demand for the drug crumpled under the same government crackdown. Jardine wrote a succession of worried letters to Bombay, warning of the "precarious state" of the once-flourishing opium traffic. "The drug market is becoming worse every day owing to the extreme vigilance of the Authorities, and we see no chance of amendment," he reported in November 1837.[29] The prospects for their trade continued to worsen into the winter, with Jardine predicting in January 1838 that "violent and determined measures on the part of the Chinese authorities, steadily persevered in, may lead to ruinous losses."[30] Still, he held out hope that the government's suppression could not last forever, if only because the officials stood to gain so much from their collusion in the trade.[31]

This dangerous turn to the trade also worried Charles Elliot, who feared an outbreak of violence between Chinese government forces and the increasingly desperate British opium traders. As early as June 1837 he had warned a contact in the Foreign Office about the changing character of Canton under free trade, especially with regard to local relations between the Chinese and British. "The altered state of this Trade," he wrote, "has filled Canton with a class of People who can not be left to their own devices amongst the natives of this Country, without the utmost risk to the safety of this Trade, and to the respectability of the national character." He worried especially about the high-handed racism of British newcomers toward the Chinese around them. "I never put my foot out of doors that I do not observe evidence of a growing dislike upon the part of the common people to our Countrymen," he wrote. "It is the fashion of the young men particularly to treat the Chinese with the most wanton insult and contumely." Without power to control them he worried that "we shall have ugly matters to deal with."[32]

As Chinese enforcement efforts continued, the foreign traffickers took greater risks, crowding more ships onto the Chinese coast to evade Deng Tingzhen's suppression efforts near Canton and Lintin. Whereas in the past no more than two or three foreign vessels had risked such journeys, by the autumn of 1837 there were more than twenty. Elliot worried that those European ships would be vulnerable to pirates, but even more dangerous were reported conflicts with the Chinese navy. "There is every reason," he warned Palmerston in November 1837, "to believe blood has been spilt in the interchange of shot . . . between them and the Mandarin boats."[33]

To make matters worse, as Chinese smugglers withdrew in the face of stronger government interdiction and foreigners took more responsibility on their own shoulders, more and more opium was carried into the inner waters of Canton, past the Tiger's Mouth to Whampoa, on the cutters of otherwise legitimate British ships. The traditional arm's-length division between the two trades—legitimate tea, silk, and cotton in the inner waters of Canton versus illegal opium at outlying Lintin and on the coast—was collapsing as the opium agents tried every angle to force their trade. The very same ships carrying aboveboard cargoes for Canton increasingly carried contraband as well, and Elliot feared there would be no way to protect the honest traders from the consequences of the lawbreakers. The Hong merchants, speaking on behalf of the governor—who himself relayed the instructions of the emperor—urged Elliot to take charge of his countrymen and banish the British drug vessels entirely from the vicinity of China. Elliot pleaded that his government had given him no such powers.[34]

Regardless of his distaste for British opium trafficking, Charles Elliot's overriding concerns were to ensure both the safety of British subjects in China and the continuance of the tea trade without interruption, imperatives that outweighed his own moral discomforts. So, absent any authority to bring the smugglers into line, he sought at least to ensure that their actions would not result in violence or the suspension of the legitimate trade. To that end, in November 1837 he suggested to Palmerston that Britain might attempt a diplomatic intervention in China—not to seek a commercial treaty as Jardine and Matheson's followers had been asking, but instead simply to reduce the risks that imperiled the tea commerce. Any delay risked "great hazard" to the immensely important trade at Canton, he warned, and it was his "strong conviction" that the rising danger posed by the aggressive traders was "an evil susceptible of early removal."[35]

Elliot could, of course, have proposed a British crackdown on smuggling, but since that would entail enforcing another country's laws for it, he chose instead to go in a direction he thought would be more palatable to the British government. Convinced as he was that Daoguang was still right on the verge of legalizing opium, he thought that Britain could do something to encourage that outcome. Specifically, he proposed that the British government send an ambassador to Beijing, accompanied by a peaceful naval force, to argue in favor of legalizing opium. Elliot knew that at least some of the emperor's advisers had been recommending this, and he thought that a tactful display of power by the British—no guns blazing, no hostility, just a respectful yet impressive parade of the tools at their command, coupled with a reminder of the importance of their tea purchases to

China's economy—might help tip the balance and make up the emperor's mind.

To dovetail with Xu Naiji's arguments about the impossibility of suppressing opium, Elliot thought the British ambassador should impress upon Daoguang that more than half of the opium coming to China was grown in free areas of India outside of British control, so the British had "neither the right nor the power" to prevent its import to China. (He also added, on a much weaker foundation, that if Britain tried to prevent the export of opium to China from its own territories by its own citizens, it would still be carried there by foreigners over whom the British had no control.) In other words, Elliot wanted the ambassador to argue that Britain was just as incapable of putting an end to the smuggling trade as China was, and therefore opium must be legalized and controlled "so that all men who visited the Empire of China might be within the control of the laws."[36] In a remarkably circular bit of reasoning, Elliot judged that since the British opium traders would then no longer be lawbreakers, their commerce would no longer be such a blight on the honor of Britain. It would of course do nothing about opium from a moral standpoint, but at least it could eliminate the danger of violence and put the regular trade back onto a safe footing.

That, however, was far more than the foreign secretary could stomach. As Palmerston understood Elliot's proposal, he was essentially recommending that the British government support the interests of opium smugglers by helping to legitimize their business. In his response, Palmerston admonished Elliot that "Her Majesty's Government" (for Victoria had by this time acceded to the throne) "cannot interfere for the purpose of enabling British subjects to violate the laws of the country to which they trade."[37] In words that would come back to haunt him, he went on to warn Elliot, "Any loss, therefore, which such persons may suffer, in consequence of the more effectual execution of the Chinese laws on the subject, must be borne by the parties who have brought that loss on themselves by their own acts." The smugglers had chosen of their own free will to flaunt Chinese laws—laws that the Chinese government had every right to enforce—and so they alone would be responsible for their losses. The British government washed its hands of them.

Palmerston's refusal to support the drug smugglers in 1838 did not mean he was sitting on his hands about China. Rather, when he wrote those words to Elliot he was in the midst of trying to pass a bill through Parliament that would finally give Elliot's position some teeth. The legislation he proposed, a "China Courts Bill," would grant Elliot (or another British official acting in a similar capacity) formal legal authority over the British subjects in south China. It called for the creation of a British court of law in Canton, under the superintendent, with jurisdiction over all British subjects within one hundred miles of the Chinese coast. If enacted, it would give Elliot authority to mediate in both civil and criminal disputes between British and other foreigners—including Chinese—as well as the power to exile lawbreaking Britons from the vicinity of Canton and Macao.[38] Palmerston's hope was that the bill would finally empower Elliot to keep the free traders in line, giving him the means to clamp down on their rising lawlessness and banish the worst offenders, thereby ensuring a peaceful trade.

In pushing to get the bill passed, Palmerston naturally sought support from his old parliamentary running mate George Staunton, the preeminent authority on China in the House of Commons. Staunton relished his acquaintance with the dashing and famous Palmerston, who in so many ways represented everything he was not: flamboyant, admired, magnetic, adored by women. (There is no evidence Staunton ever had a single romantic relationship of any kind in his life.) Palmerston's letters were among the very few that Staunton preserved in his diary and reproduced in his memoir, evidence of his proudest acquaintance. But when it came to the China Courts Bill, although he very much wanted to help Palmerston, he did spot a problem right at the outset: namely, that the bill completely ignored the judicial authority of China. After reading a draft of the bill in May 1838, Staunton advised Palmerston that it must be revised so the British court could not be construed as interfering with the jurisdiction of authorities in Canton or Beijing, unless by permission from China's government.[39] Palmerston, however, thought such permission would be impossible to gain because Britain had no ambassador at Beijing.

As he desperately wanted a means of controlling the traders, the bill went ahead as written.

Staunton's misgivings deepened as a June reading of the bill in the House of Commons approached, but Palmerston felt the deteriorating situation in China was so urgent that he could not postpone it.[40] This left Staunton in a bind: he didn't want to alienate Palmerston by defying him, but he was deeply principled on matters regarding China and could not hide his qualms. So in the end he gave Palmerston advance warning that he would have to oppose the bill in its existing form and move for an amendment requiring approval from the Chinese government. But he tempered his apparent disloyalty by pointing out that his objections would just be a formality and there didn't seem to be much other opposition to the bill in the Commons. "All I wish," he told Palmerston, "is, in fact, to place my *protest* on record; since I see it is impossible for me to do any more." But even the act of placing his protest on record, he confessed in a remarkably candid moment, was more than he really expected to do, because he was terrified to speak again in Parliament after his shattering humiliation in 1833.[41]

Staunton's fear of public speaking won out, and he did not in the end take part in the debate on the bill. But neither did he have to, for others spoke on his behalf. Palmerston's bill met with unexpectedly fierce opposition, with several lawmakers quoting George Staunton's misgivings as their primary ammunition. As one of the bill's opponents said, echoing Staunton, he "wished to ask the noble Lord [Palmerston], whether the authorities of China recognized this interference with their laws? The noble Lord was about to establish a court, whose authority he could not enforce."[42] To cries of "Hear! Hear!" he went on to argue that since China of its own volition allowed British subjects to come to Canton for trade, those British subjects "were bound to conform to Chinese usages, and not to attempt to force their own customs upon the Chinese."[43]

Remarkably, so singular was Staunton's expertise that he was also Palmerston's chief authority in *support* of the bill, with Palmerston quoting one of Staunton's books in which he wrote that the Chinese government avoided prosecuting any crimes committed by the British except for capital ones (which was indeed the case, save for the imprisonment of James Flint in 1760). Palmerston argued that since Britain and China had no formal diplomatic relations, there was no way to get permission from Beijing in advance, but since Staunton had shown that the Chinese government had effectively waived its right to prosecute foreign lawbreakers, surely it wouldn't object to the British doing it for them. His argument was not convincing, and the bill failed. Staunton, despite absenting himself from the debate, was credited as the man who sank it.

There were two conflicting issues at stake in that failed China Courts Bill. The one that caused it to fail was the applicability of Chinese law to Britons. The bill was indeed a breach of Chinese sovereignty as written, and its failure—importantly—was a testament to the British parliament's respect for that sovereignty at the time. However, the intention behind the bill was also important: Palmerston's primary hope for the court was to restrain Britons, not to impinge on the rights of the Chinese. Without such a court, Elliot would continue to be a helpless superintendent, powerless to do anything about the free traders who were throwing themselves ever more recklessly into harm's way in China and defying ever more boldly the laws of the Qing Empire, fearing no consequences at all.

Elliot was naturally disappointed when he learned the fate of the China Courts Bill—but so, significantly, was Houqua. Houqua was especially shocked that George Staunton had derailed the bill, for he could not believe that Staunton would ever hold such reservations. He insisted to Elliot that the Chinese government in fact *wanted* the British to manage the affairs of their own people in Canton, and that was exactly why they had asked them to send a taipan when the East India Company's monopoly ended. Deeply concerned (for he was the one who would bear the brunt of any frictions between the foreigners and the Chinese), Houqua asked Elliot "how it was possible to preserve the Peace, if all the English people who came to this country were to be left without control?"[44] The reason the Qing government refrained from applying most Chinese laws to outsiders, he said, was because foreigners were culturally different and it would be "unjust to subject [them] to rule made for people of totally different habits." All told, he was certain that the Chinese authorities would have preferred for Elliot to have judicial power over the British traders. But now he would not. And so thanks to the failure of the China Courts Bill, Elliot would go forward into the crucial year of 1839 as little more than a passenger—rather than captain—of the massive ship of trade as it barreled on into a darkening horizon.

Meanwhile, the Chinese debate over opium policy continued. By 1838, Xu Naiji's proposal for legalization had sat for two years without implementation. But during that time, Deng Tingzhen's efforts to enforce the existing laws had proven remarkably successful. Had the Qing government simply continued in the same pattern, and had Deng simply maintained the same pressure on domestic smugglers, it would likely have just been a matter of time before the Bombay dealers like Jamsetjee Jeejeebhoy went bankrupt and the Jardines and Mathesons of Canton were forced to give up on opium and try to make their way with cotton and other goods as best they could. But the pendulum was set to swing once more. In June 1838, a high-ranking official in the imperial court named Huang Juezi submitted a new memorial on opium, a scathing one with a dramatically different vision of how the government should break the grip of the drug on Chinese society and stop the loss of silver.

Huang Juezi's proposal, like Xu Naiji's, was entirely a domestic policy recommendation. He admitted at the outset that there was no way to block opium by embargo against foreigners who brought it from India; so much profit was at stake in the trade that any attempt to close down Canton or otherwise sever the link between foreign and domestic dealers was destined to fail. "Thus, the way to defend against this calamity," he wrote, "lies not with foreign merchants but with the wicked Chinese."[45] At the same time, he also admitted that efforts to target traffickers and dealers within China had always been crippled by the extremity of official corruption. On those counts, Huang Juezi was in agreement with Xu Naiji. But his solution was different. Whereas Xu Naiji had thrown up his hands and declared that since it was impossible to suppress the opium trade it should at least be controlled to prevent the export of silver, Huang Juezi instead recommended a newly ruthless campaign of suppression—directed this time not against the traffickers or the dealers as in the past, but against the Chinese consumers.

As Huang reasoned, if there were no common users of opium in China then there naturally would be no dealers, no traffickers, and no international smuggling trade to drain the silver out of China. So the users were the root of the problem, and if the emperor wanted to end the scourge of opium he must begin with them. Huang recommended heavy punishment for ordinary consumers of the drug—who, in recognition of how difficult it was to break their addiction to opium, would be given a grace period of one year to get clean before the full force of the law went into effect against them. Whereas the ruthlessness of Xu Naiji's proposal for legalization had been in his belief that the Chinese government should simply write off the multitude of addicts and allow them to destroy themselves, Huang's ruthlessness was of a more direct and hands-on strain: he proposed that after the one-year grace period was over, anyone left in China who still smoked opium should be executed.

It was an exceptionally harsh policy recommendation, one founded on great faith in the power of the laws and the capacity for China's fractious officials to unify and act as one. Interestingly enough, one of the arguments Huang Juezi gave in support of a death penalty for drug use was that such laws were already prevalent in the West. "Today, the opium that enters China comes from countries like England," he wrote, "and their national laws prescribe death for those who smoke opium, so each country only has people who produce the drug, and not a single person who consumes it." [46] He was completely wrong about that, of course, but this erroneous belief entered into the 1838 conversation as a given—that the reason why westerners did not use opium like the Chinese was because of their laws, not because of any difference in their social customs. (It did not, incidentally, mean that Huang saw Britain and other Western countries as models for the setting of Qing imperial policy—rather, the opposite: his implication was that if *even* the British could prevent their population from using opium, then the Qing dynasty should be able to do so easily.)

Daoguang was intrigued and sent copies of Huang Juezi's proposal to the most senior officials in the empire for comment. Twenty-nine of them responded over the summer of 1838, and while they universally deplored the spread of opium, the great majority of them (twenty-one out of twenty-nine) refused to support Huang's recommendation to execute users. Most thought punishment should still focus on dealers and traffickers, since they were less numerous and thus easier to go after. In spite of those disagreements, however, their collective backlash against Xu Naiji was unanimous: not a single one of the respondents in 1838 openly recommended legalizing opium. Their consensus advice to Daoguang was that whatever the primary target of suppression should be—whether the traffickers and dealers or the common users—it was suppression, not legalization, that should be China's course of action.[47] In light of later events, though, it is worth noting that as with Huang Juezi's original proposal, their vision of opium suppression was strictly domestic: not a single one of the twenty-nine respondents said anything about involving foreigners in a crackdown.[48]

Of the small number of officials who endorsed Huang Juezi's proposal as written, it was a man named Lin Zexu, the governor-general of Hunan and Hubei provinces in central China, who gave it the strongest and swiftest voice of approval. Lin Zexu was not an ordinary official. The son of a schoolteacher, he had passed the brutally competitive examination in the capital in 1811 at the youthful age of twenty-six, emerging as one of the best in his class. As a judge in the 1820s, he had established a reputation for fairness that earned him the nickname "Lin, Clear as Heaven" in testament to his incorruptibility. In the years that followed, on that foundation of judicial honesty he had built an even greater reputation as a pragmatic administrator deeply versed in issues of water management and flood relief— a rare kind of official who could be relied upon to put the welfare the people ahead of his own gain. By 1838 he was one of the Daoguang emperor's favorite ministers and had reached a rank comparable to Deng Tingzhen in Canton while still being ten years Deng's junior. Lin Zexu was a beacon of honesty and virtue in a time of endemic corruption. There were not many like him.

Lin Zexu's primary concerns—indeed, his sole concerns early on—had been domestic, in particular the conditions under which people lived in his jurisdictions. Foreign relations could not have been further from his mind—which was only as it should have been, for

Lin Zexu

Western trade was the exclusive business of the officials in Canton far to the south. His first taste of foreign affairs did not come until 1832 when the *Lord Amherst* arrived in a coastal province where he served as governor, carrying Hugh Hamilton Lindsay and Karl Gutzlaff on their mission to scout out new ports. Even then, he saw the problem of the *Lord Amherst* as a domestic one. He wasn't really concerned about the ship or its passengers, only that they should leave. His main concern was rather the Chinese "traitors" (as he called them) who tried to make contact with it. His efforts were spent not on combating the ship but on setting up a cordon to keep the local Chinese away from it—they, after all, were his direct responsibility. The foreigners were not.

Lin took no part in the early debates on opium and the silver drain, but he traveled in some of the same intellectual circles where it was discussed. He was quite conservative, an admirer of Bao Shichen, though his earliest thoughts on drug policy actually fit best with the legalizers: in a memorial he submitted to Daoguang in 1833, he suggested that if the primary danger from the opium trade was the drain of silver out of China, then China's farmers should be encouraged to grow poppies and process the drug themselves. If Chinese consumers could get all of their opium from local suppliers, he reasoned, then they would have no need to buy it from foreigners and the silver drain would stop. It was not a view to which he would remain wedded, but it was a typically pragmatic solution for a man concerned above all with the livelihood of peasants.

Lin Zexu's support for suppressing opium in 1838 was based on his abiding faith in moral suasion. Lin believed in the power of Confucian government to set a model for the people, to care for them and guide them. Though he had not been involved with opium policy per se prior to 1838, Huang Juezi's memorial marked a turning point for him. He seized on the issue almost as a religious crusade. In his own response, he offered the Daoguang emperor a detailed plan to support Huang's call for action. To begin, he recommended the confiscation and destruction of opium pipes and other equipment for using the drug. Local moral campaigns led by government officials would follow, ramping up in stages over the course of the grace year—including public education to teach people the evils of opium and active suppression of opium dens and corrupt officials.

Lin also recommended the provision of medical treatments to help wean addicts off their drug habits, for along with his astounding faith in the power of moral example, he also believed in the power of medicine. In an attachment to his memorial he described several methods for breaking addiction, including various recipes for pills and elixirs used to combat opium dependence. In one, patients would be given daily pills made of opium ash mixed with certain herbs and other substances to make them sick to their stomachs, with the expectation that after a full course of treatment they would be so revolted by the smell and taste of opium that they could never use it again.[49] Together, the active confiscation of drug paraphernalia, moral education, and medical treatment would—he believed—leave no more than a small fraction of users still addicted at the end of the year.

After sending his memorial in support of Huang Juezi, Lin Zexu took the initiative to put his plans into practice locally. In August 1838 he launched an intense legal and moral campaign against opium users in Hunan and Hubei. He set up hospitals to treat users, jailed dealers, and issued proclamations condemning the use of opium. He ordered local officials to round up and destroy whatever opium or opium-smoking equipment they could find. He sent reports up to the emperor detailing their successes: thousands of pipes collected through the autumn of 1838, tens of thousands of ounces of opium confiscated (though to keep some perspective, those tens of thousands of ounces of opium amounted to only about ten or twelve chests' worth, at a time when upwards of thirty *thousand* chests were being shipped to China each year). The pipes were smashed into pieces and the opium publicly burned, with the ashes thrown into a river—which was crucial, because if the destruction were not public then everyone would assume that the officials involved had just smoked the opium themselves or sold it for their own profit.[50]

Lin's reports to the throne were increasingly triumphant as he reported his successes in Hunan and Hubei. His tone also increased in urgency, arguing that such measures should not be limited to his own territories alone: in late September 1838, he declared opium to be the most fundamental problem facing the empire. "Before opium was widespread, those who smoked it only harmed themselves," he wrote to Daoguang. "The punishments of caning and exile were enough to keep them in line. But when its evil influence has penetrated into the whole country, the effect is tremendous. Laws should be put into rigid enforcement. If left in a lax state, then after a few decades, there will be no soldier in this Central Empire to fight against invaders, nor money to bear the military expenses." China would be helpless, he warned. "I have the fear," he concluded, "that if the evil be suffered to grow at this critical moment, there may be no more chance for remedy."[51]

By October 1838, Daoguang was leaning heavily in favor of suppression. Although Charles Elliot still labored under the illusion that Xu Naiji's proposal to legalize opium was right on the brink of approval, on the twenty-sixth of that month Daoguang punished Xu Naiji with a demotion in rank and removed him from office—signaling, definitively, that the legalization initiative was dead (Xu Naiji himself died soon afterward).[52] As deliberations in Beijing continued, on November 8 a Manchu named Qishan who served as governor-general of Zhili province in the north reported the largest drug seizure ever recorded in the empire. The opium was confiscated in the city of Tianjin, close to Beijing, but Qishan emphasized that it had come originally into the country through Canton, bought by Cantonese traders who shipped it north.[53] Though Huang Juezi had called for a national campaign against opium users, such a large-scale crackdown would be enormously complex and difficult to orchestrate (to say nothing of the logistics of sentencing tens if not hundreds of thousands of users to death). But as Qishan's report suggested, since all opium appeared to derive from Canton, perhaps a focused crackdown there could solve the entire empire's problem.

This, apparently, finally made up Daoguang's mind. The day after the opium seizure in Tianjin, he summoned Lin Zexu to come north to Beijing. Lin arrived in the capital on December 26, 1838, and over the course of eight audiences beginning the following day, the two men discussed the opium problem at length. On the fourth day of their meetings, Daoguang charged Lin with the singular mission of obliterating the trade at its heart in Canton.[54] Lin Zexu would travel south as an imperial commissioner, holding the power to act on Daoguang's behalf, answerable to none of the local officials. He would have command of all naval forces in the vicinity of the port. As for the governor-general on site, Deng Tingzhen, Daoguang sent him separate instructions that he should act in Lin Zexu's support.[55] And so in early January 1839, even as Charles Elliot still waited in confident expectation that the ban on opium would be lifted any day, Lin Zexu was starting on his way down to Canton with full powers to put an end to the traffic for good.

PART III

Blood-Ravenous Autumn

CHAPTER 13

Showdown

———◆———

Charles Elliot was a well-meaning man but far out of his depth at Canton. Aside from imagining that he understood more than he did about the Chinese and their government, he worried constantly about his lack of power over the British under his supposed supervision. As his anxieties mounted that the opium smugglers would provoke a crisis under his watch, his behavior became increasingly erratic. Though he had no instructions allowing him to impose order on the anarchic British free traders at Canton, out of a sense of duty (or at least out of a sense of not wanting to be blamed) he kept trying to find some way to control them. To that end he played his cards close, refusing to share his instructions from London with any of the other British and keeping all of his communications from Palmerston secret so nobody would know the truth of his limitations. The local English newspapers repeatedly asked him to clarify just what he was or was not authorized to do on behalf of the home government, but he refused to answer them.[1]

It wasn't just the small British smuggling vessels that worried him, running opium as they were into Whampoa and exchanging fire with Chinese enforcers farther afield.[2] The crews of the larger ships were also a concern. The sailors hailed from all over the British

Empire and were usually kept apart from the Chinese on land so they couldn't get into fights, but they had started causing trouble on the ships themselves, resisting the beatings used by their officers to keep them in line. After a mutiny on one British ship in the harbor, Elliot organized a naval police force of sorts, drafting regulations to give the captains the means to come to each other's aid. But even that wasn't part of his job; when Palmerston learned about it he scolded Elliot for overstepping his bounds and reminded him that "you have no power of your own authority to make any such regulations." Elliot's plan amounted to "the establishment of a system of police at Whampoa, within the dominions of the Emperor of China," said Palmerston, who told him Britain could not possibly sanction such a violation of "the absolute right of sovereignty enjoyed by independent States."[3]

By the early winter of 1838–39, it seemed increasingly likely that Governor-General Deng Tingzhen's ongoing crackdown on Chinese opium smugglers would be decisive—suggesting that even if Lin Zexu had never been sent to Canton, the trade might well have withered away without any further complications.[4] "Not a Broker to be seen, nor an Opium pipe; they have all vanished," wrote William Jardine to one of his coastal captains that December. The authorities in Canton had been especially vigilant of late, he wrote, "seizing smokers, dealers, and shopkeepers innumerable." (Ever the optimist, though, Jardine added, "We must hope for better times and brisker deliveries.")[5]

Up to that point, nothing in the Canton government's opium suppression efforts had targeted the foreign community. All of Deng Tingzhen's energies were aimed at native traffickers. Though occasional shots were fired between government boats and foreign smuggling vessels, those were isolated incidents provoked by the Europeans involved. But on December 3, a small shipment of opium was captured right inside the factory compound, carried from a boat at the riverside by two Chinese servants who quickly confessed that they worked for a British merchant. In response to that incident, Deng Tingzhen decided to make a statement to the foreign community at large. On December 12, a small body of soldiers appeared in the small dirt plaza in front of the factory buildings and hammered up a wooden cross in preparation for executing a convicted opium dealer by strangulation. The convict, the proprietor of a local opium den, was Chinese, and no foreigners were directly implicated in his crime, but Deng Tingzhen's unusual choice for the site of his execution was a clear warning to the foreigners: You, too, are responsible for this.

It was unclear in the scattered reports afterward exactly who acted first. Elliot was at Whampoa, so he didn't witness it, and the "gentlemen" traders disclaimed any responsibility. Perhaps it was sailors, they suggested. But a few foreigners who took offense at the prospect of an execution being carried out in front of their homes walked over to the scaffold and started trying to tear it down. When the Chinese soldiers did not resist, several others joined in and helped them. A crowd of Chinese formed—out of curiosity more than anything—to watch them dismantling the gallows. Everything was still peaceful until a few of the more rowdy British (here is where the sailors were blamed) started shoving their way into the Chinese crowd, hitting people with sticks to make them back up. The crowd pushed back, and grew. Someone threw the first rock. Then the riot burst out for real—open fighting between Chinese and foreigners on the plaza, a quick and furious rout that sent the British and Americans running for the gates of their factory buildings.

The angry Chinese mob grew and crowded in—several thousand people by all accounts, pelting the foreigners from outside their gates with a hail of rocks and bricks, smashing all the front-facing windows and venetian blinds in the factory buildings and tearing down fences to use as battering rams. Mercifully for the traders barricaded inside, a detachment of Chinese soldiers eventually came to their rescue and dispersed the crowd, ending the afternoon's siege. The execution scaffold was taken away. The opium dealer was strangled elsewhere. By the time Charles Elliot showed up that night, leading 120 armed sailors from the merchant ships, all was at peace again.[6]

The main thing Lord Palmerston wanted to know when he learned about the riot was not whether the British subjects at Canton needed better protection, but what had possessed them to think they had any right to try to stop the execution in the first place. On what grounds, he asked Elliot, did the traders imagine themselves "entitled to interfere with the arrangements made by the Chinese officers of justice for carrying into effect, in a Chinese town, the orders of their superior authorities"?[7] Palmerston's letter was yet another in a long list of injunctions from the British government to the residents in Canton reminding them that they had to respect the authority and jurisdiction of the Chinese government. And like all the others, it would take half a year to reach its recipient, though some of the more conscientious expatriates in Canton already saw things in the same terms. If the merchants were so offended that an opium dealer might be executed in front of their homes, wrote one correspondent to the *Canton Press*, then they should pay heed to their own fault in the matter. "The quicker the Foreign Community abandon the opium trade," he wrote, "the fewer executions may they be obliged to witness at their doors."[8]

Elliot was profoundlly shaken by the riot and redoubled his efforts to find some way to prevent the opium smugglers from causing a major crisis. He knew he wasn't supposed to interfere with them, but rationalized an intervention on the basis (as he explained to Palmerston) that the "danger and shame" of the opium trade had reached a point where it was falling "by rapid degrees into the hands of more and more desperate men" and would "stain the foreign character with constantly aggravating disgrace."[9] The riot on December 12 could just as easily have ended in a massacre, he believed—someone in the British factory had fired a pistol, and if it hadn't missed its target he feared the foreign compound would have been turned into "a terrible scene of bloodshed and ruin"—all for the sake of a handful of desperadoes who considered themselves "exempt from the operation of all law, British or Chinese."

So Elliot finally took firm action against the British smugglers. On December 18, six days after the riot, he issued a proclamation ordering all British vessels carrying opium to depart the inner waters of Canton immediately. Having no authority on his own to confiscate their cargoes or arrest them, he fell back on the power of the Chinese government: if any smugglers refused to leave the vicinity of Canton, he warned, he would personally turn them in to the Chinese. Since the smugglers had broken Chinese law in carrying their opium to Canton, he declared, parroting his recent instructions from Palmerston, "Her Majesty's Government will in no way interpose if the Chinese Government shall think fit to seize and confiscate the same."[10] A few days later, he wrote to the governor of Canton pledging his support for the local government's campaign to stop opium smuggling. "The Government of the British nation will regard these evil practices with no feelings of leniency," Elliot promised him, "but on the contrary with severity and continual anxiety."[11]

The opium traders were livid. As they saw it, Elliot, as British superintendent, was supposed to protect them, or at least stay out of their way—certainly he was not supposed to be helping the Chinese government police their trade. James Matheson complained to a correspondent that Elliot had "adopted the novel course of assisting the Government in this, against his own Countrymen."[12] The *Canton Register* condemned his "readiness to aid the local government," suggesting that "it appears to be the intention of Captain Elliot to offer himself as a kind of chief of the Chinese preventive service."[13] A week later, the same paper accused him of "lackeying the boots of the governor of Canton" and volunteering to serve China "against those whom by his office he is bound to at least endeavor to protect."[14] For Elliot, it was Guyana all over again.

In spite of all the trouble Elliot was having with his countrymen, he at least had moral support from the Americans. Robert Bennet Forbes, for one, approved fully of Elliot's efforts to drive out the opium smugglers from Whampoa, "as it is unfair that the innocent and the guilty should suffer together."[15] Forbes was shocked at how much the opium trade had changed during the six years of his absence. Far from the genteel, lazy days of his service on the *Lintin*, when the trade had been all but legal due to the regular connivance of Chinese officials and lack of enforcement, by the time he arrived back in China at the end of 1838 it had taken on a far more sinister character. Noting the government's "vigorous measures to suppress the trade in the drug," he admitted to his wife in December that the opium trade "is no doubt demoralizing the people."[16] He predicted it would not last for long.

Despite Russell & Co.'s sizable business in opium in the past, as the Lintin drug trade ground to a halt the main priority for the firm's partners was to preserve their tea and silk profits, which outweighed the diminishing share of their business that concerned risky drug consignments. To add to their pressure, in January 1839 Houqua threatened to cut off the firm's access to his tea if it didn't stop handling opium on the side.[17] Shocked by the execution of another Chinese opium dealer in front of the factories in late February 1839—this time carried out with swiftness and efficiency by a large guard of soldiers so there was no chance for anyone to protest—Robert Forbes wrote to his wife that the opium trade had devolved into a renegade commerce "carried on in spite of law & reason by a parcel of reckless individuals." The era of its being effectively legal was clearly at an end, and he and the other partners in Russell & Co. could no longer be so sanguine about their roles in it. "When the dreadful effects are brought before our very eyes," he told his wife, "we cannot compromise ourselves by dealing in it."[18] Regretting only the loss of what had been one of their greatest sources of profit in recent years, he and his partners finally did what their British counterparts would not do. On February 27, 1839, Russell & Co.—the American firm with the largest share of the Chinese drug trade—issued a public circular announcing that it would no longer do business in opium.[19]

———

William Jardine left Canton for good in late January 1839, entrusting his partner James Matheson with the business they had built over two decades. He was fifty-four years old and had been living in China for nearly twenty years, with itinerant visits dating back to his younger days as a surgeon for the East India Company. He had been planning his retirement for some time, having accumulated a great deal of wealth and wishing to enjoy it with a wife in Scotland. Conveniently, as it turned out, the timing of his departure would remove him from Canton before Lin Zexu's arrival.[20]

The *Canton Register*—a partisan source, founded as it was by his partner—pronounced Jardine's departure to be the most triumphant exit from Canton ever made by a Western merchant.[21] Jardine's only truly bad blood in the factory compound was with his chief competitor, a rival opium merchant named Lancelot Dent. Otherwise, no matter what any of the traders, missionaries, or newspapermen felt about Jardine's work and his influence from a moral standpoint, most of them respected him as the long-standing leader of their social community. Even Charles Elliot, who was so maddened by the smugglers, saw Jardine as a respectable man distinct from the rascals who were causing the most trouble—respectable enough, in fact, to give him a letter of introduction to Lord Palmerston suggesting that the foreign secretary might profit from Jardine's "perfect knowledge" of the China trade.[22]

Jardine's farewell dinner took place on the evening of January 23 in the grand dining hall of the old British factory. The pillars on its broad terrace were done up with flowers and bunting, with Jardine's initials spelled out in lanterns. It was the sunset of an era, though none of the guests had any intimation of that. More than 130 British, Parsi, and American merchants sat down to dinner that night, attended by an army of stewards and a band playing Scottish airs. The British and Americans sat inside, while the Parsis kept their own table outside on the terrace. Slowly drinking themselves silly on sherry and punch, the Anglos in the grand hall sang "God Save the Queen" and toasted the health of Queen Victoria. Hugh Hamilton Lindsay stood up to toast the president of the United States, declaring that British hearts beat with "joy and exultation" at the success of the Americans in Canton, just as "a father glories in and rejoices over the strengths, talents, and enterprize of his children." Whether or not the Americans felt patronized by this, they joined the others to sing a round of "Hail, Columbia." The crowd toasted the health of Jardine ("respected, esteemed, and beloved, even beyond your own knowledge or expectation") and sang him "Auld Lang Syne." Jardine himself got up to make a speech about his regrets on leaving. He spoke of his admiration for the courtesy of the Chinese and said he had always felt safe in Canton—safer than in any other place in the world. He defended the character of the foreign merchant community: "We are not smugglers, gentlemen!" he bellowed, to the wild applause of his audience. It was the Chinese officials and the East India Company who were the real smugglers, he said. His conscience was "quite at rest on this point."[23]

They toasted the East India Company, Charles Elliot, the future of steam power, and any number of other persons and causes, for on that one drunken night all hostilities and rivalries were forgotten (except for Lancelot Dent, who did not attend and was never toasted). They toasted the two missionaries present, who returned thanks for the financial support Jardine had given their cause. Elijah Bridgman, the frail American pastor who had once written that opium was "death to China" and still railed against it in the *Chinese Repository*, stood up to express his hope that Jardine would find happiness with "the fairest of women" when he got home. Jardine replied that he'd settle for "fat, fair and forty."[24] Robert Bennet Forbes took a raucous part in the festivities, toasting the Scots of his own blood, much to their delight, and drinking himself into oblivion with the best of them. After dinner and toasting, the party spilled out onto the terrace to drive out the Parsis, staggering men dancing in partners to "negro melodies" played by a duo from Philadelphia, guzzling more punch and champagne as they reeled around the floor. A partner in Russell & Co. named Warren Delano (whose grandson would be Franklin Delano Roosevelt) lost grip on his waltzing companion and went sailing into a flowerpot, cutting open an inch-long gash in his head. The party went past three, ending with a small group of die-hards cheering into the night under Jardine's darkened window. Robert Bennet Forbes didn't get home until 4 a.m., at which point he woke up his colleague next door, vomited profusely, and then went to sleep.[25]

———

Lin Zexu had no shortage of advice from his colleagues about how to conduct himself at Canton. Perhaps the most blunt counsel came from Qishan, the governor-general in Zhili responsible for the recent opium seizure. They met in December while Lin was on his way to the capital to see Daoguang, and Qishan warned him not to start a war with the foreigners.[26] Others were more belligerent but still advised caution. Lin's appointment as imperial commissioner was a victory for the faction of reformist Chinese scholars who had, as far back as Bao Shichen's first efforts in the 1820s, argued for taking a hard line against foreign trade. Over the years, however, their uncompromising demands to sever contact with foreigners had been tempered by a greater realism. It was clear, at least to those who had read the accounts of scholars experienced in foreign relations, what kind of military power the British and other Western countries possessed, and that direct conflict with them should be avoided. Nevertheless, there were other ways of going about things.

One prominent member of this faction, a forty-six-year-old named Gong Zizhen, wrote to Lin Zexu to offer his services as an assistant.[27] He was a member of the same literary society as Huang Juezi, the champion of the suppression policy, and he was himself rabidly anti-opium; smokers, he told Lin Zexu, should be executed by hanging, while dealers and producers should have their throats cut. Nevertheless, in writing to Lin Zexu he worried that if Lin should try to shut off the source of opium directly at Canton, then both the foreign dealers and the Chinese "traitors" who worked with them might revolt together and China wouldn't have sufficient military power to control them both.

Instead, Gong Zizhen recommended a gradual approach: first, Lin Zexu should take action simply to reduce imports, rather than trying to cut them off completely, and along with opium he should also restrict the imports of foreign durable goods like woolen products, glass, and clocks (which Gong Zizhen, like others before him, considered wasteful to China's domestic economy). Furthermore, he advised that those import restrictions should only target Chinese merchants and consumers; though Lin Zexu should be firm with the foreigners, said Gong Zizhen, he should avoid conflict with them. At the same time, though, he also recommended strengthening the military defenses around Canton. As there was no chance that China's existing naval forces could ever match the British on the high seas, he said Lin should focus his efforts entirely on coastal and inland defenses. In time, Gong implied, there would be nothing to fear from shutting out the foreign merchants completely.

Of all Lin Zexu's meetings for counsel on the way down to Canton, his most significant was with Bao Shichen himself, the conservative scholar who had been the leading voice in the calls dating back to 1820 to shut down all foreign trade in order to prevent the drain of wealth from China. Passing near Bao Shichen's home on a rainy, cold day in February during his southward journey to Canton, Lin Zexu invited the elderly political thinker onto his boat and spent a day questioning him about matters of statecraft.[28] As regarded the mission to Canton, Bao Shichen later recounted his basic advice to Lin Zexu: "To clear a muddy stream you must purify the source. To put a law into effect you must first create order within." It was a cryptic philosophy, but Lin Zexu took away a clear meaning from it. As he interpreted Bao Shichen's advice, "first create order within" meant he should begin by arresting all the government officials who had violated the ban on opium. And by "purifying the source" he understood that he must shut off completely the flow of foreign drug imports coming into Canton. After his meeting with Bao Shichen, Lin Zexu continued on down to Canton, where those twin measures—cracking down hard on the local population and severing the main artery of foreign trade—would be the pillars of his strategy to put an immediate and decisive end to China's opium problem. But even Bao Shichen, who had long before given up on the possibility of shutting down foreign trade, knew how dangerous such measures could be. Later he would say that Lin Zexu had misunderstood him completely.[29]

———

By early March 1839 the entire trading community of Canton was on edge in anticipation of Lin Zexu's arrival. Some said he was known to go among the people in disguise to gather intelligence, so it was possible he was already there. Others said he was still just crossing the mountains on his way south. They all knew how great the commissioner's powers were—literally imperial, in that he acted on behalf of Daoguang and held authority over all civil and military officials in the region—but nobody knew how he would use them.

Some even looked forward to his arrival, believing that he would soften the extreme measures Deng Tingzhen had taken against smugglers in recent months. Word in the foreign community was that if Commissioner Lin wasn't coming to legalize opium per se, he was at least going to make the trade easier than it had been in the past couple of years.[30] Some of James Matheson's Chinese contacts said that since Lin Zexu was a native of Fujian province just up the coast from Canton, and since the elites of Fujian were great connoisseurs of opium, "it is thought the Commissioner may be disposed to view it with indulgence." Others assured him that there wasn't much to worry about because Lin Zexu was said to be a "man of a mild disposition and not likely to act with harshness."[31]

They could hardly have been more wrong. Lin Zexu arrived on March 10 and immediately struck hard. He began with mass arrests of known Chinese dealers (orders for which he had issued even while still on the road). He put up proclamations announcing his mission to destroy the opium trade completely, ordering merchants to abandon the trade and calling on users to hand over their pipes to be smashed. In one such proclamation, he blamed Canton for the entire nation's opium problem.[32] His men began confiscating thousands of pounds of raw opium and tens of thousands of pipes from the local population. All told, in just three months following his arrival in March 1839, Lin Zexu would arrest five times as many people for opium crimes as Deng Tingzhen had done in the entire two years of his own suppression campaign.[33]

With his plans for the native population of Canton set in motion, Lin then broke with all precedent—as well as the advice of his colleagues—and set his sights on the foreign merchants in their little factory compound. On March 18, he issued an edict ordering the British merchants to surrender all of their opium stocks to him, giving them three days to comply. Initially it was the Hong merchants who felt the fullest brunt of his demands, even though some of them did not take part in the opium trade themselves. As the traditional mediators between the foreign community and the Chinese government, they bore the heaviest blame for allowing the traffic to continue, and when Lin Zexu began his investigations they were the first ones he brought in for interrogation—on their knees, under threat of execution if they should lie. Houqua, as their leader, was both the most responsible and the most vulnerable. At seventy years old, he suffered from failing health, and with such tremendous pressure from Lin Zexu, he confided to Robert Bennet Forbes that he wished he were already dead.[34]

The foreign merchants initially made no motion toward surrendering any of their opium. They wanted to see if Lin Zexu was really serious about using his powers against them, and Lin, who was not accustomed to being disobeyed, quickly lost patience. On March 19 he announced that no foreign merchants would be allowed to leave

the Canton factory compound until all of them had fulfilled his
orders, adding that they must also sign bonds never to sell the drug
again, under penalty of death. He threatened that if the foreigners
should continue to defy him after the three-day grace period was up,
he would execute Houqua and another of the Hong merchants on the
morning of March 22. At a hastily convened meeting with the Hong
merchants late on the night of the twenty-first, the British merchants
caved slightly and voted "under solemn protest" to hand over one
thousand chests of opium in the morning. Houqua and the others
assured them that this would be enough to prevent any executions.[35]

The chests were never handed over, though. Word came back to
the British the next day that a thousand chests wouldn't be enough and
perhaps they should try offering four thousand instead. Meanwhile,
trying a different angle, Lin began to summon the most notorious
British opium dealers individually into the walled city for interrogation. William Jardine had already left for England (and conveniently
for James Matheson, it was by Jardine's name that their firm was known
in Chinese), so the first merchant Lin summoned, on March 22,
was Jardine's rival Lancelot Dent. Dent saw no point in resisting, so
he prepared himself to go into the city and submit to questioning.
But then another foreign resident, who had done some reading in
"several old works," pointed out to him that this was just what had
happened to James Flint when he was arrested back in 1760: Flint
had been summoned alone into the city, just as Dent was, without
anyone to protect him, and he wound up in a Chinese prison for three
years. Dent changed his mind and refused to go, preferring to take his
chances with the others in the factories instead.[36]

The next morning, Houqua and another of the Hong merchants
were paraded around the square in chains with iron collars around
their necks. Lin Zexu threatened again to execute them if Dent didn't
come into the city for questioning—though by this time the merchants were starting to wonder whether his threats were just a show.
Robert Forbes, for one, noticed that Houqua's "chain" was actually so
thin it was more like a necklace.[37] And while the merchants were wary
of Lin Zexu, they were also starting to wonder how much power he
really had over them. Their opium wasn't even in Canton—it was on

ships in the outer waters and up the coast and could easily be put out of his reach—so other than shutting off the tea trade they didn't think he could do much if they refused to give it up. Some noted that the three-day deadline had come and gone without event, the handover of any opium at all lost in a vague negotiation over whether a thousand chests would be sufficient. Even Lin Zexu's threat to execute Houqua seemed like so much bluffing. It was starting to seem clear that they should take Lin Zexu's bluster with a grain of salt.[38]

That was not how Charles Elliot saw it, though. To him, it was at last the great crisis he had been dreading for so long, the realization of all his fears. He was in Macao when he first heard the news of Lin's demands on the foreigners, and he convinced himself that if Lancelot Dent should submit to Lin Zexu's interrogation, he would surely wind up getting his head chopped off—and he would be only the first. There would be a mass execution of British merchants, guilty and innocent alike. But Elliot thought he could save them. He understood the Chinese (he imagined) and he knew what to do. The last thing he wrote to Palmerston before he dashed into Canton to save the merchants was that he was certain "a firm tone and attitude" was all he needed to defuse the "unjust and menacing disposition" of Lin Zexu. He would stand up to the imperial commissioner, but also appease him, using his "best efforts for fulfilling the reasonable purposes of [the Chinese] Government." Through cooperation and respect, Elliot would make peace.[39]

Charles Elliot arrived at the Canton factory compound at sundown on March 24 in a rowboat, standing at the stern dressed in his full post captain's uniform with a cocked hat, sword in hand, to take Lancelot Dent under his personal protection. He was, as James Matheson described him, "a good deal excited."[40] He called a meeting of all foreigners of every nationality and read them a public notice. Given the "imminent hazard of life and property," he said, and given the "dark and violent" nature of Lin's threats, they should begin immediate preparations to evacuate the Canton factories.[41] If Lin Zexu refused to grant them passage from Canton to Macao within three days, Elliot said he would conclude that the Chinese intended to hold them hostage. He promised them he would intercede. He would get them passports to leave the city and would escort them to safety. He had always been willing to comply with the Chinese government, he said, "so long as their proceedings were moderate, defensible, and just," but now he had to stand his ground. He called on all the foreigners to unite as one, and grandly offered his protection to all. "I will remain with you," he shouted, "to my last gasp!"[42] They burst into cheers. For once, maybe for the first time, he was loved.

———

That night, Lin Zexu ordered all the Chinese servants out of the factory buildings. Valets, porters, cooks, compradores, linguists, and the multitudes of other attendants all packed up their belongings and left. Then he shut off supplies of fresh food to the compound. He was employing the same tactics that had been used with such success against Lord Napier in 1834, and against Baynes and his wife in 1830—namely, to isolate the unruly foreigners until they gave up.[43] At the open sides of the factory compound, he stationed lines of soldiers with drawn swords to prevent anyone from passing. The rear entrances to the factories were bricked up. The foreigners' small boats were all hauled up onto dry ground in front of the factory buildings, rudders unshipped and sails removed so they couldn't be used to escape. On the water, guard boats arranged themselves in three tight, concentric arcs to block access to the factories from the river. The only entrances left were the three little lanes packed with shops and bars—soon to be empty—that ran in gaps between the factory buildings to the street behind. Eventually, workers showed up and bricked off Hog Lane and New China Street, leaving just one lone alley—Old China Street—as the sole means of communication with the outside. It, too, stood under heavy guard.

The makeshift prison was complete in its containment of the roughly 350 British, Americans, Dutch, and Parsis trapped inside—a number that included not just the traders and their staffs but also thirty sailors on shore leave who had accidentally been caught away from their ships when the walls closed in. It was not, however, an unfriendly place. Most of the "soldiers" who guarded the compound were actually employees of the Hong merchants who had been deputized and armed for the occasion, and they were friendly to the foreigners, many of whom they knew by name. There was no molestation or menace of any kind from the professional soldiers either. (Lin Zexu had in fact given them specific orders to avoid any unnecessary violence—he wanted only to intimidate the foreign traders, not harm them or provoke a conflict.)[44]

Furthermore, the blockade of supplies was loose enough that a constant procession of capons, boiled hams, roast mutton, and baskets of bread and eggs made its way into the factories, smuggled creatively by Houqua's assistants and others. On one occasion, a Hong employee showed up for a visit at Russell & Co. with six loaves of bread stuffed into his shirtsleeves.[45] The old-timers among the merchants, some of whom could remember when supplies were cut off during Baynes's standoff over his wife in 1830, had made sure to lay in enough provisions in advance to keep their firms fed for a month at least. Matheson wrote to Jardine that their staff "not only lived comfortably all along" but also gave dinner parties for the other "inmates."[46] In all, looking back a few years later, Robert Bennet Forbes reckoned that he and the other prisoners in Canton in 1839 "suffered more . . . from absence of exercise and from over feeding than from any actual want of the necessaries of life."[47]

So nobody would starve, and—other than boredom—the greatest day-to-day annoyance was that these expatriate businessmen, who were long accustomed to being waited on hand and foot by bevies of servants, were forced to cook and clean for themselves in the factories. It didn't go very well. Class divisions prevailed for the British, with the limited number of sailors on hand being distributed among their firms to do menial work for the gentlemen. But there were hardly enough sailors to go around, so the traders still had to figure out how to build fires for themselves, wash forks, carry water from the river, sweep floors, milk cows, and make their own beds. On the upside, they could wear their pajamas all morning and nobody complained. On the downside, the food they prepared, in kitchens into which none of them had ever before set foot, was atrocious. Trying to feed the Americans of Russell & Co., Robert Forbes's first attempt at ham and eggs came out a hard black mass approximating the sole of a shoe, though his colleague Warren Delano eventually managed a passable rice pudding from a cookbook.[48]

———————

The prospect of imprisonment did not seem so amusing to Charles Elliot as it did to the merchants. Rather, it terrified him, conjuring images of starvation and mass executions. So he had already made up his mind what to do to appease Lin Zexu even before he got to Canton to "rescue" Lancelot Dent (whose partner later maintained that he really didn't need or merit rescuing).[49] On the evening of March 26, just two days after Lin Zexu closed off the compound, Elliot told a few of the merchants with whom he was on good terms that he had a plan. When he explained it to them, it was so unexpected that they had to ask him to repeat himself several times just to make sure they hadn't misunderstood him. They hadn't. The next morning, bright and early, he went around the factory compound delivering copies of a notice he had just printed up, the wording of which he had rehearsed several times the night before.[50]

The upshot was this: given his wildly exaggerated notion of the risks the British merchants were facing, Elliot had resolved that they *must* be made to cooperate with Lin Zexu and hand over every last ounce of their opium—for if they didn't, as he (and almost nobody else) seriously feared, they might all wind up dead on his watch. His plan to make them comply, which so baffled those who first heard it, was that he was going to confiscate all of their opium himself. In the name of Her British Majesty, he ordered all of the foreigners in possession of British-owned opium to surrender it to him, the superintendent of trade, in return for which he would sign promissory notes guaranteeing that the British government would pay them its fair market value.

The meaning of his offer was immediately obvious to the merchants—indeed, it seemed too good to be true. At a point of crisis when they knew the Chinese government might at any moment try to seize their illegal opium by force, here was Charles Elliot demanding (in the name of the queen!) that they turn it over to him instead, *with a promise of being paid its full value by the British government.* It was a stunning deal. Even better was the coercive nature of Elliot's plan, for the great majority of the opium under control of the traders at Canton did not actually belong to them. They worked mainly as agents to sell opium consigned to them by investors in India and England, so most of what they held wasn't theirs to give up. At the peril of their future reputations in business, they could not voluntarily hand over their clients' property—but when Charles Elliot ordered them to do so in the name of the Crown, they had no choice, and so they could never be held to blame by their consignors. From the standpoint of the opium agents, it was a perfect way out of their bind. As James Matheson explained to a worried client, "Our surrender is the most fortunate thing that could have happened."[51]

Quite happily, then, through the afternoon of March 27 the British and Parsi traders brought Elliot statements of the amount of opium under control of their firms. He, in turn, signed notes guaranteeing payment by the British government (notes that later became a form of currency in India, traded as "opium scrip").[52] Even the Americans of Russell & Co. came to see him, for while their firm had renounced its drug business a few weeks earlier, they still had more than a thousand chests of British-owned opium that they had been unable to get rid of lingering on a receiving ship at Lintin. The partners gladly signed it all over to Elliot, as did the representatives of all of the British and Parsi firms with any drug stock whatsoever. All told, their pledges came to a staggering total of 20,283 chests, with a market value of roughly $10 million, or £2 million. The editor of the *Canton Register* fully relished the absurdity of Elliot's actions, reporting in a fit of jollity the next morning that "the health of the young and lovely queen of England has been drunk, in flowing cups, on Her Majesty being at the present moment the largest holder of opium on record."[53]

Elliot's offer would turn out to be the key to everything that came after. And it was a very strange offer for him to make, not least because he had absolutely no authority to make it. Palmerston had told him explicitly that the opium smugglers must suffer their own consequences if the Chinese government should seize their wares. There was nothing at all in Elliot's instructions or his previous communications from Whitehall to give him the illusion that he could invoke the power of the British government to protect the dealers from such an outcome. It was simply a rash decision made in an episode of unbridled panic, to which Elliot was becoming increasingly prone (Robert Bennet Forbes called these moments "Elliot's mad freaks").[54] Elliot convinced himself he had saved not just the lives of his countrymen but also the economy of the empire. "I am without doubt," he wrote to Palmerston immediately afterward, "that the safety of a great mass of human life hung upon my determination."[55] Even if the merchants handed over their opium to Lin Zexu voluntarily, he rationalized, if they did so with no guarantee of being repaid it might trigger a collapse of credit in the Indian economy, a catastrophic "commercial convulsion" that would cause an "incalculable degree" of financial turmoil for Britain.

Of course, the traders themselves knew perfectly well that Charles Elliot didn't have the authority to purchase £2 million worth of opium on behalf of the Crown—but the very fact that he had been so unwilling to clarify his powers earlier meant they could plausibly claim that they took him at his word. Even if deep down they suspected that his promise was worthless (though they would *never* admit such a thing), still they signed, because they knew that even an unauthorized contract endorsed by the British superintendent, if they had signed it in good faith, would give them a strong case against the British government for compensation. Faced with a choice between having their clients' property seized by Charles Elliot or by Lin Zexu, they knew they would have far better chances of obtaining reimbursement from their own government than from China's.

Authorized or not, Elliot's offer of indemnity might also look strange on its face in that it represented a pledge from the British government to pay a group of drug dealers good money for their contraband. But on that count, Elliot's offer had a more solid precedent, which tied directly into his recent experience with slavery in Guyana, namely the means by which Britain had effected the emancipation of the slaves five years earlier. For even as the British government had condemned the institution of slavery, it also recognized that the owners had property rights and their slaves represented investments of capital. So rather than simply forcing the slave owners to give up their slaves, the government had paid them to do so—a fact that gave weight to Elliot's belief that the British and Parsis who had invested their money in opium from India, detestable as the traffic may have been to him personally, still had rights to their property.

To pay for the abolition of slavery, the British government had in 1834 created a massive compensation fund of £20 million—ten times the value of the opium in China—to reimburse the owners of emancipated slaves for their losses (though not, to be clear, to compensate the slaves themselves in any way for what they had suffered). In settling on that course of action, one of the most successful arguments had hinged on alleged widows and orphans—innocents—whose only income was derived from the titles they had inherited to slaves toiling on faraway plantations in the West Indies. If the slaves should be emancipated without compensation to their absentee owners, went the argument, the widows and orphans would starve.[56] The merchants in Canton and their supporters would try to play on identical sympathies in gaining compensation for their opium. As the editor of the *Canton Register* argued, if the British government failed to make good on Elliot's promise of payment, it would cause "the bankruptcy and utter ruin of the owners of opium consigned to China, the ruination and destitution of families, the fall in station and society, the debtor's prison, the workhouse alms, and, probably, death by starvation by many whose all was involved in speculations of opium."[57]

Elliot himself was tight-lipped on the subject, but many assumed that the slavery indemnity was what he had in mind when he signed his pledges. Even opponents of opium could support the idea. A writer in the *Chinese Repository*—which, being edited by missionaries, had always been critical of the opium trade—argued that the British government and East India Company shared the blame for encouraging the drug's production in India, so "why not then divide the loss, and let a generous government act as it did on the great question of the West Indian slavery?"[58] Others would insist that it was simply a matter of fairness. "Admitting those who deal in opium to be guilty of as grievous a sin against the law of nature—of morality, as those were who trafficked in slaves," wrote one pamphleteer in England, "what right has the one to compensation that the other has not?"[59]

Perhaps most important for what would come of this action, Charles Elliot expected—as did others, including many of the opium traders themselves—that compensation would be part and parcel with the termination of the Indian-Chinese opium trade for good.[60] Writing to Palmerston just after his arrangement to hand over the opium to Lin Zexu, Elliot said he was convinced that "the time had arrived when the merchants engaged in the trade [in opium] at Canton must resolve to forego their connexion with it."[61] He later expressed hope to Palmerston that the British navy would provide an "effectual check" to stop the opium trade; as with slavery, it appeared the detestable business of opium might finally be brought to an end by buying off those who had engaged in it.[62] And on that count, it is worth noting that the precedent of abolition does much to explain why, despite all of the controversy that Charles Elliot's actions in China would cause back home, one of the least controversial aspects was his belief that the opium traders, no matter how vile their trade, were still entitled to some kind of compensation for their lost property. The question, though, was who would pay for it.

⎯⎯⎯⎯⎯

As soon as the merchants had finished signing their opium over to Charles Elliot, he wrote to Lin Zexu promising to surrender it all to the Chinese government. Up to that point, the largest single drug seizure recorded in China had been Qishan's haul at Tianjin on the eve of Lin Zexu's appointment in 1838, which netted altogether about eighty chests' worth.[63] Lin Zexu's own anti-opium campaign in Hubei and Hunan in 1838, for which he would be famous, had only turned up something on the order of ten or twenty chests of opium all told. Even the aggressive and sustained efforts of Deng Tingzhen at Canton over the two years preceding Lin's arrival had pulled in the equivalent of less than six hundred chests.[64] Yet those successes had met with the effusive praise of the emperor, so there was no necessary reason for any official to take the risk of trying to go much higher.

When Lin Zexu first ordered the British to hand over their opium and the Hong merchants advised them that a thousand chests would be plenty, their advice made sense. With the capture of a thousand chests of opium, Lin would have confiscated more of the drug in one stroke than had been netted in all of the major campaigns to date, combined. He could, they expected, have used that seizure as grounds to declare victory to Daoguang and then leave Canton in peace. The cost of all that opium would be high—roughly half a million dollars— but the Hong merchants could absorb the loss without bankrupting themselves. They could reimburse the foreigners for their lost property, the waters would smooth, and the regular trade could return to normal as it had always done in the past. That, at least, was the most likely outcome right up to the point where Charles Elliot flung himself into the works. Lin Zexu left no record of his reaction when he first saw Elliot's total, but it is not difficult to imagine his shock upon learning that the British superintendent was volunteering to surrender more than twenty thousand chests of opium—well over a thousand tons of the unprocessed drug—with a market value of $10 million.

Lin Zexu had no sense that anything might have gone wrong. In his first dispatch to the emperor after Elliot's surrender, written a few weeks after the fact on April 12, 1839, he detailed just how successful his efforts had been. He expressed little regard for the foreigners— all of them were cunning by nature, he told Daoguang, though the opium dealers were the most treacherous of all. But he was pleased to report their swift capitulation. Elliot had agreed to hand over the British opium almost immediately, just a couple of days after Lin locked down the compound. Furthermore, Elliot complied without making any trouble (as compared to, say, Napier, who had called in gunboats when faced with a similar situation). Lin Zexu had prevailed without needing to use any military force at all, he told Daoguang; all he had to do was to confront the foreign traders with the heavenly might of the emperor's authority and "naturally they were cowed into submission."[65]

Since the most difficult part of the matter seemed to be settled, Lin advised Daoguang to show benevolence toward the newly chastened foreigners. He recommended that the emperor forgive them their past crimes, and said that he had already sent them a large gift of livestock since they were (as he imagined) running out of food in their factories. He also explained to Daoguang that since the merchants were surrendering all of their opium they would no longer have any money with which to conduct trade. In light of their submissive respect for the law, he asked Daoguang to consider sending them an imperial gift to make up for their losses.

The Hong merchants had been confident that the foreigners would eventually be reimbursed for most of the value of any opium Lin Zexu might confiscate from them, whether by Lin Zexu or by the Hong merchants themselves.[66] But that was when they were talking about a thousand chests of opium. Nobody was in a position to make good for twenty thousand chests. And as it turned out, while Lin Zexu had in fact been planning on compensation, the amount he had in mind was paltry. In writing to Daoguang after the surrender, Lin recommended that for each chest of opium the foreign merchants handed over, the emperor should reward them with a few pounds of tea. Even at the current depressed prices for opium, that would be compensation of less than a penny on the dollar. Lin expected they would be grateful to have it.[67]

Unknown to Lin Zexu at the time he wrote that dispatch in mid-April, however, Charles Elliot was not feeling so submissive anymore. He had in fact come to the end of his rope. He was deeply, furiously angry that after all he had done to arrange the surrender in late March, after all of the risk he had taken on with his own people and his own government in order to appease Lin Zexu—after putting his own personal honor on the line with the other foreigners—Lin had not immediately released the British from Canton. Rather, Lin said that he would only grant the foreigners permission to leave the factories after three-quarters of the opium had been collected, a process that would take weeks, if not months, since most of it was on ships that had been scrambled for safety to ports as far away as Singapore and Manila. And so as of April, when Lin Zexu wrote the confident report above, the lockdown at Canton still continued.

As Elliot saw it, stewing angrily in the heavily guarded factory compound with nothing to show for his flamboyant attempt at a rescue, he had tried all along to cooperate with the Chinese government. From the beginning he had deliberately distanced himself from Napier's arrogant and aggressive precedent and tried to act respectfully toward the Qing officials. He had done what he could to keep the British free traders in line, no thanks to his impotent instructions from Palmerston. He had even helped the local authorities to drive the opium smugglers out of Whampoa, for which the local English press accused him of serving the Chinese over his own people. So the anger that now boiled up within him was something like that of a lover betrayed: a sudden, explosive desire for revenge every bit as strong as his sense of injury in being scorned by the Chinese commissioner he had imagined himself helping and supporting, whose gratitude he had expected as his due.

And so on April 3, nine days before Lin Zexu would write to the emperor of his great success at Canton, Elliot had sent off a blistering secret dispatch to Palmerston begging for a naval fleet. "It appears to me, My Lord," he wrote even as Lin was taking measure of his easy victory, "that the response to all these unjust violences should be made in the form of a swift and heavy blow, unprefaced by one word of written communication." In the language of the dispatch—which was so vicious and direct that most of it would be redacted before it was ever shared with Parliament—he might as well have been channeling the ghost of Lord Napier. Elliot called for a British naval blockade of Canton and the Yangzi River. He called for the capture of the enormous island of Chusan on the eastern coast, followed by an expedition northward to demand "the disgrace and punishment" of Lin Zexu and Deng Tingzhen. He wanted Daoguang to be forced to apologize for "the indignities heaped upon the Queen," and to pay an indemnity to satisfy British losses. The time had come, wrote the once conciliatory Elliot, that the Chinese government "must be made to understand its obligations to the rest of the world." He concluded his dispatch with a warning that if the British government failed to respond decisively, if it should simply tolerate the Chinese government's actions as it had always done in the past, then Lin Zexu would think he could act with impunity and the tensions at Canton would continue to mount "till they reach a pass when such extensive measures will be necessary as would probably break up the whole fabric of society in this portion of the globe."[68]

Writing to his wife, Clara, in Macao the following day, Elliot made clear his faith that the British government would back him up. "The great point now is to get this opium delivered," he told her, "so that having fulfilled my public engagement I may make my bow to his Excellency, and all their other Excellencies till we come to Him in another sort of form, and with another kind of business in hand."[69] He focused nearly all of his anger on Lin Zexu, accusing him of treachery and cruelty in locking up the foreigners and threatening them with violence. "This wild creature from Beijing, charged with the business of mending the Emperor's watch, has done him the favor to perform that office by smashing it with a hammer," he told Clara. "All sense of security for property at Canton is broken in pieces. And I confess I am not sorry for it." Indeed, he welcomed the breach in relations, welcomed what he hoped would be a final, forceful solution to the free-trade anarchy he had worried over since he first assumed the office of superintendent. "Our good friends in Downing Street will find a more hopeful seat for trade without much difficulty," he predicted. The British could seize an island, build a settlement on it, make it their own center of trade. Canton and its idiosyncratic trading world, with its factories and gates and rules and monopoly merchants and servants and hoppos and alleyways and smugglers, would all slip away into the oblivion of history.

———

In all, the detention of the foreign population in Canton would last for six weeks, until late May 1839. It was no simple matter to get all of the promised opium into Lin Zexu's hands. Aside from much of it being on ships that had to be recalled from distant ports in Southeast Asia, some of the coastal captains read between the lines of their orders and tried to sell what they had on the way back down to Canton. By the second week of April the drug was slowly beginning to arrive at a depot Lin Zexu had established near the Tiger's Mouth forts.[70] By early May the total was getting close to what Elliot had promised, and a release of the merchants seemed imminent, but it turned out there had been errors in his original figures. Some of the distant owners refused to send their opium back for confiscation, and there were chests that had been promised twice: once by the firm that owned them, again by the firm that held them on consignment. It turned out there were not actually 20,283 chests available, and Elliot feared if he didn't make good on his pledge then Lin would never let them leave Canton. He went around the firms, begging them nervously to come up with more opium somehow. "For Heaven's sake, gentlemen," they recalled him pleading, "enable me to keep my pledge with this man, and to fulfil the whole agreement."[71] In the end, perversely enough, Elliot convinced Lancelot Dent's firm to make up for the shortfall by purchasing five hundred *more* chests of opium from a vessel that had just arrived from Bombay with the new season's crop, promising to pay them back.

If Lin Zexu had merely put the opium into storage, there might have later been a way out. Some of the traders assumed the Chinese government would sell off the confiscated drugs through a state monopoly and use the money to reimburse the traders, thus clearing the balance sheets before shutting down the trade completely.[72] In this they were encouraged when rumors said the Daoguang emperor had asked Lin Zexu to ship it all up to Beijing, and there were reports that Lin was sorting the chests according to quality (and thus price, suggesting that they would be sold at some point). But the emperor quickly reversed those orders—it would be too difficult to prevent theft during the long transport of the valuable cargo up to Beijing. Instead, he instructed Lin Zexu to dispose of it on the spot.[73] Lin obeyed.

Over the course of three weeks in June, Lin Zexu destroyed all of the British opium in a specially built site near the Tiger's Mouth. The American missionary Elijah Bridgman was on hand as a witness. Behind a palisade of sharpened bamboo stakes, the muddy compound contained three large rectangular pools about seven feet deep, with planks and piers laid across them, their insides lined with flagstones and logs. Each pool was first filled a couple of feet deep with water, then workers—under extremely close supervision—carried individual balls of opium out over the water on the planks, crushed them with their feet, and kicked them into the water. Other workers stood in the muck, stirring the thick stew of opium and water into a froth. Then they covered the whole surface with lime and salt and left it to ferment for a few days, to ensure that none of the drug could be salvaged. Each pool had a small trench with a sluice gate leading into the river, and once its load of opium was fully decomposed, the sluice

Lin Zexu destroying the opium

was opened and the vile liquid emptied into the river to be washed out to sea. In preparation for the first discharge, Lin Zexu composed a prayer for the god of the sea, apologizing for his defilement of the ocean and suggesting that the various beasts of the water might wish to move out of the way for the time being.[74]

Palmerston first learned about Elliot's confiscation of the opium not from Elliot himself but from the faster lines of communication in the merchant community—who framed it for him not as a matter of safety or national honor but of compensation. The opium traders wanted their money. On August 18, 1839, eleven days before Elliot's panicked dispatch of April 3 would reach his desk, Palmerston received a forwarded excerpt of a private letter, written by an unidentified Canton trader to his London correspondent, announcing "the astounding intelligence of Capt. Elliot having ordered the surrender to him of all opium in China, for the service of the British Government, which is pledged to surrender its full value."[75] The author of the letter urged his partner to begin working with friends in London to put pressure on the government in order to "expedite satisfactory payment in England."

The man who gave Palmerston this anonymous extract was John Abel Smith, a member of Parliament from Palmerston's Whig party who also happened to be a partner in the trading firm Magniac & Co.—which was Jardine and Matheson's correspondent firm in London (and where Jardine would take up a partnership when he arrived from China). To avoid any appearance of trying to influence Palmerston, however, Smith presented himself as a disinterested lawmaker, assuring the foreign secretary that the letter had not been written to himself, nor to his firm, so no personal interests were at stake in the urgent news it conveyed. That was a lie, though—Smith himself was the recipient of the letter, its author was James Matheson, and by forwarding the letter to Palmerston he was launching the campaign to make the government pay up.[76]

As the news rolled in from Canton, Palmerston was deluged with letters and petitions from investors in Britain and India requesting (then demanding) payment for the opium they had signed over to Charles Elliot at Canton. The international network of traders mobilized quickly—Matheson, for one, sent off a barrage of letters to correspondents in India at the same time he wrote to John Abel Smith, gearing them up to put similar pressure on the British authorities in Bombay and Calcutta. He told Jamsetjee Jeejeebhoy to "do all you can to influence your Government" to follow Elliot's plan.[77] Those Bombay merchants in turn lobbied not just the British authorities in India but the home government as well. In a particularly ominous turn, the *Canton Register* reported that two prominent Parsi merchants in Bombay had committed suicide, fearing financial ruin due to Elliot's actions. It predicted that "more suicides among the same class may be expected unless the government give prompt assurances that Captain Elliot's engagement will be redeemed."[78]

The opium traders knew what they were up against in asking to be paid for contraband, but they made their arguments in near unison. Elliot had promised compensation, they maintained, and the British government must make good on his promise. He had taken their property forcibly, ordering the agents at Canton to hand it over to him without discussion. Whether or not Elliot actually had the authority to do so, the agents had taken him at his word, their obedi- ence (as they pointed out) being proof of their loyalty to the British crown. British and Indian claimants alike argued that the East India Company had long encouraged their trade—for as everyone knew, the Company still monopolized the production of Patna opium in Bengal and sold it at auction for the sole purpose of its being resold in China. It charged transit fees on all Malwa opium exported through Bombay in order to rake in income from that realm of production as well.

Even the government back home, they argued, had sanctioned the traffic—citing as their evidence the by now much regretted statement by the House of Commons select committee in 1832 that with regard to the opium monopoly, "it does not appear advisable to abandon so important a source of revenue." (Which, in context, meant only that the Company would be financially better off keeping a monopoly over opium production rather than allowing its free cultivation by Indian growers; it was not intended as a judgment on the merits of opium itself.)

Their arguments were largely spurious. While the East India Company was indeed deeply implicated, the British government itself had scarcely supported them in any active capacity. Rather, it had done its best to ignore them, and Palmerston had disavowed the opium smugglers outright when Elliot warned they might get the other trad- ers at Canton into trouble. Furthermore, although British India had indeed milked the opium trade for all it was worth in recent years, that dependency was a fairly recent development and did not have to continue. The governor-general in Calcutta at the time, Elliot's cousin Lord Auckland, predicted that the government in British India would in the future disconnect itself from opium production, institut- ing some kind of export tax to make up for the lost revenue from the drug monopoly. In other words, the economy of British India would evolve and survive in the absence of direct involvement in opium.[79]

Elliot's pledges were just one part of the problem, though, for one major side effect of the opium crisis was that the legal, aboveboard trade had *also* been shut down since March 1839 with, as far as the British back home could tell, no end in sight. Ships full of cotton textiles from Britain were stuck at Macao, unable to sail to Canton to unload their wares. Tea shipments could not depart from Wham-poa. And so, quite separately from the narrow community of opium claimants, the much larger community of British manufacturers started lobbying Palmerston to reopen the market for their goods at Canton.

These domestic petitioners were explicit about distancing them-selves from the opium smugglers. The Londoners said they did not want "to mix up in this address the question regarding the trade in Opium," while the Bristol firms made clear that they were not "in any manner connected with the Opium Trade." Instead, they rep-resented weavers of cotton cloth and yarn in Manchester, producers of woolens in Leeds, importers of tea to Bristol—that is, firms that had benefited enormously from the end of the East India Company's monopoly in 1834, but who now found their rich markets ripped out from under them.[80] In financial terms, the group from Manches-ter alone estimated it was on track to ship £850,000 worth of cot-ton goods to China that year, that one city's production worth nearly half the value of the opium at question, all of it unsellable if Canton remained closed.[81]

Collectively, the domestic manufacturers wielded a political weight that was orders of magnitude greater than that of the opium claimants (to say nothing of being free of the moral taint that clung to them), and while they had little to say about the opium seizure itself, they did, in a coordinated voice, demand "prompt, vigorous, and decided measures" to reopen Canton and put the regular China trade "on a more secure and permanent basis."[82] In other words, they wanted a treaty—by force if necessary—to protect their markets in China from such arbitrary stoppages in the future.

With the most impeccable of timing, William Jardine arrived home in September right on the crest of the news from Canton. He, too, threw himself into lobbying for compensation, though he was not optimistic about success—mainly because he realized that ordinary people in Britain, to the extent that they knew about the opium trade at all, considered it a scandal. Politicians were loath to say anything positive about those who dealt in it, even if the matter of Lin Zexu's seizure and destruction of opium was arguably a matter of national honor for which the specific commodity at issue was irrelevant.[83]

The embarrassment of the opium trade certainly argued strongly for the government to make the whole matter disappear as quickly as possible, but the fact was that the amount of money owed to the traders for Elliot's opium pledges was enormous, and there was no obvious source from which it could be obtained. The *Times*, in its own review of the compensation question, determined, "Whether the loss is to fall on the importing merchants, the East India Company, or the exhausted Treasury of England, is, we believe, alike a matter of complete uncertainty to all."[84] In any case, the country appeared to be "wholly unprepared to meet it." Harshly critical of the speculations that had led Britain to this point, the *Times* commented that ordinary investors who had profited from the opium trade "would do well, in living upon their gains, to remember the guilty source from which they are chiefly drawn."

Buffeted from all sides, Palmerston finally turned back to the pleas for an armed expedition against China he had always rejected in the past. If the situation really were so dire as Charles Elliot made it out to be—and the urgent, loud demands for compensation from British and Indian merchants ensured that Palmerston had neither the time nor the political leeway to wait and see if Canton would right itself as it had always done before—there was an alternative waiting for him in his files.

All the way back to Macartney's aggrieved exit from China in 1793, there had been Britons who recognized the enormous advantage their navy would possess in the watery regions of coastal China where the foreign trade went on. With just a few warships, Macartney had imagined, all navigation on the Chinese coast could be destroyed, the Tiger's Mouth forts demolished, the river blockaded, the whole trade of Canton ruined, and millions of people "reduced to hunger and insurrection."[85] More recently, Palmerston had his letters from James Matheson and Hugh Hamilton Lindsay in 1836 calling on him to send a fleet to China in reprisal for Napier's death—letters arguing in detail how a small and inexpensive naval force from India could force its will on China and open a new era of trade. Their hawkish proposals had been there for him all along, lying dormant and unwanted. But in the fall of 1839, for the very first time—not just for himself but for anyone who had ever served in his office—Palmerston wondered whether the situation at Canton had deteriorated so far, and had become so acutely untenable and dangerous, that Britain might be justified in putting such a proposal into action.

Palmerston brought his thoughts on China to a cabinet meeting at Windsor Castle on October 1, 1839. It had been a little over a month since he received Elliot's secret dispatch calling for war, and the intervening weeks had been marked by intense pressure from business lobbyists demanding action. In normal times China was not a country British politicians paid attention to, other than to be glad for the large stream of revenue that derived from tea imports, and in the fall of 1839 there were other international crises that overshadowed the inconvenient events unfolding in China. There was a war in the Ottoman Empire that pitted Britain against Russia by proxy and threatened Britain's crucial routes to India and the Persian Gulf. A dispute over the border between Maine and New Brunswick was stoking tensions with the United States. An invasion of Afghanistan was under way, likewise driven by the rivalry with Russia, that would occupy much of the military force available to British India for the foreseeable future. The ministers did not want to distract themselves with China any more than was absolutely necessary.[86]

So Palmerston proposed a quick solution. At the cabinet meeting he rolled out several charts of the China coast and used them to show how a small British squadron consisting of a line-of-battle ship, two frigates, and a few steamers, properly commanded, might be able to blockade China's most crucial ports and rivers, shutting down the domestic coastal trade and the internal transport of grain in order to force a quick surrender from the Chinese government— the same kind of focused naval action Matheson and Lindsay had sketched out in their pamphlets in 1836. The resemblance wasn't lost on the other ministers, and Lord Broughton, the president of the Board of Control at the time, who left a record of the meeting in his diary, described Palmerston's plan for the distribution of force in

China as being essentially the same as what Lindsay had proposed after Napier's death. Personally, Broughton did not at first support it. He raised the issue of George Staunton's objections to Matheson and Lindsay in 1836—how such a war in China would be both unjust and uncivilized—and he shared a letter from Lord Auckland "strongly deprecating a war with China," in which the governor-general indicated that India had no forces to spare. Most of the other ministers, however, were open to the possibility of "hostile measures."[87]

The Whig prime minister at the time, Lord Melbourne, was mainly concerned that the British government should not have to pay the £2 million that it now, thanks to Charles Elliot, owed to the opium traders. It would be no simple matter for Parliament to raise a fund to pay off the opium dealers as it had done for the slave owners, not least because it had only just finished paying out most of the £20 million slave indemnity and there were no financial resources to spare. For that matter, the slave indemnity had been funded not through revenues but through the issuance of government debt—debt that piled on top of the already hideous mountain of government obligations left over from the Napoleonic Wars.[88] And since opium investors weren't nearly as widespread throughout British society as slavery investors had been, the "widows and orphans" arguments would not carry much weight.

In any case, Melbourne was an extremely unpopular prime minister and in no position to convince a hostile House of Commons that it should increase Britain's debt burden by £2 million, an amount comparable to the government's typical yearly budget *shortfall* at the time, all on account of the bizarre actions of an unhinged chief superintendent in China. As an alternative to asking Parliament for the money to pay the opium traders, the president of the Board of Trade suggested that the East India Company might be made to foot the bill. It was a reasonable suggestion, insofar as the Company had largely created the India-China opium trade in the first place. Palmerston, however, had a different option in mind, one that hadn't even occurred to the *Times* when it speculated whether the burden would fall on the government, the Company, or the merchants themselves. With voluble support from the brand-new secretary at war, Thomas Macaulay (who had just been sworn in the day before and was eager to live up to his title), Palmerston suggested that China should be made to pay for it.[89]

Despite minor disagreements, the cabinet concluded its discussion within the day, free of any complications. The matter was settled: a naval squadron of limited size would be dispatched from England to obtain reparations from China for Lin Zexu's poor treatment of Charles Elliot and the other British subjects. Instructions would also be sent to Lord Auckland that the government in India should support the China squadron as necessary, for several of the ministers worried that it was reckless to think such a small naval force could ever triumph against an empire the size of China. Nevertheless, all seemed well and the ministers left in good spirits, joking lightheartedly about how they had just made war on "the master of one third of the whole human race."[90] After the meeting let out there was still plenty of daylight left in the afternoon, so Lord Broughton went off for a two-hour horseback ride with Queen Victoria through a park and forest. It started to rain while they were out, though, and by the time they got back to the palace they were soaked through.[91]

CHAPTER 14

Will and Destiny

———◆———

Long before Charles Elliot could learn that a British fleet was on its way to Canton he had already shepherded the merchants to the brink of war. On May 21, 1839, when Lin Zexu finally lifted the restriction on foreigners leaving Canton, Eliot ordered all British subjects to abandon the factory district and move to Macao, beyond the commissioner's reach. The British and Parsis and most of the Americans followed him, emptying the factories of whatever property and important papers they could cram into their boats and spirit away to safety in Macao (along with certain less necessary items, like the 524 bottles of wine one partner in Russell & Co. managed to salvage).[1]

But tensions continued to grow even after their evacuation from Canton. In early July, a gang of drunken British sailors killed a Chinese villager in a brawl on Kowloon, a peninsula on the far side of the Pearl River delta from Macao. Lin Zexu demanded that the sailors be handed over for trial. Foreigners had always reluctantly complied with such orders in the past to avoid losing their trading privileges, but the trade at Canton was already completely shut down, for the British at least, and Elliot was emboldened by his hope that a naval fleet might be coming to his aid, so he broke with precedent and refused to surrender the sailors. Lin Zexu, however, was emboldened as well, having just received new regulations from Beijing that formally mandated the death penalty for opium users in China—and that, for the first time, prescribed execution for foreigners who sold the drug as well.[2]

To force Elliot's surrender of the murder suspects, Lin started putting pressure on Macao, where the British had thought to escape him. In August 1839 he issued orders forbidding the supply of British ships there. Servants were removed from homes, and Chinese naval junks started appearing in greater force in the harbor. To judge by warning signs written in Chinese that the British found bobbing along the shore, it appeared that someone had poisoned the springs from which their ships drew fresh water. On August 24, an English passenger on a boat near Hong Kong was set upon at night by attackers who stripped him naked, cut off his ear, and stuffed it into his mouth. Elliot thought it was the work of pirates, but others suspected Chinese loyalists acting under the influence of Lin Zexu.[3]

Facing rumors that several thousand of Lin's troops were mustering in preparation to march into Macao, on August 26 Elliot finally led the British merchants in abandoning the Portuguese city altogether. They crammed their wives and children onto a ramshackle convoy of merchant ships, removing for safety to the harbor at sparsely populated Hong Kong island, forty miles to the east of Macao on the opposite side of the Pearl River delta. Lin Zexu issued instructions for the Chinese civilians in the vicinity of Hong Kong to arm themselves and prevent shoregoers from the British merchant fleet from obtaining supplies. He authorized them to kill foreigners or take them prisoner if necessary.[4] On September 4, 1839—still a month before the British cabinet would hold its October 1 meeting to decide on sending a fleet to China, and the better part of a year before that fleet could possibly arrive—a trio of small British vessels under Elliot's command, with Karl Gutzlaff serving on board as interpreter, impulsively opened fire on a squadron of Chinese war junks that were blocking their access to fresh water, fighting them to an astonished stalemate in what would go down as the first, tentative battle of the Opium War.

As news of the opium seizure and shutdown of trade at Canton reached the British public, followed soon after by rumors of war, the press erupted with alarm. As the *Leeds Mercury* noted in September 1839, most people in Britain hadn't even known about the Chinese opium trade previously, but now it was suddenly emerging as a national crisis. The paper called on the British government to make the "righteous decision" to outlaw the trade and suppress the growth of poppies in India—for the sake not only of "the vindication of our national morality" but also "the security of our interests and the safety of our commerce." As many in the manufacturing districts saw it, opium was antithetical to British trade interests in China, both because the Chinese spent money on the drug that they might otherwise use to buy manufactured goods, and because smugglers created so much trouble for the legitimate trade. Although some might consider the British opium merchants respectable men in purely commercial terms, said the *Mercury*, "as regards morality and humanity, [they are] the pitiless agents of as cruel and detestable a system as ever was contrived by our common adversary to effect the ruin and misery of men."[5]

Antislavery activists helped lead the public outcry against the opium trade. One of the leading figures in the British abolition movement, a renowned orator named George Thompson, took up the cause of "the Opium Question," as it was called, and went on a speaking campaign during the winter of 1840, giving public lectures to overflow crowds in Leeds, Nottingham, Darlington, York, and other manufacturing centers to rally working-class support for abolishing Britain's overseas drug trade.[6] The central question, he told his audiences, was "whether we should go to war in defence of those who gained immense profits by the introduction of smuggled poisons into the Chinese empire, or abandon the idea of this unjust war, and trade with the Chinese upon fair and honourable terms."[7]

Overall, it was working-class activists who provided some of the strongest organized opposition to the war in China. The Chartist reform movement, which had been founded in 1838 to promote universal manhood suffrage, was reaching a populist peak in 1839, and its representatives identified a parallel between the oppression of Chinese with opium and the poisoning of working-class Britons with gin. With rumors of war looming, the *Northern Star*, a Chartist newspaper, printed a long, scathing editorial on British policy in China in which it called the superintendent "Mr. *Opium* Elliot" and charged that Britain's national interests "have been recklessly and shamefully sacrificed by the heartless, imbecile, and cowardly representative of a Government more heartless, more imbecile, and more cowardly, than probably any other that has ever soiled the page of history." It spoke glowingly of Lin Zexu, with unrestrained adulation for him as an "incorruptible" official "whose sterling principle and sense of moral right, placed him above the reach of British Gold."[8]

Other critics addressed the military question, warning that a war against China would not be the simple and painless affair some in Britain imagined. In *The Chinese Vindicated*, an English captain of the Hyderabad army in India warned that Great Britain should "beware how we force China to become a warlike and ambitious nation." Certainly a small British army could invade China, he wrote, and probably it could march around as it pleased for a while, but what would be the outcome of that? Conquest of such an immense empire was impossible. "What then would be gained?" he asked. "Would it restore our commerce, or give us tea?" Yet if such a war should provoke China into developing its immense resources to the full, he predicted, "the combined nations of Europe would hardly compete with her single and united power." China was "a formidable foe," he concluded, "and to attack her on such a worthless occasion as the present, savours of insanity."[9]

It wasn't just the activist press that took up the cause of opposing a war in China. The *Times*, the London political paper of record, was especially vicious in its condemnation of the cabinet's actions. Whatever "high-sounding terms" the Whig ministers might use to justify their war, it declared on March 23, 1840, the war in China was "in fact nothing less than an attempt, by open violence, to force upon a foreign country the purchase of a deadly poison prohibited by its laws."[10] In a separate editorial, the *Times* predicted that a war at Canton would cause the "utter extinction" of the China trade—Britain's only source of tea would be lost, along with the potentially vast Chinese market for its manufactured goods. The British would be saddled with the massive expense of an unnecessary foreign campaign that would cost far more than the entire value of the lost opium.[11]

Through the winter and spring of 1840, Parliament was inundated with petitions from religious groups, temperance societies, and other public organizations across England and Scotland demanding an end to the opium trade and opposing the war in China.[12] Those two elements—the smuggling trade and the war, which the government wanted to keep as distinct from each other as possible—were so obviously linked in public minds that by March 1840 critics in the British press had already taken to calling the imminent conflict "the Opium War," the derogatory name by which it would be known to posterity.[13] The sole purpose of the war, as those critics saw it, was to advance the interests of drug dealers. The *Eclectic Review* predicted it would "stand out in history as the blackest stain on the character of Britain."[14] No matter how the government ministers might try to paint it as a respectable war, said the *Spectator*, "do what they can—gloss it over as they may—THE OPIUM WAR is the name by which history will hand it down."[15]

Goaded by strong public agitation, the House of Commons finally took up the question of the war in April 1840 with a motion to censure the Whig cabinet ministers for botching their management of Britain's relationship with China—specifically, charging Palmerston with negligence for failing to give Charles Elliot the powers over other British subjects he had asked for, which might have allowed him to restrain the opium smugglers and prevent the outbreak of a war. The fact that the resolution targeted Palmerston directly and the war only obliquely was a political calculation: the Whigs in government had traditionally been the stronger party on moral issues. Meanwhile, some of their Conservative opposition (which had absorbed the earlier Tories) were certain to shy from denouncing any war alleged to be in defense of Britain's national honor. By homing in on Palmerston's conduct, the motion aimed to unite the Conservatives against Melbourne's government while convincing a sufficient number of Whigs to break with their party on moral grounds.

The author of the motion was a former Whig turned Conservative named James Graham—the same man who, when serving as First Lord of the Admiralty in 1832, responded to the calls from the

Canton traders for reprisals over their shrubbery and the king's portrait that "trade with China is our only object and conquest there would be as dangerous as defeat." His views on British relations with China had not changed since then and his resolution in 1840, despite its politically restrained language, was effectively a resolution to stop the war in China by forcing the resignation of the ministers who had launched it.[16]

To a standing-room-only audience in the cramped and poorly ventilated temporary quarters of the House of Commons (the previous chamber having burned down in 1834), James Graham began to speak on behalf of his resolution on the afternoon of April 7, 1840.[17] Politically he represented the Conservative opponents of Melbourne's Whig government, but morally he spoke on behalf of the opponents of opium and unjust war, of whom there were many on both sides of the chamber. More distinctively, though, when he spoke he represented the old view of China, the view cherished by Lord Macartney when he first set out on his hopeful embassy to Qianlong's court in 1792—the China of awe and splendor.

The truth of the Chinese empire, James Graham told his audience on April 7, was that it was "inhabited by 350,000,000 of human beings, all directed by the will of one man, all speaking one language, all governed by one code of laws, all professing one religion, all actuated by the same feelings of national pride and prejudice, tracing back their history not by centuries but by tens of centuries, transmitted to them in regular succession under a patriarchal government without interruption." The country was not just enormous and enduring and unified, he went on, but above all it was *civilized*: it was the home to a people "boasting of their education, of their printing, of their civilization, of their arts, all the conveniences and many of the luxuries of life existing there, when Europe was still sunk in barbarism, and when the light of knowledge was obscure in this western hemisphere."[18] Here was the eighteenth-century European vision of Qianlong's China, of which even Macartney had grown disillusioned, and which had largely given way to cynicism in Britain by the end of the Napoleonic Wars—China as the great civilization of the world's other side, the archetype of rational and enduring government, a model of the peaceful administration of a third of the world's population.

Awe and wonder aside, Graham also reminded his listeners how much was at stake financially if Britain's trade with China should be lost—for while the proponents of war thought it would restore trade, its opponents feared the opposite. The taxes on tea imports alone had, Graham reported, brought in nearly £3.7 million in revenue in the past year (almost 8 percent of the home government's income, and in a time of deficit no less).[19] In British India, roughly one-tenth of the government's revenue, or £2 million, derived from the China trade. Combining those and a range of more indirect sources, Graham reckoned that in total he was "guilty of no exaggeration when he stated that one-sixth of the whole united revenue of Great Britain and India depended on our commercial relations with that country." It was a fantastic sum of money at stake, far more than the value of the opium that had been destroyed, and it could all be lost if—as Macartney had once worried—the emperor should retaliate against British violence by shutting them out of China's markets for good.

Graham's resolution opened a monstrous debate that occupied the House of Commons for three full nights of expansive, exhausting speeches that went on in some cases for hours at a stretch. Supporters of the war, led by the very ministers whose conduct was under attack, offered a range of defenses. Thomas Macaulay, the secretary at war (and quintessential "Whig historian"), countered Graham's vision of Chinese grandeur with a view that Britain alone represented civilization while the Chinese were merely barbarians standing in the way of its progress. An unapologetic proponent of empire, Macaulay held that the home government should follow the lead of its agents abroad, not the reverse. He suggested that without overseas agents acting on their own initiative, independently of their instructions from home, Britain would never have achieved conquest in India. The same principle was true in China, he argued. If Charles Elliot had been so confident the Chinese government was going to legalize opium, why should Palmerston ever have issued orders for him to suppress the opium trade, knowing that it would likely be legal by the time any such instructions could reach Canton?

Palmerston, for his part, offered a sneering dismissal of the resolution as "feeble in conception, and feebly supported," a mere ploy to get the opposition into power. He defended Elliot's "zeal, courage, and patience" and denied that the superintendent had in any way contributed to the opium problem, pointing to the dispatches in which Elliot complained of his unpopularity at Canton due to his opposition to the drug trade. Palmerston insisted that the war was entirely about the security of honorable, legitimate British commerce in China, and at the climax of his speech he brandished a letter signed that day by thirty London merchant houses begging him not to let Parliament interfere with the government's plans for war—without which, they insisted, "the trade with China can no longer be conducted with security to life and property, or with credit or advantage to the British nation." The signatories of that letter—whom he treated as representatives of the entire London business community—were not supporters of the Whigs, said Palmerston proudly. In fact, he said, "the majority of them are hostile to the Government generally" and therefore their strong support for the government's war proved that it had the full and disinterested support of everyone with a stake in the China trade.[20]

(Palmerston's speech came at the end of the last night of the debate, so there was no chance for the members of the opposition to look into who exactly those thirty signatories were, but Hugh Hamilton Lindsay—one of the most long-standing champions of the war—was one of them. So were Jardine's mentor Magniac and James Matheson's nephew Alexander Matheson. Furthermore, contrary to Palmerston's claim that most of the merchants who signed the letter were normally "hostile to the government," in fact the opposite was true: twenty-five out of thirty were Whig supporters, and the few who weren't nevertheless possessed sizable claims to the opium indemnity and thus would effectively be paid with the proceeds of the war.[21] They were neither representative nor disinterested.)

Other defenders of the ministry argued that the moral and health dangers of opium were exaggerated and it was no worse than alcohol. They spoke in racial terms: the Chinese were not some simple, honest people, but rather "possessed of great shrewdness and unscrupulousness in all their proceedings."[22] They spoke of honor, charging that a censure of Palmerston would "prostrate this country at the feet of Mr. Commissioner Lin."[23] They said the war would be brief and restrained, not cruel or excessive. They insisted that it was the only way to restore peace and prosperity to the Canton trade and cement the everlasting friendship of Great Britain and China.

On the other side, lawmakers attacked the opium trade as one that "had been fostered for the love of gain, and by the misery of hundreds of thousands of human beings."[24] They quoted Palmerston's instructions to Elliot in 1838 that "Her Majesty's Government cannot interfere for the purpose of enabling British subjects to violate the laws of the country to which they trade"—instructions that Elliot had obviously ignored.[25] The Chinese were a just and kind people, they insisted, pointing to the long peace and prosperity of the Canton trade. They railed against the prospect of making war on a poorly armed, nearly defenseless nation—a war with "a people who, as Captain Elliot described them, were anxious only for justice."[26] If Britain respected its own independence, asked one speaker, "ought we not to pay some regard to that of other nations?"[27]

The most eloquent and impassioned speech of the long debate came from the young William Gladstone—later to be a four-time prime minister and one of the towering figures in nineteenth-century British politics, and at this time a thirty-one-year-old newlywed. In a debate marked to a great degree by hypocrisy and thinly veiled party spirit, Gladstone's fundamental motives were moral. As he wrote in his diary at the time, "I am in dread of the judgements of God upon England for our national iniquity towards China." His message was exceptionally controversial: that justice, in the coming war, would be on the side not of Britain but of China. Gladstone argued that Palmerston had been given more than sufficient grounds to put down the British side of the opium trade, yet neglected to do so, and as a result both the recent surge in opium imports from India and the war that seemed certain to result from that surge were Britain's fault. He questioned whether Palmerston had even read the increasingly hysterical dispatches from Elliot predicting an outbreak of violence on account of the smugglers, for the foreign secretary had consistently "refused to grant him the power necessary to control the British subjects within the dominions of China."[28]

Pointing to the many edicts from the Daoguang emperor condemning opium, and the long run-up of suppression that began under Deng Tingzhen in 1837 and ramped up steadily for two years prior to Lin Zexu's arrival, Gladstone offered that there was nothing at all "sudden" or "violent" about China's crackdown on opium. Furthermore, the mere fact that so many low-level officials in China had been complicit in the opium trade did not mean the Chinese government sanctioned it—it meant only that the Chinese government suffered from corruption within its bureaucracy, as did many countries, which was no justification for British subjects to take advantage of the ease of breaking China's laws.

In a damning conclusion, Gladstone avowed that "a war more unjust in its origin, a war more calculated in its progress to cover this country with permanent disgrace, I do not know, and have not read of." Hammering at the paradox that lay at the heart of Palmerston's war—namely, that the nation responsible so recently for abolishing slavery was now going to war in support of drug dealers—he declared that the Union Jack inspired the national pride of his countrymen because it "has always been associated with the cause of justice, with opposition to oppression, with respect for national rights, with honourable commercial enterprize." But now it would be raised in China "to protect an infamous contraband traffic." If Britain's flag should never fly again except as it was about to do in China, he concluded, "we should recoil from its sight in horror."

For George Staunton, the debate on the China war in 1840 was in many ways the event he had been preparing for his whole life (short of serving as an ambassador to China, that is, though that would never be his lot). Now—after all the hard-won Chinese language study that everyone had told him was useless, the lonely years of trade in the Canton factory, the two embassies to Beijing, the dry books on Chinese law and commerce, a lifetime spent building an unparalleled reputation for expertise on a part of the world most British found baffling and mysterious if they thought about it at all—now, almost fifty-nine years old, living on a country estate decorated with Chinese gardens and a moon bridge, Staunton was merely a quiet backbencher in Parliament, representing the naval center of Portsmouth. He had rarely spoken in the House of Commons since his humiliation in 1833 except to give brief support to the arguments of others. But the opium crisis finally brought China back to center stage in national politics, and George Staunton was—of all men in Britain, let alone in Parliament—the one person most widely trusted to judge what had gone wrong and what must be done to make it right again.

The collapse of relations with China in 1839 was Staunton's ultimate vindication. It was almost universally acknowledged, by critics and supporters of the government alike, that the problems at Canton traced back to the poorly managed ending of the East India Company's monopoly, especially the unfortunate appointment of Lord Napier.[29] Journalists and speakers in Parliament pointed back wistfully to Staunton's failed resolutions of 1833—especially his warning that if Britain should open Canton to free trade without first negotiating a new system of relations with the Chinese government, it would lead to conflict. Here, they said, was the war Staunton had predicted.

George Staunton in 1839

His words were "prophetic," said the *Times*, which reprinted his resolutions in full for its readers in January 1840.[30] In the opening speech of the China debate, James Graham said there wasn't "any authority more entitled to weight and respect" than Staunton, whose "foresight which anticipated the future must be regarded with admiration."[31]

This was his time, and in it Staunton finally found his voice. He had given a glimpse of his views two weeks earlier, during a debate on whether the government should honor Elliot's pledges, where he pronounced himself strongly anti-opium. He argued that the India-China drug trade should be abolished once and for all by an act of Parliament and by "the good feeling of the people of this country."[32] He was also sharply critical of Charles Elliot. In his view, Elliot *did* actually have the power to prohibit the opium trade—the fact that he had successfully ordered the British to evacuate Canton and remove their trade after Lin lifted the siege proved he had that power. If Elliot had simply issued that order seven months earlier, Staunton maintained, then any losses would merely have been individual ones and there would have been no claims on the British government for compensation (and thus, of course, no prospect of a war).

Late on April 7, Staunton stood in the crowded Commons Chamber to deliver his first proper speech since the one that had been cut off midstream in 1833. His fragile ego was buttressed by all of the references to him in the press as the one man in Britain who had foreseen everything that was unfolding. Due to the great importance of the debate, with a national war and the fate of the sitting government at stake, he had a larger and more attentive audience in the chamber than he had ever enjoyed before, or would again. Even in his peak of boldness, though, he was still much the same shy and awkward man he had always been. He spoke "feebly," recalled one listener on the government's side—but no matter that, for "his long residence in China gave him weight."[33] He was the expert, and they would listen.

If Staunton had one chance to stop the war, this was it. The boy who had knelt before Qianlong and delighted the legendary old sovereign by speaking to him in Chinese; the young man who had successfully defended British sailors in a Chinese court; the defender of the East India Company and the older ways in Canton against the disorder and unrestrained greed of free trade; the voice of conscience who had opposed a war of vengeance for Lord Napier's death, who declared in 1836 that to unleash Britain's might against a defenseless China would be "outrageous, and quite unparalleled in the records of the comparatively civilized warfare of modern days"—that boy, that man, now had a pulpit, and a moment, from which he could steer Britain back toward a more peaceful and respectful relationship with the Qing Empire.

Except he didn't do that.

Instead, Staunton spoke in favor of the war. He began by clarifying that he had not come to defend the smugglers who broke Chinese laws. Much less, he went on, would he ever defend the opium trade itself—indeed, he "yielded to no Member of the House in his anxiety to put it down altogether." That said, however, in his reading of the documents provided to Parliament he had come to the conclusion— reluctantly, he said, and only for this one solitary instance—that a war against China was "absolutely just and necessary." As he saw it, Lin Zexu was entirely in the wrong, and Britain could not allow him to get away with his provocations.

In two hundred years of trade, said Staunton, the worst the Chinese had ever done to the British was to suspend commerce temporarily. But Lin Zexu had come suddenly to destroy that long-standing, peaceful pattern. British merchants certainly had no right to violate China's laws, he said, but Lin had brought a "new law" to Canton all of a sudden and without warning, a new law "of a very extraordinary and severe character denouncing death against any foreigner who traded in opium." The merchants were never given a choice whether to obey that law; rather, Lin had immediately applied it to everyone who had brought their opium to China under the old system. Smugglers who by precedent should have expected deportation at worst were thus suddenly threatened with execution. This was an "atrocious injustice," Staunton insisted. In and of itself, it was sufficient to justify Britain in responding with force.[34]

The Staunton who spoke before the House of Commons on that evening might seem difficult to reconcile with the man who had tried for so long to build a more respectful opinion of China and its civilization in Britain. That Staunton, the linguist and scholar, dreamed of embassies and defended China morally against the aggression of British free traders. The Staunton who stood up to defend the war, however, had always been a part of him as well: it was the part of him that believed the East India Company kept the corrupt local authorities of Canton in "check." It was the dogmatist for protocol who had exerted so much effort to prevent Lord Amherst from performing the kowtow. Those two sides of George Staunton had always existed together, and they were not contradictory. Staunton's faith in an equal relationship between Britain and China was founded on a high respect for both—a respect that in both cases he felt personally responsible to protect. Thus he was quick to react if a British free trader like Lindsay or Matheson should disparage China and call for unwarranted violence against it. But at the same time he was equally quick to react if it seemed the Chinese were treating the British as inferiors. Britain's fundamental claim to an equal relationship with China was based, he believed, on refusing to humble itself. If Britain did not maintain what prestige it had in China—if, say, an ambassador should abase himself before the emperor, or if "atrocities" (as he saw them) against British subjects should be allowed to go unaddressed—that prestige would begin to crumble, and the relationship would fall apart.

And it was about even more than that. As Staunton went on in his speech, he argued that the British prestige that was at stake involved far more than just Lin Zexu and China. For as he (and certain others) saw it, Britain held India primarily by the force of opinion. As long as elite Indians admired British power and British institutions, they would willingly accept British dominion. A show of weakness in China, Staunton warned, could therefore shake the foundations of British control in India as well. Lin Zexu's actions at Canton were so unconscionable, he said—and, more to the point, so widely known abroad—that for the first time in all of its relations with China, Britain would have to take forceful action to restore its honor there. The implied humiliation of the kowtow had been simple enough to address through passive means, by simply refusing to perform it (or at least pretending publicly to have refused). But as he understood from Elliot's reports, Lin had used force, and had threatened worse, and such active provocations could only be countered by an equally active response. Without a powerful reaction to restore the original balance, Staunton argued, the lasting damage to British prestige would affect not just trade with China but the whole of the British Empire in Asia.

Perhaps to make up for his awkward advocacy of military action against a country whose sovereignty and dignity he had always defended, Staunton then went on at some length about how much he detested the opium trade and wished to see it brought to an end. He promised to second a motion being drafted by a lawmaker from Liverpool to ban the cultivation of poppies in British India. He insisted that the only way the drug trade could be successfully ended was if the Chinese and British were to cooperate on suppressing it—and to that end, he also suggested that the only way the two governments would cooperate on opium suppression was if they had a treaty, and given the failures of the Macartney and Amherst embassies, a treaty could probably only be gained as a result of war. Thus, by a somewhat bizarre course of reasoning, Staunton concluded that fighting a war in China might in fact be the only way to *end* the opium trade. The naval fleet on its way to Canton thus represented to him "the only prospect . . . of putting down a traffic, of which he was anxious to see the end."

In deciding to support the war, Staunton might have been entirely objective and selfless in his reasoning. He did not write down his inner thoughts at the time, so we cannot know. But behind his words one can sense an enormous measure of relief. Staunton had always been a political independent and social loner. After years of being the scorned objector, whether standing against the tide of public opinion on free trade or alienating himself from Palmerston by his objections to the China Courts Bill, he finally had a chance in his unexpected support for the war to throw off his unpopularity and be embraced for once. Given how much he still craved Palmerston's approval and friendship, the China debate was an opportunity to come to the charismatic foreign secretary's aid and regain his good graces. Staunton had begun writing to Palmerston early on in the crisis, hoping to be asked for his advice. And Palmerston, to his gratification, had responded— a fact of which Staunton was so proud that in his memoir he reprinted every short, meaningless note the great politician sent him over the weeks leading up to the debate.[35] Whatever the private forces that drove him, however, the basic fact of the matter was that in giving his full and enthusiastic support to the war, Staunton found himself for the very first time in his life firmly on the "popular" side, allied with Palmerston and the sitting government, a chamber full of rapt lawmakers hanging on his words. One hopes he didn't enjoy it too much.

And that was all there was to it. No matter how Staunton tried to salvage his moral principles by separating the issue of opium from the issue of war, denouncing the opium trade even as he defended the naval expedition, his contribution to the debate—and it was a major one—was to console any lawmakers with misgivings about the morality of Palmerston's war that it was perfectly just. Great Britain's most respected voice of authority on China, with none to rival him, gave the undecided Whigs in the House of Commons his blessing to vote their party line with a clean conscience. As the *Spectator* commented dryly afterward, "Sir George Staunton threw the weight of his experience into the Ministerial scale, and must have been almost overwhelmed with the expressions of gratitude for his help." [36]

The motion finally came to a vote at four o'clock in the morning of April 10 after three grueling nights of debate. Five hundred and thirty-three weary parliamentarians filed out into the division lobbies, and when their votes were tallied, it turned out that Palmerston had prevailed by the slimmest of margins. A majority of just nine votes—271 to 262—allowed Melbourne's government to escape censure and effectively gave Palmerston's war in China a sanction to proceed as planned. The outcome was so close that if the very cabinet ministers whose conduct was on trial had not been permitted to vote in their own favor, the motion to condemn them would have passed. For that reason it had been said that if the majority were fewer than ten votes, Palmerston and the other ministers would still agree to resign. [37] It was, but they did not.

It is impossible to measure exactly how much influence George Staunton had on that outcome, but at least seven or eight of the Whig lawmakers had openly expressed their willingness to defy their party and oppose the China war if the debate should convince them it was morally unjust.[38] If Staunton had declined to support Palmerston, or even had spoken against him, it would have taken just five of those waverers to change their votes and the entire outcome would have been reversed. James Graham's resolution of censure would have passed, Melbourne's government would have been brought down, and the Opium War might have been prevented.

An angry opposition press hunted for parties to blame. Some faulted Graham for couching his resolution in such political language of "negligence" rather than targeting the war head-on: if the Conservatives had "proposed to stop the war at all events, and to prevent every infraction of the laws of China with respect to opium—so surely would Parliament have gone along with them, in censuring the conduct of the Ministers," said the *Spectator*.[39] Another paper observed that though the ministry survived the vote of censure (barely), nevertheless "they are condemned by two hundred and sixty-two of the people's representatives, and by the nation at large the principle of the war is all but universally condemned."[40] A majority of just nine votes out of more than five hundred "would have been fatal to the existence of any preceding Administration," said one critic, "and it argues a contempt of the opinion of Parliament, and a degree of assurance never equalled, to persevere in plunging the country into war on the strength of such a vote."[41]

Any lingering hopes that the closeness of the vote in the House of Commons might still derail the war were destroyed a month later with the failure in the House of Lords of a much more explicit motion to blame the crisis on British opium traders.[42] Palmerston's Conservative antagonists had a clear majority in the upper house, and the motion was expected to pass until the elderly Duke of Wellington— the general who had defeated Napoleon at Waterloo, Britain's greatest living military hero, a former prime minister, and a Conservative— broke with his party to deliver an adamantly pro-Palmerston speech that silenced the motion's supporters and sent it to a quick death.

Wellington said he had looked into the cause of the war and was positive that "it could not be opium." The lanky, seventy-one-year-old "Iron Duke" argued that it was entirely about the protection of British lives in the far corners of the world, an unquestionably fair use of military power. The dispatch of a naval fleet was the only fitting and just response, he believed, to the rash and violent actions of Lin Zexu against Elliot and the British merchants. Wellington's one brush with China in the past had been a brief appointment as foreign secretary—just a few months in 1834, during an interim when Palmerston's party was thrown out of government and then quickly returned. But in that brief period it had been Wellington who received Lord Napier's first dispatches calling for war in China. He, in fact, was the foreign secretary who had told Napier with such snideness, "It is not by force and violence that His Majesty intends to establish a commercial intercourse between his subjects and China."

So Wellington had no natural inclination toward an aggressive policy in China—if he'd wanted one, Napier had given him a fine opening in 1834. Rather, as with Palmerston himself, and Staunton, and others who had in the past repudiated calls for violence against China but now supported the war at hand, Wellington found himself persuaded by Elliot's exaggerated reports of the "siege" at Canton and the reputed threats to execute British merchants. He was convinced that the entire nature of the situation had changed—that now, for the first time, the Chinese were vicious provocateurs, the traders were comparably innocent, and Britain had suffered "insult and . . . injuries such as he believed had never been before inflicted on this country."[43] The breakdown of relations at Canton, by this view, was not something that had been building up over time. Rather, it was so shocking and demanded such a strong response precisely because it had no precedent. After two centuries of peaceful trade, China, as he—through Elliot—saw it, had suddenly turned rabid, and if Britain wished to redeem its honor and protect its trade in the future, it had no choice but to use the navy to teach the Chinese a lesson in respect.

This, then, was the rationale for a war in China from those who would never have sanctioned such a thing even a few months earlier. War, to these recalcitrant supporters, was regrettable, and it certainly had been provoked by the irresponsible actions of British subjects, and it should have been avoided—but all that was meaningless now because the Chinese had committed themselves and so Britain must respond. Nevertheless, it should be gotten over with as quickly as possible so that peace and friendship could be restored to the two countries. Trapped by a fear of lost imperial honor, these were hardly hawks or warmongers. Few of the war's reluctant enablers in Parliament, and none of its opponents, pretended that it would result in anything resembling honor or glory for the British who fought it. They would turn out to be correct.

On the same day that Lord Wellington laid waste to the motion against the Opium War in the House of Lords, a quiet news item appeared in several local newspapers announcing the death, at age sixty-seven, of Thomas Manning. A relic of an earlier age, Manning had managed to outlive both Charles Lamb and Samuel Taylor Coleridge, to say nothing of his colleague Robert Morrison. In contrast to George Staunton's entrance into Parliament and regular involvement in various London scholarly societies, however, the once outgoing and flamboyant Manning had reversed course in his later years and lived in obscurity. After his return from China, said one obituary, "eagerly was his company sought by the noblest and most distinguished in the land," but he came to prefer solitude, and for the last few years of his life he lived alone in a small rental cottage near Dartford, England. He kept the cottage deliberately bare, with no carpets or decorations. There was no furniture save for a few chairs and his collection of Chinese books, which was reputed by some to be "the finest Chinese library in Europe."

His adventures long behind him, in his older age Manning became more and more the hermetic scholar, buried deep in his books, pottering about in his spare cottage. He had nothing to say about the run-up to war—indeed, he said nothing publicly about China at all and did not involve himself in politics. He still received visitors now and then, and did some proofreading work (for Parliament, in fact, though most recently he had worked on the papers relating to the Poor Laws, not the China war). He also gave occasional translation help to others but went to his grave without ever having published an account of his journey to Tibet. Nevertheless he was remembered, per another obituary, as "the first Chinese Scholar in Europe."[44] As if in memory of grander times, he had grown back his beard toward the end. It was no longer black as when he was a young man, but pure and white as snow, reaching down to his waist as it did when he lived in China. In a final act of the cryptic restlessness that had marked his life, shortly before his death he removed it for the last time, not with a razor but by plucking it out with his fingers, hair by hair.[45]

In 1811 Manning had spent long afternoons with his friend the half-Manchu General, listening to his stories of the old days and drinking wine as the soldiers sang to them and the General played his lute. He sat in audience with the Dalai Lama and saw in the boy such grace and beauty that he "could have wept through strangeness of sensation." It is perhaps only a cruel coincidence that in 1840 Manning's death should have come just as in the halls of Parliament, and on the larger scale of the British nation, the hope for a peaceful future with the Qing Empire was dying as well.

———

Once the war had the blessing of both houses of Parliament, lukewarm as that blessing may have been, it took on a logic of its own, building a momentum that rolled over its silenced opponents, eventually overwhelming even Charles Elliot, the man who had started it all. In none of the debates in Parliament was it ever discussed what the concrete goals of the war were to be. That was up to the cabinet, in particular Palmerston. The supporters of war talked of something brief and restrained, a polite rebuke that would return the status quo to Canton with Britain's honor intact. They called for the protection of British subjects from arbitrary attack or punishment by Chinese authorities, for redress and apologies, but those were vague and limited goals. They did not speak of what the free traders like Jardine and Matheson and Lindsay had been hoping to get from a war in China—a war for which these traders had been lobbying for years without success and were now finally being given.

The truth was that the traders at Canton didn't really much care about the events in 1839 that so preoccupied the lawmakers. They had seen through the bluster of Lin Zexu and knew that Elliot overreacted to dangers that probably didn't exist. As far as the showdown between Lin and Elliot went, all they really cared about was getting paid for their opium by the British government. Separately, how-

ever, for a very long time there had been those among them who
held grander goals for the employment of British force in China—
they wanted ports opened, they wanted free access to the coast, they
wanted treaties that protected and encouraged the expansion of their
trade. They wanted an end to the restrictions of the old Canton system that had been in place since the 1760s. They wanted what not
one single person in Parliament had called for: the opening of China.

Palmerston heard them. William Jardine got the foreign secretary's ear through his letter of introduction from Charles Elliot, aided
by the mediation of John Abel Smith. He first met with Palmerston
four days before the fateful cabinet meeting of October 1 (and gave
him several charts of the China coast that were likely the same ones
Palmerston used to make his case for a war at the meeting). Jardine
also later wrote memoranda on Chinese affairs for the Foreign Office
in which he practically sketched out a plan for the war on Palmerston's behalf, making specific recommendations on useful harbors,
on the distribution of force, even volunteering his own smuggling
fleet (and his own men!) for a deputized military role, telling Palmerston that "many of the small opium vessels might be equipped, and
placed under the Command of lieutenants of Her Majesty's Navy—
their masters, officers and crew (who are generally well acquainted
with the coast and islands) acting under them."[46] Palmerston's secret
instructions to the Admiralty that first launched the fleet to China
that November not only approximated Jardine's recommendations
for the number and size of vessels to be sent but also relayed Jardine's
offer of assistance, noting that the fleet's admiral would find in China
"a considerable number of private trading ships, built for fast sailing,
well equipped and armed" that he might wish to hire.[47]

William Jardine was even so bold as to suggest what the British
should ask for in negotiations with the Chinese government. Payment
for the opium and a treaty to prevent such collisions in the future, yes,
but also "if possible, to open the ports of the Empire to foreign commerce, or as many of them as can be obtained."[48] It was what Western
merchants had dreamed of in vain for eighty years, all the way back
to James Flint's ill-fated voyage up the coast in 1759. Jardine specified
five advantageous ports "which would bring us in more immediate

contact with the districts where our woollens are consumed, and the Teas and Silk produced."

However, Jardine did not—significantly—ask that China be made to legalize opium. In fact, he suggested that the British negotiator should tell the Chinese "it is not the usage of civilized nations to interfere with the fiscal regulations of each other," meaning that they were free to make and enforce their own laws. Jardine also said the negotiator should tell the Chinese "to bear in mind, we have never protected the opium vessels in acts of smuggling, nor complained of any aggression of the Chinese Government against them" (which was sort of true, in an exceedingly limited, technical sense). If it might appear counterintuitive for William Jardine to ask that British naval power *not* be used to force China to accept the opium trade, it is worth noting that he and Matheson had invested a great deal of money and effort in building a highly specialized fleet, and cultivating a network of Chinese contacts, specifically to dominate opium as a smuggling trade on the China coast. If it were legalized, they would lose their competitive advantage. The last thing they needed from the "Opium War" was for China to normalize the drug trade.

The ships of the British fleet began arriving off Hong Kong in early June 1840 and were fully assembled by the end of the month: sixteen men-of-war (the three largest of them carrying seventy-four guns each, more formidable than either the *Lion* or the *Alceste*), four steamers, and four thousand British and Indian troops on twenty-seven transport vessels. The admiral of the fleet, fittingly enough, was yet another of Charles Elliot's many cousins, this one named George Elliot. Palmerston made the two Elliots joint plenipotentiaries, empowering them to negotiate with the Chinese government when the time came. Even after all that had happened, even after Charles Elliot stuck the British government with a bill for £2 million worth of opium, Palmerston still trusted him. The merchants, however, were outraged when they learned he would be leading the war, one of them writing to the *Canton Register* in amazement that the Whigs would keep Elliot on after his "fearful catalogue of blunders" in China. "Where," that writer asked, "can be found such a display of incompetency as the superintendent's acts afford?"[49]

With a detachment of the fleet setting a blockade of Canton, the rest of the force sailed north to the island of Chusan, where they captured the main city, Dinghai, with hardly any effort at all. The battle for that city in early July lasted effectively for less than ten minutes before the Chinese guns went silent.[50] One of the best of those guns, they later found, bore an inscription showing it to have been cast in the year 1601.[51] The British occupied the city and set up a hasty military government for the island of Chusan in which Karl Gutzlaff—leaving behind the very last vestiges of his missionary humility—took charge as chief magistrate of the occupation government. After sending a few warships to blockade the Yangzi River and several ports along the coast, the remainder of the British fleet continued north with the two Elliots all the way to the mouth of the White River, the muddy, serpentine waterway where Macartney and Amherst had left behind the *Lion* and the *Alceste* on their respective embassies before proceeding inland on Chinese junks toward Tianjin.

The British fleet anchored a few miles off the White River on August 10, 1840, and the next morning an officer sailed in with a small convoy to deliver a letter from Palmerston, translated into Chinese, announcing the grounds of war. A Chinese official forwarded the letter to the governor-general, Qishan—the same man who had warned Lin Zexu against starting a war with the British back before Lin went to Canton. In an echo of the events eight decades earlier on the same spot when James Flint presented his translated petition from the British supercargoes to Qianlong, Qishan forwarded Palmerston's letter to the Daoguang emperor in Beijing. This time, however, the balance of strength was reversed; the British this time were not petitioners.

As Daoguang understood Palmerston's letter, it seemed that Britain's grievances were directed mainly at Lin Zexu, and so he concluded that the war was Lin's fault. In a furious edict on August 21 he blamed Lin for provoking the British and accused him of failing both in his efforts to shut down the external opium trade and to suppress its use within the country. "You are just making excuses with empty words," Daoguang wrote to his formerly favorite minister. "Nothing has been accomplished but many troubles have been created. Thinking of these things, I cannot contain my rage. What do you have to say now?"[52] In anger, Daoguang stripped Lin of his powers as imperial commissioner. He punished Deng Tingzhen as well, blaming both men for causing the war with Britain. Both would be sentenced to exile in the far western reaches of the empire.

Daoguang had never asked for, nor had he sanctioned, a war with the British. And given the much larger and more pernicious problems he faced internally in the empire, he wanted to end the external conflict as swiftly as possible. Since the root cause seemed to be Lin Zexu's actions toward the British traders, rather than anything directly involving the throne, he appointed Qishan to investigate Lin's conduct at Canton and restore peace. Qishan had long viewed Lin as a rival and was quite pleased with the appointment. He would, over time, provide Daoguang with vicious criticisms of Lin's mishandling of the foreigners at Canton, one of which centered on Lin's offer to compensate the foreigners with a few pounds of tea for each chest of opium. Lin had gotten the foreigners' hopes up so high with his hints about "rewarding" them for their surrendered opium, said Qishan, that such a measly offer of compensation was bound to provoke them into violence.[53]

On August 30, Qishan invited Charles Elliot to come meet with him at a reception tent a few miles inland from the mouth of the White River to settle terms of peace. The officials who escorted Elliot were chatty, and one remarked in passing that he liked to smoke a pipe of opium now and then.[54] Qishan himself was polished and polite, and he mentioned that he would soon be leaving for Canton to look into Lin Zexu's actions, explaining to Elliot that he and the other officials held Lin fully responsible. He even suggested the British had been right to defy him.[55] In any case, Qishan convinced Elliot that they should return to the south to settle their treaty at Canton rather than trying to do it on the spot. The change of venue would remove the immediate British threat from the vicinity of Beijing, which Elliot agreed to as a sign of good faith, but it also delayed the negotiations for several months while the fleet sailed back down the coast and Qishan made his way across the empire by the inland route. By December they would finally reconvene to negotiate an ending to what appeared at the time to have been a very brief war.

The instructions Palmerston sent Elliot to guide his negotiations were bold—much bolder than Elliot had expected—and they represented far more the avaricious desires of the free traders than the rightful claims of the British nation as Elliot understood them. Palmerston had no wish to deal with China again (indeed, so scant was his attention for the country, and so peripheral did he consider this conflict to his larger scope of responsibilities, that at least one major recent biography of him manages to skip over the Opium War entirely).[56] To make sure there would be no issues left unresolved, he threw into the hopper nearly every claim or demand the traders had nagged the British government with over the years.

This wasn't something Palmerston was coy about with Elliot. In a private note tucked in with Elliot's official instructions, Palmerston advised him to be firm in negotiations, to use the power at his disposal, and to treat the Chinese just like Europeans. The people of China might have different dress, language, and customs, he wrote, "but depend upon it, the inward man is the same all over the world." In a strikingly candid passage, the foreign secretary acknowledged that the pretext for the war was so thin that Elliot should grab everything he could possibly get "because we should not again for a small Quarrel, send a similar Force to the China Sea; and we ought to settle all our matters, now that we have on the Coast a Force which is sufficient to compel Concession to all we ask."[57] In other words, the chance would likely never come again to demand so much from the Chinese, with so much force, for so little justification.

Among Palmerston's many demands, he wanted China to pay for the opium—the "ransom," as he put it, "extorted as the price of the lives of British subjects arbitrarily imprisoned."[58] He also wanted China to pay Britain's expenses in sending a naval expedition. Then came the territorial claims. In his final instructions, which Palmerston issued shortly after meeting with Jardine, he asked Elliot to secure the outright "cession of one or more islands on the coast."[59] He wanted ports opened for trade beyond Canton, along with the right of residence in such ports for men and women alike, "freely and without restraint." He demanded an end to the monopoly of the Hong merchants, requiring that the British be able to trade with whomever they wanted. And in a particularly insidious encroachment on China's sovereignty—one that echoed the harshest criticisms of Staunton's translation of the Qing legal code—he demanded what was known as "extraterritoriality": that British subjects in China should be subject only to British laws. This meant that any British who happened to reside on Chinese soil would be accountable only to their own country's consular courts, and effectively immune to prosecution by the Chinese.

All of these demands were unknown to Parliament, for Palmerston did not share with them his instructions to Elliot. Even the speakers who most energetically supported Palmerston's war had not claimed any right for Britain to force trading concessions on China or demand access to sovereign territory from which foreigners had long been barred. The war they had argued so hard to justify and the war Palmerston decided to wage were two entirely different things.

Elliot, to his credit, refused to push for Palmerston's terms. In his first flush of anger, back when Canton was still under lockdown, he had fantasized about such things. But after having a year and a half to calm down he decided that such demands would be morally untenable. He believed that the British did have a right to demand compensation for the opium Lin Zexu had seized under duress, and that the British merchants deserved a guarantee of safety in their future trade, but beyond that he felt it would be inconsistent with "the character and dignity of England" to demand more. Specifically, he felt it would be morally wrong "to exact by fire and sword and desolation not merely ample indemnity but the means of redressing the effect of a glutted market"—particularly when that market was glutted "mainly by overproduction and overtrading in a prohibited article."[60] In other words, Britain should not use the war as an excuse to further the ends of the free traders who had caused all the trouble in the first place.

Despite the overwhelming amount of naval firepower at his disposal, Elliot was reluctant to use it to force major concessions from Qishan.[61] He worried that a protracted war would provoke the "deep hatred" of the Chinese people, and so he refrained from pressing many of his military advantages for fear of causing too many civilian casualties. Thus, although he dutifully brought up Palmerston's desired terms with Qishan, he did not push the issue when the imperial minister turned them down one after the other. Eventually Elliot backed off from nearly all the demands that involved interference in how China governed and controlled its own territory: he did not force access to new ports, or special legal status for the British in China, or any of the other wishes that derived entirely from, and mainly benefited, the private traders who had Palmerston's ear.

Instead, in his negotiations with Qishan at Canton, Elliot agreed to a settlement that seemed acceptable to himself. Britain would receive an indemnity of $6 million to cover the cost of the opium that Lin Zexu had destroyed (which Qishan indicated would be a private arrangement: the Hong merchants would pay it rather than the government in Beijing, and Daoguang would not even be notified of it).[62] The British would also be allowed to set up residence on Hong Kong—though not independently, for a Chinese customs house would be established there and the British would agree to pay the same fees and taxes on shipping at Hong Kong as they did at Canton. Finally, he and Qishan agreed that Canton would be reopened for normal trade once again.

Elliot would be utterly savaged for his "conciliation" of the Chinese, as Palmerston and the local free traders saw it. He had gained only Hong Kong—"a barren Island with hardly a House upon it," grumbled Palmerston, who was certain that it would never become a center of trade.[63] And since the Chinese government would have a customs house on Hong Kong, it seemed clear the island would not be a British colony but merely a place of residence on Chinese soil, like Macao was for the Portuguese. The indemnity of $6 million wasn't even enough to cover what Britain owed to its opium traders, let alone pay the expenses for the war as Palmerston had specified. Furthermore, Elliot had agreed that the indemnity could be paid out in installments over several years, which meant that its actual cost would probably fall on the British traders themselves, who would surely be forced to

The harbor at Hong Kong in 1843, a year after the Opium War

pay new import duties at Canton to cover the indemnity payments. Most important, there would be no change to the situation of the British merchants in China proper—they would still be restricted to trading in Canton, under nearly the same conditions as before. There would be no expansion of British trade into northern ports, no taking by force the rights Amherst and Macartney had failed to gain by diplomacy. Elliot had done nothing to open the country.

Meanwhile, to secure even those limited concessions Elliot had agreed to withdraw Britain's forces from the large and populous island of Chusan that represented their most important conquest to date and their greatest lever of influence against the emperor. With such an overwhelming advantage of military force, the British on the scene had expected Elliot and his cousin to demand far more. Equally angry about the settlement, though, was the Daoguang emperor—for even as the British government would determine that Elliot had settled for far too little, when Daoguang learned of the agreement at Canton he thought Qishan had given up far too much. Qishan quickly met the same fate as Lin Zexu. Neither government would ratify the agreement, and before long the war would resume on a larger scale.

Elliot did not last much longer than his Chinese counterparts. Palmerston took his refusal to demand greater concessions from China as a personal insult and removed him from service with a withering private letter of April 21, 1841, in which he accused Elliot of treating his instructions as "waste paper." Elliot had deliberately disobeyed his orders, said Palmerston, and dealt with Britain's national interests "according to your own Fancy." Under such circumstances, he wrote, "it is impossible that you should continue to hold your appointment in China."[64] He ordered Elliot home as soon as his replacement— a far more aggressive envoy named Henry Pottinger, with nearly forty years of experience in India, who would share none of Elliot's respect or affection for the Chinese people and would be determined to drive the war in China to its fullest and most profitable end—should arrive. In a prelude to the disgrace that awaited Elliot in Britain, there were already rumors that he had suffered a breakdown of some kind in Asia. His own cousin, Lord Minto, told a cabinet minister that Elliot "seemed to have lost his head; and, by his long residence in China, to have become more of a Chinese than an Englishman."[65]

They didn't know the half of it. Somewhere in the tumultuous cascade of events that began with his intervention to make the British merchants surrender their opium—the panicked, poorly conceived intervention that made the entire war possible—Elliot had indeed begun to lose grip on his sanity. "I have *fancied*, (and the fancy is terrible) that my mind is *not quite steady*," he wrote to his sister in May 1840, a month before the British fleet arrived. He begged her to keep his state of mind a secret. "For God's sake do not mention this," he wrote. "I have had great difficulty at times in preserving a hold, a firm hold over my thoughts."[66] The pressure had just been too great, the terror of failure too all-consuming, the whole economy and safety of the empire (as he imagined) resting on his shoulders alone. "No man has had a harder task to perform," he pleaded to his sister, "and never was a hard task more successfully worked out. *The results are before the world.*" He was positive that he had done the right thing in forcing the merchants to surrender their opium, and in provoking a national war, but he was mad with alarm that the rest of the world might not see it that way. "I shall be abused, and probably removed," he insisted, "but *I can show* that I have saved as terrible a commercial whirlwind as ever threatened British India." He was a hero, he repeated to himself, surely he was a hero.

CHAPTER 15

Aftermath

———◆———

There is no more perfect emblem of Britain's ambivalence toward the Opium War than the first medal that was struck to commemorate it. In a remarkable display of chutzpah that the designer apparently thought appropriate to the occasion, it depicted a lion wearing a crown, representing Britain, with its forepaws firmly planted on the back of a dragon, representing China, and crushing it to the ground. That was certainly how many people in the world saw the war, but it wasn't exactly the tone the British government had intended to set. So that initial design for the China campaign medal with its brazen image of subjugation was rejected in favor of a much blander design that merely shows a palm tree with some British war equipment arranged underneath—a field gun and naval cannon draped with the Union Jack, an anchor and a capstan, various rifles and priming irons—to indicate that the war was just an exercise in British arms to set the China trade back on a solid footing, not some campaign of imperial conquest. The Chinese were now our friends, it implied, not our victims. The Latin inscription across the top of the medal read *Armis Exposcere Pacem*. Loosely translated: "They demanded peace by force of arms."[1]

· · ·

In gambling that Britain could fight a focused war without invoking the combined wrath of three hundred million people, Palmerston had relied heavily on the intelligence reports Lindsay and Gutzlaff brought back from their voyage on the *Lord Amherst*—which, as it turned out, were accurate enough: China was at that time a sufficiently divided country that the people would not unify against a British attack. It was not the empire of one mind that James Graham had imagined for Parliament; there was no longer any possibility, as Macartney and others had feared, that the emperor could with a wave of his hand shut the British out of China's rich markets forever. The government simply didn't have that kind of control over its population. Far from triggering popular boycotts of British trade, the war instead opened existing fissures within Qing imperial society itself, pitting Han Chinese against Manchus, merchants against officials, abusive militia soldiers against angry locals—who, as some Chinese officials complained, were more afraid of their own country's troops than they were of the British. At times when the guns were not actively firing, the British found it relatively easy to buy their provisions from the ostensibly loyal subjects of the emperor with whom they were at war.[2]

The Qing dynasty's meager navy had barely managed to hold its own against Shi Yang's irregular pirate fleets thirty years earlier, and its land forces were still suffering from the severe funding cuts Jiaqing had implemented after the corruption of the White Lotus campaign. The soldiers' weapons were old and rusty, and, needless to say, they had no chance at all of prevailing in battle against the most powerful and modern navy in the world. And the British held nothing back, deploying even the first ironclad steamship to appear in Asia, the *Nemesis*, which proved impervious to Chinese cannons and could steam against the wind and current wherever it pleased. The outcome of any given battle was predictable as long as the fighting took place along the water—for as Lindsay and Jardine and the others who helped shape Britain's strategy knew, the empire's internal trade in the east and south depended heavily on transportation routes along inland canals and rivers, and so China's most crucial cities in the theater of war were located on the water, fully vulnerable to naval attack.

The Daoguang emperor had little clear information about what was happening in the field against the British, for many of the reports from his commanders—even from Lin Zexu and Deng Tingzhen—contained fabrications and claims of victory and destruction of British forces that never occurred.[3] Viewed from Beijing, as from London, it seemed the war could not possibly last long. And so there was no motion on the Chinese side to make a major recalibration of the empire's forces as had been done under Jiaqing against the White Lotus. Daoguang did not deem the war with Britain to be even remotely worthy of drastic measures like his ancestor Kangxi's evacuation of the coast in the seventeenth century. Chinese forces tried valiantly to defend the cities under attack, but they did not try to draw the British forces inland, away from their ships and their most crucial advantages—which they might have been advised to do, for British armies on their own were hardly invincible; in January 1842, even as China's coastal cities were falling with ease, three thousand miles to the west in Afghanistan a British army of forty-five hundred men was massacred in its entirety in the mountains outside Kabul as it tried to retreat, with only one European survivor to tell the tale. But that did not happen in China. Neither did China, as one official allegedly proposed to the emperor, muster an army of three hundred thousand soldiers and send it on campaign westward, across Russia and Europe, to sack London.[4]

As it was, the battles were generally swift and bloody and ended in Britain's favor. No amount of bravery could have changed that. In the entire course of the war China won at most one skirmish, a minor one fought by angry peasants rather than imperial forces, and they were greatly aided by foul weather. Faced with overwhelming odds despite their greater numbers, Chinese officers resorted to desperate measures like locking the gates of their forts so the soldiers couldn't run away.[5] At Ningbo, one commander purchased nineteen monkeys, intending to strap fireworks to their backs and then have someone fling them onto the British ships to set them on fire and hopefully blow up their powder magazines. But nobody dared to get close enough to throw them.[6]

Nevertheless, in spite of this drastic imbalance of military power the war still dragged on for more than three years all told, a succession of fierce, one-sided battles punctuated by long quiet seasons

British forces capturing the Tiger's Mouth forts

of waiting for instructions from London or responses from Beijing. The victories were increasingly self-defeating for British morale as their troops racked up atrocities against helpless Chinese civilians and soldiers without finding any way to compel the Qing government to surrender. A sense of mortification runs through many of the writings left by British officers in the war. One described his horror of a sea "quite blackened with floating corpses" after a battle, the inside of a fort "bespattered with brains." Another confessed in his journal that "many most barbarous things occurred disgraceful to our men." At one point in 1842, the admiral of the British fleet practically begged Lord Minto to spare his forces from having to invade any more Chinese cities because "our visitations are so calamitous to the wretched inhabitants." It was, wrote Charles Elliot in 1842 after he was no longer a part of it, "a war in which there was little room for military glory." The only path to the kind of victory Palmerston desired, he warned, was through "the slaughter of an almost defenceless and helpless people, and a people which, in a large portion of the theatre of war, was friendly to the British nation."[7]

It was one thing to oppose the war on moral grounds when it was still just an idea, but as casualty reports began to make their way home—hundreds of young British and Indian deaths caused, in most cases, not by battle but by fever and dysentery—the drumbeat of antagonism to the war in Britain began to weaken. The critics were not entirely silenced, though. The *Times*, for one, kept heaping its derision on Charles Elliot and the Whig government as the war rolled on. In April 1841, well into the fighting, it ran a satirical letter from an imaginary Chinese opium addict thanking Charles Elliot for coming to rescue him from Lin Zexu. The addict had been arrested, he said, put in the cangue, his pipes broken and his opium seized—but then came the British fleet. He was released from his prison and "bought opium of thy soldiers." He was "given back to liberty," he wrote, "and I warble forth strains of unmingled joy."[8] But even as it satirized the grounds of the war, the *Times*—joined by many of the war's former opponents—also shifted into an attack on the Whig leadership for failing to bring the conflict to an efficient close, for allowing it to drag on miserably, season after season, with no clear end in sight. That in itself, said the paper, was a separate kind of "disgraceful failure . . . an insult to our military prowess."[9]

Then came the twist: in the autumn of 1841, nearly two years after the cabinet meeting that launched the war, the Whig government fell, toppled by a successful vote of no confidence unrelated to China.[10] Palmerston was out as foreign secretary. The Conservative opposition that had so vigorously attacked the war in Parliament formed a new government. James Graham, who led their condemnation of the war in 1840, became home secretary and the most intimate adviser to Robert Peel, the new prime minister.[11] But by that time Britain was deep into a foreign campaign halfway around the world that had already gone on far longer than its instigators predicted. There were unexpectedly high numbers of British and Indian casualties, a vast squandering of funds the country could not easily spare, and nothing at all to show for it. So the Conservatives took a new approach. Rather than continuing to harangue the Whigs for their moral crime in starting the war, they attacked them instead (as the *Times* had) for letting it drag on for so long. As soon as the new ministers took power, they rapidly increased the size of Britain's forces in China. They reinforced armies and sent in more artillery, more supplies, and more ships. Since the war could no longer be prevented, they reasoned, it should at least be won.[12]

And so under the distant direction of those who had once tried to prevent it from starting, in August 1842 Henry Pottinger brought the Opium War to its close by forcing his fleet up the Yangzi River and threatening to destroy the major city of Nanjing, China's alternate capital, at which point the Qing government finally capitulated. It was a tepid victory, to be sure. Even the *Times*, which had been a strong political supporter of the Conservatives, remained ambivalent about their successful closure of this "dishonourable war," as the paper persisted in calling it.[13] In a reflective editorial after news of the peace reached England, it said that even in victory the British must not forget the disgrace by which the war was started. How galling it must be for the Whigs, the paper imagined, to see all the credit go to the Conservative ministers for concluding a war they "had not disgraced themselves by originating" and for restoring a peace with China "which they had not interrupted." The Conservatives would get the accolades for winning the war, while the Whigs would forever carry the ignominy of having started it. In the final count, though, the paper was sober as to how much celebration was merited on anyone's side. Although the end of the China war seemed certain to bring great commercial benefits to Britain, it said, nevertheless "we should be ashamed of ourselves and our principles if we allowed its intrinsic brilliancy . . . to obscure its true character, or to render us forgetful of its most questionable origin."[14]

———

The treaty that resulted from Pottinger's efforts, signed at Nanjing on August 29, 1842, was the first of what would come to be known as China's "unequal treaties." There would be many to join it over the course of the nineteenth century, for it marked a watershed in the Western discovery that one could get what one wanted from

China through violence. Its basic terms gave Britain an indemnity of $21 million, mainly to cover the destroyed opium and the costs of the war. It opened five of China's port cities to British trade and residence, including Canton (the city proper, that is), Ningbo, and, most important, Shanghai—which, being advantageously located at the confluence of the Yangzi River and the sea, would soon eclipse Canton as a center of trade and eventually become one of the largest cities in the world. The treaty gave Hong Kong to the British as a permanent colony. And it ended the monopoly of the Hong merchants—in all, effectively spelling the end of the Canton era.

One thing the Treaty of Nanjing did not do, however, was to legalize opium. It simply would have been too crass. Palmerston took great pains to deny his opponents any further ammunition to claim the war was about supporting the drug trade, and though the Conservatives were in power at the end, they basically followed Palmerston's lead. So Henry Pottinger did not demand legalization as part of the formal treaty negotiations. The only appearance of the word "opium" in the final treaty would be to describe the commodity whose value was being reimbursed with part of the indemnity. But that was only natural, for, aside from the government's own fear of ignominy, the English manufacturers and other domestic proponents of free trade who supported the war were delighted by the prospect of newly opened ports but disavowed any sympathy for drug smugglers. The traffickers themselves, meanwhile, were in no position to ask for legalization, and in any case as with Jardine and Matheson they were generally better off without the competition it would bring. The one person on the British side who had most hoped for legalization was Charles Elliot, not because he supported the opium traffickers—he very much did not—but because he thought it would remove the threat of their causing a rupture at Canton. It was now too late for that, obviously, but in similar hopes of protecting the future peace of the legal trade from the dangers of the smuggling enterprise, Palmerston did ask Henry Pottinger to see if he could quietly persuade China's government to legalize the opium traffic voluntarily—outside of the formal treaty negotiations, on its own initiative.

Pottinger obediently broached the topic of opium in a private conversation during a lull in the main negotiations at Nanjing. His

Chinese counterparts asked him why the British would not stop growing the poppy in India. Pottinger, speaking through Karl Gutzlaff, said that even if that could be done, which he doubted, it would mean nothing because others would still smuggle it. Far from acknowledging any British complicity in the traffic, he went so far as to blame the opium trade entirely on China, chastising the negotiators for their government's failure to keep its subjects in line. "If your people are virtuous," he told them, "they will desist from the evil practice; and if your officers are incorruptible, and obey their orders, no opium can enter your country." Since China obviously couldn't prevent its people from smoking opium, he told them, wouldn't it be better "to legalise its importation, and . . . thereby greatly limit the facilities which now exist for smuggling?" According to a British witness, Pottinger's Chinese counterparts were sympathetic to the logic of his proposal but said the emperor would never hear of it. Pottinger was not content to let the matter rest there, though. In a fit of liberal patronage, he went on to lecture them about how China must improve itself through free trade, drawing for them "a rapid sketch of England's rise and progress from a barbarous state to a degree of wealth and civilisation unparalleled in the history of the world," a rise he attributed mainly to "benign and liberal laws, aided by commerce."[15] It did not get him very far.

Far from the common perception that the war was fought mainly to further the opium trade, it was a genuinely open question whether Britain's direct involvement in that commerce would even survive the war. As early as September 1839, Lord Broughton, the president of the Board of Control, informed Lord Auckland, the governor-general of India, that in light of the events in China, "Doubtless, you must gradually give up the cultivation of the poppy." Shortly after the House of Commons debate he reported that he was drafting a proposal "to disconnect the government of India from the poppy cultivation." By June 1840, Broughton was insisting to Auckland that the government in India must, at the very least, "restrict the cultivation considerably," given "the monstrous outcry that has been raised against your wicked wish to poison a third of the whole human race, merely to fill your own coffers." The Company's Court of Directors resisted any measures to scale back their production of opium, but they were not unanimous—as one of them wrote to his peers in a scathing dissent, "Is there any man still so blind as not to perceive that [opium] has had a most injurious effect upon our national reputation? Can any man be found so hardy or perverse as to deny that it has led to the total derangement of our Trade with China?"[16]

The Conservative government, meanwhile, carefully avoided any appearance of supporting the opium trade after the war. Lord Aberdeen, Palmerston's successor as foreign secretary, told Henry Pottinger that even if he should convince the Chinese to legalize opium on their own terms, Britain's representatives there should still "hold themselves aloof from all connexion with so discreditable a traffic." A supplement to the Nanjing treaty would grant British subjects limited immunity to Chinese law in the treaty ports—extraterritoriality, that is—but again, the British government made it clear to Pottinger that this clause must never be invoked in the favor of drug smugglers.[17] If a British merchant chose to concern himself with opium, said Aberdeen, he "must receive no protection or support in the prosecution of his illegal sale; and he must be made aware, that he will have to take the consequences of his own conduct."[18] Aberdeen's words echoed those of Palmerston before the war, but by this time nobody could pretend they were taken by surprise if China should crack down in the same way again.

Meanwhile, anti-opium activists in Britain were trying to find a way to clear the stain of Britain's "Opium War" by agitating for a ban on the drug from their own side. George Staunton—who appears never to have had any regrets about supporting the war as one of national honor—continued to try to regain his moral footing vis-à-vis China by following up on his promise in Parliament to help end the opium traffic. He helped champion a bill in the House of Commons in 1843 that would have abolished the production of opium in British India, and in supporting it he warned that "our friendly relations with China cannot long co-exist with a large smuggling trade in opium on the coast of China under the British flag."

The end of the war could be the advent of a new era of peace and friendship between Britain and China, Staunton believed, but only if Britain stopped encouraging the smugglers by producing opium in India and selling it to them. If the opium trade were allowed to continue, he declared, the hard-won treaty with China would "be converted into a hollow truce, and probably, within a few months changed into a sanguinary war, of which no man can undertake to foretell the length or the result!" Staunton acknowledged that the campaign to suppress opium might prove to be a long and uphill battle, but he compared it hopefully to the campaign against slavery of Bishop Wilberforce, who, noted Staunton, eventually "lived to see . . . the complete triumph of his principles."[19] The bill would fail, though. And even the milder restrictions suggested by Broughton to Auckland would in time prove unnecessary as the war passed and the distant affairs of India and China slipped back into the shadows of British consciousness.

Of all those who had an individual stake in the Opium War, Lady Napier was probably the person most unreservedly delighted by it. For as she saw it, the British government had finally gotten around to avenging her husband. In March 1840, she wrote to Palmerston to convey "the joy I felt when I this day read in the newspapers that War had actually been declared against China." She reminded him that Lord Napier had been asking for just such a war in the weeks before his death in 1834. "I cannot but feel gratified that at length similar Views to those he entertained are to be acted upon," she told Palmerston. "I knew the day of Retribution must come, and I . . . shall rejoice most sincerely when the Chinese are thoroughly humbled, a lesson they have long required."[20]

Meanwhile, if there was anyone in Britain one might have expected to *denounce* a war in support of opium traffickers, it would probably be Thomas De Quincey, the famous addict who had chronicled for a generation of British and American readers his desperate attempts to break free of dependence on the drug. However, the author of *Confessions of an Opium-Eater*, apparently lacking even a threadlike sense of irony, was in fact one of the war's most rabid supporters. In an article he wrote for *Blackwood's Magazine* on "The Opium and the

China Question," he insisted that it was ridiculous to say opium had anything to do with the war in China.[21] As he reasoned, since the drug was so expensive and the peasants in China were so poor, the opium trade couldn't possibly affect the laboring classes of China like people said. And if the only users in China were wealthy elites who should choose to indulge in their own homes, well, that was their own private business—"what a chimerical undertaking, to make war upon *their* habits of domestic indulgence!" he wrote. In any case, he blamed China itself for the opium trade just as he had implicitly blamed China and the rest of the Orient for his own opium addiction: namely, because he imagined it to be the original source of a taste for the drug, by which he had been seduced and polluted. China, he wrote, was "the original tempter, inviter, hirer, clamorous suborner, of that intercourse which now she denounces."[22]

If the war wasn't about opium, then, De Quincey argued that it was instead about teaching the Chinese to respect the British—and here the old question of the "kowtow" began to emerge in a new form, touted as an indirect justification for Britain's aggressions. According to De Quincey, those British who said that Amherst and Macartney should have performed the "servile prostration" of the kowtow when they went to Beijing were "anti-national scribblers." If Amherst had kowtowed, he insisted, then surely China's next demand would have been "a requisition of the English factory of beautiful English women . . . as annual presents to the Emperor."

That was the reason for the war, in his view: national dignity, and cutting through the bigotry of the Chinese—it was the natural, inevitable consequence of the failures of the Macartney and Amherst embassies. Britain "must not any longer allow our ambassadors to be called *tribute-bearers*, as were Lords Macartney and Amherst," he wrote. "We must not any longer allow ourselves to be called *barbarians*." China, as De Quincey saw it from afar, was a country "full of insolence, full of error, needing to be enlightened." Far from condemning the drug that enslaved his own mind and precipitated the war, he instead commended the British government for standing up to the Chinese. Violence, he insisted, was "the only logic which penetrates the fog of so conceited a people."[23] The excruciating dissonance of Thomas De Quincey's position would eventually catch up with him, though. His own son would serve in the Opium War as an army lieutenant, and would die near Canton in 1842.[24]

These issues of national honor, of the "intolerable" symbolism of the kowtow, of the shabby treatment of Macartney and Amherst, gained in popularity as the war reached its end, and in the postwar era they became the hindsight logic that largely defined the war for its British defenders. For a century and more to come, apologists would say that the Opium War was destined to happen at one point or another, because China had demanded that westerners kowtow. But the kowtow had never been a serious issue. Macartney got around it in his way, and Amherst would have as well if he hadn't misplaced his letter and his fancy outfit. It was a great source of awkwardness, to be sure, but it had never been a predictor of war. In any case, the absolute and total irrelevance of past diplomatic embarrassments to the events of 1839, in contrast to the central role of opium, was obvious to those who were there at the beginning. Charles Elliot, for one, could not have put it more plainly. "The real cause of the outbreak with China in 1839," he wrote after his recall, "was the prodigiously increased supply of opium from India after the Company had lost the monopoly of regular trade in the year 1834."[25] Even George Staunton, who supported the war as one of national honor, maintained afterward that he "never denied the fact, that if there had been no opium-smuggling, there would have been no war."[26]

The war's leading proponents, meanwhile, had no want of respectability in Britain. William Jardine, Hugh Hamilton Lindsay, and James Matheson all got themselves elected to Parliament, the first two even as the war in China still carried on. Jardine entered the House of Commons in June 1841, serving until his early death in 1843 at the age of fifty-nine. In the one speech he made during that time, he argued that the first thing the government should do with its income from the China war, before covering any of the costs of the naval expedition, was to pay back the opium claimants (including himself, naturally).[27] It was a fitting enough request, insofar as the main reason the Whig government had gone to war with China in the first place was because it didn't have enough money to pay Jardine and the others what it owed them from Elliot's pledges.

Hugh Hamilton Lindsay, who would have a very successful career in the China trade after the war, served in the House of Commons from 1841 to 1847, joining with Jardine to defend the opium traders and later speaking against the failed bill in 1843 that would have abolished the drug's production in British India. In his defense of opium, he insisted that not only was it perfectly harmless to the Chinese, it actually made their minds sharper. Even in 1843 he still had faith that the Qing emperor would legalize it.[28] James Matheson succeeded in Jardine's seat after the latter's death and continued for an extended career of more than two decades in the House of Commons until his retirement in 1868 at the age of seventy-two. Matheson's service would appear to have been mainly a social engagement, though, for in the course of twenty-five years he does not seem to have made so much as a single speech. Not that he really needed to, though, for his interests had been served quite well. Funneling the vast fortune from his China trade back into real estate in Scotland, Matheson would die the second-largest landowner in the entire United Kingdom.[29]

Neither James Matheson nor William Jardine went in for significant philanthropy as John Murray Forbes's uncle Thomas Handasyd Perkins had done in Boston, but a loftier place in public memory was reserved for Jamsetjee Jeejeebhoy, Jardine's longtime associate in Bombay. With a fortune made by dominating the opium and cotton export trade of western India, Jeejeebhoy poured his own money locally into Parsi charities, famine relief, schools, hospitals, and public works, establishing himself as one of the leading figures (*the* leading figure, by some fawning accounts) who turned Bombay from a colonial backwater into a modern global metropolis. A director of banks and newspapers along with managing his business empire and funding many charitable works, Jeejeebhoy was a steadfast supporter of British rule, and on February 14, 1842, just as the war in China was nearing its end, Queen Victoria knighted him. "I feel a high, I hope a justifiable pride," he said at the time, "in the distinction of being enrolled in the knighthood of England, marked as that order has ever been by the brightest traits of loyalty and honor."[30]

Jeejeebhoy was the first Indian to become a British knight, and in 1857, Victoria would make him a baronet as well. The name of "Sir J. J.," as he is known colloquially, adorns schools and hospitals in Bombay to this day, the great philanthropist of the city's Victorian past.[31] As one Gujarati newspaper rhapsodized at the time of his death in 1859, "His hospitals, rest houses, water works, causeways, bridges, the numerous religious and educational institutions and endowments will point to posterity the man whom Providence selected for the dispensation of substantial good to a large portion of the human race."[32] Of the fact that so much of that "substantial good," dispensed to such a "large portion of the human race," was made possible by Jeejeebhoy's sale, through Jardine and Matheson, of Indian opium to Chinese smugglers, little is said.

———

Across the Atlantic in the United States, the dominant reaction to the war can be summed up as neatly as anywhere by the little girl who appeared in a story in a Boston children's magazine in 1841, nervously asking her father, "The English won't come here, will they father, and kill us if we don't buy their opium and eat it?"[33] The father reassured her they wouldn't, though the two of them agreed that the British should have sent their soldiers to China to arrest "the wicked men who sold the naughty opium" rather than "to kill [the Chinese], and burn down their houses, and destroy their cattle, and their gardens, and their fields of fruit and grain." Disillusioned, the girl in the story decided she wouldn't like Victoria so much anymore. "They say she has a little girl," the child mused. "I wonder how she would like to have it eat opium and be killed by it."

As in Britain, in America the opium question resonated with the issue of slavery. William Lloyd Garrison's newspaper, *The Liberator*, joined its abolitionist colleagues in England by taking China's side in the war. "In this quarrel," it asked in April 1840, "who can help sympathizing with the injured Chinese, and wish them success in their operations against their *Christian* opponents, whom the Chinese, with a remarkable degree of propriety, stigmatize as 'barbarians'?"[34] It ran a poem titled "Opium" that celebrated Lin Zexu as a model for Western activists, lauding his efforts to liberate China from its "fetters" of addiction:

> Let the heathen teach us! let
> Patriotic, fearless LIN!
> Show us how by man is met,
> Man-destroying, fatal sin.

> See his nation vexed and sold
> By the followers of Christ!
> Mind, the dupe of British gold,—
> Mind, unpurchased and unpriced.

> China from her slumber wakes!
> (British Christians freely scoff;)
> China, strong in virtue, breaks
> Hell's infernal fetter off.[35]

Lest the point somehow be lost on the reader that the British were trying to force opium on the Chinese, a note explained, "The opium trade is the child of the East India Company's adoption. They have employed all the resources of science, wealth, and unlimited power, to force it to its present height; and they have prostituted the means of government to an unlawful end."

Britain's hypocrisy in condemning slavery while fighting a war in support of opium traffickers was an echoing refrain in American attacks on the country's conduct in China. As one Baptist clergyman declared (and as a British opponent of the opium trade would quote him in the House of Commons in 1843), "That the government of British India should be the prime abettors of this abominable traffic, is one of the grand wonders of the nineteenth century. The proud escutcheon of the nation, which declaims against the slave trade, is thus made to bear a blot broader and darker than any other in the Christian world."[36]

There was more than one way to weigh the balance between slavery and opium, however. In the halls of Congress, John Calhoun, the proslavery senator from South Carolina, argued that the opium trade was in fact *far worse* than slavery. By his exaggerated reckoning, if Lin Zexu hadn't interrupted the British smugglers they would have shipped enough opium in 1839 to supply "thirteen or fourteen millions of opium smokers, and to cause a greater destruction of life annually than the aggregate number of negroes in the British West India colonies, whose condition has been the cause of so much morbid sympathy." Calhoun was every bit as critical of the Opium War as the abolitionists, but as a champion of slavery he turned their argument on its head. As he would have it, by enslaving and killing millions of Chinese with opium, the British had forfeited all right to pass judgment on the United States for adhering to what he saw as the comparatively minor and innocuous institution of chattel slavery.[37]

Remarkably, of all prominent Americans it was former president John Quincy Adams—no fan of the British or of slavery—who staked his reputation on endorsing the war. In a much more extensive and detailed version of Thomas De Quincey's argument about honor and the kowtow, Adams insisted that the war had nothing to do with opium and everything to do with China's disdain for free trade and its treatment of foreign ambassadors—as exemplified by its demand that Macartney and Amherst prostrate themselves before the emperor. "The cause of the war is the kowtow!" declared Adams in a speech for the Massachusetts Historical Society in the fall of 1841—"the arrogant and insupportable pretensions of China, that she will hold commercial intercourse with the rest of mankind, not upon terms of equal reciprocity, but upon the insulting and degrading forms of the relation between lord and vassal."[38] Adams believed that Britain had every right to force China to come to terms with the civilized world of free and equal commerce, and therefore the war was perfectly just and admirable. Opium, he maintained, had no more been the cause of the war in China than the tea thrown overboard into Boston Harbor had caused the American Revolution.

Adams's speech was as remarkable for its vigor and decisiveness as it was for its absolute heresy in the eyes of the American public at the time, and even as he drafted it he knew how unpopular his views would be. In his diary he noted that the lecture was "so adverse to the prevailing prejudices of the time and place that I expect to bring down a storm upon my head worse than that with which I am already afflicted."[39] His apprehensions proved correct, and though he had intended to publish his speech in the *North American Review*, the journal's editor refused to print it on account of the offensive views it contained. Adams was taken aback. "The excitement of public opinion and feeling by the delivery of this lecture far exceeds any expectation that I had formed," he wrote, "although I did expect that it would be considerable."[40] Perhaps because he was so prominent, John Quincy Adams's personal views on the Opium War would later be frequently mistaken as representing those of Americans at large. That, however, could hardly be further from the truth.

As for the American traders at Canton, in some ways they were the war's greatest beneficiaries, for they would eventually get to share most of the advantages of Britain's forced opening of China's ports without any of the violence or the lasting stain on their national character. American merchants made hay as a neutral party during the war, their trade continuing with almost no competition during the years when the British were shut out of Canton by their hostilities. (Indeed, hiring American ships became for a while the only way for private British traders to get their cargoes into Canton, and they paid dearly for it.) Even after the Chinese government allowed regular trading to resume, the British suffered from resentment and glutted backlogs, and their cherished hope that the war would result in a grand surge in their China profits was quickly dashed—the year after the treaty was signed, a year desperate private British traders had counted on to make up for their extensive losses during the war, turned out to be one of the most disastrous trading seasons they had ever experienced in China ("and it served them right," said one irate American).[41]

Beginning with Russell & Co.'s renunciation of the opium trade in February 1839, the Americans publicly distanced themselves from the British-dominated smuggling enterprise. With the war approaching, Robert Bennet Forbes led the Americans at Canton in petitioning Congress to send a naval force to protect them, but his group took pains to make clear that they had "no wish to see a revival of the opium trade," and said they had voluntarily signed a pledge to abstain from dealing in the drug in the future.[42] Heeding their call, the U.S. government sent a small squadron of two warships to China to look after them. But in a far cry from the British fleet that was so widely understood to be heading to China to protect a gang of drug smugglers, the American commodore carried instructions telling him to "impress upon the Chinese and their authorities that one great object of your visit is to prevent and punish the smuggling of opium into China."[43] The American squadron's visit to China would be friendly and—in the most welcome contrast to the British of all—uneventful.

It was the Opium War—or rather, its successful conclusion—that finally prompted the United States to send its first diplomatic mission to China. Worrying that Americans might be left out of the newly opened ports, as soon as President John Tyler learned of the Treaty of Nanjing he asked Congress for an appropriation to send an emissary to China to ensure that Americans would share the same trading rights as the British. Tyler's secretary of state, Daniel Webster, canvassed the New England China traders for their advice as to how to proceed, and John Murray Forbes responded to him on behalf of the merchants in Boston. Given the experiences of the Macartney and Amherst embassies, said Forbes, the United States should probably avoid sending regular gifts to Daoguang—they would simply be treated as "tribute" and would gain nothing. However, he did have an inspiration that the war might have opened a window of opportunity for the United States to get closer to the Qing government: the mission *could*, he believed, be an occasion for America to present itself to China as a friendly Western power, one that could act as a hedge against the aggressions of the British.[44]

Toward that end, Forbes suggested that the United States might offer to help China improve its military. Instead of more traditional gifts, he thought, the American commissioner should bring offerings of technology such as "scientific drawings and models of Steam-boats, Railroads, Cannon, and perhaps of Fortifications." A military engineer could travel with the commissioner, as well as a mechanic "thoroughly skilled in the latest mode of casting and especially boring cannon." Given that the Opium War had surely left the Daoguang emperor wary of future clashes with Great Britain and the other European naval powers, he thought that if the United States could— "in a quiet way"—help China develop the capacity to defend itself against European arms, "it would open the eyes of the Emperor to the value of an Alliance with us more than the prospect of increasing their trade a hundred fold."[45] His advice struck home.

The leader of the mission, in fitting with the small, inbred nature of the American China community, was a Massachusetts congressman named Caleb Cushing who was a relative of Forbes's older cousin John Perkins Cushing. Caleb Cushing was well aware of the history of Western diplomacy with China, and even brought along a copy of Lord Macartney's journal as well as Henry Ellis's account from the Amherst mission, but his own mission was meant to set America apart from those British precedents. So he did not bring hundreds of crates of manufactured goods to China as Macartney had done. He brought no giant lenses, no hot-air balloon, no lustres or diving bell. He did not bring any intricate watches or horse-drawn carriages. His would be a much more modest cargo, with entirely different implications. What he *did* bring, as per his instructions from President Tyler and Daniel Webster, and following on the advice of John Murray Forbes, was weaponry. He brought several "good American" Kentucky rifles to give to the Daoguang emperor, along with a collection of six-shooter pistols of varying sizes. He brought a working model of a war steamer ("armed and rigged"), along with a full model of its engine. He brought books on gunnery, fortifications, shipbuilding, and naval strategy.[46]

With China ostensibly humbled by the British, the U.S. com-missioner did not have to come seeking favor. In contrast to King George III's high-blown letter to Qianlong with its language of "tens of thousands and tens of thousands thousand years," President Tyler's message to Daoguang in 1843 was given to short, declarative sentences that might have been composed by a third grader. "I hope your health is good," he told Daoguang. "China is a great empire, extending over a great part of the world. The Chinese are numerous. You have millions and millions of subjects."[47] By way of introducing his own country, Tyler named all twenty-six states in the Union, one by one, without comment. He expressed hope for peaceful trade. At the end, he signed off, "Your good friend, John Tyler." He did not try to impress, but neither did he feel that he needed to. And while there would be no giant planetarium in Caleb Cushing's cargo that had taken thirty years to build, he did travel to China equipped with an atlas of the world, and a small globe—whose purpose, as Daniel Webster explained, was "that the Celestials may see that they are not the 'Central Kingdom.'"[48]

The Cushing mission was a success, the first diplomatic mission from any Western country to come away from China with a treaty signed in peace. One key to that success, though, was that it wasn't really necessary; by the time Caleb Cushing got to China the Daoguang emperor had already issued an edict allowing Americans to trade in the treaty ports on the same terms as the British. Qianlong, it would appear, had been quite sincere when he told Macartney that he couldn't give special trading privileges to the British because then, to be fair, he would have to give the same to all the other countries that came to trade. All the same, Cushing corralled Elijah Bridgman and two other American missionaries to be his interpreters and managed to badger his way into a series of negotiations with the imperial commissioner who had hashed out the Treaty of Nanjing with the British.

Cushing's negotiations took place at a temple in Macao (he was just as happy not to go to Beijing, as it spared him having to decide whether to kowtow). The resulting treaty between the United States and China, signed in 1844 and known as the Treaty of Wanghia, granted Americans most of the same privileges that the British had fought their atrocious and demoralizing war to secure. There were a few variations, though, which highlighted the different flavor of the American mission. One was that Cushing agreed explicitly that Americans who dealt in opium would be fully liable to Chinese law and the U.S. government would do nothing to protect them. Another was that Cushing managed to negotiate a clause allowing Americans to study Chinese legally with native teachers.[49] James Flint would have been pleased.

Nevertheless, as hopeful as the Cushing treaty might have seemed for a more equal friendship between China and the United States when viewed up close, it is somewhat more disconcerting from a wider perspective because it never would have been signed without the Opium War to precede it. But that was all part of a pattern, for the Americans in China had always enjoyed a parasitic relationship with their British rivals. Their presence at Canton in the early nineteenth century benefited the British not at all—indeed, one of the key reasons for the termination of the East India Company's monopoly, opening the era of British free trade at Canton that led ultimately to the war, had been that the Americans were sapping away Britain's full share of the China market. At the same time, however, Britain inadvertently helped carve out the spaces in which the Americans worked, and nowhere was this more apparent than in the Opium War—Americans benefited so much from the war precisely because Britain, not they, fought it. So not only could they trade without competition in the midst of it, and gain entrance to new ports and markets after its end, but it also gave them an opening to present themselves to the Chinese as a friendly and peaceful Western power in hopes of undermining the British through diplomacy. This would set a pattern of its own for the nineteenth century—one where Americans could rail against Britain's aggressive actions in China on moral grounds, while at the same time reaping great benefits from those very same actions. In essence, the more bellicose the British (and later the French) became in China, the more the Americans would profit as the neutral party. It was in their best interests for the British to keep up the very same behavior they so loudly denounced.

———————

And what did it all mean for China? When Lin Zexu was at his peak of confidence, in the summer of 1839—after all of the opium had been destroyed but before the British fleet arrived—he wrote a letter to Queen Victoria. He did so with the emperor's approval, and it was loosely modeled after Qianlong's letter to King George III. Queen Victoria herself never actually received a copy, though she might have seen it if she happened to read the *Times* on June 11, 1840, where it was published in English translation after a private merchant brought a copy back to London. In his letter, Lin Zexu chided Victoria at length for allowing her subjects to sell opium in China. It was especially unconscionable for her to do so, he said, because, as he understood, the British had banned it in their own country in recognition of "how hurtful it is to mankind." For two hundred years, he wrote, all of the wealth that made England a "rich and flourishing kingdom" had come from its trade with China. And the products that the people of China sold to the British—tea, silk, and so on—were all beneficial in some way. In fact, not only were they beneficial, they were so essential that Britain surely "could not exist a single day" without them. In that light, he asked, "By what principle of reason, then, should these foreigners send in return a poisonous drug, which involves in destruction those very natives of China?"[50]

The moral grounds of that letter were both impeccable and timeless. Aside from certain limitations of Lin's knowledge about Britain (the British did not, for example, ban opium in their own country), the basic argument that Victoria's subjects had turned a healthy and profitable commerce of two centuries into a cesspool of poison and greed was a powerful one that resonated in its own time as strongly as it does today. His letter was reprinted and quoted widely by the opponents of the Opium War in Great Britain, and it would later establish Lin Zexu in his nearly permanent position in China's historical pantheon as the voice of moral reason who stood up on behalf of his people against the imperialist drug dealers of Great Britain. That is the Lin Zexu who endures as the hero of textbooks in China, whose birthday is celebrated in Taiwan, whose statue stands vigil over New York City's Chinatown on a granite pedestal inscribed PIONEER IN THE WAR AGAINST DRUGS.

In the China of his own time, however, Lin Zexu was not a national hero by any means. To many—including the Daoguang emperor—he was a disgrace to the empire whose high-handed dealings with the British had provoked a destructive and unnecessary coastal war. The righteousness of his cause aside, that view was not without its merits;

Statue of Lin Zexu in New York City

if he had handled affairs at Canton differently, especially if he had been more welcoming of Charles Elliot's willingness to cooperate, he might have been able to do permanent damage to the opium trade without giving Britain grounds for a war of reprisal. If he had been even slightly more flexible, China might have been far better off.

The general view of Lin Zexu's peers was not that he was wrong for confiscating the opium, but rather for shutting down the legitimate trade and locking up all the foreigners in Canton for six weeks. Those actions, they believed, were what had provoked the war, not the confiscation of opium per se.[51] This was a view with strong resonance on the other side as well, for without the "siege" of Canton, the manufacturers in England would have suffered no losses and would have had no standing to lobby for reparations. Without Lin's threat of violence against British subjects—even as a bluff—the thin foundation of the British government's rationale for a war of honor (the one that George Staunton supported) would have been taken away. Palmerston's war barely made it past Parliament as it was, in spite of the scandalous fact that drug smugglers were involved; there is no way he and his supporters could possibly have sold Parliament and the public on a war whose *only* purpose was to pay back drug smugglers (even if, privately, that was his primary reason in seeking it). The insults to Elliot, the threats to execute foreigners, the shutting down of the legitimate trade at length and without warning—those were the essential "outrages" that fueled the public argument for war. Without them, no matter how many chests of opium might have been confiscated, no matter how many private smugglers might have been ruined, the Opium War simply would not have happened.

The most prominent Chinese account of the war from its own time was written by a geographer and military historian named Wei Yuan who had worked closely with Lin Zexu. Although Wei was an admirer of Lin and inclined to take his side, he saw the conflict in far less stark moral terms than its Western critics did. To him, it was not in its essence an opium war but rather a general conflict over China's management of foreign trade, one to which opium was incidental. He also saw it as having been eminently avoidable. In his judgment, Charles Elliot did not have an inherently "rebellious" nature. Wei noted that Elliot had offered early on to help find a way to end the opium smuggling trade, though Lin Zexu rebuffed him. (That, according to Wei, was one of the major mistakes of the time.) Later, Elliot went along willingly with the confiscation of property, and even though he refused to hand his men over after the murder of the villager in Kowloon, he did offer a reward to try to identify the killer. As Wei depicted him, Elliot was hardly spoiling for a fight.[52]

Wei Yuan understood the British to be motivated entirely by their desire for open trade, which he generally supported. He agreed with others that the regular commerce at Canton should never have been so suddenly cut off—it was, after all, something that could be used to strengthen the country. But he singled out for praise Lin's efforts against opium, as well as a proposal Lin made to divert funds from the Canton customs toward improving local defenses. Indeed, such improvements, to Wei's mind, were what China needed most of all for the future.

In an echo of Napoleon's warning to his Irish physician that a British war would only awaken China and cause it to start strengthening itself for revenge, Wei Yuan went on to argue that China must now begin arming itself with Western ships and cannons, and stock itself with foreign rockets and gunpowder. Those purchases could be made as exchanges through trade, he said, or even in lieu of tariffs, which would effectively redirect the millions of taels of annual customs revenue from Canton into building a modern Chinese military. By such means, he wrote, "the special skills of the Westerners would become the special skills of the Chinese." Once the naval fleets and coastal defenses of Canton were fully modernized, they could do the same in the other treaty ports up to Shanghai. It would open a new era of Chinese naval power, he predicted, such as had not been seen in a thousand years.[53] Unfortunately for his countrymen, it would be a long time before any Chinese government took such recommendations seriously.

In the final count, Wei Yuan's greatest regret about the war was that China hadn't used it as an occasion to end the importation of opium.[54] And indeed, as for the commerce in the drug, the illegal trade along the coast picked right back up again just as soon as the fighting got under way. It would soon resume its previous proportions even as the aboveboard British trade in cotton and tea was still shut down at Canton. After the war, the Daoguang emperor would issue repeated edicts calling for local officials to punish traders and users of the drug, just as he had done in the past, but those edicts would never again have the same effect they did in the years just before Lin Zexu's arrival in Canton.[55] Enforcement would be weak, corruption seeped back in, and fewer and fewer criminals were prosecuted for opium offenses, to the point that just a handful of transgressors each year appear to have been punished in China through the 1840s.[56]

For all the protestations of Palmerston and his supporters that the war was not meant to support the opium trade, it certainly proved a great boon for that commerce. In the years that followed the war, opium exports from India, mostly destined for China, surpassed their previous highs and went on to reach new ones—forty thousand chests per year by 1846, fifty thousand by 1849, more than seventy thousand by 1855.[57] As the opium trade regained steam thanks to the war, even the Americans of Russell & Co.—proving themselves more pragmatic than angelic—joined right back in again. The East India Company, meanwhile, annexed the territory of Sindh in northern India (now part of Pakistan) in 1843, which cut off the last overland route for independent producers in central India to transport their opium to the Portuguese ports of Daman and Diu, thus cementing Britain's total control over the export of the drug from the subcontinent. With the shipping of opium through non-British ports made effectively impossible, the Company sharply hiked its transit duties on Malwa opium, raising them more than three times over by 1848 to dramatically increase its income from the free growth and production of opium by independent farmers who were not British subjects.[58] British India's financial dependence on opium grew accordingly. Whereas opium revenues had made up less than a tenth of the Bengal government's income at the time of the Opium War, by the 1850s the share had risen to nearly one-sixth.[59]

Within China, opium was still technically a clandestine trade after the war (if more omnipresent than ever), but by the mid-1850s, faced with a gigantic rebellion by the quasi-Christian peasant forces of the Taiping Heavenly Kingdom—an insurrection to make the White Lotus look like a tempest in a teapot—some provincial officials resuscitated the dormant issue of legalization, proposing domestic taxes on opium to help fund the war effort.[60] And though George Staunton continued with his ineffectual efforts to force an end to Britain's involvement in opium after the war, by 1856 he conceded that such efforts were no longer necessary because the trade was by that time effectively legal in China.[61] That de facto legality would be made concrete in 1858 on the heels of another war, with Britain and France, after which the British plenipotentiary Lord Elgin would, much to his own mortification, sign a document setting a formal tariff for the import of opium into China. But already by that time, the only limit to the growth of the drug's use in the Qing Empire was its price, and Chinese farmers were responding by growing poppies and process- ing large amounts of cheap native opium to compete with the more expensive varieties coming in from India.

With the advent of a free, legal, and open Asian commerce in opium, the native merchants of India and China moved to dominate the trade, squeezing out the Europeans who had acted as go-betweens in the past. By the 1870s, the India-China opium trade was so firmly locked up in the hands of native traders on both sides that there was no longer much money to be made by the Western firms that had pioneered the "country" trade in the early part of the century. In the face of declining profits, Jardine, Matheson & Co. (now run by a slew of nephews and other descendants of the founders and their partners) pulled almost entirely out of the opium trade in 1873, joined by other large Western firms.[62] Domestic production in China, meanwhile, kept rising—ultimately to such stupendous heights that it would dwarf the continued imports of the drug from India. The dawn of the twentieth century would find China producing ten times as much opium internally as it imported from abroad, an explosive abundance of cheap domestic narcotics that would create a public health emer- gency worlds beyond even the most exaggerated estimates of what had existed in the 1830s prior to the Opium War.[63] So much for the virtues of legalization.

In spite of the best efforts of moral activists at home, the British government would ultimately do nothing to scale back the depen- dence of British India on opium revenues or otherwise try to help prevent the growth of the drug's use in China. Meanwhile, the Qing dynasty would continue in its failure to suppress or even regulate the use of opium by the general public in China, wallowing in a quagmire of official corruption it could not escape. Up to the twentieth century, though, Britain's role in that process would be dwelled upon more by westerners than by the Chinese. It was the English-speaking world that condemned it as "the Opium War" from the beginning, while

Chinese writers through the nineteenth century, including Wei Yuan, simply referred to it as a border dispute or foreign incident. To them, opium was a domestic problem and the war was a minor affair in the grand scheme of China's military history. Only after the fall of the Qing dynasty in 1912 did historians in China begin to call this war "the Opium War" in Chinese, and only in the 1920s would republican propagandists finally transform it into its current incarnation as the bedrock of Chinese nationalism—the war in which the British forced opium down China's throat, the shattering start to China's century of victimhood, the fuel of vengeance for building a new Chinese future in the face of Western imperialism, Year Zero of the modern age.

But did it have to end that way? The lasting encouragement the war gave to the opium trade, which rightfully cemented its status as an "opium war," was its effect but had never been its intention. To the contrary, the conflict marked a point where it seemed likely that the recent surge in the illegal opium trade from India could in fact be brought to an end or at least severely curtailed—and furthermore at a time when opium was still an expensive luxury good in China, when its users still numbered only in the hundreds of thousands among a population in the hundreds of millions. Such disparate figures as Lin Zexu, Wei Yuan, Charles Elliot, and George Staunton, among other significant actors in China and Britain, shared a hope that one positive outcome of this regrettable war might be the permanent elimination of the drug trade that had provoked it. Those hopes were realistic even if they were not in the end to be realized.

Nevertheless, it is important to remember just how arbitrary and unexpected the outcome of this era really was. The Opium War was not part of some long-term British imperial plan for China but rather a sudden departure from decades, if not centuries, of generally peaceful and respectful precedent. Neither did it result from some inevitable clash of civilizations. On the whole, the foreigners and Chinese who came together at Canton got along quite well over the long term, with serious conflict being the exception rather than the norm. Both the violent turn of the smuggling trade in the late 1830s and the war that it provoked were sharp aberrations from the past. Viewed in its broadest form, Canton was—when governments and navies stayed out of it—a largely peaceful intersection of civilizations, an effective center for an international trade that served as a major engine of the world's economy. Those more positive aspects of the old China trade were destined to be washed away by the bitter memories of the Opium War.

And yet. If Charles Elliot had not let his panic get the best of him when he so dramatically overreacted to Lin Zexu's threats. Or if Lin Zexu himself had been more open to working with, rather than against, Elliot; if they had cooperated on their shared interest in bringing the British opium smugglers under control. Or if just five members of the House of Commons had voted differently in the early hours of April 10, 1840—we might be looking back on very different lessons from this era.

Houqua and Forbes

———◆———

John Murray Forbes was already getting out of the China trade by the time the Opium War began. When his brothers had first gone to work in Canton for their uncle in the 1820s, and when he followed them there in 1830, it was for lack of any comparable opportunities closer to home. But once he was back in New England as a man of independent means, he found himself lured away from Russell & Co. into new directions. By the 1840s there were opportunities beginning to offer themselves in America's westward expansion that simply hadn't existed when his uncle first started sending ships to China after the Revolution, opportunities that seemed to John "better than Trade & far less troublesome"—less troublesome, that is, than the darkening clouds of Canton.[1]

Back when he was still living in China, John had savaged his older brother Robert for investing in a railroad ("cutting a paltry *dash* in a paltry city of a paltry country"), but by the time he got back to Massachusetts in the late 1830s he could see for himself the potential that rail held. By 1843 he was putting his China money into American railroad bonds, and by 1846, at a time when there were about five thousand miles of track total in the United States, he judged the field suitably mature that he entered into it himself. For an investment of $200,000, he bought a 10 percent share of the Central Railroad originating at Detroit—a line then only a quarter finished and being sold off at 70 cents to the dollar by a bankrupt state of Michigan. The investment was made possible not by the personal funds he had brought home with him from China, which were far from sufficient, but rather from the half million dollars of investment funds Houqua had entrusted to him.[2]

Forbes became president of that railroad, soon renamed the Michigan Central, which when complete would connect Lake Erie all the way to Lake Michigan. From that starting point he went on to become one of the leading railroad magnates in the antebellum United States, building a new American fortune on the foundations of the old Canton trade. He was conservative but smart about his investments, and though he let plenty of opportunities slip past (turning down, for instance, the option to buy a huge tract of land in what would eventually be the city limits of Chicago for $1.25 an acre), his holdings of land and railroad securities grew dramatically over the decades to come. He bought up land to build an expansive estate in Milton, Massachusetts, where he fashioned himself a country squire, planted twenty thousand trees, and began resettling his extended family. He bought the seven-mile-long island of Naushon next to Martha's Vineyard that is still privately held by his descendants. He invested widely in New England land mortgages and western rolling stock. He spoke of wanting to connect Boston to the Mississippi River and then build the first railroad in China.[3]

Throughout the expansion of his railroad empire, John Murray Forbes continued to invest Houqua's money in the same ventures where he put his own funds, effectively continuing the partnership they had first established in Canton when he was all of eighteen years old and Houqua sent his cargoes of tea abroad under the young Forbes's name. Their partnership had always been informal, based on trust and affection rather than contracts, and Forbes kept to its spirit assiduously as he represented Houqua's interests in the United States. In contrast to the dominant currents of the Canton trade, where the foreigners in their ships all converged on the Middle Kingdom from their far-flung nations, while the merchants of Canton sat fixed at the center and let the world revolve around them, here was evidence that the flow of capital could work just as well in the other direction, that a Chinese merchant could buy into the expanding economy of the United States. By the time John Murray Forbes began returning the funds to Houqua's heirs in the latter part of the century, the Hong merchant's U.S. investments would represent major holdings in railroad securities that read like a map of the opening of the American Midwest—the Chicago, Burlington and Quincy Railroad; the Dixon, Peoria and Hannibal; the Carthage and Burlington; the Illinois Grand Trunk Railway; the American Central.[4]

All that was yet to come, though, when John Murray Forbes wrote to Houqua in August 1843 just as the Opium War was coming to its end. In the letter, he tried to imagine what the war might ultimately mean for his old friend. The Canton system would be essentially dissolved as a result of the British treaty. Houqua's enormous fortune had come from his long success as a Hong merchant, part of the small monopoly on the Chinese side of the Canton trade, but now the British would be able to work with anyone they wished. This would remove Houqua from his centrality to China's foreign trade but it was also, Forbes noted, a blessing in its own way. Houqua had long been trapped in his position between the foreign merchants and the Chinese government, blamed for any problems that arose, regularly squeezed for massive contributions—toward the White Lotus suppression, toward the actions against pirates. Most recently, the Hong merchants had helped pay for the ransom of Canton from a threatened British occupation in the war, to which Houqua personally contributed more than $1 million.[5] His overall losses in the war would total more than $2 million all told, a figure worth billions in economic power today.[6] But Forbes, his young and trusted protégé, realized that the end of the war might actually be Houqua's liberation.

You should come to America, Forbes told him. "If when the Hong system ceases, the Mandarins continue to exact money from you, I do not see where it will end unless you will make up your mind to take one of my ships . . . for the conveyance of yourself and family and come to this country, where every man is called upon to pay his fair share of the expenses of the government."[7] Instead of having the weight of the Canton government's finances on his shoulders, Houqua could be a free man in an equal society. And if the climate in

New England might be too cold for the comfort of an elderly Chinese businessman who had spent his life in subtropical Canton, Forbes suggested he could look into buying property in Florida, or in the Caribbean, "where the climate is beautiful, and where for a small sum you could buy as much land as is covered by Canton." Houqua could live there however he pleased; he would have his own Canton, on his own terms. John said he would relish the chance to sail down from Massachusetts to visit him. Maybe he would come every winter.

Houqua died on September 4, 1843, never having gotten the letter.

Acknowledgments

As a historian, my first order of gratitude is to the librarians, curators, and archivists without whose work my own would be impossible. Those who have been most helpful to me in this project include, in no particular order: Maria Castrillo at the National Library of Scotland; Karen Robson and Mary Cockerill at the University of Southampton Archives; Rebecca Jackson at the Staffordshire Records Office; John Wells at the Cambridge University Library Department of Manuscripts; Katherine Fox and Melissa Murphy at the Harvard Business School's Baker Library; Martha Smalley, Joan Duffy, and Kevin Crawford at the Yale Divinity School Library; Adrienne Sharp and June Can at the Beinecke Rare Book and Manuscript Library; Sabina Beauchard, Anna Cook, and Thomas Lester at the Massachusetts Historical Society; Tania Quartarone at the Peabody Essex Museum; and Susan Greendyke Lachevre at the Forbes House Museum. Thank you also to Martin Barrow for permission to use the Jardine Matheson archives at Cambridge University.

It was an unexpected stroke of good fortune that just as I was starting to draft the chapters involving Thomas Manning, based on the limited and fragmentary sources then available on his life, the Royal Asiatic Society in London announced that it had discovered his personal papers and diaries languishing in an antiquarian bookseller's shop and was in the process of acquiring them. I am grateful to Ed Weech and Nancy Charley at the RAS for organizing those papers and making them available to me on remarkably short notice.

Thank you to Susanna Hoe for helping me track down the typescript she and Derek Roebuck prepared of Charles Elliot's letters, which had gone missing at the National Library of Scotland. It was an invaluable aid as I labored to decipher Elliot's atrocious handwriting, which is some of the worst I've ever seen and says quite a bit in itself about Elliot's fragile state of mind.

Sincere thanks to Lord Napier and Ettrick for sharing the diary and notebooks of his ancestor William John, the 9th Lord Napier, from his assignment to China in 1834. Thanks also to Charlie Napier of the Clan Napier Society for transcribing several more of William John Napier's letters from China that are in his possession. In all of my research for this book, there was no episode so memorable or pleasant as the early September morning I spent reading those notebooks at Lord Napier's Cambridgeshire home, eating fresh plums from the garden and watching the horses as they grazed in the pasture outside the window. As came clear from the notebooks, William John Napier was far more the author of his own fate than I had expected, but I do wish to make clear that the fact that he was so ill-suited to his position in China should not in any way reflect on the good name of the Napier clan.

Tobie Meyer-Fong, John Delury, Heather Cox Richardson, Michael Berube, and Jay Rathaus all took on the laborious work of reading my draft manuscript in its earliest form and providing corrections and suggestions that greatly improved the book. Any remaining shortcomings of substance or style are of course my own responsibility, but at least there will be fewer of them thanks to these readers.

My great debt to the many scholars whose work precedes and undergirds my own should be clear from the notes, but I would like to thank several people who provided advice and helpful conversation, vetted translations, or helped me find sources along the way, especially Robert Bickers, Chuck Wooldridge, Timothy Alborn, John Darwin, Marian Rocco, Jeffrey Wasserstrom, Joel Wolfe, Melissa Macauley, Luna Lu, Janet Theiss, Gary Chi-hung Luk, Tobias Gregory, and Lei Duan. Thanks as well to Barak Kushner for hosting me at Cambridge and giving me a tantalizing glimpse of the life of a don.

I am grateful to the National Committee on U.S.-China Relations, especially Jan Berris, for their longstanding encouragement of my work, and to the other members of the Public Intellectuals Program for the same. The history department at the University of Massachusetts has been a productive base for more than a decade now, and

I thank my colleagues—especially Joye Bowman, our chair during the years I was writing this book, who was a constant voice of support. Thanks also to Sharon Domier, our fantastic East Asian Studies librarian, and Dean Julie Hayes of the College of Humanities and Fine Arts.

The Writers' Mill in Florence, Massachusetts, provided the focused and (shall we say) industrious space in which I both started and finished writing this book; thanks to the other millworkers for making it possible. Thanks also to the staffs of Bread Euphoria, the Lady Killigrew, the Brass Buckle, and Haymarket Café for providing good coffee and energizing places to write and think.

It was a privilege and a pleasure to work again with Andrew Miller at Knopf; in this day and age, I realize how fortunate I am to have an editor who devotes such time and energy to the books he publishes. Andrew's keen insight and sense of structure helped shape and refine this book over several drafts in ways I never could have accomplished alone. The other staff at Knopf who worked on the book were amazing as always—Zakiya Harris, in particular, guided me through the many twists and turns of the production process with patience and good cheer. Great thanks to Lisa Montebello for managing the production of the book, Soonyoung Kwon for designing the text and layout, and John Vorhees for designing the jacket. Thanks as well to Paula Robbins and Terry Bush at Mapping Specialists, Ltd., for designing the maps. And of course thank you to my wonderful agent, Brettne Bloom, who helped me shape the book from the beginning and has been my steadfast champion and cheerleader all along.

Home is where I find my greatest inspiration. My son, Eliot, was born as I was starting the research for this book and he is just now learning how to read as it comes to press. The same was true of my older daughter, Lucy, for my previous book. Putting aside the question of whether I can write another book without providing them with an additional sibling, I thank both of them for the joy and perspective and sense of purpose they give me. And none of this would be possible, or even have a point, without my wife, Francie Lin, who keeps me centered and balanced and makes everything worthwhile.

Notes

INTRODUCTION   Canton

1. This description of Canton is a collage drawn from a range of sources includ-
ing, in no particular order: Valery M. Garrett, *Heaven Is High, the Emperor
Far Away: Merchants and Mandarins in Old Canton* (New York: Oxford University Press, 2002); Robert Bickers, *The Scramble for China: Foreign Devils in
the Qing Empire, 1832–1914* (London: Allen Lane, 2011); Aeneas Anderson,
A Narrative of the British Embassy to China, in the Years 1792, 1793, and 1794
(London: J. Debrett, 1795); James Johnson, *An Account of a Voyage to India,
China, &c. in His Majesty's Ship Caroline* (London: Richard Phillips, 1806); Har-
riet Low Hillard, *My Mother's Journal: A Young Lady's Diary of Five Years Spent
in Manila, Macao, and the Cape of Good Hope*, ed. Katharine Hillard (Boston:
George H. Ellis, 1900); Jürgen Osterhammel, *The Transformation of the World:
A Global History of the Nineteenth Century* (Princeton, NJ: Princeton University
Press, 2014); Samuel Kidd, "Canton," in *The Christian Keepsake, and Mission-
ary Annual*, ed. William Ellis (London: Fisher, Son, & Co., 1836), pp. 170–78;
Jonathan Spence, *God's Chinese Son* (New York: Norton, 1996); Charles God-
frey Leland, *Pidgin-English Sing-song; or, Songs and Stories in the China-English
Dialect* (London: Trübner and Co., 1876); William C. Hunter, *The 'Fan Kwae'
at Canton before Treaty Days, 1825–1844* (London: Kegan Paul, Trench & Co.,
1882); Tiffany Osmond, *The Canton Chinese: or, The American's Sojourn in the
Celestial Empire* (Boston, MA, and Cambridge, UK: James Munroe, 1849);
Anon., *An Intercepted Letter from J—T—, Esq. Writer at Canton to His Friend
in Dublin Ireland* (Dublin: M. N. Mahon, 1804); Jacques Downs, *The Golden
Ghetto: The American Commercial Community at Canton and the Shaping of American China Policy, 1784–1844* (Bethlehem, PA: Lehigh University Press, 1997);
Samuel Wells Williams, *The Middle Kingdom* (London: W. H. Allen, 1883); and
personal letters of Thomas Manning and Robert Bennet Forbes.
2. One welcome exception to this trend in general-interest books on the Opium
War is Julia Lovell's recent *The Opium War: Drugs, Dreams, and the Making of
China* (London: Picador, 2011), which is especially recommended to the reader
interested in military history as it goes into much greater detail on the events
of the war itself than the book at hand does.

PROLOGUE The Journey of James Flint

1. Hosea Ballou Morse, *The Chronicles of the East India Company Trading to China, 1635–1834* (Oxford: Clarendon Press, 1926), vol. 1, pp. 266–67; George Anson, *A Voyage Round the World, in the Years 1740–1744* (Edinburgh: Campbell Denovan, 1781), vol. 2, book 3, p. 244.

2. Charles Frederick Noble, *A Voyage to the East Indies in 1747 and 1748* (London: T. Becket and P. A. Dehondt, at the Tully's Head, 1762), p. 306; Petition of James Flint to the Court of Directors of the United East India Company (to become a supercargo), read in court February 19, 1745, British Library, East India Office Records, IOR/E/1/33.

3. "Transactions of a Voyage in the *Success* Snow from Canton to Limpo and afterwards to Tien-Tsin, 1759," British Library, East India Office Records, IOR/G/12/195 (China and Japan, Miscellaneous Papers, 1710–1814), item 12; Susan Reed Stifler, "The Language Students of the East India Company's Canton Factory," *Journal of the North China Branch of the Royal Asiatic Society* 69 (1938): 46–82, see p. 49; Robert Bennet Forbes, *Remarks on China and the China Trade* (Boston: Samuel N. Dickinson, 1844), pp. 22–23.

4. Details of Flint's voyage are taken from his journal, "Transactions of a Voyage in the *Success* Snow from Canton to Limpo and afterwards to Tien-Tsin, 1759," BL IOR/G/12/195. The White River (Chinese: Bai He) was best known to foreigners at the time as the Peiho.

5. Morse, *Chronicles*, vol. 1, p. 75.

6. *Da Qing Gaozong Chun (Qianlong) huangdi shilu* (Taipei: Taiwan Huawen shuju, 1964), *juan* 598, pp. 5a–6b.

7. As translated in the *Canton Register*, August 25, 1830; also in Anon. ("A Visitor to China"), *Address to the People of Great Britain, Explanatory of Our Commercial Relations with the Empire of China* (London: Smith. Elder and Co., 1836), pp. 62–63.

8. The edict ordering the beheading of Flint's teacher is in *Da Qing Gaozong Chun (Qianlong) huangdi shilu, juan* 598, pp. 5a–6b.

9. On Flint dying, see, for example, p. 124 of Zhang Dechang, "Qingdai yapian zhanzheng qian zhi Zhong-Xi yanhai tongshang," in Bao Zunpeng et al., eds., *Zhongguo jindaishi luncong*, part 1, vol. 3, pp. 91–132. On tofu, see Benjamin Franklin to John Bartram, January 11, 1770, in William Darlington, ed., *Memorials of John Bartram and Humphry Marshall* (Philadelphia: Lindsay & Blakiston, 1849), pp. 404–5.

10. Adam Smith, *An Inquiry into the Nature and Causes of the Wealth of Nations*, 2nd ed. (London: W. Strahan and T. Cadell, 1778), vol. 1, pp. 87–88.

11. Voltaire, *A Philosophical Dictionary*, vol. 3 of 10 (Cannibals–Councils), pp. 81–82, in series vol. 7 of *The Works of Voltaire, A Contemporary Version*, 43 vols. (Akron, OH: Werner Company, 1905).

12. A. E. Van-Braam Houckgeest, *An Authentic Account of the Embassy of the Dutch East-India Company, to the Court of the Emperor of China, In the Years 1794 and 1795* (London: R. Phillips, 1798), vol. 1, pp. v–vi.

13. Kenneth Pomeranz, *The Great Divergence: China, Europe, and the Making of*

the Modern World Economy (Princeton, NJ: Princeton University Press, 2000), pp. 36–39, 116–22.

14. Aeneas Anderson, *A Narrative of the British Embassy to China, in the Years 1792, 1793, and 1794* (London: J. Debrett, 1795), p. v.

15. Henry Defeynes (Monsieur de Monsart), *An Exact and Curious Survey of all the East Indies, even to Canton, the chiefe Cittie of China* (London: Thomas Dawson, 1615), p. 30 (changing numeral 6 to "six").

16. Lt.-Col. Sir Richard Carnac Temple, ed., *The Travels of Peter Mundy in Europe and Asia, 1608–1667* (London: Hakluyt Society, 1919), vol. 3, part 1, p. 173.

17. Ibid., vol. 3, part 1, p. 178.

18. Anon. ("A Looker-On"), *Chinese Commerce and Disputes, from 1640 to 1840. Addressed to Tea Dealers and Consumers* (London: W. Morrison, 1840), p. 8.

19. Ibid.; and Andrew Ljungstedt, *An Historical Sketch of the Portuguese Settlements in China* (Boston: James Monroe and Co., 1836), pp. 276–78.

20. Temple, *The Travels of Peter Mundy*, vol. 3, part 1, p. 191.

21. Morse, *Chronicles*, vol. 1, p. 158.

22. Michael Greenberg, *British Trade and the Opening of China, 1800–1842* (Cambridge: Cambridge University Press, 1951), p. 3.

CHAPTER 1 A Time of Wonder

1. Macartney letter to the Chairman of the East India Company, September 26, 1792, British Library, India Office Records, IOR/G/12/92. On naval preparations: William James, *The Naval History of Great Britain, from the Declaration of War by France in 1793 to the Accession of George IV* (London: Richard Bentley, 1859), vol. 1, p. 53; George Leonard Staunton, *An Authentic Account of an Embassy from the King of Great Britain to the Emperor of China* (Philadelphia: Robert Campbell, 1799), vol. 1, p. 17. In accordance with English usage of the time, "Chinese emperor" here is meant to indicate the emperor of China; it does not imply that the emperor was ethnically Chinese. The emperors of the Qing dynasty were Manchu.

2. Helen Robbins, *Our First Ambassador to China: An Account of the Life and Correspondence of George, Earl of Macartney, with Extracts from His Letters, and the Narrative of His Experiences in China, as Told by Himself, 1737–1806* (New York: Dutton and Company, 1908), p. 220.

3. Roland Thorne, "Macartney, George, Earl Macartney (1737–1806)," *Oxford Dictionary of National Biography* (Oxford: Oxford University Press, 2004–13).

4. Aeneas Anderson, *A Narrative of the British Embassy to China, in the Years 1792, 1793, and 1794* (London: J. Debrett, 1795), p. 146.

5. George Macartney, *An Embassy to China: Being the Journal Kept by Lord Macartney during His Embassy to the Emperor Ch'ien-lung, 1793–1794*, ed. J. L. Cranmer-Byng (Hamden, CT: Archon Books, 1963), p. 213.

6. U.S.-British comparison based on table for 1792 in Hosea Ballou Morse, *The Chronicles of the East India Company Trading to China, 1635–1834* (Oxford: Clarendon Press, 1926–29), vol. 2, p. 193; thirty-nine British ships visited Canton

that year (including both Company and private vessels), versus six from the United States.

7. "The China Trade," *Times*, June 8, 1791.

8. Earl H. Pritchard, "The Instructions of the East India Company to Lord Macartney on His Embassy to China," part 1, *Journal of the Royal Asiatic Society of Great Britain and Ireland*, no. 2 (April 1938): 201–30, see pp. 202–3 and 210–11.

9. Staunton, *An Authentic Account*, p. 18.

10. Ibid., p. 17 (changing "Pekin" to "Beijing").

11. William Jardine Proudfoot, *Biographical Memoir of James Dinwiddie, Ll.D., Astronomer in the British Embassy to China, 1792, '3, '4* (Liverpool: Edward Howell, 1868), p. 26.

12. William Alexander, "Journal of a voyage to Pekin in China, on board the 'Hindostan' E.I.M., which accompanied Lord Macartney on his embassy to the Emperor," British Library, Add MS 35174, fol. 86; Staunton, *An Authentic Account*, pp. 492–98; the full catalog of gifts is in the British Library, India Office Records, IOR/G/12/92, fols. 155–86.

13. *Times*, September 7, 1792, p. 2 (no article title).

14. Proudfoot, *Memoir of James Dinwiddie*, pp. 26, 27.

15. "Letter from King George III to the Emperor of China," in Morse, *Chronicles*, vol. 2, pp. 244–47.

16. Staunton, *An Authentic Account*, pp. 47–48.

17. Baring and Burges to Macartney, September 8, 1792, quoted in Pritchard, "The Instructions of the East India Company to Lord Macartney," part 1, p. 210.

18. George Leonard Staunton, *An Historical Account of the Embassy to the Emperor of China, undertaken by order of the King of Great Britain* (London: John Stockdale, 1797), p. 20.

19. Staunton, *An Historical Account*, p. 21; details of visit taken from 1792 diary of Staunton's son, in the George Thomas Staunton Papers, Rubenstein Library, Duke University, Durham, NC, accessed via Adam Matthew Digital, "China: Trade, Politics and Culture 1793–1980."

20. Macartney's journal, *An Embassy to China*, p. 231, says they were orphans or purchased; D. E. Mungello, *The Great Encounter of China and the West, 1500–1800* (Lanham, MD: Rowman & Littlefield, 1999), p. 117.

21. Hamilton letter to Staunton from Naples, February 21, 1792, Staunton Papers, Duke University; Mungello, *The Great Encounter*, p. 140.

22. Staunton, *An Historical Account*, p. 21. Macartney himself said they possessed "little energy or powers of persuasion": Macartney, *An Embassy to China*, p. 231.

23. Macartney to Chairman and Deputy Chairman of the East India Company, from near Sumatra, March 25, 1793, British Library, India Office Records, IOR/G/12/92, fols. 16–17.

24. George Thomas Staunton letter to his mother, December 9, 1792, Staunton Papers, Duke University.

25. Robbins, *Our First Ambassador*, pp. 203–4; Anderson, *A Narrative of the British Embassy to China*, pp. 27–28; George Thomas Staunton diary, February 1–2, 1793, Staunton Papers, Duke University.

26. Susan Reed Stifler, "The Language Students of the East India Company's Canton Factory," *Journal of the North China Branch of the Royal Asiatic Society* 69 (1938): 46–82, see p. 52; Macartney, *An Embassy to China*, p. 64; on Jacobus Li interpreting into Italian rather than English, see Macartney letter to Henry Dundas, November 9, 1793, British Library, India Office Records, IOR/G/12/92, fol. 35.

27. George Thomas Staunton diary for 1792–93, pp. 108, 207–9, 213–14, 223, 241; Anderson, *A Narrative of the British Embassy*, p. 54.

28. Leonard Blussé, *Visible Cities: Canton, Nagasaki, and Batavia and the Coming of the Americans* (Cambridge, MA: Harvard University Press, 2008), p. 10.

29. Anderson, *A Narrative of the British Embassy*, pp. 34, 35.

30. Macartney letter to Henry Dundas from near Hangzhou, Zhejiang province, November 9, 1793, British Library, India Office Records, IOR/G/12/92, fol. 32.

31. Macartney, *An Embassy to China*, pp. 63, 69.

32. Anderson, *A Narrative of the British Embassy*, p. 57; William Alexander diary, entries for July 9, 11, 22, and 23, 1793.

33. William Alexander diary, entry for July 17, 1793 ("it was from us few, the Chinese were to form their opinions of the English Character"); "gaining the good will": Staunton, *An Historical Account*, p. 232.

34. Staunton, *An Historical Account*, p. 234.

35. Macartney, *An Embassy to China*, pp. 69, 101.

36. Ibid., pp. 66, 74, and 75.

37. Macartney, *An Embassy to China*, p. 71; William Alexander diary, August 1, 1793; Anderson, *A Narrative of the British Embassy*, p. 63.

38. Macartney, *An Embassy to China*, pp. 77–78; "stumped along": William Alexander diary, August 9, 1793.

39. Macartney, *An Embassy to China*, p. 112.

40. Anderson, *A Narrative of the British Embassy*, p. 137; Macartney, *An Embassy to China*, p. 114; Staunton, *An Authentic Account*, vol. 2, pp. 61–62.

41. Macartney, *An Embassy to China*, p. 114; Proudfoot, *Dinwiddie*, p. 51.

42. Anderson, *A Narrative of the British Embassy*, p. 138; Staunton, *An Authentic Account*, vol. 2, p. 8.

43. Caleb Cushing to John Nelson, July 13, 1844: "It has been supposed heretofore erroneously that a great Minister of State existed at Peking [Beijing] called the 'Grand Colao' whom it was proper for foreign Governments to address." *Public Documents Printed by Order of the Senate of the United States, Second Session of the Twenty-Eighth Congress* (Washington, DC: Gales and Seaton, 1845), vol. 2, no. 67, p. 55.

44. Anderson, *A Narrative of the British Embassy*, pp. 139–41.

45. Ibid., pp. 148–49; the full thirty-two-page list of gifts given by Qianlong to the British embassy is in the British Library, India Office Records, IOR/G/12/92, fols. 317–49.

46. Staunton, *An Authentic Account*, p. 68.

47. Macartney to Dundas, November 9, 1793, British Library, India Office Records, IOR/G/12/92, fols. 56–57.

48. Staunton, *An Authentic Account*, pp. 68, 70.

49. Macartney, *An Embassy to China*, p. 118.

50. Anderson, *A Narrative of the British Embassy*, pp. 146–47.

51. Staunton, *An Authentic Account*, p. 77.

52. Ibid., p. 78.

53. The English original of the letter is in Morse, *Chronicles*, vol. 2, pp. 244–47; the Chinese translation is in *Ying shi Majiaerni fang Hua dang'an shiliao huibian* (Beijing: Guoji wenhua chuban gongsi, 1996), pp. 162–64.

54. Macartney, *An Embassy to China*, p. 124.

55. George Thomas Staunton diary for 1793–94, entry for September 14, 1793.

56. Anderson, *A Narrative of the British Embassy*, p. 148; Staunton, *An Authentic Account*, p. 78.

57. Ye Xiaoqing, "Ascendant Peace in the Four Seas: Tributary Drama and the Macartney Mission of 1793," *Late Imperial China* 26, no. 2 (December 2005): 89–113, see p. 100.

58. Macartney, *An Embassy to China*, p. 143; Anderson, *A Narrative of the British Embassy*, pp. 179–80.

59. Proudfoot, *Dinwiddie*, p. 51. Letters read: Macartney, *An Embassy to China*, p. 102; Alain Peyrefitte, *The Immobile Empire*, trans. Jon Rothschild (New York: Alfred A. Knopf, 1992), p. 271.

60. George Thomas Staunton diary, September 29, 1793.

61. Proudfoot, *Dinwiddie*, p. 53.

62. Anderson, *A Narrative of the British Embassy*, p. 171.

63. Ibid., p. 181 (changing "Pekin" to "Beijing").

64. Proudfoot, *Dinwiddie*, pp. 54–55.

65. Edict of QL58/8/6 (September 10, 1793), in *Ying shi Majiaerni fang Hua dang'an shiliao huibian*, pp. 148–49.

66. "Letter from the Emperor of China to the King of England," British Library, India Office Records, IOR/G/12/92, fols. 243–55; Qianlong's original edict of QL58/8/20 (September 24, 1793) is in *Ying shi Majiaerni fang Hua dang'an shiliao huibian*, pp. 165–66.

67. As in the paragraph above, quotations are from the translation prepared by the East India Company at the time, except for the final lines (from "Strange and costly" onward), which, because they are so well known in that form, accord to the most commonly quoted translation of this document, a much later translation found in J. O. P. Bland and Edmund Backhouse, *Annals & Memoirs of the Court of Peking (from the 16th to the 20th Century)* (Boston: Houghton, Mifflin and Company, 1914), pp. 324–25.

68. Edict of QL58/8/29 (October 3, 1793), in *Ying shi Majiaerni fang Hua dang'an shiliao huibian*, pp. 172–75; the translation prepared for the British government at the time is in the British Library, India Office Records, IOR/G/12/92, fols. 283–98.

69. Macartney, *An Embassy to China*, p. 171.

70. Ibid., pp. 170, 211.

71. Ibid., pp. 212, 213.

72. "Embassies to China," *Chinese Repository*, vol. 6 (May 1837): 17–27, see p. 18.

73. Ibid., p. 26.

74. Peter Pindar (pseudonym for John Wolcot), "Ode to the Lion Ship of War," in *The Works of Peter Pindar, Esq.* (London: J. Walker, 1809), vol. 3, pp. 348–50.

75. Macartney, *An Embassy to China*, pp. 212–13.

76. Ibid., pp. 236, 238.

77. Ibid., p. 239.

CHAPTER 2   Black Wind

1. "Hung-li," in Arthur W. Hummel, ed., *Eminent Chinese of the Ch'ing Period* (Taipei: SMC Publishing, Inc., 1991), vol. 1, p. 369; John E. Wills, *Mountain of Fame: Portraits in Chinese History* (Princeton, NJ: Princeton University Press, 1994), p. 234; Mark Elliott, *Emperor Qianlong: Son of Heaven, Man of the World* (New York: Longman, 2009), p. 8.

2. Clae Waltham, *Shu Ching: Book of History* (Chicago: Henry Regnery Company, 1971), p. 134; Ye Xiaoqing, "Ascendant Peace in the Four Seas: Tributary Drama and the Macartney Mission of 1793," *Late Imperial China* 26, no. 2 (December 2005): 89–113, see p. 105.

3. Elliott, *Emperor Qianlong*, p. 138; Ye, "Ascendant Peace in the Four Seas," pp. 105–6.

4. Elliott, *Emperor Qianlong*, p. 134; Chang Te-Ch'ang, "The Economic Role of the Imperial Household in the Ch'ing Dynasty," *Journal of Asian Studies* 31, no. 2 (February 1972): 243–73, see pp. 256–59; Preston M. Torbert, *The Ch'ing Imperial Household Department: A Study of Its Organization and Principal Functions, 1662–1796* (Cambridge, MA: Council on East Asian Studies, Harvard University, 1977), p. 100 etc.

5. Population figures from Ho Ping-ti, *Studies on the Population of China, 1368–1953* (Cambridge, MA: Harvard East Asian Series, 1959), pp. 23, 264, 270, and 278, as cited in Wang Wensheng, "White Lotus Rebels and South China Pirates: Social Crises and Political Changes in the Qing Empire, 1796–1810" (Ph.D. dissertation, University of California, Irvine, 2008), p. 35, n. 60.

6. Ssu-yü Teng, "Chinese Influence on the Western Examination System," *Harvard Journal of Asiatic Studies* 7, no. 4 (September 1943): 267–312; Voltaire, from "Essai sur les mœurs," and Montesquieu, from "De l'esprit des lois," book 8, chapter 21 (Paris, 1878), both quoted in ibid., p. 281; Derek Bodde, "Chinese Ideas in the West," prepared for the Committee on Asiatic Studies in American Education, Washington, DC, 1948.

7. Zhang Zhengmo confession, in *Qing zhongqi wusheng bailianjiao qiyi ziliao* (Suzhou: Jiangsu renmin chubanshe, 1981), vol. 5, pp. 35–36; Cecily McCaffrey gives a wonderful treatment of the rebellion in the Han River Highlands in "Living through Rebellion: A Local History of the White Lotus Uprising in Hubei, China" (Ph.D. dissertation, University of California, San Diego, 2003). I have been much influenced by her account.

8. Unless otherwise noted, following paragraphs based on Zhang's confession in *Qing zhongqi wusheng bailianjiao qiyi ziliao* (hereafter *QZQWS*), vol. 5, pp. 35–36.

9. Many times over: Wang, "White Lotus Rebels," p. 109, citing Eduard B. Ver-

meer, "The Mountain Frontier in Late Imperial China: Economic and Social Developments in the Bashan," *T'oung Pao*, 2nd series, vol. 77, livr. 4/5 (1991): 300–329, see p. 306.

10. *QZQWS*, vol. 1, p. 18.

11. Kwang-Ching Liu, "Religion and Politics in the White Lotus Rebellion of 1796 in Hubei," in *Heterodoxy in Late Imperial China*, ed. Kwang-Ching Liu and Richard Shek (Honolulu: University of Hawaii Press, 2004), p. 293.

12. Second confession of Zhang Zhengmo, *QZQWS*, vol. 5, pp. 36–41, see p. 37.

13. *QZQWS*, vol. 4, p. 165.

14. Confession of Xiang Yaoming, ibid., vol. 5, p. 4.

15. Second confession of Zhang Zhengmo, ibid., vol. 5, p. 40.

16. George Macartney, *An Embassy to China: Being the Journal Kept by Lord Macartney during His Embassy to the Emperor Ch'ien-lung, 1793–1794*, ed. J. L. Cranmer-Byng (Hamden, CT: Archon Books, 1963), p. 202; George Leonard Staunton, *An Authentic Account of an Embassy from the King of Great Britain to the Emperor of China* (Philadelphia: Robert Campbell, 1799), vol. 2, pp. 78–79.

17. Wook Yoon, "Prosperity with the Help of 'Villains,' 1776–1799: A Review of the Heshen Clique and Its Era," *T'oung Pao* 98, issue 4/5 (2012): 479–527, p. 520.

18. Harold Kahn, *Monarchy in the Emperor's Eyes: Image and Reality in the Ch'ien-lung Reign* (Cambridge, MA: Harvard University Press, 1971), p. 255.

19. On the Grand Council, see Wook Yoon, "Prosperity with the Help of 'Villains,'" pp. 483–85.

20. Staunton, *An Authentic Account*, vol. 2, p. 66.

21. Philip Kuhn and Susan Mann, "Dynastic Decline and the Roots of Rebellion," in *The Cambridge History of China*, vol. 10, *Late Ch'ing, 1800–1911, Part 1*, ed. John K. Fairbank and Denis Twitchett (Cambridge: Cambridge University Press, 1978), pp. 107–62, see pp. 127–28; David Nivison, "Ho-shen and His Accusers," in *Confucianism in Action*, ed. David Nivison and Arthur Wright (Stanford, CA: Stanford University Press, 1959), pp. 209–43, see p. 211.

22. Nivison, "Ho-shen and His Accusers," pp. 232–34.

23. Dai Yingcong, "Civilians Go into Battle: Hired Militias in the White Lotus War," *Asia Major*, 3rd series, vol. 22, part 2 (2009): 145–78, see p. 153.

24. *QZQWS*, vol. 4, pp. 164, 268; McCaffrey, "Living through Rebellion," pp. 161–62.

25. *QZQWS*, vol. 4, p. 267.

26. Ibid., p. 269.

27. Blaine Campbell Gaustad, "Religious Sectarianism and the State in Mid Qing China: Background to the White Lotus Uprising of 1796–1804" (Ph.D. dissertation, University of California, Berkeley, 1994), p. 315; Liu, "Religion and Politics in the White Lotus Rebellion," pp. 286–87, 289, 296–97, 301; Robert Eric Entenmann, "Migration and Settlement in Sichuan, 1644–1796" (Ph.D. dissertation, Harvard University, 1982), pp. 236–37.

28. On Qianlong's unwillingness to send elite Manchu banner troops, see Dai, "Civilians Go into Battle," pp. 149, 153.

29. Dai, "Civilians Go into Battle," pp. 153–55; Wang, "White Lotus Rebels," pp. 304–5.

30. Dai, "Civilians," pp. 156–58; Wang Wensheng, *White Lotus Rebels and South*

China Pirates: Crisis and Reform in the Qing Empire (Cambridge, MA: Harvard University Press, 2014), p. 142.

31. Le Bao's report, from *Jinli xin bian*, excerpted in Jiang Weiming, *Chuan-Hu-Shan bailianjiao qiyi ziliao jilu* (Chengdu: Sichuan renmin chubanshe, 1980), pp. 214–15.

32. Kahn, *Monarchy*, p. 257; Hummell, *Eminent Chinese*, p. 289; Wang, "White Lotus Rebels," pp. 282, 292–94; Beatrice Bartlett, *Monarchs and Ministers: The Grand Council in Mid-Ch'ing China, 1723–1820* (Berkeley: University of California Press, 1991), pp. 231–38.

33. Dai, "Civilians Go into Battle," pp. 159–62.

34. Zhang Xuecheng, quoted and translated by David Nivison in *The Life and Thought of Chang Hsüeh-ch'eng* (Stanford, CA: Stanford University Press, 1966), p. 268.

35. Wang Huizu, translated by David Nivison in "Ho-shen and His Accusers," pp. 216–17.

36. Nivison, *The Life and Thought of Chang Hsüeh-ch'eng*, p. 268.

37. Translation based on Wang Wensheng's in "White Lotus Rebels," p. 282.

38. Wang, "White Lotus Rebels," p. 300.

CHAPTER 3   The Edge of the World

1. Canton as third-largest city in the world in 1800: Jürgen Osterhammel, *The Transformation of the World: A Global History of the Nineteenth Century* (Princeton, NJ: Princeton University Press, 2014), p. 251. All told, Chinese cities comprised four of the top ten in the world.

2. Patrick Hanan, trans., *Mirage* (Hong Kong: Chinese University Press, 2014), p. 82 (changing "Guangdong" to "Canton").

3. George Leonard Staunton, *An Authentic Account of an Embassy from the King of Great Britain to the Emperor of China* (Philadelphia: Robert Campbell, 1799), vol. 2, p. 360. The saga of the unfortunate seal hunters on Amsterdam Island, who would remain stranded there for more than three years, is told in the memoir of Pierre François Péron, one of the Frenchmen involved, published as *Mémoires du capitaine Péron, sur ses voyages . . .* , 2 vols. (Paris: Brissot-Thivars, 1824).

4. The line-of-battle sketch in Gower's hand is in William Alexander's diary, p. 81, William Alexander, "Journal of a voyage to Pekin in China, on board the 'Hindostan' E.I.M., which accompanied Lord Macartney on his embassy to the Emperor," British Library, Add MS 35174, fol. 86.

5. Macartney to the Chairman and Deputy Chairman of the East India Company, September 4, 1794, British Library, India Office Records, IOR/G/12/92, fols. 487–88; Staunton, *An Authentic Account*, vol. 2, p. 465.

6. Quoted in James Fichter, *So Great a Proffit: How the East Indies Trade Transformed Anglo-American Capitalism* (Cambridge, MA: Harvard University Press, 2010), p. 207.

7. Herbert J. Wood, "England, China, and the Napoleonic Wars," *Pacific Historical Review* 9, no. 2 (June 1940): 139–56, see p. 141.

8. Ibid., p. 142.

9. Frederic Wakeman Jr., "Drury's Occupation of Macau and China's Response to Early Modern Imperialism," *East Asian History* 28 (December 2004): 27–34, see p. 28.

10. Ibid., p. 29.

11. George Thomas Staunton, *Memoirs of the Chief Incidents of the Public Life of Sir George Thomas Staunton, Bart.*, printed for private circulation (London: L. Booth, 1856), pp. 15–17.

12. Staunton letter to his parents, July 28, 1799, in the George Thomas Staunton Papers, Rubenstein Library, Duke University, Durham, NC, accessed via Adam Matthew Digital, "China: Trade, Politics and Culture 1793–1980." Interestingly enough, Macartney left China in 1793 with the impression that the Company supercargoes at Canton were going to start encouraging their junior staff to begin learning Chinese, though nothing seems to have come of that; Macartney to the Chairman and Deputy Chairman of the East India Company, September 4, 1794, British Library, India Office Records, IOR/G/12/92, fol. 488.

13. Staunton to his parents, July 15, 1799, Staunton Papers, Duke University.

14. Staunton to his parents, July 28, 1799.

15. Staunton, *Memoirs of the Chief Incidents*, p. 25.

16. C. H. Philips, *The East India Company, 1784–1834* (Manchester: Manchester University Press, 1940), p. 14, n. 6.

17. Jodi Rhea Bartley Eastberg, "West Meets East: British Perceptions of China through the Life and Works of Sir George Thomas Staunton, 1781–1859" (Ph.D. dissertation, Marquette University, 2009), p. 95.

18. Staunton, *Memoirs*, p. 26.

19. Staunton to his father, April 18, 1801.

20. Staunton to his father, February 26, 1801.

21. Hosea Ballou Morse, *The Chronicles of the East India Company Trading to China, 1635–1834* (Oxford: Clarendon Press, 1926), vol. 2, p. 338.

22. Staunton to his father, March 27, 1800.

23. Morse, *Chronicles*, vol. 2, p. 342 (capitalizing the "h" in "His").

24. Staunton to his father, March 27, 1800.

25. Staunton to his father, January 19, 1801; to his parents, June 27, 1800.

26. Staunton, *Memoirs*, p. 39.

27. William C. Hunter, *The 'Fan Kwae' at Canton before Treaty Days, 1825–1844* (London: Kegan Paul, Trench & Co., 1882), p. 126.

28. Thomas Noon Talfourd, *The Letters of Charles Lamb, with a Sketch of His Life* (London: Edward Moxon, 1837), vol. 1, footnote on p. 208 (Talfourd's words, not Lamb's).

29. Thomas Manning letter to Joseph Banks (draft, 1806), Manning Papers, TM/4/5, Royal Asiatic Society, London; most biographers give the year 1802 for the beginning of his plan, though Charles Lamb wrote to him in August 31, 1801, that "I heard that you were going to China": Talfourd, *Letters of Charles Lamb*, vol. 1, p. 196.

30. On the deficiency of Hager's system, see William Huttmann, "Notice of Sev-

eral Chinese-European Dictionaries which have Preceded Dr. Morrison's," in the *Asiatic Journal and Monthly Register,* vol. 12 (September 1821): 242, which lists two subsequent works explicitly written to debunk Hager's.

31. A. J. Dunkin, "Only Passport to England Signed by Napoleon I," in *Notes and Queries,* 2nd series, vol. 10 (August 25, 1860): 143–44.

32. Manning to Joseph Banks (draft, 1806), Manning Papers, TM/4/5, Royal Asiatic Society, London.

33. Charles Lamb to William Hazlitt, November 18, 1805: "Manning is come to town in spectacles, and studies physic; is melancholy, and seems to have something in his head which he don't impart." Talfourd, *The Works of Charles Lamb. To which are prefixed, His Letters, and a Sketch of His Life* (New York: Harper and Bros., 1838), vol. 1, p. 133.

34. Talfourd, *The Letters of Charles Lamb,* vol. 1, p. 242. Lamb seems to have made up the word "smouchy"—the *Oxford English Dictionary* lists this letter to Manning as the only known instance of its use.

35. Clements R. Markham, ed., *Narratives of the Mission of George Bogle to Tibet, and of the Journey of Thomas Manning to Lhasa* (London: Trübner and Co., 1876), pp. clvi–clvii.

36. Peter Auber, *China. An Outline of Its Government, Laws, and Policy: and of the British and Foreign Embassies to, and Intercourse with That Empire* (London: Parbury, Allen and Co., 1834), pp. 220–21.

37. Quoted in Edward Smith, *The Life of Sir Joseph Banks: President of the Royal Society* (London: John Lane, The Bodley Head, 1911), p. 269, n. 1; it is followed by the letter from Banks to Staunton.

38. Lamb to Manning, December 5, 1806, in Talfourd, *Letters of Charles Lamb,* vol. 1, pp. 285–89.

39. Baldwin, R. C. D. "Sir Joseph Banks and the Cultivation of Tea," *RSA Journal* 141, no. 5444 (November 1993): 813–17.

40. Susan Reed Stifler, "The Language Students of the East India Company's Canton Factory," *Journal of the North China Branch of the Royal Asiatic Society* 69 (1938): 46–82, see p. 57.

41. Eliza Morrison, *Memoirs of the Life and Labours of Robert Morrison, D.D.* (London: Longman, Orme, Brown, Green, and Longmans, 1839), vol. 1, p. 93.

42. Ibid., vol. 1, p. 98.

43. Quotations from ibid., vol. 1, pp. 94, 117–18. Preaching to ship's crew: Christopher A. Daily, *Robert Morrison and the Protestant Plan for China* (Hong Kong: Hong Kong University Press, 2013), p. 99.

44. Eliza Morrison, *Life and Labours,* vol. 1, pp. 127–31.

45. Marshall Broomhall, *Robert Morrison: A Master Builder* (Edinburgh: Turnbull & Spears, 1927), p. 52.

46. Smith, *Life of Sir Joseph Banks,* p. 271.

47. Eliza Morrison, *Life and Labours,* vol. 1, pp. 153, 162.

48. Broomhall, *Master Builder,* p. 57 (emphasis added).

49. Eliza Morrison, *Life and Labours,* vol. 1, p. 222; Stifler, "The Language Students of the East India Company's Canton Factory," p. 60.

50. Eliza Morrison, *Life and Labours,* vol. 1, p. 153.

51. On lack of smuggling: Patrick K. O'Brien, "The Political Economy of British Taxation, 1660–1815," *Economic History Review*, new series, vol. 41, no. 1 (February 1988): 1–32, see p. 26.

52. Morse, *Chronicles*, vol. 2, p. 117.

53. H. V. Bowen, *The Business of Empire: The East India Company and Imperial Britain, 1756–1833* (Cambridge: Cambridge University Press, 2006), pp. 234, 245.

54. Wakeman, "Drury's Occupation," p. 30; see also O'Brien, "The Political Economy of British Taxation," p. 15 and table 4 on p. 9 (total customs was 30 percent of income in 1810). Michael Greenberg, *British Trade and the Opening of China, 1800–1842* (Cambridge: Cambridge University Press, 1951), p. 3, provides the widely repeated figure that Chinese tea provided one-tenth of the British government's total revenue.

55. Peter Hopkirk, *The Great Game: The Struggle for Empire in Central Asia* (New York: Kodansha International, 1994), pp. 33–34.

56. Select Committee's report to Secret Committee, March 3, 1809, excerpted in Morse, *Chronicles*, vol. 3, p. 96.

57. Wakeman, "Drury's Occupation," p. 29.

58. Morse, *Chronicles of the East India Company*, vol. 3, p. 86.

59. Ibid., p. 87.

60. Stifler, "The Language Students of the East India Company's Canton Factory," p. 61; Eastberg, "West Meets East," p. 158, n. 398; Morse, *Chronicles*, vol. 3, p. 93.

61. Wakeman, "Drury's Occupation," p. 31.

62. Auber, *China*, pp. 233–34, quotation on p. 233. Referring to himself, Drury wrote that "the sword is half-out of the scabbard, and his duty forbids him making war with China": Wood, "England, China, and the Napoleonic Wars," p. 149.

63. Wakeman, "Drury's Occupation," p. 32; *Da Qing Renzong Rui (Jiaqing) huangdi shilu* (Taipei: Taiwan Huawen shuju, 1964), *juan* 202, pp. 29b–30a.

64. Wood, "England, China, and the Napoleonic Wars," p. 149; Drury to Roberts, November 8, 1808, excerpted in ibid., p. 150.

65. Wood, "England, China, and the Napoleonic Wars," pp. 150, 153.

66. Morse, *Chronicles*, vol. 3, p. 88.

67. Quoted in Wood, "England, China, and the Napoleonic Wars," p. 156.

68. Wakeman, "Drury's Occupation," p. 33, citing M. C. B. Maybon, "Les Anglais à Macao, en 1802 et en 1808," *Bulletin de l'École française d'Extrême-Orient*, tôme 6, 1906, pp. 301–25; "Sun Yu-t'ing," in Arthur W. Hummel, ed., *Eminent Chinese of the Ch'ing Period* (Taipei: SMC Publishing, Inc., 1991), vol. 2, p. 684.

CHAPTER 4   Sea and Land

1. Harold Kahn, *Monarchy in the Emperor's Eyes: Image and Reality in the Ch'ienlung Reign* (Cambridge, MA: Harvard University Press, 1971), p. 259.

2. Jiaqing edict of JQ4/zheng/16 (February 20, 1799), in *Shiliao xunkan* (Kowloon, Hong Kong: Fudi shuyuan chuban youxian gongsi, 2005), no. 6, pp. 398–401;

Wook Yoon, "Prosperity with the Help of 'Villains,' 1776–1799: A Review of the Heshen Clique and Its Era," *T'oung Pao* 98, issue 4/5 (2012): 479–527, see pp. 520–21.

3. Eight hundred million taels of silver: Wook Yoon, "Prosperity with the Help of 'Villains,'" p. 514. Total U.S. GDP in 1800 was about $350 million, as per Peter Mancall et al., "Conjectural Estimates of Economic Growth in the Lower South, 1720 to 1800," in *History Matters: Essays on Economic Growth, Technology, and Demographic Change*, ed. Timothy Guinnane (Stanford, CA: Stanford University Press, 2004), p. 396.

4. David Nivison, "Ho-shen and His Accusers," in *Confucianism in Action*, ed. David Nivison and Arthur Wright (Stanford, CA: Stanford University Press, 1959), pp. 209–43, see p. 241.

5. Benjamin Elman, *Classicism, Politics, and Kinship: The Ch'ang-chou School of New Text Confucianism in Late Imperial China* (Berkeley: University of California Press, 1990), pp. 278–82.

6. Susan Mann Jones, "Hung Liang-chi (1746–1809): The Perception and Articulation of Political Problems in Late Eighteenth Century China" (Ph.D. dissertation, Stanford University, 1971), p. 162.

7. Ibid., p. 158.

8. Elman, *Classicism Politics, and Kinship*, pp. 287–90; Jones, "Hung Liang-chi," pp. 159–60; Nivison, "Ho-shen and His Accusers," p. 242.

9. Elman, *Classicism Politics, and Kinship*, p. 289, citing Jones, "Hung Liang-chi," p. 160, and Nivison, "Ho-shen and His Accusers," p. 243.

10. Jiaqing edict of JQ4/1/4 (February 8, 1799), in Wang Xianqian, ed., *Shi chao donghua lu* (1899), vol. 33, Jiaqing *juan* 7, p. 19b; also excerpted in *Qing zhongqi wusheng bailianjiao qiyi ziliao*, vol. 3, pp. 103–4 (hereafter *QZQWS*).

11. Wang Wensheng, *White Lotus Rebels and South China Pirates: Crisis and Reform in the Qing Empire* (Cambridge, MA: Harvard University Press, 2014), p. 140.

12. "E-le-teng-pao," in Arthur W. Hummel, ed., *Eminent Chinese of the Ch'ing Period* (Taipei: SMC Publishing, Inc., 1991), vol. 1, pp. 222–24; Pamela Crossley, *The Wobbling Pivot: China since 1800, an Interpretive History* (Malden, MA: Wiley-Blackwell, 2010), pp. 21–22.

13. Gong Jinghan, "Ping zei yi," in *QZQWS*, vol. 5, pp. 169–78; heavy loads as per *QZQWS*, vol. 5, p. 179.

14. Daniel Mark McMahon, "Restoring the Garden: Yan Ruyi and the Civilizing of China's Internal Frontiers, 1795–1805" (Ph.D. dissertation, University of California, Davis, 1999), p. 168.

15. *QZQWS*, vol. 3, p. 170.

16. Ibid., p. 171.

17. Dai Yingcong, "Broken Passage to the Summit: Nayancheng's Botched Mission in the White Lotus War," in *The Dynastic Centre and the Provinces: Agents and Interactions*, ed. Jeroen Duindam and Sabine Dabringhaus (Leiden: Brill, 2014), pp. 49–73, see pp. 69–70. On Eldemboo's reputation for suffering hardship, see John Fairbank's review of Suzuki Chūsei's *Shinchō chūkishi kenkyū* in the *Far Eastern Quarterly* 14, no. 1 (November 1954): 104–6.

18. Cecily McCaffrey, "Living through Rebellion: A Local History of the White Lotus Uprising in Hubei, China" (Ph.D. dissertation, University of California,

San Diego, 2003), p. 229; Philip Kuhn and Susan Mann, "Dynastic Decline and the Roots of Rebellion," in *The Cambridge History of China*, vol. 10, *Late Ch'ing, 1800–1911, Part 1*, ed. John K. Fairbank and Denis Twitchett (Cambridge: Cambridge University Press, 1978), p. 142.

19. On the *jianbi qingye* system, see Philip Kuhn, *Rebellion and Its Enemies in Late Imperial China: Militarization and Social Structure, 1796–1864* (Cambridge, MA: Harvard University Press, 1971), pp. 37–63.

20. Gong Jinghan, "Jianbi qingye yi," in *QZQWS*, vol. 5, pp. 178–84.

21. A February 13, 1800, edict mentioned that 448 of the *baozhai* in Shaanxi were built through local funding, while just 93 were built by officials; *QZQWS*, vol. 2, p. 293.

22. Wei Yuan, *Sheng wu ji* (1842), *juan* 10, p. 34a.

23. See edict of JQ8/7/15 (August 31, 1803), in *QZQWS*, vol. 3, pp. 344–46.

24. Hummel, *Eminent Chinese*, pp. 222–24; Crossley, *The Wobbling Pivot*, pp. 21–22.

25. Wei Yuan, *Sheng wu ji*, *juan* 10, p. 39b.

26. Dian Murray, "Cheng I Sao in Fact and Fiction," in *Bandits at Sea: A Pirate Reader*, ed. C. R. Pennell (New York: New York University Press, 2001), pp. 253–82. The comparison to the Spanish Armada is Murray's; see p. 275.

27. Owen Rutter, ed., *Mr. Glasspoole and the Chinese Pirates: Being the Narrative of Mr. Richard Glasspoole of the Ship Marquis of Ely: Describing His Captivity . . .* (London: The Golden Cockerel Press, 1935), p. 57.

28. Wang Wensheng, "White Lotus Rebels and South China Pirates: Social Crises and Political Changes in the Qing Empire, 1796–1810" (Ph.D. dissertation, University of California, Irvine, 2008), pp. 147–48, 151–52.

29. Quoted in David Faure, *Emperor and Ancestor: State and Lineage in South China* (Stanford, CA: Stanford University Press, 2007), p. 173.

30. Faure, *Emperor and Ancestor*, pp. 277–78.

31. Robert J. Antony, "State, Continuity, and Pirate Suppression in Guangdong Province, 1809–1810," *Late Imperial China* 27, no. 1 (June 2006): 1–30, see pp. 7–10.

32. Chung-shen Thomas Chang, "Ts'ai Ch'ien, the Pirate King Who Dominates the Seas: A Study of Coastal Piracy in China, 1795–1810" (Ph.D. dissertation, University of Arizona, 1983), p. 37; Dian Murray, *Pirates of the South China Coast, 1790–1810* (Stanford, CA: Stanford University Press, 1987), pp. 101–5.

33. Robert J. Antony, "Piracy and the Shadow Economy in the South China Sea, 1780–1810," in *Elusive Pirates, Pervasive Smugglers: Violence and Clandestine Trade in the Greater China Seas*, ed. Robert J. Antony (Hong Kong: Hong Kong University Press, 2010), pp. 99–114, see p. 111.

34. Rutter, *Narrative of Mr. Richard Glasspoole*, p. 55; Murray, "Cheng I Sao in Fact and Fiction," p. 259.

35. Antony, "Piracy and the Shadow Economy," p. 109.

36. John Turner, *A Narrative of the Captivity and Sufferings of John Turner . . . among the Ladrones or Pirates, on the Coast of China . . . in the year 1807* (New York: G. & R. Waite, 1814), p. 12.

37. Ibid., p. 33.

38. "Substance of Mr. Glasspoole's Relation, upon his return to England, respect-

ing the Ladrones," in *Further Statement of the Ladrones on the Coast of China: Intended as a Continuation of the Accounts Published by Mr. Dalrymple*, ed. Anon. (London: Lane, Darling, and Co., 1812), pp. 40–45, see p. 40.

39. Rutter, *Narrative of Mr. Richard Glasspoole*, pp. 36–39.

40. Jiaqing edict of JQ10/2/7 (March 7, 1805), in *Qingdai waijiao shiliao* (Beijing: Gugong bowuyuan, 1932–33), Jiaqing *juan* 1, pp. 21b–22a.

41. Jiaqing edict of JQ10/10/17 (December 7, 1805), in *Qingdai waijiao shiliao*, Jiaqing *juan* 1, p. 33a.

42. Wang, "White Lotus Rebels," pp. 498, 501.

43. Dian Murray, "Piracy and China's Maritime Transition," in *Maritime China in Transition, 1750–1850*, ed. Wang Gung-wu and Ng Chin-keong (Wiesbaden: Harrassowitz Verlag, 2004), pp. 43–60, see p. 58.

44. Hosea Ballou Morse, *The Chronicles of the East India Company Trading to China, 1635–1834* (Oxford: Clarendon Press, 1926), vol. 3, p. 117.

45. Ibid., vol. 3, p. 118.

46. J. H. and Edith C. Hubback, *Jane Austen's Sailor Brothers: Being the Adventures of Sir Francis Austen, G.C.B., Admiral of the Fleet and Rear-Admiral Charles Austen* (New York: John Lane, 1906), p. 219; Morse, *Chronicles*, vol. 3, p. 121.

47. Quoted in Hubback and Hubback, *Jane Austen's Sailor Brothers*, p. 220.

48. Hubback and Hubback, *Jane Austen's Sailor Brothers*, p. 220; Morse, *Chronicles*, vol. 3, p. 122.

49. Yuan Yonglun, *Jing haifen ji* (Guangzhou: Shanyuan tang, 1830), vol. 2, p. 5a, translation adapted from Charles Friedrich Neumann, *History of the Pirates Who Infested the China Sea from 1807 to 1810* (London: Oriental Translation Fund, 1831), p. 59.

50. Rutter, *Glasspoole and the Chinese Pirates*, p. 56.

51. Yuan Yonglun, *Jing haifen ji*, vol. 2, pp. 11a–12a, trans. Neumann, *History of the Pirates*, pp. 71–72.

52. Ibid., vol. 2, p. 21b, trans. Neumann, *History of the Pirates*, p. 88.

53. Murray, "Cheng I Sao in Fact and Fiction," p. 260.

54. The figure of two hundred million taels for the White Lotus suppression is from McCaffrey, "Living through Rebellion," p. 196, and Wang, "White Lotus Rebels," p. 104. Roger Knight, in *Britain against Napoleon: The Organization of Victory, 1793–1815* (London: Allen Lane, 2013), p. 386, gives the figure of £830 million for the total financial cost of the Napoleonic Wars to Britain between 1793 and 1815; he also gives £578 million for the size of the debt that was run up to pay for the war. Paul Kennedy, in *The Rise and Fall of British Naval Mastery* (Malabar, FL: R. E. Krieger Pub. Co., 1982), p. 139, puts the cost of the war at double that: £1.657 billion; at the standard exchange of three taels to one pound sterling, £830 million was worth 2.49 billion taels.

55. Linda Colley, "Britishness and Otherness: An Argument," *Journal of British Studies*, vol. 31, no. 4 (October 1992): 309–29, see p. 323.

56. Dai Yingcong, "Civilians Go into Battle: Hired Militias in the White Lotus War," *Asia Major*, 3rd series, vol. 22, part 2 (2009): 145–78, see pp. 176–77.

57. Rutter, *Glasspoole and the Chinese Pirates*, p. 19; Morse, *Chronicles*, vol. 3, pp. 144–45.

CHAPTER 5 Points of Entry

1. George Thomas Staunton to Charles Grant, November 20, 1809, Staunton Papers, Rubenstein Library, Duke University, Durham, NC, accessed via Adam Matthew Digital, "China: Trade, Politics and Culture 1793–1980."
2. George Thomas Staunton, *Memoirs of the Chief Incidents of the Public Life of Sir George Thomas Staunton, Bart.*, printed for private circulation (London: L. Booth, 1856), pp. 42–43.
3. William Foster, *The East India House: Its History and Associations* (London: John Lane, 1924), pp. 139–40.
4. Staunton, *Memoirs of the Chief Incidents*, p. 44.
5. George Thomas Staunton, trans., *Ta Tsing Leu Lee; being the Fundamental Laws, and a Selection from the Supplementary Statutes, of the Penal Code of China* (London: T. Cadell and W. Davies, 1810), p. i.
6. John Barrow, *Some Account of the Public Life and a Selection from the Unpublished Writings, of the Earl of Macartney*, 2 vols. (London: T. Cadell and W. Davies, 1807).
7. See "Staunton's Translation of the Penal Code of China," *Critical Review*, Series the Third, vol. 21, no. 4 (December 1810): 337–53, pp. 338–39.
8. Staunton, *Ta Tsing Leu Lee*, p. xi.
9. George Staunton, review of J. Marshman, *A Dissertation on the Characters and Sounds of the Chinese Language*, in *Quarterly Review* (May 1811): 372–403, see p. 396; in the latter quote he is himself citing a contemporary geographer.
10. Staunton, *Ta Tsing Leu Lee*, p. 493.
11. "Ta Tsing Leu Lee; or, The Laws of China," *Quarterly Review* 3, no. 6 (May 1810): 273–319.
12. "Penal Code of China," *Edinburgh Review*, no. 32 (August 1810): 476–99, quote on pp. 481–82.
13. "Staunton's Translation of the Penal Code of China," *Critical Review*.
14. "Penal Code of China," *Edinburgh Review*.
15. For an in-depth study of British ideas on Chinese law in the era leading up to the Opium War, see Chen Li, *Chinese Law in Imperial Eyes: Sovereignty, Justice, and Transcultural Politics* (New York: Columbia University Press, 2016). The best long-range history of extraterritoriality in China, post–Opium War, is Pär Cassell's *Grounds of Judgment: Extraterritoriality and Imperial Power in Nineteenth-Century China and Japan* (New York: Oxford University Press, 2012).
16. Eliza Morrison, *Memoirs of the Life and Labours of Robert Morrison, D.D.* (London: Longman, Orme, Brown, Green, and Longmans, 1839), vol. 1, p. 136.
17. William Johns, *A Sermon, Preached in the Meeting-House of the Baptist Society in Salem . . . for the Benefit of the Translations of the Scriptures into the Languages of India and China* (Boston: Lincoln & Edmands, 1812), p. 14.
18. William W. Moseley, *The Origin of the First Protestant Mission to China* (London: Simpkin and Marshall, 1842), pp. 9, 12.
19. Ibid., pp. 20, 24, 53–63, 108, 109, n. 1; see also A. C. Moule, "A Manuscript Chinese Version of the New Testament (British Museum, Sloane 3599)," *Journal of the Royal Asiatic Society of Great Britain and Ireland*, no. 1 (April 1949): 23–33.

20. Marshall Broomhall, *Robert Morrison: A Master Builder* (Edinburgh: Turnbull & Spears, 1927), p. 39.

21. William Brown to the directors of the London Missionary Society, April 12, 1806, quoted in Christopher A. Daily, *Robert Morrison and the Protestant Plan for China* (Hong Kong: Hong Kong University Press, 2013), p. 96.

22. Broomhall, *Master Builder*, p. 59.

23. "Memoir of the Rev. Robert Morrison," *Asiatic Journal and Monthly Register*, vol. 11, new series (January–April 1835): 198–220, see pp. 199–200. As to Morrison's guilt, his diary from January 10, 1809, reads, "I spent the evening with Mr. Morton and family. By not applying to my studies my mind is uncomfortable." Two days later: "I spent the evening with the family of the Mortons. Scarcely so devoted as I ought to be." Eliza Morrison, *Life and Labours*, vol. 1, pp. 247–49 (which has error of "June" for "January").

24. George Thomas Staunton, *Memoirs of the Chief Incidents*, p. 37. Staunton notes that he studied for different purposes, and "much less exclusively and assiduously" than Morrison, who "attained ultimately to a much greater degree of proficiency."

25. Eliza Morrison, *Life and Labours*, vol. 1, pp. 163, 168.

26. Ibid., vol. 1, pp. 212, 245.

27. Hosea Ballou Morse, *The Chronicles of the East India Company Trading to China, 1635–1834* (Oxford: Clarendon Press, 1926), vol. 3, p. 103, says Manning's translations were nearly unintelligible; "very imperfectly": Clements R. Markham, ed., *Narratives of the Mission of George Bogle to Tibet, and of the Journey of Thomas Manning to Lhasa* (London: Trübner and Co., 1876), p. 260.

28. William Milne, *A Retrospect of the First Ten Years of the Protestant Mission to China* (Malacca: Anglo-Chinese Press, 1820), p. 79.

29. Morse, *Chronicles*, vol. 3, p. 134; Laurence Kitzan, "The London Missionary Society in India and China, 1798–1834" (Ph.D. dissertation, University of Toronto, 1965), p. 84; Susan Reed Stifler, "The Language Students of the East India Company's Canton Factory," *Journal of the North China Branch of the Royal Asiatic Society* 69 (1938): 46–82, see p. 62.

30. Stifler, "Language Students," p. 62.

31. Eliza Morrison, *Life and Labours*, vol. 1, p. 288.

32. Ibid., vol. 1, pp. 286, 295 (quotation on p. 286).

33. Lo-shu Fu, *A Documentary Chronicle of Sino-Western Relations (1644–1820)* (Tucson: Published for the Association for Asian Studies by the University of Arizona Press, 1966), vol. 1, pp. 397–98.

34. Stifler, "Language Students," p. 64; Kitzan, "The London Missionary Society in India and China," pp. 87–88.

35. Eliza Morrison, *Life and Labours*, vol. 1, pp. 414–17; Kitzan, "The London Missionary Society in India and China," pp. 88–89.

36. Peter Auber, *China. An Outline of Its Government, Laws, and Policy: and of the British and Foreign Embassies to, and Intercourse with That Empire* (London: Parbury, Allen and Co., 1834), pp. 221–22; Thomas Manning to his father, William Manning, February 12, 1808, Manning Papers, TM/1/1/44, Royal Asiatic Society, London; "veiled mysteries": Manning to his father, August 18, 1808, Manning Papers, TM/1/1/46.

37. Soup: Markham, *Narratives*, p. 230.
38. Manning to his father from Canton, March 1, 1809, Manning Papers, TM/1/1/49.
39. Morse, *Chronicles*, vol. 3, p. 72.
40. "The Late Mr. Thomas Manning," obituary in *Asiatic Journal and Monthly Register*, vol. 33, new series (September–December 1840), part 2, pp. 182–83.
41. Manning to his father from Calcutta, April 28, 1810, Manning Papers, TM/1/1/51.
42. Zhao Jinxiu's deposition, as parsed in Matthew William Mosca, "Qing China's Perspectives on India, 1750–1847" (Ph.D. dissertation, Harvard University, 2008), p. 274.
43. Manning to Lamb, October 11, 1810, in *The Letters of Thomas Manning to Charles Lamb*, ed. Gertrude Anderson (London: Martin Secker, 1925), p. 114.
44. According to a letter Manning sent just before his departure, much of that intervening year was wasted in waiting for passports to travel through Bhutan, which made him so miserable he couldn't even write to his friends. ("I gasp and breathe hard when I think how I waste my time here," he wrote.) Manning to George Tuthill from Rangpur, August 27, 1811, Manning Papers, TM/2/3/7.
45. Markham, *Narratives*, p. 215. The original manuscript of Manning's narrative of his journey to Lhasa is in the Thomas Manning Papers at the Royal Asiatic Society in London. As Markham's publication of that manuscript differs little from the original (entailing mainly minor changes in wording and the elimination of some of Manning's constant judgments on the wine he drank), I will generally cite the published version below.
46. Ibid., p. 217.
47. Ibid., pp. 217, 242.
48. Manning manuscript narrative, part 1, p. 9, Manning Papers, TM/10.
49. Markham, *Narratives*, p. 230; Manning manuscript narrative, part 2, p. 7.
50. Markham, *Narratives*, p. 260.
51. Ibid., pp. 255, 256.
52. Ibid., p. 259.
53. Ibid., pp. 264–65. Description of audience hall based also on Sarat Chandra Das, *Journey to Lhasa and Tibet* (London: John Murray, 1902), pp. 166–67.
54. Markham, *Narratives*, pp. 265, 266–67.
55. Ibid., pp. 275–76.
56. Ibid., pp. 238, 258, 275–76.
57. *Da Qing Renzong Rui (Jiaqing) huangdi shilu* (Taipei: Taiwan Huawen shuju, 1964), *juan* 251, p. 14b.
58. Markham, *Narratives*, p. 278.
59. *Da Qing Renzong Rui (Jiaqing) huangdi shilu* (Taipei: Taiwan Huawen shuju, 1964), *juan* 251, pp. 14b–15a.
60. Markham, *Narratives*, p. 293. He was not executed, but was exiled to Yili in the far northwest. See Mosca, "Qing China's Perspectives on India," p. 274.
61. See Manning's deposition from May 17, 1821, in "Third Report from the Select Committee appointed to consider the means of improving and maintaining the Foreign Trade of the Country. East Indies and China," House of Commons, July 10, 1821, pp. 355–57.

62. Murray A. Rubinstein, *The Origins of the Anglo-American Missionary Enterprise in China, 1807–1840* (Lanham, MD: Scarecrow Press, 1996), p. 95.

63. Ibid., p. 114.

64. Elphinstone to the Court of Directors, November 11, 1812, quoted in Su Ching, "The Printing Presses of the London Missionary Society among the Chinese" (Ph.D. dissertation, University of London, 1996), p. 48.

65. Su, "Printing Presses," p. 48.

66. Robert Morrison, *A Dictionary of the Chinese Language, in Three Parts* (Macao: The Honourable East India Company's Press, 1815), vol. 1, part 1, dedication page.

67. Ibid., vol. 1, part 1, pp. 746–85.

68. Prospectus for Morrison's dictionary in the *Literary Panorama and National Register,* September 1818, cc. 1137–38.

69. "Morrison's Dictionary of the Chinese Language," *Asiatic Journal and Monthly Register* 2, no. 9 (September 1816): 258–65, quotation on p. 265.

70. "Missionary Chinese Works," *Quarterly Review* (July 1816): 350–75, quotation on p. 371.

CHAPTER 6   Hidden Shoals

1. Staunton's £20,000 salary: C. H. Philips, *The East India Company, 1784–1834* (Manchester: Manchester University Press, 1940), p. 14, n. 6; "rather high play": George Thomas Staunton, *Memoirs of the Chief Incidents of the Public Life of Sir George Thomas Staunton, Bart.,* printed for private circulation (London: L. Booth, 1856), p. 40.

2. Lord Castlereagh instructions to Lord Amherst ("General Instructions on Undertaking the Embassy to China"), January 1, 1816, UK National Archives, Public Record Office, Foreign Office records (hereafter PRO FO), 17/5/18.

3. Hosea Ballou Morse, *The Chronicles of the East India Company Trading to China, 1635–1834* (Oxford: Clarendon Press, 1926), vol. 3, pp. 214–19.

4. Amherst's instructions: Ibid., vol. 3, p. 281.

5. Douglas M. Peers, "Amherst, William Pitt, First Earl Amherst of Arracan (1773–1857)," *Oxford Dictionary of National Biography* (Oxford: Oxford University Press, 2004–13).

6. Thomas Handasyd Perkins (in Boston) to Perkins & Co., Canton, July 15, 1814, in Thomas Greaves Cary, *Memoir of Thomas Handasyd Perkins; containing Extracts from his Diaries and Letters* (Boston: Little, Brown, 1856), p. 298.

7. George Thomas Staunton, *Miscellaneous Notices Relating to China, and Our Commercial Intercourse with That Country* (London: John Murray, 1822), p. 240.

8. *Da Qing Renzong Rui (Jiaqing) huangdi shilu* (Taipei: Taiwan Huawen shuju, 1964), *juan* 299, pp. 30b–31a.

9. Morse, *Chronicles,* vol. 3, pp. 259–60.

10. Staunton to his mother, July 12, 1816, George Thomas Staunton Papers, Rubenstein Library, Duke University, Durham, NC, accessed via Adam Matthew Digital, "China: Trade, Politics and Culture 1793–1980."

11. George Thomas Staunton, *Notes of Proceedings and Occurrences, during the British*

Embassy to Pekin, in 1816 (London: Habant Press, for private circulation, 1824), pp. 5–8.

12. Staunton to his mother, July 12, 1816, Staunton Papers, Duke University.

13. Thomas Noon Talfourd, ed., *The Works of Charles Lamb* (New York: Harper and Bros., 1838), vol. 1, p. 173.

14. Matthew Mosca, "Qing China's Perspectives on India, 1750–1847" (Ph.D. dissertation, Harvard University, 2008), p. 313.

15. Staunton, *Notes of Proceedings and Occurrences*, p. 9; "natural indolence": John Davis, quoted in Clements R. Markham, ed., *Narratives of the Mission of George Bogle to Tibet, and of the Journey of Thomas Manning to Lhasa* (London: Trübner and Co., 1876), p. clix.

16. "Embassy to China," *British Review and London Critical Journal* 11, no. 21 (February 1818): 140–73, quotation on p. 141.

17. Henry Ellis, *Journal of the Proceedings of the Late Embassy to China* (London: John Murray, 1817), p. 39.

18. Ibid., pp. 440, 491.

19. Robert A. Morrison, *A Memoir of the Principal Occurrences during an Embassy from the British Government to the Court of China in the Year 1816* (London, 1819), p. 16.

20. "Abel's Journey in China," *Quarterly Review* 21, no. 41 (January 1819): 67–91, quotation on p. 74.

21. Lord Amherst dispatch of April 21, 1817, PRO FO 17/3/128.

22. John M'Leod, *Narrative of a Voyage in His Majesty's Late Ship Alceste to the Yellow Sea* (London: John Murray, 1817), pp. 27–47 (quotation modified from "I don't know who ye are; what business have ye here?").

23. Ellis, *Journal of the Proceedings of the Late Embassy*, pp. 72, 91–92 etc.

24. Quotation from Amherst's instructions, PRO FO 17/3/21.

25. Jiaqing's instructions, dated July 16, 1816, are in *Wenxian congbian quanbian* (Beijing: Beijing tushu chubanshe, 2008), vol. 11, p. 352 (Jiaqing 21 nian Ying shi lai pin an, p. 20b).

26. Amherst to George Canning, February 12, 1817, PRO 17/3/59; Jiaqing's witnessing of Macartney's kowtow is also mentioned in Staunton, *Notes of Proceedings*, p. 96.

27. Ellis, *Journal of the Proceedings of the Late Embassy*, pp. 154, 157–58; Morrison, *Memoir of the Principal Occurrences*, p. 35. Beale's aviary: Peter Fay, *The Opium War, 1840–1842: Barbarians in the Celestial Empire in the Early Part of the Nineteenth Century and the War by Which They Forced Her Gates Ajar* (Chapel Hill: University of North Carolina Press, 1975), p. 26.

28. Amherst to Canning, February 12, 1817, PRO FO 17/3/59.

29. Staunton diary 1793–94, entry for September 14, 1793, Staunton Papers, Duke University.

30. Staunton diary 1793–94, entry for September 17, 1793; on Qianlong's birthday being the occasion on which Jiaqing saw Macartney kowtow, see Ellis, *Journal of the Proceedings of the Late Embassy*, p. 110.

31. George Macartney, *An Embassy to China: Being the Journal Kept by Lord Macartney during His Embassy to the Emperor Ch'ien-lung, 1793–1794*, ed. J. L. Cranmer-Byng (Hamden, CT: Archon Books, 1963), p. 131.

32. As Amherst explained in his report to George Canning in February 1817, well after the fact, "I have since been given to understand that on an occasion subsequently to his first audience, Lord Macartney multiplied his bow nine times in conformity to the usual number of prostrations made by the Chinese." Amherst to Canning, February 12, 1817, PRO FO 17/3/59.

33. Lord Amherst to George Canning from Batavia, February 20, 1817, PRO FO 17/3/83.

34. Lord Amherst dispatch of April 21, 1817, PRO FO 17/3/128; Amherst to George Canning, August 8, 1816, PRO FO 17/3/50; Amherst to Canning, February 12, 1817, PRO FO 17/3/62–65; Ellis, *Journal of the Proceedings of the Late Embassy*, pp. 93–97.

35. Morrison, *Memoir of the Principal Occurrences*, pp. 32, 33.

36. Amherst to Canning, February 20, 1817, PRO FO 17/3/86.

37. Staunton, *Notes of Proceedings*, p. 99; Ellis, *Journal of the Proceedings of the Late Embassy*, p. 153.

38. Staunton, *Notes of Proceedings*, pp. 102–3.

39. Ibid., p. 103.

40. English draft of Amherst's letter, PRO FO 17/3/88–89; Amherst to Canning, February 20, 1817, PRO FO 17/3/86; Staunton, *Notes of Proceedings*, p. 103.

41. Amherst to Canning, August 8, 1816, PRO FO 17/3/51.

42. John F. Davis, "Sketches of China," supplement to *The Chinese: A General Description of China and Its Inhabitants* (London: Charles Knight & Co., 1846), p. 86; Amherst to Canning from Batavia, March 8, 1817, PRO FO 17/3/90.

43. Staunton, *Notes of Proceedings*, p. 112.

44. Clarke Abel, *Narrative of a Journey in the Interior of China, and of a Voyage to and from That Country in the Years 1816 and 1817* (London: Longman, Hurst, Rees, Orme, and Brown, 1818), p. 104.

45. Ellis, *Journal of the Proceedings of the Late Embassy*, p. 178.

46. Abel, *Narrative of a Journey in the Interior of China*, p. 106.

47. Amherst to Canning, Batavia, March 8, 1817, PRO FO 17/3/92.

48. Abel, *Narrative*, p. 107; Ellis, *Journal of the Proceedings of the Late Embassy*, pp. 179–80.

49. Morse, *Chronicles*, vol. 3, p. 306; M'Leod, *Narrative of a Voyage in His Majesty's Late Ship Alceste*, pp. 136–37. Staunton claimed that nobody was killed by the *Alceste*: see Staunton, "Extract of a Letter upon the Propositions entertained relative to the China Trade, in 1819," in *Miscellaneous Notices*, p. 313.

50. M'Leod, *Narrative of a Voyage in His Majesty's Late Ship Alceste*, pp. 137, 144, 140.

51. Abel, *Narrative*, p. 111.

52. Jiaqing edict of JQ21/7/8 (August 30, 1816), in *Da Qing Renzong Rui (Jiaqing) huangdi shilu, juan* 320, pp. 6b–9a.

53. Jiaqing edict of JQ21/7/3 (August 25, 1816), in *Wenxian congbian quanbian*, vol. 11, p. 357 (Qing Jiaqing 21 nian Ying shi lai pin an, p. 30a).

54. M'Leod, *Narrative of a Voyage in His Majesty's Late Ship Alceste*, p. 140.

55. Jiaqing edict of JQ21/7/8 (August 30, 1816), in *Da Qing Renzong Rui (Jiaqing) huangdi shilu, juan* 320, pp. 4b–6b (quotation on 6b); translation adapted from that of George Staunton, published in *The Gentleman's Magazine*, vol. 89 (September 1819), as "Letter from the Emperor of China," pp. 264–65.

56. "The Late Embassy to China," *Times*, August 11, 1818.
57. "Chinese Embassy and Trade," *Edinburgh Review* 29, no. 58 (February 1818): 433–53; Staunton, *Memoirs of the Chief Incidents*, p. 72.
58. "Embassy to China," *Quarterly Review* 17, no. 34 (July 1817): 464–506, quotations on pp. 464, 465.
59. "Chinese Drama—Lord Amherst's Embassy," *Quarterly Review* 16, no. 32 (January 1817): 396–416, quotation on p. 412.
60. *Monthly Review*, vol. 83 (June 1817): 222–23.
61. Barry E. O'Meara, *Napoleon in Exile; Or, A Voice from St. Helena. The Opinions and Reflections of Napoleon on the Most Important Events of His Life and Government, in His Own Words* (London: W. Simpkin and R. Marshall, 1822), vol. 1, p. 471.
62. Ibid., vol. 1, p. 472. Clarke Abel, Amherst's physician, who met Napoleon shortly after this exchange, described how Napoleon's eyes would seem to shift color during conversation. When serious and earnest he had what seemed, in Abel's words, "a very dark eye." Abel, *Narrative*, p. 316.

CHAPTER 7   Boom Times

1. John Murray Forbes, *Reminiscences of John Murray Forbes*, ed. Sarah Forbes Hughes (Boston: George H. Ellis, 1902), vol. 1, p. 139. Forbes says "fifteen or twenty ships," but H. B. Morse gives a more precise size for the fleet as sixteen. Hosea Ballou Morse, *The Chronicles of the East India Company Trading to China, 1635–1834* (Oxford: Clarendon Press, 1926), vol. 4, p. 231.
2. Peter C. Holloran, "Perkins, Thomas Handasyd," *American National Biography Online* (Oxford University Press, 2000).
3. Forbes, *Reminiscences of John Murray Forbes*, vol. 1, p. 90.
4. Thomas T. Forbes to John M. Forbes, Canton, Jane 30, 1828, in Forbes, *Reminiscences*, vol. 1, pp. 92–95.
5. His seat was Mitchell, Cornwall, which was abolished by the Reform Act of 1832.
6. George Thomas Staunton, *Memoirs of the Chief Incidents of the Public Life of Sir George Thomas Staunton, Bart.*, printed for private circulation (London: L. Booth, 1856), pp. 74–77.
7. Thomas Noon Talfourd, ed., *The Works of Charles Lamb* (New York: Harper and Bros., 1838), vol. 1, p. 262.
8. Lindsay Ride, *An East India Company Cemetery: Protestant Burials in Macao* (Hong Kong: Hong Kong University Press, 1996), p. 253. Description of aviary and parrot: Harriet Low Hillard, *Lights and Shadows of a Macao Life: The Journal of Harriett [sic] Low, Traveling Spinster*, ed. Nan P. Hodges and Arthur W. Hummel (Woodinville, WA: The History Bank, 2002), vol. 1, p. 120.
9. Marshall Broomhall, *Robert Morrison: A Master Builder* (Edinburgh: Turnbull & Spears, 1927), pp. 127–30.
10. *Canton Register*, November 15, 1830.
11. Hosea Ballou Morse, *The Chronicles of the East India Company Trading to China, 1635–1834* (Oxford: Clarendon Press, 1926), vol. 4, pp. 254–55; specifically,

there were twenty members of the Company's factory, thirty-two private British traders, twenty-one Americans, and forty-one Parsis.

12. William W. Wood, *Sketches of China* (Philadelphia: Carey & Lea, 1830), p. 64.

13. "The Opium Trade," *Canton Register,* April 12, 1828. Money-changing shops: Jonathan Spence, "Opium Smoking in Ch'ing China," in *Conflict and Control in Late Imperial China,* ed. Frederic Wakeman Jr. and Carolyn Grant (Berkeley: University of California Press, 1975), p. 162.

14. Paul A. Van Dyke, "Smuggling Networks of the Pearl River Delta before 1842: Implications for Macao and the American China Trade," in *Americans and Macao: Trade, Smuggling, and Diplomacy on the South China Coast,* ed. Paul A. Van Dyke (Hong Kong: Hong Kong University Press, 2012), pp. 49–72, see p. 63.

15. Robert Forbes made $30,000 in 1831 alone. See Jacques Downs, "American Merchants and the Opium Trade, 1800–1840," *Business History Review* 42, no. 4 (Winter 1968): 418–42, see 436, n. 65. Comparison in value as per calculator on Measuringworth.com.

16. Daniel Defoe, *The Farther Adventures of Robinson Crusoe; Being the Second and Last Part of His Life* (London: W. Taylor, 1719), pp. 249, 274.

17. Morse, *Chronicles,* vol. 1, p. 215.

18. Ibid., vol. 2, p. 239.

19. Clements R. Markham, ed., *Narratives of the Mission of George Bogle to Tibet, and of the Journey of Thomas Manning to Lhasa* (London: Trübner and Co., 1876), p. 238.

20. Robert A. Morrison, *A Memoir of the Principal Occurrences during an Embassy from the British Government to the Court of China in the Year 1816* (London: 1819), p. 197; Clarke Abel, *Narrative of a Journey in the Interior of China, and of a Voyage to and from That Country in the Years 1816 and 1817* (London: Longman, Hurst, Rees, Orme, and Brown, 1818), pp. 213–14.

21. John F. Davis testimony to the Committee of the House of Commons on the East India Company's Affairs, 1830, in *Parliamentary Papers Relating to the Opium Trade . . . 1821 to 1832* (Collected for the use of the Committee of the House of Commons on China Trade, 1840), p. 30.

22. Amar Farooqui, *Opium City: The Making of Early Victorian Bombay* (Gurgaon, India: Three Essays Collective, 2006), p. 39.

23. David Edward Owen, *British Opium Policy in China and India* (New Haven, CT: Yale University Press, 1934), p. 87.

24. Ibid., pp. 69–72, 80–101; Carl Trocki, *Opium, Empire and the Global Political Economy: A Study of the Asian Opium Trade, 1750–1950* (New York: Routledge, 1999), p. 94.

25. Michael Greenberg, *British Trade and the Opening of China, 1800–1842* (Cambridge: Cambridge University Press, 1951), pp. 81, 88–90, 105, 106; Richard J. Grace, *Opium and Empire: The Lives and Careers of William Jardine and James Matheson* (Montreal and Kingston: McGill-Queen's University Press, 2014), p. 92, citing Paul A. Van Dyke, *The Canton Trade: Life and Enterprise on the China Coast, 1700–1845* (Hong Kong: Hong Kong University Press, 2005), pp. 126–41. My data is taken from Charles Marjoribanks's "Statement of British trade at the port of Canton, for the Year ending 30th June 1828," submitted as

part of his 1830 testimony to the House of Commons select committee on the affairs of the East India Company. See *First Report from the Select Committee on the Affairs of the East India Company (China Trade)*, House of Commons, July 8, 1830, pp. 56–57. Specifically, the value of all British imports in the year ending June 1828 was $20,364,600. Of that, Patna and Malwa opium together were worth $11,243,496. The Company's tea exports that year were 5,756,872 taels, or $7,656,640.

26. Trocki, *Opium, Empire and the Global Political Economy*, p. 95.

27. Each chest of raw opium contained about 100 catties by weight (133 pounds), which would render half that amount in smokable extract, so 50 catties. A catty was equivalent to 16 taels by weight, so each chest contained roughly 800 taels of smokable opium extract. Anecdotal accounts from this era generally put the amount of opium smoked by regular users in a range from 0.1 taels/day for light smokers up to one full tael per day for the most inveterate addicts. For more precise figures, in 1869 the Scottish physician John Dudgeon, director of the London Missionary Society's hospital in Beijing, reported his conclusions after observing several hundred opium smokers over the course of five years. According to his study, the breakdown of their daily usage was as follows: 20 percent of smokers in the study used 0.05 taels per day, 20 percent used 0.1 taels, 20 percent used 0.2 taels, 30 percent used 0.3–0.4 taels, and 10 percent used a full tael or more. By his numbers, the average smoker thus used 0.28 taels per day. A chest of opium with its 800 taels of smokable extract would have been sufficient to supply the annual needs of eight regular users, and the nearly 19,000 chests imported by 1830–31 would have been enough to supply a little over 150,000 habitual daily users throughout China. See J. Dudgeon, M.D., "On the Extent and Some of the Evils of Opium Smoking," *The Chinese Recorder and Missionary Journal*, February 1869, pp. 203–4. Zheng Yangwen cites these statistics as a "benchmark" in *The Social Life of Opium in China* (Cambridge: Cambridge University Press, 2005), p. 158. A similar figure for average daily usage (0.3 taels) was also found in a study by Robert Hart of China's Imperial Customs Service in 1879; see Frank Dikötter, Lars Laamann, and Zhou Xun, *Narcotic Culture: A History of Drugs in China* (Chicago: University of Chicago Press, 2004), p. 53.

28. Scholars constantly refer to the opium trade with China as being "the" largest commodity trade of its time, an exaggeration that traces back to a statement on p. 104 of Michael Greenberg's often-cited *British Trade and the Opening of China* that opium was "probably the largest commerce of the time in any single commodity." Greenberg misread his own source, though, which was a treatise from 1836 that only implied opium was *one* of the largest. See John Phipps, *A Practical Treatise on the China and Eastern Trade* (London: Wm. H. Allen and Co., 1836), p. viii.

29. Richard Grace, "Jardine, William (1784–1843)," *Oxford Dictionary of National Biography* (Oxford: Oxford University Press, 2004–13); Maggie Keswick, ed., *The Thistle and the Jade: A Celebration of 175 Years of Jardine Matheson* (London: Frances Lincoln, 2008), p. 14.

30. Grace, *Opium and Empire*, pp. 94, 99–100, 106 and passim.

31. In 2016, Jardine Matheson had 440,000 employees and revenues of $37 billion:

http://beta.fortune.com/global500/jardine-matheson-273 (accessed February 21, 2017).

32. Richard Grace, "Matheson, Sir (Nicholas) James Sutherland, first baronet (1796–1878)," *Oxford Dictionary of National Biography;* Grace, *Opium and Empire,* p. 104.

33. E. J. Rapson, "Jeejeebhoy, Sir Jamsetjee, first baronet (1783–1859)," *Oxford Dictionary of National Biography.* Orphaned: Cooverjee Sorabjee Nazir, *The First Parsee Baronet, Being Passages from the Life and Fortunes of the Late Sir Jamsetjee Jeejeebhoy Baronet* (Bombay: The Union Press, 1866), pp. 5–7. Jeejeebhoy's account of the capture of the *Brunswick* is in the *Bombay Courier,* April 19, 1806.

34. Nazir, *The First Parsee Baronet,* pp. 27–28.

35. On Jeejeebhoy's charity starting in 1822, see ibid., pp. 30–72.

36. William Wood, *Sketches of China,* p. 68.

37. John Murray Forbes journal, Forbes Family Business Records, vol. F-2, Baker Library, Harvard Business School.

38. He Sibing, "Russell and Company, 1818–1891: America's Trade and Diplomacy in Nineteenth-Century China" (Ph.D. dissertation, Miami University, Ohio, 1997), p. 60.

39. The figure of 5 percent is from Hao Yen-p'ing, "Chinese Teas to America," in *America's China Trade in Historical Perspective,* ed. Ernest R. May and John K. Fairbank (Cambridge, MA: Harvard Studies in American–East Asian Relations, 1986), pp. 11–31, see p. 28.

40. There are many accounts of the diverse range of goods scoured from across the oceans by American merchants to sell in Canton, but James Fichter's chapter on "America's China and Pacific Trade," in *So Great a Proffit: How the East Indies Trade Transformed Anglo-American Capitalism* (Cambridge, MA: Harvard University Press, 2010), pp. 205–31, is especially good.

41. Hao, "Chinese Teas to America," pp. 22–23, 25.

42. Meriwether Lewis journal entry of January 9, 1806, in Reuben Gold Thwaites, ed., *Original Journals of the Lewis and Clark Expedition, 1804–1806* (New York: Dodd, Mead & Company), vol. 3, p. 327, cited in Fichter, *So Great a Profitt,* p. 213.

43. J. R. Child, logbook of the *Hunter,* pp. 47, 129–30, Massachusetts Historical Society, Boston.

44. This account of a typical American ship based in part on Roger Houghton's summary in his capacious exploration of the *Canton Register* in the 1830s (and beyond), which he has made available online at http://www.houghton.hk; see in particular Houghton's entry for the *Canton Register* of August 2, 1830. He Sibing, "Russell and Company," pp. 90–92.

45. Hao Yen-p'ing, *The Commercial Revolution in Nineteenth-Century China: the Rise of Sino-Western Mercantile Capitalism* (Berkeley: University of California Press, 1986), p. 215.

46. "The Opium Trade," *Canton Register,* April 12, 1828.

47. "Foreign Vessels Visiting China," *The Canton Register,* Apr. 19, 1828.

48. As William Wood observed in 1830, "captures of opium boats are unfrequent, and seldom accomplished without a severe contest": Wood, *Sketches of China,* p. 208.

49. Ibid., p. 209.

50. Jardine to R. Rolfe, April 6, 1830, quoted in Grace, *Opium and Empire*, p. 108.

51. Dr. Duncan, *Wholesome Advice Against the Abuse of Hot Liquors, Particularly of Coffee, Chocolate, Tea, Brandy, and Strong-Waters* (London, H. Rhodes and A. Bell, 1706), p. 15.

52. Anon., *An Essay on the Nature, Use, and Abuse, of Tea, in a Letter to a Lady; with an Account of its Mechanical Operation* (London: J. Bettenham, 1722), pp. 30 and 39.

53. Ibid., p. 44.

54. Anon., *An Essay on Modern Luxuries* (Salisbury, UK: J. Hodson, 1777), pp. 7, 13, 14, 26–27.

55. Mike Jay, *Emperors of Dreams: Drugs in the Nineteenth Century* (Sawtry, UK: Dedalus, 2000), p. 73.

56. Robert Bennet Forbes, *Personal Reminiscences* (Boston: Little, Brown, 1882), p. 17.

57. Thomas De Quincey, *Confessions of an English Opium-Eater*, 3rd ed. (London: Taylor and Hessey, 1823), p. 91.

58. On Lamb's aid in getting De Quincey published, see the introduction to the 1888 edition of *Confessions* (London: George Routledge and Sons, 1888), p. 7. It was, incidentally, rumored at the time that the true author of the work might be Charles Lamb himself, or even Samuel Taylor Coleridge: see the review of *Confessions* in the *Monthly Review* for March 1823, p. 296.

59. De Quincey, *Confessions* (1823), pp. 4–5.

60. Ibid., pp. 171, 172–73.

61. Ibid., p. 169.

62. M. H. Abrams, *The Milk of Paradise* (New York: Octagon Books, 1971), p. x. The original manuscript is in the British Library, Add. MS 50847.

63. Thomas Talfourd, ed., *The Works of Charles Lamb, with A Sketch of His Life and Final Memorials* (New York: Harper and Bros., 1875), vol. 1, p. 437.

64. Grevel Lindop, "Quincey, Thomas Penson De (1785–1859)," *Oxford Dictionary of National Biography*.

65. Eliza Morrison, *Memoirs of the Life and Labours of Robert Morrison, D.D.* (London: Longman, Orme, Brown, Green, and Longmans, 1839), vol. 2, p. 203.

66. Wood, *Sketches of China*, pp. 206–7.

67. Michael C. Lazich, "E. C. Bridgman and the Coming of the Millennium: America's First Missionary to China" (Ph.D. dissertation, SUNY Buffalo, 1997), p. 259.

68. John P. Cushing memo to Thomas T. Forbes respecting Canton Affairs, March, 1828, Forbes Family Papers, Massachusetts Historical Society.

69. John Murray Forbes's impressions: *Reminiscences of John Murray Forbes*, vol. 1, p. 140; "a man of remarkable ability": Robert Forbes, *Personal Reminiscences*, pp. 370–71; There are many examples of Houqua's avoidance of opium, but see, for example, Michael D. Block, "New England Merchants, the China Trade, and the Origins of California" (Ph.D. dissertation, University of Southern California, 2011), pp. 386–87; "only one bad man": John D. Wong, "Global Positioning: Houqua and his China Trade Partners in the Nineteenth Century" (Ph.D. dissertation, Harvard University, 2012), p. 133.

70. Sydney Greenbie, "Houqua of Canton—A Chinese Croesus," *Asia*, vol. 25 (October 1925): 823–27 and 891–95, quotation on p. 823.

71. The figure for Houqua's fortune comes from William C. Hunter, *The 'Fan Kwae' at Canton before Treaty Days, 1825–1844* (London: Kegan Paul, Trench & Co., 1882), p. 48. Astor's New York real estate holdings would be worth around $20 million upon his death in 1848, which as a share of the U.S. GDP was equivalent to a fortune of about $116 billion today (and it should be noted that Astor's accumulation of real estate was funded in part by his early domination of the fur trade to Canton, another reminder of how much wealth could be derived from China in this era). Anna Youngman, "The Fortune of John Jacob Astor: II," *Journal of Political Economy* 16, no. 7 (July 1908): 436–41, see p. 441. "The Wealthiest Americans Ever," *New York Times*, July 15, 2007.

72. Elma Loines, "Houqua, Sometime Chief of the Co-Hong at Canton (1769–1843)," *Essex Institute Historical Collections* 89, no. 2 (April 1953): 99–108, description on pp. 99–100.

73. State Street Trust Company, *Old Shipping Days in Boston* (Boston: Walton Advertising & Printing Co., 1918), p. 24.

74. As Houqua wrote to young Forbes in one letter, "I find that you enter into and assist my view much more readily than any other foreigner": Houqua to John Murray Forbes, January 25, 1834, Forbes Family Business Records, vol. F-5, p. 56, Baker Library, Harvard Business School.

75. John Murray Forbes, *Reminiscences of John Murray Forbes*, vol. 1, pp. 141–42.

76. Robert B. Forbes to Thomas Handasyd Perkins, October 25, 1831, Forbes Family Papers, Massachusetts Historical Society.

77. Henry Greenleaf Pearson, *An American Railroad Builder: John Murray Forbes* (Boston: Houghton, Mifflin and Company, 1911), p. 6; Forbes, *Reminiscences of John Murray Forbes*, vol. 1, p. 142.

CHAPTER 8   Fire and Smoke

1. This account based on Susan Naquin, *Millenarian Rebellion in China: The Eight Trigrams Uprising of 1813* (New Haven, CT: Yale University Press, 1976), pp. 166–84; also Arthur W. Hummel, ed., *Eminent Chinese of the Ch'ing Period* (Taipei: SMC Publishing, Inc., 1991), vol. 2, p. 574.

2. Leo Tolstoy, *War and Peace*, trans. Leo Weiner, vol. 6 of *The Complete Works of Count Tolstoy* (London: J. M. Dent & Co., 1904), vol. 2, p. 537; Walter Barlow Stevens, *Missouri: The Center State, 1821–1915* (Chicago–St. Louis: S. J. Clarke Publishing Co., 1915), vol. 2, p. 545; Elizabeth Rusch, "The Great Midwest Earthquake of 1811," *Smithsonian*, December 2011; Naquin, *Millenarian Rebellion*, pp. 89, 314.

3. *Da Qing Renzong Rui (Jiaqing) huangdi shilu* (Taipei: Taiwan Huawen shuju, 1964), *juan* 274, pp 8a–9b; translation based on Robert Morrison, *Translations from the Original Chinese, with Notes* (Canton: P. P. Thoms, The Honorable East India Company's Press, 1815), pp. 4–8.

4. January 29, 1814 (changing "Peking" to "Beijing"), as transcribed by Roger

Houghton at http://www.houghton.hk/?p=84. It is unclear exactly which Indian newspaper was his source.

5. Zheng Yangwen's translation in *The Social Life of Opium in China* (Cambridge: Cambridge University Press, 2005), p. 57 (changing "yan" to "smoke").

6. Based on Zheng Yangwen's translation in ibid., p. 57; see the same for her argument that this cannot represent a tobacco pipe.

7. Hu Jinye, *Zhongguo jinyan jindu shi gang* (Taipei: Tangshan chubanshe, 2005), p. 6.

8. Paul Howard, "Opium Suppression in Qing China: Responses to a Social Problem, 1729–1906" (Ph.D. dissertation, University of Pennsylvania, 1998), p. 40.

9. Hu Jinye, *Zhongguo jinyan jindu shi gang*, pp. 6–13; Howard, "Opium Suppression," pp. 77–80; Zhu Weizheng, *Rereading Modern Chinese History*, trans. Michael Dillon (Boston: Brill, 2015), p. 178; David Bello, *Opium and the Limits of Empire: Drug Prohibition in the Chinese Interior, 1729–1850* (Cambridge, MA: Harvard University Asia Center, 2005), p. 118.

10. Zheng, *Social Life of Opium*, p. 58.

11. *Da Qing Renzong Rui (Jiaqing) huangdi shilu, juan* 227, pp. 4a–b.

12. Ibid., *juan* 270, p. 12a.

13. Edict dated DG2/12/8 (January 19, 1823), in Yu Ende, *Zhongguo jinyan faling bianqian shi* (Shanghai: Zhonghua shuju, 1934), p. 40. N.b.: Yu Ende has the Western-conversion year wrong for this document.

14. Zheng, *Social Life of Opium*, p. 66.

15. See note 27 in chapter 7 for general calculations on opium usage. Assuming 0.28 taels/day for an average daily user of the drug, and 800 taels of smokable opium extract in a typical chest of opium, five thousand chests per year would be enough to support about forty thousand regular opium smokers. A light smoker would use only about 0.1 taels per day, though that was considered a small enough dose that it did not damage the health of the user in any noticeable way; serious addicts used much more. See W. H. Medhurst, "Remarks on the Opium Trade," *North-China Herald*, November 3, 1855.

16. Jonathan Spence, "Opium Smoking in Ch'ing China," in *Conflict and Control in Late Imperial China*, ed. Frederic Wakeman Jr. and Carolyn Grant (Berkeley: University of California Press, 1975), p. 145.

17. Medhurst, "Remarks on the Opium Trade."

18. Lin Man-houng, "Late Qing Perceptions of Native Opium," *Harvard Journal of Asiatic Studies* 64, no. 1 (June 2004): 117–44, see pp. 119–20.

19. Paul A. Van Dyke, *The Canton Trade: Life and Enterprise on the China Coast, 1700–1845* (Hong Kong: Hong Kong University Press, 2005), pp. 122–23.

20. Melissa Macauley, "Small Time Crooks: Opium, Migrants, and the War on Drugs in China, 1819–1860," *Late Imperial China* 30, no. 1 (June 2009): 1–47, see p. 40.

21. Lin, "Late Qing Perceptions of Native Opium," p. 118–19, 128.

22. Zheng, *Social Life of Opium*, pp. 71–86.

23. Bello, *Opium and the Limits of Empire*, pp. 1–2.

24. Zheng, *Social Life of Opium*, pp. 65, 71–86.

25. Hollingworth Magniac testimony to the Committee of the House of Lords

relative to the Affairs of the East India Company, 1830, in *Parliamentary Papers Relating to the Opium Trade . . . 1821 to 1832* (Collected for the use of the Committee of the House of Commons on China Trade, 1840), p. 25.

26. *Da Qing Xuanzong Cheng (Daoguang) huangdi shilu* (Taipei: Taiwan Huawen shuju, 1964), *juan* 163, p. 18b.

27. Memorial from Lu Yinpu et al., in Qi Sihe et al., eds., *Yapian zhanzheng* (Shanghai: Xin zhishi chubanshe, 1955), vol. 1, pp. 413–15, quotation on p. 414.

28. These 1831 memorials are reprinted in Qi, *Yapian zhanzheng* (hereafter *YPZZ*), vol. 1, pp. 411–48.

29. Spence, "Opium Smoking," p. 162.

30. William W. Wood, *Sketches of China* (Philadelphia: Carey & Lea, 1830), pp. 208–10.

31. Macauley, "Small Time Crooks," pp. 6, 7, 8, 22.

32. Joyce Madancy, *The Troublesome Legacy of Commissioner Lin: The Opium Trade and Opium Suppression in Fujian Province, 1820s to 1920s* (Cambridge, MA: Harvard University Asia Center, 2003), p. 52.

33. The foregoing section is heavily indebted to Melissa Macauley, "Small Time Crooks."

34. Yu Ende, paraphrasing Tao Zhu in *Zhongguo jinyan faling bianqian shi* (Shanghai: Zhonghua shuju, 1934), p. 51; Tao Zhu was the Liangjiang governor-general at the time.

35. "Pao Shih-ch'en," in Hummel, ed., *Eminent Chinese*, vol. 2, pp. 610–11; William T. Rowe, *Speaking of Profit: Bao Shichen and Reform in Nineteenth-Century China*, prepublication book manuscript, chapter 1.

36. Susan Mann's translation in *The Talented Women of the Zhang Family* (Berkeley: University of California Press, 2007), p. 251, n. 83.

37. My profile of Bao Shichen is much indebted to William Rowe, *Speaking of Profit*, chapter 1.

38. Philip Kuhn, *Origins of the Modern Chinese State* (Stanford, CA: Stanford University Press, 2002), pp. 19–20.

39. William Rowe, "Bao Shichen and Agrarian Reform in Early Nineteenth-Century China," *Frontiers of History in China* 9, no. 1 (2014): 1–31, see p. 9.

40. Rowe, "Bao Shichen and Agrarian Reform," p. 15.

41. Bao Shichen, "Gengchen zazhu er," in *Bao Shichen quan ji (guanqing sanyi, qimin sishu)*, ed. Li Xing (Hefei: Huangshan shushe, 1997), pp. 209–13, see p. 213.

42. Rowe, "Bao Shichen and Agrarian Reform," p. 17.

43. Bao Shichen, "Gengchen zazhu er."

44. Ibid.

45. Guan Tong, "Jin yong yanghuo yi," in Hu Qiuyuan, ed., *Jindai Zhongguo dui Xifang ji lieqiang renshi ziliao huibian* (Taipei: Academia Sinica, Modern History Institute, 1972) (hereafter *JDZGDXF*), vol. 1, pp. 819–20.

46. Guan Tong, "Jin yong yanghuo yi," pp. 819–820.

47. Biographical note on Cheng Hanzhang in *JDZGDXF*, vol. 1, p. 817; Inoue Hiromasa, "Wu Lanxiu and Society in Guangzhou on the Eve of the Opium War," trans. Joshua Fogel, *Modern China* 12, no. 1 (January 1986): 103–15, see pp. 110–12; Cheng Hanzhang, "Lun Yanghai," in *JDZGDXF*, vol. 1, p. 817.

48. Cheng Hanzhang, "Lun Yanghai," p. 817.

49. Bao Shichen, "Da Xiao Meisheng shu," in *JDZGDXF*, vol. 1, p. 800.
50. Biographical note on Xiao Lingyu in *JDZGDXF*, vol. 1, p. 766.
51. Xiao Lingyu, "Yingjili ji," in *YPZZ*, vol. 1, pp. 19–30.
52. For a wonderful study of Qing perceptions of India, see Matthew W. Mosca, "Qing China's Perspectives on India, 1750–1847" (Ph.D. dissertation, Harvard University, 2008), later revised and published as *From Frontier Policy to Foreign Policy: The Question of India and the Transformation of Geopolitics in Qing China* (Stanford, CA: Stanford University Press, 2013).
53. Bao Shichen, "Da Xiao Meisheng shu," p. 800.
54. Xiao Lingyu, "Yingjili ji," p. 22.
55. This is actually a fairly accurate rendition of Amherst's response, which Henry Ellis relates in his account of the embassy. See Ellis, *Journal of the Proceedings of the Late Embassy to China* (London: John Murray, 1817), p. 412.

CHAPTER 9   Freedom

1. Harriet Low Hillard, *Lights and Shadows of a Macao Life: The Journal of Harriett [sic] Low, Traveling Spinster*, ed. Nan P. Hodges and Arthur W. Hummel (Woodinville, WA: The History Bank, 2002), vol. 1, p. 196.
2. Hosea Ballou Morse, *The Chronicles of the East India Company Trading to China, 1635–1834* (Oxford: Clarendon Press, 1926), vol. 4, pp. 199–21.
3. In Hillard, *Journal of Harriett Low*, vol. 1, p. 73, Low calls her the prettiest woman in Macao ("she is a *beauty*").
4. Ibid., pp. 110, 141; William C. Hunter, *The 'Fan Kwae' at Canton before Treaty Days, 1825–1844* (London: Kegan Paul, Trench & Co., 1882), p. 120.
5. Hillard, *Journal of Harriett Low*, vol. 1, pp. 141–42.
6. Ibid., vol. 2, p. 435.
7. Low complained to her sister of being left behind, writing of a woman she feared would join the others in Canton, "I do hope she will not go this season to C[anton], for we shall be alone if she does." Hillard, *Journal of Harriett Low*, vol. 1, p. 110.
8. Morse, *Chronicles*, vol. 4, p. 236.
9. Ibid., p. 237.
10. Ibid., pp. 237–38.
11. Hillard, *Journal of Harriett Low*, vol. 1, p. 193.
12. Ibid., vol. 1, pp. 193, 194.
13. Hunter, *The 'Fan Kwae' at Canton*, p. 120.
14. "China Trade: Copy of a Petition of British Subjects in China . . . ," House of Commons, March 20, 1833; the petition is also reproduced in Alain Le Pichon, ed., *China Trade and Empire: Jardine, Matheson & Co. and the Origins of British Rule in Hong Kong, 1827–1843* (Oxford: Oxford University Press for the British Academy, 2006), appendix IV, pp. 553–59.
15. On claims of governor, see Morse, *Chronicles*, vol. 4, p. 286; on the position of the two portraits in the great hall, see Gideon Nye, *The Morning of My Life in China* (Canton, 1873), p. 20.

16. "Resolutions of the British Merchants of Canton," May 30, 1831, in Morse, *Chronicles*, vol. 4, p. 311.

17. Secret letter from the Select Committee to the Court of Directors, June 18, 1831, in *Papers Relating to the Affairs of the East India Company, 1831–32* (House of Commons, 1832), pp. 6–10.

18. Robert Bennet Forbes to John Perkins Cushing, June 30, 1831, Forbes Family Papers, Massachusetts Historical Society.

19. Robert Bennet Forbes to Thomas H. Perkins, December 21, 1831, ibid.

20. On September 5, 1832, she described him as "my *recherché* admirer, Gutzlaff." Hillard, *Journal of Harriett Low*, vol. 2, p. 435.

21. Issachar Roberts in 1839, as quoted in Jessie Lutz, *Opening China: Karl F. A. Gutzlaff and Sino-Western Relations, 1827–1852* (Grand Rapids, MI: William B. Eerdmans, 2008), p. 20.

22. Charles (Karl) Gutzlaff, *Journal of Three Voyages along the Coast of China* (London: Frederick Westley and A. H. Davis, 1834), p. 71.

23. Lutz, *Opening China*, p. 72.

24. Gutzlaff, *Journal*, pp. 68, 69, 70, 88.

25. Ibid., pp. 73, 128, 107.

26. Ibid., pp. 132–33.

27. Ibid., p. 151.

28. *Hansard's Parliamentary Debates*, 3rd series (London: T. C. Hansard), HC Deb., June 28, 1831, vol. 4, quotations from cc. 432, 433, and 435.

29. *Hansard*, HL Deb., December 13, 1831, vol. 9, quotations from cc. 211, 212.

30. Quoted in Capt. T. H. Bullock, *The Chinese Vindicated, or Another View of the Opium Question* (London: Wm. H. Allen and Co., 1840), pp. 8, 10.

31. Charles Stuart Parker, *Life and Letters of Sir James Graham, Second Baronet of Netherby, P.C., G.C.B., 1792–1861* (London: John Murray, 1907), vol. 1, p. 150.

32. Anthony Webster, *The Twilight of the East India Company* (Woodbridge, Suffolk, UK: Boydell Press, 2009), p. 62.

33. "East India Company—China Question," *Edinburgh Review*, January 1831, pp. 281–322, quotation on p. 311.

34. Yukihisa Kumagai, "The Lobbying Activities of Provincial Mercantile and Manufacturing Interests against the Renewal of the East India Company's Charter, 1812–1813 and 1829–1833" (Ph.D. dissertation, University of Glasgow, 2008), p. 133.

35. John Slade, *Notices on the British Trade to the Port of Canton* (London: Smith, Elder, and Co., 1830), pp. 65–68.

36. Webster, *Twilight of the East India Company*, p. 98.

37. Bates testimony, March 15, 1830, in *Reports from the Select Committee of the House of Commons Appointed to Enquire into the Present State of the Affairs of the East India Company, together with the Minutes of Evidence, and Appendix of Documents, and a General Index* (London: Printed by order of the Honourable Court of Directors, 1830), pp. 332–56.

38. John Murray Forbes, *Reminiscences of John Murray Forbes*, ed. Sarah Forbes Hughes (Boston: George H. Ellis, 1902), vol. 1, p. 154.

39. C. H. Philips, *The East India Company, 1784–1834* (Manchester: Manchester

University Press, 1940), pp. 289, 291–292; Webster, *Twilight of the East India Company*, pp. 99–100; "The Directors are labouring": Charles Marjoribanks to Hugh Hamilton Lindsay from St. Helena, April 19, 1832, Lindsay Papers, D(W)1920-4/1, Staffordshire Records Office, Stafford, England.

40. George Thomas Staunton diary, November 17, 1831, Staunton Papers, Rubenstein Library, Duke University, Durham, NC, accessed via Adam Matthew Digital, "China: Trade, Politics and Culture, 1793–1980."

41. Staunton diary, December 10, 1831.

42. George Staunton, "To the Freeholders of the County of Southampton," and "To the Freeholders and other Electors of South Hants" (n.d., newspaper clippings contained in Staunton diary for 1831–37).

43. "slipshod and untidy": George W. E. Russell, *Collections and Recollections* (New York and London: Harper & Brothers, 1903), p. 138, cited in Antonia Fraser, *Perilous Question: Reform or Revolution? Britain on the Brink, 1832* (New York: PublicAffairs, 2013), p. 59.

44. George Thomas Staunton, *Memoirs of the Chief Incidents of the Public Life of Sir George Thomas Staunton, Bart.*, printed for private circulation (London: L. Booth, 1856), pp. 124–27; David Brown, *Palmerston: A Biography* (New Haven, CT: Yale University Press, 2010), pp. 170–74.

45. Staunton, *Memoirs*, p. 77.

46. "Sir George Staunton, we find, has postponed his motion on the China trade . . . ," *Times*, April 1, 1833.

47. George Thomas Staunton, *Corrected Report of the Speeches of Sir George Staunton, on the China Trade, in the House of Commons, June 4, and June 13, 1833* (London: Edmund Lloyd, 1833), pp. 6, 9.

48. Staunton's mumbling: untitled clipping in Staunton's diary for 1831–37 (Staunton Papers), in which Buckingham refers to "the low tone of voice in which the hon. baronet addressed the house," which the reporters could not hear, so that his entire speech was reduced to just a few lines in the papers the next day; "It could not be expected": *Hansard*, HC Deb., June 4, 1833, vol. 18, c. 378.

49. Ibid., June 13, 1833, vol. 18, c. 708.

50. William James Thompson in London to Jardine, Matheson & Co. in Canton, April 8, 1833 (and allowing six months for the letter's arrival in Canton). In Le Pichon, *China Trade and Empire*, p. 180.

CHAPTER 10   A Darkening Turn

1. Eliza Morrison, *Memoirs of the Life and Labours of Robert Morrison, D.D.* (London: Longman, Orme, Brown, Green, and Longmans, 1839), vol. 2, p. 505.

2. Houqua to John Murray Forbes, January 25, 1834, Forbes Family Business Records, vol. F-5, pp. 56–57, Baker Library Historical Collections, Harvard Business School.

3. Basil Lubbock, *The Opium Clippers* (Glasgow: Brown, Son & Ferguson, Ltd., 1933), pp. 4, 13 passim; A. R. Williamson, *Eastern Traders: Some Men and Ships of Jardine, Matheson & Company* (S.l.: Jardine, Matheson & Co., 1975), p. 191.

4. William Jardine to James Matheson, January 28, 1832, in Alain Le Pichon, ed., *China Trade and Empire: Jardine, Matheson & Co. and the Origins of British Rule in Hong Kong, 1827–1843* (Oxford: Oxford University Press for the British Academy, 2006), pp. 143–45, quotation on p. 144.

5. Harriet Low Hillard, *Lights and Shadows of a Macao Life: The Journal of Harriett [sic] Low, Traveling Spinster*, ed. Nan P. Hodges and Arthur W. Hummel (Woodinville, WA: The History Bank, 2002), vol. 2, p. 590.

6. Hugh Hamilton Lindsay, *Report of Proceedings on a Voyage to the Northern Ports of China, in the Ship Lord Amherst*, 2nd ed. (London: B. Fellowes, 1834), pp. 10–11.

7. Ibid., p. 44.

8. *Ship Amherst: Return to an Order of the Honourable the House of Commons, dated 17 June 1833* . . . (Printed by order of the House of Commons, June 19, 1833), p. 4.

9. "A Brief Account of the English Character," original English as reproduced in Ting Man Tsao, "Representing 'Great England' to Qing China in the Age of Free Trade Imperialism: The Circulation of a Tract by Charles Marjoribanks on the China Coast," *Victorians Institute Journal* 33 (2005): 179–96; an English version also appeared in the *Canton Register*, July 18, 1832; the Chinese version is in *Yapian zhanzheng dang'an shiliao* (Shanghai: Renmin chubanshe, 1987), vol. 1, pp. 118–20.

10. "Voyage of the Amherst to Northern China," *Eclectic Review*, October 1833, p. 332, cited in Ting Man Tsao, "Representing China to the British Public in the Age of Free Trade, c. 1833–1844" (Ph.D. dissertation, SUNY Stony Brook, 2000), p. 51.

11. "Mr. Gutzlaff's Voyages along the Coast of China," *Times*, August 26, 1834.

12. For example, "The Chinese," *Farmer's Cabinet*, Amherst, New Hampshire, December 7, 1832.

13. For example, the *Evangelical Magazine and Missionary Chronicle*, vol. 12, new series (September 1834): 381.

14. *Ship Amherst*, p. 5.

15. Robert Bickers, "The *Challenger*: Hugh Hamilton Lindsay and the Rise of British Asia, 1832–1865," *Transactions of the Royal Historical Society*, vol. 22 (December 2012): 141–69, see pp. 146, 152–57.

16. William Jardine to James Matheson, January 28, 1832, in Le Pichon, *China Trade and Empire*, pp. 143–45.

17. "Voyage of the 'Sylph,'" *Canton Register*, May 31, 1833.

18. "Political Economy," *Canton Register*, May 13, 1831.

19. "Prize Essay," *Canton Register*, June 18, 1831.

20. These are listed in Alexander Wylie, *Memorials of the Protestant Missionaries to the Chinese* (Shanghai: American Presbyterian Mission Press, 1867), pp. 56–66.

21. For example, in a letter of June 1834, Gutzlaff said he was dedicating his next book (a history of China) to William Jardine, praising the opium baron for having "greatly assisted in the promotion of a free intercourse with the Chinese Empire, of which we may expect the greatest results both for religion, science and commerce." Gutzlaff to William Jardine, Canton, June 20, 1834, in Le Pichon, *China Trade and Empire*, pp. 216–17.

22. "Letter from Mr. Gutzlaff," *Boston Recorder,* April 5, 1834.

23. "Mission to China," *Boston Recorder,* May 31, 1834.

24. "[W]e are glad," proclaimed the Society's mission statement, "to engage in a warfare, where we are sure the victors and the vanquished will meet only to exult and rejoice together." "Society for the Diffusion of Useful Knowledge," *Chinese Repository,* December 1834, p. 380; Report of a meeting of the Society, as "Supplement to the Canton Register," *Canton Register,* October 20, 1835.

25. "Barbarism. Civilisation," *Canton Register,* December 30, 1834.

26. As observed by George Staunton in *Miscellaneous Notices Relating to China, and Our Commercial Intercourse with That Country,* 2nd ed. (London: John Murray, 1822–50), p. 155.

27. Quoted in Anne Bulley, *The Bombay Country Ships, 1790–1833* (Richmond, Surrey: Curzon Press, 2000), p. 172.

28. Much to the *Canton Register* editor's outraged disbelief, Staunton told the House of Commons that the Chinese were "an industrious, intelligent race" and that their government, "however despotic and arbitrary, is not practically oppressive." "British Merchants' Petition to Parliament," *Canton Register,* August 16, 1832. Later, in the December 5, 1833, issue of the paper, the editor noted that Staunton was mainly remembered in Canton for his "violent opposition" to the merchants' petition.

29. "A funeral sermon, occasioned by the death of the Right Honorable William-John, Lord Napier, his Britannic Majesty's chief superintendent in China," *Chinese Repository* 3, no. 6 (October 1834): 271–80.

30. Diary of William John, 9th Lord Napier, entry for October 26, 1833, manuscript in private possession of Lord Napier and Ettrick.

31. Before his departure, King William confided to Napier, "I can tell you I fought a hard Battle for you—if it had not been for me, you would never have got it." William John Napier diary, Christmas Day 1833.

32. William John Napier, "Letters to Earl Grey, Lord Palmerston and Others. 1833–1834. China," manuscript notebook in private possession of Lord Napier and Ettrick.

33. Viscount Palmerston to Lord Napier, January 25, 1834, in *Correspondence relating to China. Presented to both Houses of Parliament, by Command of Her Majesty, 1840* (London: T. R. Harrison, 1840), pp. 4–5.

34. Harriet Low Hillard, *My Mother's Journal: A Young Lady's Diary of Five Years Spent in Manila, Macao, and the Cape of Good Hope,* ed. Katharine Hillard (Boston: George H. Ellis, 1900), p. v.

35. Palmerston to Napier, January 25, 1834, UK National Archives, Public Record Office, Foreign Office records (hereafter PRO FO), 17/5/87–89.

36. Napier diary, February 25, 1834.

37. William John Napier, "Remarks and Extracts relative to diplomatic relations with China," personal notebook kept during voyage to China. In private possession of Lord Napier and Ettrick.

38. Ibid.

39. Ibid.

40. Heat wave reported in the *Commercial Advertiser,* January 19, 1835.

41. Eliza Morrison, *Life and Labours,* vol. 2, p. 524.

42. As Palmerston wrote to Napier's widow in 1840, "I think Lord Napier misconceived the Instruction to go to Canton; which meant only that he should go thither in the usual manner, and was not intended to imply that he should go up from Macao without the ordinary Formalities of Passports, etc." Palmerston to Elizabeth Napier, April 5, 1840. Palmerston Papers, GC/NA/20/enc 1, University of Southampton.

43. Eliza Morrison, *Life and Labours*, vol. 2, p. 526.

44. As related in memorial from Lu Kun, DG14/8/28 (September 30, 1834), in Qi Sihe et al., eds., *Yapian zhanzheng* (Shanghai: Xin zhishi chubanshe, 1955), vol. 1, p. 119.

45. Napier to Palmerston, August 8, 1834, in *Correspondence relating to China* (1840), p. 8.

46. Ibid., p. 9.

47. George Thomas Staunton, *Remarks on the British Relations with China, and the Proposed Plans for Improving Them* (London: Edmund Lloyd, 1836), p. 38.

48. *Correspondence relating to China* (1840), pp. 25, 47, 62, 65 (capitalization changed for consistency).

49. Napier to Margaret Heron Maxwell, August 6, 1834, letter in possession of the Clan Napier Society.

50. Napier to Charles Grant, August 14, 1834, in Napier notebook, "Letters to Earl Grey, Lord Palmerston and Others."

51. Napier to Palmerston, August 14, 1834, in *Correspondence relating to China* (1840), pp. 11–15, see p. 12.

52. Ibid., pp. 12–14.

53. Napier to Palmerston, August 27, 1834, in *Correspondence relating to China* (1840), p. 29.

54. "Present state of relations between China and Great Britain—Interesting to the Chinese merchants—A true and official Document," in *Correspondence relating to China* (1840), p. 33.

55. Per account given in Johnston to Astell, October 11, 1834, PRO FO 17/12/180–85.

56. Napier letter for communication to the Chinese authorities and Hong merchants, September 8, 1834, in *Correspondence relating to China* (1840), pp. 35–36.

57. Duke of Wellington to Lord Napier, February 2, 1835, PRO FO 17/8/2. Wellington was serving briefly as foreign secretary after a change of government, though after yet another change Palmerston would soon be returned to the position.

58. John F. Davis to George Staunton, October 20, 1834, PRO FO 17/12/101–3. In his eyewitness account, Davis said each vessel fired 350 rounds of shot.

59. James Goddard, *Remarks on the Late Lord Napier's Mission to Canton; in Reference to the Present State of our Relations with China*, printed for private circulation (London, 1836), pp. 8–9.

60. Napier to Palmerston (postscript), August 17, 1834, in *Correspondence relating to China* (1840), pp. 15–16, quotation on p. 16.

61. Napier's widow was especially angry at the other British for turning against her husband. Lord Napier's negotiations, she wrote in a letter home, would have succeeded "had not selfish interests and party spirit interfered, and given the

Chinese courage to hold out by showing them that disunion prevailed among the British merchants." Their refusal to support Napier, she added, "is well known here." Lady Napier to Alexander Hunter, November 4, 1834, PRO FO 17/12/191–95.

CHAPTER 11   Means of Solution

1. Joyce Madancy, *The Troublesome Legacy of Commissioner Lin: The Opium Trade and Opium Suppression in Fujian Province, 1820s to 1920s* (Cambridge, MA: Harvard University Asia Center, 2003), p. 51, citing Lin Renchuan, "Qingdai Fujian de yapian maoyi," *Zhongguo shehui jingji yanjiu*, vol. 1 (Xiamen: Fujian xinwen): 62–71, see pp. 63–65.
2. Philip Kuhn, *Rebellion and Its Enemies in Late Imperial China: Militarization and Social Structure, 1796–1864* (Cambridge, MA: Harvard University Press, 1971), pp. 106–7; "Yin bingding xishi yapian zhishi lianzhou jinbing buneng deli zhaozhong chu Li Hongbing deng shangyu," in *Yapian zhanzheng dang'an shiliao* (Shanghai: Renmin chubanshe, 1987), vol. 1, p. 130; James Polachek, *The Inner Opium War* (Cambridge, MA: Council on East Asian Studies/Harvard University Press, 1992), p. 109.
3. "Formosa," *Canton Register*, October 24, 1833.
4. "Formosa," *Chinese Courier and Canton Gazette*, March 22, 1832.
5. Philip Kuhn and Susan Mann, "Dynastic Decline and the Roots of Rebellion," in *The Cambridge History of China*, vol. 10, *Late Ch'ing, 1800–1911, Part 1*, ed. John K. Fairbank and Denis Twitchett (Cambridge: Cambridge University Press, 1978), pp. 107–62 and passim; Ts'ui-jung Liu, "A Retrospection of Climate Changes and their Impacts in Chinese History," in *Nature, Environment and Culture in East Asia: The Challenge of Climate Change*, ed. Carmen Meinert (Leiden: Brill, 2013), pp. 107–36, see p. 132.
6. Lin Man-houng, *China Upside Down: Currency, Society, and Ideologies, 1808–1856* (Cambridge, MA: Harvard University Asia Center, 2006), p. 107.
7. Ibid., pp. 86–87.
8. William T. Rowe, "Money, Economy, and Polity in the Daoguang-Era Paper Currency Debates," *Late Imperial China* 31, no. 2 (December 2010): 69–96, see p. 70.
9. Hosea Ballou Morse, *The Chronicles of the East India Company Trading to China, 1635–1834* (Oxford: Clarendon Press, 1926), vol. 4, pp. 259–60. On the melting down of sycee in London, see John Phipps, *A Practical Treatise on the China and Eastern Trade* (London: Wm. H. Allen and Co., 1836), p. 168.
10. Richard von Glahn, "Cycles of Silver in Chinese Monetary History," in *The Economy of Lower Yangzi Delta in Late Imperial China*, ed. Billy K. L. So (New York: Routledge, 2013), pp. 17–71, see pp. 45–46.
11. Ibid., p. 54; Rowe, "Money, Economy, and Polity," pp. 71–72.
12. Lin, *China Upside Down*, pp. 107–14. According to Lin, by the 1850s China's own silver supplies would recover, even as far more opium was by then being purchased from abroad, lending weight to the argument that the opium trade had in fact been only incidental to the monetary crisis of the 1830s.

13. Daoguang edict of DG14/9/3 (October 5, 1834), in *Da Qing Xuanzong Cheng (Daoguang) huangdi shilu* (Taipei: Taiwan Huawen shuju, 1964), *juan* 256, pp. 3b–5b, quotation on p. 4b.

14. Lu Kun memorial of DG14/10/3 (November 3, 1834), in Qi Sihe et al., eds., *Yapian zhanzheng* (Shanghai: Xin zhishi chubanshe, 1955) (hereafter *YPZZ*), vol. 1, pp. 118–19.

15. Liang Tingnan, *Yifen wenji*, in *YPZZ*, vol. 6, pp. 1–104, see p. 7.

16. Wu Lanxiu, "Mihai," in Liang, *Yifen wenji*, in *YPZZ*, vol. 6, pp. 6–7.

17. Liang, *Yifen wenji*, in *YPZZ*, vol. 6, p. 7.

18. Paul Howard, "Opium Suppression in Qing China: Responses to a Social Problem, 1729–1906" (Ph.D. dissertation, University of Pennsylvania, 1998), pp. 104–5.

19. *Report from the Select Committee of the House of Commons on the Affairs of the East-India Company, 16th August, 1832* (London: J. L. Cox and Son, 1833), p. 89. Staunton registered his "entire disapproval" of that resolution in George Staunton, *Corrected Report of the Speech of Sir George Staunton, on Sir James Graham's Motion on the China Trade* (London: Edmund Lloyd, 1840), p. 10.

20. *Hansard's Parliamentary Debates*, 3rd series (London: T. C. Hansard), HC Deb., June 13, 1833, vol. 18, c. 770.

21. Charles Marjoribanks, *Letter to the Right Hon. Charles Grant, President of the Board of Controul, on the Present State of British Intercourse with China* (London: J. Hatchard and Son, 1833), p. 16.

22. Ibid., p. 17.

23. As Gutzlaff wrote in 1838, "The illicit trade in opium cannot be excused in any way. The drug is destructive of health, and highly demoralizing to the consumer; thousands, by a momentary enjoyment, lose the happiness of a whole life, and find a premature grave." Charles (Karl) Gutzlaff, *China Opened* (London: Smith, Elder and Co., 1838), vol. 2, p. 73.

24. Robert Philip and Thomas Thompson, *No Opium! or: Commerce and Christianity Working Together for Good in China* (London: Thomas Ward and Co., 1835); the pamphlet was anonymous, but authorship is given in a memoir of Robert Philip by his son. See Robert Philip, *Manly Piety: A Book for Young Men* (London: William P. Nimmo, 1879), p. 36.

25. Phipps and Thompson, *No Opium!*, p. 7.

26. Ibid., pp. 10, 13.

27. Ibid., p. 56.

28. "The Petition of the Undermentioned British Subjects at Canton," December 9, 1834, UK National Archives, Public Record Office, Foreign Office records (hereafter PRO FO), 17/12/251–52.

29. Houqua to John Perkins Cushing, October 10, 1834, Forbes Family Business Records, vol. F-5, p. 98, Baker Library, Harvard Business School.

30. John Murray Forbes to Joshua Bates, September 20, 1834, ibid., vol. F-6, p. 23.

31. John Murray Forbes to John Perkins Cushing, December 22, 1834, ibid., vol. F-6, n.p. (changing "Viceroy" to "governor-general").

32. John Barrow to John Backhouse (private), March 13, 1834, PRO FO 17/12/172–73.

33. John F. Davis, trans., *The Fortunate Union: A Romance* (London: Printed for the Oriental Translation Fund, 1829), p. vi.

34. Palmerston to Napier, January 25, 1834, states that any vacancies in the committee should be filled with other members of the former Company factory; PRO FO 17/5/69.

35. John F. Davis to George Staunton, October 20, 1834, PRO FO 17/12/101–2.

36. Davis to Palmerston, January 19, 1835, in *Correspondence relating to China. Presented to both Houses of Parliament, by Command of Her Majesty, 1840* (London: T. R. Harrison, 1840), pp. 78–80, quotation on p. 80.

37. Davis to Palmerston, January 2, 1835, ibid., p. 76.

38. "Imperial Edict, against extortions of Hong Merchants under the name of Duties, and against incurring debts to Foreigners," enclosure to ibid., p. 77.

39. Lady Napier to Alexander Hunter, Macao, November 4, 1834, PRO FO 17/12/194.

40. Richard J. Grace, *Opium and Empire: The Lives and Careers of William Jardine and James Matheson* (Montreal and Kingston: McGill–Queen's University Press, 2014), p. 166.

41. Matheson to Jardine from London, July 8, 1835, Jardine Matheson Archive, JM B-10, Cambridge University.

42. See, for example, her letter to Palmerston of April 20, 1835, PRO FO 17/12/257–59.

43. Lady Napier to Palmerston, Castle Craig, July 14, 1835, PRO FO 17/12/346–48.

44. Matheson to Jardine, August 24, 1835, in Alain Le Pichon, ed., *China Trade and Empire: Jardine, Matheson & Co. and the Origins of British Rule in Hong Kong, 1827–1843* (Oxford: Oxford University Press for the British Academy, 2006), p. 271.

45. Matheson to Jardine from London, August 1, 1835, Jardine Matheson Archive, JM B-10, Cambridge University.

46. Lady Napier to Hugh Hamilton Lindsay, January 18, 1836, Lindsay Papers, D(W)1920-4-1, Staffordshire Records Office, Stafford, England.

47. Le Pichon, *China Trade and Empire*, p. 376, n. 65.

48. James Matheson, *The Present Position and Prospects of the British Trade with China* (London: Smith, Elder and Co., 1836), p. 1.

49. Ibid., quotations from pp. 5, 6, and 79–80.

50. Hugh Hamilton Lindsay, *Letter to the Right Honourable Viscount Palmerston on British Relations with China* (London: Saunders and Otley, 1836), quotations from pp. 3, 4, 6, and 19.

51. George Staunton, *Remarks on the British Relations with China, and the Proposed Plans for Improving Them* (London: Edmund Lloyd, 1836), quotations from pp. 1, 7, 11, and 24.

52. Ibid., p. 28.

53. Xu Naiji, "Yapian yan lijin yuyan liubi yuda yingji qing biantong banli zhe," in Qi Sihe, ed., *Huang Juezi zoushu, Xu Naiji zouyi hekan* (Beijing: Zhonghua shuju, 1959), pp. 216–18.

54. Dai Xueji, ed., *Yapian zhanzheng renwu zhuan* (Fuzhou: Fujian jiaoyu chubanshe, 1985), p. 38; "Teng T'ing-chen," in Arthur W. Hummel, ed., *Emi-*

nent Chinese of the Ch'ing Period (Taipei: SMC Publishing, Inc., 1991), vol. 2, pp. 716–17.

55. Deng Tingzhen memorial in response to Xu Naiji, in *Chouban yiwu shimo*, ed. Wen Qing et al. (Beijing: Gugong bowuyuan, 1929–30), Daoguang *juan* 1, pp. 5b, 6b.

CHAPTER 12   The Last Honest Man

1. Charles Elliot report of March 7, 1832, from Office of Protector of Slaves, in *Papers Presented to Parliament, by His Majesty's Command, in Explanation of the Measures Adopted by His Majesty's Government for the Melioration of the Condition of the Slave Population in His Majesty's Possessions in the West Indies, on the Continent of South America, and at the Mauritius* (Printed by order of the House of Commons, August 8 1832), pp. 241–44, see p. 244. On Elliot's becoming an abolitionist: as he wrote to a friend in government in 1832, "What should be given to the Slaves is *such a state of FREEDOM as they are now fit for.*" Charles Elliot to Lord Howick, 1832, excerpt, in Kenneth Ball and W. P. Morrell, eds., *Select Documents on British Colonial Policy, 1830–1860* (Oxford: Clarendon Press, 1928), p. 382.

2. Charles Elliot to his sister Emma Hislop, January 25, 1834, Minto Papers, MS 13135, National Library of Scotland.

3. Ibid.

4. Elliot to his sister, May 10, 1834, ibid.

5. Elliot's promotion: "Official Notification," *Canton Register,* October 28, 1834. Strong liking: as Elliot bragged to his sister, "Our intercourse has been very intimate, and publicly *very confidential*": Elliot to his sister, January 19, 1835, Minto Papers, MS 13135, National Library of Scotland. "Duck my head": Elliot to George Lenox-Conyngham, March 18, 1837, UK National Archives, Public Record Office, Foreign Office records (hereafter PRO FO), 17/20/56–57. Resigned preemptively: John F. Davis to George Staunton, October 20, 1835, PRO FO 17/12/101–3. Right kind of "temper": Davis to Palmerston, December 9, 1834, PRO FO 17/6/222. Better if Elliot had been superintendent: Davis to John Barrow, November 8, 1834, PRO FO 17/12/176. "Uneasy for the state of affairs": Davis to Palmerston, June 26, 1835, PRO FO 17/12/341.

6. Elliot to George Lenox-Conyngham, January 28, 1836 (rec'd at Foreign Office June 6, 1836), PRO FO 17/15/7–13, see fol. 13; W. C. Costin, *Great Britain and China, 1833–1860* (Oxford: Clarendon Press, 1937), p. 32.

7. Petition from the "East India and China Association," June 29, 1836, PRO FO 17/16/142–44.

8. Palmerston to the Treasury, November 8, 1836, PRO FO 17/17/160–64.

9. Elliot to his sister, April 28, 1835, Minto Papers, MS 13135, National Library of Scotland; Susanna Hoe and Derek Roebuck, *The Taking of Hong Kong: Charles and Clara Elliot in China Waters* (Richmond, Surrey: Curzon Press, 1999), p. 46.

10. Daoguang's edict approving of Elliot coming to Canton under the taipan regulations, dated DG17/zheng/18 (February 12, 1838), is in *Yapian zhanzheng dang'an shiliao* (Shanghai: Renmin chubanshe, 1987), vol. 1, p. 226.

11. Elliot to Palmerston, December 14, 1836 (rec'd May 1, 1837), in *Correspondence relating to China. Presented to both Houses of Parliament, by Command of Her Majesty, 1840* (London: T. R. Harrison, 1840), p. 139.

12. Clara Elliot to Emma Hislop, November 4, 1839, Minto Papers, MS 13137, National Library of Scotland.

13. Elliot to Palmerston, January 25, 1836 (rec'd June 6, 1836), PRO FO 17/15/3–7, quotation on fol. 5.

14. Elliot to Palmerston, February 2, 1837 (rec'd Jul. 17, 1837), in *Correspondence relating to China* (1840), p. 153.

15. PRO FO 17/24 is fully dedicated to Gutzlaff's reports from 1835 to 1837.

16. "Remarks on the Opium Trade with China," *Chinese Repository* 5, no. 6 (November 1836): 300.

17. "If my private feelings were of the least consequence," he wrote to Palmerston at one point, ". . . I might justly say, that no man entertains a deeper detestation of the disgrace and sin of this forced traffic on the coast of China than the humble individual who signs this despatch." He saw "little to choose between it and piracy." Elliot to Palmerston, November 16, 1839, in *Additional Papers Relating to China. Presented to both Houses of Parliament by Command of Her Majesty, 1840* (London: T. R. Harrison, 1840), pp. 3–5, quotation on p. 5.

18. Elliot to Palmerston, February 21, 1837, in *Correspondence relating to China* (1840), pp. 189–90.

19. William C. Hunter, *Bits of Old China* (London: Kegan Paul, Trench & Co., 1885), p. 270.

20. Harriet Low Hillard, *Lights and Shadows of a Macao Life: The Journal of Harriett [sic] Low, Traveling Spinster*, ed. Nan P. Hodges and Arthur W. Hummel (Woodinville, WA: The History Bank, 2002), vol. 1, pp. 14–15.

21. John Murray Forbes to his wife, Sarah Forbes, February 20, 1835, in *Reminiscences of John Murray Forbes*, ed. Sarah Forbes Hughes (Boston: George H. Ellis, 1902), vol. 1, p. 192.

22. John Murray Forbes to Sarah Forbes, July 11, 1835, in John Murray Forbes, *Letters (supplementary) of John Murray Forbes*, ed. Sarah Forbes Hughes (Boston: George H. Ellis, 1905), vol. 1, p. 22.

23. John Murray Forbes to Sarah Forbes, March 25, 1836, in ibid., vol. 1, p. 26.

24. Robert Bennet Forbes to Thomas Handasyd Perkins, October 25, 1831, Forbes Family Papers, Massachusetts Historical Society.

25. John Murray Forbes to Sarah Forbes, August 1836, describes Houqua as "horror struck" when John tells him he will return home. *Reminiscences of John Murray Forbes*, vol. 1, p. 227; see ibid., p. 273, for "moderate competency."

26. Forbes, *Reminiscences of John Murray Forbes*, vol. 1, pp. 245–47. The figure of $100,000 is from John Murray Forbes's letter to Robert Bennet Forbes, June 19, 1836, Forbes Family Papers, Massachusetts Historical Society. Half a million of Houqua's money: *Reminiscences of John Murray Forbes*, vol. 1, p. 273.

27. Wu Yixiong, "Deng Tingzhen yu Guangdong jinyan wenti," *Jindaishi yanjiu* (2008, no. 5): 37–55, see p. 41.

28. Jardine to Capt. Rees on the *Austen*, April 25, 1837, Jardine private letterbook, JM C4/6, Jardine Matheson Archive, Cambridge University.

29. Jardine to Jamsetjee Jeejeebhoy, November 27, 1837, Jardine private letter-book, JM C4/6.

30. Jardine to Jamsetjee Jeejeebhoy, January 8, 1838, Jardine private letterbook, JM C4/6.

31. Jardine to H. Fawcett in Bombay, February 21, 1838, Jardine private letter-book, JM C4/7.

32. Extract of letter from Charles Elliot to George Lenox-Conygnham, June 12, 1837, PRO FO 17/28/269–70.

33. Elliot to Palmerston, November 19, 1837, in *Correspondence relating to China* (1840), pp. 241–42.

34. Elliot to Palmerston, November 18, 1837, in ibid., p. 233.

35. Elliot to Palmerston, November 19, 1837, in ibid., p. 242.

36. Ibid., p. 245.

37. Palmerston to Elliot, June 15, 1838, in ibid., p. 258.

38. A draft of the China Courts Bill is in PRO FO 17/28/48–49.

39. Staunton to Palmerston, May 3, 1838, Palmerston Papers, GC/ST/36, University of Southampton.

40. Staunton to Palmerston, June 10, 1838, Palmerston Papers, GC/ST/37; Palmerston to Staunton, June 10, 1838, Palmerston Papers, GC/ST/46.

41. "I have not forgotten the *counting out* I experienced five years ago," he confided to Palmerston, "and am still less disposed than I was then, to address an unwilling audience." Staunton to Palmerston, June 12, 1838. Palmerston Papers, GC/ST/38.

42. *Hansard's Parliamentary Debates*, 3rd series (London: T. C. Hansard), HC Deb., July 28, 1838, vol. 44, c. 744.

43. *Hansard*, HC Deb., July 28, 1838, vol. 44, c. 745; audience response as per report in *Canton Register*, December 11, 1838.

44. Elliot to Palmerston, January 2, 1839, in *Correspondence relating to China* (1840), p. 342.

45. Huang Juezi memorial of DG18/*run*4/10 (June 2, 1838), in *Yapian zhanzheng dang'an shiliao*, vol. 1, pp. 254–57, quotation on p. 255.

46. Ibid., p. 256.

47. Yang Guozhen, *Lin Zexu zhuan* (Beijing: Renmin chubanshe, 1995), p. 197.

48. Mao Haijian, *Tianchao de bengkui: yapian zhanzheng zai yanjiu* (Beijing: Sanlian shudian, 2012), p. 94.

49. "Jie yan fang," addendum to Lin Zexu memorial of DG18/5/19 (July 10, 1838), in *Yapian zhanzheng dang'an shiliao*, vol. 1, p. 274–77. The memorial itself is in ibid., pp. 270–74. Ironically, according to one recent historian the opium ash used in many of these recipes had essentially been processed into heroin, so the treatment was far worse than the original habit; see Zhu Weizheng, *Rereading Modern Chinese History*, trans. Michael Dillon (Boston: Brill, 2015), p. 172.

50. Yang, *Lin Zexu zhuan*, p. 195.

51. Lin Zexu memorial of DG8/8/2 (September 20, 1838), in *Lin Zexu quan ji*, ed. Mao Linli et al. (Fuzhou: Haixia wenyi chubanshe, 2002), vol. 3, zouzhe, pp. 76–79, quotation on p. 79. Translation is that of P. C. Kuo in *A Critical Study of the Anglo-Chinese War, with Documents* (Taipei: Ch'eng Wen Publishing Co., 1970), p. 85.

52. Dai Xueji, ed., *Yapian zhanzheng renwu zhuan* (Fuzhou: Fujian jiaoyu chuban-she, 1985), p. 32.

53. Mao Haijian, *Tianchao de bengkui*, pp. 92–93.

54. Lin Zexu diary entries for December 27, 1838, through January 3, 1839 (DG18/11/11 to DG18/11/18), in *Lin Zexu quan ji*, vol. 9, riji, pp. 363–64.

55. Chang Hsin-pao, *Commissioner Lin and the Opium War* (New York: Norton, 1964), p. 120.

CHAPTER 13   Showdown

1. Robert Inglis testimony in *Report from the Select Committee on the Trade with China; together with the Minutes of Evidence taken before Them* (Printed by order of the House of Commons, June 5, 1840), pp. 17–18.

2. In April 1838, Elliot reported, "In the course of the last two months the num-ber of English boats employed in the illicit traffic between Lintin and Canton has vastly increased, and the deliveries of opium have frequently been accom-panied by conflict of fire-arms between those vessels and the Government pre-ventive craft." Elliot to Palmerston, April 1, 1838, in *Correspondence relating to China. Presented to both Houses of Parliament, by Command of Her Majesty, 1840* (London: T. R. Harrison, 1840), p. 299.

3. Palmerston to Elliot, March 23, 1839, in ibid., pp. 317–18.

4. Charles Elliot, for one, was convinced that if the Chinese government had just kept up its pressure on domestic users as it had been doing prior to Lin Zexu's arrival, the British merchants of opium "would have been for the most part ruined." In that case, there would have been no grounds for a war. Charles Elliot notes, n.d., defending his conduct in China, Minto Papers, MS 21218, National Library of Scotland. Jardine and others, incidentally, would later claim that the only smooth trade in the drug at the time had been conducted by Deng's own men in the Pearl River, but there is no evidence that Deng himself was involved. See Jardine testimony in *Report from the Select Committee on the Trade with China* (1840), p. 101.

5. Jardine to Capt. Jauncey, December 10, 1838, Jardine private letterbook, JM C4/7, Jardine Matheson Archive, Cambridge University.

6. John Slade, *Narrative of the Late Proceedings and Events in China* (Canton: Can-ton Register Press, 1839), p. 3A–3C; Elliot to Palmerston, December 13, 1838, in *Correspondence relating to China* (1840), p. 324; Robert Forbes to Rose Forbes, December 18, 1838, in *Letters from China: The Canton-Boston Correspondence of Robert Bennet Forbes, 1838–1840*, ed. Phyllis Forbes Kerr (Mystic, CT: Mystic Seaport Museum, 1996), p. 76; William C. Hunter, *The 'Fan Kwae' at Can-ton before Treaty Days, 1825–1844* (London: Kegan Paul, Trench & Co., 1882), pp. 73–77 (with incorrect date); *Canton Register*, "Extra" of December 13, 1838.

7. Palmerston to Elliot, April 15, 1839, in *Correspondence relating to China* (1840), p. 325.

8. "To the editor of the Canton Press," *Canton Press*, February 27, 1839, in *Canton*

Press: Communications and Notes Relating to Chinese Customs, 1826–1840 (n.p.: 1826–40), p. 55.

9. Elliot to Palmerston, January 2, 1839, in *Correspondence relating to China* (1840), pp. 326–329.

10. "Public Notice to Her Majesty's Subjects," December 18, 1839, in ibid., pp. 332–33.

11. Capt. Elliot to the Governor of Canton, December 23, 1838, in ibid., p. 333.

12. Matheson to James A. Stewart-Mackenzie (then governor of Ceylon), January 26, 1839. Matheson private letterbook, JM C5/3, Jardine Matheson Archive, Cambridge University.

13. *Canton Register,* December 18, 1838.

14. *Canton Register,* December 25, 1838.

15. Robert Bennet Forbes to Rose Forbes, December 20, 1838, in Forbes, *Letters from China,* p. 77.

16. Robert Bennet Forbes to Rose Forbes, December 2, 1838, in ibid., pp. 72–73.

17. Robert Bennet Forbes to Samuel Russell, January 12, 1839, cited in He Sibing, "Russell and Company, 1818–1891: America's Trade and Diplomacy in Nineteenth-Century China" (Ph.D. dissertation, Miami University, Ohio, 1997), p. 108.

18. Robert Bennet Forbes to Rose Forbes, February 27, 1839, in Forbes, *Letters from China,* pp. 98–99.

19. Jacques Downs, "American Merchants and the Opium Trade, 1800–1840," *Business History Review* 42, no. 4 (Winter 1968): 418–42, see p. 441.

20. Jardine to A. Thomson, March 20, 1838, makes mention of Jardine's plans to leave the following January; Jardine private letterbook, JM C4/7, Jardine Matheson Archive. Deng Tingzhen would send a rather self-serving report to the emperor that Jardine, whom he described as being responsible for most of the foreign opium vessels, had gone home because he was afraid of Deng's crackdown on smuggling. See Lin Zexu's memorial of DG19/3/21 (May 4, 1839) confirming Jardine's departure, in *Lin Zexu quan ji,* ed. Mao Linli et al. (Fuzhou: Haixia wenyi chubanshe, 2002), vol. 3, zouzhe, pp. 139–40.

21. *Canton Register,* January 29, 1839.

22. Elliot letter of introduction to Palmerston for William Jardine, January 26, 1839, UK National Archives, Public Record Office, Foreign Office records (hereafter PRO FO), PRO FO 17/30/236–37.

23. "Public Dinner to Mr. Jardine, on the occasion of his departure for Europe," *Canton Register,* January 29, 1839.

24. Robert Bennet Forbes to Rose Forbes, January 25, 1839, in *Letters from China,* p. 88.

25. *Canton Register,* January 29, 1839; Richard J. Grace, *Opium and Empire: The Lives and Careers of William Jardine and James Matheson* (Montreal and Kingston: McGill-Queen's University Press, 2014), pp. 224–26; Robert Bennet Forbes to Rose Forbes, January 25, 1839, in *Letters from China,* pp. 87–90.

26. Lei Jin, "Rongcheng xianhua," in Qi Sihe et al., eds., *Yapian zhanzheng* (Shanghai: Xin zhishi chubanshe, 1955), vol. 1, p. 314.

27. Gong Zizhen, "Song qinchai dachen houguan Lin gong xu," in Hu Qiuyuan,

ed., *Jindai Zhongguo dui Xifang ji lieqiang renshi ziliao huibian* (Taipei: Academia Sinica, Modern History Institute, 1972), vol. 1, pp. 824–25.

28. Lin records the date and weather in his diary entries for February 15, 1839, and dates surrounding, *Lin Zexu quan ji*, vol. 9, riji, p. 375.

29. Bao Shichen, "Zhi qian Sichuan dubu Su Gong shu," in *Anwu si zhong* (n.p., 1888), *juan* 35, p. 24b.

30. Testimony of Capt. Thacker, *Report from the Select Committee on the Trade with China* (1840), p. 60.

31. Matheson to Henderson, February 13, 1839, and Matheson to Chas. Smith, February 11, 1839, both in Matheson private letterbook, JM C5/3, Jardine Matheson Archive.

32. Lin Zexu, "Xiaoyu Yuesheng shi shang jun min ren deng su jie yapian gaoshi gao," in *Lin Zexu quan ji*, vol. 5, wenlu, p. 107.

33. Chang Hsin-pao, *Commissioner Lin and the Opium War* (New York: Norton, 1964), p. 129.

34. Robert Bennet Forbes to Rose Forbes, March 11, 1839, in *Letters from China*, p. 105.

35. Minutes of the meeting are in John Slade, *Narrative of the Late Proceedings and Events in China* (Canton: Canton Register Press, 1839), pp. 42–46. Abiel Abbot Low, an American who was there at the time, said that everyone knew to take Lin Zexu's edicts with a grain of salt; see Elma Loines, *The China Trade Post-Bag of the Seth Low Family of Salem and New York, 1829–1873* (Manchester, ME: Falmouth Publishing House, 1953), pp. 68–69.

36. Abiel Abbot Low to Harriet Low, April 17, 1839, in Loines, *China Trade Post-Bag*, p. 68; also Slade, *Narrative*, p. 49.

37. Robert Bennet Forbes to Rose Forbes, March 25, 1839, in *Letters from China*, p. 109.

38. Ibid., p. 110.

39. Elliot to Palmerston, March 22, 1839, in *Correspondence relating to China* (1840), p. 349.

40. His arrival is described in a letter from Matheson to Jardine, May 1, 1839, Matheson private letterbook, JM C5/4, Jardine Matheson Archive. Sword detail is from A. A. Low's letter in Loines, *China Trade Post-Bag*, p. 69.

41. Elliot's notice, and his informal comments afterward, are in Slade, *Narrative*, pp. 53–54.

42. Slade, *Narrative*, p. 54 (exclamation point added in place of period, based on his having "exclaimed" this phrase according to Slade).

43. Lin referred to the blockade of Canton as a past precedent for dealing with such situations in his memorial of April 12, 1839, reporting the surrender of the opium. See *Lin Zexu quan ji*, vol. 3, zouzhe, p. 132.

44. Lin Zexu memorial of DG19/2/29 (April 12, 1839), in *Lin Zexu quan ji*, vol. 3, zouzhe, pp. 131–34, see p. 132.

45. W. C. Hunter, "Journal of Occurrances at Canton, during the Cessation of Trade at Canton, 1839," ed. E. W. Ellsworth, *Journal of the Royal Asiatic Society Hong Kong Branch*, vol. 4 (1964): 9–36, see p. 15.

46. Robert Inglis testimony in *Report from the Select Committee on the Trade with China* (1840), p. 22; Grace, *Opium and Empire*, p. 236.

47. Robert Bennet Forbes, *Remarks on China and the China Trade* (Boston: Samuel N. Dickinson, 1844), p. 49.

48. Robert Bennet Forbes, *Personal Reminiscences* (Boston: Little, Brown, 1882), p. 147; Robert Bennet Forbes to Rose Forbes, March 25, 1839, in *Letters from China*, p. 111; rice pudding: Robert Bennet Forbes to Rose Forbes, March 29, 1839, in ibid., p. 113.

49. Robert Inglis testimony in *Report from the Select Committee on the Trade with China* (1840), pp. 7–9.

50. Ibid., pp. 14–15.

51. Matheson to Middleton, April 9, 1839, Matheson private letterbook, JM C5/4, Jardine Matheson Archive.

52. "Private Correspondence," *Times*, November 1, 1839. ("Captain Elliot's receipts for the opium delivered have appeared in the Calcutta money market, under the head 'Opium Scrip,' and some were lately sold by public auction at 355 rupees.")

53. *Canton Register*, March 26, 1839 (publication delayed to March 27).

54. Robert Bennet Forbes to Rose Forbes, January 31, 1840, in *Letters from China*, p. 205.

55. Elliot to Palmerston, March 30, 1839 (rec'd August 29, 1839), *Correspondence relating to China* (1840), p. 357.

56. Nicholas Draper, *The Price of Emancipation: Slave-Ownership, Compensation and British Society at the End of Slavery* (Cambridge: Cambridge University Press, 2010), pp. 75–113.

57. Slade, *Narrative*, p. 46.

58. "Remarks on the Opium Question," *Chinese Repository* 8, no. 3 (July 1839): 120.

59. Samuel Warren, *The Opium Question* (London: James Ridgway, 1840), p. 92.

60. Even John Murray Forbes, in America at the time, assumed that Britain's future trade in China would not include opium, on which count he worried about the effect on the United States of a resumed drain of silver specie into China. John Murray Forbes to Robert Bennet Forbes, December 20, 1839, Forbes Family Business Records, vol. F-8, p. 50, Baker Library, Harvard Business School.

61. Elliot to Palmerston, April 6, 1839, in *Correspondence relating to China* (1840), p. 386. As Elliot explained privately to his sister, "I was so sensible, that the opium ground was untenable, that I offered *to abandon it entirely* for the sake of peace and the transaction of the regular trade": Elliot to his sister Emma Hislop, February 23, 1840, Minto Papers, MS 13135, National Library of Scotland.

62. Elliot to Palmerston, July 18, 1839, in *Correspondence relating to China* (1840), p. 431.

63. Mao Haijian, *Tianchao de bengkui: yapian zhanzheng zai yanjiu* (Beijing: Sanlian shudian, 2012), pp. 92–93. Qishan had confiscated 130,000 taels of the drug. A chest of opium contained about 100 catties, or 1,600 taels, of the unprocessed drug (which, after processing, would render about 800 taels of smokable extract).

64. Mao, *Tianchao*, p. 103. Deng confiscated about 460,000 taels of smokable extract, equivalent to 576 chests of raw opium.

65. Lin Zexu memorial of DG19/2/29 (April 12, 1839), in *Lin Zexu quan ji*, vol. 3, zouzhe, pp. 131–34.

66. A. A. Low letter to Harriet Low, April 17, 1839, in Loines, *China Trade Post-Bag*, p. 71.
67. Lin Zexu memorial of DG19/2/29 (April 12, 1839); he specifically recommended 5 *jin* (nearly 7 pounds) of tea as compensation for each 133-pound chest of opium. Under normal circumstances opium was at least ten times as costly as tea by weight.
68. Elliot to Palmerston (secret), April 3, 1839. PRO FO 17/31/113–17.
69. Elliot to his wife, Clara, April 4, 1839, Minto Papers, MS 13140, National Library of Scotland (changing "Peking" to "Beijing").
70. The deliveries are recorded in Lin Zexu's diary for April and May 1839, *Lin Zexu quan ji*, vol. 9, riji, pp. 386–91.
71. Robert Inglis testimony, *Report from the Select Committee on the Trade with China* (1840), p. 26.
72. James Matheson to Jamsetjee Jeejeebhoy, May 3, 1839, Matheson private letterbook, JM C5/4, Jardine Matheson Archive.
73. The emperor's reversal is noted in Lin Zexu's diary for DG19/4/13–18 (May 25–30, 1839), *Lin Zexu quan ji*, vol. 9, riji, p. 392.
74. Lin Zexu describes the process in a memorial of DG19/5/25 (July 5, 1839), *Lin Zexu quan ji*, vol. 3, zouzhe, p. 160. Elijah Bridgman's eyewitness description of the destruction site is in the *Chinese Repository* 8, no. 2 (June 1839): 70–77. Lin Zexu's prayer is described in his diary entry for DG19/4/20 (June 1, 1839), *Lin Zexu quan ji*, vol. 9, riji, p. 392.
75. Letter extract enclosed in John Abel Smith to Palmerston, August 18, 1839, in PRO FO 17/35/14–17.
76. Matheson's letter to John Abel Smith of April 4, 1839, is noted in Matheson's private letterbook, JM C5/4. Though the letterbook only summarizes the Smith letter, it describes it as being nearly identical to a fully recorded letter written the same day to Jamsetjee Jeejeebhoy in Bombay, which contained identical language to the ostensibly anonymous extract given to Palmerston by Smith.
77. James Matheson to Jamsetjee Jeejeebhoy, April 4, 1839, Matheson private letterbook, JM C5/4, Jardine Matheson Archive.
78. *Canton Register*, July 21, 1840.
79. "As regards India," wrote Auckland when he learned of the surrender of opium at Canton, "we must for the present look upon the opium revenue as annihilated." "This will bear heavy on us," he continued, "but . . . I have always great confidence in the growing resources of India and I would still look cheeringly at our financial prospects." Auckland to Hobhouse, June 6, 1839, quoted in Glenn Melancon, *Britain's China Policy and the Opium Crisis: Balancing Drugs, Violence and National Honour, 1833–1840* (Aldershot, UK: Ashgate, 2003), p. 99.
80. London petition: PRO FO 17/35/109–10. Bristol petition: PRO FO 17/35/190–91.
81. These petitions are scattered throughout PRO FO 17/35; the Manchester data is at PRO FO 17/35/102.
82. Quotes are from the Manchester petition (PRO FO 17/35/104–5), the Blackburn, Lancashire, petition (PRO FO 17/35/188–89), and the Leeds petition (PRO FO 17/35/120–21).

83. Jardine complained in a letter to Matheson that "many people [here] are for doing nothing; they, very foolishly, mix up the insult & violence with the illicit trade, & are for remaining quiet, pocketing the insult, and refusing to pay for the opium." Jardine to Matheson, September 25, 1839, quoted in Melancon, *Britain's China Policy and the Opium Crisis*, p. 102.
84. Editorial beginning "Proceeding with our view of the 'opium question,'" *Times*, October 23, 1839.
85. George Macartney, *An Embassy to China: Being the Journal Kept by Lord Macartney during His Embassy to the Emperor Ch'ien-lung, 1793–1794*, ed. J. L. Cranmer-Byng (Hamden, CT: Archon Books, 1963), p. 211.
86. David Brown, *Palmerston: A Biography* (New Haven, CT: Yale University Press, 2010), pp. 217–25; Grace, *Opium and Empire*, p. 248.
87. Lord Broughton diary, entry for October 1, 1839, British Library, Add. MS 56561.
88. Draper, *The Price of Emancipation*, pp. 106–8.
89. Lord Broughton diary, entries for September 30–October 1, 1839, British Library, Add. MS 56561.
90. Broughton diary, entry for October 1, 1839.
91. John Cam Hobhouse, Baron Broughton, *Recollections of a Long Life, by Lord Broughton (John Cam Hobhouse)*, ed. Lady Dorchester (London: John Murray, 1911), vol. 5, p. 229.

CHAPTER 14 Will and Destiny

1. William C. Hunter, *The 'Fan Kwae' at Canton before Treaty Days, 1825–1844* (London: Kegan Paul, Trench & Co., 1882), pp. 89–90.
2. Lin Zexu's diary entry for DG19/5/26 (July 6, 1839) records his receipt of the new regulations. A later entry, for DG/5/19 (July 19, 1839), notes that foreign dealers will be subject to execution. *Lin Zexu quan ji*, vol. 9, riji, pp. 396, 398.
3. Elliot to Palmerston, August 27, 1839, in *Correspondence relating to China. Presented to both Houses of Parliament, by Command of Her Majesty, 1840* (London: T. R. Harrison, 1840), p. 434; Astell, Braine et al. to Elliot, August 25, 1839, in ibid., p. 436.
4. Lin Zexu proclamation of August 31, 1839, trans. John Robert Morrison, in *Correspondence relating to China* (1840), p. 456.
5. *British Opium Trade with China*, a pamphlet containing reprints from the *Leeds Mercury*, 1839–40 (Birmingham, UK: B. Hudson, n.d.), pp. 3–4.
6. Anna Stoddart, *Elizabeth Pease Nichol* (London: J. M. Dent, 1899), p. 93.
7. "The Opium Question," *Northern Star*, February 22, 1840.
8. "The 'Shopkeepers;' Their 'Profit' and Our 'Loss,'" *Northern Star*, January 18, 1840 (changing "principal" to "principle").
9. T. H. Bullock, *The Chinese Vindicated, or Another View of the Opium Question* (London: Wm. H. Allen and Co., 1840), pp. 111–16.
10. Editorial beginning "The war against China . . . ," *Times*, March 23, 1840.
11. Editorial beginning "The reckless negligence and gross incapacity of the Queen's Ministers . . . ," *Times*, April 7, 1840.

12. A great number of such petitions are listed in the *Mirror of Parliament* for 1840, vols. 1–4.

13. "The Opium War," *Spectator*, March 28, 1840; "The Opium War," *Northern Star*, April 4, 1840; "Opium War with China," *Times*, April 25, 1840.

14. "The Opium Trade and War," *Eclectic Review*, vol. 7 (June 1840): 699–725, quotation on pp. 709–10.

15. "The Opium War," *Spectator*, March 28, 1840.

16. The *Times* clearly interpreted it that way: "If the war with China be not stopped, if the criminals who have entailed it on us be not disgraced and dispossessed of power," they wrote in Graham's support, "the Chinese quarrel will be but a drop in the vast sea of our calamities." See editorial beginning "The reckless negligence . . . ," *Times*, April 7, 1840.

17. The cornerstone for the new (current) House of Commons chamber was laid just a few weeks after the start of this debate. Description of temporary chamber from T. H. S. Escott, *Gentlemen of the House of Commons* (London: Hurst and Blackett, Ltd., 1902), vol. 2, pp. 303–4.

18. Graham's full speech is in *Hansard's Parliamentary Debates*, 3rd series (London: T. C. Hansard), HC Deb., April 7, 1840, vol. 53, cc. 669–704.

19. The chancellor of the exchequer reported to the House of Commons on May 15, 1840, that the government's revenue for the coming year would be £46.7 million, and expenditures £49.4 million, for a deficit of nearly £3 million. See *Hansard*, HC Deb., May 15, 1840, vol. 54, c. 130; also reported in the *Canton Register* for September 1, 1840.

20. *Hansard*, HC Deb., April 9, 1840, vol. 53, cc. 925–48.

21. Letter to the editor of the *Morning Post*, April 31, 1839, reprinted in the *Canton Register* of August 18, 1840.

22. *Hansard*, HC Deb., April 8, 1840, vol. 53, c. 829.

23. Ibid., c. 828.

24. *Hansard*, HC Deb., April 9, 1840, vol. 53, c. 856.

25. *Hansard*, HC Deb., April 7, 1840, vol. 53, c. 694, and April 8, 1840, vol. 53, c. 775.

26. *Hansard*, HC Deb., April 7, 1840, vol. 53, c. 737.

27. *Hansard*, HC Deb., April 8, 1840, vol. 53, c. 836.

28. "I am in dread": Roy Jenkins, *Gladstone* (New York: Random House, 1997), p. 60; a full transcript of Gladstone's speech is in *Hansard*, HC Deb., April 8, 1840, vol. 53, cc. 800–825.

29. As one paper described Napier at this time, he was "as hot-headed, ignorant, presumptuous, and prejudiced a Captain of the Navy, as was ever by virtue of noble birth thrust into an office, for which he was wholly unfit." See "Narrative of the events which led to the steps taken by the Chinese government for the suppression of the opium-trade," *Colonial Gazette*, reprinted in *Spectator*, March 28, 1840.

30. "The Chinese Question," *Times*, January 27, 1840.

31. *Hansard*, HC Deb., April 7, 1840, vol. 53, cc. 675, 676.

32. *Hansard*, HC Deb., March 24, 1840, vol. 53, c. 8.

33. John Cam Hobhouse, Baron Broughton, *Recollections of a Long Life, by Lord*

Broughton (John Cam Hobhouse), ed. Lady Dorchester (London: John Murray, 1911), vol. 5, p. 257.

34. Staunton's speech is in *Hansard*, HC Deb., April 7, 1840, vol. 53, cc. 738–45.

35. George Thomas Staunton, *Memoirs of the Chief Incidents of the Public Life of Sir George Thomas Staunton, Bart.*, printed for private circulation (London: L. Booth, 1856), pp. 88–90.

36. "News of the Week," *Spectator*, April 11, 1840.

37. "Sir James Graham's Motion," *Manchester Courier*, April 11, 1840.

38. "Letter to Lord Palmerston," from the *Morning Post*, reprinted in *Canton Register*, August 18, 1840.

39. "The Whigs and the Tories on the China Question," *Spectator*, April 4, 1840.

40. Editorial beginning "The House of Commons has been engaged . . . ," *Hampshire Advertiser*, April 11, 1840.

41. "News of the Week," *Spectator*, April 11, 1840.

42. *Hansard*, HL Deb., May 12, 1840, vol. 54, c. 26.

43. Ibid., c. 35.

44. "The Late Mr. Thomas Manning," *Friend of India*, July 30, 1840, reprinted in *Asiatic Journal and Monthly Register*, vol. 33, new series (November 1840): 182–83.

45. "Thomas Manning, Esq.," *Gentleman's Magazine*, vol. 14, new series (July 1840): 97–100.

46. Jardine to Palmerston, October 27, 1839, Minto Papers, MS 12058, National Library of Scotland.

47. Palmerston to Admiralty (secret), November 4, 1839, UK National Archives, Public Record Office, Foreign Office records (hereafter PRO FO), 17/36/76.

48. Jardine to Palmerston, October 26, 1839, PRO FO 17/35/281–83.

49. Letter to editor, *Canton Register*, July 21, 1840.

50. Julia Lovell, *The Opium War: Drugs, Dreams, and the Making of China* (London: Picador, 2011), p. 110.

51. Rick Bowers, ed., "Lieutenant Charles Cameron's Opium War Diary," *Journal of the Royal Asiatic Society Hong Kong Branch*, vol. 52 (2012): 29–61, see p. 37.

52. Daoguang edict of August 21, 1840 (DG20/7/24), trans. Chang Hsin-pao in *Commissioner Lin and the Opium War* (New York: Norton, 1964), p. 212.

53. Qishan's memorial is in Qi Sihe et al., eds., *Yapian zhanzheng* (Shanghai: Xin zhishi chubanshe, 1955), vol. 1, p. 387.

54. Lord Jocelyn, *Six Months with the Chinese Expedition; or, Leaves from a Soldier's Note-book* (London: John Murray, 1841), p. 110.

55. Ibid., p. 116.

56. David Brown, *Palmerston: A Biography* (New Haven, CT: Yale University Press, 2010).

57. Palmerston to Elliot, January 24, 1840, Palmerston Papers, GC/EL/29/1-2, University of Southampton.

58. Palmerston to Elliot, November 4, 1839 (rec'd April 9, 1840), in *Papers Relating to China (Private and Confidential) 1839–40 and 1841*, p. 3, Minto Papers, MS 21216A, National Library of Scotland.

59. Palmerston to Plenipotentiaries, February 20, 1840, ibid., p. 9.

60. Charles Elliot to Lord Palmerston, July 20, 1842, Minto Papers, MS 21218, National Library of Scotland.

61. As Elliot wrote to Palmerston, to notify him that he would be departing from his instructions on negotiation, that "if I can secure so much without a blow" it would be better to settle for minor concessions rather than "to cast upon the country the burden of a distant war . . . with its certain consequences of deep hatred." Quoted in Lovell, *Opium War,* p. 129.

62. W. C. Costin, *Great Britain and China, 1833–1860* (Oxford: Clarendon Press, 1937), p. 87.

63. Palmerston to Elliot, private (draft), April 21, 1841, PRO FO 17/45/36–56, see fol. 43.

64. Palmerston to Elliot, private (draft), April 21, 1841, PRO FO 17/45/36–56.

65. Hobhouse, *Recollections of a Long Life,* vol. 6, p. 14; even Queen Victoria expressed bewilderment at Elliot's behavior, writing to her uncle, "*All* we wanted might have been got, if it had not been for the unaccountably strange conduct of Charles Elliot . . . who completely disobeyed his instructions and *tried* to get the *lowest* terms he could." Queen Victoria to Leopold, the King of the Belgians, April 13, 1841, in *The Letters of Queen Victoria* (New York: Longmans, Green, and Co., 1907), vol. 1, p. 329.

66. Elliot to his sister Emma Hislop, May 12, 1840, Minto Papers, MS 13135, National Library of Scotland.

CHAPTER 15   Aftermath

1. John Horsley Mayo, *Medals and Decorations of the British Army and Navy* (Westminster: A. Constable, 1897), pp. 255–256; George Tancred, *Historical Record of Medals and Honorary Distinctions Conferred on the British Navy, Army & Auxiliary Forces from the Earliest Period* (London: Spink & Son, 1891), pp. 270–71. A copy of the original medal is held at the Fitzwilliam Museum in Cambridge, England.

2. Mao Haijian, *Tianchao de bengkui: yapian zhanzheng zai yanjiu* (Beijing: Sanlian shudian, 2012), pp. 416–17; Julia Lovell, *The Opium War: Drugs, Dreams, and the Making of China* (London: Picador, 2011), p. 162 and passim; D. MacPherson, M.D., *Two Years in China. Narrative of the Chinese Expedition from its Formation in April, 1840, till April, 1842* (London: Saunders and Otley, 1842), pp. 230–31; Keith Stewart Mackenzie, *Narrative of the Second Campaign in China* (London: Richard Bentley, 1842), p. 28; Mark C. Elliott, "Bannerman and Townsman: Ethnic Tension in Nineteenth-Century Jiangnan," *Late Imperial China* 11, no. 1 (June 1990): 36–74.

3. Lovell, *Opium War,* p. 116.

4. As reported by Karl Gutzlaff, based on an uncited source, in *The Life of Taoukwang, Late Emperor of China* (London: Smith, Elder and Co., 1852), p. 180.

5. W. H. Hall, *Narrative of the Voyages and Services of the Nemesis, from 1840 to 1843,* ed. W. D. Bernard (London: Henry Colburn, 1844), vol. 1, p. 334.

6. Bei Qingqiao, "Duoduo yin," in Qi Sihe et al., eds., *Yapian zhanzheng* (Shanghai: Xin zhishi chubanshe, 1955), vol. 3, p. 198.

7. "quite blackened," "bespattered": McPherson, *Two Years in China*, pp. 73, 74; "many most barbarous things: Journal of Henry Norman, quoted in David McLean, "Surgeons of the Opium War: The Navy on the China Coast, 1840–42," *English Historical Review* 121, no. 491 (April 2006): 487–504, see p. 492; "our visitations": Sir William Parker to Lord Minto, July 30, 1842, quoted in ibid., pp. 497–98; "a war in which": Charles Elliot to Earl of Aberdeen, January 25, 1842, Minto Papers, MS 21218, National Library of Scotland.

8. "Letter of Hyu-Ly (Opium-Eater) to Captain Elliot" (reprinted from the *Charivari*), *Times*, April 17, 1841.

9. Editorial beginning "While the public are abundantly convinced . . . ," *Times*, June 14, 1841.

10. Glenn Melancon, *Britain's China Policy and the Opium Crisis: Balancing Drugs, Violence and National Honour, 1833–1840* (Aldershot, UK: Ashgate, 2003), p. 129.

11. Jonathan Parry, "Graham, Sir James Robert George, second baronet (1792–1861)," *Oxford Dictionary of National Biography* (Oxford: Oxford University Press, 2004–13).

12. As per the orders of Lord Stanley, the secretary of state for war and the colonies, the new government wished "to increase the force which has been hitherto employed upon the coasts of China, and to make preparations for an early and vigorous prosecution of the war." Lord Stanley to the Board of Control, extract, December 31, 1841, in *China. Return to two addresses of the Honourable The House of Commons, dated 3 August 1843* (Printed by order of the House of Commons, August 21, 1843), p. 23; see also pp. 20–24, 28, and 32–33 of ibid. for details on troop numbers.

13. Christmas editorial, beginning "At the present season . . . ," *Times*, December 24, 1842.

14. Editorial beginning "We were scarcely aware of the pain we were inflicting . . . ," *Times*, November 28, 1842.

15. Capt. Granville G. Loch, *The Closing Events of the Campaign in China: The Operations in the Yang-tze-kiang; and Treaty of Nanking* (London: John Murray, 1843), pp. 173–74.

16. Hobhouse to Auckland, September 22, 1839, in Broughton Correspondence, British Library, MSS EUR F.213.7, fol. 189; Hobhouse to Auckland, May 4, 1840, in ibid., fol. 342; Hobhouse to Auckland, June 4, 1840, in ibid., fol. 364; Henry St. George Tucker, as quoted in George Thomas Staunton, *Miscellaneous Notices Relating to China, and Our Commercial Intercourse with That Country*, 2nd ed., enlarged (London: John Murray, 1822–50), p. 35; Glenn Melancon, "Honour in Opium? The British Declaration of War on China, 1839–1840," *International History Review* 21, no. 4 (December 1999): 855–74.

17. As Lord Stanley explained in the House of Commons, "the merchants had been warned that if they chose to violate the laws of China, either by the introduction of prohibited goods into a legalised port, or the introduction of any goods whatever into ports not legalised, they must not expect the protection of the British Government; but must be exposed to the penalties inflicted by the laws of China." *Hansard's Parliamentary Debates*, 3rd series (London: T. C. Hansard), HC Deb., February 10, 1844, vol. 72, c. 473.

18. Aberdeen to Pottinger, December 29, 1842, as quoted by Robert Peel in *Hansard*, HC Deb., April 4, 1843, vol. 68, c. 464.

19. Staunton's full speech on the suppression of the opium trade is in *Hansard*, HC Deb., April 4, 1843, vol. 68, cc. 411–24.

20. Lady Napier to Palmerston, March 12, 1840, Palmerston Papers, GC/NA/18, University of Southampton.

21. Thomas De Quincey, "The Opium and the China Question," *Blackwood's Edinburgh Magazine* 47, no. 296 (June 1840): 717–38; Cannon Schmitt, "Narrating National Addictions: De Quincey, Opium, and Tea," in *High Anxieties: Cultural Studies in Addiction*, ed. Janet Brodie and Marc Redfield (Berkeley: University of California Press, 2002): 63–84. The article was not printed under De Quincey's name, but confirmation that he was the author can be found in David Masson, *The Collected Writings of Thomas De Quincey* (Edinburgh: Adam and Charles Black, 1890), vol. 14, footnote on p. 146.

22. Thomas De Quincey, "Postscript on the China and the Opium Question," *Blackwood's Edinburgh Magazine* 47, no. 296 (June 1840): 847–53, quotation on p. 849.

23. De Quincey, "The Opium and the China Question," pp. 723, 728, 735, 738.

24. Grevel Lindop, "Quincey, Thomas Penson De (1785–1859)," *Oxford Dictionary of National Biography* (Oxford: Oxford University Press, 2004).

25. Charles Elliot, undated notes in his own defense, 1840s, Minto Papers, MS 21218, National Library of Scotland.

26. *Hansard*, HC Deb., April 4, 1843, vol. 68, c. 417.

27. *Hansard*, HC Deb., March 17, 1842, vol. 61, c. 786.

28. *Hansard*, HC Deb., April 4, 1843, vol. 68, cc. 453–57.

29. Richard J. Grace, *Opium and Empire: The Lives and Careers of William Jardine and James Matheson* (Montreal and Kingston: McGill-Queen's University Press, 2014), p. 299.

30. "Sir Jamsetjee Jeejeebhoy, the First Indian Knight," *Asiatic Journal and Monthly Miscellany*, vol. 38, new series (August 1842): 376.

31. Gyan Prakash, *Mumbai Fables: A History of an Enchanted City* (Princeton, NJ: Princeton University Press, 2010), pp. 37, 51.

32. *Rast Goftar*, April 17, 1859, as translated and quoted by Jesse Palsetia in "Merchant Charity and Public Identity Formation in Colonial India: The Case of Jamsetjee Jeejeebhoy," *Journal of Asian and African Studies* 40, no. 3 (2005): 197–217, see pp. 199–200.

33. "English Outrage in China," *Youth's Companion* (Boston), March 26, 1841, p. 183, cited by Dael Norwood in "Trading in Liberty: The Politics of the American China Trade, c. 1784–1862" (Ph.D. dissertation, Princeton University, 2012), p. 255.

34. "China," *Liberator*, April 24 1840 (from the "Mer. Journal").

35. "Opium," *Liberator*, April 10, 1840 (reprinted from the *Boston Weekly Magazine*, March 28, 1840).

36. Howard Malcom, *Travels in South-Eastern Asia* (Boston: Gould, Kendall, and Lincoln, 1839), vol. 2, p. 160, quoted by Lord Ashley in debate on suppression of opium trade; see *Hansard*, HC Deb., April 4, 1843, vol. 68, c. 390.

37. John C. Calhoun, *Speeches of John C. Calhoun* (New York: Harper & Brothers, 1843), p. 389.

38. John Quincy Adams, "Lecture on the War with China, delivered before the Massachusetts Historical Society, December, 1841," *Chinese Repository*, vol. 11 (May 1842): 274–89, quotation on p. 288 (changing "kotow" to "kowtow").

39. Charles Francis Adams, ed., *Memoirs of John Quincy Adams* (Philadelphia: J. B. Lippincott, 1876), vol. 11, p. 30.

40. Ibid., p. 31.

41. Memoir of John Heard (typescript), Heard Family Business Records, vol. FP-4, p. 36, Baker Library, Harvard Business School.

42. "Merchants of the United States at Canton, China," rec'd January 9, 1840, House of Representatives, 26th Congress, 1st Session, Doc. no. 40.

43. An extract from the commodore's instructions is in "Memorial of Lawrence Kearny, a Captain in the United States Navy," U.S. Senate, 35th Congress, 1st session, Mis. Doc. no. 207, pp. 34–35, quoted in Norwood, "Trading in Liberty," p. 273.

44. John Murray Forbes, *Letters and Recollections of John Murray Forbes*, ed. Sarah Forbes Hughes (Boston: Houghton, Mifflin and Company, 1899), vol. 1, p. 115.

45. John Murray Forbes to Daniel Webster, April 29, 1843, in *Letters (supplementary) of John Murray Forbes*, ed. Sarah Forbes Hughes (Boston: George H. Ellis, 1905), vol. 1, pp. 40–41 (changing "an hundred" to "a hundred").

46. "List of Articles for the Legation to China," April 11, 1843, in Kenneth E. Shewmaker, ed., *The Papers of Daniel Webster; Diplomatic Papers, Volume 1: 1841–1843* (Hanover, NH: University Press of New England, 1983), p. 907.

47. William J. Donahue, "The Caleb Cushing Mission," *Modern Asian Studies* 16, no. 2 (1982): 193–216, see pp. 200–201.

48. "List of Articles for the Legation to China," April 11, 1843, in Shewmaker, *Papers of Daniel Webster*, pp. 907–10.

49. Donahue, "The Caleb Cushing Mission," pp. 202–16.

50. "China: The High Commissioner's Second Letter to the Queen of England," *Times*, June 11, 1840.

51. This is the "common view" (*shi su*) as described by Wei Yuan in *Yi sou ru kou ji* (Taipei: Guangwen shuju, 1974, duplicate of undated manuscript), p. 33.

52. Wei Yuan, *Yi sou ru kou ji*, pp. 6 and 31.

53. Ibid., p. 32.

54. Ibid., p. 33.

55. Zhu Weizheng, *Rereading Modern Chinese History*, trans. Michael Dillon (Boston: Brill, 2015), p. 171.

56. John K. Fairbank, "The Legalization of the Opium Trade before the Treaties of 1858," *Chinese Social and Political Science Review* 17, no. 2 (July 1933): 215–63, see pp. 222–24.

57. "Tabular View of the Quantity of Opium Exported from Bengal and Bombay," *North-China Herald*, November 3, 1855.

58. Amar Farooqui, *Opium City: The Making of Early Victorian Bombay* (Gurgaon, India: Three Essays Collective, 2006), p. 39; J. Y. Wong, "British Annexation of

Sind in 1843: An Economic Perspective," *Modern Asian Studies* 31, no. 2 (May 1997): 225–44.

59. Table in Wong, "British Annexation of Sind," p. 240.

60. Fairbank, "The Legalization of the Opium Trade," pp. 230–33.

61. George Thomas Staunton, *Memoirs of the Chief Incidents of the Public Life of Sir George Thomas Staunton, Bart.*, printed for private circulation (London: L. Booth, 1856), p. 93.

62. Edward Le Fevour, *Western Enterprise in Late Ch'ing China: A Selective Survey of Jardine, Matheson and Company's Operations, 1842–1895* (Cambridge, MA: East Asia Research Center, Harvard University, 1968), p. 25.

63. Lin Man-houng, "Late Qing Perceptions of Native Opium," *Harvard Journal of Asiatic Studies* 64, no. 1 (June 2004): 117–44, see p. 120.

CODA Houqua and Forbes

1. John L. Larson, *Bonds of Enterprise: John Murray Forbes and Western Development in America's Railway Age* (Cambridge, MA: Harvard University Graduate School of Business Administration, 1984), p. 22.

2. John Murray Forbes, *Letters and Recollections of John Murray Forbes*, ed. Sarah Forbes Hughes (Boston: Houghton, Mifflin and Company, 1899), vol. 1, pp. 101, 118–19.

3. Larson, *Bonds of Enterprise*, pp. 21–24; Forbes, *Letters and Recollections*, vol. 1, pp. 105–6, 120.

4. John D. Wong, "Global Positioning: Houqua and his China Trade Partners in the Nineteenth Century" (Ph.D. dissertation, Harvard University, 2012), pp. 262–66.

5. Elma Loines, "Houqua, Sometime Chief of the Co-Hong at Canton (1769–1843)," *Essex Institute Historical Collections* 89, no. 2 (April 1953): 99–108, see p. 106.

6. Figure of $2 million: Houqua to Plowden, April 2, 1843, in Letterbook of Houqua (1840–1843), Massachusetts Historical Society.

7. John Murray Forbes to Houqua, August 5, 1843, in *Letters (supplementary) of John Murray Forbes*, ed. Sarah Forbes Hughes (Boston: George H. Ellis, 1905), vol. 1, pp. 45–47 (changing "Co Hong" to "Hong system").

Bibliography

Abel, Clarke. *Narrative of a Journey in the Interior of China, and of a Voyage to and from That Country in the Years 1816 and 1817.* London: Longman, Hurst, Rees, Orme, and Brown, 1818.

Ainger, Alfred, ed. *The Letters of Charles Lamb.* 2 vols. London: Macmillan, 1904.

Anderson, Aeneas. *A Narrative of the British Embassy to China, in the Years 1792, 1793, and 1794.* London: J. Debrett, 1795.

Anderson, Gertrude A., ed. *The Letters of Thomas Manning to Charles Lamb.* London: Martin Secker, 1925.

Andrade, Tonio. *The Gunpowder Age: China, Military Innovation, and the Rise of the West in World History.* Princeton, NJ: Princeton University Press, 2016.

Anon. ("A Visitor to China"). *Address to the People of Great Britain, Explanatory of Our Commercial Relations with the Empire of China.* London: Smith, Elder and Co., 1836.

Anon. ("A Looker-On"). *Chinese Commerce and Disputes, from 1640 to 1840. Addressed to Tea Dealers and Consumers.* London: W. Morrison, 1840.

Anon. *An Essay on Modern Luxuries.* Salisbury, UK: J. Hodson, 1777.

Anon. *An Essay on the Nature, Use, and Abuse, of Tea, in a Letter to a Lady; with an Account of its Mechanical Operation.* London: J. Bettenham, 1722.

Anon., ed. *Further Statement of the Ladrones on the Coast of China: Intended as a Continuation of the Accounts Published by Mr. Dalrymple.* London: Lane, Darling, and Co., 1812.

Anon. *An Intercepted Letter from J—T—, Esq. Writer at Canton to His Friend in Dublin Ireland.* Dublin: M. N. Mahon, 1804.

Anson, George. *A Voyage Round the World, in the Years 1740–1744.* 2 vols. Edinburgh: Campbell Denovan, 1781.

Antony, Robert J. *Like Froth Floating on the Sea: The World of Pirates and Seafarers in Late Imperial South China.* Berkeley: Institute of East Asian Studies, University of California, 2003.

———. "State, Continuity, and Pirate Suppression in Guangdong Province, 1809–1810." *Late Imperial China* 27, no. 1 (June 2006): 1–30.

———, ed. "Piracy and the Shadow Economy in the South China Sea, 1780–1810." In *Elusive Pirates, Pervasive Smugglers: Violence and Clandestine Trade in the Greater China Seas.* Hong Kong: Hong Kong University Press, 2010.

Auber, Peter. *China. An Outline of Its Government, Laws, and Policy: and of the British and Foreign Embassies to, and Intercourse with That Empire.* London: Parbury, Allen and Co., 1834.

Baldwin, R. C. D. "Sir Joseph Banks and the Cultivation of Tea." *RSA Journal* 141, no. 5444 (November 1993): 813–17.

Ball, Kenneth, and W. P. Morrell, eds. *Select Documents on British Colonial Policy, 1830–1860.* Oxford: Clarendon Press, 1928.

Bao Shichen. *Anwu si zhong* (Four works by Anwu [Bao Shichen]). 36 *juan.* N.p., 1888.

———. *Bao Shichen quan ji* (The complete works of Bao Shichen). Edited by Li Xing. Hefei: Huangshan shushe, 1997.

Bao Zunpeng et al., eds. *Zhongguo jindaishi luncong* (Essays on modern Chinese history). Taipei: Zhengzhong shuju, 1956–59.

Barrow, John. *Some Account of the Public Life and a Selection from the Unpublished Writings, of the Earl of Macartney.* 2 vols. London: T. Cadell and W. Davies, 1807.

Bartlett, Beatrice. *Monarchs and Ministers: The Grand Council in Mid-Ch'ing China, 1723–1820.* Berkeley: University of California Press, 1991.

Baumler, Alan, ed. *Modern China and Opium.* Ann Arbor: University of Michigan Press, 2001.

Beaty, Frederick L., ed. *The Lloyd-Manning Letters.* Bloomington: Indiana University Press, 1957.

Bello, David. *Opium and the Limits of Empire: Drug Prohibition in the Chinese Interior, 1729–1850.* Cambridge, MA: Harvard University Asia Center, 2005.

Bickers, Robert. *The Scramble for China: Foreign Devils in the Qing Empire, 1832–1914.* London: Allen Lane, 2011.

———. "The *Challenger:* Hugh Hamilton Lindsay and the Rise of British Asia, 1832–1865." *Transactions of the Royal Historical Society,* vol. 22 (December 2012): 141–69.

Blake, Clagette. *Charles Elliot R.N., 1801–1875: A Servant of Britain Overseas.* London: Cleaver-Hume Press, 1960.

Blake, Robert. *Jardine Matheson: Traders of the Far East.* London: Weidenfeld & Nicolson, 1999.

Block, Michael D. "New England Merchants, the China Trade, and the Origins of California." Ph.D. dissertation, University of Southern California, 2011.

Blussé, Leonard. *Visible Cities: Canton, Nagasaki, and Batavia and the Coming of the Americans.* Cambridge, MA: Harvard University Press, 2008.

Bodde, Derek. "Chinese Ideas in the West." Prepared for the Committee on Asiatic Studies in American Education, Washington, DC, 1948.

Bourne, Kenneth. *The Foreign Policy of Victorian England, 1830–1902.* Oxford: Clarendon Press, 1970.

Bowen, H. V. *The Business of Empire: The East India Company and Imperial Britain, 1756–1833.* Cambridge: Cambridge University Press, 2006.

Bowers, Rick, ed. "Lieutenant Charles Cameron's Opium War Diary." *Journal of the Royal Asiatic Society Hong Kong Branch,* vol. 52 (2012): 29–61.

British Opium Trade with China (pamphlet containing reprints from the *Leeds Mercury,* 1839–40). Birmingham, UK: B. Hudson, n.d.

Broomhall, Marshall. *Robert Morrison: A Master Builder.* 2nd impression. Edinburgh: Turnbull & Spears, 1927.

Broughton, John Cam Hobhouse, Baron. *Recollections of a Long Life, by Lord Broughton (John Cam Hobhouse).* Edited by Lady Dorchester. 6 vols. London: John Murray, 1911.

Brown, David. *Palmerston: A Biography.* New Haven, CT: Yale University Press, 2010.

Bulley, Anne. *The Bombay Country Ships, 1790–1833.* Richmond, Surrey: Curzon Press, 2000.

Bullock, Capt. T. H. *The Chinese Vindicated, or Another View of the Opium Question.* London: Wm. H. Allen and Co., 1840.

Canton Press: Communications and Notes Relating to Chinese Customs, 1826–1840. N.p., 1826–40.

Cary, Thomas Greaves. *Memoir of Thomas Handasyd Perkins; containing Extracts from his Diaries and Letters.* Boston: Little, Brown, 1856.

Cassell, Pär. *Grounds of Judgment: Extraterritoriality and Imperial Power in Nineteenth-Century China and Japan.* New York: Oxford University Press, 2012.

Chang, Chung-shen Thomas. "Ts'ai Ch'ien, the Pirate King Who Dominates the Seas: A Study of Coastal Piracy in China, 1795–1810." Ph.D. dissertation, University of Arizona, 1983.

Chang Hsin-pao. *Commissioner Lin and the Opium War.* New York: Norton, 1964.

Chang Te-Ch'ang. "The Economic Role of the Imperial Household in the Ch'ing Dynasty." *Journal of Asian Studies* 31, no. 2 (February 1972): 243–73.

Chatterton, E. Keble. *The Old East Indiamen.* Greenwich, UK: Conway Maritime Press, 1970.

Chen Li. *Chinese Law in Imperial Eyes: Sovereignty, Justice, and Transcultural Politics.* New York: Columbia University Press, 2016.

Cheong, W. E. *Mandarins and Merchants: Jardine, Matheson, & Co., a China Agency of the Early Nineteenth Century.* London: Curzon Press, 1979.

Chouban yiwu shimo (A complete account of our management of foreign affairs). Edited by Wen Qing et al. Beijing: Gugong bowuyuan, 1929–30.

Colley, Linda. "Britishness and Otherness: An Argument." *Journal of British Studies* 31, no. 4 (October 1992): 309–29.

Correspondence relating to China. Presented to both Houses of Parliament, by Command of Her Majesty, 1840. London: T. R. Harrison, 1840.

Costin, W. C. *Great Britain and China, 1833–1860.* Oxford: Clarendon Press, 1937.

Crossley, Pamela. *The Wobbling Pivot: China since 1800, an Interpretive History.* Malden, MA: Wiley-Blackwell, 2010.

Cushman, Richard David. "Rebel Haunts and Lotus Huts: Problems in the Ethnohistory of the Yao." Ph.D. dissertation, Cornell University, 1970.

Da Qing Gaozong Chun (Qianlong) huangdi shilu. (The veritable records of the Qing dynasty, Qianlong reign). 30 vols. Taipei: Taiwan Huawen shuju, 1964.

Da Qing Renzong Rui (Jiaqing) huangdi shilu (The veritable records of the Qing dynasty, Jiaqing reign). 8 vols. Taipei: Taiwan Huawen shuju, 1964.

Da Qing Xuanzong Cheng (Daoguang) huangdi shilu. (The veritable records of the Qing dynasty, Daoguang reign). 12 vols. Taipei: Taiwan Huawen shuju, 1964.

Dai Xueji, ed. *Yapian zhanzheng renwu zhuan* (Biographical sketches of figures involved in the Opium War). Fuzhou: Fujian jiaoyu chubanshe, 1985.

Dai Yingcong. "Civilians Go into Battle: Hired Militias in the White Lotus War." *Asia Major,* 3rd series, vol. 22, part 2 (2009): 145–78.

———. "Broken Passage to the Summit: Nayancheng's Botched Mission in the White Lotus War." In *The Dynastic Centre and the Provinces: Agents and Interactions,* edited by Jeroen Duindam and Sabine Dabringhaus. Leiden: Brill, 2014.

Daily, Christopher A. *Robert Morrison and the Protestant Plan for China.* Hong Kong: Hong Kong University Press, 2013.

Darlington, William, ed. *Memorials of John Bartram and Humphry Marshall.* Philadelphia: Lindsay & Blakiston, 1849.

Das, Sarat Chandra. *Journey to Lhasa and Central Tibet.* London: John Murray, 1902.

Davis, John Francis. *The Chinese: A General Description of China and Its Inhabitants.* 3 vols. and supplement, "Sketches of China." London: Charles Knight & Co., 1846.

———, trans. *The Fortunate Union: A Romance.* 2 vols. London: Printed for the Oriental Translation Fund, 1829.

Defeynes, Henry (Monsieur de Monsart). *An Exact and Curious Survey of all the East Indies, even to Canton, the chiefe Cittie of China.* London: Thomas Dawson, 1615.

De Quincey, Thomas. *Confessions of an English Opium-Eater.* 3rd ed. London: Taylor and Hessey, 1823.

Dikötter, Frank, Lars Laamann, and Zhou Xun. *Narcotic Culture: A History of Drugs in China.* Chicago: University of Chicago Press, 2004.

Donahue, William J. "The Caleb Cushing Mission." *Modern Asian Studies* 16, no. 2 (1982): 193–216.

Downs, Jacques. "American Merchants and the Opium Trade, 1800–1840." *Business History Review* 42, no. 4 (Winter 1968): 418–42.

———. *The Golden Ghetto: The American Commercial Community at Canton and the Shaping of American China Policy, 1784–1844.* Bethlehem, PA: Lehigh University Press, 1997.

Draper, Nicholas. *The Price of Emancipation: Slave-Ownership, Compensation and British Society at the End of Slavery.* Cambridge: Cambridge University Press, 2010.

Duncan, Dr. *Wholesome Advice Against the Abuse of Hot Liquors, Particularly of Coffee, Chocolate, Tea, Brandy, and Strong-Waters.* London: H. Rhodes and A. Bell, 1706.

Eames, James Bromley. *The English in China.* London: Curzon Press, 1909.

Eastberg, Jodi Rhea Bartley. "West Meets East: British Perceptions of China through the Life and Works of Sir George Thomas Staunton, 1781–1859." Ph.D. dissertation, Marquette University, 2009.

Elliott, Mark C. "Bannerman and Townsman: Ethnic Tension in Nineteenth-Century Jiangnan." *Late Imperial China* 11, no. 1 (June 1990): 36–74.

———. *Emperor Qianlong: Son of Heaven, Man of the World.* New York: Longman, 2009.

Ellis, Henry. *Journal of the Proceedings of the Late Embassy to China.* London: John Murray, 1817.

Elman, Benjamin, *Classicism, Politics, and Kinship: The Ch'ang-chou School of New Text Confucianism in Late Imperial China.* Berkeley: University of California Press, 1990.

Entenmann, Robert Eric. "Migration and Settlement in Sichuan, 1644–1796." Ph.D. dissertation, Harvard University, 1982.

Fairbank, John King. "The Legalization of the Opium Trade before the Treaties of 1858." *Chinese Social and Political Science Review* 17, no. 2 (July 1933): 215–63.

Farooqui, Amar. *Opium City: The Making of Early Victorian Bombay.* Gurgaon, India: Three Essays Collective, 2006.

Faure, David. *Emperor and Ancestor: State and Lineage in South China.* Stanford, CA: Stanford University Press, 2007.

Fay, Peter. *The Opium War, 1840–1842: Barbarians in the Celestial Empire in the Early Part of the Nineteenth Century and the War by Which They Forced Her Gates Ajar.* Chapel Hill: University of North Carolina Press, 1975.

Fichter, James R. *So Great a Proffit: How the East Indies Trade Transformed Anglo-American Capitalism.* Cambridge, MA: Harvard University Press, 2010.

Forbes, John Murray. *Letters and Recollections of John Murray Forbes.* Edited by Sarah Forbes Hughes. 2 vols. Boston: Houghton, Mifflin and Company, 1899.

———. *Letters (supplementary) of John Murray Forbes.* Edited by Sarah Forbes Hughes. 3 vols. Boston: George H. Ellis, 1905.

———. *Reminiscences of John Murray Forbes.* Edited by Sarah Forbes Hughes. 3 vols. Boston: George H. Ellis, 1902.

Forbes, Robert Bennet. *Remarks on China and the China Trade.* Boston: Samuel N. Dickinson, 1844.

———. *Personal Reminiscences.* 2nd ed. Boston: Little, Brown, 1882.

———. *Letters from China: The Canton-Boston Correspondence of Robert Bennet Forbes, 1838–1840.* Edited by Phyllis Forbes Kerr. Mystic, CT: Mystic Seaport Museum, 1996.

Foster, William. *The East India House: Its History and Associations.* London: John Lane, 1924.

Fraser, Antonia. *Perilous Question: Reform or Revolution? Britain on the Brink, 1832.* New York: PublicAffairs, 2013.

Fu, Lo-shu. *A Documentary Chronicle of Sino-Western Relations (1644–1820).* 2 vols. Tucson: Published for the Association for Asian Studies by the University of Arizona Press, 1966.

Garrett, Valery M. *Heaven Is High, the Emperor Far Away: Merchants and Mandarins in Old Canton.* New York: Oxford University Press, 2002.

Gaustad, Blaine Campbell. "Religious Sectarianism and the State in Mid Qing China: Background to the White Lotus Uprising of 1796–1804." Ph.D. dissertation, University of California, Berkeley, 1994.

Goddard, James. *Remarks on the Late Lord Napier's Mission to Canton; in Reference to the Present State of our Relations with China.* Printed for private circulation. London, 1836.

Grace, Richard J. *Opium and Empire: The Lives and Careers of William Jardine and James Matheson.* Montreal and Kingston: McGill-Queen's University Press, 2014.

Grant, Frederic Delano. *The Chinese Cornerstone of Modern Banking: The Canton*

Guaranty System and the Origins of Bank Deposit Insurance, 1780–1933. Leiden: Brill, 2014.

Greenberg, Michael. *British Trade and the Opening of China, 1800–1842.* Cambridge: Cambridge University Press, 1951.

Guan Shijie. "Chartism and the First Opium War." *History Workshop,* no. 24 (Autumn 1987): 17–31.

Gutzlaff, Charles (Karl). *Journal of Three Voyages along the Coast of China, in 1831, 1832, & 1833, with Notices of Siam, Corea, and the Loo-Choo Islands.* London: Frederick Westley and A. H. Davis, 1834.

———. *China Opened: or, A Display of the Topography, History, Customs, Manners, Arts, Manufactures, Commerce, Literature, Religion, Jurisprudence, etc., of the Chinese Empire.* 2 vols. London: Smith, Elder and Co., 1838.

———. *The Life of Taou-kwang, Late Emperor of China.* London: Smith, Elder and Co., 1852.

Haddad, John Rogers. *The Romance of China: Excursions to China in U.S. Culture, 1776–1876.* New York: Columbia University Press, 2008.

Hall, Captain Basil. *Account of a Voyage of Discovery to the West Coast of Corea, and the Great Loo-Choo Island.* London: John Murray, 1818.

Hall, Commander W. H. *Narrative of the Voyages and Services of the Nemesis, from 1840 to 1843.* Edited by W. D. Bernard. 2 vols. London: Henry Colburn, 1844.

Hanan, Patrick, trans. *Mirage.* Hong Kong: Chinese University Press, 2014.

Hansard's Parliamentary Debates. 3rd series. London: T. C. Hansard.

Hao Yen-p'ing. "Chinese Teas to America." In *America's China Trade in Historical Perspective,* edited by Ernest R. May and John K. Fairbank. Cambridge, MA: Harvard Studies in American–East Asian Relations, 1986.

———. *The Commercial Revolution in Nineteenth-Century China: The Rise of Sino-Western Mercantile Capitalism.* Berkeley: University of California Press, 1986.

He Sibing. "Russell and Company, 1818–1891: America's Trade and Diplomacy in Nineteenth-Century China." Ph.D. dissertation, Miami University, Ohio, 1997.

Hevia, James. *Cherishing Men from Afar: Qing Guest Ritual and the Macartney Embassy of 1793.* Durham, NC: Duke University Press, 1995.

Hillard, Harriet Low. *My Mother's Journal: A Young Lady's Diary of Five Years Spent in Manila, Macao, and the Cape of Good Hope.* Edited by Katharine Hillard. Boston: George H. Ellis, 1900.

———. *Lights and Shadows of a Macao Life: The Journal of Harriett [sic] Low, Traveling Spinster.* Edited by Nan P. Hodges and Arthur W. Hummel. 2 vols. Woodinville, WA: The History Bank, 2002.

Hilton, Boyd. *A Mad, Bad, and Dangerous People?: England, 1783–1846.* Oxford: Clarendon Press, 2006.

Ho Ping-ti. *Studies on the Population of China, 1368–1953.* Cambridge, MA: Harvard East Asian Series, 1959.

Hoe, Susanna, and Derek Roebuck. *The Taking of Hong Kong: Charles and Clara Elliot in China Waters.* Richmond, Surrey: Curzon Press, 1999.

Hopkirk, Peter. *The Great Game: The Struggle for Empire in Central Asia.* New York: Kodansha, 1994.

Houckgeest, A. E. Van-Braam. *An Authentic Account of the Embassy of the Dutch East-India Company, to the Court of the Emperor of China, In the Years 1794 and 1795.* 2 vols. London: R. Phillips, 1798.

Howard, Paul. "Opium Suppression in Qing China: Responses to a Social Problem, 1729–1906." Ph.D. dissertation, University of Pennsylvania, 1998.

Hu Jinye. *Zhongguo jinyan jindu shi gang* (A historical survey of the suppression of opium and other drugs in China). Taipei: Tangshan chubanshe, 2005.

Hu Qiuyuan, ed. *Jindai Zhongguo dui Xifang ji lieqiang renshi ziliao huibian* (Compiled historical materials on China's understanding of the West and the great powers in the modern era). 5 vols. Taipei: Academia Sinica, Modern History Institute, 1972.

Hubback, J. H., and Edith C. Hubback. *Jane Austen's Sailor Brothers: Being the Adventures of Sir Francis Austen, G.C.B., Admiral of the Fleet and Rear-Admiral Charles Austen.* New York: John Lane, 1906.

Hummel, Arthur W., ed. *Eminent Chinese of the Ch'ing Period.* 2 vols. Taipei: SMC Publishing, Inc., 1991.

Hunter, William C. *The 'Fan Kwae' at Canton before Treaty Days, 1825–1844.* London: Kegan Paul, Trench & Co., 1882.

——. *Bits of Old China.* London: Kegan Paul, Trench & Co., 1885.

——. "Journal of Occurrances at Canton, during the Cessation of Trade at Canton, 1839." Edited by E. W. Ellsworth. *Journal of the Royal Asiatic Society Hong Kong Branch*, vol. 4 (1964): 9–36.

Inoue Hiromasa. "Wu Lanxiu and Society in Guangzhou on the Eve of the Opium War." Translated by Joshua Fogel. *Modern China* 12, no. 1 (January 1986): 103–15.

James, William. *The Naval History of Great Britain, from the Declaration of War by France in 1793 to the Accession of George IV.* 6 vols. London: Richard Bentley, 1859.

Janin, Hunt. *The India-China Opium Trade in the Nineteenth Century.* Jefferson, NC: McFarland & Co., 1999.

Jay, Mike. *Emperors of Dreams: Drugs in the Nineteenth Century.* Sawtry, UK: Dedalus, 2000.

Jenkins, Roy. *Gladstone.* New York: Random House, 1997.

Jiang Weiming. *Chuan-Hu-Shan bailianjiao qiyi ziliao jilu* (Historical materials on the White Lotus uprisings in Sichuan, Hubei, and Shaanxi). Chengdu: Sichuan renmin chubanshe, 1980.

Jocelyn, Lord. *Six Months with the Chinese Expedition; or, Leaves from a Soldier's Notebook.* London: John Murray, 1841.

Johnson, James. *An Account of a Voyage to India, China, &c. in His Majesty's Ship Caroline.* London: Richard Phillips, 1806.

Johnson, Kendall, ed. *Narratives of Free Trade: The Commercial Cultures of Early US-China Relations.* Hong Kong: Hong Kong University Press, 2012.

Jones, Susan Mann. "Hung Liang-chi (1746–1809): The Perception and Articulation of Political Problems in Late Eighteenth Century China." Ph.D. dissertation, Stanford University, 1971.

Kahn, Harold. *Monarchy in the Emperor's Eyes: Image and Reality in the Ch'ien-lung Reign.* Cambridge, MA: Harvard University Press, 1971.

Keay, John. *The Honourable Company: A History of the East India Company.* New York: Macmillan, 1991.

Kennedy, Paul. *The Rise and Fall of British Naval Mastery.* Malabar, FL: R. E. Krieger Pub. Co., 1982.

Keswick, Maggie, ed. *The Thistle and the Jade: A Celebration of 175 Years of Jardine Matheson.* London: Frances Lincoln, 2008.

Kitzan, Laurence. "The London Missionary Society in India and China, 1798–1834." Ph.D. dissertation, University of Toronto, 1965.

Knight, Roger. *Britain against Napoleon: The Organization of Victory, 1793–1815.* London: Allen Lane, 2013.

Kuhn, Philip. *Rebellion and Its Enemies in Late Imperial China: Militarization and Social Structure, 1796–1864.* Cambridge, MA: Harvard University Press, 1971.

———. *Origins of the Modern Chinese State.* Stanford, CA: Stanford University Press, 2002.

Kuhn, Philip, and Susan Mann. "Dynastic Decline and the Roots of Rebellion." In *The Cambridge History of China,* vol. 10, *Late Ch'ing, 1800–1911, Part 1.,* edited by John K. Fairbank and Denis Twitchett. Cambridge: Cambridge University Press, 1978.

Kumagai, Yukihisa. "The Lobbying Activities of Provincial Mercantile and Manufacturing Interests against the Renewal of the East India Company's Charter, 1812–1813 and 1829–1833." Ph.D. dissertation, University of Glasgow, 2008.

Kuo, P. C. *A Critical Study of the Anglo-Chinese War, with Documents.* Taipei: Ch'eng Wen Publishing Co., 1970 (reprint of 1935 Shanghai edition).

Lamas, Rosmarie W. N. *Everything in Style: Harriet Low's Macau.* Hong Kong: Hong Kong University Press, 2006.

Larson, John Lauritz. *Bonds of Enterprise: John Murray Forbes and Western Development in America's Railway Age.* Cambridge, MA: Harvard University Graduate School of Business Administration, 1984.

Lazich, Michael C. "E. C. Bridgman and the Coming of the Millennium: America's First Missionary to China." Ph.D. dissertation, SUNY Buffalo, 1997.

Le Fevour, Edward. *Western Enterprise in Late Ch'ing China: A Selective Survey of Jardine, Matheson and Company's Operations, 1842–1895.* Cambridge, MA: East Asia Research Center, Harvard University, 1968.

Leland, Charles Godfrey. *Pidgin-English Sing-song; or, Songs and Stories in the China-English Dialect.* London: Trübner and Co., 1876.

Le Pichon, Alain, ed. *China Trade and Empire: Jardine, Matheson & Co. and the Origins of British Rule in Hong Kong, 1827–1843.* Oxford: Oxford University Press for the British Academy, 2006.

Lindsay, Hugh Hamilton. *Report of Proceedings of a Voyage to the Northern Ports of China, in the Ship Lord Amherst.* 2nd ed. London: B. Fellowes, 1834.

———. *Letter to the Right Honourable Viscount Palmerston on British Relations with China.* London: Saunders and Otley, 1836.

Lin Man-houng. "Late Qing Perceptions of Native Opium." *Harvard Journal of Asiatic Studies* 64, no. 1 (June 2004): 117–44.

———. *China Upside Down: Currency, Society, and Ideologies, 1808–1856.* Cambridge, MA: Harvard University Asia Center, 2006.

Lin Qingyuan. *Lin Zexu ping zhuan* (A critical biography of Lin Zexu). Nanjing: Nanjing daxue chubanshe, 2000.

Lin Renchuan. "Qingdai Fujian de yapian maoyi" (The opium trade in Qing-era Fujian). *Zhongguo shehui jingji yanjiu*, vol. 1 (Xiamen: Fujian xinwen): 62–71.

Lin Zexu. *Lin Zexu quan ji* (The complete works of Lin Zexu). Edited by Mao Linli et al. 10 vols. Fuzhou: Haixia wenyi chubanshe, 2002.

Litzinger, Ralph A. "Making Histories: Contending Conceptions of the Yao Past." In *Cultural Encounters on China's Ethnic Frontiers*, ed. Stevan Harrell. Seattle: University of Washington Press, 1995.

Liu, Kwang-Ching. "Religion and Politics in the White Lotus Rebellion of 1796 in Hubei." In *Heterodoxy in Late Imperial China*, ed. Kwang-Ching Liu and Richard Shek. Honolulu: University of Hawaii Press, 2004.

Liu, Ts'ui-jung. "A Retrospection of Climate Changes and Their Impacts in Chinese History." In *Nature, Environment and Culture in East Asia: The Challenge of Climate Change*, ed. Carmen Meinert. Leiden: Brill, 2013.

Ljungstedt, Andrew. *An Historical Sketch of the Portuguese Settlements in China*. Boston: James Monroe and Co., 1836.

Loch, Capt. Granville G. *The Closing Events of the Campaign in China: The Operations in the Yang-tze-kiang; and Treaty of Nanking*. London: John Murray, 1843.

Loines, Elma. *The China Trade Post-Bag of the Seth Low Family of Salem and New York, 1829–1873*. Manchester, ME: Falmouth Publishing House, 1953.

Lovell, Julia. *The Opium War: Drugs, Dreams, and the Making of China*. London: Picador, 2011.

Lubbock, Basil. *The Opium Clippers*. Glasgow: Brown, Son & Ferguson, Ltd., 1933.

Lutz, Jessie G. *Opening China: Karl F. A. Gutzlaff and Sino-Western Relations, 1827–1852*. Grand Rapids, MI: William B. Eerdmans, 2008.

Macartney, George. *An Embassy to China: Being the Journal Kept by Lord Macartney during His Embassy to the Emperor Ch'ien-lung, 1793–1794*. Edited by J. L. Cranmer-Byng. Hamden, CT: Archon Books, 1963.

Macauley, Melissa. "Small Time Crooks: Opium, Migrants, and the War on Drugs in China, 1819–1860." *Late Imperial China* 30, no. 1 (June 2009): 1–47.

McCaffrey, Cecily Miriam. "Living through Rebellion: A Local History of the White Lotus Uprising in Hubei, China." Ph.D. dissertation, University of California, San Diego, 2003.

Machin, Ian. *The Rise of Democracy in Britain, 1830–1918*. New York: St. Martin's Press, 2001.

Mackenzie, Keith Stewart. *Narrative of the Second Campaign in China*. London: Richard Bentley, 1842.

McLean, David. "Surgeons of The Opium War: The Navy on the China Coast, 1840–42." *English Historical Review* 121, no. 491 (April 2006): 487–504.

McMahon, Daniel Mark. "Restoring the Garden: Yan Ruyi and the Civilizing of China's Internal Frontiers, 1795–1805." Ph.D. dissertation, University of California, Davis, 1999.

McMahon, Keith. *The Fall of the God of Money: Opium Smoking in Nineteenth-Century China*. Lanham, MD: Rowman & Littlefield, 2002.

McPherson, D., M.D. *Two Years in China. Narrative of the Chinese Expedition from its Formation in April, 1840, till April, 1842*. London: Saunders and Otley, 1842.

Madancy, Joyce. *The Troublesome Legacy of Commissioner Lin: The Opium Trade and Opium Suppression in Fujian Province, 1820s to 1920s.* Cambridge, MA: Harvard University Asia Center, 2003.

Malcom, Howard. *Travels in South-Eastern Asia.* 2 vols. Boston: Gould, Kendall, and Lincoln, 1839.

Mandler, Peter. *Aristocratic Government in the Age of Reform: Whigs and Liberals, 1830–1852.* Oxford: Clarendon Press, 1990.

Mann, Susan. *The Talented Women of the Zhang Family.* Berkeley: University of California Press, 2007.

Mao Haijian. *Tianchao de bengkui: yapian zhanzheng zai yanjiu* (The collapse of the heavenly dynasty: a reexamination of the Opium War). Beijing: Sanlian shudian, 2012.

Marjoribanks, Charles. *Letter to the Right Hon. Charles Grant, President of the Board of Controul, on the Present State of British Intercourse with China.* 2nd ed. London: J. Hatchard and Son, 1833.

Markham, Clements R., ed. *Narratives of the Mission of George Bogle to Tibet, and of the Journey of Thomas Manning to Lhasa.* London: Trübner and Co., 1876.

Matheson, James. *The Present Position and Prospects of the British Trade with China.* London: Smith, Elder and Co., 1836.

Medhurst, W. H. *China: Its State and Prospects.* London: John Snow, 1838.

Melancon, Glenn. "Honour in Opium? The British Declaration of War on China, 1839–1840." *International History Review* 21, no. 4 (December 1999): 855–74.

———. *Britain's China Policy and the Opium Crisis: Balancing Drugs, Violence and National Honour, 1833–1840.* Aldershot, UK: Ashgate, 2003.

Menzies, Nicholas Kay. "Trees, Fields and People: The Forests of China from the Seventeenth to the Nineteenth Centuries." Ph.D. dissertation, University of California, Berkeley, 1988.

Miles, Steven B. *The Sea of Learning: Mobility and Identity in Nineteenth-Century Guangzhou.* Cambridge, MA: Harvard University Asia Center, 2006.

Milne, William. *A Retrospect of the First Ten Years of the Protestant Mission to China.* Malacca: Anglo-Chinese Press, 1820.

Mitchell, Peter M. "Wei Yüan (1794–1857) and the Early Modernization Movement in China and Japan." Ph.D. dissertation, Indiana University, 1970.

———. "The Limits of Reformism: Wei Yüan's Reaction to Western Intrusion." *Modern Asian Studies* 6, no. 2 (1972): 175–204.

M'Leod, John. *Narrative of a Voyage in His Majesty's Late Ship Alceste to the Yellow Sea.* London: John Murray, 1817.

Mody, Jehangir R. P. *Jamsetjee Jejeebhoy: The First Indian Knight and Baronet (1783–1859).* Bombay: R.M.D.C. Press, 1959.

Monteith, Robert. *Reasons for Demanding Investigation into the Charges against Lord Palmerston.* Glasgow: William Collins & Co., 1840.

Morley, John. *The Life of William Ewart Gladstone.* 3 vols. New York: Macmillan, 1904.

Morrison, Eliza. *Memoirs of the Life and Labours of Robert Morrison, D.D.* 2 vols. London: Longman, Orme, Brown, Green, and Longmans, 1839.

Morrison, Robert. *Translations from the Original Chinese, with Notes.* Canton: P. P. Thoms, The Honorable East India Company's Press, 1815.

————. *A Dictionary of the Chinese Language, in Three Parts*. 6 Vols. Macao: The Honourable East India Company's Press, 1815–1823.

————. *A Memoir of the Principal Occurrences during an Embassy from the British Government to the Court of China in the Year 1816*. London, 1819.

Morriss, Roger. *The Foundations of British Maritime Ascendancy: Resources, Logistics and the State, 1755–1815*. Cambridge: Cambridge University Press, 2011.

Morse, Hosea Ballou. *The Chronicles of the East India Company Trading to China, 1635–1834*. 5 vols. Oxford: Clarendon Press, 1926–29.

Mosca, Matthew William. "Qing China's Perspectives on India, 1750–1847." Ph.D. dissertation, Harvard University, 2008.

Moseley, William W. *The Origin of the First Protestant Mission to China*. London: Simpkin and Marshall, 1842.

Moule, A. C. "A Manuscript Chinese Version of the New Testament (British Museum, Sloane 3599)." *Journal of the Royal Asiatic Society of Great Britain and Ireland*, no. 1 (April 1949): 23–33.

Mungello, D. E. *The Great Encounter of China and the West, 1500–1800*. Lanham, MD: Rowman & Littlefield, 1999.

Murray, Dian. *Pirates of the South China Coast, 1790–1810*. Stanford, CA: Stanford University Press, 1987.

————. "Cheng I Sao in Fact and Fiction." In *Bandits at Sea: A Pirates Reader*, ed. C. R. Pennell. New York: New York University Press, 2001.

————. "Piracy and China's Maritime Transition." In *Maritime China in Transition, 1750–1850*, ed. Wang Gung-wu and Ng Chin-keong. Wiesbaden: Harrassowitz Verlag, 2004.

Murray, John Fisher. *The Chinese and the Ministry: An Inquiry into the Origins and Progress of our Present Difficulties with China, and into the Expediency, Justice, and Necessity of the War*. London: T. Cadell, 1840.

Naquin, Susan. *Millenarian Rebellion in China: The Eight Trigrams Uprising of 1813*. New Haven, CT: Yale University Press, 1976.

Nazir, Cooverjee Sorabjee. *The First Parsee Baronet, Being Passages from the Life and Fortunes of the Late Sir Jamsetjee Jeejeebhoy Baronet*. Bombay: The Union Press, 1866.

Newman, R. K. "Opium Smoking in Late Imperial China: A Reconsideration." *Modern Asian Studies* 29, no. 4 (October 1995): 765–94.

Nivison, David. "Ho-shen and His Accusers: Ideological and Political Behavior in the Eighteenth Century." In *Confucianism in Action*, ed. David Nivison and Arthur Wright. Stanford, CA: Stanford University Press, 1959.

————. *The Life and Thought of Chang Hsüeh-ch'eng*. Stanford, CA: Stanford University Press, 1966.

Noble, Charles Frederick. *A Voyage to the East Indies in 1747 and 1748*. London: T. Becket and P. A. Dehondt, at the Tully's Head; and T. Durham, at the Golden Ball, 1762.

Norwood, Dael A. "Trading in Liberty: The Politics of the American China Trade, c. 1784–1862." Ph.D. dissertation, Princeton University, 2012.

Nye, Gideon. *The Morning of My Life in China*. Canton, 1873.

O'Brien, Patrick K. "The Political Economy of British Taxation, 1660–1815." *Economic History Review*, new series, vol. 41, no. 1 (February 1988): 1–32.

O'Meara, Barry E. *Napoleon in Exile; Or, A Voice from St. Helena. The Opinions and Reflections of Napoleon on the Most Important Events of His Life and Government, in His Own Words.* 2 vols. London: W. Simpkin and R. Marshall, 1822.

Osmond, Tiffany. *The Canton Chinese: or, The American's Sojourn in the Celestial Empire.* Boston, MA, and Cambridge, UK: James Munroe, 1849.

Osterhammel, Jürgen. *The Transformation of the World: A Global History of the Nineteenth Century.* Princeton, NJ: Princeton University Press, 2014.

Owen, David Edward. *British Opium Policy in China and India.* New Haven, CT: Yale University Press, 1934.

Palsetia, Jesse S. "Merchant Charity and Public Identity Formation in Colonial India: The Case of Jamsetjee Jejeebhoy." *Journal of Asian and African Studies* 40, no. 3 (2005): 197–217.

———. *Jamsetjee Jejeebhoy of Bombay: Partnership and Public Culture in Empire.* Oxford: Oxford University Press, 2015.

Papers Presented to Parliament, by His Majesty's Command, in Explanation of the Measures Adopted by His Majesty's Government for the Melioration of the Condition of the Slave Population in His Majesty's Possessions in the West Indies, on the Continent of South America, and at the Mauritius. Printed by order of the House of Commons, August 8, 1832.

Papers Relating to China (Private and Confidential) 1839–40 and 1841. N.p., n.d. In Minto Papers, MS 21216A, National Library of Scotland.

Parker, Charles Stuart. *Life and Letters of Sir James Graham, Second Baronet of Netherby, P.C., G.C.B., 1792–1861.* 2 vols. London: John Murray, 1907.

Parry, Jonathan. *The Rise and Fall of Liberal Government in Victorian Britain.* New Haven, CT: Yale University Press, 1993.

Pearson, Henry Greenleaf. *An American Railroad Builder: John Murray Forbes.* Boston: Houghton, Mifflin and Company, 1911.

Peyrefitte, Alain. *The Immobile Empire.* Translated by Jon Rothschild. New York: Alfred A. Knopf, 1992.

Philip, Robert, and Thomas Thompson. *No Opium! or: Commerce and Christianity Working Together for Good in China.* London: Thomas Ward and Co., 1835.

Philips, C. H. *The East India Company, 1784–1834.* Manchester: Manchester University Press, 1940.

Phipps, John. *A Practical Treatise on the China and Eastern Trade.* London: Wm. H. Allen and Co., 1836.

Polachek, James M. *The Inner Opium War.* Cambridge, MA: Council on East Asian Studies/Harvard University Press, 1992.

Pomeranz, Kenneth. *The Great Divergence: China, Europe, and the Making of the Modern World Economy.* Princeton, NJ: Princeton University Press, 2000.

Prakash, Gyan. *Mumbai Fables: A History of an Enchanted City.* Princeton, NJ: Princeton University Press, 2010.

Pritchard, Earl H. *The Crucial Years of Early Anglo-Chinese Relations, 1750–1800.* New York: Octagon Books, 1970.

Proudfoot, William Jardine. *Biographical Memoir of James Dinwiddie, Ll.D., Astronomer in the British Embassy to China, 1792, '3, '4.* Liverpool: Edward Howell, 1868.

Qingdai waijiao shiliao Jiaqing Daoguang chao (Historical materials on Qing foreign relations during the Jiaqing and Daoguang reigns). 10 vols. Beijing: Gugong bowuyuan, 1932–33.

Qing zhongqi wusheng bailianjiao qiyi ziliao (Historical materials on the White Lotus uprisings in five provinces in the mid-Qing era). 5 vols. Suzhou: Jiangsu renmin chubanshe, 1981.

Qi Sihe, ed. *Huang Juezi zoushu, Xu Naiji zouyi hekan* (A joint publication of the memorials of Huang Juezi and Xu Naiji). Beijing: Zhonghua shuju, 1959.

Qi Sihe et al., eds. *Yapian zhanzheng* (The Opium War [a collection of historical documents]). 6 vols. Shanghai: Xin zhishi chubanshe, 1955.

Report from the Select Committee of the House of Commons on the Affairs of the East-India Company, 16th August, 1832. London: J. L. Cox and Son, 1833.

Report from the Select Committee on the Trade with China; together with the Minutes of Evidence taken before Them. Printed by order of the House of Commons, June 5, 1840.

Reports from the Select Committee of the House of Commons Appointed to Enquire into the Present State of the Affairs of the East India Company, together with the Minutes of Evidence, and Appendix of Documents, and a General Index. London: Printed by order of the Honourable Court of Directors, 1830.

Ride, Sir Lindsay. *An East India Company Cemetery: Protestant Burials in Macao.* Hong Kong: Hong Kong University Press, 1996.

Robbins, Helen. *Our First Ambassador to China: An Account of the Life and Correspondence of George, Earl of Macartney, with Extracts from His Letters, and the Narrative of His Experiences in China, as Told by Himself, 1737–1806.* New York: Dutton and Company, 1908.

Rowe, William T. "Money, Economy, and Polity in the Daoguang-Era Paper Currency Debates." *Late Imperial China* 31, no. 2 (December 2010): 69–96.

———. "Bao Shichen and Agrarian Reform in Early Nineteenth-Century China." *Frontiers of History in China* 9, no. 1 (2014): 1–31.

———. *Speaking of Profit: Bao Shichen and Reform in Nineteenth-Century China.* Cambridge, MA: Harvard University Asia Center, forthcoming.

Rubinstein, Murray A. *The Origins of the Anglo-American Missionary Enterprise in China, 1807–1840.* Lanham, MD: Scarecrow Press, 1996.

Rutter, Owen, ed. *Mr. Glasspoole and the Chinese Pirates: Being the Narrative of Mr. Richard Glasspoole of the Ship Marquis of Ely: Describing His Captivity . . .* London: The Golden Cockerel Press, 1935.

Schell, Orville, and John Delury. *Wealth and Power: China's Long March to the Twenty-First Century.* New York: Random House, 2013.

Schmitt, Cannon. "Narrating National Addictions: De Quincey, Opium, and Tea." In *High Anxieties: Cultural Studies in Addiction,* ed. Janet Brodie and Marc Redfield. Berkeley: University of California Press, 2002.

Shiliao xunkan (A periodical publication of historical documents). 13 vols. Kowloon, Hong Kong: Fudi shuyuan chuban youxian gongsi, 2005. (Reprint of original edition published in Beijing by the National Palace Museum, 1930.)

Ship Amherst: Return to an Order of the Honourable the House of Commons, dated 17 June 1833 . . . Printed by order of the House of Commons, June 19, 1833.

Slade, John. *Notices on the British Trade to the Port of Canton.* London: Smith, Elder and Co., 1830.

————. *Narrative of the Late Proceedings and Events in China.* Canton: Canton Register Press, 1839.

Smith, Adam. *An Inquiry into the Nature and Causes of the Wealth of Nations.* 2nd ed. 2 vols. London: W. Strahan and T. Cadell, 1778.

Smith, Edward. *The Life of Sir Joseph Banks: President of the Royal Society.* London: John Lane, The Bodley Head, 1911.

Spence, Jonathan. "Opium Smoking in Ch'ing China." In *Conflict and Control in Late Imperial China,* ed. Frederic Wakeman Jr. and Carolyn Grant. Berkeley: University of California Press, 1975.

————. *God's Chinese Son.* New York: Norton, 1996.

Staunton, George Leonard. *An Historical Account of the Embassy to the Emperor of China, undertaken by order of the King of Great Britain.* London: John Stockdale, 1797.

————. *An Authentic Account of an Embassy from the King of Great Britain to the Emperor of China.* 2 vols. Philadelphia: Robert Campbell, 1799.

Staunton, George Thomas. *Ta Tsing Leu Lee; being the Fundamental Laws, and a Selection from the Supplementary Statutes, of the Penal Code of China.* London: T. Cadell and W. Davies, 1810.

————. *Miscellaneous Notices Relating to China, and Our Commercial Intercourse with That Country.* London: John Murray, 1822.

————. *Miscellaneous Notices Relating to China, and Our Commercial Intercourse with That Country.* 2nd ed., enlarged. London: John Murray, 1822–50.

————. *Notes of Proceedings and Occurrences, during the British Embassy to Pekin, in 1816.* Printed for private circulation. London: Habant Press, 1824.

————. *Corrected Report of the Speeches of Sir George Staunton, on the China Trade, in the House of Commons, June 4, and June 13, 1833.* London: Edmund Lloyd, 1833.

————. *Remarks on the British Relations with China, and the Proposed Plans for Improving Them.* London: Edmund Lloyd, 1836.

————. *Corrected Report of the Speech of Sir George Staunton on Sir James Graham's Motion on the China Trade in the House of Commons, April 7, 1840.* London: Edmund Lloyd, 1840.

————. *Memoirs of the Chief Incidents of the Public Life of Sir George Thomas Staunton, Bart.* Printed for private circulation. London: L. Booth, 1856.

Stevens, Walter Barlow. *Missouri: The Center State, 1821–1915.* 2 vols. Chicago and St. Louis, S. J. Clarke Publishing Co., 1915.

Stifler, Susan Reed. "The Language Students of the East India Company's Canton Factory." *Journal of the North China Branch of the Royal Asiatic Society* 69 (1938): 46–82.

Su Ching. "The Printing Presses of the London Missionary Society among the Chinese." Ph.D. dissertation, University of London, 1996.

Talfourd, Thomas Noon. *The Letters of Charles Lamb, with a Sketch of His Life.* 2 vols. London: Edward Moxon, 1837.

————. *The Works of Charles Lamb. To which are prefixed, His Letters, and a Sketch of His Life.* 2 vols. New York: Harper and Bros., 1838.

————. *The Works of Charles Lamb, with A Sketch of His Life and Final Memorials.* 2 vols. New York: Harper and Bros., 1875.

Temple, Lt.-Col. Sir Richard Carnac, ed. *The Travels of Peter Mundy in Europe and Asia, 1608–1667.* 5 vols. London: Hakluyt Society, 1919.

Teng, Ssu-yü. "Chinese Influence on the Western Examination System." *Harvard Journal of Asiatic Studies* 7, no. 4 (September 1943): 267–312.

———. *Chang Hsi and the Treaty of Nanking, 1842.* Chicago: University of Chicago Press, 1944.

Thoms, P. P. *Dialogues and Detached Sentences in the Chinese Language; with a Free and Verbal Translation into English.* Macao: The Honorable East India Company's Press, 1816.

Torbert, Preston M. *The Ch'ing Imperial Household Department: A Study of Its Organization and Principal Functions, 1662–1796.* Cambridge, MA: Council on East Asian Studies, Harvard University, 1977.

Townsend, William John. *Robert Morrison: The Pioneer of Chinese Missions.* London Missionary Society's edition. London: S. W. Partridge & Co., 1888.

Trocki, Carl. *Opium, Empire and the Global Political Economy: A Study of the Asian Opium Trade, 1750–1950.* New York: Routledge, 1999.

Tsao, Ting Man. "Representing China to the British Public in the Age of Free Trade, c. 1833–1844." Ph.D. dissertation, SUNY Stony Brook, 2000.

———. "Representing 'Great England' to Qing China in the Age of Free Trade Imperialism: The Circulation of a Tract by Charles Marjoribanks on the China Coast." *Victorians Institute Journal* 33 (2005): 179–96.

Turner, John. *A Narrative of the Captivity and Sufferings of John Turner . . . among the Ladrones or Pirates, on the Coast of China . . . in the year 1807.* New York: G. & R. Waite, 1814.

Van Dyke, Paul A. *The Canton Trade: Life and Enterprise on the China Coast, 1700–1845.* Hong Kong: Hong Kong University Press, 2005.

———. *Merchants of Canton and Macao: Politics and Strategies in Eighteenth-Century Chinese Trade.* Hong Kong: Hong Kong University Press, 2011.

———. "Smuggling Networks of the Pearl River Delta before 1842: Implications for Macao and the American China Trade." In *Americans and Macao: Trade, Smuggling, and Diplomacy on the South China Coast,* ed. Paul A. Van Dyke. Hong Kong: Hong Kong University Press, 2012.

Vermeer, Eduard B. "The Mountain Frontier in Late Imperial China: Economic and Social Developments in the Bashan." *T'oung Pao,* 2nd series, vol. 77, livr. 4/5 (1991): 300–329.

Victoria, Queen of Great Britain. *The Letters of Queen Victoria.* Edited by Arthur Christopher Benson and Viscount Esher. 3 vols. New York: Longmans, Green, and Co., 1907.

von Glahn, Richard. "Cycles of Silver in Chinese Monetary History." In *The Economy of Lower Yangzi Delta in Late Imperial China,* ed. Billy K. L. So. New York: Routledge, 2013.

Wakeman, Frederic Jr. *The Fall of Imperial China.* New York: Free Press, 1975.

———. "Drury's Occupation of Macau and China's Response to Early Modern Imperialism." *East Asian History* 28 (December 2004): 27–34.

Waley, Arthur. *The Opium War Through Chinese Eyes.* Stanford, CA: Stanford University Press, 1968.

Waley-Cohen, Joanna. *The Culture of War in China: Empire and the Military under the Qing Dynasty*. London: I. B. Tauris, 2006.

Waltham, Clae. *Shu Ching: Book of History*. Chicago: Henry Regnery Company, 1971.

Wang Wensheng. "White Lotus Rebels and South China Pirates: Social Crises and Political Changes in the Qing Empire, 1796–1810." Ph.D. dissertation, University of California, Irvine, 2008.

———. *White Lotus Rebels and South China Pirates: Crisis and Reform in the Qing Empire*. Cambridge, MA: Harvard University Press, 2014.

Wang Xianqian, ed. *Shi chao donghua lu* (Court records from the Donghua gate, for ten reigns). 62 vols. 1899.

Warren, Samuel. *The Opium Question*. 3rd ed. London: James Ridgway, 1840.

Webster, Anthony. *The Twilight of the East India Company: The Evolution of Anglo-Asian Commerce and Politics, 1790–1860*. Woodbridge, Suffolk, UK: Boydell Press, 2009.

Webster, Daniel. *The Papers of Daniel Webster; Diplomatic Papers, Volume 1: 1841–1843*. Edited by Kenneth E. Shewmaker. Hanover, NH: University Press of New England, 1983.

Wei, Betty Peh-T'i. *Ruan Yuan, 1764–1849: The Life and Work of a Major Scholar-Official in Nineteenth-Century China before the Opium War*. Hong Hong: Hong Kong University Press, 2006.

Wei Yuan. *Sheng wu ji* (A record of the Qing dynasty's military campaigns). Daoguang 22 (1842).

———. *Yi sou ru kou ji* (A record of the invasion by foreign ships). Taipei: Guangwen shuju, 1974 (facsimile of undated manuscript).

Wenxian congbian (Collected publications of historical materials). 46 vols. Beijing: Gugong bowuyuan wenxian guan, 1930–1943.

Wenxian congbian quanbian (Complete publications of historical materials). 12 vols. Beijing: Beijing tushu chubanshe, 2008.

Williams, Samuel Wells. *The Middle Kingdom*. 2 vols. London: W. H. Allen, 1883.

Williamson, Capt. A. R. *Eastern Traders: Some Men and Ships of Jardine, Matheson & Company and their Contemporaries in the East India Company's Maritime Service*. S.l.: Jardine, Matheson & Co., 1975.

Wills, John E. *Mountain of Fame: Portraits in Chinese History*. Princeton, NJ: Princeton University Press, 1994.

Wong, J. Y. "British Annexation of Sind in 1843: An Economic Perspective." *Modern Asian Studies* 31, no. 2 (May 1997): 225–44.

Wong, John D. "Global Positioning: Houqua and his China Trade Partners in the Nineteenth Century." Ph.D. dissertation, Harvard University, 2012.

Wood, Herbert J. "England, China, and the Napoleonic Wars." *Pacific Historical Review* 9, no. 2 (June 1940): 139–56.

Wood, William W. *Sketches of China*. Philadelphia: Carey & Lea, 1830.

Wu Yixiong. "Deng Tingzhen yu Guangdong jinyan wenti" (Deng Tingzhen and the problem of opium suppression in Guangdong province). *Jindaishi yanjiu* (2008, no. 5): 37–55.

Wylie, Alexander. *Memorials of the Protestant Missionaries to the Chinese*. Shanghai: American Presbyterian Mission Press, 1867.

Yang Guozhen. *Lin Zexu zhuan* (Biography of Lin Zexu). Beijing: Renmin chuban-she, 1995.

Yapian zhanzheng dang'an shiliao (Archival sources on the Opium War). Zhongguo diyi lishi dang'an guan (comp.). 7 vols. Shanghai: Renmin chubanshe, 1987-.

Ye Xiaoqing. "Ascendant Peace in the Four Seas: Tributary Drama and the Macart-ney Mission of 1793." *Late Imperial China* 26, no. 2 (December 2005): 89–113.

Ying shi Majiaerni fang Hua dang'an shiliao huibian (Collected archival sources on the British envoy Macartney's visit to China). Zhongguo diyi lishi dang'an guan (comp.). Beijing: Guoji wenhua chuban gongsi, 1996.

Yoon, Wook. "Prosperity with the Help of 'Villains,' 1776–1799: A Review of the Heshen Clique and Its Era." *T'oung Pao* 98, issue 4/5 (2012): 479–527.

Yu Ende. *Zhongguo jinyan faling bianqian shi* (A history of the changes in China's opium suppression laws). Shanghai: Zhonghua shuju, 1934.

Yuan Yonglun. *Jing haifen ji* (A record of the pacification of the pirates). 2 vols. Guangzhou: Shanyuan tang, 1830. Translated by Charles Friedrich Neumann as *History of the Pirates Who Infested the China Sea from 1807 to 1810*. London: Oriental Translation Fund, 1831.

Zheng Yangwen. *The Social Life of Opium in China*. Cambridge: Cambridge University Press, 2005.

Zhu Weizheng. *Rereading Modern Chinese History*. Translated by Michael Dillon. Boston: Brill, 2015.

Index

Page numbers in *italics* refer to illustrations.

ILLUSTRATION CREDITS

213 Image copyright © The Metropolitan Museum of Art. Image source: Art Resource, NY

215 Courtesy of the Forbes House Museum, Milton, MA

223 Wellcome Library, London

228 Wellcome Library, London

247 George Chinnery (English, 1774–1852), *Portrait of Harriet Low, 1833.* Peabody Essex Museum, museum purchase with partial funds donated by The Lee and Juliet Folger Fund and Joan Vaughan Ingraham, 2001. © Peabody Essex Museum, Salem, MA. Photography by Mark Sexton

255 iStock.com / GeorgiosArt

267 Courtesy of the Yale Center for British Art, Paul Mellon Collection

274 Wellcome Library, London

301 Courtesy of the Beinecke Rare Book and Manuscript Library, Yale University

311 Wellcome Library, London

351 Courtesy of the Yale Center for British Art

382 *Commissioner Lin Zexu (1785–1850) Overseeing the Destruction of Opium at Canton in 1839.* / Pictures from History / Bridgeman Images

400 Wellcome Library, London

417 Courtesy of the Yale Center for British Art, Paul Mellon Collection

423 Courtesy of the Beinecke Rare Book and Manuscript Library, Yale University

442 iStock.com / SeanPavonePhoto

Stephen R. Platt is a professor of Chinese history at the University of Massachusetts, Amherst. His last book, *Autumn in the Heavenly Kingdom*, was a *Washington Post* Notable Book, a *New York Times Book Review* Editors' Choice, and won the Cundill History Prize. Platt lives with his wife and children in Northampton, Massachusetts.

A NOTE ON THE TYPE

This book was set in Janson, a typeface long thought to have been made by the Dutchman Anton Janson, who was a practicing typefounder in Leipzig during the years 1669–1687. However, it has been conclusively demonstrated that these types are actually the work of Nicholas Kis (1650–1702), a Hungarian, who most probably learned his trade from the master Dutch typefounder Dirk Voskens. The type is an excellent example of the influential and sturdy Dutch types that prevailed in England up to the time William Caslon (1692–1766) developed his own incomparable designs from them.

Composed by North Market Street Graphics,
Lancaster, Pennsylvania

Printed and bound by Berryville Graphics,
Berryville, Virginia

Designed by Soonyoung Kwon